W9-CZU-836

THE TRAVEL BOOK

CONSUMER INFORMATION SERIES

The Consumer Health Information Source Book
by Alan M. Rees and Blanche A. Young

The Travel Book: A Guide to the Travel Guides
by Jon O. Heise

THE TRAVEL BOOK

GUIDE TO THE TRAVEL GUIDES

JON O. HEISE
with Dennis O'Reilly

R. R. BOWKER COMPANY
New York & London, 1981

Published by R. R. Bowker Company
1180 Avenue of the Americas, New York, NY 10036

Printed and bound in the United States of America

Library of Congress Cataloging in Publication Data

Heise, John O.
The travel book.

(Consumer Information Series)
Includes indexes.
1. Voyages and travels—1951- —Guide-books—Bibliography. I. O'Reilly, Dennis, joint author.
II. Title. III. Series: Consumer Information Series (New York)
Z6011.H4 [G153.4] 016.910'2'02 80-39598
ISBN 0-8352-1337-4

CONTENTS

PREFACE

Travel guidebooks in the most traditional sense have been a substitute for an in-person guide. Their purpose has been to identify sights and describe them for travelers. Perhaps the most classic of all travel guidebooks is the Baedeker series, one volume of which recently was reprinted (*Baedeker's Egypt*) and is reviewed in this book. Although many current travel guides continue the tradition of explanation and education, several new types of guides are now being published that reflect changes in our contemporary world.

The largest new category of travel guides is the *accommodation and restaurant guides*, providing the traveler with specific details, including address, prices, a description of services, hours, telephone number, and a variety of other practical information. Whether because journeys are now likely to be thought of in terms of days or weeks rather than months, or because the choice of accommodations and restaurants is now more complex, or because today's traveler is older and/or less adventurous than earlier travelers, the number and success of accommodation and restaurant guides is clearly a contemporary fact.

Perhaps one of the fastest growing types of travel guides is the *specialty guide* group. These are guides for a specific group of travelers, such as women, the handicapped, or single travelers; for a specific type of travel style, such as hiking, rail travel, or cruises; or for a specific travel interest, such as music festivals, shopping, or wine tours.

Those guides that provide descriptions of sights, coupled with accommodation and restaurant information and frequently also more specialized information, are reviewed in this book under the category of *comprehensive guides*. These are the guides that try to include everything necessary for the traveler in one book.

Other types of travel books include books of photographs, bibliographies, and compilations of addresses.

The choice of guide type is a decision a traveler must make. Although some books endeavor to be all things to all people, few succeed. Travelers desiring a guide that accomplishes several specific purposes may find themselves using two or more books. Others may wish to revert to an earlier time, when more risk and responsibility were taken on by the traveler, who regarded taking care of the practicalities of travel as part of the personal adventure.

HOW TO USE THIS BOOK

For the most part, the guides reviewed in *The Travel Book* were published after 1976, although some earlier guides whose content continues to be relevant for today's traveler are also included. Publishers were asked to submit copies of travel guides for review, and only those guides received from the publishers were reviewed. Most major, and indeed most lesser-known, publications are reviewed, although there are some exceptions. Reviews of the guides are descriptive and evaluative; still careful examination of each guide is advisable before the traveler places total dependence on any guide as a travel companion.

Bibliographic information given for each guide includes title, author, place of publication, publisher, U.S. distributor (if not published in the United States), year or frequency of publication, number of pages, and price. Whenever available, British and Canadian price information is also provided.

The Travel Book is divided into seven parts: The World, Africa, Asia, Australia and the Pacific, Europe, Latin America and the Caribbean, and North America. Titles (including series) covering more than one continent are listed under The World. Also listed there are those specialty guides that have no specific geographic frame of reference. For each of the continents, guides covering the entire continent are listed first, followed by the guides that cover specific countries. In North America, under Canada and the United States, regional and provincial or state guides are listed after the guides that cover the country as a whole.

Each guide is listed under the geographic heading that reflects the broadest scope of its coverage. A book on California and Nevada, for instance, is listed under The West, rather than under California, or Nevada, or the United States. (Cross references are provided to facilitate location of the review for titles covering more than one state or region.) Also, although city, state, and regional sections list only guides to a specific area, in many cases books covering the country or continent as a whole also have information on those areas.

Readers desiring information on a specific geographic area or on a specific travel interest should approach the book through the contents. Title/author and broad subject access are provided by the Index. The

Directory of Publishers includes all of the U.S., British, and Canadian publishers listed in the book.

ACKNOWLEDGMENTS

A great number of people are responsible for the realization of this book. Most importantly, it would not have been possible without the extremely capable and untiring assistance of Dennis O'Reilly in reviewing the guides. Jessica Vintner also assisted in the review process. To them, and to Shirley Wharton for her help with the typing, I owe a great debt of gratitude. And to the publishers who so generously provided their books, making this work possible, I would like to offer my special thanks.

THE WORLD

Comprehensive Guides

A to Z World Travel Guides. Robert S. Kane. Garden City, NY: Doubleday & Co. 200-500 pp. $6.95-9.95. Revised periodically.

Robert Kane, prolific writer and veteran traveler, has written this series, dating from the 1963 *Asia A to Z* to the most recent guide, the 1977 *Italy A to Z: Grand Tour of the Classic Cities.* Selective major cities are emphasized, with minimal inclusion of rural and more out-of-the-way places. Historical and cultural background and practical information are given, along with hotel and restaurant suggestions. Kane's travel style is centered around "creature comforts"; he addresses travelers with budgets ranging from moderate to luxurious; his books are geared to both first-time and veteran travelers.

Evaluation: Although the guides vary in organization and emphasis, Kane's particular style appears to be the evocation of travel in the manner of the eighteenth-century Grand Tour of the Continent (note especially *Grand Tour A to Z: The Capitals of Europe).* The advantages of Kane's A to Z guides are similar to those of Myra Waldo's Travel Guides (see below); their personal style allows the reader to gauge the author's personal opinion on a large number of areas. Kane, unlike Myra Waldo, promotes an increasingly popular notion: the idea of travel with a theme, which perhaps renders his guides more successful.

Included in the series: Africa A to Z; Asia A to Z; Canada A to Z; Eastern Europe A to Z; Grand Tour A to Z: The Capitals of Europe; Hawaii A to Z; Italy A to Z: Grand Tour of the Classic Cities; London A to Z; Paris A to Z; South America A to Z; South Pacific A to Z.

Blue Guide Series. Chicago, IL: Rand McNally & Co.; London: Ernest Benn. approx. 403 pp. pap. $5.95-$17.95. Revised periodically.

The Blue Guide: Scotland is an example of the Blue Guide series, well known and respected throughout Europe. Extensive background and practical information are provided in the first part of the guide. The second section divides Scotland into ten geographic areas, which includes an introduction to the area as well as a wide range of sights. The accommodation listings should appeal to travelers of all budgets. Numerous motoring routes, planned to include all areas of interest to tourists, give route numbers, distances, scenery, and many other features. There is an atlas as well as town plans and a full index, all of which add to the usefulness and extensive scope of this guide.

Evaluation: The Blue Guide: Scotland attempts to guide and inform travelers, not to cajole them or create artificial enthusiasm. Information is complete, compact, and well organized, and the compact format makes the guide easy to use on the road. While motoring routes are included, information is useful for all types of traveling. Like all the Blue Guides, this guide succeeds in its goal of providing a wealth of information for the serious traveler.

Included in the series: The Adriatic Coast; Athens and Environs; Belgium and Luxembourg; Bernese Oberland; Crete; Denmark; England; Greece; Holland; Ireland; London; Lucerne; Malta; Northern Italy; Northwestern France; Paris; Rome and Environs; Scotland; South of France; Southern Italy; Southern Spain; Wales; Yugoslavia.

Fodor's Area Guides. New York: David McKay Co., 1980. approx. 500 pp. $12.95 & $13.95, pap. $7.95–$10.95. London: Hodder & Stoughton, 1980. £3.95-£6.95. Revised regularly.

The first section of these books provides all the necessary information for planning a trip to the regions covered. Brief country descriptions, travel costs, climate, transportation options, suggested itineraries, and many more topics are concisely presented. Longer essays in the second section, on culture, history, creative arts, and other topics, provide a feeling for the areas. A variety of authors provide the information specific to each country that fills the third and major portion of each book. The lengthy entries for each country contain extensive background information and descriptions of areas and cities and an abundance of practical information in summary form. Costs, best times for travel, local events, visas and customs, money, shopping, night life, hotels, restaurants, and local transportation are some of the many details covered.

Evaluation: Travelers looking for extensive and detailed hotel and restaurant information have the wrong book if they select a Fodor Area Guide, although these topics are covered. But for those who want to be knowledgeable travelers, both in background information and practical know-how, there is no substitute for these thorough and readable guides. While not for the quickie, picture-taking tourist stopover, the well-organized Fodor books will serve the intelligent traveler well, facilitating an informed and well-planned trip.

Included in the series: Australia, New Zealand, and the South Pacific; Caribbean, Bahamas, and Bermuda; Europe; Europe on a Budget; India and Nepal; Scandinavia; South America; South-East Asia.

Fodor's City Guides. New York: David McKay Co. approx. 350 pp. $13.95; pap. $6.95. London: Hodder & Stoughton. £3.50. Revised annually.

Starting with pretravel planning and a basic introduction to each city in the series, followed with an extensive look at various historical points, buildings, gardens, schools, monuments, and other noteworthy locations, Fodor's City series takes an exhaustive look at each city. It is doubtful that even a native would be able to tell you as much about as many things as can one of these guides. Even such remote and obscure locations as the Paris site of an observatory built in 1654 by a royal finance minister, the location of the building where Van Gogh first exhibited, and the street on which King Henri IV was assassinated in 1610 are included. Hotels and restaurants are grouped by price category and contain the minimum necessary details, but no actual prices are given in the very brief descriptions.

Evaluation: Whereas some guidebooks are written by a regular staff who cover all countries, Fodor uses a staff of area specialists. Therefore the various sections of the books are uneven, but all are highly informative. The books are of most use to potential residents of the cities or long-term visitors who have the time to use the extraordinary wealth of detail; typical short-term tourists could be buried in detail. If they do use the Fodor City Guides, however, they will be especially well informed.

Included in the series: London; Paris; Peking; Rome.

Fodor's Country Guides. New York: David McKay Co. approx. 550 pp. $12.95 & $13.95; pap. $9.95 & $10.95. London: Hodder & Stoughton. £3.95-£5.95. Revised annually.

Everything you ever wanted to know about a country is conveniently squeezed into these books. The many contributing writers and editors discuss the countries as a whole, as well as their regions, cities, culture, transportation, history, and numerous other topics, in useful to almost overwhelming detail. Practical information on hotels, restaurants, schools, entertainment, retirement possibilities, visa requirements, roads, and even trailer parks is provided.

Evaluation: It is difficult to imagine a more complete guide to any country. Travelers of all incomes and ages can find exactly what they need in Fodor's Country Guide series. Aimed at those who will spend some time in a country and want to understand what they see, these books take a broad look at the countries they cover, as well as listing more-than-ample details. The only thing left to other guidebooks is details about specific tourist-oriented sights and more extensive coverage of restaurants and hotels, to supplement the brief but accurate details given by Fodor. These well-organized guides should be used by all travelers who want to comprehend what they are seeing.

Included in the series: Austria; Belgium and Luxembourg; Bermuda; Brazil; Czechoslovakia; Egypt; France; Germany; Great Britain; Greece; Holland; Iran; Ireland; Israel; Italy; Jordan and the Holy Land; Portugal; Spain; Switzerland; Tunisia; Turkey; Yugoslavia.

Holiday Guides. New York: Random House. 127 pp. pap. $2.95. Revised periodically.

As an example of this series, *The Holiday Guide to Spain* offers the traveler a concise and informative guide to cities and towns throughout Spain. Preparatory and practical information and major sites are given, with special emphasis on their historical background. Hotels and restaurants from expensive to budget are provided in a separate section and are organized under alphabetic listings of various towns and cities. Transportation is oriented toward travel by car, but information is applicable to other modes of travel.

Evaluation: This handy pocketbook-sized guide offers a brief but informative introduction to travel in Spain. Its special emphasis on history is very informative, as is the information on culture, architecture, and sports. Black-and-white photographs are scattered throughout the book, and the chapter on the Spanish language is also helpful. Since its coverage is not comprehensive, this guide is best used in conjunction with a more detailed guide, especially an accommodation and restaurant guide. It is perhaps most useful for inexperienced travelers, both for pretravel reading and for use on the road.

Included in the series: Britain; London; The Caribbean and the Bahamas; France; Paris; Greece and the Aegean Islands; Hawaii; Ireland; Israel; Italy; Mexico; Scandinavia; Spain; West Germany.

Myra Waldo's Travel Guides. Myra Waldo. New York: Macmillan Publishing Co. 500 pp. pap. $7.95. Revised biennially.

As an example of these guides, *The Orient and Asia* covers 14 countries. The capital cities, described in detail, are used as points of departure, and various excursions from the capitals cover some of the lesser-traveled areas. The ample introduction is quite thorough for the traveler with an unrestricted budget, but lacks tips and information for the budget-conscious traveler. A great deal of attention is paid to background information, sights, and so on. As in Ms. Waldo's other guides, hotel and restaurant information does not contain addresses or telephone numbers. Ms. Waldo also supplies information on shopping and sports. Walking and riding tours are suggested and briefly described.

Evaluation: Myra Waldo's Travel Guide to the Orient and Asia is clearly the best of her series. She provides introductory travel information that is difficult to find in other Asian guides, such as information on weather, the International Date Line, etc. The descriptions of sights and areas disclose information that is not easily found elsewhere. Myra Waldo's style of writing is somewhat discursive and glib, but the information is well organized and easy to find. While accommodations and restaurants are well beyond rock-bottom and moderate budget travelers, *Myra Waldo's Travel Guide to the Orient and Asia* is helpful for travel planning and preparation for all budgets.

Included in the series: Northern Europe; Southern Europe; South America; South Pacific.

Accommodations and Restaurants

Dollars a Day Guides. Arthur Frommer. New York: Arthur Frommer (dist. by Simon & Schuster). 400-700 pp. pap. $4.50. Revised annually.

Frommer's Dollars a Day Guides to various countries provide a wide selection of low- to moderate-budget accommodations and restaurants for the general sightseer interested in saving money, while still traveling in relative comfort. The basic format for the series is the same, although the writers differ. The figures in the title indicate travel budget for accommodation and meals; transportation, sightseeing, and entertainment are extra. Coverage sticks to the major cities.

Evaluation: The goal of this series is to provide a handy collection of budget restaurants and accommodations. Like other Frommer guides, the Dollars a Day series specifically concentrates on the practical aspects of where to eat and sleep; it is very brief on what to see. Travelers interested in historical and cultural information should supplement the series with other guides. As with other accommodations guides sold in large numbers, it directs travelers to places where they are likely to encounter large numbers of others who have also purchased the book.

Included in the series: Australia on $15 a Day; England on $15 a Day; Europe on $15 a Day; Greece on $10 and $15 a Day; Hawaii on $20 a Day; Ireland on $15 a Day; Israel on $15 a Day; Mexico and Guatemala on $10 and $15 a Day; New York on $15 and $20 a Day; New Zealand on $10 and $15 a Day; Scandinavia on $20 a Day; South America on $10 and $15 a Day; Spain and Morocco (plus the Canary

Islands) on $10 and $15 a Day; Turkey on $10 and $15 a Day; Washington, D.C. on $15 a Day.

International Youth Hostel Handbook: Vol. 1—Europe and Mediterranean Countries; Vol. 2—Africa, America, Asia, and Australia. Herts, England: International Youth Hostel Federation (dist. in the U.S. by American Youth Hostels Inc. and American Youth Hostels across the country). 192 pp. pap. $5 (£0.65). Revised annually.

The International Youth Hostel Federation provides simple, inexpensive lodgings for its members around the world. This handbook lists all youth hostels alphabetically by country. Specifics on costs, sizes, telephone numbers, and available facilities are given in three languages. Also included are AYHA regulations, information on how to obtain a Youth Hostel membership card, and how to book accommodations in advance. Background information for each country, such as language, currency, and so on, is briefly covered.

Evaluation: This handbook manages to condense much of the basic information a hosteler needs into pocket-sized form. The information is concise, complete, and, once the symbols are mastered, easy to understand. Included is a map that graphically illustrates hostel locations and major routes. This pocket-sized guide will prove invaluable for hostelers.

Pretravel Reading

ADVENTURE

Adventure Holidays. Oxford, England: Vacation-Work. 231 pp. pap. $6.95. Revised annually.

When "vacation" means an interesting change of activities, *Adventure Holidays* provides information for the reader seeking exciting and sometimes demanding activities as varied as ballooning, orienteering, falconry, or goat keeping. Divided by activities, and within these activities by geographic location, the entries contain addresses, phone numbers, names of program directors, number of years in business, dates, prices, lists of equipment needed, accommodation and meal information, age requirements, whether experience is necessary, and reservation information.

Evaluation: Printed in Great Britain, this catalog of adventure vacations makes the reader rethink what the term *vacation* means. The activities listed for new experiences worldwide are clearly described, with all the information needed in a minimum amount of space. While the adventures are worldwide, there are more listed for Great Britain than for other areas, which are widely spread as the Arctic, the Pacific

Ocean, and Africa. More of a catalog than *Off the Beaten Track* (see below), it resembles the *Worldwide Adventure Travel Guide* (see below), which emphasizes United States adventures. As with both these two books, *Adventure Holidays* is highly recommended for those looking for a change in their traditional vacation activities.

Francis Galton's Art of Travel. Francis Galton. North Pomfret, VT: David & Charles, 1872 (reprinted 1971, 1979). 354 pp. $18.50.

So many people were traveling adventurously in the last century that in 1855 this how-to book was written. It went through eight editions before 1893, attesting to its popularity and usefulness. The author put into his books a huge quantity of information that is important, and often critical, for life in the "wild countries." Topics, each covered in great detail, include preparation for travel, medicine, equipment, fire, domestic animals, guns, signals, management of savages, building materials, and a large variety of others.

Evaluation: This predecessor to today's how-to books on camping and outdoor life is a fascinating journey into the past. While many of the topics covered are no longer of use (how to resilver a sextant glass), some are still current in scout manuals (how to start a fire without matches). The main use of this 1872 book, however, is the sheer pleasure and fascination it offers. It makes excellent fireside reading and affords a good idea of the rigors facing Victorian travelers. It makes an ideal gift for the armchair adventurer.

Off the Beaten Track: A Wexas Travel Handbook. Ingrid Cranfield and Richard Harrington, eds. New York and London: Wexas International, 1977. 255 pp. pap. $9.95.

If you are planning an expedition or want to join one, *Off the Beaten Track* is the book you've been searching for. Wexas, the World Expeditionary Society, was founded in London in 1970 to provide an information and travel service for expeditions. *Off the Beaten Track,* compiled by various authors, tackles practically every aspect of expedition planning imaginable. Additionally, it provides lists of adventure trip operators in the United Kingdom, expeditions, and an annotated bibliography of books and periodicals concerned with off-the-beaten-track travel.

Evaluation: Although Wexas has both a New York and a London base, this guide is distinctly British-oriented. Its British bias is well justified, however, since many of the best expeditions do, in fact, originate in England. This well-written and complete guide provides thorough and interesting information on expedition planning. The individual chapters are written by experts in the field, who contribute firsthand experience in such diverse facets of expedition planning as fund raising, map reading, and government bureaucracies. This guide is not directed toward independent travelers, although some of this information will apply. Sections on health care and photography will be of interest to all out-of-the-way travelers.

Worldwide Adventure Travel Guide. Seattle, WA: American Adventures Association, 1980. 608 pp. pap. $9.95.

Worldwide Adventure Travel Guide is a comprehensive guide to varying forms of adventure travel throughout the world. Included are 3,000 descriptions of adventure trips for land, air, water, and underwater, from skiing to trekking safaris and scuba diving. Chapters are headed by adventure types, listing various adventure trips under individual country headings. Brief descriptions, addresses, telephone numbers, costs and dates for clubs, organizations, and rental agencies are given. This is not a how-to guide, but rather a compilation of some of the adventure trips available around the world.

Evaluation: For the independent traveler seeking unique and adventurous travel alternatives, the *Worldwide Adventure Travel Guide* is an excellent source for ideas about options in adventure travel. This guide lists only the various types of adventure trips available and does not include preparation information or specifics on the trips. The concise descriptions give the reader a sense of what to expect from the trips listed, and the numerous addresses for further information provide the initial steps to planning an adventure trip. The guide is highly recommended for any traveler. Included are exciting excursions to remote areas, which can add spice to anyone's vacation, and not all of the trips described require experience.

BACKPACKING

Travel Light Handbook. See the review of this title in the chapter on North America under United States, Backpacking.

DANCE

The Dance Horizons Travel Guide to Six of the World's Dance Capitals. Sally and Eric Jacobson. Brooklyn, NY: Dance Horizons (dist. in the U.K. by Dance Books, London), 1978. 316 pp. pap. $7.95 (£5).

A new and unique guide, *The Dance Horizons Travel Guide* is devoted entirely to the dance. Six of the world's best-known dance capitals—New York, Washington, D.C., London, Paris, Moscow, and Leningrad—are covered. Each chapter, written by a different author, includes a section on orientation; where, when, and what to see; festivals; dance museums; shopping; publications; and many other dance-related attractions. Addresses and telephone numbers and sometimes seating charts are provided for theaters. The guide is oriented toward dancers, dance aficionados, and any traveler interested in dance.

Evaluation: For professional dancers or those with amateur interest in dance, this indispensable guide presents a great deal of dance-related information in a compact and organized format. It is designed to be used in conjunction with a practical travel guide and is highly recommended for pretravel planning and on-the-road usage.

EMPLOYMENT

Overseas Summer Jobs—1980. C. J. James, ed. Oxford, England: Vacation-Work (dist. in the U.S. by Writer's Digest Books; in Canada by Henry Fletcher Services), 1980. 168 pp. pap. $6.95.

Like other Vacation-Work summer job directories, this book lists a variety of temporary jobs in 41 European, African, North American (minus the United States), and Middle Eastern countries. Most of the jobs are for clerks, custodians, housekeepers, and restaurant help, although many skilled and semiskilled opportunities are included. The entries are divided by country and include the name and address of the employer, positions available, short descriptions, qualifications necessary, and deadlines for applications. Special sections include notes on applying for a job; *au pair;* paying guests and exchange visits; visa, residence, and work regulations for each country; a list of useful publications; and a short section on jobs in England, Scotland, and Wales.

Evaluation: The book gives complete information on finding a job in areas all over the world. The jobs are not always well paying, and most are unglamorous, but they do provide an income for travelers who may lack funds but are interested in an extended visit to a particular area. The information in the job entries is clear and accessible, although the entries lack the details of the job descriptions in the *Directory of Summer Jobs in Britain* (see under Great Britain, Summer Employment). They are meant only as a first step for anyone searching for employment overseas. The book is an excellent pretravel reference to temporary employment opportunities in many parts of the world.

Whole World Handbook: A Student Guide to Work, Study, and Travel Abroad. See the review of this title under Pretravel Reading, Learning Vacations.

GENERAL

Encyclopedia of World Travel: Vol. 1—U.S., Canada, Mexico, Central America, Bermuda, Caribbean, South America; Vol. 2—Europe, Africa, the Middle East, the Pacific. Nelson Doubleday and C. Earl Cooley, eds. Garden City, NY: Doubleday & Co., 4th ed., 1979. 1,290 pp. $16.95.

This two-volume reference work gives brief background information on the countries and major cities of North, Central, and South America, Europe, Africa, Asia, and the Pacific. The countries are arranged alphabetically by continent. Each entry includes descriptions of the country's land, climate, people, agriculture, industry, sports and recreation, special events, dining, and shopping, along with short descriptions of major cities and population areas. Maps are provided of each major area, and many photographs are included among the entries.

Evaluation: What the book lacks in detail it makes up in scope. Every area of the world except Greenland and Antarctica is covered in the entries, and the information, although brief, gives a solid overview of the basic characteristics of each different country. The book was meant as a travel reference such as those frequently found in libraries. In this capacity, it serves well, but as practical travel literature, its use is limited by the emphasis on general inclusion.

44 lbs. or Size and Piece. Virginia Jansen. Pinedale, CA: Jansen Publishing (dist. by Caroline House Publishers), 1978. 58 pp. pap. $3.50.

Everyone packs when traveling. *44 lbs. or Size and Piece* makes that an understandable process. In it, the author discusses the appropriate number and size of bags, and the advantages of various styles of luggage and other bags. What to put into the bags is carefully covered, with a focus on clothing, shoes, and travel paraphernalia. A myriad of tips on how to pack are included, as are checklists for pretravel activities and what to take.

Evaluation: For the novice traveler, *44 lbs. or Size and Piece* will bring peace of mind well worth the price. While the author assumes that her readers are mostly middle-class adult women, the information the book contains is equally useful to all travelers. The reader should not be put off by the overly cute writing style. Much of value is here. For the first-time traveler, all the basic details are included. See also the review of *The Best European Travel Tips* under Europe, Pretravel Reading, for a similar book.

International Meet-the-People Directory. Washington, DC: International Visitors Information Service, 1980. 23 pp. pap. $1.

This directory, compiled by the International Visitors Information Service (IVIS), lists addresses in 34 countries around the world for meet-the-people and other comparable programs and provides a brief description of programs in each country. For those travelers seeking unique experiences and wishing to see how people all around the world live, this style of travel will be of much interest. The *International Meet-the-People Directory* will prove invaluable to them.

1001 Sources for Free Travel Information. Jens Jurgen. King's Park, NY: Travel Information Bureau, 1978. 144 pp. pap. $5.50.

1001 Sources for Free Travel Information was written as a pretravel reference providing addresses for tourist offices of every country, state, province, and territory. The book begins with a checklist of available literature and maps, followed by information on developing a travel library, help from airlines, travel films, and a confusing discussion on how to get the airlines to pay for your expenses. The lists of addresses that make up most of the book are arranged alphabetically by country, state, and province and sometimes include embassy, mission, and national airline addresses. Special sections include information on moving within the United States and abroad, tips on travel preparation, U.S. government publications, information for students, a list of major hotel/motel chains, travel to the Middle East and China, and how to use scheduled stopovers to see more on your trip for no extra charge.

Evaluation: For travelers who are willing to put in hours of pretravel research to save a few dollars on their trip, the book could be useful. But much of the information, apart from the long lists of addresses, can be found in other more complete travel guides, and in a much clearer manner. The sections on cutting costs are confusing, incomplete, and patronizing, with the word *free* appearing time and again in bold, over-sized print. The information in the different sections nearly always ends with a reference to where more thorough information can be acquired, so that the book is only the beginning of the research. Travelers with time on their hands and a compulsion for saving money may find the book worthwhile, though they should note that it is far from free.

Pan Am's World Guide: The Encyclopedia of Travel. New York: McGraw-Hill Book Co., 25th ed., 1980. 1,118 pp. $8.95.

As an authoritative reference for the prospective traveler to any part of the world, Pan Am's encyclopedia covers 162 countries. Its all-encompassing nature necessitates brevity. The country chapters are composed of general background information and statistics; information on currency and restaurant accommodations; sightseeing recommendations; entertainment; sports; shopping; and practical information such as customs regulations and airport information. Pan Am routes and air travel times serve as transportation information to specific countries. Directed at the commercial airline user, the book suggests prices that fall into the moderate to expensive range.

Evaluation: Considering the scope of the book, the material is well organized, concise, and complete. The information, however, does not go beyond a traditional tourist or business visitor orientation. This guide should well suffice for a stopover or short visit to major cities. More specialized guides should be consulted for longer stays or journeys to nonurban areas.

Rand McNally Traveler's Almanac: The International Guide. Nancy Meyer, ed. Los Angeles, CA: Bill Muster (dist. by Rand McNally & Co.). 320 pp. pap. $7.95. Revised annually.

The *Traveler's Almanac* is a planning guide, not a guidebook. It is composed of a series of articles treating subjects ranging from air travel to vagabonding, and it attempts to fulfill the needs of wealthy and budget-conscious travelers alike. In addition to chapters on different travel modes and philosophies, the worldwide touring guide chapter details the practicalities of travel to some 200 destinations and includes general information on transportation, accommodations, food, and entertainment.

Evaluation: Pan Am's World Guide (see above) presents a good deal more specific information on individual countries than does *Rand McNally Traveler's Almanac.* Pan Am, however, does not include the series of articles introducing different travel possibilities, such as vagabonding. For the novice voyager, the *Traveler's Almanac* presents a wide range of such travel modes. Helpful features are the thorough index and the specific book suggestions for further information.

Time Off: A Psychological Guide to Vacations. See the review of this title in the chapter on North America under United States, Pretravel Reading.

Traveling the World Abroad. Wilson Strand, ed. Holland, MI: Travelwise. 120 pp. pap. $6.95. Revised annually.

This book, like its companion, *Traveling in Greece and Cyprus,* contains references to travel articles published in a variety of magazines. It features synopses of a large number of articles published in the year preceding the book's publication date and lists many others published earlier. Listings are divided by country, and all the magazines referred to can be found in a medium-sized library. The book on Greece and Cyprus contains very brief personal recommendations to sights, hotels, and restaurants.

Evaluation: Traveling the World Abroad is an excellent source for pretravel reading, specialized and general, old and new, for all travelers. This is the first guide of its kind, and it provides travelers a service not found elsewhere. It includes a large variety of articles.

Information presented is brief, but adequate for library research, and is presented clearly. The book has one underlying goal—to provide a complete source of free travel background information. And to this end it is very successful.

Included in the series: Traveling in Greece and Cyprus.

Worldwide What and Where: Geographic Glossary and Traveler's Guide. Ralph De Sola. Santa Barbara, CA: Clio Press, 1975. 720 pp. $13.65.

Worldwide What and Where is an unusual reference for travelers. It lists countries, cities, mountains, natural wonders, foreign words and phrases, international abbreviations, parks, rivers, lakes, geographic terms, and many other odds and ends, all arranged alphabetically. Listings for the Netherlands are found between "nephology" (the study of clouds) and "neu" (German, "new"), while information on Amsterdam is located 360 pages away between "Amritsar" (a city in Pakistan) and "Amu Darya" (the name of a river in Central Asia). It is obvious that the practicality of this method of organization for someone seeking travel information is severely limited.

Evaluation: Because the book is in glossary form and the information in the entries is kept to skeletal descriptions, it is most useful as a reference to common and obscure geographic place-names, small cities in small countries, and other odd bits of information. The book has little value to travelers other than as a pretravel reference; much more detailed practical and background information could be acquired more easily from other sources.

HANDICAPPED TRAVELERS

Access to the World: A Travel Guide for the Handicapped. Louise Weiss. New York: The Chatham Square Press, 1977. 178 pp. $7.95.

Access to the World: A Travel Guide for the Handicapped is an indispensable reference for the handicapped traveler. Its purpose is to inform the handicapped traveler of various travel options. There are separate chapters on transportation options, including accessibility of airports, specific airlines, and other forms of transportation. Facilities and accessibility of various hotels and motels are listed, with addresses, for major cities, and an extensive bibliography for guidebooks and pamphlets is also included. Another chapter is devoted to travel agencies and special tours. Although the majority of coverage focuses on the United States, other worldwide destinations are also included.

Evaluation: Access to the World is a valuable, well-organized reference for the handicapped traveler. It is very sensitive to the problems and hesitations facing a handicapped traveler and successfully dispels doubts and fears by providing a positive and informative basis for pretravel planning. The author further stresses the fact that a handicapped traveler can travel independently. This guide is highly recommended for pretravel planning for any handicapped person.

HEALTH

How to Travel and Stay Healthy. Duff Henry Pfanner. Smithtown, NY: Exposition Press, 1979. 67 pp. pap. $5.

The purpose of the book is to "inform the traveler of the precautions he can take to prevent the diseases he will be likely to encounter in his journeys." It is geared primarily to international travelers and includes information on prescriptions, vaccinations, food and water, basic first aid kits, and diseases currently encountered by travelers. There is a discussion of prevention and a long list of basic first aid advice on the most frequently occurring problems (insect bites, burns, blisters, and so on). The book is meant as pretravel reading and possibly as a reference on the road.

Evaluation: One rarely thinks about falling ill on an overseas trip, but it definitely happens. *How to Travel and Stay Healthy* discusses the occurrence of all types of ailments, common and exotic, that a traveler may encounter. It is a relatively expensive book for its size, and much of the information could be gleaned from other free sources, but many may find it convenient to have all the necessary information in one place. Whether this book would be useful to a particular traveler depends on the travel style and the length of the stay. For those on long trips to lightly traveled areas, the book should be required reading. Others may find that common sense will suffice.

The Year-Round Travelers' Health Guide. Patrick J. Doyle, M.D., M.P.H., and Janet E. Banta, M.D., M.P.H. Washington, DC: Acropolis Books, 1978. 144 pp. pap. $4.95.

Written by two well-traveled doctors, this guide attempts to answer all health-related travel questions. The purpose, as stated in the introduction, is "to serve as a guide to good general health habits" for the traveler. The book is geared to those with or without specific health problems and includes advice on traveling with children, the handicapped, and senior citizens, immunization, first aid and medicine, and health tips for campers. It is organized into three sections: "Going There," "Over There," and "Back Home."

Evaluation: The Year-Round Travelers' Health Guide is an indispensable source for dispelling travelers' doubts and insecurities regarding health questions while traveling. It can be useful for at-home planning as well as on-the-road reference. The guide is organized thematically by chapters, such as "Traveling with Children." Such a broad chapter title consists of a little more than one page. This brevity is typical of most chapters; the advice given, however, is all useful and practical. It is written by doctors who understand travel anxieties and deal with them in a reassuring and professional manner.

HEALTH SPAS

The Health Spas: World Guidebook to Health Spas, Mineral Baths, and Nature-Cure Centers. Robert Yaller and Raye Yaller. Santa Barbara, CA: Woodbridge Press Publishing Co. (dist. in the U.K. by Thorsons Publishers), 1974. 158 pp. pap. $2.95 (£1.95).

The emphasis of the book is on health maintenance and natural cures through therapeutic use of mineral water, along with other nonmedicinal remedies such as fasting, hydrotherapy, electrotherapy, massage, high colonics, fresh air, sunshine, recreation, rest, pleasant surroundings, and exercise. The book is divided into four parts. The first is an introduction to the spas, describing the similarities and differences among them and giving the philosophy behind nature-cure centers; the second section discusses special kinds of spas—for diet, for nutrition, and for treating chronic diseases. Spas in 11 European countries, the United States, Mexico, the Soviet Union, Israel, and Japan are described in the third section, with references to specific diseases treated, special facilities, and addresses for more information. The last section is a short list of special information on who treats what, health spa terminology, and typical spa menus.

Evaluation: This book takes a much different approach to therapeutic bathing from other "hot water" guides. It covers a much larger area, but includes much less information on each spa (most of the entries are merely descriptions, with references to a variety of common and exotic diseases) and lists only selected sites. The entries include no practical information on the spas, and the information is unevenly distributed (Czechoslovakian spas are described in detail, Italian spas are listed with the address only). The book serves as an introduction to health spas and nature-cure centers, but more information than is provided in this book will be needed before picking one to visit.

ISLANDS OF THE WORLD

The Islands Series. North Pomfret, VT and Devon, England: David & Charles, 1973-1979. approx. 200 pp. $9.95–$18.95 (£1.75-£4.95).

The islands described in the series differ so much in size, location, physical setting, and history that it seems the only thing they have in common is that they are all islands. Yet the books that describe them share many characteristics; all emphasize history and descriptions of the past and present cultures that have developed on the islands. All include references to their geography, geology, climate, wildlife, and economy, and all feature many pages of photographs showing scenes of urban and rural life. Long bibliographies and complete indexes are included in the back of each book.

Evaluation: The series provides detailed background information on a wide range of subjects pertaining to the islands—so detailed that only readers with an unquenchable interest in the different characteristics of the islands can slug their way through the slow-moving text. The descriptions include many obscure scientific and historic references that mean very little to the average traveler, and probably not much more to scholars in different fields. The books are most useful as pretravel references, although the detail in the entries is much more than most travelers need. On the road, a guide with more practical travel information should be used.

Included in the series: The Aran Islands; Canary Islands: Fuerteventura; Corsica; Cyprus; Dominica; The Falkland Islands; Grand Bahama; Harris and Lewis Lundy; The Isle of Arran; The Isle of Mull; The Maltese Islands; Orkney; Puerto Rico; St. Kilda and the Other Hebridean Outliers; The Seychelles; Shetland; Singapore; Skye; The Solomon Islands; Vancouver Island.

LEARNING VACATIONS

Learning Vacations. See the review of this title under North America, Learning Vacations.

Whole World Handbook: A Student Guide to Work, Study, and Travel Abroad. Council on International Educational Exchange. New York: CIEE and Frommer/Pasmantier Publishing Corp. 368 pp. pap. $3.95. Revised biennially.

In its fourth edition and new compact size, the *Whole World Handbook* remains an important clearinghouse of information, ideas, and addresses for short-term or long-term travel, work, and study abroad. Directed to students, the *Handbook* is organized by area with essential information and specifics on individual countries. It is not a guidebook as such; travel is only one of the topics it covers.

Evaluation: Intended to be used in the United States before leaving, the *Whole World Handbook* is packed with information and is well organized and comprehensive. A resource for literally hundreds of names and addresses, the *Whole World Handbook* is one of the best books available on work, study, and travel opportunities around the world. The authors put forth a wide range of suggestions without pretending to have all the answers. For student travelers, the *Handbook* is a topflight reference to other guidebooks.

World Study and Travel for Teachers. Richard J. Brett. Washington, DC: American Federation of Teachers. 64 pp. pap. $1.50. Regularly revised.

Prepared in cooperation with the American Federation of Teachers, *World Study and Travel for Teachers* lists worldwide educational trips and sabbaticals sponsored by universities in 28 states. The 352 programs offered include, among others, ancient Greek drama, culture in Hawaii, kibbutz education, silversmithing, Soviet politics, health professions, a variety of art and social studies programs, languages, volcanology, tropical marine biology, and the music of Bach. The entries are divided into summer and nonsummer programs and are arranged by continent and field of study (arts, education, science, and so on). Each entry includes the specific subject areas, countries included, college credit available, cost (other than tuition), U.S. departure point, dates, deadlines, restrictions or prerequisites, an address for more information or reservations, and a brief description of the program. In the back of the book are indexes of the colleges and universities, the countries for which programs are listed, and the subject areas.

Evaluation: Although the book was intended to be used primarily by teachers, the variety of programs listed in all parts of the world will be of interest to anyone looking for a thinking vacation. The information in the book is fairly complete and easy to find, and the frequent editions insure that it is as up-to-date as possible. However, the descriptions of the programs do not all list parallel information. Some include no mention of costs, some do not give definite dates, and some merely refer to an address. The detail of the descriptions also varies from entry to entry. *Learning Vacations* (see under North America, Learning Vacations) is a little older and contains fewer entries, but it covers outdoor activities, lists many trips in the United States, and distributes the information more evenly. However they may differ, both books serve equally as pretravel references for the scholastically inclined.

LOW-BUDGET TRAVEL

The Art and Adventure of Traveling Cheaply. Rich Berg. Berkeley, CA: And/Or Press, 1979. 226 pp. pap. $4.95.

The Art and Adventure of Traveling Cheaply is a compilation of pretravel advice for the independent young traveler interested in rock-bottom traveling. It is directed toward travel in underdeveloped countries, away from modern conveniences. Hitchhiking is the most-emphasized mode of transportation but other alternatives are offered as well. Alternative accommodations, such as army barracks and monasteries, are recommended. This guide also contains information on medical problems and treatment, food, bargaining in markets, and profiting on the black market. Emphasis is on traveling slowly to attain the most cultural appreciation and to make the most cultural contact while spending the least amount of money.

Evaluation: Traveling Cheaply contains lots of practical advice derived from firsthand experiences. However, some of the advice on how to save money is rather underhanded, to the point sometimes of taking advantage of underdeveloped countries. The author's attitude at times would seem to further the distrust that many underdeveloped countries have toward tourists. Much of the advice is insightful and offers good suggestions and anecdotes for off-the-beaten-track travelers.

How to Travel without Being Rich. Norman D. Ford. Floral Park, NY: Harian Books, 1978. 160 pp. pap. $4.95. Revised periodically.

How to Travel without Being Rich is a guide for worldwide travel, filled with low-cost travel tips. Norman Ford, author of many travel guidebooks, advocates cheap travel on age-old trade and caravan routes. He provides the how-to's for finding travel bargains and supplies information for transatlantic travel as well as Central American and U.S. travel. Many different transportation alternatives are given. In addition, itineraries for continental and around-the-world travel are suggested.

Evaluation: This guidebook fills a gap in travel literature by providing low-cost travel tips that cross geographic and continental boundaries. The same glib, overconfident style that characterizes most Ford/Harian publications is evident here, but it is balanced by much useful, practical information. While low-cost hotels are briefly mentioned, no specifics on accommodations are provided, and information on food and restaurants is not included. However, this useful guide certainly will be of interest for pretravel planning for worldwide, U.S., and transcontinental travelers.

Vagabonding. Ed Buryn. New York: Random House—The Bookworks, 1973. 247 pp. pap. $5.95.

Students going to Europe often want to travel in the rock-bottom category. For them *Let's Go: The Budget Guide to Europe* (see under Europe, Comprehensive Guides) and *Whole World Handbook* (see above, under Learning Vacations) were written. But for people who desire a still rockier bottom, *Vagabonding* was written. *Vagabonding* begins with a discussion of the travel style from which it takes its name, followed by chapters on where to get further information, when to go (when you have the money), how to get there and with whom, packing, hitchhiking, walking, bicycling, trains, cars, camping, accommodations (or lack thereof), how to meet people, and other miscellaneous information. Near the end of the book, two or three paragraphs are given to sketch a quick image of the countries of eastern and western Europe. Addresses and bibliographic references are amply provided throughout.

Evaluation: Self-described as an underground classic, *Vagabonding* was written in a style that appeals to those who feel outside the mainstream of culture. The information provided, however, is sound and accurate—or at least it was in 1973. Readers should regard fondly prices that are now almost ten years old; this financial antiquity is one of the serious drawbacks of the book. On the other hand, for the inexperienced traveler, whether alternative life-style or middle-class student, this is an excellent book. The pretravel information is much more extensive than either *Whole World Handbook* or *Let's Go: Europe* is able to provide, and in spite of its self-conscious attempt to be "underground" and alternate, it is a thorough pretravel preparation book that would be useful to all rock-bottom travelers. Unfortunately, the time-related information has not been changed to protect the innocent. Still, the work may be regarded as a classic, even for those above ground. A more updated collection of travel hints can be found in *The Best European Travel Tips* (see under Europe, Pretravel Reading). While that title and text style may not appeal to those who see themselves as vagabonds, its information is more up-to-date and just as inclusive. The combination of both books would be like a million dollars' worth of insurance. Take your pick. Both are highly recommended as pretravel reading.

LUXURY TRAVEL

Travel at Its Best. Al Schwartz. Brookline, MA: Branden Press, 1978. 280 pp. pap. $9.95.

Travel at Its Best is not a travel guide, but rather a compilation of travel destinations based on the author's selection of "the most exciting places one might ever hope to visit." Out-of-the-way, rural spots are stressed, with only the most expensive hotels and restaurants listed. The book is divided into three sections, the first containing brief introductory information on the author's personal favorites. The second section tells how to select the best California and French wines, and the third section is a collection of the author's favorite recipes from various restaurants. The descriptions of individual countries are sketchy, and food and restaurants are emphasized. Color photographs are scattered throughout the book.

Evaluation: Geared to only those with luxury travel in mind, *Travel at Its Best* could appeal to a very limited audience. Most of the book consists of the author's subjective impressions and personal experiences, and hence would only be useful as light, pretravel reading, offering an introduction to those looking for different travel options. For the price, there is not enough information to make it worth the money.

You Can See the World in 40 Days. Leland T. Waggoner. New York: Arco Publishing Co., 1978. 240 pp. $5.25; pap. $2.45.

You Can See the World in 40 Days is the author's account of his travels from Los Angeles to New York via various stops in parts of the South Pacific, Australia, Indonesia, Asia, and southern Europe. His approach is based on preplanned, group travel for the high-budget traveler. Emphasis is given to charter flights, and information on the advantages of travel agencies and charter flights is given, a now-unfortunate inclusion since charters are no longer as advantageous as they once were. Brief descriptions of the author's impressions and experiences in each country or city along with historical and cultural background make up the majority of the book. "World-famous" hotels and restaurants are suggested by the author, with lists of the most-visited sights.

Evaluation: More of a personal narrative than a travel guidebook, this book may be useful for pretravel reading for first-time travelers, providing orientation and suggestions to the lesser-traveled vacation spots for conventional travelers. Little practical information is given, and descriptions and information are scanty and subjective. No addresses are given for hotels, restaurants, or sights. A more informative and all-encompassing guide would be more useful.

OLDER ADULT TRAVELERS

Now It's Your Turn to Travel. Rosalind Massow. New York: Collier Books, Macmillan Publishing Co., 1976. 339 pp., pap. $4.95.

This travel guide is for "mature people," for the frankly 40 to the energetic 70- or 80-year-olds. Coverage includes selective popular destinations around the world, including the United States and Canada. Travel style is oriented toward ease and comfort, and travel with a theme, such as art, music, wildlife, or retracing one's ethnic roots, is advocated. Travel preparations, health tips, suggested tours and excursions, and various transportation alternatives are covered, as well as descriptions of various cities and sights.

Evaluation: For the older, inexperienced traveler, this guide will be a good source of travel possibilities with a minimum of difficulty. Information is very selective and general, and coverage for each country is not uniform. *Now It's Your Turn to Travel* is not designed for on-the-road use, but rather as pretravel planning. Once a trip is planned, a more extensive and detailed travel guide will be necessary. The book is one of the few travel guides geared to elderly travelers.

OVERLANDING

Overland. Peter Fraenkel. North Pomfret, VT and Devon, England: David & Charles, 1975. 156 pp. $14.50 (£4.95).

Overland attempts to answer the questions of travelers planning a long journey on four wheels. The author's experience includes over 100,000 miles of overland travel on three continents, and he calls upon this experience and that of other travelers to describe planning, preparation, equipment, maintenance and repairs, hazards, navigation, camping, food, water, and emergencies. Although no specific routes are included, the book emphasizes travel in Africa, Asia, and Europe and is intended primarily for British travelers. Many cost-cutting tips are included, as well as advice on avoiding certain problems. Special sections include checklists for equipment and information, how to record the journey, a bibliography and appendixes on personal and communal equipment, vehicle documents, medical kits, useful addresses, and basic vocabularies.

Evaluation: Even though the book is over five years old, most of the information included is as useful now as it was when it was written. The book emphasizes planning, preparation, and problem avoidance, leaving the particulars of the journey up to the traveler or other guidebooks. The information included is complete, easy to find, and very useful, but it would be necessary to supplement this information with more current practical travel information on the road. Other guidebooks to overland travel are more up-to-date and include more essential on-the-road information, but few can match the quality and detail of the preparatory information in this guide.

Overlanding: How to Explore the World on Four Wheels. John Steele Gordon. New York: Harper & Row, Publishers, 1975. 328 pp. pap. $4.95.

"Overlanding is the land-lover's equivalent of sailing; the long, slow crossing of large areas of the world" by motor vehicle, preferably one with four-wheel drive. This challenging mode of travel is for only the adventurous and hardy. *Overlanding* is packed with instructions on preparation and execution of long-distance voyages. Not a guide to specific places, the book concentrates on practicalities that apply to all countries.

Evaluation: As much a philosophy of travel as a transportation guide, the book covers both the practical and subjective aspects of overlanding. Not many guides exist for this special mode of travel, and this guide is extremely well researched and documented in all aspects of overlanding. Especially good are sections on preparation. Unfortuately, inflation has rendered the prices listed obsolete. Nonetheless, *Overlanding* is invaluable for potential overlanders, both for pretravel reading and reference once on the road.

RAILWAYS

Eurail Guide: How to Travel Europe and All the World by Train. Marvin L. Saltzman and Kathryn Saltzman Muileman. Malibu, CA: The Saltzman Cos. (dist. in the U.K. by Lascelles [Roger]). 816 pp. pap. $9.95 (£4.50). Revised annually.

The Saltzman family publishes this guide annually for inexperienced and experienced travelers alike. All aspects of train travel, from Eurailpasses to the Trans-Siberian Express, are handled in this small but thick pocket book. This guide concentrates on showing the reader how to manage on one's own traveling by train and includes preparation and helpful hints for train travel. Detailed itineraries, approximate train schedules and rates, one-day excursions, and scenic train routes are some of the topics covered. The guide is organized by individual countries, including a chapter on train travel in the United States. Some sights are included.

Evaluation: This informative guide should be of special interest to the neophyte traveler who intends to cover a lot of territory by train; it describes many aspects of train travel. Especially helpful are the chapters on valuable train travel tips and descriptions of train travel in individual countries. Experienced independent travelers might want to scan this guide before taking off; more inexperienced travelers might read it carefully and take it along in addition to a sights/accommodations guide. While its major focus is on the European countries, other destinations are also covered.

Fodor's Railways of the World. New York: David McKay Co., 1977. 374 pp. pap. $9.95.

Fodor's Railways of the World is a guide to train travel in 101 countries around the world, including the United States and Canada. The advantages of train travel are given, as well as pretravel planning. Description of train travel, suggestions for train passes, and train routes are included. Special scenic train routes are given in addition to various destination routes such as the San Francisco Zephyr, or Le Mistral in France. Train stations are cited for some of the countries along with taxi and bus service from the station to downtown areas. Description of speed, types of engines, services available, and sometimes historical background are also provided. Railway museums around the world are also included.

Evaluation: Anyone considering train travel in any part of the world will be better informed after consulting *Fodor's Railways of the World.* This guide's main use is for pretravel planning, and the book is geared mainly to first-class train travel. The information is not uniform since it is a compilation by different authors. Some countries, like the United States, are described in great detail, and others have mainly general introductions and descriptions. However, this guide is well organized and informative and allows the intrepid traveler to expand itinerary possibilities.

SHIP TRAVEL

Fodor's Cruises Everywhere. Eugene Fodor and Robert C. Fisher, eds. New York: David McKay Co. 366 pp. $12.95; pap. $9.95. London: Hodder & Stoughton. £6.50. Revised annually.

Fodor's Cruises Everywhere 1977 is the first edition of an annually revised guide to cruises. Although cruising is probably out of the price range of the student or low-to-moderate-budget traveler, Fodor's cruise guide properly suggests that the average cruise cost of $50–$70 a day (including three-plus gourmet meals) is best compared to costs for an elegant land-based resort. For those who can foot that bill, *Cruises Everywhere* is a complete guide to the waterways of the world and the ships that cruise them. The one area not covered is Africa, since the editors felt that political conditions and cruise itineraries were too uncertain at the time of writing to warrant inclusion in the present edition.

Evaluation: Like other Fodor's guides, *Cruises Everywhere* is well researched and thorough. Its 90-page introduction includes helpful information on planning, money-saving ideas, and an excellent picture of luxurious shipboard life—a feature helpful to those who are still deciding on whether to choose a cruise. The introduction also addresses the concerns of the single cruise traveler and of retired persons. In a section entitled "World Cruise Areas," *Fodor's Cruises Everywhere* gives an overview of costs, the best time of year to go, and what ports to visit for each of the cruise areas identified. Another section describes representative cruises. The guide concludes with extensive sections on individual ports, shipping lines and their ships, and a schedule of cruises for the year. Expected yearly updates should keep this a current and useful volume, especially when supplemented with a guide to the ports to be visited.

Ford's Freighter Travel Guide. Merrian E. Clark, ed. Woodland Hills, CA: Ford's Travel Guides. 152 pp. pap. $4.95. Revised semiannually.

Published semiannually, *Ford's Freighter Travel Guide* is the complete guide to worldwide freighter travel. The introduction acclimates travelers to life aboard ship, with information on living quarters, food, medical aid, preparation, itineraries, clothing, sea jargon, and weather. The trips are listed by the ports of departure, with the different ports arranged geographically. The entries include descriptions of the routes, passenger fares, restrictions, and addresses for further information. Special sections are included on the Alaska Marine Highway System, foreign government tourist offices, a ports-of-call index, an index of passenger-carrying freighters, a directory of travel agents handling freighter passenger business, and an index of steamship lines.

Evaluation: The book provides a service not to be found elsewhere. The information is complete, well organized, and very easy to find. The introductory section offers travelers a brief glimpse of what freighter travel can be like and gives useful background for travelers unfamiliar with sea-going vessels. The many indexes and cross-references make the book relatively easy to use, though it may call for plenty of page turning. Many photographs, maps, and illustrations complement the text. The book is an excellent pretravel reference for anyone interested in a vacation aboard a freighter.

Ford's International Cruise Guide. Merrian E. Clark, ed. Woodland Hills, CA: Ford's Travel Guides. 160 pp. pap. $5.95. Revised 4 times/yr.

Like its sister publication on freighter travel (see above), *Ford's International Cruise Guide* describes cruises around the world and the ships that make them possible. It begins with questions and answers for travelers planning their first cruise and a list of travel agents specializing in cruise travel. Photographs and descriptions are provided of 84 cruise ships, listing the size and facilities of each. The cruises are divided geographically by their port of departure. Most of the trips described originate from North American ports, though many other countries, including those in Europe and the Mediterranean, are well represented. The entries include a description of the route, sailing dates, cruise fares, and addresses of steamship lines. A cruise ship calendar is included for each area. Many photographs, illustrations, and advertisements are included, as well as ports of call and cruise ship indexes.

Evaluation: Because it is published quarterly, it would be difficult to find a cruise guide as up-to-date as this. The information for first-time travelers is not as complete as that provided in the guide to freighter travel, but one of the features of a cruise vacation is that less intensive preparation is necessary. The information in the entries for the individual cruises is clear and fairly complete, though no information is included on shipboard activities or entertainment. The book is very useful as a pretravel reference for anyone contemplating a cruise vacation.

Vacation at Sea: A Travel Guide for Cruises. Else Daniels and Bennet Daniels. New York: Cornerstone Library (dist. by Simon & Schuster), 1979. 178 pp. pap. $5.95.

Vacation at Sea is a full description of what cruise vacations are like, from packing and reservations to debarkation. The book shows a cruise as a very social activity, and it emphasizes how to make the most of the trip for all travelers, young and old, rich and less rich. It begins by comparing a cruise vacation with a trip to heaven and becomes more optimistic with every page. The authors try to dispel some common apprehensions of noncruisers, describing this style of travel as soothing, peaceful, economical, safe, and memorable. Sections are included on reviewing the passenger list, selecting and booking a particular cruise, the deck plan, travel agents, packing, embarkation, on-board activities, a glossary of nautical terms, the crew, cuisine, health, tipping, ports-of-call shopping and sightseeing, and the return. Special sections are included for young travelers, the handicapped, technology buffs, and photographers.

Evaluation: The emphasis on descriptions in the entries suggests that the book's best use is as pretravel reading to provide a feel for what cruise vacations are about. The preparatory and background information is presented clearly and includes all the necessary particulars. In the past, cruise vacations were solely for those with means and plenty of time. Now, however, this method of travel has been opened up to those with limited funds and on regimented schedules. The quality and completeness of the preparatory information make this guide an excellent complement to a book with full information on the cruise lines and schedules, such as *Ford's International Cruise Guide* (see above).

SOLO TRAVELERS

Everywoman's Guide to Travel. Donna Goldfein. Millbrae, CA: Les Femmes Publishing, 1977. 128 pp. $3.95.

Everywoman's Guide to Travel is a short guide containing practical information and travel tips from a seasoned traveler for women traveling alone on business trips or short vacations. The majority of this guide offers a practical approach to organization of time, wardrobe, and attitude, all taken care of by proper and in-depth planning. Emphasis is on comfort, and Goldfein stresses that with proper planning one need not sacrifice comfort for economy. While this guide is not geared to those traveling on a low budget, travel tips are given that can cut down on costs.

Evaluation: Intended as a pretravel guide to planning and organization for women, *Everywoman's Guide* is filled with practical information for taking the stress out of travel for women who are bothered by such things as having dinner alone and who feel that travel imposes too many inconveniences. Travel tips are geared to those staying at conventional hotels. For those women who travel frequently on short business trips or take occasional short holidays alone, this guide would be beneficial.

A Guide for Solo Travel Abroad. Eleanor Adams Baxel. Stockbridge, MA: The Berkshire Traveller Press, 1979. 231 pp. pap. $5.50.

The title indicates that this book is for those traveling alone, but the information it contains can be used by all travelers, with a few exceptions. In a conversational style, Eleanor Baxel presents the reader with ideas on what is involved in traveling alone, followed by information regarding expenses, travel options, travel agents, luggage and packing, theft, car rental and purchase, travel practicalities, restaurant information, relationships with the opposite sex, and shopping hints.

Evaluation: Definitely a pretravel book for first-time travelers, this volume should reassure and encourage the timid. It provides an almost endless list of tips and anecdotes written in a style that makes the reading more like listening to a well-traveled friend. *Solo Travel Abroad* is very similar to *The Best European Travel Tips* by John Whitman (see under Europe, Pretravel Reading). While Whitman is better organized, *Solo Travel Abroad* covers more areas of the world. Whitman includes information on more topics, but *Solo Travel Abroad* is more fun to read. An accommodation and restaurant guide and a sights guide will definitely be needed on the road; this book should be read, appreciated, and left at home.

TRAVEL WRITING

The Travel Writer's Handbook. Louise Purwin Zobel. Cincinnati, OH: Writer's Digest Books, 1980. 274 pp. $11.95.

The Travel Writer's Handbook discusses many ways of turning travel experiences into marketable copy. It stresses that previous writing experience is helpful but far from necessary. Sections are included on how to think like a travel writer, what to look for while traveling, pretravel research, how best to use a library, proper marketing, defining an audience, preparation, special equipment necessary, how to put it all together, selling material before and after it is written, writing queries to editors, interviewing techniques, photography, tax deductions, and the special role of a travel writer. Many story and article ideas are included, as well as useful addresses, reference works, a number of tips on how best to prepare for a trip, and, most importantly, useful tips on how to sell ideas.

Evaluation: The advice and helpful tips given by the author offer valuable short-cuts for would-be travel writers. The book makes it possible to avoid many common problems and helps writers define their goals and their audience, prepare for the unexpected, and arrive home to a waiting editor ready to buy the article before it is written. The information is presented clearly and covers many different aspects of travel writing. The sections on how to deal with editors and the 12 most popular types of travel articles are particularly useful to those with little or no professional writing experience. The book is an excellent introduction to the field of travel writing, although its optimism about the readiness of editors to buy whatever may cross their desks should be tempered a little.

AFRICA

COMPREHENSIVE GUIDES

Africa A to Z. See A to Z World Travel Guides under The World, Comprehensive Guides.

Africa Guide. Essex, England: D. Jamieson & Associates (dist. in the U.S. by Rand McNally & Co.). 366 pp. pap. $16.95 (£6.95). Revised annually.

Africa Guide is an annual publication that aims to provide a comprehensive and up-to-date presentation of important issues and facts about contemporary Africa. It is not a travel guide in the traditional sense; it is directed primarily at businesspeople, but also addresses government officials, journalists, researchers, and travelers. The guide begins with a series of articles concerning African political development, economy, social affairs, and travel. The "Country-by-Country" section includes a summary of the history, economy, and political affairs of each country and a section concerned with travel and business.

Evaluation: Although the *Africa Guide* is directed principally toward businesspeople, the information contained would be of interest to other travelers as well. The guide has great value as an annual publication, keeping abreast of conditions in an area where radical changes occur frequently. Its greatest asset is the section concerned with contemporary political Africa; the travel sections are somewhat brief and limited in scope.

HITCHHIKING

Africa for the Hitchhiker. Fin Biering-Sorensen and Torben Jorgense. Copenhagen: Bramsen and Hjort (dist. in the U.S. by the Council on International Educational Exchange), 1974. 159 pp. pap. $4.95.

Africa for the Hitchhiker is chiefly concerned with the practicalities of rock-bottom travel in Africa. "Hitchhiking" is assumed to mean more than bumming rides; for the author, it implies a very close contact with people in the countries where one travels. Other modes of travel such as trains and buses are therefore covered as well. A thorough introductory chapter is followed by six brief possible itineraries and a complete rundown on all countries in Africa.

Evaluation: The focus on cheap travel excludes cultural, historical, and social information. This is a guide to practical matters; the 1974 publication date jeopardizes its accuracy. Yet the authors convincingly convey the possibility of rock-bottom travel in Africa, and a good deal of information might still be relevant. The book is good for pretravel reading; its small, compact format makes it easily portable for travel as well.

Egypt

Baedeker's Egypt. Karl Baedeker. North Pomfret, VT and Devon, England: David & Charles, 1974 (reprint of 1929 ed.). 672 pp. $17 (£6).

Although guidebooks existed before Baedeker, the late 1800s saw the introduction of *the* classic guide, to which all other guides were destined to be compared. The first English version of the *Baedeker's Egypt* was published in 1878, in response to the growing interest of Europeans and Americans in the Middle East. During the next 50 years, the book was revised seven times, to keep up with the rapidly changing times. The 1929 version, reviewed here, was an update to include the then-recently opened tomb of Tutankhamen.

Not stinting on information, Baedeker managed to squeeze 106 maps and plans and 56 woodcuts into this book, the text of which fills 672 pages with tiny print. In this classic guide, practical information regarding travel is given briefly in a section called "preliminary information," which includes currency, tour routes and times, transportation options, postal information, and conversation with the local people. One short paragraph assures the reader that hotels do exist; restaurants are not mentioned at all.

In pages numbered from I to CCIV (1 to 204), geographic and ethnological "notes" are provided, covering geography, origin and present condition of various groups of people, the Nile, geology, agriculture, climate, Islam, history, hieroglyphics, religion, art, and architecture. The text proper consists of detailed notes and descriptions of locations and journeys. These are divided into four categories: Lower Egypt; Upper Egypt; Lower Nubia; and Upper Nubia and the Sudan. The location descriptions are extremely detailed, so that the traveler will see *everything* worth seeing and will know dates, square footages, histories, and so on. Tours of museums are described showcase by showcase. Maps and illustrations are profuse. The difference between columns and pillars is explored. No point of interest is missed. Journeys between points are similarly described, mile by mile. Admitting that the detail may overwhelm the reader, Baedeker has set the text in two type sizes; the larger is for points of general interest, and the smaller is for more detailed information.

Evaluation: This classic guidebook was a substitute for an in-person guide. It points things out and explains them. Actual living and travel arrangements are left to the resourcefulness of the traveler. The modern use of a guidebook as an accommodation and restaurant guide is more a comment on today's traveler and today's life-style than on guidebooks. For guidebook aficionados, those who are historically inclined, and those who want to encounter a classic, this guide will be well worth its rather hefty price.

Egypt. See Fodor's Country Guides under The World, Comprehensive Guides.

Egypt Observed. Henri Gougand and Colette Gouvion. New York: Oxford University Press, 1979. approx. 160 pp. $19.95.

As an example of other, totally European guides in this series, *Egypt Observed*, covering both old and new Egypt, is "a richly rewarding prologue to a visit and a memorable souvenir"; it provides interesting historic and cultural background of the country and its unusual and ancient sights. Sixty-one full-color and 64 beautiful black-and-white photographs and six itineraries are included. This is not a travel guide, but rather pretravel reading.

Evaluation: This rather large but beautiful picture guide to Egypt provides selective in-depth information on various aspects of Egypt, but none on actual travel in the country. It is well suited for both those interested in traveling to Egypt and those with a general interest in the country, its past and present, and its peoples.

Included in the series: Florence Observed; France Observed; Paris Observed; Greece Observed; Moscow and Leningrad Observed; Spain Observed.

Morocco

Europe's Wonderful Little Hotels and Inns. See the review of this title under Europe, Accommodations and Restaurants.

Let's Go: The Budget Guide to Europe. See the review of this title under Europe, Comprehensive Guides.

Morocco. See The Traveller's Guide series under Europe, Comprehensive Guides.

Spain and Morocco (plus the Canary Islands) on $10 and $15 a Day. See Dollars a Day Guides under The World, Accommodations and Restaurants.

The Seychelles

The Seychelles. See The Islands series under The World, Pretravel Reading, Islands of the World.

Tunisia

Europe's Wonderful Little Hotels and Inns. See the review of this title under Europe, Accommodations and Restaurants.

Tunisia. See Fodor's Country Guides under The World, Comprehensive Guides.

ASIA

COMPREHENSIVE GUIDES

All-Asia Guide. Michael Lynch, ed. Hong Kong: Far Eastern Economic Review (dist. in the U.S. by Charles E. Tuttle Co.), 1978 (10th ed.). 584 pp. pap. $5.95.

The *All-Asia Guide* is just that. It covers 27 Asian countries, including China and Mongolia. For each country, history, immigration information, customs and traditions, climate, language, food, transportation, tours, hotels, shopping, sports, and holidays are listed. The guide has a great deal of information for seeing the sights of each country, arranged for easy touring; addresses, telephone numbers, and rates are listed for the accommodations, which are rated by the guide. No equivalent restaurant information is provided.

Evaluation: The *All-Asia Guide* is a well-organized and informative guide and is the most complete in-depth guide to Asia. It is sponsored by the Far Eastern Economic Review, which in part explains its expense-account budget. Indeed, most of the accommodations suggested are beyond a student's budget. Because of the quality and quantity of information contained, this book is highly recommended for use by all travelers in Asia. Students will want to supplement it with a more budget-oriented accommodation guide such as *The Budget Traveler's Asia* (see below) or *The On-Your-Own Guide to Asia* (see below).

Asia A to Z. See A to Z World Travel Guides under The World, Comprehensive Guides.

The Budget Traveler's Asia. David Jenkins. New York: E. P. Dutton. 414 pp. pap. $4.95. Revised annually.

Formerly titled *The Student Guide to Asia, The Budget Traveler's Asia* is a youth-oriented guide to 26 Asian countries, including China. It is geared to modest, but not necessarily rock-bottom budgets. This guide provides a capsule history of each country, followed by its vital statistics, transportation, and sights. A directory of accommodations is concentrated in one section; local foods are discussed, but specific restaurants are rarely given.

Evaluation: This is an excellent survey guide to Asia. It suffers from many of the problems and offers many of the advantages of the European *Let's Go* (see under Europe, Comprehensive Guides). Since such a large geographic area is covered, many aspects of travel in these countries are not covered. Further readings on individual countries would be helpful; bibliographies are provided for suggested reading, and many useful addresses are given. Overall, *The Budget Traveler's Asia* provides a good basis and summation for travel in the expensive Asian countries.

Myra Waldo's Travel Guide to the Orient and Asia. See Myra Waldo's Travel Guides under The World, Comprehensive Guides.

The On-Your-Own Guide to Asia: The Budget Handbook to East and Southeast Asia. Alison Davis, ed. Stanford, CA: Volunteers in Asia; Rutland, VT: Charles E. Tuttle Co., 1979. 347 pp. pap. $3.95.

The On-Your-Own Guide to Asia draws upon the experiences of dozens of young travelers who, as members of Volunteers in Asia (VIA), have lived and worked in Asian countries for extended periods of time. This guide is directed to other students traveling on limited budgets and concentrates on essential information for low-cost travel to ten countries in east and southeast Asia. Both urban and rural areas are covered, and relevant information on history, culture, sights, language, food, and specific low-budget hotel and restaurant listings as well as transportation information is provided.

Evaluation: A very informative and sensible guide to Asia, this compact book provides the essentials for low-cost travel in Asia. Especially helpful are the maps, bibliographies, and directions for major airports. This guide pleasantly eschews traditional tourist jargon for straightforward, practical advice. As it covers only ten Asian countries, it often provides more thorough and in-depth information than *The Budget Traveler's Asia* (see above). This guide is useful for both pretravel and travel use.

Pan Am's Guide to the Pacific. New York: Pan American Airways, 1976. 219 pp. pap. $2.

Pan Am's Guide to the Pacific emphasizes basic but comprehensive coverage of all aspects of travel in the areas described, which include all the Pacific Islands, Australia, New Zealand, Japan, South Korea, India, Sri Lanka, Taiwan, Thailand, Bangladesh, Afghanistan, the People's Republic of China, and Nepal. The entries for each country concentrate on practical travel information, such as its setting, climate, currency, entry and customs requirements, banks, shopping, and health. Transportation to and in the areas, entertainment, food and restaurants, sports, sights, and sources for more information are briefly mentioned. In the beginning sections there are general discussions of pretravel paperwork, health, money, insurance, packing, electricity, and photography. The book serves travelers on moderate and more than moderate budgets planning a trip to a number of areas in the Pacific.

Evaluation: Because the book emphasizes practical travel information, it is necessary for that information to be up-to-date. It isn't. The book was published in 1976, and since that time many changes have occurred that make much of the information either inaccurate or unreliable. The book includes very little background, transportation, and accommodation information, and the sights listings are sketchy and brief. The book's best features are the inclusion of practical and preparatory information on a very large area and its low cost. Its worst features are its age, the basic quality of the information, and the lack of descriptions in the accommodations and sights listings.

OVERLANDING

Across Asia on the Cheap. Tony Wheeler. South Yarra, Victoria, Australia: Lonely Planet Publications (dist. in the U.S. by Bradt Enterprises; dist. in the U.K. by Lascelles [Roger]), 1978. 256 pp. pap. $3.95 (£1.95). Revised periodically.

Across Asia on the Cheap is an overlanding guide for those traveling by vehicle across Asia toward Europe. "Overlanding" implies moving your vehicle and possessions much the same as the covered wagons that moved early settlers across North America. This guide for rock-bottom budgets is essentially a how-to guide containing a large amount of practical information. Inexpensive yet adequate hotels and restaurants are listed, though they are not always followed with essential information such as addresses and telephone numbers. Information on the 26 countries covered includes principal sights, history and background information, and transportation suggestions, all based on firsthand information. *Across Asia on the Cheap,* written by an Australian, is versatile enough to be useful for anyone interested in an overland trip.

Evaluation: This guide, based on the author's own travel adventures, is useful for pretravel reading as well as on the road. Many of the details are left up to the individual; more often than not the traveler is directed to an area with the largest number of inexpensive hotels, rather than to specific hotels. This guide advocates a rock-bottom travel style, but can be a useful source for practical information on Asia for any type of travel. *Across Asia on the Cheap* makes for interesting reading and is a good introduction to overland travel, but should be paired with a more comprehensive guide of the area. Suggested bibliographies are given throughout the book.

Asia Overland: A Practical Economy-Minded Guide to the Exotic Wonders of the East. Dan Spitzer and Marzi Schorin. New York: The Stonehill Publishing Co., 1978. 333 pp. pap. $5.95.

Asia Overland is intended for students or young people traveling overland through Asia from Turkey to Indonesia. It is basically a how-to guide and provides a substantial amount of preparatory information and travel tips for overland traveling. The author captures many aspects of Asian culture and its people, and stresses the importance of a Westerner's blending in with diverse cultures and customs. While the purpose of the guide is to aid one to travel economically, it does not advocate rock-bottom travel or scrounging. Hotels, pensions, hostels, and inexpensive restaurants are covered as well as various means of transportation.

Evaluation: Asia Overland contains excellent advice on health, laws, customs, and many other aspects of budget travel in Asia for both experienced and novice travelers. The sections on culture and budgeting time and money to get the most out of a trip to Asia with the least amount of problems are particularly good.

PRETRAVEL READING

Sunset Travel Guide to the Orient. Menlo Park, CA: Lane Publishing Co. 192 pp. pap. $5.95. Revised periodically.

Sunset Travel Guide to the Orient covers the countries of Japan, South Korea, Taiwan, Hong Kong, Macau, and China. Not a guidebook in the strictest sense, this guide provides interesting, thoroughly researched background information on the areas covered. Coverage includes history, geography, culture, and other background information, augmented by numerous black-and-white photographs. Other features include sights, maps and town plans, festivals and events, nightlife, shopping, and so on. General information on accommodations, restaurants, and transportation for each country is also given.

Evaluation: Interesting and easy to read, the *Sunset Travel Guide to the Orient* is a good source for pretravel reading; its rather large size would make it difficult for on-the-road usage. The suggested reading list is also very helpful and suggests some comprehensive guides such as the *All-Asia Guide* (see above). For informative armchair reading offering a good introduction to the Orient, the *Sunset Travel Guide* will prove very helpful.

A Travel Guide to the Orient and the South Pacific. Ted Kosoy. New York: St. Martin's Press, 1977. 266 pp. pap. $4.95.

A Travel Guide to the Orient and the South Pacific provides a superficial coverage of 25 countries. Included is practical information, a calendar of events, sights, and sections on sports and shopping. Few accommodations are listed, with no specific information such as addresses or prices. Descriptions of local foods are given, but no restaurants are listed. Because of the limited amount of information and lack of details, this guide is more of a pretravel guide than one for use on the road.

Evaluation: Ted Kosoy's *Travel Guide to the Orient and the South Pacific* suffers from many of the same things as *A Kosoy Travel Guide to Europe* (see under Europe, Sightseeing)—that is, it is too general and nonspecific. It would be useful only to those who know nothing about the Orient or South Pacific and need some good but limited pretravel information.

THEATER

Brandon's Guide to Theatre in Asia. James R. Brandon. Honolulu, HI: The University Press of Hawaii, 1976. 178 pp. pap. $3.95.

Brandon's Guide to Theatre in Asia covers various dramatic art forms in fourteen Asian countries. Descriptions of regional dances, operas, plays, and musical performances are given for each country, including cities and rural areas. Both performances and theaters are rated, and background information on historical origins is provided. Festivals, best seasons, information sources, and general transportation information are also included. A chapter on theater lists at the end of the guide includes addresses, general directions (including means of transportation), hours of attractions, telephone numbers, and rates.

Evaluation: For anyone interested in theater in Asia, *Brandon's Guide to Theatre in Asia* is an excellent pretravel and on-the-road guide. There is enough introductory information and description to render this guide useful to both the amateur and the connoisseur of Asian theater. It is a well-written, well-organized, and informative guide. For anyone traveling in Asia, the widely accessible and inexpensive performances of Asian theater could be an important part of experiencing the culture and people of the countries covered.

Southeast Asia

South-East Asia on a Shoestring. Tony Wheeler. South Yarra, Victoria, Australia: Lonely Planet Publications (dist. in the U.S. by Two Continents; dist. in the U.K. by Lascelles [Roger]), 1977. 238 pp. pap. $2.50 (£1.95).

South-East Asia on a Shoestring is a handy little guide to rock-bottom travel in eight southeast Asian countries. It complements and continues the tradition of another guide by the same author, *Across Asia on the Cheap* (see above, under Asia, Overlanding). The guide contains background information on history and sights, with emphasis on practical information, including visas, hotel and restaurant suggestions, money, and a variety of other topics.

Evaluation: Although budget concerns are a priority, Tony Wheeler manages to include some cultural and historical information as well as solid information on rock-bottom travel in Asia. Among the book's assets are its portability and low cost. It is an Australian publication, perhaps not as well known worldwide as other publications, but its contents are applicable to practically everyone traveling on a restricted budget. Some of the information, however, is sketchy, and addresses are often incomplete. This guide would make a good supplement to a more inclusive culture- and sight-oriented guide such as the *All-Asia Guide* (see above, under Asia, Comprehensive Guides).

China

American's Tourist Manual. John E. Felber. Newark, NJ: International Intertrade Index, 1979. 224 pp. pap. $5.95. Revised annually.

The *American's Tourist Manual* to China, like the similar publication for the USSR (see under USSR), is basically a sightseeing guide to the cities of China. It also contains preparatory, background, and practical information. Cities are listed alphabetically, and much of the information has been taken directly from tours in travel brochures of the China Travel Service (CTS). Accommodations and restaurants are not covered, since these aspects of travel are arranged by the CTS. Various maps, temperature and currency information, and many other items of practical information are also provided.

Evaluation: The *American's Tourist Manual* to China is an excellent guide to the sights and cities of China. Historical and cultural background information is extensive. However, since the material has been taken from the CTS, it is not oriented to the needs of American travelers in particular. This is not necessarily a drawback, but further information on travel in this country would be helpful. No information is given on what to expect of the hotels, transportation, food, or the difficulties one might expect to arise in traveling in this extensive and very different country. This guide is recommended for use along with a more comprehensive guide, such as *The China Guidebook* (see below).

The China Guidebook: A Traveler's Guide to the People's Republic of China. Arne J. de Keijzer and Fredric M. Kaplan. Fairlawn, NJ: Eurasia Press, 1979. 304 pp. $12.95.

The China Guidebook is divided into three major sections: background and preparation, practical travel information, and tours of cities and sites. A short introduction gives advice on a variety of subjects pertaining to travel in China, its people, and its politics. The background and preparatory section emphasizes recent changes in Chinese travel that have diminished previous restrictions. It describes exchange groups, official visitors, travel to China from particular Western countries, application procedures, what to pack, and what not to pack. China friendship associations around the world are listed, as well as China's foreign trade corporations and overseas diplomatic missions of the People's Republic of China. The second section lists complete practical travel information, including climate, language, currency, communication, transportation, and behavior. The last section describes 35 major cities, with history, description, sights, accommodations, and food listings for each. Special features include a detailed bibliography, Chinese phrases, a multicolored fold-out map, and sections on China's health care facilities, schools, art and archaeological sites, and the Chinese export commodities fair.

Evaluation: The practical information in *The China Guidebook* is complete, clear, and up-to-date. It includes all the necessary preparatory information and much knowledgeable advice for inexperienced travelers. Although recent years have seen a relaxing of many of the travel restrictions, a trip to China is still controlled by the government, and it can be very expensive. A large amount of preparation, both mental and physical, is necessary to get the most out of the trip, and *The China Guidebook* is an excellent first step. It is a wide-ranging, complete, and informative guide to a relatively unknown land.

China Travel Guide. Peking, China: China International Travel Service and Cartographic Publishing House (dist. in the U.S. by China Books), 1976. pap. $2.50.

The *China Travel Guide* is a series of multicolored maps, photographs, illustrations, and short descriptions of 34 cities and regions in the People's Republic of China. The cities and areas are arranged roughly by size and importance, with the entries including many references to changes that have occurred since the 1949 revolution. The book includes no practical travel information and should be used with a more comprehensive guide to China.

Evaluation: The book is perhaps the most beautiful travel guide ever published, with striking scenes of urban and rural development and incredibly vivid, hand-painted maps. However, this is the extent of its usefulness. The short descriptions are filled with political references and many self-congratulations on the advancement of the "revolutionary struggles." The maps and photographs in the book cannot be matched by any other guide, but travelers will need much more information than the book provides.

Going to China. Mary Chiang. Burlingame, CA: China Publications, 1972. 56 pp. pap. $2.95.

The book is an intensive introduction to modern Mandarin, the national language of the People's Republic of China. It is intended for businesspeople, tourists, and students and may be used along with a tape cassette that can be purchased separately. The first section is a pronunciation guide that discusses tones, vowels, and special pronunciation problems. The word lists are divided into 11 sections: everyday words and expressions, numbers and dates, nouns and verbs, at the hotel desk, in the hotel room, at the restaurant, the guide arrives, some conversational gambits, a tailor is called, at the hospital, and departing. Each section lists the English word or phrase, the Romanized Mandarin spelling, and the Chinese character. The final 21 pages are a short English-Mandarin dictionary listing about 500 vocabulary items.

Evaluation: Although it gives only simplified coverage of the Mandarin language, the book is very useful to China travelers as an introduction to the language they will encounter on their trip. The information is presented clearly and is easy to find. It covers all the basic phrases for common travel situations and takes into consideration the limited language ability of the average reader. Many travelers to the People's Republic of China find knowing any native language unnecessary, but others will find that a little language background will give them a degree of independence and will allow them to gain a greater appreciation for the area they are visiting.

Peking. See Fodor's City Guides under The World, Comprehensive Guides.

Indonesia

Indonesian Handbook. Bill Dalton. Berkeley, CA: Moon Publications, 1979. 486 pp. pap. $8.50.

The *Indonesian Handbook* is a comprehensive guide to the islands of Indonesia. It has a lengthy, detailed introduction covering such topics as geography, history and politics, religion, language, customs, and many more. Coverage of individual islands includes background, accommodations, transportation and food, along with culture, sights, archaeology, etc. Folk music, drama, dance, and crafts are also covered in detail. Maps of the individual islands and cities can be found throughout the book. Special consideration is given to those traveling on a budget, and there are many helpful tips for budget travel. However, this guide can be useful to any type of traveler on any kind of budget.

Evaluation: Very few travel guidebooks have the expansive scope and detailed coverage of the *Indonesian Handbook*. It is well organized and easy to use, as well as being in a handy, compact size. The general orientation and travel philosophy is geared to young, budget travelers, but information is extensive and versatile enough to be of use to any budget. An extensive bibliography is provided for pretravel reading. Cultural considerations, customs, and so on are covered in detail, and information into the diverse and unusual peoples and land of Indonesia is provided. This guide is a must for anyone traveling in Indonesia, for its complete and detailed coverage as well as the cultural awareness conveyed by the author.

Iran

Iran. See Fodor's Country Guides under The World, Comprehensive Guides.

Israel

Europe's Wonderful Little Hotels and Inns. See the review of this title under Europe, Accommodations and Restaurants.

Israel. See Fodor's Country Guides under The World, Comprehensive Guides.

Israel on $15 a Day. See Dollars a Day Guides under The World, Accommodations and Restaurants.

Let's Go: The Budget Guide to Europe. See the review of this title under Europe, Comprehensive Guides.

Japan

Exotic Japan. Boye De Merte. Phoenix, AZ: Phoenix Book Publishers, 1976. 159 pp. pap. $3.

Exotic Japan provides background descriptions of many facets of travel in the country. The first section describes its physical setting, with references to Japanese mythology, the geography of the islands, and scenic areas. The climate and seasons are then described, with emphasis on how they are perceived by the Japanese and how the climate compares with that of other regions of the world. The section on the Japanese people discusses the growth and development of religion and philosophy and the hospitality of the people toward foreign visitors. The most useful section of the book for travelers is the last, "Pleasures." It describes nightlife, bars and cabarets, Japanese cuisine, the coffee-shop culture, theater, baths, Japanese inns and hotels (description only), hot-spring spas, gardens, parks, travel by train and car, and annual festivals.

Evaluation: Although little practical travel information is included, the book is very useful pretravel reading for all travelers planning a vacation in Japan. The deep feeling the author has for the country is clearly evident in the colorful descriptions and the wide range of topics discussed. The book provides a feel for the area that could not be gleaned from other sources. It is entertaining and informative reading, the best introduction to Japan currently available to travelers.

Japan: A Traveler's Companion. Lensey Namioka. New York: Vanguard Press, 1979. 253 pp. pap. $7.95.

Japan: A Traveler's Companion features detailed background information, sights, and activities throughout the islands. Japan's climate and geographic characteristics are described briefly, and many different methods of transportation are discussed (walking, driving, taxis, street cars, subways, trains, ferries, and domestic flights), but little practical transportation information is included. An entire chapter is devoted to language: pronunciation, calligraphy, sociolinguistic constraints, and a glossary of basic words and phrases. Sections are included on food, housing, baths and toilets, amusements, sports, arts and crafts, castles and samurai, and churches, shrines, and temples. All of the above sections provide background information, with a minimal amount of practical information (addresses, prices, etc.). The final chapter discusses social misconceptions and the problems of generalization. Appendixes include a description of major historical periods, a list of useful words in kanji, hiragana, and katakana scripts, addresses for more information, and titles for suggested reading.

Evaluation: The book introduces the reader to the country's two distinct personalities—the new and the old—and tells how the two combine to form modern Japan. The background information on the country, its people, and their past is informative and highly entertaining. The sections on language, food, and the folly of cross-cultural generalizations are particularly useful to travelers planning their first visit. The book provides background information on travel in Japan with a detail and style unmatched by other guides. With accommodation and preparatory information taken from another book, the traveler will find that this is the only guide needed.

Kites, Crackers and Craftsmen. Carry Gordon and Kimiko Nagasawa. Tokyo: Shufunotomo (dist. in the U.S. by I.S.B.S.), 1974. 144 pp. pap. $6.95.

The lures of the 50 Tokyo specialty and craft shops described in the book are the tradition and family ties, the emphasis on quality and craftsmanship over profit, and the fact that most of the shops, while not hidden, lie well off the beaten tourist path. Items in which the shops specialize include *geta* (Japanese thongs), rice crackers, fans for all seasons, handmade stationery and paper products, *koh* (incense), fabrics, lanterns, knives, and woodcrafts. The entries are organized by neighborhood, with the location of each shop shown on a map that accompanies each section. Each entry includes the name, address, hours, and telephone number, the shop's specialty, the date it was founded, the owner, a description of the shop, its history, the price range, and shopping hints. A full page of color photographs of the shop and its wares follows each entry. Special features include Japanese phrases for shoppers, a historical chronology, and a glossary and index.

Evaluation: The book invites travelers to discover the traditional Japan through its crafts and craftspeople. Few guides open up an area's culture to visitors as clearly as this one. The practical information on the shops is complete and very accessible, and the descriptions, along with the color photographs and illustrated maps, bring the wares and their creators to life. When used with a more comprehensive guide to Japan, the book is one of the best ways to explore and discover the unique charms of the country.

Reading Your Way around Japan. Boye De Merte. Phoenix, AZ: Phoenix Book Publishers, 1978. 120 pp. pap. $3. Tokyo: Lotus Press, 1978. 750 yen.

Independent travel in Japan can be a trying experience for those without some knowledge of Japanese script. The kanji characters may be aesthetically pleasing, but the inability to understand them can detract from the overall enjoyment of a trip. *Reading Your Way around Japan* lists hundreds of street signs travelers are likely to encounter, with the kanji symbols, their Romanized spelling, and a phonetic representation of each. Included are signs at airports, hotels, and post offices, in restaurants, shops, subways, taxis, theaters, and trains, warning and traffic signs, city names, and common signs in Tokyo and Osaka. Special sections include Tokyo and Osaka subway maps, how to pronounce Japanese, and a brief description of Japanese calligraphy.

Evaluation: The book provides a very useful service for travelers to Japan who wish to explore on their own, but who lack any background in the Japanese language. The signs, their English translation, and phonetic representation are presented clearly and are organized so that each can be found quickly. Many of the traffic and warning signs are shown in color, and the fold-out subway map is clear and uncomplicated. The book is a unique and worthwhile investment for travelers planning a trip to any of Japan's urban areas.

Jordan

Jordan and the Holy Land. See Fodor's Country Guides under The World, Comprehensive Guides.

Mongolia

Mongolia Today: A Travellers Guide. Henry Field, ed. and comp. Miami, FL: Field Research Projects (dist. by Mongolia Society), 1978. 71 pp. pap. $5.

Perhaps the least traveled area in the world, Mongolia gives travelers a chance to visit the eighteenth century. The articles in this guide were all written by Mongolians and adapted by the editor to serve travelers as armchair reading and as a practical travel guide. Sections are included on the land (both descriptive and scientific), wonders of nature, nature reserves, hunting, museums, Ulan Bator, hospitality and customs, tourism, and wilderness preservation. Most of the articles have a slightly technical quality, but all can be read easily by laypeople. Of particular interest are the sections on the "Birth of a City" (showing the pattern of development in the country), the growth of tourism in the area, and the descriptions of native customs.

Evaluation: The book cannot be compared with other travel guides because of the unique nature of the area and the country's relatively undeveloped tourist industry. The articles on the natural characteristics of the country are clear and very descriptive, with many references to the area's wildlife and the efforts to guarantee their survival. The technical information is presented in a clear and uncomplicated manner, and the reading is surprisingly fluid. The book is an excellent introduction to the country's people, places, and past.

Nepal

Trekking in the Himalayas. Stan Armstrong. South Yarra, Victoria, Australia: Lonely Planet Publications (dist. in the U.S. by Bookpeople; dist. in the U.K. by Lascelles [Roger]), 1979. 192 pp. pap. $3.95 (£1.50).

Hardy and adventurous travelers will find *Trekking in the Himalayas* a helpful guide to the most mountainous region of the world. This book describes the various ways one can prepare for a trek in Nepal through trekking agencies. General information on preparation, historical and cultural background, currency, and climate, along with other practical information, is included. Day-by-day route descriptions, with maps for the more interesting treks, are provided. Armstrong's approach is not rock bottom, but rather encourages trekkers to contribute to the local Nepalese economy and use discretion and insight when dealing with the Nepalese.

Evaluation: Trekking in the Himalayas is a very useful guide for trekkers and offers an unspoiled view of Nepal, its land and culture. The author points out that this type of travel is not for everyone. He stresses good physical condition and a proper attitude toward the local population. Very worthwhile for pretravel preparation and on-the-road use, this guide offers a refreshing alternative to more conventional travel modes. Those interested in more conventional transportation, hotels, or rock-bottom travel will not find this book useful, as it specializes in trekking only.

Singapore

Singapore. See The Islands series under The World, Pretravel Reading, Islands of the World.

Thailand

Thailand: A Complete Guide. William Duncan. Rutland, VT: Charles E. Tuttle Co., 1976. 384 pp. pap. $7.50.

Thailand: A Complete Guide is a comprehensive guide to Thailand, subtitled "From Bangkok to Backroads with Walking Tours." The focus is on seeing all of Thailand, from the cities to the hill villages of the north. The guide is organized regionally, including a separate section on Bangkok, which is preceded by a lengthy and detailed introduction covering various aspects of traveling in Thailand such as language, climate, holidays and festivals, transportation, and accommodations.

The major focus of this guide is sights. Historical and cultural background and interest, with hours of admissions, prices, and directions, are some of the aspects covered. No specific budget group is addressed, and hotel and restaurant listings have a wide price range.

Evaluation: The detailed coverage of the culture and sights of Thailand makes William Duncan's guide a worthwhile purchase. It does not have many individual hotel and restaurant listings, but it does contain sufficient background information on these areas. *Thailand: A Complete Guide* provides an interesting and complete description of the interesting and diverse sights throughout Thailand.

Turkey

Let's Go: The Budget Guide to Europe. See the review of this title under Europe, Comprehensive Guides.

Turkey. See Fodor's Country Guides under The World, Comprehensive Guides.

Turkey on $10 and $15 a Day. See Dollars a Day Guides under The World, Accommodations and Restaurants.

AUSTRALIA AND THE PACIFIC

COMPREHENSIVE GUIDES

Pan Am's Guide to the Pacific. See the review of this title under Asia, Comprehensive Guides.

Practical Guide to the South Pacific. Nicole Roucheux. Privately published (dist. in the U.S. by Charles E. Tuttle Co.), 1978. 224 pp. pap. $6.95.

The *Practical Guide to the South Pacific* is called "practical" because it does not include anecdotes or photographs and emphasizes the facts on each of the areas described. The entries for each area include the history, geography, climate, flora and fauna, transportation and practical information, entertainment, duty-free shopping, food, tours, restaurants, and hotels. Major cities are described in slightly more detail, with some informal driving tours and a few short excursions. A number of advertisements and maps are interspersed throughout the entries. Along with the major South Pacific Islands, a special section is included on Sydney, Australia.

Evaluation: The book includes brief but wide-ranging practical travel information on the areas described, but finding it is quite a challenge. There is no index, no table of contents, and no obvious method of organization. Much space is given to advertisements. This book, as well as the author's guide to New Zealand, is available in both French and English; it can only be hoped that the French edition is easier to use than this. The information on the countries and areas is fairly complete and useful to travelers, but even the best tool is useless if the material cannot be found. Most of the same information, along with more complete background and some photographs, can be found in the *South Pacific Handbook* (see below).

Other books in the series: Practical Guide to New Zealand.

South Pacific A to Z. See A to Z World Travel Guides under The World, Comprehensive Guides.

South Pacific Handbook. Bill Dalton and David Stanley. Berkeley, CA: Moon Publications, 1979. 352 pp. pap. $8.50.

The *South Pacific Handbook* is a comprehensive guide to the 12 major island groups in the South Pacific. Major as well as minor islands are covered. Similar to its counterpart, the *Indonesian Handbook* (see under Indonesia), in format and style, this guide has the same detailed and extensive coverage. The lengthy introduction provides background information on the people, language, customs, history, geography, and so on. Coverage of individual islands includes customs, health, people, transportation, accommodations, food, and sights. Numerous maps, illustrations, and photographs are found throughout the book. Travel style and budget range from moderate to low, and the authors encourage travelers to "be integrated into the island culture." High-priced tourist accommodations and restaurants are left out of the guide for this reason.

Evaluation: For both background information and travel information on the South Pacific, the *South Pacific Handbook* is hard to beat. Its emphasis is on mingling with the people, rather than the traditional tourist approach. Many different transportation and accommodation alternatives are included, such as staying with families or traveling by motorcycle or "le truck." Walking and mountain-climbing information as well as many other alternatives are given. Well organized and easy to use, this guide is highly recommended for not only the budget traveler, but anyone traveling in the South Pacific.

South Pacific Travel Digest. Charles Jacobs and Babette Jacobs. Palm Desert, CA: Travel Digests, Paul Richmond & Co., 1978 (4th ed.). 175 pp. pap. $7.95.

The book features basic coverage of the major tourist areas in Australia, New Zealand, Papua New Guinea, and most of the South Pacific islands. The entries are arranged geographically, with brief sections on transportation by sea and air, practical travel information, and special activities in many of the areas covered. For each area there is a description of major tourist sights, a list of restaurants (with addresses, phone numbers, and short descriptions), transportation and shopping information, a calendar of events, information on climate, money, language, and laws, and a directory of hotels and motels that lists addresses, price ranges, and short descriptions of the facilities. Many photographs and illustrations are included in the entries, along with a few advertisements.

Evaluation: Many factors contribute to make this less than the complete travel guide to the South Pacific. The book emphasizes practical travel information in the entries, but much of the information is out-of-date, incomplete, and difficult to find. Only the most frequently visited areas are described, and the entries do little to introduce the reader to the inhabitants or their land. Much of the book discusses travel in Australia and New Zealand, but the information is narrow in scope and unevenly distributed. Very few rural areas are described. Travelers looking for more reliable and accessible practical information and more colorful and detailed background information should look for another guide.

Travel Guide to the Orient and the South Pacific. See Myra Waldo's Travel Guides under The World, Comprehensive Guides.

A Travel Survival Kit Series. Tony Wheeler. South Yarra, Victoria, Australia: Lonely Planet Publications (dist. in the U.S. by Bookpeople), 1979. pap. $3.95.

Like other Lonely Planet publications, the *Travel Survival Kit* books to Australia, New Zealand, and Papua New Guinea emphasize travel on a rock-bottom budget. The books differ slightly in format, with many more accommodations and restaurants in the first two books and more background and history in the Papua New Guinea guide. Each of the books in the series includes complete preparatory information on transportation, lodging, dining possibilities, paperwork, language, and geography. They list a wide variety of sights and outdoor activities, again emphasizing little or no cost. Special references are included for student discounts and bargain air fares to and around the different areas.

Evaluation: The author's years of experience with rock-bottom travel have left him with an in-bred cost-avoidance mechanism that finds inexpensive alternatives to the costliest of vacation expenditures. Many of his suggestions call for advanced planning or the sacrifice of comfort, but some more expensive alternatives are included as well. The books take an honest approach to the subject, giving a well-rounded view of travel in the different areas and including some less than positive aspects. The information is complete but less detailed than either *The Maverick Guide* (see below, under Australia), or the *South Pacific Handbook* (see above). It is organized well. Travelers on low to nonexistent budgets are served well by this series.

Included in the series: Australia; New Zealand; Papua New Guinea.

Australia

Australia: A Travel Survival Kit. See A Travel Survival Kit series above, under Comprehensive Guides.

Australia on $15 a Day. See Dollars a Day Guides under The World, Accommodations and Restaurants.

The Maverick Guide to Australia. Robert W. Bone. Gretna, LA: Pelican Publishing Co., 1979. 308 pp. pap. $7.95.

This is the second in the Maverick series, and, like the author's *Maverick Guide to Hawaii* (see under United States, State Guides), it is as complete in scope as any travel guide. It is most useful to travelers on a long visit to a large area of the country, on a modest or more than modest budget. The first 100 pages deal with history, transportation to and around the country, language, and a broad spectrum of practical information. This is followed by entries for the seven states and territories, with information on all facets of travel in the areas. The book should be read while planning a trip to make the most use of the travel tips included and should also be referred to on the road.

Evaluation: The portrait of Australia painted by the author in his *Maverick Guide* is one of strange contrast to the world up over. He begins by asking, "Have you been to another planet yet?" With the wide range and completeness of the information in the book, it very well could be a guide to an entirely unknown land. For most travelers, that is exactly what Australia is. The author's years of experience as a writer for Fielding's guides are evident in the entertaining and very readable text. Like the *Maverick Guide to Hawaii,* the book's best feature is also its worst. The amount of information may be more than many travelers would need. But when traveling to another planet, it is best to be prepared.

Easter Island

Easter Island. Bob Putigny. New York: The Two Continents Publishing Group, 1976. 128 pp. pap. $5.95.

Primarily a picture book about "the navel of the world," *Easter Island* contains a text that covers the discovery of the island by the Dutch and its early encounters with Europeans and Chileans. The section on current life on Easter Island matches pictures with written material covering the capital, the inhabitants, agriculture, the sea, tourism, recreation, sculpture, and the mysterious history of the famous statues.

Evaluation: For those who have been there, *Easter Island* will serve as an excellent reminder of the trip. So, too, will it be a foretaste for those who might be interested in going. But the book perhaps serves best the armchair traveler. The many excellent photographs give the reader an excellent view of the island. The text covers the areas most people want to know about in an interesting and well-written manner. But it is the photographs that make this book special.

New Zealand

New Zealand on $10 and $15 a Day. See Dollars a Day Guides under The World, Accommodations and Restaurants.

New Zealand: A Travel Survival Kit. See A Travel Survival Kit series under Australia and the Pacific, Comprehensive Guides.

Practical Guide to New Zealand. See *Practical Guide to the South Pacific* under Australia and the Pacific, Comprehensive Guides.

Papua New Guinea

Papua New Guinea: A Travel Survival Kit. See A Travel Survival Kit series under Australia and the Pacific, Comprehensive Guides.

Solomon Islands

The Solomon Islands. See The Islands series under The World, Pretravel Reading, Islands of the World.

EUROPE

COMPREHENSIVE GUIDES

Fodor's Europe. Eugene Fodor and Robert C. Fisher, eds. New York: David McKay Co. 807 pp. pap. $9.95. Revised annually.

Fodor's Europe has a more refreshing, international approach than many other generalized European guides. Directed to Canadian and Australian travelers in addition to those from the United States, this guide offers practical information, sightseeing information, and accommodation and restaurant listings for 34 eastern and western European countries, as well as the USSR. Although listings range from inexpensive to deluxe, the guide is geared toward travelers with above-average means. *Fodor's Europe* also includes suggestions for more unusual, directed travel for those with special interests.

Evaluation: Whereas the Fielding guides take a "family" approach to travel writing, Fodor's receives contributions from area specialists, a fact that may make it slightly more uneven than its Fielding rival, but is at the same time one of its strengths. Fodor's places less emphasis on accommodation and restaurant listings and instead provides more complete, comprehensive treatment of sights and transportation.

Grand Tour A to Z: The Capitals of Europe. See A to Z World Travel Guides under The World, Comprehensive Guides.

Let's Go: The Budget Guide to Europe. Harvard Student Agencies, Rogers Brubaker, ed. New York and London: E. P. Dutton. 735 pp. pap. $4.95 (£1.95). Revised annually.

Written by students for students, *Let's Go* is chiefly concerned with inexpensive travel. Its wide coverage includes all major western and eastern European countries as well as Israel, Turkey, Morocco, and the USSR. The book emphasizes less frequently traveled areas, and individual exploration and experimentation, rather than group tours, are encouraged. The text is filled with practical information, succinctly stated, covering all matters of concern to the small spender.

Evaluation: With budget travel its major priority, this important student guide occasionally gives short shrift to comfort and cleanliness.

These disadvantages, however, are usually compensated for by considerable savings. The chief advantages of *Let's Go* are its all-inclusive European coverage and its listings of rock-bottom price accommodations and student discounts. For young adults (and others) who are really serious about absolute minimum budget travel, and who are willing to explore on their own, this is *the* book.

Other titles in the series: Let's Go: France; Let's Go: Great Britain and Ireland; Let's Go: Italy; Let's Go: U.S.A.

Letts Guide (City Series). Frederick Tingey. London, Edinburgh, Munich, New York: Charles Letts & Co., 1976, 1980. 87 pp. pap. $2.95 (£1.25).

As an example of this series, *Letts Guide—Paris* is a brief but comprehensive guide to the city's sights, history, restaurants, and hotels. Sections are included on transportation to the city (from London) and in the city (by Métro, bus, car, and foot), with references to the best time to visit, the city's physical setting, and how to cope with the maze of streets. The book describes many different Parisian neighborhoods, pointing out sights and buildings of interest, and includes short histories of most. The hotel and restaurant sections are short and emphasize low and moderately priced rooms and meals, with addresses, telephones, price ratings, and very brief descriptions. Special sections include museums, shopping, Paris by night, parks, gardens, excursions, and a list of useful addresses. Many large, clear maps of the city are featured in the back of the book.

Evaluation: With the exception of the hotel and restaurant entries, the information in the book is complete, clearly presented, and extremely useful to travelers on either their first or their fortieth visit to the city. A city such as Paris offers so much for travelers to do and see that it is often difficult to sort through it all to find that which is of most interest to a particular traveler. *Letts Guide* does an admirable job in highlighting the unique features of the sights and activities without becoming lost in information. Although some travelers may wish to supplement the hotel and restaurant information, the book is a worthwhile investment for travelers planning a short visit to Paris.

Included in the series: Letts Guide—Amsterdam; Letts Guide—London; Letts Guide—Paris; Letts Guide—Rome.

Letts Guide (Country Series). Frederick Tingey. London, Edinburgh, Munich, New York: Charles Letts & Co., 1979, 1980. 96 pp. pap. $2.95 (£1.25).

Letts Guide to England and Wales, as an example of the series, lists sites of interest throughout both countries, emphasizing their more rural aspects. The book begins with general descriptions of the British

Isles for the benefit of North American visitors. It then describes different types of vacations and various transportation alternatives, though little practical information, aside from useful addresses, is included. Accommodation possibilities are discussed, with references to sources for more complete information, and a comparison of prices is provided. A section on practical travel information gives health, emergency, telephone, tipping, mail, and customs information, along with essential addresses. A brief historical overview precedes the listings of sights in 46 different areas of England and Wales, with short descriptions but no directions or practical information (hours, admissions, and so on).

Evaluation: This short guide gives a brief but comprehensive view of the outlying districts in the countries described. The background and practical information sections are complete and clear, with a wide range of information provided on a number of topics. The book is well organized, though the alphabetic listings of the towns and districts may cause some confusion for those unfamiliar with the area. When supplemented with more complete accommodation and transportation information, the book is the only guide to sights needed by travelers planning a tour of the rural areas of England and Wales.

Included in the series: Austria; Costa Brava; Costa del Sol; Denmark; England and Wales; France; Germany; Greek Islands; Greek Mainland; Holland; Italy; Norway and Sweden; Portugal; Spain; Spanish Islands; Switzerland; Yugoslavia.

Myra Waldo's Travel Guide: Northern Europe with Motoring Routes and **Southern Europe with Motoring Routes.** See Myra Waldo's Travel Guides under The World, Comprehensive Guides.

Rand McNally Pocket Guides. Carole Chester. Chicago, IL: Rand McNally & Co., 1980. 96 pp. pap. $3.95.

In very small print, Rand McNally manages to squeeze into 96 pages an amazing number of facts. An introduction to Germany, for example, its way of life, its arts and sciences, transportation, practical information, sports, and spas are all included in the first 25 pages. The remainder of the book provides facts about the cities and towns throughout the five regions into which Rand McNally has divided Germany. Smaller towns are briefly described, with tourist highlights indicated. The distance from the nearest large city is always given, as is a map reference point. Additionally, larger city descriptions include accommodations (first class), restaurants, nightlife, culture, sports, sights, and more information.

Evaluation: This is an excellent book for the visitor making a quick trip; only essential information is presented. The writing style is highly factual and encyclopedic, with no personal notes, observations, or recommendations. The size and weight of the book do indeed assure that it is a pocket book that can be taken along. The cost of recommended restaurants and accommodations is considerably above that which the budget-minded might seek. For both pretravel and on-the-road use for the hasty traveler, however, it is an excellent reference work.

Included in the series: France; Germany; Italy; London; Spain.

The Traveller's Guide Series. Sylvie Nickels. London: Jonathan Cape (dist. in the U.S. by Merrimack Book Service), 1977. 240 pp. $10.95.

As an example of the entire series, *The Traveller's Guide to Finland* offers thorough information in a pocket-sized form, covering many aspects of traveling in Finland, as well as historic, geographic, and cultural background information. Preparatory and practical information, sights, restaurants, and accommodations of varying price ranges are also covered. Three motoring routes are given, along with distances, maps, principal sights, and other important information.

Evaluation: The extensive information in this guide is presented in a well-organized and easily accessible format. Its scope incorporates sports, festivals, language, music, and so on, as well as many of the practical aspects of travel. Maps, town plans, marked travel routes, and a selected bibliography add to the usefulness of the book. Useful for both pretravel preparation and for on the road, it is recommended for varying travel styles and budgets.

Included in the series: The Channel Islands; Corfu and Other Ionian Islands; Crete; Cyprus; Elba and the Tuscan Archipelago; Finland; Malta and Gozo; Morocco; Rhodes and the Dodecanese; Sardinia; Sicily; Tunisia; Turkey; Yugoslavia.

The Uncommon Guide to Europe. John Whitman. New York: St. Martin's Press, 1978. 532 pp. pap. $5.95.

The book is called "uncommon" because the author tries to list sights, restaurants, and hotels that are usually not visited by American tourists and that exhibit a uniquely European charm. A short introduction discusses small hotels and restaurants in major cities, transatlantic plane travel, hotel reservations, maps, and communications, with lists of information sources, travel reports, and international airlines. The countries are listed alphabetically, with a brief description of major sights, weather, informal travel suggestions, and lists of hotels and restaurants in each country. The hotels make up the majority of the entries. They are arranged by city, with the cities organized alphabetically. The address and telephone number of each hotel are given, with a short description and price classification. Maps that show the location of major cities of each country are provided.

Evaluation: A guide to the areas in western Europe not often visited by U.S. travelers is a good idea, but many features detract from this book's overall usefulness. The information is incomplete. The listings of sights do not include their location or any other practical information, and the descriptions are brief and unclear. The hotels are listed without references to facilities, size, or services, and the descriptions are too short to be of any use. There is no transportation or background information, no information on language, and very little preparatory travel information. The book must be used with a more complete and comprehensive guide to be useful at all.

Whitman's Off Season Travel Guide to Europe. John Whitman. New York: St. Martin's Press, 1976. 692 pp. pap. $6.95.

Whitman's Off Season Travel Guide claims to introduce travelers to "Europe at its best from September to May." The 25 individual country chapters are divided regionally, with information on towns, weather, hotels, and restaurants. There is more rural coverage compared to most other European guides; all entries are brief and superficial, intended to give the reader a general background on what to expect. Off-season activities such as skiing, wine and music festivals, and hunting are included, and there is information on scenery, flowers, and animals. Minimal information on transportation and preparation is provided. Although off-season travel usually implies bargain or inexpensive rates, the majority of the accommodations and restaurants cater to those with ample budgets.

Evaluation: Unfortunately, this book does not live up to its potential as an off-season European travel guide. Perhaps one problem is that the author attempts to cover too much of Europe. The result is a quick, generalized approach that precludes in-depth treatment of the advantages and disadvantages of off-season travel. The author does attempt to lead the reader away from the big tourist crowds and major cities, into rural Europe, and also stresses mingling with the culture and people. Another good feature is the chapter on ski resorts in Europe, which could, however, be further expanded.

ACCOMMODATIONS AND RESTAURANTS

AA Budget Guide to Europe. Basingstake, Hampshire, England: Automobile Association (dist. in the U.S. by Standing Orders). 194 pp. pap. $8.95. Revised annually.

The *AA Budget Guide to Europe* lists over 5,000 low-cost accommodations, such as hotels, guesthouses, pensions, farmhouses, and inns, for 12 continental European countries. Published by Great Britain's Automobile Association, the guide also contains helpful preparatory information and motoring tips, reflecting the fact that it is geared mainly to motorists. The book is organized by country, with cities and towns listed alphabetically. Most towns and cities listed are marked in the handy 42-page atlas. A section on the vineyards of Bordeaux is also included.

Evaluation: This is a practical and handy guide to AA-recommended low-cost accommodations for the budget-minded traveler. Coverage and completeness of listings vary from country to country. Both capital cities and towns are given, but capital cities are especially weak. These drawbacks are reduced if the guide is used along with a guide oriented to major cities. Another slight drawback for non-British readers is that the practical information is directed to British regulations and standards; again this is not difficult to overcome.

AA Guesthouses, Farmhouses and Inns in Europe. Basingstoke, Hampshire, England: Automobile Association (dist. in the U.S. by Standing Orders). 256 pp. pap. $8.95. Revised annually.

The *AA Guesthouses, Farmhouses and Inns in Europe* includes listings of 5,000 moderately priced accommodations for 14 European countries. Like the other AA guides (see *AA Budget Guide to Europe*, above), geared mainly to the motorist, this one contains preparatory information for pretravel planning and helpful, practical tips for the motorist. The chapters on individual countries include only accommodation listings, no background or sights information. For each entry the town and map location are given as well as such specific details as telephone numbers, addresses, facilities, and so on. A 56-page atlas is provided for finding the location of the entries.

Evaluation: The information provided in this guide is well organized and easy to use. For the motorist looking for alternative accommodations to the major hotels, it will prove invaluable. However, a comprehensive guide covering sights, background, and so on is necessary to complement this and other AA guides.

AAA European Accommodations. Falls Church, VA: American Automobile Association. 407 pp. pap. $5. Revised biennially.

Published by the AAA as a service for its members, *AAA European Accommodations* is the intended companion to *AAA Travel Guide to Europe.* It is a directory of accommodations and restaurants for 30 European countries, oriented to motorists of adequate financial means. Hotel and restaurant listings are organized alphabetically by country and city and include essential information, brief descriptions, and the AAA stamp of approval.

Evaluation: This directory provides a substantial compilation of AAA-approved hotels and restaurants, especially useful for the motorist. Listings for both major cities and innumerable small towns add to its usefulness. Based on the strict AAA standards, the information is sure to be reliable.

Other books in the series: AAA Travel Guide to Europe.

Castle Hotels of Europe. Robert P. Long. East Meadow, NY: Robert P. Long (dist. by Hastings House Publishers), 1977. 180 pp. pap. $4.95.

Castle Hotels of Europe includes listings of castle hotels in 19 west European countries. Each listing includes the castle's name, address, location, and a brief description including sports facilities, countryside, and room and food facilities. The hotels are also categorized according to rates; although most castle hotels are over $25 per person, a surprising number are under $15. Some castle restaurants are also included. Most of the listings are accompanied with a small photograph of the castle hotel.

Evaluation: Castle Hotels of Europe will be of interest to those interested in exploring the ancient abbeys and accessible castle homes of western Europe. The variety of price ranges makes this guide useful to travelers of all budget ranges. The descriptions for each listing are brief but adequate, and maps for each country with locations of major towns and castle hotels facilitate planning. This guide is highly recommended for interesting alternative accommodations while traveling in Europe, although the publication date may render prices obsolete.

Country Inns and Back Roads, European Edition. Norman T. Simpson. Stockbridge, MA: Berkshire Traveller Press, 1978. 383 pp. pap. $6.95.

Covering Austria, Denmark, England, France, Germany, Ireland, Italy, the Netherlands, Norway, Scotland, Spain, and Sweden, Norman Simpson leads readers along a travel route he took seeking inns and small hotels. Each country chapter begins with notes describing inn-type accommodations, driving tips, reservation methods, car rentals, maps, and the author's itinerary. In a conversational format, each inn is described, with references to history, atmosphere, size, food available, rooms, and personal anecdotes provided by the author. Drawings of many inns are included. Each description ends with a paragraph of practical information regarding the inn name, address, size, telephone, meals provided, special features, rates, and the innkeeper's name. Rough driving directions are sometimes provided.

Evaluation: Reading *Country Inns and Back Roads* is like talking to a friend who has just returned from Europe. Stories and facts about the accommodations are delightfully mixed in a manner that makes the reader confident that staying in an inn is easy, and certainly preferable to a large hotel. For travelers to the cities and towns covered, the book provides an excellent though small group of accommodation suggestions. Since only about 20 inns are included for each country, travelers will also need a more extensive guidebook. Likewise, a guide to the sights and culture of each area will also be necessary.

Other books in the series: Country Inns and Back Roads, Britain and Ireland; Country Inns and Back Roads, North America.

DollarWise Guides. New York: Frommer/Pasmantier Publishing Co. (dist. by Simon & Schuster). pap. $4.95-$5.95. Revised periodically.

These guidebooks give specific, practical suggestions for hotels and restaurants, sightseeing attractions, and nightlife in the major cities and towns of six European countries. They enhance the appeal of budget travel, revealing that it is not always necessary to pay excessive prices to enjoy a country's charm, comforts, and food. Although the audience is defined as travelers on all budgets, the guides will appeal most to travelers on a medium or above-average budget.

Evaluation: The DollarWise Guides delve a little more deeply into outer provinces and regions than does the more traditional and more general *Europe on $15 a Day* (see below). The DollarWise inclusion of deluxe hotels and restaurants and concentration on moderate budgets distinguish the guides from the Dollars a Day series. Different countries are covered by each of these guides. Like all Frommer guides, of which these are a part, the strength is the many hotel and restaurant suggestions.

Included in the series: DollarWise Guide to England/Scotland; DollarWise Guide to France; DollarWise Guide to Germany; DollarWise Guide to Italy; DollarWise Guide to Portugal.

Europe on $15 a Day. Arthur Frommer. New York: Frommer/Pasmantier Publishing Co. (dist. by Simon & Schuster). 706 pp. pap. $5.95. Revised annually.

Europe on $15 a Day is primarily a guide to inexpensive accommodations and restaurants in 17 major cities in Europe. The self-imposed budget includes accommodations and restaurants, but not transportation, sights, or shopping, all of which are included in the guide. In addition to the major cities, information on 100 other cities and towns is condensed into one chapter of readers' selections. Throughout the guide, readers' selections provide additional insight into various accommodations and restaurants.

Evaluation: For low-cost accommodations and restaurants, Frommer is hard to beat. Almost an institution, already a corporation, it has one disadvantage: many of the recommended lodgings are filled with other tourists toting *$15 a Day*. And because it concentrates on cities, it leaves out much of the vital and inexpensive part of the experience of traveling in Europe. There is also no information on visas and passports. Coupled with a more well-rounded country-by-country guide, Frommer's *Europe on $15 a Day* would provide a very good source for traveling cheaply in Europe.

See also the review of Dollars a Day Guides, under The World, Accommodations and Restaurants.

Europe's Wonderful Little Hotels and Inns. Hillary Rubinstein. New York: E. P. Dutton, 1979. 383 pp. $10.95; pap. $5.95.

Europe's Wonderful Little Hotels and Inns is a collection of firsthand accounts from various travelers of unusual and quaint hotels and inns throughout Europe. The main focus is England and Ireland, but 22 other European countries, as well as North Africa and Israel, are given. There are no specific price ranges, but most are geared to comfort and elegance. Information includes addresses, telephone numbers, prices, facilities, and a personal impression of the establishment.

Evaluation: This guide provides a good collection of refreshing alternatives to the larger, more commercial hotels in Europe. The selections are not presented in any particular order, which makes it hard to use. Comments vary in focus, and most are quite subjective. If one can sift through the limited comments of some of the entries, this guide can offer good suggestions for those interested in staying away from the larger hotels. It is recommended for the traveler of moderate to above-average means.

Fielding's Europe. Temple Fielding. New York: Fielding Publications, 1979. 1,148 pp. pap. $10.95. Revised annually.

The oldest of the Fielding family publications, this guide was originally published under the name *Fielding's Travel Guide to Europe*. It has evolved into a major guide emphasizing the practicalities of travel in Europe. While sights are briefly mentioned, the greater part of the text describes restaurants, hotels, nightlife, and shopping. Membership in the high-income bracket seems necessary for the style of travel presented in this book. Serious economizers are directed to *Fielding's Low-Cost Europe* (see below).

Evaluation: A classic, due in part to its continued publication since 1948, *Fielding's Europe* now seems a bit dated in attitude and approach. There is very little information on sights and none at all on history and culture. Remarks about the natives concern themselves with attitudes toward tourists and tales of local rackets. The selective accommodation and restaurant listings lack precise addresses and prices. The Fieldings have a devoted following who can consistently enjoy the Fielding way of travel: a style that caters to high standards of comfort and doesn't make concessions merely in order to save a few dollars.

Fielding's Favorites: Hotels and Inns, Europe. Dodge Temple Fielding. New York: Fielding Publications. 474 pp. pap. $4.95. Revised annually.

Fielding's Favorites: Hotels and Inns, Europe, written by Dodge Temple Fielding, son of the renowned Fieldings, is written for "the cosmopolitan North American traveler." It is a guide to some of Europe's most exclusive hotels and inns. It ranks some 300 hotels as "Fielding's Favorites" and offers an additional 500 alternatives. Handy charts contain all specific information, and symbols denote what kind of travelers—businesspeople, families, or those seeking urban or rural settings—the various hotels and inns are likely to attract.

Evaluation: Although this guide purports to address a wide range of travel budgets, most hotels listed are in the range of $50 per double/per night or above. This is definitely a guide for those with well-padded wallets and a taste for luxury. While information on the "Favorites" is easy to find and extensive, the "alternates" do not have complete information on addresses or price range.

Fielding's Low-Cost Europe. Nancy Fielding and Temple Fielding. New York: Fielding Publications. 845 pp. pap. $9.95. Revised annually.

Fielding's Low-Cost Europe is compiled by the Fielding staff and contains firsthand bargain and money-saving tips for travel in 18 European countries. It offers much of the same general information and travel philosophy as the *Fielding's Europe* (see above), but with a slant toward the inexpensive. This guide is geared to both students (there are sections with suggestions for students) and other travelers. Many cities and towns are described briefly, and for major cities, accommodations (including hotels, hostels, and camping), restaurants, nightspots, and so on are covered. Listings include budgets from low to expensive.

Evaluation: Fielding's Low-Cost Europe is for bargain hunters intent on seeing the Continent cheaply with a maximum of comfort. The same general drawbacks of the other Fielding guides apply here: no information on history or culture, with stress on major cities, and practically nothing on out-of-the-way places. On the other hand, full addresses and telephone numbers are included for accommodations and restaurants—a big improvement over the other Fielding guides. When out-of-the-way places are given, there are very few specifics. General maps of both countries and cities aid in orientation. *Fielding's Low-Cost Europe* is thus superior to *Fielding's Europe* for those who desire specific information on accommodations, restaurants, and night-life, while also wishing to stretch their travel dollars without sacrificing too much comfort.

Michelin Red Guides. Paris: Michelin Co. (dist. in the U.S. by Michelin Guides and Maps). $9.95–$11.95; pap. $2.95. Revised annually.

The annually revised, multilingual Red Guides to accommodations and restaurants are intended as companion volumes to the Michelin Green Guides (see below, under Sightseeing), which are sightseeing guides. Aimed at the motorist, the Red Guides offer a rated selection of hotels and restaurants. A wide range of information is included for each country, presented through a system of symbols. The Red Guides also provide such information as years of the best local wines and addresses of reputable garages. Detailed maps including regions, cities, and towns are also provided. Coverage is organized alphabetically, including major as well as minor cities and towns.

Evaluation: A Michelin star of approval usually guarantees excellent fare and lodging. The Michelin Red Guides are highly recommended for all types of travelers, from the one-time, tourist-oriented traveler to the professional. Through the wide range of accommodations and restaurants presented, the guides serve budget traveler and big spender alike. Similar extensive and detailed coverage cannot be found in other accommodation and restaurant guides.

Included in the series: Hardcover: *Benelux (Belgium, Netherlands, Luxembourg); France; Germany; Great Britain and Ireland; Italy; Spain and Portugal.* Paperback: *Camping in France; Greater London; Paris.*

Rand McNally Economy Guide to Europe: A Comprehensive Guide to Twenty Major Cities. Petern Verstoppen. Chicago, IL: Rand McNally & Co., 1979-1980. 681 pp. pap. $6.95.

Rand McNally Economy Guide to Europe is basically a hotel and restaurant guide to 20 major cities in Europe. It is not a low-budget guide, but rather one containing lots of advice for getting the most for your money without sacrificing comfort. Information is plentiful and fairly versatile, addressing not only the standard middle-income tourist, but also students and families. Accommodations and restaurants are in chart form, listing all the important information and brief descriptions; recommendations provide further information. In addition, there is information on sights and tips for saving money on transportation.

Evaluation: Written for both Americans and British, *Rand McNally Economy Guide to Europe* contains a myriad of good tips for stretching money while traveling in Europe. Although geared more to high budgets than to low, it contains information that can be applied to any budget, except rock bottom. It is well organized and easy to use. Background information for out-of-the-way places is rarely given, although excursions from each city are included. Despite some limitations, this guide is a good contribution to the library of travel guidebooks to Europe, especially for those following the Grand Tour approach.

AUTOMOBILE TRAVEL

AA Guide to Motoring on the Continent. Basingstoke, Hampshire, England: Automobile Association (dist. in the U.S. by Standing Orders), 1978. 352 pp. pap. $8.50 (£2.95).

Complete motoring information and long listings of accommodations for all of western Europe are provided in the *AA Guide to Motoring on the Continent*. The introductory sections include comprehensive preparatory, practical, and emergency information on all facets of motor travel in the different areas. The sections for each country discuss how to get there, AA port agents and emergency centers, emergency and practical driving information, holidays and annual events, toll roads and bridges, and tourist information offices. The listings of hotels and garages for each country are organized by city, with the cities arranged alphabetically. Each hotel is rated on a five-star system, with the address, telephone, rates, and facilities listed for each. Many city and area maps are included, as well as a five-language vocabulary list and metric conversion tables. The book is intended primarily for residents of Great Britain and serves motorists on modest and above-average budgets.

Evaluation: The quality and completeness of the preparatory and emergency information make the book useful to all Continental motorists, although many may be disappointed by the meager accommodations information. The book lists many hotels in the different countries, but the information provided for each is sparse. The complicated use of symbols in the entries and the alphabetical organization of the towns make the book difficult to use. The book's major feature is the comprehensive road information and the quality maps, both of which are very valuable to motorists. However, it is recommended that a more complete and easier to use sights/accommodations guide be used along with it.

Enjoy Europe by Car. William J. Dunn. New York: Charles Scribner's Sons, 1976. 303 pp. pap. $5.95.

Enjoy Europe by Car is not a guide to specific routes, places, accommodations, or restaurants. Its goal is to show American tourists "how to travel in Europe as the Europeans do" and "how to make your own decisions." The guide is organized into three main parts; the first is devoted to general preparation and practical information concerning motoring in Europe. Part 2 consists of introductory information on 22 western and southern European countries. A series of appendixes make up the third part, and a good deal of practical information, charts, and conversion tables are packed into a concise format.

Evaluation: Dunn sets out to cover everything you need to know about motoring in Europe, and he succeeds fairly well; this book is loaded with useful information and motoring tips. The organization of this guide is somewhat rambling, as is the writing style, which sometimes makes it difficult to locate information. But overall, this guide will prove to be a great asset, especially for novice motorists who want to be well informed, and particularly for pretravel planning.

Europa Touring: Motoring Guide of Europe. Bern, Switzerland: Hallwag Verlag (dist. in the U.S. by American Map Co.; dist. in the U.K. by Collins [William] Sons & Co.). 796 pp. $32.20 (£7.75). Revised annually.

This multilingual "bible" of motoring in Europe is published by the prestigious map company Hallwag. Maps for 26 countries and 97 cities are followed by international motoring tips. More specific motoring information is included in separate country sections, in addition to background information on history, geography, sights, sports, shopping, and so on. *Europa Touring* presents information on each area, with an extensive alphabetical directory of towns and a list of hotel accommodations. This Hallwag guide is directed to the international motorist with a moderate to deluxe budget.

Evaluation: The detailed maps and extensive motoring tips provided by *Europa Touring* are essential to anyone motoring in Europe. Information is very accessible and well organized, although the size of the book and the small type interfere somewhat with its ease of use. Despite these problems, the guide contains a vast amount of useful information, and as an atlas it is difficult to surpass.

Rand McNally Road Atlas of Europe. Chicago, IL: Rand McNally & Co., 1978. pap. $4.95.

Regional and city maps of both western and eastern European countries make up this book. An index, key to maps, types of roads (motorways, toll roads, scenic routes), sights, distances, and other information add to the usefulness of this atlas.

Evaluation: As a comprehensive road atlas of Europe, the Rand McNally version is excellent. The format is easy to follow and countries and towns are easy to locate.

CAMPING

AA Guide to Camping and Caravanning in Europe. Basingstoke, Hampshire, England: Automobile Association (dist. in the U.S. by Standing Orders). 288 pp. pap. $8.95 (£2.95). Revised annually.

AA Guide to Camping and Caravanning in Europe includes 5,000 entries for 19 European countries. A brief section of practical information is followed by chapters on individual countries. Each country has a brief introduction followed by listings of approved campsites. Each listing includes telephone number, location and general directions, and opening dates. A general description is provided, and many useful details of available facilities are included. A 70-page atlas helps pinpoint location of sites.

Evaluation: Like the *AA Guide to Camping and Caravanning in Britain* (see below, under Great Britain, The Outdoors), this guide contains a complete and detailed listing of approved campsites, with extensive, easy-to-find information. A more comprehensive guide to Europe, such as *Let's Go: The Budget Guide to Europe* (see above, under Comprehensive Guides), *Europa Touring* (see above, under Automobile Travel), or *Fodor's Europe* (see above, under Comprehensive Guides), will make a good complement to this book, as it has very little introductory material to Europe and none on sights.

Europe under Canvas: A Guide to Camping for Singles, Couples, or Families. Patricia Foulke and Robert Foulke. Englewood Cliffs, NJ: Prentice-Hall, 1980. 181 pp. pap. $4.95.

The book deals primarily with camping preparation, with sections on planning the route, estimating expenses, insurance, air fares to Europe, clothing, equipment, packing, information sources, transportation on the road, problems that may arise, and tips for enjoying and relaxing while camping. There is a long section on food, which discusses campsite cooking, local wines and beers, cooking by computer, and sample menu plans. Twelve pages of recipes are also featured, all of which can be made fairly easily on an open fire. Suggested itineraries for trips in England, Scotland, Scandinavia, and central Europe are included, describing trips of 10 to 35 days. Many sights of interest and suggested camping areas are mentioned in the entries, although practical information on them is not included.

Evaluation: The preparatory information in the book is as complete as can be found in any European camping guide, but the lack of any practical travel information severely limits the book's usefulness on the road. The information is presented clearly, and the lists of books for further reading suggest a number of on-the-road camping guides that describe particular campsites and gives their exact location (which this guide neglects). *Europe under Canvas* is a good pretravel reference; also describes food alternatives and local cuisine and menus (no restaurants). More complete transportation, sights, and campground information should be acquired before leaving.

How to Camp Europe by Train. Lenore Baken. Mercer Island, WA: Ariel Publications, 1977. 384 pp. pap. $5.95. Revised biennially.

How to Camp Europe by Train provides just what its title promises.

This revised edition also includes a car-camping supplement and a rundown of the advantages and disadvantages of both modes of camping. It is aimed primarily at campers who want to save money by avoiding escalating gasoline prices and car rental fees. A substantial portion of the guide is devoted to travel preparation, train and motoring information, food, shopping strategies, and so on. Chapters on 15 western European countries describe selected towns and cities and nearby campsites. Maps are included, as are sightseeing and restaurant suggestions.

Evaluation: Lenore Baken proposes a viable and inexpensive way to see Europe for Eurailpass or student rail pass users. Although smaller towns receive ample coverage, the emphasis is on the Grand Tour, major city approach. Especially helpful are the numerous maps, the specific directions to campsites from train stations, and the information for families traveling with children. One drawback is the apparent random selection of areas covered. Overall, this handy and informative guide is a very useful source for camping in Europe.

Rand McNally European Campground Guide. Chicago, IL: Rand McNally & Co., 1977. 352 pp. pap. $6.95.

Rand McNally's multilingual directory lists over 4,700 campsites for 32 European countries. Campsite listings are arranged in tabular form across two pages, facilitating comparison with other campsites. Forty-one points of information on each site are given, including addresses, telephone numbers, activities, description of grounds, facilities, fees, and so on. Instead of an alphabetical listing, the towns are listed in the order in which you would reach them if you traveled the main tourist routes. Excellent maps are provided, along with a map reference for each site, facilitating location.

Evaluation: This guide is exclusively a directory for campsites, with excellent maps that indicate location of campsites and also a detailed road map. However, it needs to be supplemented with a guide for advice on camping and trailer travel in addition to background information and description of countries. The travel-route organization and tabular format may be confusing at first, but once mastered render the book a useful tool for pretravel planning and on-the-road consultation.

MUSIC

Music Festivals in Europe and Britain. Carol Price Rabin. Stockbridge, MA: Berkshire Traveller Press, 1980. 163 pp. pap. $5.95.

Music festivals can be either the center of any trip to Europe or an exciting highlight. Carol Rabin seeks to turn that possibility into a reality by providing the necessary information. *Music Festivals in*

Europe and Britain describes 91 festivals in 21 countries. Each festival entry gives the name in English and the local language, the city and approximate dates, and length of the festival. A brief description provides the history, flavor, and setting of the festival, along with the names of the most noted musicians performing. Specific information is provided for ticket ordering, prices, telephone numbers, customary concert dress, and for further information. Addresses are provided for obtaining information on accommodations.

Evaluation: Music Festivals in Europe and Britain is obviously written by a music festival enthusiast. The author describes the history and ambience of each festival and festival community accurately, but with the verve of a paid publicity agent. Festivals are listed by festival name in each country, which might be a problem for the traveler who has a set itinerary and is looking for festivals in a specific geographic area. Musical travelers should also be aware of The Music Guide series by Elaine Brody and Claire Brook (see below). These books provide the same practical information about the same festivals as Ms. Rabin's book, but are more evaluative (and sometimes critical) about the performances. The difference between *Music Festivals* and The Music Guide series is that *Music Festivals* is more personal and enthusiastic and covers more countries, while The Music Guide series is more crisp and professional; it also contains vastly more musically related information (in vastly more space) for $10. *Music Festivals* is $5.95. But for only $15.95, the reader can have both.

The Music Guide Series. Elaine Brody and Claire Brook. New York: Dodd, Mead & Co., 1976-1978. approx. 230 pp. $10. London: Hall, 1976-1978. £5.50.

The books in this series provide extensive information for the musical traveler. Each book is organized on the same format, offering an introductory essay for each country followed by detailed practical information for major musical cities. Covered are guides and services, opera houses and concert halls, concert series, libraries and museums, conservatories and schools, musical landmarks, musical organizations, music business dealers, instrument makers, and periodicals. In all categories, all necessary practical information is given regarding addresses, phone numbers, seating capacities, seasons, hours, and so on. To make the book applicable over a long period, exact dates have not been listed. Following major cities, the entire country is covered, with entries as appropriate for smaller cities and events.

Evaluation: It is difficult to imagine a more helpful or complete series of guides for music lovers traveling in western Europe, be they performers, researchers, or audience. The vast amount of information is presented in a uniform and tight organizational format, making it highly accessible. The geographical organization of the books makes trip planning easy; those interested in particular instruments or music types are less well served, even by the index. The scholarship and immense amount of hard work represented in these books make them a valuable resource. The publishing dates (1975 for Austria and Germany and Great Britain; 1977 for Belgium, Luxembourg, Holland, and Switzerland; and 1978 for Italy) should not deter the potential reader, since the information is not time-bound. New information will naturally not be in these particular editions. The forthcoming editions for France, Spain, and Portugal and for Scandinavia will be an excellent addition to this very useful series. The books will, of course, have to be supplemented by a more general guidebook, since only musically related material is given.

Included in the series: The Music Guide to Austria and Germany; The Music Guide to Belgium, Luxembourg, Holland and Switzerland; The Music Guide to Great Britain: England, Scotland, Wales and Ireland; The Music Guide to Italy.

PRETRAVEL READING

The Best European Travel Tips. John Whitman. Minnetonkar, MN: Meadowbrook Press, 1980. 212 pp. pap. $3.95.

This book contains *everything* a potential first-time traveler would need in the nature of pretravel information. Enormous numbers of details are listed under the topic headings of travel documents, travel partners, itineraries, lodging, packing, money matters, eating and drinking, communicating, health, and many more.

Evaluation: "Don't leave for Europe without this book," claims the back cover. For the first-time traveler going to Europe (or even another place), this is excellent advice. Writing in a friendly but concise style, the author manages to convey huge amounts of information to travel novices with only rare lapses into patronizing text. A larger set of pretravel hints exists nowhere. This book is highly recommended as pretravel reading for first-time travelers of all ages, budgets, and travel styles.

Travellers Survival Kit: Europe. Roger Brown. Oxford, England: Vacation-Work (dist. in the U.S. by Writer's Digest Books; dist. in Canada by Henry Fletcher Services), 1980. 208 pp. $6.95 (£2.95); pap. $2.95 (£1.95).

The Travellers Survival Kit: Europe lists complete practical information for 37 eastern and western European countries. Topics covered in the entries for each country include population, weather, politics, language (but no glossaries), passports and visas, customs, money and banking, shopping, tipping, taxes, brief but comprehensive transportation information, a description of accommodation possibilities, mail, telephone, and telegram information, health, emergencies, entertainment, the law, public holidays, and many addresses for more information. The countries are divided into eastern and western groups and are arranged alphabetically. Special references are included in the introduction on the European telephone system, English-language newspapers, and British radio programs that can be picked up on the Continent.

Evaluation: The completeness and accessibility of the practical information in the book make it an ideal pretravel guide, particularly for businesspeople planning a visit to a number of European countries or those who are frequent travelers to Europe. The book covers all areas of Europe, and although the entries are brief, they include a wide range of information on a variety of topics. When combined with an accommodations and sights guide (and perhaps more background information), the book is sure to answer the practical questions of travelers of all budgets and travel styles.

RAILWAYS

Baxter's Eurailpass Travel Guide. Robert Baxter. Alexandria, VA: Rail-Europe. 503 pp. pap. $7.95. Revised annually.

Baxter's Eurailpass Travel Guide is a guide to rail travel for holders of Eurailpasses. The 16 European countries covered by the Eurailpass are included in this guide. Coverage includes suggested tours and itineraries and special Eurailpass uses such as ferries, buses, trolleys, and so on. For many major cities, descriptions of train stations, hotels near train stations, and principal sights are given, as well as a variety of walking tours, excursions, and much more. The prices in Baxter's guide are geared to moderate-budget travelers, but there are some references to low-cost accommodations.

Evaluation: All holders of Eurailpasses will find this guide useful, especially in the bigger cities. The travel philosophy tends toward Grand Tour traveling, so that coverage of out-of-the way places is minimal. Underwritten by Icelandic Airlines, the guide contains a special section for inexpensive stopovers in Iceland and Luxembourg and also the Bahamas. In addition to a more comprehensive European travel guide, this guide would be an indispensable reference for on-the-road usage and also very helpful for pretravel planning, especially for planning an itinerary for Eurailpass holders.

Eurail Guide: How to Travel Europe and All the World by Train. See the review of this title under The World, Pretravel Reading, Railways.

Europe by Eurail. George Wright Ferguson. Columbus, OH: George Wright Ferguson. pap. $6.95. Revised annually.

Europe by Eurail provides a pragmatic approach to train travel, explaining such things as train schedules and making reservations. This guide promotes a base city–day excursion method of travel through Europe, whereby travelers establish a base in a city from which to make numerous day trips. The guide focuses on 20 base cities and includes such practical information as schedules for arrivals and departures, types of trains available, how to locate the money exchanges, and sights. Hotel and restaurant suggestions are left to other guides. *Europe by Eurail* is oriented toward experienced and inexperienced travelers alike.

Evaluation: Europe by Eurail presents a viable, interesting mode of European travel. Coupled with the Eurailpass, this method of travel is unharried and relaxed and helps make maximum use of the pass. The guidelines of this book are flexible enough to allow for independence and exploration. *Europe by Eurail* is good for pretravel planning as well as on the road, but its format necessitates additional use of another guidebook; a helpful bibliography is provided.

Europe by Rail and Backpack. Doug Smith. Corvallis, OR: Doug Smith, 1979. 104 pp. pap. $3.

Designed for the backpack and youth hostel approach to Europe, *Europe by Rail and Backpack* offers advice on how to travel in Europe on a limited budget. It is also geared to Eurailpass holders. The author provides preparatory information as well as brief chapters on 12 European countries and London. Various rated sights and description of train travel are covered.

Evaluation: Doug Smith's brief guide would be good pretravel reading for students planning an itinerary for a first-time trip to Europe, but his information, while helpful, is too brief to be of use for extensive traveling. His comments on some sights—especially beaches—are rather sexist, and the ratings of the sights and cities are quite subjective. Using it with discretion and in conjunction with a more comprehensive budget guide, such as *Let's Go: The Budget Guide to Europe* (see above, under Comprehensive Guides), the first-time traveler will have ample suggestions for itinerary planning.

SHOPPING

Fielding's Selective Shopping Guide to Europe. Temple Fielding and Nancy Fielding. New York: Fielding Publications (dist. by William Morrow & Co.), 1979. 318 pp. pap. $4.95.

Fielding's Selective Shopping Guide to Europe is a guide to selected department stores, specialty shops, boutiques, antique shops, flea markets, and various other shopping spots in European countries. Emphasis is on top quality and is directed to those with sizable pocketbooks. Shopping locations, along with addresses and in some cases proprietors, are listed under types of goods, which in turn are listed under the major cities of each country. Types of goods range from diamonds and furs to toys and handicrafts. Information on mail orders is also covered. The guide also contains helpful hints on distinguishing quality goods from shoddy merchandise.

Evaluation: This guide is indispensable for anyone planning to do extensive shopping in Europe with few or no financial limitations. As the title states, it is a selective guide, and recommendations given by the authors may be of no interest to others. Other than this drawback, *Fielding's Selective Shopping Guide to Europe* is filled with helpful advice on shopping in Europe, written by two experienced European travelers and shoppers.

SIGHTSEEING

Castles in Color. Anthony Kemp. New York: Arco Publishing Co., 1977. 208 pp. $8.95. Poole, Dorset, England: Blanford Press, 1977. £3.75.

Anthony Kemp, a military historian, provides the reader with a historical account of the architecture, uses, and societies surrounding European castles. In addition there are color photographs of 121 castles throughout Europe, with plate descriptions. Various illustrations are also provided. Castle hotels are not covered. The emphasis is on Europe, but some castles from the Middle East are included.

Evaluation: For castle buffs planning an extensive visit of castles in Europe, Kemp's *Castles in Color* provides interesting pretravel reading. Emphasis is on castles as military fortifications; hence the book may appeal to a very limited audience. The glossary of technical terms and the bibliography will prove helpful.

Fielding's Sightseeing Guide to Europe. Margaret Zellers. New York: Fielding Publications, 1978. 496 pp. pap. $9.95.

The new *Fielding's Sightseeing Guide to Europe* complements *Fielding's Europe* (see above, under Accommodations and Restaurants). While the latter focuses on accommodations and restaurants of major European cities, the *Sightseeing Guide* devotes itself to off-the-beaten-track spots and selected highpoints of lesser-known sights in 19 European countries. Sights are given ample coverage, with addresses, directions, and hours of attractions, along with historical and cultural background. Transportation alternatives to and in the rural areas and suggested walking routes ("rambles"), with specifics for on-the-road usage, are included. Practical and preparatory information is also left up to *Fielding's Europe*. The travel style is geared to no particular budget, but slants toward moderate or above.

Evaluation: As with most Fielding guides, the personal preferences of the authors are particularly noticeable. The travel style in the *Sightseeing Guide*, however, is less superficial than other Fielding guides and is geared to those traveling through Europe at a leisurely pace to get exposure to European history and culture. However, coverage is not uniform and is scanty for some countries. *Fielding's Sightseeing Guide* will be a useful supplement to more conventional European travel guides, since it contains much additional information. Those traveling by car and those interested in walking routes will find this guide the most beneficial.

A Guide to Magical and Mystical Sites: Europe and the British Isles. Elizabeth Pepper and John Wilcock. New York: Harper & Row, Publishers, 1977. 304 pp. pap. $4.95. London: Weidenfeld & Nicolson, 1977. £6.50. London: Sphere Books, 1977. pap. £2.50.

Is the oracle at Delphi still spouting ambiguous prophecies? What became of the race of giants that once populated the British Isles? And where was it that Johannes Faust first made his pact with Mephistopheles? *A Guide to Magical and Mystical Sites* describes places throughout Europe and the British Isles where history, myth, and magic are intertwined. The book is divided into three parts: the first covers Greek, Roman, and Egyptian sites; the second, sites on the Continent (Spain, France, and Germany); the third, sites in Great Britain and Ireland. The cities and areas featured in the book include Ephesus, Atlantis, Delos, Delphi, Malta, Rome, Pompeii, Toledo, southern Germany, the Basque country, Chartres, Brittany, Cornwall, London, Stonehenge, and the western isles. A long bibliography is included in the back of the book, along with a complete index.

Evaluation: The text of the entries is in story form, mixing what has been accepted by historians as fact with myths, legends, and some rather bizarre folklore on the regions' past inhabitants, human and otherwise. The book provides background information on the sites not to be found in other guides, in a lively, informative, and very entertaining style. It is not a substitute for a complete travel guide to the areas described, but the information provided is certain to add to the enjoyment of the trip. The stories in the book make excellent armchair reading for all travelers, whether they travel by traditional means or simply in their imagination.

A Kosoy Travel Guide to Europe. Ted Kosoy. Toronto: Kosoy Travel Guides, 1979. 256 pp. pap. $5.95.

This guide contains very brief and generalized information for 16 major European countries, focusing on the major cities. Coverage for each country averages six pages. Information includes transportation, sights, and practical information. Little or no background information is given, and the listing of accommodations is very limited. There are brief descriptions of local foods, but no restaurants.

Evaluation: This guide could perhaps be of use for pretravel reading as an introduction to Europe for a totally naive traveler. In this respect the practical information and listing of sights are two of the book's stronger points. But beyond this basic information it provides minimal help.

Michelin Green Guides. Paris: Michelin Co. (dist. in the U.S. by Michelin Guides and Maps; dist. in the U.K. by Michelin Tyre Co.). approx. 225 pp. pap. $6.95 (£1.00-2.50). Revised periodically.

The Michelin guides, published by the Michelin Tyre Company, were among the first travel guides written primarily for the motorist. Since then, Michelin Green Guides, translated from French, have earned a well-deserved reputation for providing thorough and intelligent discussions of the history, art, architecture, and sights of many areas. The guides for countries and areas include maps, suggested itineraries, and tours, as well as introductory and practical information. More specific information, Michelin-rated sights, and cities are covered alphabetically.

Evaluation: Michelin guides provide interesting historical and cultural background for travelers interested in in-depth coverage of an area, as well as a broad overview. The books are lightweight and slim, thus being excellent complements to accommodation and restaurant guides such as the Michelin Red Guides (see above under Accommodations and Restaurants). They are also well organized and easy to read. Michelin Green Guides are highly recommended for both pretravel reading and on-the-road use.

Included in the series: Austria; Brittany; Chateaux of the Loire; Dordogne; French Riviera; Germany; Italy; London; New York City; Normandy; Paris; Portugal; Provence; Rome; Spain; Switzerland.

Youth Hosteler's Guide to Europe. Youth Hostel Association. New York: Macmillan Publishing Co., 1977. 494 pp. pap. $3.95. London: Y.H.A. Services, 1977. pap. £2. Revised periodically.

The *Youth Hosteler's Guide to Europe* is the intended companion to the *International Youth Hostel Handbook*, Volume 1 (see under The World, Accommodations & Restaurants), which lists vital information, addresses, and prices for youth hostels in Europe. The *Youth Hosteler's Guide* provides travel information and itineraries for hostelers traveling by foot or bicycle. Advice on basic preparation and transportation to Europe is left to other guides, but facts on flora, fauna, history, literature, and art are featured for the 21 European countries covered.

Evaluation: This guide succeeds in achieving the Youth Hostel Association's aim of getting beyond traditional sightseeing. It is a culturally sensitive, broad survey introduction to the countries and peoples of Europe. Although it is specifically directed to hostelers, the touring routes may be of interest to motorists and train travelers who wish to explore beyond the well-worn, heavily traveled tourist routes. Combine it with its companion volume and you have all the basic information for a hostel or an off-the-beaten-track adventure in Europe.

SOLO TRAVELERS

Travel and the Single Woman—Europe. Shirley Van Campen. Wheaton, IL: Merton House Publishing Co., 1977. 213 pp. pap. $4.95.

Travel and the Single Woman—Europe is oriented toward women traveling alone in Europe, interested in meeting people—especially men. The author calls this "togetherness." She includes preparatory information and practical tips for the woman traveler. Coverage of nine European countries includes selective cities, towns, and sights; the author provides sightseeing tours, shopping, and very selective accommodations, restaurant, and nightspot listings.

Evaluation: Written in a wordy style, this guide has very limited uses. Coverage is not uniform. Sections describing European men are indicative of the orientation of the guide and an implied sexism. Some useful information can be found, but a more comprehensive guide is recommended.

WALKING TOURS

Walk Straight through the Square. Juliann V. Skurdenis and Lawrence J. Smircich. New York: David McKay Co., 1976. 206 pp. pap. $4.95.

Walk Straight through the Square is a guidebook with a very specific, limited goal: to provide an alternative to Grand Tour European travel by letting the reader walk through and experience some of Europe's lesser-known towns. Twelve towns, "more typically European than the bustling metropolises," are provided for France, Switzerland, Austria, Italy, and Yugoslavia. Sixteen detailed walking tours, with maps, cover directions, sights and their historical background, and some side excursions.

Evaluation: Walk Straight through the Square is a unique guide, covering lesser-traveled towns in Europe and encouraging exploration of the more typical and picturesque areas that convey the national flavor of the countries included. Ample background information for sights, primarily from the medieval period, is provided. This guide is recommended as a supplement to more comprehensive guides and also as a source book for potential side trips.

Another book in the series: More Walk Straight through the Square (Germany, England, Holland, Belgium, and Spain).

Austria

Austria. See Fodor's Country Guides under The World, Comprehensive Guides, and Michelin Green Guides under Europe, Sightseeing.

Letts Guide—Austria. See Letts Guide (Country Series) under Europe, Comprehensive Guides.

The Music Guide to Austria and Germany. See The Music Guide series under Europe, Music.

Belgium

Belgium and Luxembourg. See Blue Guide series and Fodor's Country Guides under The World, Comprehensive Guides.

Benelux. See the Michelin Red Guides under Europe, Accommodations and Restaurants.

The Music Guide to Belgium, Luxembourg, Holland and Switzerland. See The Music Guide series under Europe, Music.

Cyprus

Cyprus. See The Islands series under The World, Pretravel Reading, Islands of the World, and The Traveller's Guide series under Europe, Comprehensive Guides.

Czechoslovakia

Czechoslovakia. See Fodor's Country Guides under The World, Comprehensive Guides.

Eastern Europe A to Z. See A to Z World Travel Guides under The World, Comprehensive Guides.

Denmark

Denmark. See Blue Guide series under The World, Comprehensive Guides.

Letts Guide—Denmark. See Letts Guide (Country Series) under Europe, Comprehensive Guides.

Scandinavia on $20 a Day. See Dollars a Day Guides under the The World, Accommodations and Restaurants.

France

COMPREHENSIVE GUIDES

France. See Fodor's Country Guides and Holiday Guides under The World, Comprehensive Guides, and Rand McNally Pocket Guides under Europe, Comprehensive Guides.

France Especially for Women. For a review of a title in the Especially for Women series, see *Mexico Especially for Women* in the chapter on Latin America and the Caribbean, under Mexico, Comprehensive Guides.

Let's Go: France. See *Let's Go: The Budget Guide to Britain and Ireland* below, under Great Britain, Comprehensive Guides.

Letts Guide: France. See Letts Guide (Country Series) under Europe, Comprehensive Guides.

ACCOMMODATIONS AND RESTAURANTS

DollarWise Guide to France. See DollarWise Guides under Europe, Accommodations and Restaurants.

France. See Michelin Red Guides under Europe, Accommodations and Restaurants.

CAMPING

Camping in France. See Michelin Red Guides under Europe, Accommodations and Restaurants.

SIGHTSEEING

France Observed. For a review of a title in this series, see *Egypt Observed* under Africa, Egypt.

Regional Guides

Brittany. See Michelin Green Guides under Europe, Sightseeing.

Corsica. See The Islands series under The World, Pretravel Reading, Islands of the World.

Dordogne. See Michelin Green Guides under Europe, Sightseeing.

French Riviera. See Michelin Green Guides, under Europe, Sightseeing.

Chateaux of the Loire. See Michelin Green Guides under Europe, Sightseeing.

Normandy. See Michelin Green Guides under Europe, Sightseeing.

Northwestern France. See Blue Guide series under The World, Comprehensive Guides.

Provence. See Michelin Green Guides under Europe, Sightseeing.

South of France. See Blue Guide series under The World, Comprehensive Guides.

Paris

Paris. See Blue Guide series, Fodor's City Guides, and the Holiday Guides under The World, Comprehensive Guides; Letts Guide (City Series) under Europe, Comprehensive Guides; Michelin Green Guides under Europe, Sightseeing; and Michelin Red Guides under Europe, Accommodations and Restaurants.

Paris A to Z. See A to Z World Travel Guides under The World, Comprehensive Guides.

Paris Observed. For a review of a title in this series, see *Egypt Observed* under Africa, Egypt.

Paris on $500 a Day. For a review of a title in this series, see *Los Angeles on $500 a Day* in the chapter on North America, under California, Los Angeles and Vicinity.

ParisWalks. Alison and Sonia Landers. Washington, DC: New Republic Books, 1975, 1979. 238 pp. pap. $5.95.

Many city walking guides try to cover the entire city and emphasize directions rather than descriptions in the entries. They may concentrate on architecture, history, or general points of interest on the tours, but the only benefit most travelers will receive from them is exercise. The five walks described in *ParisWalks*, however, are different. Their purpose is to introduce the reader to the subtle, almost invisible characteristics that distinguish the area and reveal its past. The five neighborhoods described are LaHuchette, St. Julien le Pauvre, St. Germain des Près, Mouffetard, and the Place des Vosges. Along with detailed descriptions and background of each area, the walks include the location and which Métro and bus to take to the starting point. The streets covered on the walk are described, and the route of each walk is shown on a large, clear map. Special sections include brief transportation information, advice on tipping and shopping, telephones, newspapers, pharmacies, recipes, selected hotel and restaurant entries, and a historical chronology.

Evaluation: The inclusion of hotel and restaurant, transportation, and practical and emergency information broadens the scope of the book, but the most important feature of the book is the walks. The lively and informative descriptions seem to bring out each neighborhood's most carefully guarded secrets. The amount of information on each route goes far beyond that found in other city walking guides. Even with the added hotel and transportation information, however, the guide is best used with a more comprehensive guide to the city, especially by inexperienced travelers or those making their first trip to Paris. But whether alone or paired, no guide to the city brings its history and uniqueness to life as clearly and simply as *ParisWalks*.

Germany

DollarWise Guide to Germany. See DollarWise Guides under Europe, Accommodations and Restaurants.

Germany. See Fodor's Country Guides under The World, Comprehensive Guides; Michelin Green Guides under Europe, Sightseeing; Rand McNally Pocket Guides under Europe, Comprehensive Guides; and Michelin Red Guides under Europe, Accommodations and Restaurants.

The Music Guide to Austria and Germany. See The Music Guide series under Europe, Music.

Letts Guide—Germany. See Letts Guide (Country Series) under Europe, Comprehensive Guides.

Great Britain

COMPREHENSIVE GUIDES

Britain. See Holiday Guides under The World, Comprehensive Guides.

DollarWise Guide to England/Scotland. See DollarWise Guides under Europe, Accommodations and Restaurants.

England. See Blue Guide series under The World, Comprehensive Guides.

England and Wales. See Letts Guide (Country Series) under Europe, Comprehensive Guides.

England Especially for Women. For a review of a title in the Especially for Women series, see *Mexico Especially for Women* in the chapter on Latin America and the Caribbean, under Mexico, Comprehensive Guides.

Great Britain. See Fodor's Country Guides under The World, Comprehensive Guides.

Let's Go: The Budget Guide to Britain and Ireland. Ruth U. Whaley, ed. New York and London: E. P. Dutton. 558 pp. pap. $5.50 (£1.95). Revised annually.

Let's Go: The Budget Guide to Britain and Ireland is a comprehensive guide for the budget traveler, covering a wide range of information for England, Scotland, Wales, and Ireland. A lengthy chapter is devoted to London; both cities and the countryside are covered throughout the guide. For each city or town, practical information, addresses for tourist information, budget accommodations and restaurants, principal sights, sports, and various special features are given. As this guide is oriented toward students, information on working or studying abroad is included.

Evaluation: Like its counterpart, *Let's Go: The Budget Guide to Europe* (see under Europe, Comprehensive Guides), *Let's Go: Britain and Ireland* presents a broad range of information and in-depth coverage of the countries covered. The travel style of the British guide is geared to a slower and more in-depth coverage, for those planning an extensive stay in a limited geographic area; hence the rock-bottom, sometimes sacrificial philosophy of the European guide is not as prevalent. As a result accommodations are slightly more expensive, but many low-cost hostels, rooms, and so on are suggested. This guide emphasizes independent and exploratory traveling and is a must for the student or budget traveler.

Other books in the series: Let's Go: France; Let's Go: Italy; Let's Go: USA.

Scotland. See Blue Guide series under The World, Comprehensive Guides.

Wales. See Blue Guide series under The World, Comprehensive Guides.

ACCOMMODATIONS AND RESTAURANTS

AA Guesthouses, Farmhouses and Inns in Britain. Basingstoke, Hampshire, England: Automobile Association (dist. in the U.S. by Standing Orders). pap. $8.95 (£1.95). Revised annually.

AA Guesthouses, Farmhouses and Inns in Britain includes moderate to inexpensive accommodations in England, Scotland, and Wales. Like all AA approved listings, quality standards are guaranteed. Entries are listed alphabetically under individual countries, and information includes location, classification of accommodation (such as guesthouse or inn), a map reference, and specific details such as telephone number, hours of operation, facilities, and so on. Also included are a 16-page location atlas and plans of larger holiday towns and cities. Entries are not rated, as they are in the *AA Guide to Hotels and Restaurants* (see below), but there is a section on "Guesthouses of the Year."

Evaluation: For those seeking relatively inexpensive alternatives to hotels, *AA Guesthouses, Farmhouses and Inns* is an excellent reference. Information is complete and extensive, and coverage includes both urban and rural accommodations. Information is well organized and easy to use.

AA Guide to Hotels and Restaurants. Basingstoke, Hampshire, England: Automobile Association (dist. in the U.S. by Standing Orders). 616 pp. pap. $8.95 (£3.25). Revised annually.

The *AA Guide to Hotels and Restaurants* includes nearly 5,000 AA-approved hotels and restaurants in Great Britain and Ireland. Hotel and restaurant listings range from moderately priced to luxury accommodations. The well-researched listings for hotels include such information as addresses, telephone numbers, rates, facilities and services available, and hours for dinner and entertainment, along with much other descriptive information. Restaurant listings include addresses, telephone numbers, description of décor, hours of operation, and so on. The guide is organized by ratings, and entries then are listed alphabetically by name. The handy, detailed maps indicate locations of hotels and restaurants.

Evaluation: This easy-to-use, all-inclusive guide to hotels and restaurants is the guide to use for anyone with high standards for comfort and service who is traveling extensively in Great Britain and Ireland. The sections on the history of hotel accommodations, Middle Eastern dining, and the Quick Reference List are also helpful. Used along with a guide covering sights, historical background, and so on, the *AA Guide to Hotels and Restaurants* will be invaluable.

AA Guide to Self-Catering Holiday Accommodations. Basingstoke, Hampshire, England: Automobile Association (dist. in the U.S. by Standing Orders). pap. $6.95. 189 pp. + maps. Revised annually.

The *AA Guide to Self-Catering Holiday Accommodations* lists over 12,000 AA-inspected and approved houses, cottages, chalets, bungalows, and flats with kitchen facilities in England, Scotland, and Wales. Listings are organized alphabetically by country and include a short description of each accommodation, followed by specific information on facilities, when accommodations are available, and so on. Addresses, telephone numbers, and addresses for booking the self-catering accommodations are included, as well as many other useful details. Practical information for self-catered holidays is also included. A 50-page location atlas provides invaluable information for choosing and locating accommodations.

Evaluation: The extensive information and details provided in the *AA Guide to Self-Catering Holiday Accommodations* are more than adequate for finding an acceptable self-catering accommodation for a wide range of audiences. The guide is very well organized, and the wealth of information is easy to find and use. This guide is recommended for anyone interested in alternative accommodation in England, Scotland, or Wales.

Country Inns and Back Roads, Britain and Ireland. See *Country Inns and Back Roads, European Edition* under Europe, Accommodations and Restaurants.

Egon Ronay's Lucas Guide to Hotels, Restaurants and Inns, Great Britain and Ireland. Egon Ronay. New York: Penguin Books, 1978. 828 pp. pap. $8.95. London: Seymour Press, 1978. pap. £3.20.

Egon Ronay's Lucas Guide is a directory of hotels, inns, pensions, pubs, wine bars, and restaurants of Great Britain and Ireland. Accommodation listings range from "bargains" to "deluxe," and all are graded on facilities, service and cleanliness, and comfort, according to Egon Ronay's high professional standards. Restaurants are also rated according to quality of food and service. Addresses, telephone numbers, hours, approximate prices, and a brief description of the décor and the menu are provided for each entry; in the case of restaurants, the quality wine list is also included. Each entry has a map code number for easy location on the maps provided.

Evaluation: The Egon Ronay Organization is a group of professional inspectors with high standards of comfort and luxury. While it has some inexpensive listings, this guide will be primarily useful for those looking for comfort and luxury and with a budget able to support the high life. Organization is by city and town rather than by alphabetical order, which makes it easy to find listings; good maps locating hotels, inns, and so on help further. Lucas is a British corporation, and advertisements for it and other big corporations are scattered throughout the book, which detracts from information. This guide is for those less adventurous travelers who like organization and conventional accommodations.

England on $15 a Day. See Dollars a Day Guides under The World, Accommodations and Restaurants.

Great Britain and Ireland. See Michelin Red Guides under Europe, Accommodations and Restaurants.

Just a Bite: Egon Ronay's Lucas Guide 1978 for Gourmets on a Family Budget. Egon Ronay. New York and London: Penguin Books, 1979. 371 pp. pap. $3.95 (£1.50).

Just a Bite is a guide to restaurants throughout England (including a separate chapter on London), Scotland, Wales, and the Channel Islands. Restaurants, wine bars, cafés, tea shops, and many other types of unusual eateries are given for both large cities and towns. The guide is oriented toward "gourmets on a budget," although entries are not rated for price, except with a few examples of prices from menus. Organization is by alphabetical listings of city or town, followed by all the necessary information, including a description of atmosphere, décor, and specialties.

Evaluation: Egon Ronay's carefully inspected entries cater to the gourmet, and the term "budget" is relative—it is not rock bottom. There is a wealth of various types of restaurants, and information is complete, well organized, and easily accessible. For anyone with a taste for gourmet food and good wine, who wants to shy away from very expensive restaurants in Britain, this guide will be very useful.

AUTOMOBILE TRAVEL

Services on and off the Motorways. Jimmy Young. North Pomfret, VT and Devon, England: David & Charles, 1979. pap. $4.95 (£1.95).

Simply by driving 6,274 miles of British motorways (the equivalent of U.S. interstate highways), and turning off at every major junction, the author has identified the existence of every pub, restaurant, café, hotel, and garage within three miles of the junction. The simple and clear maps, similar to the American Automobile Association (AAA) Triptik maps, pinpoint the locations of off-the-road services. Individual entries are extremely abbreviated and are listed in geographic order along the motorways. Each two pages feature a map with reference numbers, the services offered, their hours, and addresses.

Evaluation: The abbreviations take some getting used to, but once the poorly explained system has been figured out and mastered, the book is not too difficult to use. However, because every restaurant, café, pub, hotel, and garage is listed, with no evaluative comment, the reader is left with a directory to the unknown. The author states that motorway services leave something to be desired. Whether or not any particular off-the-road service offers that certain something is unclear. Perhaps it can be said that the chances are better in Britain than in the United States. The services at least give travelers a chance to get off the motorway for a time while checking out the local offerings. The sturdy book is therefore useful to those in need of a break while traveling the British motorways.

CRAFTS

A Visitor's Guide to Scottish Craft Workshops. Mary Gladstone. Edinburgh: Scottish Development Agency. 60 pp. pap. free.

Travelers visit Scotland for its beauty, but the trip will be longer remembered if Scottish crafts are taken home as a part of that journey. In a booklet, rather than a book, 18 crafts are described as they are practiced in Scotland; each is followed by a listing, by craft, of men and women engaged in these activities—some of the 1,290 craft workers listed with the Scottish Development Agency. Each entry includes the name, address, and phone number of the artist, a brief summary of the products, and symbols indicating whether the public may observe the work as it is being done, whether commissions are accepted, and whether a showroom exists.

Evaluation: It must be presumed that members of the Scottish Craft Centre are all high-quality workers. No evaluation of skill is provided, nor are prices even hinted at. The map and corresponding locations in the text make individual workshops easy to locate by region. For the traveler interested in any of the 18 crafts, this book will be sure to please. It contains material not found elsewhere.

LITERARY TOURS

A Literary Tour Guide to England and Scotland. Emilie C. Harting. New York: William Morrow & Co., 1978. 191 pp. pap. $4.95.

A Literary Tour Guide to England and Scotland is a collection of homes, estates, and museums associated with some of England and Scotland's main authors. The first section contains alphabetical listings of sites throughout England and Scotland, except London, which has its own section. The information includes location, directions, road numbers, seasons and visiting hours, along with historical and literary background and descriptions of what to see. Some additional sights, such as cathedrals and castles with which the various authors have been associated, are given. Detailed maps and photographs are included for additional information and orientation.

Evaluation: For any traveler with an interest in the literary aspects of England and Scotland, this guide provides an informative and well-organized addition to the travel library. Since England and Scotland are rich areas of literary history, a guide such as this is a valuable asset to travel in these countries. The section on London is particularly detailed and includes various streets, homes, cathedrals, inns, and so on; it is especially good for walking tours. This guide is recommended as a companion to a good comprehensive guide to England and Scotland, such as the Michelin Red Guide (see under Europe, Accommodations and Restaurants), Fodor's guide (see under The World, Comprehensive Guides), or Frommer's Dollars a Day guide (see under The World, Accommodations and Restaurants).

MUSIC

The Music Guide to Great Britain: England, Scotland, Wales and Ireland. See The Music Guide series under Europe, Music.

NATIONAL PARKS

Britain's National Parks. Mervyn Bell, ed. North Pomfret, VT and Devon, England: David & Charles, 1975. 160 pp. $16.95 (£4.95).

The history, geology, geography, and wildlife of Britain's ten national parks (all in England and Wales) are described in detail in this guide. The introduction discusses the processes that led to the formation of the National Parks Commission and the work of the commission to preserve and protect the different park areas. The section for each park lists the areas; altitude; population; directions to the parks by train, bus, and car; vantage points; the address of the park information center and other visitor centers; and the administrators for the park, along with the detailed descriptions and background information. Special sections include a short description of natural areas in Scotland and problems jeopardizing the future of the parks. A short bibliography and complete index are included in the back of the book.

Evaluation: Because the book emphasizes background and description in the entries, it is most useful as a pretravel reference or as armchair reading. The lack of accommodation and camping information and the incomplete transportation information suggest that the book be used along with a more practical guide to a particular area. The background information gives a vivid picture of past developments in the parks, and the detailed descriptions provide a solid impression of the parks' physical characteristics. The book was published in England and is intended primarily for use by Britons. North American travelers and others unfamiliar with the different areas will have a hard time finding the parks from the information included in the entries.

THE OUTDOORS

AA Guide to Camping and Caravanning in Britain. Basingstoke, Hampshire, England: Automobile Association (dist. in the U.S. by Standing Orders). 256 pp. pap. $8.95 (£1.95). Revised annually.

AA Camping and Caravanning in Britain provides practical information and campsite listings for England and Scotland. Information on British laws for camping and driving, vehicle information and maintenance, and other useful information on the practical matters of planning a camping or caravaning trip is followed by an alphabetical listing of campsites for each country. All the sites have been AA-inspected and approved, and standards are guaranteed. Information includes addresses, telephones, map references for finding locations of sites, general descriptions, sizes, seasons, facilities, and many other details. Picnic sites and country parks, bridges, tunnels, and ferries are also listed. The 16-page atlas is very helpful for locating sites.

Evaluation: AA Camping and Caravanning in Britain is an invaluable guide for anyone camping and caravaning in Britain. The extensive information is well organized and easy to use, as with other AA guides. A chapter on orienteering, a new and different sport developing in England, provides an interesting possibility for travelers in Britain. When used in conjunction with a sights-oriented guide, *AA Camping and Caravanning in Britain* is highly recommended.

Caves and Caving in Britain. Edmund J. Mason. London: Robert Hale (dist. in the U.S. by Transatlantic Arts), 1977. 208 pp. $12 (£4.50).

The beauty and wonder of a cave cannot be appreciated by everyone, but for those who enjoy the dark stillness of an underground cavern, there is now *Caves and Caving in Britain*. The book describes cave explorations throughout the country and gives detailed background and physical characteristics of caves in general. It takes a scholastic approach to the subject, with many references to past cave explorations, archaeology, geology, mineralogy, and life in the caves (bats, fish, insects, and so on). Many photographs are included of the caves described, and a list of British caving clubs, a long bibliography, and complete index are featured at the back of the book.

Evaluation: The technical quality of the information may deter some readers, but it is presented clearly and can be understood by those with little science background. The detail of the entries is sure to please travelers with a deep interest in caves and cave formation. Whether travelers will find the book useful depends on their degree of interest in caves.

Long Distance Paths of England and Wales. T. G. Millar. North Pomfret, VT and Devon, England: David & Charles, 1977. 160 pp. $15.50 (£4.95).

Long Distance Paths features descriptions of eight hiking routes in England and Wales. The first section discusses the history and general characteristics of the paths, with references to their origins, their changing conditions, and the irregularity of signposts on the trails. This is followed by brief preparatory information on maps, overnight accommodations, and common hiking courtesy. The entries for each hike include the length, the date it was opened, the location of National Park Information Centers, and detailed descriptions of each route. Large, clear maps are provided of each path (although more-detailed hiking maps should be acquired), and many photographs and illustrations are interspersed throughout the entries. A complete bibliography and index are also included.

Evaluation: The book covers the same general area as *Walking in the Countryside* (see below), but the two books differ greatly in emphasis. *Long Distance Paths* emphasizes descriptions of the hiking routes and includes very little preparatory information on equipment, hazards, and so on. *Walking in the Countryside*, on the other hand, gives only brief descriptions of the paths, but includes detailed information on preparation and safety. Both books succeed in their purpose; whether a particular hiker uses one or the other depends on the degree of expertise and the length of the visit to a particular area. Travelers planning to combine more traditional vacation activities with their hiking should look for a more comprehensive travel guide to the area, to use along with this one.

Scottish Mountain Climbs. Donald Bennet. North Pomfret, VT and London, England: B. T. Batsford (dist. in the U.S. by Hippocrene Bks.) 1979. 192 pp. $14.95.

Travelers unfamiliar with the British Isles may have a hard time believing that the mountains shown in the many excellent photographs and described in the entries of this book are actually in Scotland. The scenes are reminiscent of the Colorado Rockies or even the Andes. The variety of climbing experiences available in the area is amazing. The book describes 40 different climbing routes, most of which are near the country's western shore. The descriptions include references to the types of rock to be encountered, particular hazards along each route, and seasonal differences in the climbs. The book serves as armchair reading and as a practical climbing guide for experienced mountaineers.

Evaluation: The entries for each climb describe the routes in great detail, sometimes devoting long sections to a space of five or six yards. However, this is the extent of the information. The book includes no preparatory or equipment information, no emergency information, and no information on anything other than the mountains. The text is clear and fluid, and the entries are very enjoyable reading, but the narrow scope of the book limits its usefulness to experienced climbers and armchair travelers.

Walking in the Countryside. David Sharp. North Pomfret, VT and Devon, England: David and Charles, 1978. 192 pp. $12.95 (£4.95).

The most striking feature of the book is the detailed preparatory hiking information. The author covers every aspect of hiking except how to tie one's shoe laces. The book begins with a historical and geological description of the major British hiking areas, followed by a long discussion of trespassing and rights of way, and general hiking do's and don'ts. Weather, obstructions, disappearing paths (erosion), fences, bulls, mud, deterrent notices, and other hazards are described, and the use of maps and compasses is discussed in detail. Other topics include clothing, equipment, hiking clubs, and brief descriptions of major hiking areas. Long lists of useful organizations, books of interest to hikers, maps, and guides are included in the back of the book, along with a complete index.

Evaluation: The emphasis on preparation and problem avoidance limits the book's usefulness to pretravel reading as a description of hiking possibilities in the country. The information is complete and so detailed that many hikers will find much of the information unnecessary. But for beginning hikers, the information is sure to answer all but the most obvious questions. Because the descriptions of the hiking areas are short, it would be best to use the book along with a guide that includes more thorough coverage of the hiking trails, such as *Long Distance Paths of England and Wales* (see above).

PRETRAVEL READING

Landscapes of North Wales. Roy Millward and Adrian Robinson. North Pomfret, VT and Devon, England: David & Charles, 1978. 207 pp. $18.95 (£7.50; pap. £4.95).

The book details the history, geology, and geography of North Wales through text, photographs, and illustrations. The beginning sections describe general characteristics of the area's seascapes and land formations, followed by individual studies of 12 particular areas. Along with the descriptions, the entries for each area include suggested itineraries by car for viewing the features highlighted in the text. Long lists for further reading and map references are included at the back of the book, along with a complete index.

Evaluation: Because the book covers such a small area, it is useful only to residents of North Wales or travelers planning an extended visit to the area. The detailed science and historical references and the lack of any practical travel information limit the book's usefulness to pretravel reading for those with more than a passing interest in the area's natural and social setting. Travelers planning a short visit to the area or those interested in more traditional vacation activities should look for another guide.

PUBS

The Best of British Pubs. Peter Earle and David Colbeck. New York and London: Charles Letts Co., 1980. 197 pp. pap. $6.95 (£1.95).

Although it emphasizes vendors of spirits, *The Best of British Pubs* also lists restaurants and some inns throughout England, Scotland, Wales, and the Channel Isles. The entries are divided into 17 geographic areas and are listed by city, with the cities in each area arranged alphabetically. Each entry lists the name of the pub, its architectural style, the availability of parking, whether dogs and children are allowed or specifically catered to, the music and atmosphere, the availability of food, beer, cider, snacks, and wine, a rating of the class, the prices, and the service, and a short description of the clientele. Maps of each area are provided, and a glossary of terms is included for the benefit of foreign readers.

Evaluation: The number of pubs and restaurants listed in the book is amazing. Well over a thousand establishments are described, located from the major cities to the smallest towns. The entries include all the necessary practical information on the pubs, but the complicated system of symbols employed takes some getting used to. The glossary of British drinking terms is especially helpful for North American visitors who are planning a pub crawl. How else would they be able to tell their scrumpy from their shandy? When used with a more comprehensive guide to the area (one that includes accommodation and transportation information), *The Best of British Pubs* ensures a full belly and high spirits for travelers throughout Britain.

Egon Ronay's Raleigh Pub Guide. Egon Ronay. New York: Penguin Books, 1980. 328 pp. pap. $4.95. London: Ronay Organization, 1980. £2.95.

Egon Ronay's Raleigh Pub Guide lists and assesses cocktail bars and pubs, their food, and, in some cases, their accommodations, for England, Scotland, Wales, and the Channel Islands. The major cities as well as smaller towns are covered; London has a separate chapter. Information for each pub in this guide includes address, telephone number, a description of all of the available facilities, as well as a description of atmosphere, history, décor, and food. Entries are listed alphabetically under city or town, and lists for pub restaurants, waterside pubs, cheeseboards, and cocktail bars are given. Recommended "bed and breakfasts" are also organized by cities and towns for easy location.

Evaluation: Information for each entry is complete and well organized, and *Egon Ronay's Raleigh Pub Guide* offers travelers interesting alternatives to traditional accommodation and food. The purpose of this guide is to evaluate food and accommodations, and ratings of entries are based on this. The major emphasis is for England; entries for other countries are substantially smaller. This guide will be useful to bar-frequenters and back-road travelers in Great Britain.

SIGHTSEEING

AA Guide to Stately Homes, Castles and Gardens. Basingstoke, Hampshire, England: Automobile Association (dist. in the U.S. by Standing Orders). 282 pp. pap. $6.95. Revised annually.

The *AA Guide to Stately Homes, Castles and Gardens* is the only sightseeing guide published by the Automobile Association. England, Scotland, and Northern Ireland are included, and historic homes, castles, and gardens as well as cathedrals, museums, zoos, and nature reserves are covered, along with other points of interest. This guide is organized by sections of the country, such as Cornwall, Devon, or Great London, and entries are listed alphabetically. Symbols and maps marking sights included provide quick access to information. This includes description, historic interest, hours of operation, admission, and telephone, along with other useful information. Coverage is extensive—over 2,000 entries are included.

Evaluation: Like the other AA guides, this is a comprehensive and complete guide to many interesting and historic sights in Britain. Information is well organized and easy to find, and the book is recommended to travelers of any style or budget. The 52 pages of location maps and the index to towns and places of interest are extremely useful.

Colourful Britain. London: British Tourist Authority (dist. in the U.S. by Merrimack Book Service), 1980. 128 pp. $19.95.

Great Britain possesses many treasures, chief among which, at least from the traveler's vantage point, are its buildings, both great and small, and its scenery. The British Tourist Authority dipped into several photographic libraries to bring these treasures to readers of *Colourful Britain*. Each page features a large and beautiful photograph of a British scene, building, or person. Texts of varying lengths accompany each picture, with longer comments on England, Wales, and Scotland. Interesting historical facts are often included.

Evaluation: For those who enjoy splendid color photographs and have a fancy for Britain, this is an ideal book. For the traveler who has been there, it is a wonderful memory book. For those going, it will help them capture the mood of different areas of Britain. And for the armchair traveler, it is what dreams are made of. It is, of course, not a guidebook; it is a feast for the eye.

A Guide to the National Trust in Devon and Cornwall. Peter Laws. North Pomfret, VT and Devon, England: David & Charles, 1978. 173 pp. $13.95 (£4.95).

The extensive Devon and Cornwall properties owned by the National Trust are carefully cataloged in this book. Each chapter deals with a particular type of property. Land along the north and south coastlines of Devon and Cornwall is covered in the first four chapters. The great houses of Devon and Cornwall occupy the next two chapters, the inland landscapes also taking two chapters. Miscellaneous buildings owned by the Trust, as described in the next chapter, include cottages available for holiday rental, although no particulars are given. A chapter on archaeological sites of the industrial age lists these properties. A final chapter lists Trust-owned prehistoric sites. Poor-quality black-and-white photographs appear throughout the book.

Evaluation: The carefully prepared book is fondly recommended to the public via a publisher's note, which states that it is for everyone making serious acquaintance with Devon and Cornwall. Indeed, one must be serious to read this book. It appears to be a highly accurate catalog of Trust-owned properties, rather than an inviting guide to an exciting area. The descriptions of the great houses come closer to reader-oriented text than the rest of the book. Perhaps the author is depending upon the booklets and leaflets recommended in the book to spark interest in the individual locations. The earnest traveler could use this book when planning a contemplative trip to Cornwall and Devon, but the casual traveler definitely needs a different guidebook.

SUMMER EMPLOYMENT

Directory of Summer Jobs in Britain. Susan Griffith, ed. Oxford, England: Vacation-Work (dist. in the U.S. by Writer's Digest Books;

dist. in Canada by Henry Fletcher Services). 159 pp. $6.95 (£1.95). Revised annually.

Although restaurant, housekeeping, and clerical jobs make up the majority of entries, the *Directory of Summer Jobs in Britain* also lists a variety of pastime employment opportunities in England, Scotland, and Wales. Some of the more unusual jobs include tennis coaches, English tutors, hairdressers, celery packers, kennel assistants, bird scarers, caving instructors, and forestry workers. The jobs are listed by geographic area and are divided into eight categories: business and industry, children, holiday centers and resorts, hotels and catering, medical, outdoor, sport, and teaching. Each entry includes the name, address, and telephone number of the establishment, followed by a short description of the position, skills or experience necessary, and to whom applications may be sent. Special sections include notes on applying for a job, visa and work permit regulations, voluntary work, *au pair*, paying guest and exchange visits, and a list of useful publications.

Evaluation: The book provides a valuable service to students, teachers, and others looking for summer employment in Britain. It lists a variety of jobs throughout the British Isles (with the exception of Ireland) and is updated annually to ensure reliability of the information. The entries include all the necessary practical information, presented clearly and organized well. The book is an excellent pretravel reference for anyone interested in a working vacation.

TRANSPORTATION

Baxter's BritRail Guide: Britain by Car, Bus, Rail. Robert Baxter. Alexandria, VA: Rail-Europe. 231 pp. pap. $7.95. Revised periodically.

Mainly a guide to transportation, *Baxter's BritRail Guide* covers many aspects of travel in Britain by car, bus, and especially train. It begins with preparatory information and travel tips, including transportation options and special fares, such as the BritRail pass. This is followed by sections on 19 cities and towns organized geographically from south (beginning in London) to north (Scotland), with a brief section on Wales. For each city and town there is a description of the train station and public transportation for the largest cities, hotel and restaurant suggestions, as well as sights, walking tours, and excursions.

Evaluations: This guide would be useful for those travelers holding a BritRail pass, since the majority of information is geared to train travel. Organization is somewhat haphazard, and coverage of each city or town is not consistent. However, the author provides very useful information, and the walking tours are one of the guide's strong points. This guide is recommended for the train traveler, coupled with a more comprehensive guide to Britain.

Inland Waterways. Charles Hadfield. North Pomfret, VT and Devon, England: David & Charles, 1978. 126 pp. $6.95 (£2.50).

Inland Waterways is somewhere on the border between travel guidebooks and leisure time hobby books. For those who like quiet and are not in a hurry, this book will draw them out of their cars and onto the canals of England. An introduction to the activity called canalling discusses types of boats and how to get acquainted with them. A brief discussion of where to go canalling is followed by helpful comments on the best months for travel, clothing, locks, courtesies, tunnels, maps, and the practicalities of boat handling. There is one sketchy map showing all the English waterways. The majority of the book is a series of essays on canals, their history, and their current operations. A brief section outlines canalling outside Britain. Helpful appendixes provide bibliographies and addresses, which will enable the intrigued to become actual canal travelers.

Evaluation: More of an introduction to canalling than a guidebook, *Inland Waterways* will serve as an excellent starting point for those interested in this relaxing mode of travel. Written in a comfortable style, the book leads the reader into the world of canalling, leaving the actual details to other publications, all of which are listed and referenced here. For the potential water traveler, this is an excellent book to start with.

Island Guides

The Channel Islands. See The Traveller's Guide series under Europe, Comprehensive Guides.

Harris and Lewis Lundy. See The Islands series under The World, Pretravel Reading, Islands of the World.

The Isle of Arran. See The Islands series under The World, Pretravel Reading, Islands of The World.

The Isle of Mull. See The Islands series under The World, Pretravel Reading, Islands of The World.

Orkney. See The Islands series under The World, Pretravel Reading, Islands of the World.

Shetland. See The Islands series under The World, Pretravel Reading, Islands of The World.

St. Kilda and the Other Hebridean Outliers. See The Islands series under The World, Pretravel Reading, Islands of the World.

Skye. See The Islands series under The World, Pretravel Reading, Islands of The World.

London

The Book of London. Michael Cady, ed. Basingstoke, Hampshire, England: Automobile Association (dist. in the U.S. by Hutchison Publishing), 1979. 191 pp. $16.95.

The Book of London is delightful. It features beautiful color photographs, maps, and illustrations throughout the entries and includes practical travel information on a variety of topics. Sections are included on royal London, London history, the Thames, cultural London, London's churches, shops and markets, parks, pubs, and restaurants. Twelve walking tours are described through every part of the city. At the back of the book are 17 pages of large, multicolored maps and a detailed index.

Evaluation: It is a truly remarkable book, combining the best features of practical, descriptive, and photographic guides into a beautiful and useful tool for exploring London. The information is complete and presented very clearly. The maps provided in the book would be the envy of Michelin. Although its large size may make it cumbersome to travel with, the book is sure to please all travelers and may even surprise lifelong residents of London with the depth of coverage it provides. Anyone interested in discovering London will find the book the key to that discovery and an invitation to a very memorable vacation.

Greater London. See Michelin Red Guides under Europe, Accommodations and Restaurants.

Letts Guide—London. See Letts Guide (City Series) under Europe, Comprehensive Guides.

London. See Blue Guide series, Fodor's City Guides, and Holiday Guides under The World, Comprehensive Guides; Michelin Green Guides under Europe, Sightseeing; and Rand McNally Pocket Guides under Europe, Comprehensive Guides.

London A to Z. See A to Z World Travel Guides under The World, Comprehensive Guides.

London on $500 a Day. For a review of a title in this series, see *Los Angeles on $500 a Day* in the chapter on North America, under California, Los Angeles and Vicinity.

The London Theatre Scene. Susan Elms, ed. Chistlehurst, Kent, England: Frank Cook Travel Guides, 1979. 175 pp. pap. $3.95.

The London theater tradition extends back at least 400 years, and the city is well known for the quality and diversity of its theatrical presentations. Fifty-six major theaters and concert halls are described in detail in *The London Theatre Scene*, with entries that include box office hours, telephone numbers, dining services, seating, credit cards accepted, directions by train and bus, auditorium outline plans, and short histories of the theaters with references to memorable past performances. The introduction gives an intensive history of London theater life, with a section on Theatreland Tours and a list of useful information on booking, ticket agencies, dress, tipping, and so on. Special sections include short descriptions and practical information on a number of hotels and restaurants, nightlife, dancing, pubs and wine bars, shopping, information centers, and major sites. There is also an Underground and Inter-City Rail map and a series of street maps at the back of the book that show the locations of theaters, hotels, and restaurants, sites of interest, underground and rail stations, tourist information centers, and parking areas.

Evaluation: The inclusion of hotel, restaurant, sights, shopping, and transportation information makes this the only London guide many travelers will need. The entries in these sections lack the depth of coverage provided in other guides to London, but the information is complete and very accessible. The descriptions and practical information for theaters and concert halls, along with the illustrations and auditorium plans in the entries, give an incredibly vivid picture of the theaters' past histories and their physical settings. Whether used alone or along with another guide containing more comprehensive accommodation and sights information, the book is sure to please all theatergoers planning a visit to the city.

Greece

COMPREHENSIVE GUIDES

Greece. See Blue Guide series and Fodor's Country Guides under The World, Comprehensive Guides.

Letts Guide—Greek Mainland. See Letts Guide (Country Series) under Europe, Comprehensive Guides.

ACCOMMODATIONS AND RESTAURANTS

Greece on $10 and $15 a Day. See Dollars a Day Guides under The World, Accommodations and Restaurants.

PRETRAVEL READING

TravelAid Guide to Greece. Michael von Haaz and Neville Lewis. London: Travel Aid Services (dist. in the U.S. by the Two Continents Publishing Group), 1979. 256 pp. pap. $7.50.

Hotels, restaurants, and taverns are briefly listed in the last nine pages of this book. Practical travel information is presented in eighteen pages at the front and two pages at the back. The main purpose of the book is to describe Greece: its culture, its people, its history, its geography, its architecture, its mood, and its special sights. Walking and driving directions, history, authors' stories, and information are included in a nonstop running text.

Evaluation: The text is interrupted only when the authors shift from one to another of the 18 geographic areas into which they have divided Greece. Headings in the margins identify the themes of the paragraphs, which include a startling variety of topics. The reader is unable to turn directly to any particular topic, such as history, art, or travel directions, since they are all hopelessly divided and scattered through the never-ending text. Despite these serious organizational problems, the authors' love of and knowledge of Greece show through. For those travelers seeking a good introduction to Greece in pretravel reading, this book offers the past and present as an existing whole. Its use on the road is limited by its organizational problems.

Traveling in Greece and Cyprus. See *Traveling the World Abroad*, under The World, Pretravel Reading, General.

SIGHTSEEING

Greece Observed. For a review of a title in this series, see *Egypt Observed* in the chapter on Africa, under Egypt.

Regional and Island Guides

The Adriatic Coast. See Blue Guide series under The World, Comprehensive Guides.

Corfu. See The Travellers' Guide series under Europe, Comprehensive Guides.

Crete. See Blue Guide series under The World, Comprehensive Guides, and The Traveller's Guide series under Europe, Comprehensive Guides.

The Greek Islands. Robin Mead. North Pomfret, VT and London: B. T. Batsford, 1979. 157 pp. $19.95.

The descriptions of the many islands and island groups that lie off the coast of Greece emphasize the major characteristics of each. Some, such as Corfu, are popular tourist spots, and the entries for them highlight their more touristy aspects; others, such as Patmos and Leros, are relatively undeveloped and offer travelers peaceful, uncrowded settings. The descriptions of the different islands include many references to their history, culture, sites of interest, and tavernas and suggestions for excursions, boat and car tours, and other activities. A special section is included on food and shopping, and maps are provided of the major islands.

Evaluation: Because the book emphasizes descriptions in the entries and excludes any practical travel information, it is useful only as a pretravel guide to vacationing on the islands. In this guise it serves very well. The entries capture the various charms of the islands and highlight their most interesting features. They provide a feel for the different areas that evokes a succession of peaceful, colorful images of vacationers lounging on a deserted beach, arriving at a noisy, crowded harbor, or exploring the ruins of an ancient Dionysian temple. The author's style is clear and descriptive, making the book read extraordinarily well. It is an excellent guide to the islands of Greece for all travelers, but most will need to acquire complete practical travel information to use along with it.

Letts Guide—Greek Islands. See Letts Guide (Country Series) under Europe, Comprehensive Guides.

Rhodes. See The Traveller's Guide series under Europe, Comprehensive Guides.

Athens

Athenian Odyssey. William M. Taylor. Corte Madera, CA: Omega Books, 1977. 90 pp. pap. $4.50.

Athenian Odyssey is much more than a guide to historic sites in ancient Athens. It gives detailed background on the history and mythology behind the ruins, describes each site through text, illustrations, and photographs, quotes from the works of Athenian dramatists, philosophers, and historians, and discusses the psychological and philosophical significance of the sites and the people who lived and died among them. The first chapter is a general overview of the city, introducing the reader to sites described in more detail in following sections. These include the Agora, the Panathenaic Road, the Acropolis, the Pnyx, the Theatre of Dionysus, and the Kerameikos (Cemetery of the Heroes). Complete reference notes and a short bibliography are included in the back of the book.

Evaluation: The book gives a feel for the area it describes not to be found in other guides. The detailed descriptions, the many literary and historical references, and the intellectual discussions of the significance of the city's past residents on modern thinking combine to make the book a unique learning experience for both travelers planning a trip to the area and those whose travels will be limited to their own imagination. When used along with a guide that includes practical travel information, the book will be the key to a vacation of discovery and intellectual stimulation.

Athens and Environs. See Blue Guide series under The World, Comprehensive Guides.

Iceland

Baxter's Eurailpass Travel Guide. See the review of this title under Europe, Railways.

Ireland

The Aran Islands. See The Islands series under The World, Pretravel Reading, Islands of the World.

Ireland. See Blue Guide series and Fodor's Country Guides under The World, Comprehensive Guides.

Ireland on $15 a Day. See Dollars a Day Guides under The World, Accommodations and Restaurants.

Let's Go: The Budget Guide to Britain and Ireland. See the review of this title in the chapter on Europe, under Great Britain, Comprehensive Guides.

Italy

DollarWise Guide to Italy. See DollarWise Guides under Europe, Accommodations and Restaurants.

Italy. See Fodor's Country Guides under The World, Comprehensive Guides; Michelin Green Guides under Europe, Sightseeing; Michelin Red Guides under Europe, Accommodations and Restaurants; and Rand McNally Pocket Guides under Europe, Comprehensive Guides.

Italy A to Z. See A to Z World Travel Guides under The World, Comprehensive Guides.

Italy Especially for Women. For a review of a title in the Especially for Women series, see *Mexico Especially for Women* in the chapter on Latin America and the Caribbean, under Mexico, Comprehensive Guides.

Let's Go: Italy. See *Let's Go: The Budget Guide to Britain and Ireland* in the chapter on Europe, under Great Britain, Comprehensive Guides.

Letts Guide—Italy. See Letts Guide (Country Series) under Europe, Comprehensive Guides.

Music Guide to Italy. See The Music Guide series under Europe, Music.

Regional and Island Guides

Malta. See Blue Guides series under The World, Comprehensive Guides.

Malta and Gozo. See The Traveller's Guide series under Europe, Comprehensive Guides.

The Maltese Islands. See The Islands series under The World, Pretravel Reading, Islands of the World.

Northern Italy. See Blue Guide series under The World, Comprehensive Guides.

Sardinia. See The Traveller's Guide series under Europe, Comprehensive Guides.

Sicily. See The Traveller's Guide series under Europe, Comprehensive Guides.

Southern Italy. See Blue Guide series under The World, Comprehensive Guides.

Florence

Florence Observed. For a review of a title in this series, see *Egypt Observed* under Africa, Egypt.

Rome

Letts Guide—Rome. See Letts Guide (City Series) under Europe, Comprehensive Guides.

Rome. See Fodor's City Guides under The World, Comprehensive Guides, and Michelin Green Guides under Europe, Sightseeing.

Rome and Environs. See Blue Guide series under The World, Comprehensive Guides.

Luxembourg

Belgium and Luxembourg. See Blue Guide series and Fodor's Country Guides under The World, Comprehensive Guides.

Benelux. See Michelin Red Guides under Europe, Accommodations and Restaurants.

The Music Guide to Belgium, Luxembourg, Holland and Switzerland. See The Music Guide series under Europe, Music.

Netherlands

Benelux. See Michelin Red Guides under Europe, Accommodations and Restaurants.

Holland. See Blue Guide series and Fodor's Country Guides under The World, Comprehensive Guides.

Letts Guide—Amsterdam. See Letts Guide (City Series) under Europe, Comprehensive Guides.

Letts Guide—Holland. See Letts Guide (Country Series) under Europe, Comprehensive Guides.

The Music Guide to Belgium, Luxembourg, Holland and Switzerland. See The Music Guide series under Europe, Music.

Norway

Letts Guide—Norway and Sweden. See Letts Guide (Country Series) under Europe, Comprehensive Guides.

Scandinavia on $20 a Day. See Dollars a Day Guides under The World, Accommodations and Restaurants.

Portugal

DollarWise Guide to Portugal. See DollarWise Guides under Europe, Accommodations and Restaurants.

Letts Guide—Portugal. See Letts Guide (Country Series) under Europe, Comprehensive Guides.

Portugal. See Fodor's Country Guides under The World, Comprehensive Guides, and Michelin Green Guides under Europe, Sightseeing.

Spain

COMPREHENSIVE GUIDES

Spain. See Fodor's Country Guides under The World, Comprehensive Guides, and Rand McNally Pocket Guides under Europe, Comprehensive Guides.

Spain and Portugal. See Michelin Red Guides under Europe, Accommodations and Restaurants.

ACCOMMODATIONS AND RESTAURANTS

Spain and Morocco (plus the Canary Islands) on $15 a Day. See Dollars a Day Guides under The World, Accommodations and Restaurants.

Spain and Portugal. See Michelin Red Guide under Europe, Accommodations and Restaurants.

PRETRAVEL READING

Spain. Jan Morris. New York: Oxford University Press, 1979. 155 pp. $10.95.

Jan Morris's *Spain* is not a travel guidebook but rather a description of the unique and interesting character of this country. Historical and cultural aspects of the various regions and cities of Spain are covered, as well as geography, architecture, customs, and the people. The book offers an insightful picture of this complex and unusual country.

Evaluation: Spain provides a well-written and unique account of some of the more subtle qualities, both good and bad, of Spain. By reading this book, the reader can gain a unique perspective of the customs and peoples of Spain. It is excellent pretravel reading, especially for those travelers interested in more than a touristy, sightseeing approach.

SIGHTSEEING

Spain. See Michelin Green Guides under Europe, Sightseeing.

Spain Observed. For a review of a title in this series, see *Egypt Observed* under Africa, Egypt.

Regional and Island Guides

Canary Islands: Fuerteventura. See The Islands series under The World, Pretravel Reading, Islands of the World.

Letts Guide—Costa Brava, Costa del Sol, Spanish Islands. See Letts Guide (Country Series) under Europe, Comprehensive Guides.

Southern Spain. See Blue Guide series under The World, Comprehensive Guides.

Sweden

Letts Guide—Norway and Sweden. See Letts Guide (Country Series) under Europe, Comprehensive Guides.

Scandinavia on $20 a Day. See Dollars a Day Guides under The World, Accommodations and Restaurants.

Switzerland

Bernese Oberland. See Blue Guide series under The World, Comprehensive Guides.

The Inn Way . . . Switzerland. Margaret Zellers. Stockbridge, MA: Berkshire Traveller Press, 1978. 126 pp. pap. $4.95.

The Inn Way . . . Switzerland is a guide to quaint, out-of-the-way inns and hotels personally visited and evaluated by the author; it offers accommodation alternatives to larger hotels overrun by tourists. The guide is organized by region, covering 12 tourist regions and the principality of Lichtenstein. The entries include addresses, telephone numbers, number of rooms, and a paragraph describing atmosphere, architecture, dining facilities, sports, and many other aspects. The last part of the guide is devoted to practical information on traveling in Switzerland.

Evaluation: The Inn Way . . . Switzerland is a good source for unique accommodations, useful for both pretravel and on-the-road usage. Addresses for more specific information such as prices and reservations are very helpful. The country receives a brief introduction, but a more comprehensive guide including more background information, transportation, etc., is needed in addition to this guide.

Letts Guide—Switzerland. See Letts Guide (Country Series) under Europe, Comprehensive Guides.

Lucerne. See Blue Guide series under The World, Comprehensive Guides.

The Music Guide to Belgium, Luxembourg, Holland and Switzerland. See The Music Guide series under Europe, Music.

Switzerland. See Fodor's Country Guides under The World, Comprehensive Guides and Michelin Green Guides under Europe, Sightseeing.

Union of Soviet Socialist Republics

American's Tourist Manual for the U.S.S.R. John E. Felber. Newark, NJ: International Intertrade Index, 1979. 225 pp. pap $6.95.

The fourteenth edition of John E. Felber's *American's Tourist Manual for the U.S.S.R.* is a guide to the sights and attractions of the major cities in the Soviet Union. It also includes practical information such as preparation, currency, weather, and transportation. Cities are covered alphabetically, listing major sights and places of cultural and historical importance. Each of the major cities has listings with specific information for sights, hotels, restaurants, entertainment, and excursions. Moscow and Leningrad, the largest Soviet cities, are covered more extensively than others; in fact, the coverage is taken directly out of separate publications. Useful mileage charts, various maps, and useful Russian expressions, along with other helpful illustrations, provide additional information.

Evaluation: This guide is limited by the restrictions put on travelers by Intourist, such as where to stay, what to see, and why one should see it. Coverage of the cities reads like a travel brochure, as much of the information is taken directly from these sources. The alphabetical city listings are disorienting for such a large and relatively unfamiliar geographic area. There is very little background information, and very little on the various cultural differences within the country. Overall, however, the usefulness of the information in this book outweighs the limitations. Felber provides a helpful, though not all-inclusive, guide for traveling in the Soviet Union.

Moscow and Leningrad Observed. For a review of a title in this series, see *Egypt Observed* in the chapter on Africa, under Egypt.

The Soviet Union—Guide and Information Handbook. V. Ludvikova and L. Shokan. New York: Rand McNally & Co., 2d ed., 1976. 198 pp. pap. $4.95. Northamptonshire, England: Collet's Holdings, 1976. pap. £2.

Rand McNally's *The Soviet Union* is primarily an information handbook and motoring guide. Included are historical, geographic, and economic data and eight assigned motor routes covering approximately 12,500 kilometers. Important on-the-road information is also given, such as gasoline and service stations, distances, directions, and maps. Hotels, motels, and camping sites are listed in relation to the given routes. Cities are listed alphabetically and include background information. Restaurants are always included in packaged tours, and food prices are given for campers. There is little preparatory information.

Evaluation: All of the factual information provided serves as good introductory pretravel reading, but very little of it would be useful for traveling in the Soviet Union. The motor routes, which include all those available to the tourist, are useful, but there is not enough detail to supplement them. This guide is limited by the fact that travel in the Soviet Union is confined to designated places and also to possible travel styles. The book is translated into English from Czech, so information is not geared to the American tourist. In fact, much of the contents seems to be taken from a geography book. The alphabetical rather than geographic order of the city listings is somewhat disorienting, especially since such an extensive geographic area is covered. This guide is not recommended for anyone except those interested in seeing the Soviet Union by car, and even then, a more comprehensive guide is needed.

Yugoslavia

Eastern Europe A to Z. See A to Z World Travel Guides under The World, Comprehensive Guides.

Letts Guide: Yugoslavia. See Letts Guide (Country Series) under Europe, Comprehensive Guides.

Yugoslavia. See Blue Guide series and Fodor's Country Guides under The World, Comprehensive Guides, and The Traveller's Guide series under Europe, Comprehensive Guides.

LATIN AMERICA AND THE CARIBBEAN

COMPREHENSIVE GUIDES

Along the Gringo Trail: A Budget Travel Guide to Latin America. Jack Epstein. Berkeley, CA: And/Or Press, 1977. 484 pp. pap. $6.95.

Along the Gringo Trail is a low-budget guide to Mexico and the countries of Central America, South America, and the West Indies. It is geared to students or young travelers and those interested in independent travel. The Gringo Trail is an actual trail, and the author has given those countries through which the trail passes more coverage than those off the trail, so that coverage is uneven. Practical and background information is abundant, and brief sections for each country include a few accommodation suggestions, a description of regional foods (specific restaurant listings are infrequent), and brief descriptions of selected sights.

Evaluation: The strong points of this guide are the abundant preparatory information and cultural and political background information. The style is rather specific, geared to the typical counter-culture traveler. The guide is filled with jargon and emphasizes drugs, "hippie harassment," and the "police situation." *Along the Gringo Trail* could best be used for pretravel reading, and a guide containing more specific information on transportation, accommodation, and so on, such as *The South American Handbook* (see under South America, Comprehensive Guides), would be necessary for on-the-road travel.

The Budget Traveler's Latin America. Council on International Educational Exchange. New York: E. P. Dutton, 1979-1980. 250 pp. pap. $4.95.

The Budget Traveler's Latin America, formerly *The Student Guide to Latin America,* offers the budget traveler some of the basics for traveling in the countries of Mexico, Central America, South America, and the Caribbean islands. All countries are in alphabetical order and include only the essential information. Historical and cultural background information, getting there and getting around, and sights are briefly covered.

Evaluation: The Budget Traveler's Latin America is not an all-encompassing guide, nor is it meant to be. However, it provides a good orientation to Latin America and also tells the reader how to approach travel in these countries with a low budget. Addresses for further information and a bibliography are provided and are highly recommended. The quotations inserted throughout the book, which are firsthand accounts from students, provide many good tips and suggestions. A more detailed guide is recommended to complement this guide, such as *The South America Handbook* (see under South America, Comprehensive Guides), which the author suggests.

Pan Am's Guide to Latin America. New York: Pan American Airways, 1976. 178 pp. pap. $2.

Pan Am's Guide to Latin America emphasizes basic but comprehensive coverage of all aspects of travel in the countries described. The entries for each country concentrate on practical travel information, such as its setting, climate, currency, entry and customs requirements, banks, shopping, and health. Transportation to and in the country, entertainment, food and restaurants, sports, sights, and sources for further information are briefly mentioned in each entry. In the beginning sections there are general discussions of pretravel paperwork, health, money, insurance, packing, electricity, and photography. The book serves travelers on moderate and above-average budgets planning a trip to a number of Latin American countries.

Evaluation: Because the book emphasizes practical travel information, it is necessary that the information be as up-to-date as possible. It is not. The book was published in 1976, and since that time many changes have occurred that make much of the information either inaccurate or unreliable. The book includes very little background, transportation, or accommodations information, and the sights listings are sketchy and brief. The book's best features are the inclusion of practical and preparatory information on all Latin American countries and its low cost. Its worst features are its age, the basic quality of information, and the lack of descriptions in the accommodations and sights listings.

The Caribbean

COMPREHENSIVE GUIDES

The Budget Traveler's Latin America. See the review of this title above, under Latin America & the Caribbean, Comprehensive Guides.

Pilots' Guide to the Lesser Antilles. Paul Fillingham. New York: McGraw-Hill Book Co., 1977. 377 pp. $15.95.

It is not necessary to be a pilot, or even to travel by plane in the area to use the book, although flyers are those it was originally intended to serve. The book provides detailed coverage of a variety of aspects of travel on the islands that form a crescent between Puerto Rico and Trinidad and Tobago. The introduction gives basic historical and political background, describes the islands and their major airfields, and discusses flight and en-route planning. Following this are descriptions of and practical travel information on the 24 different islands and island groups, including flight approaches, background, sights, activities, selected hotels and restaurants (descriptions only), sports, and excursions by car and on foot. The appendixes list preparatory and emergency information for pilots, measurement conversion tables, a long list for further reading, repair stations and authorized inspectors, air taxi operators, and 30 pages of flight charts that only a pilot could decipher.

Evaluation: The book is geared to travelers on moderate and above-average budgets planning a trip to a number of the islands described. It includes a wide range of travel information, but very few low-cost alternatives. The information is complete and easy to find, and the background and historical references provide an excellent feel for the social and physical characteristics of the different islands. Many travelers will find that the book is the only guide they need, but others with more budget restrictions and those planning an extended visit to a particular Caribbean island should look for another guide.

The South American Handbook. See the review of this title below, under South America, Comprehensive Guides.

ACCOMMODATIONS AND RESTAURANTS

Caribbean Hideaways. Ian Keown. New York: Harmony Books, 1978. 370 pp. pap. $5.95.

Caribbean Hideaways is a guide to 130 accommodations in out-of-the-way spots on the islands of the Caribbean and parts of southern Mexico. Intended as a hideaway guide for lovers of "all inclinations," the accommodations focus on quiet, secluded places. Emphasis is given to comfort and luxury. Accommodations are rated for romantic atmosphere, food and service, sports facilities, and cost. The author states that the ratings are highly subjective. Budgets for the listed accommodations range from moderate (the lowest being $50) to very high.

Evaluation: For a diverse and unusual selection of quiet and secluded accommodations in the Caribbean, Ian Keown's *Caribbean Hideaways* is a good reference, informative and complete. However, the author is writing for a very select group (that is, lovers), and his writing style is at times tasteless and pretentious, which interferes with the effectiveness of the book. For those travelers looking for a quiet Caribbean resort vacation and not restricted by budget limitations, this guide could offer some reasonable suggestions; a more inclusive guide, however, would be of more value.

Fielding's Caribbean Including Cuba. Margaret Zellers. New York: Fielding Publications, 1979. 73 pp. pap. $10.95.

Fielding's Caribbean Including Cuba, like other Fielding guides, is primarily a guide to accommodations, restaurants, and nightspots. Coverage includes 20 Caribbean islands. The travel style is geared to those who enjoy Fielding's travel approach, which emphasizes creature comforts and first-class traveling. Although the guide claims to include all price ranges, it is geared to those with ample pocketbooks. Coverage includes the major tourist spots and the major sights, shopping and sports, and some cultural and historical background, including political descriptions for each country.

Evaluation: For those interested in preplanned, all-inclusive resort vacations, *Fielding's Caribbean Including Cuba* will be of use. It would be more useful for pretravel reference to hotels and restaurants than as an on-the-road guide. While the author is well acquainted with the Caribbean, some of the information is superfluous, with the author's personal injections and opinions. Cities, hotels, and sights are selective, and coverage is not always uniform for each country. Independent travelers and those who are interested in the sights will need a more comprehensive guide. Transportation around the islands and to and from the islands is not covered at all.

The Inn Way . . . The Caribbean. Margaret Zellers. Stockbridge, MA: Berkshire Traveller Press, 1978. 192 pp. pap. $4.95.

The Inn Way . . . The Caribbean lists small inns, hotels, estates, and resorts in 18 countries of the Caribbean. Address, telephone number, description and number of rooms, and so on, are given for each entry, as well as a lengthy paragraph describing atmosphere, distinctive features, scenery and surrounding areas, dining, and entertainment. Information regarding many kinds of sports available at the accommodations, such as snorkeling, scuba diving, horseback riding, and golf, is also provided. Exact prices are not given, but are regarded by the author as modest. They are not rock bottom, however; such things as creature comforts, dining, and entertainment are included. Many entries can be both complete resort vacations and simple accommodations for touring and sightseeing.

Evaluation: For pretravel accommodation or resort vacation planning to the Caribbean, Margaret Zellers's book will be of great help. She provides a good introduction to what is available and addresses for specifics such as prices and reservations. Listings for each country are preceded by a brief introduction to the country, but a more in-depth guide is necessary. Transportation and practical information is also not included.

Bahamas

Baxter's Eurailpass Travel Guide. See the review of this title under Europe, Railways. (A section in the book discusses the Bahamas.)

Grand Bahama. See The Islands series under The World, Pretravel Reading, Islands of the World.

Bermuda

Bermuda. See Fodor's Country Guides under The World, Comprehensive Guides.

Cuba

The Complete Travel Guide to Cuba. Paula DiPerna. New York: St. Martin's Press, 1979. 275 pp. pap. $4.95.

The rules and restrictions involved in traveling to a Communist country require extensive preplanning, usually through the country's office of tourism, and such travel is rarely inexpensive. *The Complete Travel Guide to Cuba* outlines all the necessary preparatory information and includes complete information on the country's vital statistics, immigration regulations, tours and tour operators, money, transportation, and communication. The city entries are organized alphabetically and follow a long history and social profile of the country. History, sights, transportation, and accommodations are listed for the larger cities. The entries for the smaller towns are limited to a paragraph or two of descriptions. The entries include many well-drawn maps. There is also a glossary of common Spanish terms at the back of the book.

Evaluation: The book gives a complete overview of travel in Cuba as well as a full description of the country before and after the Revolution. Tourist facilities have remained relatively unchanged in the last 20 years, but the author notes that many changes in the tourist industry are in progress. The information is complete, particularly the extensive background and history sections, but because the city entries (two-thirds of the book) are arranged alphabetically instead of regionally, it is difficult to figure out exactly where they are. Still, this is a very useful guide for all travelers to Cuba, and not just because it is the only one.

Dominica

Dominica. See The Islands series under The World, Pretravel Reading, Islands of the World.

Virgin Islands

Country Inns and Back Roads. See the review of this title under North America, Accommodations and Restaurants.

Central America

Four Keys to Guatemala. Vera Kelsey and Lilly de Jongh Osborne. New York: Thomas Y. Crowell Co., 11th ed. 1978. 255 pp. pap. $5.95.

The book gives extensive coverage of all aspects of travel in Guatemala, showing it as a country that has much to offer travelers, whether experienced or not. The information is divided into three sections. The first lists practical data on the country, sports and outdoor activities, and a brief history. Small and large cities, areas of historic interest, and picturesque rural areas are described in the second section; the third details the customs, folk cultures, and arts of the country. Photographs are included of many sites in the country, and a complete index is found at the back of the book.

Evaluation: The feel the book provides for the country and its inhabitants shows the author's respect and admiration for them. The information is presented clearly and includes all necessary practical information on transportation, accommodations, sights, and activities. The background on Guatemala's history and culture gives an excellent overview of life in the country. The book is the only travel guide necessary for an enjoyable and enlightening trip to a relatively undiscovered area.

Mexico and Central America: A Handbook for the Independent Traveller. Frank Bellamy. New York: The Two Continents Publishing

Group, 1977. 224 pp. pap. $6.95. London: Wilton House Gentry, 1977. £5.95.

For the independent, rock-bottom budget traveler with a spirit of adventure and tolerance, *Mexico and Central America* provides a detailed itinerary and set of instructions. Assuming that the reader has not traveled south of the border, the book begins with a discussion of costs, the suggested itineraries, health, visa requirements, insurance, and luggage. Historical, cultural, and practical travel concerns are covered extensively. Detailed travel instructions follow, enabling the traveler to duplicate the author's journey through Mexico and Central America, including its final segment from Miami to El Paso, Texas.

Evaluation: Readers under 30 who want (or need) detailed itineraries and instructions for a rock-bottom trip in Mexico and Central America will find this book helpful. Even for this restricted audience, however, the 1977 publishing date renders many of the prices, bus schedules, and perhaps even addresses out of date. Both the strength and weakness of this book is that it follows a strict itinerary and provides information only on the one hotel in each location where the author stayed. No others are mentioned; neither are there any references to restaurants. The entire book reads like a revision of detailed and accurate notes taken in a travel diary. It can inspire the young with empty pockets to travel, however.

Mexico and Guatemala on $10 and $15 a Day. See Dollars a Day Guides under The World, Accommodations and Restaurants.

Mexico

COMPREHENSIVE GUIDES

Living Easy in Mexico: A New Guide to Traveling and Living in Marvelous Mexico. Hayes C. Schlundt. Santa Barbara, CA: Woodbridge Press Publishing Co., 1978. 208 pp. pap. $3.95.

Living Easy in Mexico is divided into two sections—living in Mexico and traveling in Mexico. The first section concentrates on selecting a home, housekeeping, what to expect, descriptions of various cities and towns, and so on. The second section, on traveling, is geared to those traveling by car (road numbers and directions are given). Cities and towns are organized regionally. Coverage is rather selective, with the author recommending locations and hotels. Hotel listings include rates and brief descriptions with nonspecific directions. Other entries include restaurants, some sights and shopping, and descriptions of road conditions.

Evaluation: As a travel guide, *Living Easy in Mexico* is not very useful, since coverage is very selective, based on the author's personal experiences and individual recommendations. A more comprehensive guide, including sights, transportation, and so on, is necessary. However, for those considering living in Mexico, this guide will be useful for a general background. Information is not specific, and no addresses for further details are given. The book is more for the armchair reader who is vaguely considering living in Mexico.

Mexico and Central America: A Handbook for the Independent Traveller. See the review of this title above, under Central America.

Mexico Especially for Women. Gerie Tully. New York: Abelard-Schuman, 1976. 421 pp. $9.95.

Gerie Tully's *Mexico Especially for Women,* as an example of her series, is directed primarily to women traveling alone. It contains preparatory and practical information for pretravel planning, background information, accommodations, restaurants, sights, shopping, and many other aspects of travel in Mexico. The major cities and tourist attractions as well as many smaller cities and towns are covered. The guide is mainly oriented to those with ample budgets, as budgeting is not considered. All of the essential information on accommodations and restaurants is given, along with a description of clientele, rooms, and available facilities. Nightlife, entertainment, and sports events are also included.

Evaluation: While some parts of this guide concerning women travelers deal with somewhat superficial concerns, *Mexico Especially for Women* does have some important practical information for women traveling alone. Coverage of cities and towns, especially hotels, restaurants, sights, and events, is detailed and complete. Transportation, however, is slighted, while shopping is covered in great detail. For women traveling alone, with a bent toward luxury and the high life, this guide provides a good comprehensive approach to travel throughout the country of Mexico.

Included in the series: England Especially for Women; France Especially for Women; Italy Especially for Women; Mexico Especially for Women.

The Moneywise Guide to North America. See the review of this title under North America, Comprehensive Guides.

The People's Guide to Mexico. Carl Franz. Santa Fe, NM: John Muir Publications (dist. in the U.S. by Bookpeople; dist. in the U.K. by Selpress Books, London). 625 pp. pap. $9. (£5.75). Revised periodically.

The People's Guide to Mexico, as the author states, is a book about

Mexico; a "sort of guidebook" rather than the traditional accommodation and restaurant guide. This guide is a compilation of the author's travel experiences in Mexico, offering practical information on preparation, what to expect while traveling in Mexico, and many other aspects of Mexican travel such as customs, public transportation, shopping, camping, renting a car, and many others. The intended audience is those traveling cheaply, such as students, rather than those interested in comfort or luxury.

Evaluation: This guide contains practical tips and suggestions for budget travelers and will be of more use for pretravel reading than on the road. No information regarding hotels, restaurants, or sights is provided, there is nothing on cities and towns, and no addresses or specific bus or train schedules. The author interjects personal experience and anecdotes that are of little use to the reader, but comply with the author's casual and rambling writing style. Despite this, the guide offers unusual insight into many aspects of traveling in Mexico and into the people and the country.

The Wilhelms' Guide to All Mexico. John Lawrence and Charles Wilhelm. New York: McGraw-Hill Book Co., 1978. 484 pp. $12.50.

The Wilhelms' Guide to All Mexico is a guide to principal cities and resort areas in Mexico. Historical background, hotels, restaurants, and nightclubs, as well as principal sights, sports, and shopping, are covered for each area. Transportation information is limited and generalized, although there is a chapter on travel by car. The authors state that this guide was "written for the traveler on a budget as well as the luxury minded." Hotel and restaurant listings range from very expensive to bargain.

Evaluation: For the first-time traveler, and as a hotel and restaurant guide, this guide would be useful. Information provided is sketchy and general, and there is not much information on the Mexican people and their culture. The hotels and restaurants and listings of principal sights are the book's strong points. The guide, although it includes low-budget accommodations and restaurants, is principally geared to the traveler on a moderate budget.

ACCOMMODATIONS AND RESTAURANTS

Mexico and Guatemala on $10 and $15 a Day. See Dollars a Day Guides under The World, Accommodations and Restaurants.

DRIVING TOURS

Offbeat Baja. Jim Hunter. San Francisco, CA: Chronicle Books, 1977. 156 pp. pap. $4.95.

It would be very difficult to get any farther off the beaten track than onto the roads and trails described in *Offbeat Baja.* Many of the routes described in the book are passable with "the family car," but the degree of exploration suggested by the author almost makes a four-wheel drive vehicle mandatory. The trips are divided geographically, with general descriptions of the areas and detailed mileage charts that give landmarks for navigation, possible campsites, and natural points of interest. Special sections are included on motorcycle and four-wheel drive vehicle maintenance, photography, the road-log and classification system used by the author, a reading list, and a particularly useful section called "Between Friends" that gives a variety of helpful tips on traveling on the Baja peninsula.

Evaluation: The number of roads described provide weeks of exploration in one of the most rugged areas in North America. The information is as complete as possible for the area, but the changing availability of supplies and conditions of the routes calls for some previous experience in this method of travel. The maps included are large and clear, but no guarantee against becoming lost in the lightly traveled areas. A trip to the back country of the Baja peninsula requires a large amount of preparation, and travelers on their first or fortieth visit will find this book a good beginning.

HANDICAPPED TRAVELERS

The Wheelchair Traveler. See the review of this title in the chapter on North America under United States, Handicapped Travelers.

HISTORY AND ARCHAEOLOGY

A Guide to Ancient Mexican Ruins. C. Bruce Hunter. Norman, OK: University of Oklahoma Press, 1977. 261 pp. $10.95; pap. $5.95.

A Guide to Ancient Mexican Ruins details the pre-Columbian history of Mexico and describes through text, illustrations, and photographs the many artifacts of the different cultures. The introduction discusses the general history of the different groups and describes basic characteristics of their buildings, stonework, and jewelry. The area is then divided into five major valleys in southern and central Mexico, with detailed descriptions of the ancient civilizations of each and what survives of their cities. Special sections include suggestions for reaching archaeological zones and a long list of suggested reading. The book serves all travelers with more than a passing interest in the archaeological history of Mexico; it should be read before leaving and referred to on the road.

Evaluation: The author succeeds in presenting a wide range of information on the archaeological history of the area in a fairly nontechnical style, though some previous knowledge is useful. The beautiful photographs, in color and black and white, and the high-quality illustrations are excellent complements to the text. The book is extremely well presented and clearly organized. The information it contains offers months of exploration, but travelers should supplement it with a more comprehensive guide to the area. It is an invaluable asset for those wishing to discover the world of ancient Mexico on their own.

A Travel Guide to Archaeological Mexico. Robert D. Wood. New York: Hastings House Publishers, 1979. 158 pp. $10.95; pap. $6.95.

This guide is intended as an on-the-road guide to seeing the profuse archaeological sites in Mexico by car. It is for those with no other prerequisite than interest. Twelve motor routes are given, which include information on sites, their accessibility and location, and distances between locations (given in kilometers and miles). Three other sections of the book provide alphabetical listings of archaeological sites, ancient cultures, and archaeological regions. In addition, there is a very brief section of practical information.

Evaluation: Although limited in its coverage, this guide provides sufficient information to fulfill its intriguing aims. However, directions are somewhat vague and can be disorienting. Details are left for the tourist to dig up via tourist offices (no addresses or telephone numbers are given). Coupled with a more comprehensive guide that includes accommodations, food, and budget information, this guide could be the door to an exciting experience.

ROAD ATLASES

Rand McNally Road Atlas. See the review of this title under North America, Road Atlases.

South America

COMPREHENSIVE GUIDES

Brazil. See Fodor's Country Guides under The World, Comprehensive Guides.

Fodor's South America. Eugene Fodor and Robert C. Fisher. New York: David McKay Co. 621 pp. pap. $9.95. London: Hodder & Stoughton. £6.95. Revised annually.

Fodor's South America tackles the 13 countries of South America in an assiduously thorough guide. A substantial introduction to the continent and a practical section on pretrip planning are followed by material introducing each of the individual countries. Although most of the information is geared to the moderate- and high-budget traveler, care is also taken to include those on a low budget.

Evaluation: The tone of the introductory and background material in *Fodor's South America* is more tourist-oriented and chatty than the rather scholarly *South American Handbook* (see below). Fodor's reliance on country specialists to write the individual country chapters invites a wide range of opinion. All in all, *Fodor's South America* is a very good introduction to this less-traveled continent and is highly recommended. It is especially useful for background information and as a guide to larger and capital cities; it is somewhat weaker on smaller cities.

Myra Waldo's Travel Guide: South America. Myra Waldo. New York: Macmillan Publishing Co. 392 pp. pap. $7.95. Revised periodically.

Myra Waldo candidly offers her own subjective guide to South America. This is not a guide for student or budget travelers, but for first- to tourist-class plane travelers. Coverage of the South American countries focuses on capital cities with excursions. Information is limited, briefly covering background, practical information, cities, and sights.

Evaluation: Myra Waldo attempts to cover a large amount of information on South America, but provides only a superficial and limited outline. Restaurant and hotel listings do not include addresses. Her travel style is oriented toward the tourist with an ample budget, rather than the inquisitive or independent budget traveler. For inexperienced travelers not interested in an in-depth travel approach, *Myra Waldo's Travel Guide: South America* may prove useful, but for those interested in a more in-depth and objective approach, both *The South American Handbook* (see below) and *Fodor's South America* (see above) are far superior.

Other books in the series: Myra Waldo's Travel Guide: Southern Europe with Motoring Routes; Myra Waldo's Travel Guide: Northern Europe with Motoring Routes; Myra Waldo's Travel Guide: Orient and Asia; Myra Waldo's Travel Guide: South Pacific.

South America A to Z. See A to Z World Travel Guides under The World, Comprehensive Guides.

The South American Handbook. John Brooks. Bath, England: Trade & Travel Publications (dist. in the U.S. by Rand McNally & Co.). 1,200 pp. $19.75 (£6.95). Revised annually.

Published in England but adapted for American travelers, *The South American Handbook* addresses all visitors, whether sightseers or businesspeople. Coverage includes not only all the South American countries, but also all of Mexico, Central America, and the Caribbean Islands. This well-organized guide contains a wealth of information, covering every practical detail for travel in these countries, as well as a rundown on their peoples, history, and present forms of government.

Evaluation: Although very expensive, *The South American Handbook* is invaluable for travelers who desire more than the standard tourist-oriented jargon and are headed to the lesser-known areas and islands. This guide is exceptional in its breadth of coverage; a maximum of information is packed into a relatively small format. While low-budget accommodations are included, the general orientation and travel philosophy leans toward moderate to high budgets. The editors warn of escalating inflation, which render most prices obsolete. *The South American Handbook* is highly recommended for all travelers, especially those desiring a knowledge of the history and cultural composition of each country and a greater appreciation of contemporary Latin America.

South American Survival: A Handbook for the Independent Traveller. Maurice Taylor. London: Wilton House Gentry (dist. in the U.S. by Transatlantic Arts), 1977. 272 pp. $18.

South American Survival is geared to travelers on low to moderate budgets traveling from Europe or North America and wishing to discover independently the many different environments of the continent. The first section discusses preparation and pretravel routines, documents, language, clothing and equipment, money, and health. Next there is a discussion of weather, food, drink, transportation, types of accommodations, security, wild animals, and local dress and customs. The countries are listed in the order in which they were visited by the author, and the entries are organized so that the author's route can be followed exactly. The information on each country includes descriptions of the physical setting, history, people, and economics, followed by descriptions of major cities and suggested routes between them. Many excerpts from the author's journal are included, along with some color photographs and appendixes that list American Express offices, approximate costs, Trail Finders' offices, and a short bibliography. Of particular use are the 68 pages of carefully drawn maps at the back of the book.

Evaluation: The practical and preparatory information in the book is complete and very useful, though it includes few higher-cost alternatives. The unique organization of the countries is slightly confusing, but the book is generally easy to use, with the information presented clearly. The author features descriptions of the more rural aspects of different areas and includes only minimal coverage of major cities. Travelers wishing to see and experience the countries as their inhabitants do will be served well by this book. Those looking for a more traditional vacation in the area should look for another guide.

South American Travel Digest. Charles and Babette Jacobs. William Doughty, ed. Palm Desert, CA: Travel Digests, Paul Richmond & Co., 12th ed. 1979. 178 pp. pap. $7.95.

Geared to travelers on moderate and above-average budgets, the *South American Travel Digest* includes travel information on all South American countries. The introductory sections feature a route planner that describes possible itineraries, a discussion of Amazon touring, information on land and air travel to major South American cities, a cruise guide, and brief practical information on entry requirements, money, clothing, and climate. The countries are arranged in no discernible order and include information on transportation, sights, hotels and restaurants, shopping, and annual events. The entries concentrate on major cities, with special descriptive sections on the land of the Incas, islands off the Pacific and Atlantic coasts, the Panama Canal Zone, and other areas of historic and natural interest. Many photographs of industrious Indians, smiling visitors, city street scenes, exotic meals, and natural wonders are included, along with a number of advertisements.

Evaluation: The book's best features are the air travel information, the abundance of practical information on all South American countries, and the listings of sights and activities in major cities. Areas in which the book falls short include accommodation information, background, practical travel information, transportation, and organization. The entries include little information for the budget minded and emphasize broad but superficial coverage. Nearly all topics pertaining to travel in South America are touched upon, but few are detailed. More comprehensive information, with some cost considerations, can be found in either *The South American Handbook* (see above) or *A Traveler's Guide to El Dorado and the Inca Empire* (see below).

A Traveler's Guide to El Dorado and the Inca Empire. Lynn Meisch. New York: Penguin Books, 1977. 446 pp. pap. $8.95.

A Traveler's Guide to El Dorado and the Inca Empire contains a vast amount of information on preparing for a trip to South America and also on various aspects of the past and present cultures of Colombia, Ecuador, Peru, and Bolivia, the countries of the Inca Empire. Information on the "continuity of pre-Columbian civilizations and modern Indian cultures," archaeology, folk art and handicrafts, native markets, music, festivals, and many other points are covered. Practical information and traveling tips such as descriptions of food, accommodations, transportation, "how things work," health, and many others are also covered in substantial detail.

Evaluation: A Traveler's Guide to El Dorado and the Inca Empire is a unique and indispensable guide to experiencing Colombia, Peru, Ecuador, and Bolivia. All information on preparation, practical traveling and history, culture, archaeology, and so on is presented in a well-written, well-organized, and intelligent style. An extensive bibliography is given, and the author highly recommends pairing her book with *The South American Handbook* (see above), which would provide an excellent combination of a basic how-to guide and an in-depth descriptive guide such as this. This guide is useful to travelers through all of South America, not only those interested in the Inca civilizations.

ACCOMMODATIONS AND RESTAURANTS

South America on $15 a Day. See Dollars a Day Guides under The World, Accommodations and Restaurants.

PRETRAVEL READING

The Falkland Islands. See The Island series under The World, Pretravel Reading, Islands of the World.

NORTH AMERICA

COMPREHENSIVE GUIDES

The Moneywise Guide to North America. Michael von Haag and Anna Crew, eds. London: Travelaid Publishing (dist. in the U.S. by Hippocrene Books), 15th ed. 1980. 354 pp. pap. $3.50 (£2.50).

This Travelaid publication is aimed at the limited-budget foreign traveler in the United States who might also be interested in side trips to Canada and Mexico. The background provided for the United States (and Canada and Mexico) contains visa information, transoceanic transportation information, notes on climate, packing tips, comments on national character, information on parks, health, accommodations, and food, a discussion of financial matters, and a huge variety of other practical topics. After this general background information, the seven regions of the United States are introduced briefly, each followed with similarly brief discussions of states. Within each state, listings are found for cities appropriate as bases for exploration and also other interesting cities and towns through which one might pass. For each, accommodations, food, sites of interest, entertainment possibilities, information, and transportation follow a short general description. More extensive information is available for the larger cities. Similar but much shorter sections are provided for Canada and Mexico.

Evaluation: Because the book covers such a large number of smaller towns as well as major cities, the information provided has been cut to the bare necessities. It is adequate for the tourist on the move, however. Hotels and restaurants are selected with a firm eye on prices, which will be welcomed by the cost-conscious. The notes on what to see list major tourist attractions but not much else. If one is going to travel extensively in Canada or Mexico, a different guide is in order. For the limited-budget foreign traveler, this no-nonsense guide will be of great value on the road across the entire United States. It is the only guide that most short-term foreign visitors will need.

ACCOMMODATIONS AND RESTAURANTS

AAA TourBook Series. Falls Church, VA: The American Automobile Association. pap. free to members. State editions revised annually.

Available only to AAA members, the state editions of the TourBook series provide extensive listings of sights, activities, accommodations, and restaurants. The introduction explains how to use the book and includes information on other motoring services provided by AAA. The information is organized by city, with sights listed separately from the accommodation and restaurants entries and the cities arranged alphabetically. The entries are brief, with simple descriptions of facilities and a complete listing of practical information that includes all prices. For accommodations, the guides use a rating system much like the Michelin Guide Stars. A number of advertisements are included, as well as special listings of state and national parks and the location of AAA offices.

Evaluation: AAA has been dispensing practical travel information to motorists for years. The guides in the TourBook series provide complete listings of sights and accommodations and make up in scope what they lack in detail. The information is complete, but because of the alphabetical organization of the cities and towns, and the lack of an index, the books may be difficult to use. Low-budget accommodations are not frequently included, although moderate ones abound. The inclusion of advertisements and the AAA rating system make it easier to choose from the accommodations listed. With a good set of maps, also available to members from AAA, the books in the series are the only guides most motorists would need, though those wanting more comprehensive background information on a particular area should look for another guide to use along with them.

Included in the series: Guides for each U.S. state and Canadian province, some grouped by twos or threes.

Country Inns and Back Roads. Norman T. Simpson. Stockbridge, MA: Berkshire Traveller Press. 365 pp. pap. $4.95. Revised annually.

Since the first edition in 1966, *Country Inns and Back Roads* has been as concerned with the quality of the service and hospitality in the inns as with the quality of the inns' furnishings and table fare. Rather than providing an exhaustive list of North American country inns, it emphasizes those selected few that offer much more than simply rural accommodations. Inns in twenty-five states, five Canadian provinces, and the Virgin Islands are described, with entries that include the address and telephone number, meal plans, operating dates, nearby recreation, and complete directions, along with the complete and colorful descriptions of the inns and innkeepers. The inns are arranged by state, with the states divided into geographic regions. The location of the inns is shown on a large, hand-drawn map of each area. An ink drawing of each inn is included, and many of the entries feature descriptions of some of the small towns in which the inns are situated. Travelers looking for the finest country inns from coast to coast will find them in this book.

Evaluation: Other guides to country inns include a larger number and wider variety of inns, but they often become indistinguishable from one another and may vary in emphasis. Some describe the inns, some their history, others the areas around them, but it sometimes seems as if they have all shared the same notes. *Country Inns and Back Roads* is immediately recognizable as a guide that stands apart, that is unique, and that has been refined through the years into the guide against which the others are compared. The introductions to the innkeepers, and the stories of how they found themselves in the inn business, more than any other trait set the guide apart. The book should be required reading for anyone with even a slight interest in country inns of North America.

ADVENTURE

Adventure Travel: A Source Book of Exciting Trips, Outdoor Challenges, and Thrilling Vacations in North America. Pat Dickerman. New York: Thomas Y. Crowell Co. (dist. by Berkshire Traveller Press), 1978. 240 pp. pap. $5.95. Revised biennially.

The purpose of the book is to provide a reference for all kinds of outdoor activities for travelers with little or no previous experience in them. The types of trips described include hiking, mountaineering, cattle drives, bicycling, jet boating, canoeing, snorkling and scuba diving, dog sledding, ski touring, snowshoeing, ballooning, and hang gliding. The trips are divided by travel style (on foot, on/in water, in the air, and so on) and by state, with each entry including all the practical information and a brief description of the services. All the trips are supervised, and many of the establishments listed will supply all the necessary food and equipment. Special sections are included for youth adventures, river runs and outfitters, and an extensive bibliography.

Evaluation: The work that began as a supplement to a past edition of *Farm, Ranch, and Country Vacations* by the same author has blossomed into a complete and easy-to-use reference guide to outdoor vacations of every type throughout North America. The information is not detailed and is meant only to provide ideas about the many outdoor vacation possibilities available. More concrete information should be requested from the different groups by writing the addresses included in each entry. The wide range of activities for all four seasons guarantees something for everyone. Camping will never be the same.

CAMPING

Rand McNally Campground and Trailer Park Guide. Chicago, IL: Rand McNally & Co., 1979. 624 pp. pap. $7.95.

The book lists thousands of campsites in North America. It opens with instructions on how to use the guide, followed by an extensive guide to buying and using all types of recreational vehicles. The introductory section ends with a tent guide, mileage charts, rules of the road, toll road information, fish and game law information, a list of supplier-sponsored camping clubs, state park information, and tips on crossing international borders. The campgrounds are listed in tables that give all the necessary information about the campsites and park services. Anyone doing a large amount of camping in a number of areas will find this a valuable book.

Evaluation: The book is as complete and well organized as *Camper's Park Guide* (see under U.S. Regional Guides, The East) and covers a wider area. It includes more preparatory information and a longer transportation section than *Woodall's Campground Directory* (see below), though Woodall's includes a wider selection of campsites. The tables in the book are organized and presented well, and the symbols employed are legible, but the print goes from small to minuscule. This is necessary because of the number of entries, but it may be a problem for some. Also, the large size of the book may make it difficult to handle. Overall, the book is as complete and clear a camping guide as will be found.

Woodall's Campground Directory: North American Edition. Highland Park, IL: Woodall Publishing Co. (dist. by Simon & Schuster), 1,528 pp. pap. $8.95. Revised annually.

Intended primarily for trailer and recreational vehicle campers, the North American edition of *Woodall's Campground Directory* lists 17,000 private and public camping sites in the United States and Canada. The book begins with sections on how to read the condensed entries, an explanation of the rating system, an index of advertisers, a description of camping possibilities in 21 major U.S. cities, a catalog of camping gadgets, road regulations, tollway and turnpike information for the different states and provinces, a discussion of maintenance and recreational vehicles of the future, and a long list of border-crossing tips. The entries are arranged by city, with the cities organized alphabetically by state. Each entry can be located on an accompanying state map; it includes directions, facilities, nearby recreation, and the overall Woodall rating. Advertisements for private campgrounds, recreational vehicle dealerships, and service centers are included, as well as four pages of money-saving coupons.

Evaluation: The book's strongest feature is obviously the number of camping sites described and the large area covered in the single column. The information on the campgrounds is fairly complete, but the brevity in the entries and the complicated rating system make it difficult to find the necessary information. The sections on road regulations and recreational vehicle maintenance are less complete than the information in the *Rand McNally Recreational Vehicle Handbook* (see under United States, Recreational Vehicles), but some recreational vehicle campers may want to have all the camping information in one volume (Rand McNally's is a separate book). Both Woodall's and the Rand McNally campground guides cover about the same area and information and are of comparable price, though the two use different formats and systems of evaluation. Which is chosen by a particular recreational vehicle camper is a matter of style and convenience.

HANDICAPPED TRAVELERS

The Wheelchair Traveller. See the review of this title under United States, Handicapped Travelers.

LEARNING VACATIONS

Learning Vacations. Gerson G. Eisenberg. Washington, DC: Acropolis Books (dist. in the U.K. by Paul Maitland), 2nd ed. 1978. 191 pp. pap. $5.95 (£3.25).

The purpose of the book is to provide meaningful ways for people to spend their leisure time. The variety of thinking vacations described in the book is amazing. Included are college seminars, museum tours, conferences on a number of topics, outdoor activities, intellectual journeys to five continents, photography, crafts, music, art, and folk festivals. The different activities are divided by type and listed by state. Each entry includes the name and address of the organizers, the location, title, dates, cost, course content, accommodations, meals, facilities for children, nearby recreational and cultural activities, a short comment, and an address for further information. Nearly all the trips are in North America, though some are overseas. The activities are indexed by state, by institution, and by subject. The book is especially useful to students looking for college credit while on vacation, but it is worthwhile for anyone searching for unusual vacation ideas.

Evaluation: The book is unique in its approach to vacations. It provides a wide range of activities for every interest and budget. Though the second edition has seen the information updated and expanded, it should be noted that many of the activities included (nearly all of which occur in the summer) change yearly. To be certain of particulars, it is necessary to write for more current information. The book is well organized and easy to use. It can be the key to many vacations of discovery and enlightenment.

MUSEUMS

Directory of Unique Museums. Bill Truesdell. Kalamazoo, MI: Creative Communications, 1979. 100 pp. pap. $3.50.

You won't find the Smithsonian listed in this directory, but after reading it you'll never pass through Newton, Iowa, again without stopping at the Maytag Washer Historical Center. Over 200 specialized museums are described in the book, from those containing antique musical instruments to sports halls of fame. Not all the museums described are as rural as the Maytag Historical Center, but most are well off the beaten tourist path of the United States and Canada. The entries are arranged alphabetically by state or province and include the address, telephone, and hours of each, with descriptions of the museums and their contents. Sixteen pages of photographs are included, and the many subjects are indexed in the back of the book.

Evaluation: The author's purpose, as stated in the introduction, is to provide a complete catalog of one-of-a-kind museums and to alert travelers to the possibilities so often overlooked in their own state or province. To this end he has succeeded admirably. The incredible variety of museums in all parts of the United States and Canada can be matched by no other guide. The information in the entries is as complete as necessary, and the museum descriptions stimulate the imagination, almost as if a part of the museum itself were on the page. The lack of a geographic index detracts slightly from the book's overall usefulness, but the entries are well organized and the information is presented clearly. The book is a unique and very useful pretravel reference for travelers looking for a break from the too predictable tourist routine.

RAILWAYS

North America by Rail. Inez Morris and David Morris. Indianapolis, IN: The Bobbs-Merrill Co., 1977. 227 pp. pap. $5.95.

Train travel has long been a popular means of transportation for vacationers in Europe and Asia, but it is a distant fourth to automobile, bus, and air travel in the United States and Canada. This is not as much a matter of choice as one of accessibility and cost. *North America by Rail* promotes travel by train as economical, safe, and sociable. The first two-thirds of the book deal with the history of the railway systems in North America and describe the authors' many trips to all parts of the continent. The last third conveys practical information on all facets of train travel, with special sections on dining, travel with children, customs, combining train and auto travel, photography, and train tours. The last section is a selling of the railroads, giving all the reasons for choosing trains over other transportation methods. However convincing the authors may be, train travel in North America is currently more expensive than most of the alternatives and calls for a moderate to high budget. The narrative style suggests the book's best use is pretravel reading.

Evaluation: It is regrettable that the authors did not take a more formal approach to the subject, this being the only guide of its kind. The only routes and train stations described are those they visited, and these are in story form. The practical information section is complete for available train services, but the only list of possible routes is on a cluttered map. The guide is a good beginning for a trip by train, but more information should be acquired from Amtrak before making concrete plans.

ROAD ATLASES

Rand McNally Road Atlas. Chicago, IL: Rand McNally & Co. 128 pp. pap. $3.95. London: E. P. Group of Companies. £2.45. Revised annually.

The granddaddy of North American road atlases, the *Rand McNally Road Atlas,* in its fifty-fifth annual edition, provides large, clear, and usually uncluttered maps of all 50 states, Canada, and Mexico. The maps open up to a full 21″ × 14″, which is as large as most reference atlases and allows plenty of room for the inclusion of the smallest towns (all indexed in the back), historic sites and monuments, national parks and forests, camping areas, Indian reservations, airports, recreation areas, military bases, colleges, springs and wells, ports of entry, roadside parks, golf and country clubs, and general points of interest. The state maps are arranged alphabetically, though many neighboring states are shown on adjoining pages. Special insert maps are included for close to 200 metropolitan areas. Other special features include mileage charts, a U.S. interstate map, motor, fish, and game law information, and a telephone area code map. The book is invaluable to anyone planning a motoring vacation in North America.

Evaluation: To the dismay of some travel guidebook publishers, many travelers find that the *Rand McNally Road Atlas* is the only guide they need. It includes the clearest, most detailed, and most up-to-date maps and road information available, but two features detract slightly from the book's overall usefulness. The alphabetic arrangement of the states and provinces calls for much page turning at state lines, though this is a problem all atlases share. The other problem is the book's size; it is too large to store conveniently, and it quickly becomes a mass of irregular folds after a few days on the road. For a slight added cost, a plastic folder is available to avoid this problem. Of course, the large size of the book is both a positive and a negative aspect, depending on the circumstances. The *Rand McNally Road Atlas* is the best North American road atlas currently available.

SKIING

Skiing the Great Resorts of North America. See the review of this title under United States, Skiing.

Canada

COMPREHENSIVE GUIDES

Canada: A Candid Travel Guide. Gerald Hall and John Brehl. New York: William Morrow & Co., 1978. 274 pp. pap. $6.95.

Canada: A Candid Travel Guide is a candid travel guide in that it presents more or less a total picture and includes some opinions of Canada (voiced mostly by past and present U.S. citizens) that are less than positive. The authors also point out particular places and circumstances to avoid. The book emphasizes travel by car and is targeted primarily for visitors from the United States on a moderate to high budget with at least some past travel experience. Travelers crossing along the Trans-Canadian Highway will be very pleased with the histories and descriptions of the prairies and Western Provinces. The guide includes a wide variety of indoor and outdoor activities and a calendar of special annual events. It is of most use to people traveling through Canada by car.

Evaluation: The authors bring a refined wit and almost apologetic honesty to the task of guiding tourists through the giant country. They give a view of Canada as Canadians see and live it. The people of the different areas, particularly in the east, are introduced to the reader as old friends. The reading is fluid and the information accessible if not always detailed. The format works well for the Maritime, Plains, and Western Provinces, but the text seems cluttered in the longer Ontario and Quebec sections.

Canada A to Z. See A to Z World Travel Guides under The World, Comprehensive Guides.

A Cozy Getaway. See the review of this title under United States, Comprehensive Guides.

A Kosoy Travel Guide to Canada. Ted Kosoy. Washington, DC: Acropolis Books, 3rd ed. 1979. 323 pp. pap. $5.95.

Kosoy guides are basic in their approach. They provide a great amount of practical information and are directed to a wide audience. This book includes an extensive pretravel section, which mentions trip preparation, travel agents, packing, traveler's checks and credit cards, climate and clothing, weather, and travel-style information. Special sections include student travel, tips for international visitors, ferry services, travel photography, car rental and drive-away services, and a French conversation guide. The entries for the provinces give short histories and descriptions, some short tours (with major points of interest), sports, museums, theaters, travel routes, and shopping. Accommodations and restaurants are listed separately by city with short descriptions.

Evaluation: The Kosoy guide to Canada is a good basic guide to a large area. Because of the size of the country, it is difficult to bring together the many different areas and the possibilities for travel that they present. The author has done an admirable job, minimizing the dry information to keep it manageable while including a good representation of the wide range of activities. The large amount of pretravel and practical information may seem unnecessary to some, but because of the basic approach of the book, its inclusion is justified. The book gives less of a feel for the different areas than do other Canadian tour guides, such as *Canada: A Candid Travel Guide* (see above), but the completeness and accessibility of the information outshine most other guides. This guide serves a wide audience, but would be of most use to people with little or no previous travel experience.

ACCOMMODATIONS AND RESTAURANTS

AAA TourBook Series. See the review of this series under North America, Accommodations and Restaurants.

America's Wonderful Little Hotels and Inns. See the review of this title under United States, Accommodations and Restaurants.

Country Bed and Breakfast Places in Canada. John Tompson. Stockbridge, MA: Berkshire Traveller Press, 1979. pap. $4.95.

The book lists close to 200 homes throughout Canada that offer meals and inexpensive accommodations. They are usually farmhouses whose owners open their homes to a small number of guests. Each listing includes the name of the owner, the address, phone, the seasons it is open, the number of rooms (rarely more than five), rates, directions, a comment by the owner, and comments of past visitors. Though the entries cover all but the northernmost sections of Canada, nearly half the entries are in the Maritime Provinces. The book serves travelers looking for inexpensive rural accommodations. It should be read before leaving on a trip, because almost all the homes require reservations.

Evaluation: The information in the entries is complete and clear, but finding a particular home would be difficult. There is no index, no table of contents, and no page numbers. The descriptions of the homes are by the owners and are far from consistent. Some are very good, pointing out special features, activities, and describing the nearby area. Others are not. The maps and directions make locating the homes simple, but the emphasis on travel by car necessitates the acquisition of a good road map. The book is most useful when paired with a guide that includes sights, transportation, and practical information.

Country Inns and Back Roads. See the review of this title under North America, Accommodations and Restaurants.

Mobil Travel Guide Series. See the review of this series under United States, Accommodations and Restaurants.

ADVENTURE

Adventure Travel: A Source Book of Exciting Trips, Outdoor Challenges, and Thrilling Vacations in North America. See the review of this title under North America, Adventure.

CAMPING

Rand McNally Campground and Trailer Park Guide. See the review of this title under North America, Camping.

Woodall's Campground Directory: North American Edition. See the review of this title under North America, Camping.

HANDICAPPED TRAVELERS

The Whole Hiker's Handbook. See the review of this title under United States, Hiking, Walking, and Running.

HIKING

The Whole Hiker's Handbook. See the review of this title under United States, Hiking, Walking, and Running.

LEARNING VACATIONS

Learning Vacations. See the review of this title under North America, Learning Vacations.

MUSEUMS

Directory of Unique Museums. See the review of this title under North America, Museums.

RAILWAYS

North America by Rail. See the review of this title under North America, Railways.

ROAD ATLASES

Hammond Road Atlas and Vacation Guide. See the Review of this title under United States, Road Atlases.

Rand McNally Road Atlas. See the review of this title under North America, Road Atlases.

SKIING

Skiing the Great Resorts of North America. See the review of this title under United States, Skiing.

REGIONAL GUIDES

Eastern Canada

A Guide to Atlantic Canada. Frederick Pratson. Old Greenwich, CT: Chatham Press, 1973. 160 pp. pap. $3.95.

Travelers looking for an inexpensive outdoor vacation in a rugged environment need look no further than Canada's eastern shoreline. *A Guide to Atlantic Canada* promotes an understanding of the area's history, culture, and physical splendor. The introductory sections describe the area's past and present and include transportation (though the book emphasizes travel by car), currency, language, and emergency information. The sections for each of the four provinces include travel routes, restaurants, a description of accommodation possibilities, cruise ships, parks, a calendar of events, sporting activities, and addresses for further information. There is a special listing of golf courses at the back.

Evaluation: The completeness of the information makes it an ideal on-the-road guide for first-time travelers to the area. The information is kept brief, is well organized, and serves a variety of interests. The scant accommodation sections (little more than a name) and the short city entries make the book most useful to campers and travelers on low to moderate budgets. *Canada: A Candid Travel Guide* (see above, under Comprehensive Guides) gives a better feel for the area, but includes much less practical information.

Rand McNally Campground and Trailer Parks Guide—Eastern. See the review of this title under United States, The East, Camping.

Western Canada

The Milepost. See the review of this title under United States, Alaska, Comprehensive Guides.

Rand McNally Campground and Trailer Parks Guide—Western. See the review of this title under United States, The West, Camping.

PROVINCIAL GUIDES

Alberta

AAA TourBook: Alberta. See the AAA TourBook series under North America, Accommodations and Restaurants.

British Columbia

AAA TourBook: British Columbia. See the AAA TourBook series under North America, Accommodations and Restaurants.

British Columbia. Harry P. McKeever. San Francisco, CA: Chronicle Books, 1978. 192 pp. pap. $5.95.

This book is a series of essays describing the outdoor attractions of the province. Its focus is on travel by car through the many parks in the area, as well as campsites and trail directions. The book examines a wide range of outdoor activities and describes the history and geography of the different areas. The province is divided into nine regions, with a section on the city of Vancouver that is long on narrative and short on practical information. The large size of the book and its essay style suggest its best use as pretravel reading.

Evaluation: The mix of information and the easy essay style make for enjoyable reading. But the outdoor emphasis of the book and the lack of practical information make it worthwhile only for experienced campers. Noncampers should look for a more comprehensive guide to the area.

Country Inns of the Far West. See the review of this title under United States, The West, Accommodations and Restaurants.

A Guide to the Queen Charlotte Islands. Neil G. Carey. Anchorage, AK: Alaska Northwest Publishing Co., 3rd ed. 1978. 74 pp. pap. $2.95.

This short book gives an extremely clear picture of the islands. Since the nature of the islands precludes a touristy vacation, the book emphasizes the outdoors—camping, canoeing, fishing, and hiking in an unspoiled environment. A pull-out map is included, along with weather information, transportation, Native American crafts, gas stations, and hunting regulations. The volume of information and detail covered in the book restricts its usefulness to travelers spending more than a day or two on the islands.

Evaluation: The book has all the information needed for a trip to the Queen Charlotte Islands. It gives a modest overview of the small area, with the expected histories and descriptions. The combination of brevity and thoroughness makes for a very usable guide.

Vancouver Island. See The Islands series under The World, Pretravel Reading, Islands of the World.

Winery Tours in Oregon, Washington, Idaho, and British Columbia. See the review of this title under United States, Pacific Coast, Wine Tours.

Manitoba

AAA TourBook: Manitoba. See the AAA TourBook series under North America, Accommodations and Restaurants.

New Brunswick

AAA TourBook: New Brunswick. See the AAA TourBook series under North America, Accommodations and Restaurants.

New Brunswick Inside Out. Colleen Thompson. Ottawa, ON: Waxwing Productions (dist. in the U.S. by Berkshire Traveller Press; dist. in Canada by Burns & MacEachern), 1977. 226 pp. pap. $3.50.

Complete is the word for this guide. Along with the detailed background and descriptions of all parts of the province, it lists complete information on transportation to and in the area, accommodations (with rates), camping, restaurants, shopping, sights and activities for a variety of interests, driving tours, a calendar of annual events, emergency telephone numbers, nightlife and liquor stores, sports, guided tours, and information offices. Sections are included on the province's three largest cities, including street maps and walking tours plus the information listed above. Other features include a list of

New Brunswick expressions, crafts and antiques, and poems and folk songs written in or about the area.

Evaluation: Anyone planning a trip to New Brunswick is strongly advised to take this guide along. It includes all the necessary practical travel information, organized well and presented very clearly. The most striking feature of the book is the lively and entertaining stories of the province's history and past and present residents. It serves both as pretravel reading and as a guide to be used on the road, though visitors traveling by car should acquire a good set of road maps to use along with it. The book is as fun to read as it is useful and is a valuable companion for all visitors to New Brunswick.

Newfoundland

AAA TourBook: Newfoundland. See the AAA TourBook series under North America. Accommodations and Restaurants.

Northwest Territories

AAA TourBook: Northwest Territories. See the AAA TourBook series under North America, Accommodations and Restaurants.

Nova Scotia

AAA TourBook: Nova Scotia. See the AAA TourBook series under North America, Accommodations and Restaurants.

Exploring Halifax. See *Exploring Toronto* below, under Ontario.

Ontario

AAA TourBook: Ontario. See the AAA TourBook series under North America, Accommodations and Restaurants.

Woodall's Ontario Campground Directory. See *Woodall's Campground Directory: State Editions* under United States, Camping.

Niagara-on-the-Lake

Exploring Niagara-on-the-Lake. See *Exploring Toronto,* below.

Point Pelee

Point Pelee: Canada's Deep South. Darryl Steward and Don Ross. Detroit, MI: Wayne State University Press, 1977. 112 pp. pap. $5.95.

The small area described in the book is in a unique position. Jutting southward into Lake Erie, it is the natural first stop for birds migrating across the lake in the spring and fall. This, along with other features, makes it a naturalist's haven. The book is a full description of the wildlife in the area. The introduction describes the natural setting of the park, seasonal changes, and the climate. Sections are included on the birds, mammals, reptiles and amphibians, fish, and insects, along with a short history of the park, visiting restrictions, a checklist of birds, and a reading list. The entries include many color photographs and illustrations. The technical quality of the text limits the book's usefulness to those with a science background. It should be read before leaving and used as a reference on the trip.

Evaluation: The book is an ornithologist's delight. Its best feature is the detailed descriptions of the great variety of birds that may be found in the park at any one time and tips on how and where to find them. The book has a narrower scope and covers a smaller area than most science guides and uses more technical terms. The lack of any practical travel information calls for it to be used with a more inclusive guide. Canada's Deep South is a long way from Dixie, but this guide shows that it is well worth a visit.

Toronto

Canada's Capital Inside Out. See *Montreal Inside Out* under Quebec.

Exploring Toronto: Its Buildings, People, and Places. The Toronto Chapter of Architects. Toronto, ON: Greey de Pencier Publications, 1977. 125 pp. pap. $3.95.

Exploring Toronto divides Toronto into 12 areas and provides at least one walking tour for each. It opens with a short introduction that gives some history and describes architectural trends of the city's past and present. The tours themselves could be taken comfortably in an afternoon. The entries include descriptions of the buildings and neighborhoods, suggested spots to stop and rest, and places to shop along the way. The tours cover a wide area of the city, from downtown to the suburbs and along the river. There is also a short list of points of interest in the city not mentioned in any of the tours at the back of the book, along with the architectural credits.

Evaluation: The book has a definite architectural bias, which is understandable when you consider that it was written by architects. But it mentions much more than the buildings of the city. It includes insights, an abundance of local flavor, parks, and shopping. It highlights the sights of the city and briefly gives the stories behind them. The tour directions are clear and the maps are fairly easy to read, though the authors suggest the readers use a street map along with those included. The book is an excellent complement to a more general guide for anyone spending more than a day in Toronto.

Other books in the series: Exploring Halifax; Exploring Montreal; Exploring Niagara-on-the-Lake.

Toronto Guidebook. Alexander Rodd, ed. Toronto, ON: Key Publishers, 1977. 254 pp. pap. $3.95.

Toronto Guidebook is a comprehensive guide to the city. It was written for travelers with or without means and includes special sections for children, singles, students, and foreign visitors. It opens with a description and history of the city and features a transportation section, walking and driving tours, a calendar of events, parks, art galleries, shopping, and nightlife. The hotel and restaurant entries include all the necessary practical information (including rates) and sparkling descriptions. They cover every imaginable price range from soup kitchens and crash pads to the royal suite. There is a wide variety of sporting activities listed (to participate in and to watch) and a section on moving to Toronto.

Evaluation: This is an excellent guidebook. The union of information and style makes for consistently smooth and clear reading. The book is very well organized and the information is complete. If any parts of the book could be said to surpass other guides, they would be the hotel and restaurant sections. The book's completeness, style, and consistency make it a model city guide. It serves every travel budget and belongs close at hand when in Toronto.

The Very Best of Metropolitan Toronto . . . Affectionately Yours. Mary Conway and Harry Setchwell. Detroit, MI: J. Well, 1979. 32 pp. pap. $2.25.

The Very Best of Metropolitan Toronto was written primarily for residents of the cities in the Great Lakes region and is intended as a guide for short trips to the city. As in their guide to Detroit, the authors concentrate on restaurant information; restaurant menus, with complete descriptions and listings of practical information, make up over half of the book. Most of the restaurants in this section are on the expensive side, but less expensive alternatives are provided in the long lists of specialty restaurants and stores. The book begins with a chart that lists the services and facilities of 13 Toronto hotels, with the address, telephone number, and a brief comment on each. The locations of the hotels are shown on a large map of the downtown area. Other sections discuss transportation to and in the city, a short list of practical travel information (laws, banking, holidays, and so on), a calendar of events, a brief description of major sights and activities, and short sections on theater, nightlife, sports, and shopping. The book is useful to travelers with moderate or above-average budgets who are planning a short visit to Toronto.

Evaluation: The authors' specialty is restaurants. This is abundantly clear both in the high-quality restaurant listings and in the secondary treatment of the hotel, sights, and transportation information. It almost seems as if the inclusion of the later was an afterthought, although the information in these sections is complete enough for short trips. For travelers whose vacation activities are centered around great dining, the book is sure to please. Travelers looking for a more comprehensive view of the city and more complete travel information will find it in the *Toronto Guidebook* (see above).

Prince Edward Island

AAA TourBook: Prince Edward Island. See the AAA TourBook series under North America, Accommodations and Restaurants.

Quebec

AAA TourBook: Quebec. See the AAA TourBook series under North America, Accommodations and Restaurants.

Montreal

Exploring Montreal. See *Exploring Toronto* above, under Ontario.

Great Montreal Walks. Bonnie Buxton and Betty Guernsey. Ottawa, ON: Waxwing Productions (dist. in the U.S. by Berkshire Traveller Press), 1976. 176 pp. pap. $3.50.

Sixteen walks of various lengths are described in this book. Each walk has a theme and is shown on a clear, hand-drawn map. The walks feature the residents and buildings of the neighborhoods, with less architecture and more directions than books such as *Exploring Toronto* (see above, under Ontario). Options are given throughout for longer or shorter trips.

Evaluation: Each of the walks is loaded with information of all kinds. The entries are much longer than those in other city walking guides, which makes for nearly as much reading as walking. The directions are italicized in the book and are easy to follow. Its best use is as a complement to a more comprehensive city guide, such as *Montreal Inside Out* (see below), by the same authors.

Montreal Inside Out. Bonnie Buxton and Betty Guernsey. Ottawa, ON: Waxwing Productions (dist. in the U.S. by Berkshire Traveller Press), 1976. 282 pp. pap. $3.95.

Opening with a general discussion of Montreal, the book examines its history, geography, city transportation, and vantage points. The brief hotel section lists famous guests of each establishment, if there were any. Some tourist homes are listed. The more extensive restaurant section provides ample helpful information, classifying restaurants into useful groups such as "sidewalk cafés" and "big splurge." Spots of tourist interest are mentioned, including museums, China Town, the zoo, parks, and tours. An "On the Town" section will help the visitor find bars, theaters, music, and coffeehouses. Sports possibilities are also well covered. Fully half of *Montreal Inside Out* is given to listings and descriptions of stores, shops, galleries, boutiques, and other places to acquire goods and services. The book closes with a very complete section of practical information, including driving information, emergency repairs, French lessons, health information, libraries, and emergency phone numbers.

Evaluation: Montreal Inside Out is perhaps more valuable to the Montreal resident than to the traveler. Information regarding landscape architects, for example, is hardly what the usual tourist wants. The book clearly is a consumer's book, intended for those seeking goods and services. Its use as a general guide for the traveller is somewhat limited; the Montreal resident, however, is sure to be pleased with it.

Other titles in the series: Canada's Capital Inside Out.

Saskatchewan

AAA TourBook: Saskatchewan. See the AAA TourBook series under North America, Accommodations and Restaurants.

Yukon Territory

AAA TourBook: Yukon Territory. See the AAA TourBook series under North America, Accommodations and Restaurants.

United States

COMPREHENSIVE GUIDES

A Cozy Getaway. Cozy Baker. Washington, DC: Acropolis Books, 1976. 184 pp. pap. $3.95.

The lure of the 41 vacation spots described in *A Cozy Getaway* is their detachment from the bustling tourist routine, and relaxation is the key to enjoying them. The areas featured in the book include small coastal towns and large cities, rugged, back-country areas, and islands off the beaten path. Most of the sites are on or near the Atlantic coast of the United States and Canada, though some western spots are included. The entries for each area emphasize descriptions and histories, with irregular mention of nearby sights, accommodations, and restaurants. A special section describes eleven unique travel destinations around Washington, D.C. The book is intended as pretravel reading to provide ideas for those planning a trip.

Evaluation: The colorful descriptions and lively style of the entries make the book enjoyable armchair reading; the practical travel information in the entries is limited. The book is useful only as a description of potential out-of-the-way travel destinations. The entries provide a feel for the different areas not to be found in other guides. Of particular interest to travelers planning a trip to Washington, D.C., are the entries describing rural areas within a few hours of the capital by car. The book is an excellent pretravel reference, though more comprehensive guides to the particular areas should be used on the road.

Let's Go: USA. For a review of a title in the Let's Go series, see *Let's Go: The Budget Guide to Britain and Ireland* under Europe, Great Britain, Comprehensive Guides.

Minivacations. Karen Cure. Chicago, IL: Follett Publishing Co., 1976. 216 pp. pap. $6.95.

With the advent of long holiday weekends and the rising cost of transportation, there has been an emphasis on vacations close to home. *Minivacations* describes hundreds of trips in areas throughout the United States that can be easily reached from major population centers. The book divides the country into five regions and lists a variety of vacation destinations in each area. Each entry includes detailed descriptions of sights and activities in the area, including prices and seasonal restrictions. Accommodation possibilities are mentioned for each area, and addresses for further information are included. Lists of backpacking, bike, and canoe trips for each region are provided, along with a long calendar of annual events. The entries also include large, clear maps and photographs of many of the sights.

Evaluation: Most of the vacation spots described in the book are major tourist areas, with many entries for amusement parks, historical villages, beach resorts, and national parks and monuments. This means that travelers looking for out-of-the-way vacation destinations would be served better by another guide. However, the majority of travelers will find exactly the spot they are looking for in the entries, which include all the necessary preparatory information, given in a smooth and informative style. The great number of photographs and illustrations, the clear use of symbols, and the complete index make the book attractive and easy to use. The book serves as a pretravel reference only. On the road, more complete travel information (transportation, accommodation) will be necessary.

Pan Am's U.S.A. Guide. New York: McGraw-Hill Book Co., 1980. 666 pp. $7.95.

Written for foreign visitors, *Pan Am's U.S.A. Guide* is an overview of travel in the 50 states and U.S. territories. The introductory sections cover large amounts of practical information, including, among other things, visa requirements and customs regulations, government, language, currency, clothing, tipping, banks, communication, and transportation. The states and territories are divided by area and include a brief description and history of each, followed by a discussion of sights and accommodations throughout the area. More detailed information is included on the major cities, including restaurants, shopping, sports, a calendar of events, and nearby sights. The accommodations sections list names, telephone numbers, and rates only. For each state there are addresses for further information.

Evaluation: The information in the book is superficial, describing many of the travel possibilities but rarely examining any one facet in detail. The practical information is scant. For each area, a few sights and accommodations will be mentioned without addresses and with very short descriptions. The book is useful only to foreign visitors on moderate and above-average budgets who will be making a number of short visits throughout a large area of the country. Most travelers would be better off with more comprehensive state or regional guides that provide a more complete description of travel possibilities in the different areas.

Rand McNally Vacation and Travel Guide. Chicago, IL: Rand McNally & Co. 276 pp. pap. $6.95. Revised annually.

The *Rand McNally Vacation and Travel Guide* highlights from one to seven areas of particular interest to travelers in each of the 50 states. The states are divided into nine geographic areas, with short descriptions of each state preceding the entries. The areas described in the entries include large cities and small towns, rugged coastal areas, some national parks, and areas of general interest to travelers. The entries list points of interest and mention nearby attractions in each area, but very little practical travel information is included. The book provides a variety of vacation ideas for travelers of all budgets and travel styles with an urge but without a destination.

Evaluation: The majority of areas described are popular tourist attractions, and visitors—especially in the summer—should prepare for crowds. However, many points of interest are included that are well worth a visit and are found well off the beaten track. The entries are more suggestions than comprehensive descriptions of the various travel possibilities in each state, and the information is meant only as the first step in planning a trip to one of the areas. Like the other Rand McNally travel guides, the book is very well organized and presented, with a complete index and the usual high-quality maps. Other sight-seeing guides, such as *American Travelers' Treasury* (see below under Museums and Historical Sights), list many more sights in each state, but include less information on each. The book provides a wide assortment of vacation ideas of interest to a variety of travelers.

Very Special Places: A Lover's Guide to America. Ian Keown. New York: Collier Books, Macmillan Publishing Co., 1978. 360 pp. pap. $4.95.

For some people, romance is wherever you find it. A dingy city street can be transformed into paradise in the right company. Others look for just the right setting, and anything less is not good enough. For these people there is *Very Special Places*, which describes romantic inns, hotels, resorts, and other hideaways throughout the continental United States, with an emphasis on the east and west coast states. The entries are divided into 13 regions, with each entry including a detailed description of the establishment's facilities and furnishings, restaurant specialties, and the location of the best rooms. Complete practical information (address, directions, rates, telephone, meals, and entertainment) is listed for each, as well as diversions and some nearby attractions. The book serves couples on moderate and above-average budgets looking for lodgings with a flair.

Evaluation: The completeness of the practical information and the wide area covered make *Very Special Places* an excellent accommodations guide for all travelers looking for a quiet but memorable vacation. The book's special feature is the colorful and informative descriptions of the different lodgings that highlight the unique charms of each of the hotels and inns. The title of the book has been changed since the first edition—it seems *A Lover's Guide to America* had immoral overtones for some. Make no mistake; the places described in the book were chosen for their quality service and facilities as well as their romantic qualities. Travelers should supplement the information in this book with sights and transportation information for a particular area.

ACCOMMODATIONS AND RESTAURANTS

American Youth Hostels Handbook. Delaplane, VA: American Youth Hostels Inc. 192 pp. pap. $1.75 (free to members). Revised annually.

This book is a guide to youth hostels in America. Travelers must be members of a youth hostel association to use the facilities listed in the book, and hostels do not allow automobiles. The guide contains complete information on applying for membership, rules and regulations, a description of the different types of hostels, how the system works, tips on planning a trip, an equipment checklist, clothing, and first aid. There is a special section for traveling by bicycle and addresses of the International Youth Hostel Federations are listed at the back. The entries for each hostel are divided by state and include a store of practical information: address, phone, directions, opening dates, reservations, groups, types of facilities, shopping, transportation, churches, and special attractions. The extensive preparation sections make the book ideal as a reference for first-time campers, whether hosteling or not.

Evaluation: The shining features of the book are its organization and the completeness of the basic information. Hosteling and low-budget traveling go hand in hand. Those on a rock-bottom budget will find membership in AYH a good method of cutting expenses. But the *AYH Handbook* is of most use when paired with a guide that includes sights and adventures in a particular area. The book uses complicated symbols that are hard to see and harder to decipher. Some include hand-drawn maps that are at times good and at times impossible. Except for its preparation section, the book's usefulness is restricted to travelers committed to hosteling in North America.

America's Favorite Restaurants and Inns. Bob Christopher and Ellen Christopher. New York: William Morrow & Co., 7th ed. 1980. 1,024 pp. pap. $8.95.

This new book was formerly published under the title *America on $8 and $16 a Night.* Beginning with an extensive and stern warning about the necessity of advanced reservations, the introductory material discusses motel facilities in general and how to check out a room before renting. All accommodation chains are described, listing locations, rates, reservation methods and toll-free numbers, services and facilities, and credit cards accepted. The main body of the books lists, alphabetically by city, state by state, chain and franchise motels and individually owned restaurants. For motels, addresses, road directions, and phone numbers are given. For restaurants, descriptions range from complete practical information regarding prices, hours, and so on to extensive descriptions, provided by a large number of correspondents who report to the authors. Price ratings of motels and restaurants are provided in a series of symbols. Franchise and fast-food restaurants are listed in a summary at the end of each state section.

Evaluation: This more than two-inch-thick paperback is a curious mixture of an excellent and thorough guide to chain motels throughout the United States, both inexpensive and expensive, and a less thorough guide to privately owned restaurants. Travelers seeking privately owned motels (or chain restaurants) will have to look elsewhere. Coverage of the chain motels is detailed and accurate, facilitating the often repeated admonition to make reservations in advance. Restaurant coverage is very uneven, with some descriptions long and chatty, others basic and factual. The choice seems to be up to the large number of correspondents who select their own personal favorites, rather than the most unusual or best a town has to offer. The restaurant price symbols are not explained anywhere in the book, making them ineffective. For travelers seeking an accommodations guide that includes all the budget chains as well as the more expensive, this is the best book to be found. While the restaurant information is not wrong, it certainly does not present as thorough coverage. Nevertheless, *America's Favorite Restaurants and Inns* could serve travelers as the only accommodations guide they need.

America's Wonderful Little Hotels and Inns. Barbara Crossette, ed. New York: Thomas Congdon Books, E. P. Dutton, 1980. 352 pp. pap. $8.95 ($6.95 in Canada).

The new companion volume to *Europe's Wonderful Little Hotels and Inns* (see under Europe, Accommodations and Restaurants), the book lists hundreds of establishments whose only similarity is that they offer something special to travelers. It may be tranquility, beauty, luxury, homeyness, haute cuisine, or outdoor or social activities, but whatever it is, it is special. The entries are divided into eight geographic areas, covering all of the United States and much of Canada. The hotels and inns are listed by city and state and include the address, telephone number, dates of operation, number of rooms, prices, credit cards accepted, a short listing of special features, and foreign languages spoken, along with descriptions of the establishments by past guests. Illustrations of many of the inns are included in the entries, and 16 pages of maps are provided at the back of the book.

Evaluation: A variety of accommodation possibilities throughout North America is described in the book, all in the moderate and above-average price range. The establishments tend to be located more often in rural areas than in major cities and finding them may be difficult for those unfamiliar with a particular area. The entries include all the necessary practical information about the hotels and inns, organized well and clearly presented. Because the descriptions of the establishments have been solicited from past guests, they do not all follow a set pattern or include the same information on the facilities and services provided, but they usually give a clear picture of the hotel or inn they describe. The book lists a wider range of rural accommodations than most guides to country inns and is easier to use than many, but it covers a smaller price range (few inexpensive places are included) and lacks consistency in the descriptions.

Arthur Frommer's City Guide Series. New York: Frommer/Pasmantier Publishing Co. approx. 200 pp. pap. $2.50. Revised semiannually.

The strength of Arthur Frommer's City Guides is the extensive hotel and restaurant listings. The entries in these two sections cover all price ranges and styles in the cities and nearby areas. The hotel entries include complete listings of rates and descriptions of the facilities, as well as nearby attractions and items of special interest. The restaurant entries feature a wide variety of eateries that include connoisseur's choices, international specialties, special settings, delicatessens, pizza shops, lunch counters, and soup kitchens. Sections are also included for sights, transportation, entertainment, nightlife, shopping, and nearby excursions. The books in the series are recommended for travelers on a modest and above-average budget who are planning short visits to the different cities.

Evaluation: The quality and completeness of the accommodations and restaurant sections make Frommer's City Guides ideal for travelers whose primary concerns are where they will stay and what they will eat. Most other city guides include more background information and more detailed practical information on a wider range of subjects pertaining to the city. The Frommer series is very brief on transportation to and around the cities, and the sights listed are limited to the major tourist attractions. Travelers planning an extended visit to a particular city, or those looking for more complete background and transportation information, should consult a more comprehensive guide to that city.

Included in the series: Boston; Honolulu; Las Vegas; Los Angeles; New York; Philadelphia; San Francisco; Washington, D.C.

Best Restaurants Series. San Francisco, CA: 101 Productions, 1978. approx. 223 pp. pap. $3.95.

The Best Restaurants Series was written by authors who know the restaurants of their cities well. The books feature restaurants in a wide price range with three major classifications: under $10, $10 to $20, and over $20, for "an average dinner with appetizer, entree, dessert, and coffee." The restaurants are arranged geographically, with each entry including a page-long description of the atmosphere, specialties, and service. It also lists the address, phone number, hours, credit cards accepted, reservations, parking, and drinks. A major feature of the entries is that each includes a copy of the menu. The restaurants are indexed by specialty and price. Because of the number and variety of restaurants, the books in the series are most useful to residents and travelers on an extended stay.

Evaluation: The descriptions of the restaurants and their specialties are clear and inviting. The authors include a variety of information about the eateries and sparkling descriptions of the meals. The solid organization and indexes make the books very easy to use. The Best Restaurants Series offers a full spectrum of great dining experiences in the different cities, but travelers on short visits will find the information is more than they need. The restaurant listings in a more inclusive city guide should serve them better.

Included in the series: Chicago; Florida; Los Angeles and Southern California; New York; Pacific Northwest; Philadelphia; San Francisco and Northern California; Texas.

Country Inns and Back Roads. See the review of this title under North America, Accommodations and Restaurants.

Country Inns of America Series. Los Angeles, CA: The Knapp Press, 1980. 96 pp. pap. $6.95.

The most striking feature of the books in this series is the beautiful color photographs of the inns, their furnishings, and rural scenes in the areas around them. But although the photography is what first catches the eye, the colorful and detailed descriptions and histories of the inns, and the stories of some of their past owners and visitors, are by no means negligible. Each volume in the series is organized by state, except for the California edition, which is by area, and the inns are listed alphabetically for each state or area. Along with the many photographs and background information, the entries for each inn list its address, telephone number, innkeepers, number of rooms, other facilities, meals served, dates of operation, rates, credit cards accepted, nearby shops and points of interest, and directions from nearby cities. Each book includes a map on which the locations of the inns are shown, and other inns in the area are described in less detail at the back of each book.

Evaluation: Other guides to country inns include more establishments, cover larger geographic areas, and give more detailed background, but no other guide provides the feel for the different inns found in this series. The many color photographs that surround the entries do more to sell the inns to perspective lodgers than the most detailed descriptions. The books devote much more space to photography than text, but the entries for the inns include all the necessary information and enough historical background to pique the reader's interest. The series' major drawback is the small number of inns described and the lack of listings for more economical inns. Only the most popular (and usually most expensive) inns are described. Travelers looking for a wider variety of inns in a larger geographic area should use another guide.

Included in the series: California, by Peter Andrews and George Allen; *Lower New England,* by Peter Andrews, George Allen, and Tracy Ecclesine; *Upper New England,* by Peter Andrews, George Allen, and Tracy Ecclesine; *New York & Mid-Atlantic,* by Peter Andrews and Tracy Ecclesine.

Country Inns Series. Anthony Hitchcock and Jean Lindgren. New York: Burt Franklin & Co., 1979. approx. 200 pp. pap. $3.95.

The most striking feature of the Burt Franklin Country Inns series is the number of inns included and the large area covered by the series. The five books in the series describe hundreds of inns in 45 states. The inns are divided by city and state, with short background information on each state that includes addresses for complete travel information. There are also descriptions of the cities and towns in which the inns are located, which include references to nearby parks and other attractions. The entries for the inns list addresses, telephone numbers, the names of the innkeepers, and the seasons of operation. Each entry describes the inn and the area around it, as well as its furnishings and table fare, and gives rates and driving directions. The books serve travelers on moderate and above-average budgets looking for a variety of rural accommodations.

Evaluation: The entries emphasize descriptions of the inns and their neighborhoods and give only brief historical information. Other inn guides such as *Country Inns and Back Roads* (see under North America, Accommodations and Restaurants), introduce the reader to the innkeepers and give a recent history of the establishment. The Burt Franklin series describes more inns and covers a wider area than other inn guides and includes more information on nearby sights and activities; however, it would still be necessary to supplement these books with more complete sightseeing and transportation information. The practical information on the inns is complete and fairly accessible, and the descriptions are clear and inviting. Travelers looking for more background information on the inns and the innkeepers will find another guide more useful.

Included in the series: Country New England Inns: The Compleat Traveler's Companion (Connecticut, Massachusetts, Rhode Island, Vermont, New Hampshire, Maine); *Country Inns: Lodges and Historic Hotels of the Middle Atlantic States* (New York, Pennsylvania, New Jersey, Maryland, West Virginia); *Country Inns: Lodges and Historic Hotels of the Midwest and Rocky Mountain States* (Ohio, Illinois, Indiana, Michigan, Wisconsin, Missouri, Minnesota, Iowa, South Dakota, North Dakota, Nebraska, Kansas, Idaho, Colorado, Wyoming, Montana); *Country Inns: Lodges and Historic Hotels of the South* (Virginia, North Carolina, South Carolina, Georgia, Florida, Kentucky, Tennessee, Mississippi, Louisiana, Arkansas, Texas); *Country Inns: Lodges and Historic Hotels of the West and Southwest* (California, Washington, Oregon, Utah, Nevada, Arizona, New Mexico).

Hosteling U.S.A.: The Official American Youth Hostel Handbook. Charlotte, NC: Fast & McMillan Publishers, 1979. 219 pp. pap. $5.95.

Like its sister publications, the annual editions of the AYH handbooks to different areas of the world, *Hosteling U.S.A.* includes complete listings of all the hostels in the 50 states. What makes this book different is the inclusion of basic information on preparation, bicycling, canoeing, ski touring, and backpacking. There is also information on the history and operation of AYH, an equipment checklist, and a list of resource materials. This is the first edition that has been made available to the general public, but the facilities described in the book can be used only by AYH members. Although the preparatory information may be useful to all campers, nonmembers will find much of the same information in other camping guides, such as *Rand McNally Backpacking and Outdoor Guide* (see below, under Backpacking).

Evaluation: The information on the hostels and regulations governing them is complete and well organized, but the system of symbols employed and the hand-drawn maps make the book difficult to use. The sections describing outdoor recreation possibilities try hard to be as basic as possible, but in the end they are merely confusing and less than complete. Much better information on a variety of sports is available in other guides. The book is very useful—even essential—for hostelers, but other outdoor travelers would find camping or field guides to a particular area much more useful.

Mobil Travel Guide Series. Chicago, IL: Rand McNally & Co. approx. 300 pp. pap. $4.95. Revised annually.

Moderately priced accommodations and restaurants make up the majority of the entries in the Mobil Travel Guide series. The seven regional books include entries for small and large towns throughout the area they cover. Each town entry includes a short description, a listing of sights and activities, annual events, motels, hotels, resorts, and restaurants. The accommodations and restaurant listings include a five-star rating system, addresses and telephone numbers, directions, rates, credit cards accepted, and a brief but complete description of the facilities. Large maps are provided of each of the states and large cities, as well as a number of discount coupons. Special sections include tips for handicapped travelers, emergency information, and a short section on car care. The series serves motor travelers on a moderate budget, particularly those visiting lightly traveled areas.

Evaluation: Apart from the accommodations and restaurant listings, the larger, more populated areas are covered superficially. The series' strength lies in the comprehensive coverage of the small towns in each of the different areas. The information is well organized and presented clearly, but it is complete only for food and lodging. Sights, background, and transportation information are all secondary. The Mobil series provides a broader range of practical information than the *AAA Tourbook* series (see under North America, Accommodations and Restaurants), but the latter includes more sights, is more compact in size, and is free to AAA members. The Mobil Travel Guide series is useful to travelers covering a larger area on their vacation, who will be looking for moderately priced accommodations outside of the major cities.

Included in the series: California and the West (Arizona, California, Nevada, Utah); *Great Lakes Area* (Illinois, Indiana, Michigan, Ohio, Wisconsin, Ontario); *Middle Atlantic States* (Delaware, District of Columbia, Maryland, New Jersey, North Carolina, Pennsylvania, South Carolina, Virginia, West Virginia); *Northeastern States* (Connecticut, Maine, Massachusetts, New Hampshire, New York, Rhode Island, Vermont, Quebec, Canadian Atlantic Provinces); *Northwest and Great Plains States* (Idaho, Iowa, Minnesota, Montana, Nebraska, North Dakota, Oregon, South Dakota, Washington, Wyoming, Alberta, British Columbia, Manitoba, Ontario, Saskatchewan); *Southeastern States* (Alabama, Florida, Georgia, Kentucky, Mississippi, Tennessee); *Southwest and South Central Area* (Arkansas, Colorado, Kansas, Louisiana, Missouri, New Mexico, Oklahoma, Texas).

National Directory of Budget Motels, 1979-80. Raymond Carlson, ed. New York: Pilot Books, 1979. 64 pp. pap. $2.95.

The book is very simply a listing of budget motels. It defines a budget motel as one offering overnight accommodations costing between $10 and $15 for a single, one-bed occupancy. The motels are listed alphabetically by city and state. Each entry includes name, address (or location), and telephone number. It should be noted that these motels are found much more often in the south and west than in the north or east. The majority of entries are of national budget motel chains (Days Inn, Motel 6, Red Roof, and so on). The book is of most use to anyone who will be spending a long time on the road and who is interested in inexpensive accommodations.

Evaluation: There is very little to the book; it is simply a list. The entries do not include prices, directions, or descriptions. Most travelers would be as well off with the motel listings to be found in a more complete guide, such as *Where to Stay U.S.A.* (see below).

Other books in the National Directory series: *Free Tourist Attractions; Free Vacation and Travel Information; Low-cost Tourist Attractions; Theme Parks and Amusement Areas.*

Roadfood. Jane Stern and Michael Stern. New York: Random House, 1980. 368 pp. pap. $7.95.

For those who are prisoners of the highway, but are not willing to surrender to the fast-food franchises, *Roadfood* presents a guide to edible national treasures. The eateries described in this book feature real, local cooks preparing real, local food. The establishments are listed by regions of the United States and by state and town within state. The towns covered are mostly small and have intriguing names like Krumsville, Ishpeming, and Ozona, although there are a very few large cities like Dallas. The maps at the beginning of each U.S. region pinpoint the locations of the restaurants included—a very helpful feature. The food is all inexpensive and plainly good.

Evaluation: The chatty style of the text does much to make the restaurants seem inviting and familiar. The detail provided about both the food and the establishment allows the reader to have a good idea of what to expect. The reviews are frank and honest, making *Roadfood* a real treat for the frequent traveler looking for a good, inexpensive meal. Few restaurant guides cater to the old-fashioned traveler who is willing to spend time for well-prepared food, but is not willing to spend the money for fancy cuisine. For those travelers, this book is highly recommended.

The Vegetarian Times Guide to Dining in the U.S.A. Eds. of *Vegetarian Times,* Kathleen Moore, comp. New York: Atheneum/SMI, 1980. 314 pp. pap. $8.95.

The life of a vegetarian in a meat-eating world is not an easy one. Dining out can be a series of disappointments; the salad arrives sprinkled with bacon bits, the pita bread is warmed on a grill used to cook shish-kabob, and a seat near the kitchen sends the smell of scorched pork wafting across the table. Until recently, vegetarians either ate at home or went hungry. Now there is the *Vegetarian Times Guide to Dining in the U.S.A.*, which lists restaurants in 45 states and the District of Columbia that cater wholly or in part to vegetarian diners. The editors do not get involved in the debate about exactly what constitutes vegetarianism. They simply describe the restaurants and let the reader decide. The restaurant entries are divided by state, with the states listed alphabetically. Each entry includes the name, address, and telephone number of the restaurant, with a short description, a list of services and facilities, hours and days of operation, the price range, and directions by car. Special sections include a glossary of foods and "what to do if you can't find a Vegie restaurant."

Evaluation: The book is going to make a lot of diners very, very happy. Vegetarian dining is almost always ignored in other restaurant guides, and even when it is mentioned it is merely in passing. The information on the restaurants is complete, accessible, and clearly presented. The descriptions are short, but serve as introductions to the restaurants and proprietors. The book covers a wide price range and lists a variety of restaurants, from cafeterias and lunch counters near college campuses to the most elegant dining rooms in major cities. The book opens an entirely new world for many diners, and it is sure to advance the trend toward meatless dining from coast to coast.

Where to Eat In America. William Rice and Burton Wolf, eds. New York: Random House, 1979. 567 pp. pap. $7.95.

Where to Eat in America is a thorough examination of fine eating in 50 of North America's most visited cities. It is unique in both the variety of dining experiences included and the method of organizing the restaurants. The entries for each city begin with a general description and history of its eating establishments. The restaurants are organized under a variety of subheadings. First are the "Big Deals," worth it and not worth it. These are the restaurants with the best reputations; whether they live up to them is clearly pointed out. Other subheadings are for international cuisine, specialty cooking (delis, steakhouses, vegetarian, and so on), and restaurants for individual needs, which is a unique and useful subgrouping. Here are found the best hotel meals, business breakfasts and lunches, fast, good food, the best wine lists, drinks, late-night service, and so on. There are special listings for restaurants in the suburbs, markets, and gift foods. The book best serves frequent travelers over a large area of the country on modest and above-average budgets.

Evaluation: No restaurant guide comes close to matching the broad scope and usability of this guide. The restaurant descriptions are clear and complete, with all the expected practical information. The unique organization greatly facilitates the book's usage. Traveling gourmands and gourmets could not ask for a better guide. The wide price range and the special sections on restaurant owners and wines in restaurants make it ideal for those searching for a way out of the fast-food rut. Unfortunately, the quality of the food is not described or rated—an important oversight in a restaurant guide. Nevertheless, it is a most serviceable guide, and one that can make any trip in North America a diner's delight.

Where to Stay U.S.A. Marjorie A. Cohen; Margaret E. Sherman, ed. New York: Frommer-Pasmantier Publishing Co., 5th ed. 1980. 360 pp. pap. $4.95.

The author's purpose is to enable as many people as possible to enjoy an American experience on a limited budget. The book opens with a small transportation section that explains the many different ways of getting from here to there. Along with the more popular methods, it includes drive-away cars, car rentals, ride sharing, buying a used car, and, briefly, walking and boating. This is followed by a chapter on extended stays, which includes youth hostels, YMCA's International Houses, dormitories, tourist homes and guesthouses, "crashing," low-cost motel chains, and camping. These entries do not list places to stay, but rather describe the possibilities. Throughout the book, addresses for further information are included. The book also includes a long chapter for foreign visitors, loaded with practical and emergency information, survival tips, money and banking, laws, and medical advice. In the major portion of this book, more than 1,700 different accommodations are listed by state and include address, phone, and rates. All accommodations are listed by state and include address, phone, and rates. All accommodations are $20 a night or lower. Fourteen cities have been selected for more detailed coverage, including restaurants, sightseeing, and transportation, as well as the usual inexpensive accommodations.

Evaluation: The book provides a great amount of information on all types of low-budget travel in the United States. The information in the opening sections is both complete and clear, with a wide range of low-cost travel possibilities presented. The accommodations entries are unevenly distributed across the country, not through the fault of the author, but because these types of hotels and motels tend to be concentrated much more in the south and west. For the low-budget traveler in the United States, this is clearly the book that will make it all possible. It will save its users many times its purchase price in a short time.

ADVENTURE

Adventure Travel: A Source Book of Exciting Trips, Outdoor Challenges, and Thrilling Vacations in North America. See the review of this title under North America, Adventure.

BACKPACKING

Guide to Backpacking in the United States. Eric Meves. New York: Collier Books, Macmillan Publishing Co., 1979. 789 pp. pap. $5.95.

Guide to Backpacking in the United States is the complete reference guide to backpacking areas in all 50 states. Along with the descriptions of the hiking areas, sections are included on equipment and techniques, trip planning, a checklist of supplies, hiking ethics, a description of major backpacking environments, general hiking background, and safety tips. The backpacking area entries are divided into six geographic regions, with maps provided of each region showing the location of the hiking areas described. Included are national and state forests, wildlife refuges, and wilderness areas, as well as many other sites. The geographic characteristics of each area are described in the entries, and addresses for more information and trail maps are included. Irregular references are made to camping areas, but visitors will need more information when on the trip than is provided in the entries. A very useful feature is the physiographic cross-reference that lists mountains, deserts, low-elevation forests, coastal areas, grasslands, marshes, and floodplains. A short bibliography and complete index are included at the back of the book.

Evaluation: The book describes a wider variety of hiking areas than can be found in any other hiking guide and includes preparatory and practical information for beginners. The emphasis on descriptions in the entries and the many addresses listed for more information are very useful to hikers while planning their trips. On the road, a more complete guide to a particular area (with transportation and campsite information) should be used. The clear descriptions and the physiographic cross-reference make it relatively easy to find areas that meet the criteria of hikers with a variety of interests and at all levels of expertise.

Rand McNally Backpacking and Outdoor Guide. Richard Dunlop. Chicago, IL: Rand McNally & Co., 4th ed. 1979. 194 pp. pap. $5.95.

While many guides to outdoor sports stress "adventure," the *Rand McNally Backpacking and Outdoor Guide* takes a slightly more relaxed approach to the outdoor activities covered. The beginning sections are informal discussions of the basic characteristics of the sports, which include camping, backpacking and trail riding, wilderness survival, biking, orienteering, bike hiking and camping, rock hounding, canoeing and rafting, boating and boat camping, sport diving, and conservation and wildlife. These sections mix information on equipment and safety precautions with past experiences of the author and others. This is followed by state listings of where these sports can be enjoyed. The states are divided into seven regions, with the location of each activity divided by sport. The entries list only the location of each and very brief descriptions of the area. The book serves as a pretravel reference for travelers with little or no previous experience in the sports.

Evaluation: The topics covered in the book are comparable to those in *Adventure Travel* (see under North America, Adventure), but the two books differ mostly in emphasis. The *Backpacking and Outdoor Guide* includes much less practical information on the sports and in the entries, but it has much more background and serves as a better introduction to the sports. The book is more a discussion of outdoor travel possibilities than a practical camping or adventure guide. The scope of the sports included is slightly narrower and for the most part less challenging. A wider range of topics and more thorough coverage of preparation is provided in *The Whole Hiker's Handbook* (see below, under Hiking, Walking, and Running).

Travel Light Handbook. Judy Keene. Chicago, IL: Contemporary Books, 1979. 91 pp. pap. $3.95.

The first rule of backpacking is that you carry what you don't pay for. This is, the lighter the equipment, the higher the cost. And on the trail, extra ounces can turn an enjoyable vacation into a chore. The purpose of this book is to provide information to campers in general and backpackers in particular on the different types of trail equipment, additional supplies, food and food preparation, packing, an equipment checklist, and a list of suppliers. Much of the equipment described is more expensive than average, but there are plenty of tips throughout on how to cut costs in other areas, such as food from grocery stores as opposed to the more expensive freeze-dried trail food. The book is particularly useful to travelers preparing for their first backpacking trip who are not severely limited by a tight budget.

Evaluation: This short and relatively inexpensive book can save hours of frustration on the trail. The preparatory information is complete and easy to use, covering all the necessary angles. Though it is intended primarily for backpackers, all styles of campers would gain from the advice in the book—especially the food, food preparation, and doubling-up (using one item for two or more purposes) sections. The author's advice is consistently on the nose. It is quite a useful little book.

CAMPING

Rand McNally Campground and Trailer Park Guide. See the review of this title under North America, Camping.

Woodall's Campground Directory: North American Edition. See the review of this title under North America, Camping.

Woodall's Campground Directory: State Editions. Highland Park, IL: Woodall Publishing Co. pap. $1.95. Revised annually.

The state editions of *Woodall's Campground Directory* include the same introductory sections as the North American directory, with the addition of sections on city descriptions and basic travel tips (most frequently forgotten items, avoiding squeaks, severe traveling conditions, and so on), and background on each of the areas. The state campground listings are taken directly from those in the North American edition. The lower price and more manageable size of the state editions make them more suitable for campers covering a small area on their trips.

Evaluation: The books' strongest feature is obviously the number of camping sites described for each state. The information on the campgrounds is fairly complete, but the brevity in the entries and the complicated rating system make it difficult to find the necessary information. The sections on the road regulations and recreational vehicle maintenance are less complete than the information in the *Rand McNally Recreational Vehicle Handbook* (see below, under Recreational Vehicles), but some recreational vehicle campers may want to have all the camping information in one volume (Rand McNally's is a separate book).

Included in the series: Woodall's Arizona Campground Directory; Woodall's Arkansas/Missouri Campground Directory; Woodall's California Campground Directory; Woodall's Colorado Campground Directory; Woodall's Delaware/Maryland/Virginia/District of Columbia Campground Directory; Woodall's Florida Campground Directory; Woodall's Idaho/Oregon/Washington Campground Directory; Woodall's Illinois/Indiana Campground Directory; Woodall's Kentucky/Tennessee Campground Directory; Woodall's Michigan Campground Directory; Woodall's New England States Campground Directory; Woodall's New Jersey/New York Campground Directory; Woodall's North Carolina/South Carolina Campground Directory; Woodall's Ohio/Pennsylvania Campground Directory; Woodall's Ontario Camp-

ground Directory; Woodall's Texas Campground Directory; Woodall's Wisconsin Campground Directory.

CANOEING

Canoe Trails Directory. James C. Makens. Garden City, NY: Doubleday & Co., 1979. 360 pp. pap. $5.95.

Hundreds of canoe trips down rivers in every state and Puerto Rico are described in the *Canoe Trails Directory* (formerly titled *Makens Guide to U.S. Canoe Trails*). After a disclaimer and explanation of the abbreviations used in the entries, there are 33 pages of trail indexes arranged alphabetically and regionally. Why the indexes appear before the entries is unclear. The rivers and creeks are listed by state, with the states arranged alphabetically. For most rivers, a number of different trips are described, varying in length and, sometimes, difficulty. Each entry includes the counties and national forests through which the rivers pass, a difficulty rating, the characteristics of the rivers (size, speed of current, and so on), put-in and take-out spots, portage points, possible hazards along the route, and the time and distance of each leg of the trail. References to camping areas and descriptions of the shore lines are irregularly included. Special sections include suggestions on recording a canoe trip and a long list of sources and addresses for further information.

Evaluation: The entries for each river are short and loaded with abbreviations, but they manage to give a feel for the distinct characteristics of the different trips. The book includes no preparatory, safety, or equipment information, and the author gives very little advice to novices other than warnings of areas to avoid. Because of the inclusion of complete indexes, the book compares favorably in ease of use with *Canoeing and Rafting* (see below), though both books cover the same general areas and include the same information on the rivers. Which one is used depends on the preferences of the particular traveler.

Canoeing and Rafting: The Complete Where-To Guide to America's Best Tame and Wild Rivers. Sara Pyle. New York: William Morrow & Co., 1979. 363 pp. pap. $5.95.

Canoeing and Rafting provides complete descriptions of water routes in 49 states (Hawaii is not included). The introduction discusses guides and maps to specific areas, river classification, river safety, and environmental conservation, and lists canoeing clubs and how-to manuals. The entries divide the trips by state, and include locations, directions, put-in and take-out spots, descriptions of the route, camping, fishing, the river classifications, the best times for a trip, and addresses for further information. For each state there is a list of rental services, outfitters, park service addresses, and publications on canoeing in the state. The book describes short and long trips for canoeists of all levels of expertise.

Evaluation: The wide range and completeness of the information make this an excellent reference book to canoe and rafting trips from coast to coast. It is very well organized, with a complete index, and the information is as up-to-date as possible. The descriptions lack detail, but they are meant only to give the reader an impression of what the particular trip is like. The addresses for further information and the lists of other sources provide the means for acquiring more thorough detail.

CHILDREN

Traveling with Children in the U.S.A. Leila Hadley. New York: William Morrow & Co., 1977. 480 pp. pap. $4.95.

The purpose of the book is to provide a variety of sights and activities for short trips in all fifty states. The introduction discusses transportation possibilities, ways of cutting costs, inexpensive and/or unusual family accommodations, pets and other hazards, and tips for foreign visitors. The activities are arranged by city and state, and include addresses, short descriptions, hours, and whether or not an admission is charged. Most of the entries are parks and museums, though some unusual vacation ideas are included. Annual festivals are listed separately at the end of each state section. Special information is included on adventure trips, maps, and free sources of information, most often from government offices. The book serves families on modest (and above) budgets traveling over a large area of the country.

Evaluation: The narrow scope and the sketchy information limit the book's usefulness. Because it lists only sights and activities, it would be necessary to use a more complete transportation/accommodation guide along with it. The lack of an index and the unbroken text make the book very difficult to use. It covers a large geographical area and a wide range of sights and activities, which suggests that the book could be used many times over. However, the incompleteness of the information and the difficulty in finding it detract from the book's serviceability.

DRIVING TOURS

America by Car. Norman D. Ford. Floral Park, NY: Harian Books (dist. by Grosset and Dunlap), 1979 (18th ed.). 263 pp. pap. $4.95.

Geared to first-time travelers looking for regimented itineraries, *America by Car* describes 30 travel routes covering many different areas in North America. The introductory sections discuss ways of cutting costs, provide a list of what to do before leaving, give driving tips, and list a number of tourist information sources. The tours range from 5 to 18 days, with one Grand Tour of 73 days. The entries for each tour list directions and include short descriptions of the area covered. The towns and cities are listed as they are found on the tour (first day, second day, and so on) and include brief descriptions and a few selected sights. A special section in the book lists where to eat and stay in each of the cities visited, with an emphasis on low and moderately priced accommodations and restaurants.

Evaluation: The basic quality of the information in the book and the drill-sergeant-style of touring will not appeal to many travelers. The entries concentrate on the standard tourist routine, with selected sights in each area. The information is incomplete, the directions are confusing, and most of the cost-cutting advice in the introductory sections would be obvious to travelers with even the slightest experience. The structured itineraries, limited scope of information, and poor organization all detract from the book's usefulness. Travelers will find little discovery or adventure outside of well-worn tourist paths in the trips described in this book.

EXTENDED RETIREMENT VACATIONS

Where to Retire on a Small Income. Norman D. Ford. Floral Park, NY: Harian Books (dist. by Grosset and Dunlap), 1979 (22nd ed.). 274 pp. pap. $4.95.

Although it does not qualify as a travel guide in a strict sense, *Where to Retire on a Small Income* does offer some important information on housing and activities of particular interest to retirees. This information may be used as a retirement guide or as a guide to an extended vacation to one of the many areas described in the book. The first three chapters discuss monetary and health considerations, precautions in choosing the right spot, different types of accommodations, and buying versus renting. Most of the cities included are in the Sun Belt, though some areas in New England, the Rocky Mountain states, the Pacific Northwest, and outlying islands are included as well. The city entries (arranged alphabetically by state or area) describe the climate and recreational facilities of each town, as well as nearby housing possibilities. Special sections include areas free from hay fever, how to keep active, and a list of America's most livable, worry-free towns.

Evaluation: The book's relative benefits as a retirement guide will not be discussed here. What is important is its use to retirees as a guide to low-cost vacation accommodations and comfortable travel destinations. Along these lines, the book serves very well. The information is fairly complete, and the descriptions of the different areas are detailed enough to give a clear picture of what they are like. A wide variety of towns is included: small and large, rural and urban, quiet and jumping. The book is most useful to travelers planning an extended vacation, as a reference to a variety of possible travel destinations.

FARMS AND RANCHES

Farm, Ranch, and Country Vacations. Pat Dickerman. New York: Farm & Ranch Vacations (dist. by Berkshire Traveller Press), 1979. (30th ed.) 1979. 222 pp. pap. $5.95.

From rustic lodges in the Alaska wilderness to a small family farm in rural Pennsylvania, *Farm, Ranch, and Country Vacations* describes rural vacation spots for spectators and participants of every travel budget. The thirtieth anniversary edition has seen the amount of information for each of the entries expanded and the addition of appendixes that list the farms and ranches by special services and facilities. The introduction discusses the development of this style of travel and includes information on rates, reservations, and selecting the vacation spot that best suits a particular traveler. The entries include short descriptions of the farms with testimonies from past visitors, complete information on services, rates, and the degree of supervision, as well as addresses, telephone numbers, and seasons of operation. The book serves as a pretravel reference for all travelers, particularly families who want to get back to the land.

Evaluation: The variety of rural vacations described and the wide area covered make this guide a valuable source book for anyone looking for an alternative to the well-worn tourist paths. The information in each of the entries is complete, and the solid organization and detailed appendixes make the book easy to use. Although the entries do mention some nearby attractions, more complete travel information on a particular area should be acquired before setting out.

HANDICAPPED TRAVELERS

Access to the World: A Travel Guide for the Handicapped. See the review of this title under The World, Handicapped Travelers.

Rollin' On. Maxine H. Atwater. New York: Dodd, Mead & Co., 1978. 290 pp. $9.95.

Rollin' On opens with chapters on basic travel tips for the traveler in a wheelchair. Air, train, bus, car, and taxi transportation and hotel facilities and reservations are included. The main portion of the book focuses on wheelchair visits in eight cities: Chicago, Honolulu, New

York, Philadelphia, San Antonio, San Diego, San Francisco, and Washington, D.C. For each there is a general description, planning suggestions, notes on accessibility in general, hotel descriptions, comments on what to see and do, and restaurant suggestions—all with an eye for the traveling wheelchair. Three to six day-long detailed tours are provided for each city, planned for variety, ease of accomplishment, location of restrooms, and general interest. In- and outdoor activities are included. A chapter near the end of the book briefly covers an additional six cities. An excellent travel guidebook bibliography for the handicapped concludes the book.

Evaluation: Rollin' On is an ideal match to other guidebooks for the handicapped. Its daily itineraries make visiting the cities included easy. What the *Wheelchair Vagabond* (see below) does for the camper and nonurban traveler, *Rollin' On* does for the city visitor. Since *Rollin' On* is largely a collection of carefully planned daily tours, the practicalities of traveling in a wheelchair are more extensively covered in *Travelability* (see below). A broader variety of hotels and restaurants around the United States is given in *The Wheelchair Traveler* (see below). There are two assumptions made in *Rollin' On* of which the reader should be aware. First, the traveler should have the means to afford a rather expensive vacation: the cities included are expensive, and most of the restaurants and accommodations are midrange or above. Second, since many points on the itinerary are out of doors, summer will be the best time for using the book. The author's enthusiasm for travel and the care with which she has checked her details make the book a very exciting one. This may excuse the overuse of words such as "fabulous," "elegant," "stunning," and "fascinating." They do, however, capture the excitement the wheelchair traveler can get in the cities included.

Travelability: A Guide for Physically Disabled Travelers in the United States. Lois Reamy. New York: Macmillan Publishing Co., 1978. 298 pp. $9.95.

This book is geared to handicapped persons who want to travel, but who lack the know-how. It describes a variety of travel methods, detailing through text and illustrations travel by car (rented and owned), by bus, by train, by air, and aboard ship. Sections are included on travel in Hawaii, outdoor vacations, a complete source list of state and regional publications on handicapped travel, a description of a typical stay in a hotel with addresses and descriptions of major hotel and motel chains, complete preparatory and practical travel information (money, weather, insurance, and so on), and medical questions and answers. Other sections discuss figuring out the physical limits of a particular traveler, planning a trip with a travel agent, and a long list of the international references.

Evaluation: The transporatation information in the book is more detailed and is presented much more clearly than the comparative sections in other handicapped-travel guides. These sections escort the readers through all the necessary procedures from predeparture planning to postarrival enjoyment. The many photographs illustrate these procedures and help greatly to familiarize travelers with the different routines. The preparatory and practical travel information is complete, clear, and accessible, with many addresses for further information included. The book is most useful as a pretravel reference and is worthwhile to all handicapped individuals, whether traveling or not. It opens areas and styles of travel that previously seemed inaccessible and helps make travelers feel at home wherever they may be.

The Wheelchair Traveler. Douglass R. Annand. Milford, NH: The Wheelchair Traveler, 1979. pap. $8.25.

The book lists hotels and restaurants throughout North America that are accessible to wheelchair travelers. A short introduction discusses trip preparation and transportation possibilities and gives advice to travelers on a variety of subjects. The entries are arranged alphabetically by city and state, or sometimes by region and state, and include the address, location, telephone numbers, and services of each hotel and restaurant. A complex system of abbreviations is used to give a rating of the suitability of the establishment for wheelchair travelers, the facilities, rates, and services provided. Hospitals and barrier-free rest areas are listed for each state, and selected sights are occasionally included in the entries. A long list of directories and other useful addresses is included at the back of the book, but there is no index and the pages are not numbered.

Evaluation: Although it includes very little preparatory information, *The Wheelchair Traveler* provides an invaluable service to handicapped travelers in North America. The information on the hotels and restaurants is complete and, apart from the complicated abbreviations and the lack of headings to separate the entries, clearly presented. The book emphasizes travel by car, which suggests *Wheelchair Vagabond* (see below) as the logical complement to this book for more detailed preparation and the irreplaceable inspiration it provides. Canada, Mexico, and parts of the Caribbean are also covered in the listings, but by far the best coverage is provided for areas in the United States. The book is a worthwhile companion for all handicapped travelers planning a trip in the United States.

Wheelchair Vagabond. John G. Nelson. Santa Monica, CA: Project Press, 1975. 132 pp. $7.95. pap. $4.95.

Wheelchair Vagabond was written as "a guide and a goad for the handicapped traveler." It concentrates not only on how to travel but why, and works to alleviate possible psychological problems handicapped travelers may have. The beginning sections of the book describe the author's past travel experiences, discussing how he overcame some basic problems and telling of some unexpected rewards gained from his journeys. More practical information includes how to cut the costs of food and shelter, choosing and modifying the right vehicle, a complete list of equipment, directions on how to pack it, travel preparation, and a discussion of camping facilities, cooking, and housekeeping. The book also includes a complete list of tourist information sources, camping equipment catalogs, recreational vehicle and camping publications, and publications relating to the handicapped.

Evaluation: The author's insights into the unique problems of handicapped travelers and how to overcome them is an invaluable service to all those for whom travel heretofore seemed an impossibility. The practical preparatory information is fairly complete and wide ranging, but the major feature of the book is in providing the incentive for handicapped people to try to expand the limits of their world and thereby increase their self-reliance. The conversational style of the book makes for smooth and clear reading, and the wide range of subjects provides at least minimal coverage of nearly every facet of handicapped travel. Other guides for handicapped travelers include more complete and up-to-date accommodations and transportation information (*The Wheelchair Traveler,* for one; see above), but they tend to include much less information on preparation.

HIKING, WALKING, AND RUNNING

Traveler's Guide to Running in Major American Cities. Randy Sloane and Mary-Jo Carroll. Harrisburg, PA: Stackpole Books, 1978. 219 pp. pap. $4.95.

What can match the despair of a runner in a strange city, feet wrapped in leather Pumas, palms moist with anticipation, gaze void of expression, ready to run six miles in a half hour, but without the slightest idea where. For runners there is now the *Traveler's Guide to Running in Major American Cities.* Jogging routes in twenty U.S. cities are described in the book, with an average of three routes included for each area. The entries for each city are arranged alphabetically and include description of the climate, the dates and lengths of annual races, and addresses for more information, along with descriptions of the running routes. The descriptions sometimes include references to other points of interest in the various areas, although running is definitely emphasized; hand-drawn maps are provided for each route described. Special sections include short descriptions of running areas in 24 additional cities and a running travelog.

Evaluation: Traveling runners no longer have to worry about missing their daily enjoyment while visiting a strange city. The information on the routes is clear and fairly complete, though little information on anything other than the jogging areas is included. The inclusion of weather and climate information helps prepare for whatever obstacles Mother Nature may conjure up. However, not all of the references in the entries may be trusted. Many Great Lakes freighter pilots, for instance, will be surprised to learn that the Detroit River empties into Lake St. Clair. This may be a small error, but it makes the book's reliability suspect. When used with a more comprehensive guide to a particular city, the book is useful to runners who wish to stay in shape while on the road.

Walking Tours of America. Louise Feinsot, ed. New York: Collier Books, Macmillan Publishing Co., 1979. 381 pp. pap. $7.95.

Who better to compile a guide to walks in 24 states and the District of Columbia than a shoe manufacturing company? In an effort to promote physical fitness in America, the Kinney Shoe Corporation has gathered together these tours from writers all over the country, and though all are in or near urban areas, the variety in the tours is representative of the diversity of the nation. The walks are arranged into seven geographic regions. Each trip is described in detail, with points of historic and natural interest highlighted. Large, clear maps show the route of each tour, and the locations of the buildings and areas described in the text. Many of the entries include references to other sites and activities in the different areas.

Evaluation: The large area covered by the book suggests that its best use is by travelers planning a number of visits to many different areas or as a pretravel reference for visitors to a particular city. The information in the entries emphasizes points of historic interest, but many sights and activities of interest to children are also included. The large maps make each of the routes easy to follow. The walks are an excellent way to discover the unique features of the many small and large towns described in the book.

The Whole Hiker's Handbook. William Kemsley, Jr., ed. New York: William Morrow & Co., 1979. 442 pp. pap. $9.95.

The Whole Hiker's Handbook is a series of articles compiled from *Backpacker* magazine on a wide range of subjects pertaining to the outdoors. It was written as a source book particularly for novice hikers and includes sections on food and equipment, physical fitness, navigation in the field, hazards and safety, family hiking and hiking alone, winter camping and sports, the hiker as naturalist and photographer; articles on hiking and mountain climbing in many areas of the world; and environmental conservation. Many of the articles deal strictly with practical and emergency information, others are descriptions and essays, and some are in the form of interviews. The variety and quality of the articles guarantees something of interest to all outdoor enthusiasts. The book should be consulted while planning a trip to make the most of the wide range of information.

Evaluation: The book is unique in both the scope of information it includes and its approach to the subject. The many different areas are covered clearly and completely in a narrative, essay style and in a more basic how-to fashion. The firsthand accounts of outdoor adventures in many North American areas may not include practical information about the trips, but they provide something that is just as important: inspiration. The book is an excellent reference for all hikers and campers, though it is no substitute for a practical field or camping guide on the road.

LEARNING VACATIONS

Learning Vacations. See the review of this title under North America, Learning Vacations.

LITERARY TOURS

Exploring Literary America. Marcella Thum. New York: Atheneum, 1979. 316 pp. $11.95.

The book emphasizes biographical information on 62 men and women of literary importance and the sites from their past that can still be visited. The entries are arranged in an informal chronology, from Captain John Smith to John Steinbeck. Each entry averages five pages in length and includes, along with the short biographies, the location of homes, buildings, and other sites of importance in the lives of the writers, with directions to each, and whether an admission is charged. Many photographs and illustrations of the authors, their homes, and other sites associated with them are interspersed throughout the text, with detailed captions that explain their relevance. Geographic, author-title, and subject indexes are included at the back of the book.

Evaluation: The entries in the book are much less detailed than those in the Literary Tour Guide series (see below), emphasizing biographical information over the significance of the sites to the writers and their works. The biographies are clear and direct, but the information on the different sites is incomplete and unevenly distributed. The book is useful as a source for short biographies of the men and women of American *belles lettres,* but its use as a travel guide is severely limited. Most travelers will find the information in the Literary Tour Guide series more complete and much more useful on the road.

A Literary Tour Guide to the United States Series. New York: William Morrow & Co., 1978 & 1979. approx. 220 pp. $8.95 and $9.95; pap. $4.95 and $5.95.

The Northeast volume is a series of descriptions of the homes and hangouts from Maine to Delaware of the men and women of American literature. Among the entries are the home of Mark Twain in Connecticut, Walt Whitman's home on Long Island, the home that was the setting for Eugene O'Neill's *Long Day's Journey into Night,* and the memorial to Edgar Allan Poe in Baltimore. The addresses and hours of attractions are included, along with other points of interest in the area. The other books in the series are similar, although they also describe many historic sites not directly associated with American literature.

Evaluation: The descriptions are an interesting blend of the histories of the buildings and those of their occupants. Historical odds and ends are sewn together to form the simplest of biographies, concentrating on the time spent at that residence or the significance of the building or area on the life and works of the author. The book can be used as pretravel reading and as a reference on the trip. It offers insights for the student of literature not to be found elsewhere, in a style that is both pleasurable and informative.

Included in the series: A Literary Tour Guide to the United States: South and Southwest, by Rita Stein (1979); *A Literary Tour Guide to the United States: West and Midwest,* by Rita Stein (1979); *A Literary Tour Guide to the United States: Northeast,* by Emilie C. Harting (1978).

MUSEUMS AND HISTORIC SIGHTS

American Jewish Landmarks Series. Bernard Postal and Lionel Koppman. New York: Fleet Press Corp. Vol. 1: 1977. 672 pp. $18.50; pap. $8.50. Vol. 2: 1979. 334 pp. $13.95; pap. $7.50. Vol. 3: To be published in 1981.

The three books in this series give in-depth descriptions of sites and areas throughout the United States of particular significance to American Jewish history. The states in each of the three volumes are arranged alphabetically, with a discussion of the development of Jewish communities in each state preceding the listings of sites in many different cities. The sites described include synagogues, memorials, college and university buildings, parks, community centers, libraries, cemeteries, and many other buildings of historical significance. Many of the entries list only the address or location of the site, while others include more detailed descriptions. Practical information (such as telephone numbers or hours) is severely limited.

Evaluation: The series serves a double purpose. First, the books can be used as travel guides, describing sites and areas of interest to many travelers that are not listed in other guides. Second, they are worthwhile as background reading, opening an area of U.S. history of which few of its citizens are aware. However, the information on the areas described in the books is unevenly distributed, and the lack of practical travel information suggests that their best use is in conjunction with a more thorough guide to a particular area. As a travel guide, the series leaves much to be desired. But as background reading, the books provide information not to be found elsewhere, in an informative and very readable style.

Included in the series: Northeast (Vol. 1); *South and Southwest* (Vol. 2); *Middle West and West* (Vol. 3).

American Traveler's Treasury: A Guide to the Nation's Heirlooms. Suzanne Lord. New York: William Morrow & Co., 1977. 588 pp. pap. $5.95.

No guide can match this book for variety, number of sights, and the large area covered. The entries are organized alphabetically by state and city and include museums of every kind, homes of famous Americans, folk arts, cemeteries, archaeological sites, gardens, sculptures, musical instruments, Indian cultural centers, and churches. The book also includes walking tours, state and national parks, and tourist office addresses for all 50 states. The entries are rarely longer than a line or two and include addresses, hours, and admission charges. The book serves all travel budgets and styles, but particularly those interested in viewing American history firsthand.

Evaluation: When used with an accommodations/transportation guide, this book is all a traveler should need for an informative and enjoyable vacation. The variety of sights and activities described guarantees something for everyone. A problem with the book is the lack of an index. It is difficult—almost impossible—to find a particular entry among the thousands included. In this case, perseverance pays. This is a book that can be used many times over and one that increases in value with each use.

Art Museums of America: A Guide to Collections in the United States and Canada. Lila Sherman. New York: William Morrow & Co., 1980. 416 pp. $12.95.

Art museums of every size and description, in every state, province, and the District of Columbia, are described in detail in the book. The museums and galleries included are all "non-profit . . . with permanent collections maintained for the purpose of the exhibition, not sale, of art work," emphasizing paintings, prints, and sculptures over crafts and historical displays (artifacts). The museums are listed by city and state, which in turn are listed alphabetically. Each entry includes the address, dates and hours of operation, parking information, directions by car, and whether an admission fee is charged. The entries also include short histories of the museums, descriptions of the interiors and exteriors, special collections on exhibit, the location of shops, special exhibitions planned, classes and lectures sponsored, and art works on display of particular interest. Photographs of many of the museums are included, along with a list of where to find special collections, and a complete index.

Evaluation: This is the first guide to compile practical information and complete descriptions of North America's art museums, and the quality and completeness of the entries guarantees its warm reception by the traveling public and its continuing success. The information is presented clearly and is easy to find. The variety of museums described and the large area covered by the book make it an invaluable reference for researchers, students, teachers, and anyone else who appreciates art, fine or otherwise. It is the key to many enjoyable afternoons of quiet contemplation.

Directory of Unique Museums. See the review of this title under North America, Museums.

Historic Homes and Sights of Revolutionary America. See the review of this series below, under Regional Guides, The East, Sightseeing.

Restored Towns and Historic Districts of America. Alice Cromie. New York: E. P. Dutton, 1979. 384 pp. $17.50; pap. $10.95.

This book is a listing of historic places in the United States, with a small section on Canada. The author divides the United States into 14 areas, and within each of these areas lists states. Selected towns are listed alphabetically within states. The towns selected contain usually lesser-known historical sites. The well-known places such as Williamsburg or Greenfield Village are included, but space given to them is limited, on the grounds that they have adequate publicity and orientation programs for visitors. Most towns selected have several historic buildings, each of which is described briefly, with a snatch of history and architectural comments. Addresses are given (no directions), but the author thinks prices and hours fluctuate too often to merit inclusion.

Evaluation: This extensive listing of historic sites and museums will well serve the traveler who wants to see a bit of history while traveling in the United States. Most of the entries are locally noteworthy, but, with some exceptions, are not worth an individual excursion. The geographic organization of the text and the vast number of inclusions throughout the United States will make it very easy for natives and foreign visitors alike to savor the past. This is a good book to keep in the car while traveling if you have any inclination toward the past.

MUSIC FESTIVALS

A Guide to Music Festivals in America. Carol Price Rabin. Stockbridge, MA: Berkshire Traveller Press, 1979. 199 pp. pap. $4.95.

Everybody likes some kind of music, but usually the only music travelers hear while on vacation comes out of the box on the dashboard. Finding a music festival in an unfamiliar area was strictly a matter of chance until now. *A Guide to Music Festivals in America* covers every type of music festival (except rock and roll) in 30 states. The festivals and concerts are arranged by type of music and by state, with an emphasis on the classics, though jazz, ragtime, Dixieland, bluegrass, folk and traditional are well represented. The entries give the approximate dates of the festivals (nearly always in the summer), a description and history of each, and addresses for ticket and accommodation information. There is also a suggested reading list at the back of the book.

Evaluation: It would be entirely possible to build an entire vacation around music festivals, though most travelers will want to supplement this guide with a more inclusive travel book. It is very well organized, easy to read, and complete. Particulars about the festivals change yearly, so it is necessary to plan in advance. The book is unique for the subject and can be used many times over. Why hasn't it been thought of sooner?

NATIONAL PARKS

Exploring Our National Parks and Monuments. Devereux Butcher. Ipswitch, MA: Gambit, 7th ed. 1976. 373 pp. pap. $7.95.

Since its first edition in 1947, *Exploring Our National Parks and Monuments* has been considered by many as the best source of information on the areas under the control of the National Park Service. It describes all the National Parks, as well as 32 national nature monuments and 17 national archaeological monuments. The introductory sections discuss some of the mistakes of the past and emphasize the fragility of the many areas and the care necessary to protect them.

The parks are arranged alphabetically, with each entry describing the formation and physical characteristics of the park, available park services, directions to the park, and an address for further information. The National Monuments are listed separately and include the same information. Special sections include descriptions of other nature reserves in the United States, threats to the preservation of the parks, a copy of the National Park Service declaration of policy, and a detailed reading list. The book is worthwhile reading for all travelers to the national park areas.

Evaluation: Exploring Our National Parks includes less practical information on park facilities than either the *Rand McNally National Park Guide* (see below) or *Traveling and Camping in the National Park Areas* (see below), but the detailed descriptions, colorful background, and emphasis on preservation make the book a much better introduction to the parks and how best to enjoy them. The many photographs and illustrations, the smooth style of the text, and the many special features make the book enjoyable reading. It is most useful as a pretravel reference. A guide with more complete camping or accommodations information should be used on the road.

Rand McNally National Park Guide. Michael Frome. Chicago, IL: Rand McNally & Co., 1980 (14th ed.). 212 pp. pap. $6.95.

Comprehensive descriptions and perhaps the most up-to-date information on all the National Park areas are found in the *National Park Guide*. The introduction discusses how best to use the parks, with brief information on planning, equipment and clothing, special services, and traveling for the handicapped. The parks are listed alphabetically. Each entry includes a short description and history, a list of practical information on sights, camping, nearby attractions and accommodations, the seasons, recommended reading, and an address for further information. Special sections are included on Washington, D.C., archaeological and historical areas, natural and recreational areas, the environments of the parks, and bird watching. The book is most useful as a pretravel reference for anyone planning a trip to one or more of the National Park areas.

Evaluation: The practical information in the entries is wide ranging and fairly complete. While the book provides travel ideas, a guide with more complete transportation and accommodations information will be necessary on the road. *National Park Guide* is well organized, with information easy to find. The many maps and photographs in color and black and white add greatly to the book's appeal. The guide covers a larger geographic area and includes more information than

Traveling and Camping in the National Park Areas (see below). Although *Exploring Our National Parks and Monuments* (see above) gives a better feel for the parks, it is a few years older. The Rand McNally guide is worthwhile reading—especially for those planning their first visit to a National Park.

Traveling and Camping in the National Park Areas (Mid-America and Western States). David L. Scott and Kay Woefel Scott. Chester, CT: The Globe Pequot Press, 1978. 167 pp. (Mid-America), 173 pp. (Western States). pap. $4.95.

The two books in this series describe 76 western and 82 mid-American national parks, monuments, seashores, and historic sites, all administered by the National Park Service. The western edition covers the seven Far West states, Alaska, and Hawaii. The mid-American edition includes all the other states west of the Mississippi, as well as Wisconsin, Illinois, and Mississippi. The entries are arranged alphabetically by state and include descriptions and brief histories of the areas, facilities, camping, and fishing. Each of the areas is shown on an accompanying map that points out park offices, visitor's centers, picnic areas, and trails. The books are useful to experienced campers planning a trip to a number of National Park areas in the western United States.

Evaluation: The descriptions of the park areas and the facilities they provide are clear, but they lack the detail of other National Park guides. The entries include no information on transportation to the areas, nearby sights, or natural points of interest. The different parks are grouped together, though they vary greatly in size, facilities, and emphasis (historical significance, scenic areas, and so on). Because of the lack of an index, the geographic grouping of the parks, and the sameness of the entries, it is difficult to find the information the books provide. Most travelers will want more background and a wider range of practical travel information than can be found in these guides.

PRETRAVEL READING

Forgotten Pleasures. Ruth Rudner. New York: Penguin Books, 1978. 243 pp. pap. $3.95.

The book has little to do with travel, but it is useful to travelers as a guide to activities in the outdoors that can be enjoyed at home or on the road. It takes a seasonal approach to outdoor pastimes and describes a wide variety of activities for a number of interests. The author describes the variations in the seasons through walks in a forest near her home. Springtime activities described include bird watching, kite flying, rock hunting, canoeing, and walking. In the summer there is berrying, caving, horseback riding, rafting, musseling, and body surfing. Orienteering, skipping stones, gathering nuts, and watching hawks are all activities for the fall, and wintertime is a time for sledding, tracking, snowshoeing, skating, ice fishing, ski touring, and going for walks. The entries for each activity are merely descriptions, with lists of sources for more information and organizations following each activity. A special section is included on the night, and appendixes list national recreation areas and national recreation trails.

Evaluation: The major use of the book for travelers is as a pretravel description of a variety of inexpensive outdoor activities for all seasons. The author's descriptive powers sometimes get the best of her, and most of the entries consist primarily of recollections of her experiences, which are more poetic than practical. The book provides a wide variety of vacation ideas, and the lists of books following each entry are very useful for those whose interest is piqued by the colorful and relaxed descriptions. Again, the book is not a travel guide, but it is useful to travelers as a description of seasonal outdoor activities.

Lakeside Recreation Areas. Bill and Phyllis Thomas. Harrisburg, PA: Stackpole Books, 1977. 160 pp. pap. $6.95.

The book is a guide to lakes created by the U.S. Army Corps of Engineers. There are 101 lakes and reservoirs listed in 40 states. The book opens with a short introduction that tells a little about the history of the Corps and the way it operates. The entries are arranged alphabetically by state. Each is about a page long and includes a description, directions, fishing, hunting, camping, other activities, area attractions, and addresses for additional information. One of the main features of the lakes is that they are usually located near urban areas and are easily accessible.

Evaluation: There are many problems with this book. The first is that it does not mention boating at all. The entries emphasize sporting activities around the lakes and spend little time on history, nature, or hiking. The information included is incomplete. The book tries to cover too wide an area. It should have fewer entries or perhaps regional editions, with more information on each. It is unlikely that anyone would travel 3,000 miles to visit a man-made lake. Unless you have a great interest in the U.S. Army Corps of Engineers, pass this one by.

Sunset Pictorial Series. Editors of Sunset Books and *Sunset* magazine. Menlo Park, CA: Lane Publishing Co., 2nd and 3rd eds. 1977. pap. $6.95.

The Sunset Pictorial series offers pages and pages of beautiful photographs, in color and black and white, of scenes in the areas covered by the series. A brief introduction describes general characteristics of each area, but the major story is told through pictures—dramatic coastlines, snow-clad peaks, and scenes of urban and rural life. The practicality of the series as travel literature is limited to pretravel reading, providing a feel for the different areas, or as an excellent collection of pictures the traveler might never manage to get.

Evaluation: All the books in the series provide a glimpse of the scenic beauty of the different areas, though some include more practical and background information than others. The first three books listed below concentrate almost exclusively on photographs, while the last four include a wider range of information. Still, none could be called complete travel guides. They were meant to provide a sampling of travel possibilities in each of the areas. On the road, more comprehensive travel guides should be used.

Included in the series: Alaska; Beautiful California; Beautiful Hawaii; Beautiful Northwest; California Coast; California Missions; Ghost Towns of the West.

Time Off: A Psychological Guide to Vacations. Stephen A. Shapiro, Ph.D., and Alan J. Tuckman, M.D. Garden City, NY: Anchor Press, Doubleday & Co., 1978. 102 pp. $5.95.

This is a guide for travelers whose past vacations turned out to be less than they anticipated. It is also useful to those with vacation anxiety or who simply have no idea how to plan and prepare for a vacation. The introduction discusses how important vacations are in the modern world and the difficulty some travelers have in enjoying themselves on the road. Topics discussed in the book include knowing who you are, knowing your travel companions, recognizing your type of travel style (planned or impulsive), travel goals for different age groups, relaxation versus activity, the culture quest, seeking sex, shopping, self-indulgence, using a travel agent, getting in shape, setting the rhythm for a trip, health precautions, knowing when not to go, and the last-minute blues. An entire chapter is devoted to "the spoilers," the feelings and emotions that can sabotage a good time.

Evaluation: It can only be hoped that most travelers will not need this guide. Nevertheless, not all those who travel have an enjoyable time. The book's discussion of preparation, both physical and psychological, will be useful to anyone who has trouble making pretravel plans, and the section on knowing what kind of traveler you are and what type of vacation you are most likely to enjoy will help simplify some basic travel perplexities. Travelers who find themselves backing out of a long-planned trip will reconsider after reading the final section on trip spoilers. The book may help some travelers get more out of their vacation time, but it is hoped that most will find it unnecessary.

Traveling the United States. Dr. Wilson Strand and Professor Gisela Strand, eds. Holland, MI: Travelwise, 1978. pap. free.

Traveling the United States is a reference to travel articles published in a variety of magazines. It provides listings of article titles, dates, pages, and the magazines in which they are found. Listings are divided by state, and all magazines cited can be found in a medium-sized library. The book is an excellent source for pretravel reading, specialized and general, old and new, for all travelers.

Evaluation: This is the first guide of its kind, and it provides a service to travelers not to be found elsewhere. It offers a wide range of articles on all areas covered. The information is brief, but adequate for library research, and is clearly presented. It has as its goal the provision of a complete source of free travel background information. And to this end it is very successful.

RAILWAYS

North America by Rail. See the review of this title under North America, Railways.

RECREATIONAL VEHICLES

Rand McNally Recreational Vehicle Handbook. Connie B. Howes. Chicago, IL: Rand McNally & Co., 2nd ed. 1978. 96 pp. pap. $2.95.

The *Rand McNally Recreational Vehicle Handbook* provides complete preparatory information on all facets of RV (recreational vehicle) camping. Written primarily for travelers unfamiliar with RV travel, the book discusses the benefits of owning and renting, the differences between trailers, pickups, and motor homes, and gives special driving and towing tips. The book features a long section on RV maintenance, with many photographs and illustrations that help clarify the instructions. Special sections include winter camping, tips on traveling in Canada, Mexico, and Europe, a short history of RV travel, and a complete checklist and index. The book is most useful to new and potential RV campers as pretravel reading and as a reference on the road.

Evaluation: The information is much more complete and more readily accessible than that provided in *Woodall's Campground Directory* (see under North America, Camping). Also, because it is in a separate book and is much less expensive, many travelers will find the *Recreational Vehicle Handbook* more convenient to use. The sections on maintenance and driving safety and the thorough preparatory information are particularly useful. Because the book includes no practical information on campgrounds or road services, it should be used along with a camping and motoring guide. The book is the best currently available how-to manual for RV travelers.

The Twelve Best RV Trips in America. Charles L. Cadieux. Highland Park, IL: Woodall Publishing Co. (dist. by Simon & Schuster), 1977. 136 pp. pap. $2.95.

What makes these 12 recreational vehicle trips the best in America is unknown, and the author includes no information that explains why these 12 routes were selected out of the infinite number possible. Five of the trips are in the Southwest; the others are in the Canadian Rockies, Yellowstone, Florida, North Carolina, Virginia, and Vancouver Island, and one reaches from Pennsylvania to Quebec. The entries for each trip average eight pages and blend directions with sights and histories. Thirty-two pages of color photographs are included, as well as skeleton maps. The book is meant to be used while planning a trip.

Evaluation: The style of the book is lively enough, but there are many mysteries about it. What makes the 12 trips described of particular interest to recreational vehicle campers? Why is there no mention of roadside services or emergency information? Why are some of the trips so much longer than others, with no clue as to the approximate time needed to complete them? Aside from the descriptions of the areas, there is little in the book to make it worthwhile. Perhaps it can be useful when used with a camping guide, but only by recreational vehicle travelers who are looking for a regimented itinerary. The *Rand McNally Recreational Vehicle Handbook* (see above) will be more helpful to RV owners.

ROAD ATLASES

Hammond Road Atlas and Vacation Guide. Maplewood, NJ: Hammond, 1979. 48 pp. pap. $1.50.

The *Hammond Road Atlas and Vacation Guide* includes many special features, such as a highway mileage chart, C.B. information, and lists of sights in each state, but the most important feature of any road atlas is the maps. Those in the *Hammond Road Atlas* are divided by area, rather than by state, and are arranged roughly from northeast to southwest, including the southernmost areas of Canada. The maps show state and national parks, monuments and historical sites, and highlight scenic roads in each area. A cities index and a small geographic map are included along with the listings of major tourist sites in each area. Special maps are also provided for major U.S. cities.

Evaluation: The *Hammond Atlas* covers a smaller area and its maps are less detailed than the *Rand McNally Road Atlas* (see under North America, Road Atlases), but it is less clumsy to use, is less expensive, and includes many features, such as the sights listings, not found in other atlases. The maps themselves are very clear and uncluttered, but they use small print, and, again, lack the detail of other road atlases. Many smaller cities are not listed. Travelers looking for an inexpensive and easy-to-use atlas should use this one or the *Hammond Glove Compartment Road Atlases* (which uses the same maps reduced in size and does not list sights). Those looking for larger and more detailed maps should use Rand McNally's.

Rand McNally Road Atlas. See the review of this title under North America, Road Atlases.

SCIENCE

Field Guide Series. Dubuque, IA: Kendall/Hunt Publishing Co., 1977. approx. 150 pp. pap. $4.95–$6.95.

As an example of the many Field Guides in the series, *The Southern Colorado Plateau* is a science guide that relies more on observations in the field than on comprehensive geological information. It is meant primarily to be used by high school and college students as part of a class in introductory geology, but it is also useful to travelers interested in the geological characteristics of northeastern Arizona and northwestern New Mexico. The information is organized around a series of automobile tours along backroads and highways throughout the area. The introduction briefly discusses general characteristics of the region; a short geological history, with charts and illustrations, precedes the tours. Five major routes are described in the back, with side trips included for each tour. The different routes range from 50 to 350 miles in length, though all can easily be modified to suit particular needs. A mile-by-mile log is used to point out the natural characteristics along each route. Hiking trails and scenic vistas are also highlighted in the tours, and many photographs and illustrations are included in the entries. Other features include a complete glossary of terms and a long reference list.

Evaluation: Because the book emphasizes observation more than detailed geological information, it is easier for travelers to use than other science guides. That is not to say there are no geological references in the entries (there are many), but they are not as prominent as those in the Roadside Geology series, for example (see below). The routes described in the book are easy to follow from the maps provided and from the directions in the mileage logs, and the illustrations included help clarify the information in the text. Travelers with an interest in geology but with little or no science background will find the books very useful.

Included in the series: New England; Greater Metropolitan New York; Upstate New York; Chesapeake Bay; Appalachian Region; Southern Florida; Southern Great Lakes; Southern Ohio, Indiana and Northern Kentucky; Northern Great Lakes; St. Louis Area; Southern Rockies; North Texas and Southern Oklahoma; Southwest Texas; Northern Colorado Plateau; Southern Colorado Plateau; Western Washington and Oregon; Northern California; Southern California; Coastal Southern California.

Roadside Geology Series. Missoula, MT: Mountain Press Publishing Co., 1975-1979. approx. 275 pp. pap. $6.95 and $7.95.

This is a series of science guides with a much narrower scope than most, dealing exclusively with the geological history of the different states and areas. It is organized in a series of highway tours between two designated spots that are usually 50 to 125 miles apart. A map is included with each tour that shows both the route and the geological characteristics of the area. The accompanying text deals strictly with geology. The photographs, glossary, and detailed illustrations give the book a scholarly appearance, though it is readable and was intended to be read by those with little science background.

Evaluation: The books in the Roadside Geology series were written primarily for residents of the different areas who have more than a passing interest in the earth-shaping processes. They are written in an informal, nontechnical style, but 275 pages of pure geology is enough to lull even the most enraptured rockhound to sleep. Few people other than residents would be able to use the amount of information included in the series. The books would be much more useful in a high school natural science class than in a travel library.

Included in the series: Roadside Geology of Colorado, by Halka Chronic; *Roadside Geology of Northern California,* by David D. Alt and Donald W. Hyndman; *Roadside Geology of the Northern Rockies,* by David D. Alt and Donald W. Hyndman; *Roadside Geology of Oregon,* by David D. Alt and Donald W. Hyndman; *Roadside Geology of Texas,* by Robert Sheldon.

SHOPPING

Factory Outlet Shopping Guide Series. Jean Bird. Oradell, NJ: F. O. S. G. Publications, 1979. approx. 100 pp. pap. $2.95.

The stores listed in the Factory Outlet Shopping Guide series vary greatly in size, type and quality of merchandise, and location, but they all have one thing in common—discounts. The entries sometimes read like post-Christmas advertisements, with claims of 50 to 75 percent savings in nearly every entry. Over 500 outlets and discount stores are included in each book. The entries are arranged alphabetically and include addresses, hours, telephone numbers, credit cards accepted, parking, directions, and brief descriptions of the stores and their specialties. The stores are indexed by type of merchandise and by state. Special features in the book include general shopping tips, a glossary of outlet shopping terms, how to shop for particular items, complaints, and how to use the Small Claims Court (!). The books are most useful to residents of the different areas, though many traveling shoppers would jump at the opportunity to save money while on vacation.

Evaluation: The books in the series cover a larger area and include more factory outlets than the *Factory Store Guide to All New England* (see under New England, Shopping) though the descriptions of the stores are less detailed. The information is complete and clear, and the indexes make it easy to use. The introductory sections help introduce those unfamiliar with factory outlet shopping to the basic differences between outlets and retail stores. The comparatively low prices of the books makes them worthwhile for all shoppers with an eye on their pennies. These are some of the few books from which it is possible to make a profit.

Included in the series: Factory Outlet Shopping Guide: New England States; Factory Outlet Shopping Guide: New Jersey and Rockland County; Factory Outlet Shopping Guide: New York, Long Island, and Westchester; Factory Outlet Shopping Guide: North and South Carolina; Factory Outlet Shopping Guide: Pennsylvania; Factory Outlet Shopping Guide: Washington, D.C., Maryland, Virginia, Delaware.

SKIING

Cross-Country Skiing: A Guide to America's Best Trails. Lucy M. Fehr. New York: William Morrow & Co., 1979. 198 pp. pap. $6.95.

Like the other books in the Americans-Discover-America series, *Cross-Country Skiing* emphasizes broad but basic coverage. The introduction briefly discusses the growth in the ski touring industry, describes the trail rating system used in the entries, gives a brief description of equipment, and lists basic safety tips. The 37 states that are covered are arranged alphabetically, and the ski touring areas are listed by city. Each entry includes the name of the park or trail, directions by car, the total distance of marked trails, equipment rental, the number of routes for novice, intermediate, and expert skiers, hours and dates of operation, instructions, facilities, whether a fee is charged, and addresses for more information. Major ski areas, such as Aspen and Sun Valley, are described in more detail. References to camping and accommodation possibilities are included irregularly.

Evaluation: The information in the entries is complete, though some areas are described in more detail than the rest, and information listed in some entries is missing from others. The book is organized well and the information is easy to find. The book serves as a pretravel reference for skiers planning a trip to any part of the country, whether experienced or not. The large area covered and the number of entries cannot be matched by other ski-touring guides, which usually cover a particular area and include more equipment and safety information. This is not a how-to guide, but it provides a service to cross-country skiers not to be found elsewhere.

Skiing the Great Resorts of North America. Wendy Williams. Chicago, IL: Contemporary Books, 1978. 270 pp. pap. $5.95.

"Great" resorts, in this case, translates into most expensive. The book is a guide to the best ski runs in North America, but skiers can expect to pay top dollar for the privilege. Most of the resorts included are in the American Rockies, and nearly all are west of the Mississippi. The entries concentrate on the slopes of the areas and describe lodging, dining, and nightlife possibilities. Also included is practical information (addresses, phone numbers, and so on). The author includes safety tips, ski schools (though the emphasis is on experienced skiers), and some nearby attractions in the entries and a preparation checklist in the back.

Evaluation: The book is for skiers looking for the best—the most challenging runs, the plushest accommodations, and the hangouts of North America's skiing elite. The descriptions of the slopes and the areas around them are colorful and complete, including all the necessary information. But the accommodation and dining sections give a very small selection and limited information. The book includes fewer ski areas than *Skiing U.S.A.* (see below) and is harder to use, but it has better descriptions of the lodges and is written in a much more lively and entertaining style. It is a worthwhile book for those with few budget restrictions looking for the best skiing North America has to offer.

Skiing U.S.A.—A Guide to the Nation's Ski Areas. Lucy M. Fehr. New York: William Morrow & Co., 1977. 211 pp. pap. $4.95.

The major feature of this book is the number of entries and the wide area covered—more than 700 ski areas in 39 states. The entries include the address and telephone number of each area, its location, the number and types of lifts, rates (low, medium, or high), ski schools, and remarks that include dining, après-ski activities, rentals, special services, slope lengths, and the availability of nearby accommodations. For each state there is an address for further information. The book is intended for both novice skiers and experts and provides listings of ski areas for all budgets.

Evaluation: The author takes a no-nonsense approach to the subject. The information in the book is kept short and clear, with each entry less than a half page in length. The book's strength is the number and variety of ski areas listed. Its weakness is the lack of detail. The book is very easy to use, and the information on the slopes and ski facilities is complete. This is the most useful to skiers as a reference to the variety of slopes in the country and can be used many times over.

SUMMER EMPLOYMENT

Summer Employment Directory of the United States. Sally Davidow, Lynne Lapin, Leslie Burke Wilson, eds. Cincinnati, OH: Writer's Digest Books. 213 pp. pap. $6.95. Revised annually.

The temporary employment opportunities listed in this directory are mostly clerical, housekeeping, restaurant, or summer camp positions, although a few other less common jobs are included. The pay rates are generally low, and rarely is previous experience necessary. The jobs are listed by state, with the states arranged alphabetically. The information on the jobs comes directly from the employers and includes the name of the company, its location, description of the jobs, the number of positions available, special skills or experience required, school credit available, the pay rate, the deadline for applicaltions, and the address to which applications should be sent. Special sections include how to apply for a job, working for the federal government, a section listing businesses and organizations with summer job openings across the country, internships, and information for foreign visitors.

Evaluation: The book serves students, teachers, and others looking for temporary summer employment, but the types of jobs listed are not necessarily the kind that stir the imagination. Still, they do offer a temporary income and a chance to experience a totally different physical environment. The information in the entries is clear and complete, and the sections on finding and applying for a particular job will be useful to those with little employment experience. The large number of listings in the book suggests that summer jobs are available even during an economic downturn, though the variety of job openings suffers.

TOURIST ATTRACTIONS

Free Tourist Attractions. See *National Directory of Budget Motels, 1979-80* under United States, Accommodations and Restaurants.

Low-Cost Tourist Attractions. See *National Directory of Budget Motels, 1979-80* under United States, Accommodations and Restaurants.

Theme Parks and Amusement Areas. See *National Directory of Budget Motels, 1979-80* under United States, Accommodations and Restaurants.

Weird America—A Guide to Places of Mystery in the United States. Jim Brandon. New York: E. P. Dutton, 1978. 257 pp., pap. $4.95.

This guide is not for everyone. Here, the rules of sciences are, if not broken, slightly bent. See the spot where a full-grown alligator fell from the sky miles from any swamp or airplane path, or visit Bigfoot's lair in the shadow of a nuclear power plant. More mundane sights include ancient Amerindian burial grounds, Charles Manson's "hole-in-the-earth," the Lake Michigan Triangle, areas frequently visited by UFOs, and, of course, plenty of haunted houses. Entries are included describing strange areas and occurrences in every state, though many particular spots may be hard to find because of lack of clear directions. A number of photographs and illustrations are included, as well as a complete bibliography. Travelers with more than a passing interest in the unexplained will find many subjects to ponder in this book.

Evaluation: Although its use as a practical travel guide is severely limited by the narrow scope of information, *Weird America* offers many unique vacation goals and lists sights not to be found in other guides. The different stories surrounding the strange sights and occurrences leave the reader with a thousand unanswered questions. It is certain that such a book will fascinate some and bore others. Skeptics will scoff at the wild and extravagant descriptions and stories, but this is not the book for them. Travelers interested in visiting the areas described in the book should supplement the information it contains with more comprehensive travel information.

REGIONAL GUIDES

The East

CAMPING

Camper's Park Guide. Robert Shosteck. McLean, VA: EPM Publications, 1978. 663 pp. pap. $9.95.

The book lists 888 campsites in 19 states along the Atlantic Coast. It opens with a short introduction that explains how to use the guide, tips on planning a trip, when to visit, facilities, sports and activities, and children. The entries for the campsites employ symbols to denote such things as showers, electric hookups, drinking water, pets, recreational vehicles, supply stores, cabins, and restaurants. This helps keep the entries short and easy to read without sacrificing any pertinent information. The entries are organized geographically and briefly describe the park or site, tell what to do there (fishing, hiking, points of interest, and so on), mention nearby attractions, and give directions. As there is little information in the book on camping preparation, it would be of most use to experienced campers.

Evaluation: The book is organized extremely well. The listings are complete and very easy to use. Everything an experienced camper should need to know about the campsites is included. Because of the high cost of the book, it is suggested only for those who make regular camping trips along the East Coast. The book is an overall excellent camping guide.

Rand McNally Campground and Trailer Parks Guide—Eastern. Chicago, IL: Rand McNally & Co. 320 pp. pap. $5.95. Revised annually.

Complete campground information on all eastern states and Canada is included in this volume of the *Rand McNally Campground and Trailer Parks Guide*. Along with the campground listings, the book features an extensive recreational vehicle buyer's guide, a section on recreational vehicle camping clubs and caravans, a long section discussing tents, and a great number of advertisements. The states and provinces are organized alphabetically, with public and private campground entries listed on crowded charts that provide all the necessary practical information at a squint. Special features include mileage charts, road regulations and toll road information, fish and game laws, an abundance of specialized maps, and a list of where to rent recreational vehicles. The book is useful for all trailer and recreational vehicle campers traveling over a large area of the country.

Evaluation: The camping information in the *Rand McNally Campground and Trailer Parks Guides* is complete and broad in scope, but the complex systems of symbols and the small print make it difficult to use. However, once the system has been mastered, travelers will find the tables easier to use than the entries in *Woodall's Campground Directory* (see under North America, Camping). Apart from the maintenance sections in Woodall's and the quality maps and special features in Rand McNally, both books cover the same area and have the same emphasis (trailer and recreational vehicle campers), though Woodall's is in one volume and Rand McNally comes in an eastern and a western volume. The major difference between the two directories is in the way the camping information is presented. Which one a traveler uses is a matter of style and convenience.

RESTAURANTS

The Traveler's Directory of Fast-Food Restaurants—Eastern Edition. Kathleen M. Gruber. New York: Pilot Books, 1979. 72 pp. pap. $3.50.

For travelers with a less-developed palate there is now *The Traveler's Directory of Fast-Food Restaurants—Eastern Edition.* This handy guide lists the location of the restaurants from Maine to Maryland of 58 fast-food chains. The selection is not strictly limited to burgers. Donuts, hot dogs, ice cream, chicken, sausage, root beer, and chopped steaks round out the specialties of the restaurants included. The restaurants are listed by city and state, with only the name and address of each included. Neon will have to guide travelers to their doors through the dark of night. The book serves residents and frequent visitors to the East who seek a meal in a moment.

Evaluation: Restaurant guides most often include restaurants because of the quality of the food and service or the uniqueness of the establishments. Convenience is rarely a major criterion. However, many meals eaten away from home are of the fast-food variety, and a guide such as this may be useful to frequent travelers who are not looking for any surprises. The lack of information other than the names and addresses of the restaurants makes the book difficult to use, but as a rule, fast-food restaurants are rarely hidden, and many fast-food diners may feel the book is not necessary. Of course, for travelers to New York City who want to have lunch in a different McDonald's every day during their three-month stay, no other guide will do.

SCIENCE

Field Guide Series: Appalachian Region. See the review of this series under United States, Science.

SIGHTSEEING

Made in America: A Guide to Tours of Workshops, Farms, Mines, and Industries—Northeast Edition. Susan Farlow. New York: Hastings House Publishers, 1979. 304 pp. pap. $7.95.

What better way to relax on a vacation than to watch others work? *Made in America* describes tours of factories, farms, mines, and workshops of every kind from Maine to Pennsylvania. See a television station or a sawmill. Visit a fish hatchery or a vineyard. Or tour a nuclear power plant. Hundreds of tours are described in every part of the states included. Each entry includes location, company and tour descriptions, cost (usually free), length of tour schedule, restrictions, mementos, and on-site stores. Each state section includes a special listing of maple orchards and sugar houses. The book is most useful to residents of the Northeast, but it can be used as a pretravel reference for all travelers visiting the area.

Evaluation: The practical information on each of the tours is complete, though some descriptions are more detailed than others. The variety of tours described is rather amazing. The book is certain to provide something for every interest. The solid organization and detailed table of contents make the book easy to use, but more complete travel information for a particular area should be acquired from other sources. The book offers a variety of free vacation activities that can be both enjoyable and enlightening.

Middle Atlantic

ACCOMMODATIONS AND RESTAURANTS

Country Inns: Lodges and Historic Hotels of the Middle Atlantic States. See Country Inns series under United States, Accommodations and Restaurants.

Country Inns of America: New York and Mid-Atlantic. See Country Inns of America series under United States, Accommodations and Restaurants.

Mobil Travel Guide: Middle Atlantic States. See Mobil Travel Guide series under United States, Accommodations and Restaurants.

CAMPING

Woodall's Campground Directory: State Editions. See the review of this series under United States, Camping.

HISTORY

America's Freedom Trail. M. Victor Alper. New York: Collier Books, Macmillan Publishing Co., 1976. 562 pp. $12.95.

This book lists colonial and Revolutionary War sites in Massachusetts, New York, New Jersey, and Pennsylvania. The information for each state is divided into major historical areas. For each area described there is a brief Revolutionary War history, followed by the location of visitors' centers, the availability of public transportation, and a listing of the major historical sites. These listings include the address, hours, and admission charge of each site, along with detailed historical descriptions. The information in the entries is complemented by a number of photographs and maps. Nearby points of interest and some walking and driving tours are included irregularly. Special sections include a list of state facts, motel and hotel information (with address, phone, directions, number of rooms, rates, and credit cards accepted), and information for foreign visitors.

Evaluation: The amount of historical information included is enough to keep the most energetic historian occupied for many weeks. Most of the sites are old homes and historic buildings, although museums, monuments, and battle sites are also included. The practical travel information in the entries is sparse and uneven, with few references to transportation between the sites. The accommodation listings rely heavily on nationwide chains, and the information is at least four years old. For these reasons, and because of the book's high cost, it is suggested only when one wants a historical reference for trips on the East Coast. More comprehensive and up-to-date travel information for the different areas should be acquired before setting out.

SHOPPING

Factory Outlet Shopping Guide: Washington, D.C., Maryland, Virginia, Delaware. See the review of this series under United States, Shopping.

SIGHTSEEING

Historic Homes and Sights of Revolutionary America: The Middle Atlantic. See the review of this series under Regional Guides, New England, Sightseeing.

The Midwest and The Great Lakes Region

COMPREHENSIVE GUIDES

The Great Lakes Guidebook Series. George Cantor. Ann Arbor, MI: The University of Michigan Press, 1980. 200 pp. pap. $5.95.

The books in this series combine histories, descriptions, and sights in the entries, covering all the areas surrounding the Great Lakes. The introductions describe the distinct personalities of the lakes and give a brief history of each. The entries are divided into many geographic regions, with history, background, descriptions of many different sights and side trips, some informal driving tours, and camping areas and parks listed in each area. Many photographs and maps are included in the entries, along with irregular information on trains, ferry services, and scenic roads. Special sections are included on major cities that are more descriptive than practical. Each book in the series also includes a complete bibliography and index.

Evaluation: The background information provided in the books gives a feel for the different areas not to be found in other guides. The entries inform and entertain, with smooth, colorful descriptions blended with practical information on the sights and activities listed. This blending sometimes makes it difficult to find the information, but the solid organization of the books and the detailed indexes are very helpful. The books cover the less-populated areas much better than the major cities and are most useful to those planning a rural vacation in the area. The inclusion of camping information makes the books the only guides necessary for some travelers, though others will need more complete transportation and accommodations information.

Included in the series: Lake Huron and Eastern Lake Michigan; Lakes Ontario and Erie; Lake Superior and Western Lake Michigan.

ACCOMMODATIONS AND RESTAURANTS

Country Inns: Lodges and Historic Hotels of the Midwest and Rocky Mountain States. See Country Inns series under United States, Accommodations and Restaurants.

Mobil Travel Guide: Great Lakes Area. See Mobil Travel Guide series under United States, Accommodations and Restaurants.

CAMPING

Traveling and Camping in the National Park Areas (Mid-America). See the review of this book under United States, National Parks.

Woodall's Campground Directory: State Editions. See the review of this series under United States, Camping.

CANOEING AND RAFTING

Whitewater; Quietwater. Bob Palzer and Jody Palzer. Two Rivers, WI: Evergreen Paddleways, 3rd ed. 1977. 160 pp. pap. $7.95.

This is a how-to book for anyone interested in canoeing, kayaking, or rafting. Over 40 rivers of Wisconsin, upper Michigan, and northeast Minnesota are listed, usually with a few day-long trips for each. Most entries include large, clear maps, but the authors suggest that forest service maps be obtained before setting out. The book has everything a beginner should know and tips for experts. The beginning of the book deals extensively with equipment, technique, hazards, and safety tips. Other areas covered include boating organizations, how to transport a boat, competition, boat building, ratings of the rivers, hydrology, seasonal changes, and knowing your limits. The book also emphasizes the preservation of the wild state of the rivers with a complete section on wild river legislation and the responsibility of users.

Evaluation: The authors try hard to simplify the subject as much as possible. They even include a glossary of technical terms. The book has more practical information and is more complete for the beginner than *Canoeing and Rafting* (See under United States, Canoeing), but the amount of technical information makes it difficult to sort out at times. The book is useful as an introduction to canoeing and as a general river guide to the upper Midwest.

LITERARY TOURS

A Literary Tour Guide to the United States: West and Midwest. See the review of this series under United States, Literary Tours.

MOUNTAIN CLIMBING

Fifty Short Climbs in the Midwest. Alan Bagg. Chicago, IL: Contemporary Books, 1978. 234 pp. pap. $6.95.

Mountain climbing in the Midwest? That's like surfing in Pennsylvania, right? Not quite. It is true that the area is not known for its spectacular peaks, but *Fifty Short Climbs* shows that there are plenty of climbing opportunities to be found in six states of the upper Midwest (minus Indiana). Nearly all the climbs are in Illinois, Iowa, and Wisconsin. The book includes all the necessary information for beginners: a description of the "modified" Sierra Club classification, a glossary of terms, a thorough equipment section, a list of equipment suppliers, and information on ordering topographic sheets. Fifty hikes are divided by state. For each there is a description of the area and the climbing site, a list of campgrounds and other sights, and a map. Special sections include a list and description of climbing clubs and schools throughout the country, a detailed reading list, and a discussion of bouldering and "buildering."

Evaluation: The book opens an entirely new area of weekend trips for outdoor enthusiasts in the Midwest. The information is organized well and is complete for both novice and expert. With the proper preparation and equipment, mountain climbing is a much safer sport than it would seem and one whose popularity is greatly increasing. Nonresidents interested in climbing in the area as part of a more traditional vacation should use the book along with a more complete sights/accommodation guide.

SCIENCE

Field Guide Series. See the review of this series under United States, Science.

SIGHTSEEING

American Jewish Landmarks: Middle West and West. See American Jewish Landmarks series under United States, Museums and Historic Sights.

New England

ACCOMMODATIONS AND RESTAURANTS

Country New England Inns: The Compleat Traveler's Companion. See Country Inns series under United States, Accommodations and Restaurants.

Country Inns of America: Lower New England. Country Inns of America: Upper New England. See Country Inns of America series under United States, Accommodations and Restaurants.

Guide to the Recommended Country Inns of New England. Suzy Chapin and Elizabeth Squier. Chester, CT: The Globe Pequot Press, 5th ed. 1979. 295 pp. pap. $4.95.

Over 120 inns are listed covering a fairly wide price range. Most of the entries include a photograph or drawing of the inn, rates, address, directions, food plans, short descriptions of the inns, special features, and a closing tip from each of the authors. It should be noted that an inn, by the authors' definition, must provide food and lodging year-round. This would exclude many inns in the area. The list is by no means exhaustive.

Evaluation: The information is both concise and complete, each entry being less than two pages long. The book offers a wider selection than *Country Inns and Back Roads* (see under North America, Accommodations and Restaurants), but the latter gives a better feel for the inns and the people who run them. The number of vacationers foregoing the hotel/motel grind in favor of inns is increasing, and the need for a book such as this increases with it. This one is a solid introduction to the variety of inns in the area.

Mobil Travel Guide: Northeastern States. See Mobil Travel Guide series under United States, Accommodations and Restaurants.

The New England Guest House Book. Corinne Madden Ross. Charlotte, NC: The East Woods Press, East & McMillan Publishers, 1979. 192 pp. pap. $6.95.

When is an inn not an inn? When it's a guesthouse! In the continuing semantic debate about just what constitutes an inn, a new term arises to confuse the issue completely. A guesthouse, by the author's definition, is usually smaller than an inn and basically provides only lodging, though many of the establishments included in this guide offer some meals for an extra charge. The guesthouses are arranged by state, with a short introduction to each state and a map that shows the location of the guesthouses described. The areas in which the guesthouses are found are also briefly described, with some historical references and a few nearby points of interest mentioned. The entries for the guesthouses include complete descriptions of the homes and their furnishings and listings of the addresses, directions, rates, facilities, and dates of operation. The houses are also indexed by city and state. The book serves travelers looking for inexpensive, rural accommodations in New England.

Evaluation: The descriptions of the guesthouses and the areas around them are colorful and inviting. The author points out the unique features and services of each house in a style that is both informative and entertaining. The practical information on the guesthouses is complete and easy to find. This book compares favorably with guides to New England country inns, though it can be argued that they cover different areas. The only discernible difference is the lack of meals provided, but even this is not uniform. Whether this guide or a guide to New England country inns is used by a particular traveler is mostly a matter of style.

ARCHITECTURE

A Primer on New England's Colonial Architecture. Isabella Hagelstein. Boston, MA: Herman Publishing, 1977. 32 pp. pap. $1.95.

A Primer on New England's Colonial Architecture describes very clearly through text and illustrations the architectural trends of seventeenth- and early eighteenth-century New England. It shows interior and exterior design patterns of early one-room structures, the Cape Cod house, and Georgian colonials. European influences and colonial innovation are briefly described, as are changes wrought by weather and the availability of material. The book also includes a bibliography and a glossary of terms. The audience for this book can be defined as those with little knowledge of but more than a passing interest in colonial architecture.

Evaluation: The book was not intended as a travel guide, but it has use for travelers interested in New England colonial life. The information is complete, but very narrow in scope, dealing only with the design of early New England structures. Because it is a short and relatively inexpensive book, it is useful as a complement to a more comprehensive guide to New England for architecture and history enthusiasts.

CAMPING

Woodall's Campground Directory: State Editions. See the review of this series under United States, Camping.

LITERARY TOURS

A Literary Tour Guide to the United States: Northeast. See the review of this series under United States, Literary Tours.

OUTDOOR RECREATION

Country New England Recreation and Sports. Anthony Hitchcock and Jean Lindgren. New York: Burt Franklin & Co., 1978. 186 pp. pap. $3.95.

Country New England Recreation and Sports is an overview of the many outdoor recreation possibilities in the area. Sports activities for all four seasons are included, with references to downhill and cross-country skiing, beaches and state parks, riding stables, hiking trails, picnic areas, boating, canoeing, fishing and hunting, golf courses, racquet clubs, tennis resorts, and bicycling. The entries are arranged by city and state, with the six states divided into different regions and the cities organized alphabetically. Each entry includes its address or location, a short description of the area and/or services provided, and rates. Telephone numbers, rental services, camping information, and addresses for further information are included irregularly. The book is most useful to New England residents and as pretravel reading for travelers planning a variety of outdoor activities while on vacation in the area.

Evaluation: The book is no substitute for a complete camping, hiking, or outdoor guide to New England. The entries provide suggestions for many types of outdoor recreation, but more information is necessary for most of them before concrete plans can be made. Like other books in the Country New England series, the alphabetical organization of the towns and the lack of a subject index suggest that the book's best use is as a pretravel reference to the outdoor recreation possibilities of the area for travelers who will be combining some outdoor activities with a more traditional vacation. Those concentrating on one particular activity (campers, hikers, canoeists) should use a more complete guide to that sport for the area.

Included in the series: Country New England Antiques, Crafts, and Factory Outlets; Country New England Historical and Sight-Seeing Guide; Country New England Inns: The Compleat Traveler's Companion.

Twenty-Five Ski Tours Series. Somersworth, NH: New Hampshire Publishing Co., 1978. 128 pp. pap. $4.95.

The books in the Twenty-Five Ski Tours series list cross-country ski trails in western New England. Each tour includes the distance, difficulty, and a sketch of the trail. The entries describe the trails and give directions to the starting points, tips on outdoor etiquette, possible hazards, and advice for novices. The authors suggest strongly that all skiers use contour maps on the trails. They tell how to order U.S. Geological Survey (U.S.G.S.) topographic sheets, and on which U.S.G.S. map each of the trails can be located. The books should be read before leaving on a trip and consulted en route. They were written primarily for intermediate skiers and include no preparatory material (clothing, equipment, emergency information, and so on).

Evaluation: The information in the entries is kept simple and clear. The directions are easy to follow, and descriptions are meant only to help skiers stay on or near the trails. The lack of preparatory and emergency information limits the book's usefulness to skiers with some previous experience.

Included in the series: Twenty-Five Ski Tours in Connecticut, by Stan Wass with David Alvord; *Twenty-Five Ski Tours in the Green Mountains,* by Sally Ford and Daniel Ford; *Twenty-Five Ski Tours in the White Mountains,* by Sally Ford and Daniel Ford; *Twenty-Five Ski Tours in Western Massachusetts,* by John Frado, Richard Lawson, and Robert Coy.

SCIENCE

Field Guide Series: New England. See the review of this series under United States, Science.

A Guide to New England's Landscape. Neil Jorgensen. Chester, CT: The Pequot Press, 1977. 256 pp. pap. $4.95.

The book is both a textbook and a travel guide. It describes the area geologically, geographically, and botanically and includes sections on the effect of the glaciers, the peculiarities of the different mountain ranges, the lakes, the geography of the forests, and identification of New England's flora. It is a thinking person's guide in that the reader is expected to take an active role in discovering particular traits described in the book. Take your boots!

Evaluation: The book is unique in its approach. It is a good mix of the science, history, and interesting natural phenomena of the New England area. The technical material included is organized in a way that is both informative and fairly easy to understand. The author avoids becoming bogged down in data. The book promotes an ecological awareness of the area that can be appreciated by visitors and residents alike.

The Northeastern Outdoors: A Field and Travel Guide. Steve Berman. Boston, MA: Stone Wall Press, 1977. 287 pp. pap. $7.95.

This is a book for anyone on the way back to nature. Written by an escapee from the city, it was originally entitled *A Cheap and Lazy*

Person's Guide to Nature. The emphasis is on the outdoors in the Northeast for the layman. The book is divided into two sections. The first is a series of essays whose topics include birds, insects, flowers, trees, animals, vegetables, minerals, weather, beaches (not necessarily for swimming or girl watching), stars, and pests. The second section is a listing of hikes in the area. They are divided by state, with a special entry for the Appalachian Trail. The entry for each hike is rarely longer than two paragraphs and includes a short description of the area, a little history, and directions to the starting points. All the hikes included are day trips. The book is intended for hikers, naturalists, campers, backpackers, or any combination of the above.

Evaluation: The Northeastern Outdoors takes a broader approach than either *A Guide to New England's Landscape* (see above) or the *Sierra Club Naturalist's Guide* (see below). The scientific material is primarily written for people with little science background. The information does not include entries for hunting or fishing, but rather emphasizes discovery. The author writes in an easy, conversational style, which points to the book's best use as pretravel reading (with the exception of the hikes). The book should be paired with either a camping or an accommodation guide.

Sierra Club Naturalist's Guide: Southern New England. Neil Jorgensen. San Francisco, CA: Sierra Club Books, 1978. 417 pp. pap. $9.95.

The Sierra Club Naturalist's guides all have the same underlying purpose: to introduce the reader to the environment and to nurture a degree of understanding and respect for it. The books in the series differ in format and in emphasis, depending on the nature of the area they describe. The *Naturalist's Guide: Southern New England* deals more with the plant and animal life of the area than with geology. The author begins by explaining how to look and by listing precautions in field explorations. The book then describes in detail the geography, history, and ecology of the many types of forests in the region. Following are descriptions and explanations of the sand plain and wetlands communities and finally a long section on the animal life in the area. Lists for further reading and useful addresses are included, as well as a complete index.

Evaluation: The quality and detail of the science information makes this book an excellent home reference as well as a field guide. The information is presented in a way that can be enjoyed and appreciated by both novice and experienced naturalists, but the great amount of information and the relatively high price of the book make it useful only for those who can plan to use it many times over. Experienced campers and hikers can enjoy many weeks of outdoor adventure with this guide alone, although beginners or those looking for more traditional vacation activities should supplement this book with a more complete camping guide.

SHOPPING

Country New England Antiques, Crafts, and Factory Outlets. Anthony Hitchcock and Jean Lindgren. New York: Burt Franklin & Co., 1978. 156 pp. pap. $3.95.

Antique shops make up the majority of the entries in the book. As the authors state, the days of wresting valuable antiques from the attics of unwary farmers are over, and today it is the buyer who must beware. The entries are divided by city and state and include annual craft festivals, craft shops, factory outlets, and specialty stores throughout New England. Each entry includes the address or location of the store, its telephone number, hours, and a brief description of its specialties. Photographs of some items are included, and each city mentioned is shown on a map of the state. There is an index of cities, as well as addresses for further travel and antique information. The book is suggested for New England residents and travelers on an extended visit with more than a passing interest in antiques.

Evaluation: More antique and craft shops are listed in the book than in other New England shopping guide, but there are few budgetary considerations and less information included on each. Because of the lack of an index of stores and the organization of the stores by city, the book is difficult to use even for those familiar with the area. The book is most useful as a pretravel reference for travelers interested in a shopping excursion or two while on vacation. Traveling shoppers hunting for bargains should use one of the factory store outlet guides to the area (see below).

Factory Outlet Shopping Guide: New England States. See Factory Outlet Shopping Guide series under United States, Shopping.

Factory Store Guide to All New England. A. Miser and A. Pennypincher. Chester, CT: The Pequot Press, 1977. 204 pp. pap. $3.50.

The book is a compilation of over 250 places in which to shop cheaply for almost every imaginable item sold in New England. The objects found in various factory stores and outlets include candles, pottery, stoves, watches, curtains, fabrics, toys, jewelry, clocks, and luggage. The authors begin by describing the benefits of a factory store and a little of what to expect there. The entries are arranged by state and include addresses, phones, hours, credit cards accepted, and, briefly, the peculiarities of the stores. Each is indexed in the back of the book by its specialty.

Evaluation: The book is well organized and the information is presented briefly and clearly with an emphasis on saving money. A visitor to the area using the book would probably need a more comprehensive guide, particularly one with maps. It is most useful to residents of the area who can shop and take their purchases home. A traveler would be forced to lug purchases around for the rest of the trip. But if this does not present a problem, the book presents a unique opportunity to save money while on vacation.

Only in New England. J. Chandler Hill, ed. Chester, CT: The Pequot Press, 1977. 158 pp. pap. $4.95.

Folk arts and crafts, antiques, sports equipment, handmade clothing, maple syrup, marine outfitters, old-style housewares, book binderies, gardening equipment—nearly every product or service that can be associated with New England and a few that generally are not are included in this catalog to shopkeepers and small manufacturing businesses in the Northeast. The entries are not arranged in any particular order, but are indexed geographically in the back of the book. Each entry includes a description of the product and/or the store, with an address and usually an accompanying photograph or illustration. Some entries take up more than a page, while others may be less than a paragraph long. The book is enjoyable armchair reading for anyone interested in the folk arts and crafts of New England.

Evaluation: While the practical travel value of the book may be negligible, it still can be useful as pretravel reading for first-time travelers to the area, to provide a feel for New England folk traditions and the people who keep them alive and growing. Still, the book's major purpose is as a mail-order catalog, and the practical information included is meant only for that purpose. Whether the shops and outlets can be visited is not clear from the entries, but it is unlikely that more than a few would rely completely on mail-order sales. Although it was not intended to be used as a travel guide, the book includes information on New England folk arts and crafts not to be found in the more traditional guides to New England.

SIGHTSEEING

American Jewish Landmarks: Northeast. See American Jewish Landmarks series under United States, Museums and Historic Sights.

Country New England Historical and Sight-Seeing Guide. Anthony Hitchcock and Jean Lindgren. New York: Burt Franklin & Co., 1978. 228 pp. pap. $3.95.

The scope of the *Country New England Historical and Sight-Seeing Guide* goes beyond that of many other guides to historical points of interest, to include such events as bathtub races on Cape Cod, baroque music festivals in New Hampshire, fish hatcheries in Rhode Island, and barn dances in Maine, in addition to the expected number and variety of old homes and museums. The sights are organized by city and state, with cities listed alphabetically. There is a short introduction to each state, which includes brief background information and addresses for more information. Each entry includes the address or location of the sight, a short description (one or two lines), hours, and admission charges. Telephone numbers are included in some of the entries, but are missing from others. The book serves all budgets and travel styles and should be read while planning a trip.

Evaluation: Like the other books in the Country New England series, the *Historical and Sight-Seeing Guide* emphasizes the quantity of entries and sacrifices detail. The practical information on the sights is irregular, with many references to where more information may be acquired. The descriptions are too short to give a very clear impression of the sights. Also, the alphabetical organization of the towns and cities and the lack of a subject index make the book difficult to use. For these reasons it is recommended as a pretravel reference to the variety of sights in the area. On the road a more complete transportation/accommodation guide should be used.

Historic Homes and Sights of Revolutionary America: New England. Adelaide Hechtlinger. Gretna, LA: Pelican Publishing Co., 1976. 128 pp. pap. $3.95.

This book lists sights of historical significance in the American Revolution. The entries are organized by state. Each state section begins with a short history (less than a page) covering the time from the first European settlements to the ratification of the Constitution. Each sight is listed under the town in which it is found, with the towns arranged alphabetically. The entries are rarely longer than two paragraphs and some are as short as a single line. There are some parks and outdoor sites included, but the vast majority of the entries are homes, inns, churches, taverns, or meeting houses, almost all of which are open to the public. The listings emphasize the historical significance of the buildings with little mention of their architectural significance. Each includes its address, hours, and whether an admission is charged.

Evaluation: Most of the entries in the book read like the back of a postcard; there is just not much to them. The books would be more useful if they had fewer entries and more detail. For the most part, the author neglects to point out why a particular building would be worth visiting. It is hard to discern any difference in the buildings from the entries.

Other volumes planned for the series: The Middle Atlantic; The South.

New England Cemeteries. Andrew Kull. Brattleboro, VT: The Stephen Greene Press, 1975. 253 pp. pap. $5.95.

The book lists 262 cemeteries in the six New England states. The entry for each graveyard includes its location, a description, historical references, interesting monuments and epitaphs both comical and reverent. The author uses symbols in the entries to denote interesting carvings, famous people, unusually picturesque cemeteries, and grand styles. The book is geared to travel by car. It is probably most useful to residents of the areas as the basis for some uncommon weekend trips.

Evaluation: The short entries, the clear style, and the unambiguous use of symbols make the book easy to use. Each cemetery is easy to locate from the directions and maps in the book. Because of the narrow scope of the book, it would be best to use it as a complement to an accommodation/sights guide. The entries mix history, humor, and tragedy in storyteller fashion.

New England Gardens Open to the Public. Rolce Redard Payne. Boston, MA: David R. Godine, Publisher, 1979. 230 pp. $17.50.

The gardens described in the book include arboreta, farms, nature centers and wildlife sanctuaries, museum and university grounds, and many historic homes and buildings. Gardens in all six New England states are listed, with the address, telephone, hours, operating dates, admission charges, and wheelchair accessibility included for each. The descriptions of the gardens include many colorful references to the different personalities of the gardens, seasonal changes, and the stories of their development. Symbols are used to show the best seasons for viewing the gardens, and a glossary of special terms and plant names is included, along with a long bibliography and complete index.

Evaluation: The variety of gardens in the book, the colorful descriptions, and the completeness of the practical information on the gardens make this book the definitive guide to the gardens of New England. The book is very well organized and the information is presented clearly. It serves as an introduction to the New England area in general as well as to its gardens. The glossary of terms is particularly useful to travelers with little background in botany. The book is an excellent guide for New England residents and visitors to the area with even a passing interest in New England gardens.

Pacific Coast

ACCOMMODATIONS AND RESTAURANTS

Best Restaurants: Pacific Northwest. See Best Restaurants series under United States, Accommodations and Restaurants.

Mobil Travel Guide: Northwest and Great Plains States. See Mobil Travel Guide series under United States, Accommodations and Restaurants.

CAMPING

Woodall's Campground Directory: State Editions. See the review of this series under United States, Camping.

DRIVING TOURS

Backroad Journeys of the West Coast States. David Yeadon. New York: Harper & Row, Publishers, 1979. 232 pp. pap. $6.95.

Intended primarily for residents of the West, *Backroad Journeys of the West Coast States* describes 15 trips of varying length, though most are overnight trips. The importance of the routes is not the destination, but the trip itself: through small, rural towns, around the shoulder of a volcano, and in the shade of a redwood glen on a bluff overlooking the Pacific. A map is provided for each tour that shows the route, towns in which provisions and accommodations can be found, mountains and lakes, wilderness areas, and general points of interest. The entries for the tours combine histories, descriptions, directions, and anecdotes from the author's journeys through the areas. Beautiful illustrations of many scenes along the route are included, as well as a list of backroad travel tips and a complete index.

Evaluation: The book has much longer entries, includes more information, covers a larger area, and describes longer trips than *Roaming the Back Roads* (see under California, Driving Tours), but the unique charms of the areas are less evident from the entries in this guide. The descriptions of the routes include all the necessary information, but the directions are blended into the text, so that finding them can be very difficult. The maps of the routes are clear and uncomplicated, and the ink sketches included add greatly to the book's eye appeal. Travelers planning backroad trips through the West looking for detailed background and descriptions should use this guide. Those looking for a wider variety of shorter trips in California will find *Roaming the Back Roads* more useful.

HOT SPRINGS AND POOLS

Hot Springs and Pools of the Northwest. See the review of this title under Regional Guides, The West, Hot Springs and Pools.

PRETRAVEL READING

Sunset Pictorial Series: Beautiful Northwest. See Sunset Pictorial series under United States, Pretravel Reading.

WINE TOURS

Winery Tours in Oregon, Washington, Idaho, and British Columbia. Tom Stockley. Mercer Island, WA: The Writing Works, 1978. 124 pp. pap. $3.95.

There are 32 tours in the book, the majority of them in Oregon. The book opens with a short history and description of the wineries in the area, followed by the tours themselves, grouped by state. Before each state listing is a short description of the state's wineries in general. Each tour includes a map, a copy of the vineyard label, address, telephone number, and a page-long description. The text of the entries introduces the owners, gives a short history, explains the types of wines in each vineyard, and briefly tells how they are produced. The book offers inexpensive travel ideas to those looking for an out-of-the-way vacation.

Evaluation: The wine industry in the Northwest is very young, and most of the wineries are less than 20 years old. The author compares the area to the more popular wine country in California at the turn of the century. It is a relatively undiscovered and unspoiled area—far away from tourist congestion. The book is well organized, with the information kept simple and clear. Some may want to use the book along with a more complete guide (with accommodations, restaurants, and so on), while others will find it is all they need for a relaxing vacation in a relatively peaceful area.

Rocky Mountains

ACCOMMODATIONS AND RESTAURANTS

Country Inns: Lodges and Historic Hotels of the Midwest and Rocky Mountain States. See Country Inns series under United States, Accommodations and Restaurants.

CAMPING

Woodall's Campground Directory: State Editions. See the review of this series under United States, Camping.

SCIENCE

Field Book Series. See the review of this series, which includes *The Big Horn Range, The Teton Range and the Gros Ventre Range, The Wind River Range*, and *Yellowstone Park and the Absaroka Range*, under Wyoming.

Field Guide Series: Southern Rockies. See the review of this series under United States, Science.

Roadside Geology of the Northern Rockies. See Roadside Geology series under United States, Science.

The South

COMPREHENSIVE GUIDES

A Kosoy Travel Guide to Florida and the South. See the review of this title under Florida, Comprehensive Guides.

ACCOMMODATIONS AND RESTAURANTS

Country Inns: Lodges and Historic Hotels of the South. See Country Inns series under United States, Accommodations and Restaurants.

Country Inns of the Old South. Robert W. Tolf. San Francisco, CA: 101 Productions, 1978. 180 pp. pap. $4.95.

What sets this book apart from many other guides to country inns is the variety in both types of inns and price ranges. The entries are much more detailed than those in other inn guides and include all the necessary practical information, as well as clear directions to each of the inns. Most include a drawing of the inn and mention nearby attractions. The inns included provide either food or lodging or both and can be found in the cities and the country. Sixty-two inns are described in Virginia, West Virginia, North Carolina, South Carolina, Florida, Georgia, Tennessee, Kentucky, Alabama, Mississippi, Louisiana, and Arkansas.

Evaluation: This book gives a better feel for the inns and the areas around them than many other inn guides and includes a wider variety than most. The descriptions of the furnishing of the inns and their physical settings sparkle. The text smoothly blends histories with descriptions of the inns and their past and present residents. The practical information is complete and accessible. As in other inn guides, the historical references in the entries serve as excellent introductions to the areas for first-time travelers.

Mobil Travel Guide: Southeastern States. See Mobil Travel Guide series under United States, Accommodations and Restaurants.

CAMPING

Woodall's Campground Directory: State Editions. See the review of this series under United States, Camping.

HISTORY

America's Heritage Trail. M. Victor Alper. New York: Collier Books, Macmillan Publishing Co., 1976. 323 pp. $12.95.

America's Heritage Trail lists colonial and Revolutionary War sites in the Carolinas and Virginia. The information for each state is divided into major historical areas. For each there is a brief Revolutionary War history, followed by the location of visitors' centers, the availability of public transportation, and a listing of the major historical sites. These listings include the address, hours, and admission charge of each site, along with detailed historical descriptions. The information in the entries is complemented by a number of photographs and maps. Nearby points of interest and some walking and driving tours are included irregularly. Special sections include a list of state facts, motel and hotel information (with address, phone, directions, number of rooms, rates, and credit cards accepted), and information for foreign visitors.

Evaluation: The amount of historical information included is enough to keep the most energetic historians occupied for many weeks. Most of the sites are old homes and historic buildings, though museums, monuments, and battle sites are also included. The practical travel information in the entries is sparse and uneven, with few references made to transportation between the sites. The accommodation listings rely heavily on nationwide chains, and the information included is at least four years old. For these reasons, and because of the book's high cost, it is suggested only as a historical reference for trips on the east coast. More comprehensive and up-to-date travel information for the different areas should be acquired before setting out.

LITERARY TOURS

A Literary Tour Guide to the United States: South and Southwest. See the review of this series under United States, Literary Tours.

SCIENCE

Field Guide Series: Chesapeake Bay. See the review of this series under United States, Science.

SIGHTSEEING

American Jewish Landmarks: South and Southwest. See American Jewish Landmarks series under United States, Museums and Historic Sights.

Historic Homes and Sights of Revolutionary America: The South. See the review of this series under Regional Guides, New England, Sightseeing.

The Southwest

ACCOMMODATIONS AND RESTAURANTS

Mobil Travel Guide: Southwest and South Central Area. See Mobil Travel Guide series under United States, Accommodations and Restaurants.

CAMPING

Woodall's Campground Directory: State Editions. See the review of this series under United States, Camping.

HOT SPRINGS AND POOLS

Hot Springs and Pools of the Southwest. See *Hot Springs and Pools of the Northwest* under Regional Guides, The West, Hot Springs and Pools.

LITERARY TOURS

A Literary Tour Guide to the United States: South and Southwest. See the review of this series under United States, Literary Tours.

NATIONAL PARKS

Your National Park System in the Southwest. Earl Jackson. Globe, AZ: Southwest Parks and Monuments Assn., 1978. 66 pp. pap. $3.00.

What sets this guide apart from other guides to outdoor sights in the Southwest is the accuracy striven for in the short park entries and the directions to each. The author worked closely with the National Park Service in compiling the information, and the many revisions from the first (1976) edition keep it as up-to-date as possible. The book covers all of Utah, Arizona, Colorado, New Mexico, and Texas, with one park each in Nevada, Kansas, and Oklahoma. The parks are arranged alphabetically, with each entry on one large page accompanied by a color photograph of the area. The entries are mostly histories and descriptions of the parks, which irregularly include campgrounds, provisions, park services, and wildlife. Each ends with an address for further information. The large size of the book, the beautiful photography, and the short entries all suggest that the book's best use is as pretravel reading.

Evaluation: The information in the book is up-to-date but unevenly distributed. Some entries include camping, and some do not. Some list the location of park offices; others do not. The book serves as a description of the many outdoor sights in the area and the travel possibilities they present. The short entries and the large photographs almost make it a picture book with long captions. The book is recommended to travelers planning their first trip to the Southwest. On the road a more practical camping/accommodations/transportation guide should be used.

SCIENCE AND THE OUTDOORS

Canyon Country Series. See the review of this series, which includes *Camping, Canyon Country Exploring, Geology for the Layman and Rockhound, Hiking and Natural History, Off-Road Vehicle Trails*, and *Paddles*, under United States, State Guides, Utah.

Sierra Club Naturalist's Guide: The Deserts of the Southwest. Peggy Larson. San Francisco, CA: Sierra Club Books, 1977. 286 pp. pap. $5.95.

The major difference between *The Deserts of the Southwest* and the other Sierra Club guides is the inclusion of complete camping, emergency, and preparatory information along with the detailed science information. This addition makes it a much more well-rounded guide, one that can be used alone when planning a trip to the area. The book begins by describing the general physical characteristics of the four major deserts and their plant and wildlife. Each of the deserts is then described in more detail, with the usual high-quality maps, charts, and illustrations. Like the other guides in the series, there is an extensive reading list and complete index. The guide to the deserts is shorter and less expansive than the other Sierra Club guides, but it has the same quality and completeness of information, and, when judged strictly as a travel guide, is more practical.

Evaluation: The quality and detail of the science information makes this book excellent as a home reference as well as a field guide. The information is presented in a manner that can be enjoyed and appreciated by both novice and experienced naturalists. Campers and hikers can enjoy many weeks of outdoor adventure with this guide alone.

SIGHTSEEING

American Jewish Landmarks: South and Southwest. See the review of this series under United States, Museums and Historic Sights.

The West

ACCOMMODATIONS AND RESTAURANTS

Country Inns: Lodges and Historic Hotels of the West and Southwest. See Country Inns series under United States, Accommodations and Restaurants.

Country Inns of the Far West. Jacqueline Killeen, Charles C. Miller, and Rachel Bard. San Francisco, CA: 101 Productions, 1979. 228 pp. pap. $4.95.

What sets this book apart from many other guides to country inns is the variety in both types of inns and price ranges. The entries are much more detailed than those in other inn guides and include all the necessary practical information, as well as clear directions to each of the inns. Most include a drawing of the inn and mention nearby attractions. The inns included provide either food or lodging or both and can be found in the cities and the country. Seventy-five inns are described in California, Oregon, Washington, and British Columbia.

Evaluation: This book gives a better feel for the inns and the area around them than many other inn guides and includes a wider variety than most. The descriptions of the furnishing of the inns and their physical settings sparkle. The text smoothly blends histories with descriptions of the inns and their past and present residents. The practical information is complete and accessible. As in other inn guides, the historical references in the entries serve as excellent introductions to the areas for first-time travelers.

Mobil Travel Guide: California and the West. See Mobil Travel Guide series under United States, Accommodations and Restaurants.

Mobil Travel Guide: Northwest and Great Plains States. See Mobil Travel Guide series under United States, Accommodations and Restaurants.

CAMPING

Rand McNally Campground and Trailer Parks Guide—Western. Chicago, IL: Rand McNally & Co. 224 pp. pap. $4.95. Revised annually.

Complete campground information on all western states and Canada is included in this volume of the *Rand McNally Campground and Trailer Parks Guides*. Along with the campground listings, the book features an extensive recreational vehicle buyer's guide, a section on recreational vehicle camping clubs and caravans, a long section discussing tents, and a great number of advertisements. The states and provinces are organized alphabetically, with public and private campground entries listed on crowded charts that provide all the necessary practical information at a squint. Special features include mileage charts, road regulations and toll road information, fish and game laws, an abundance of specialized maps, and a list of where to rent a recreational vehicle. The book is useful for all trailer and recreational vehicle campers traveling over a large area of the country.

Evaluation: The camping information in the *Rand McNally Campground Guides* is complete and broad in scope, but the complex system of symbols and the small print make it difficult to use. However, once the system has been mastered and a magnifying glass acquired, travelers will find the tables easier to use than the entries in *Woodall's Campground Directory* (see under North America, Camping). Apart from the maintenance sections in Woodall's and the quality maps and special features in Rand McNally, both books cover the same area and have the same emphasis (trailer and recreational vehicle campers), though Woodalll's is in one volume and Rand McNally comes in an eastern and a western volume. The major difference between the two directories is in the way the camping information is presented. Which one a traveler uses is mostly a matter of style and convenience.

HOT SPRINGS AND POOLS

Hot Springs and Pools of the Northwest and **Hot Springs and Pools of the Southwest.** Jayson Loam. Santa Barbara, CA: Capra Press, 1980. 159 pp. (*Northwest*), 189 pp. (*Southwest*). pap. $7.95.

The two books in this series describe hot springs, resorts, thermal pools, and ranches with primitive or developed bathing areas in the Northwest and in the Southwest. The introductions discuss characteristics of the area and its natural springs and pools, water temperature and mineral content, bathhouses, gas-heated city-water pools, laws, rules and customs, and geothermal energy. The listings of the pools are divided by state, with a general description of bathing in the state preceding the entries. Inns, hotels, motels, campgrounds, resorts, and trailer parks with therapy pools, mineral baths, or whirlpools are listed with name, address, phone, and the type of pool available. The entries for the hot springs and some resorts are slightly more detailed, with descriptions of the area and the facilities, directions, and credit cards accepted along with the information listed above. The location of each area described is shown on a large map of each state, and many photographs of springs, streams, pools, and contented bathers are interspersed throughout the text.

Evaluation: The two books cover a larger area and describe more bathing spots than *Hot Springs and Spas of California* (see under California, Spas and Hot Springs), but the latter gives a much better feel for the areas and serves as a better introduction to therapeutic bathing in general. The information in the entries is condensed, incomplete, and sometimes difficult to find. Some areas are described in more detail than others, and many different types of bathing experiences are grouped together. The books' strengths are the large area covered and the number of pools and springs listed. Their major weakness is the lack of detail in the descriptions and the incompleteness of the practical information in the entries. States included in the Northwest book are Colorado, Oregon, Washington, Idaho, Utah, Montana, and Wyoming. States covered in the Southwest book are California, Nevada, Arizona, and New Mexico.

LITERARY TOURS

A Literary Tour Guide to the United States: West and Midwest. See the review of this series under United States, Literary Tours.

NATIONAL PARKS

National Parks of the West. Dorothy N. Krell, ed. Menlo Park CA: Lane Publishing Co. (dist. in the U.K. by Lunesdale Publishing Group), 1980. 255 pp. $8.95 (£7.50).

Twenty-six western U.S. National Parks are included in this "pictorial interpretation," including some of the most famous, such as Yellowstone and the Grand Canyon. Parks are listed from the Northwest, California, the Southwest, the Rocky Mountains, Alaska, and Hawaii. Each park is described clearly and helpfully, with mention of its geography, climate, wildlife, plant life, history, special features, and facilities. For larger parks with a variety of areas, each area is described separately. Clear and understandable illustrations explain the natural origin of the terrain, variety of plant zones, and other interesting facts. Relief maps of each park are provided, indicating all roads and trails. All pertinent facts, along with the park information office address, are included in a "park facts" summary at the beginning of each park description. More than 200 color photographs are included, along with a sprinkling of antique pictures giving flavor to the historical information.

Evaluation: Readers familiar with Sunset books expect outstanding photographs. And readers familiar with the National Parks in the American West expect outstanding sights. *National Parks of the West* meets both expectations easily. The close-up pictures and the scenic views are inspiring. It is a pleasure to find that the text is as easy to take as the pictures—it is informative without being dull. Potential travelers could well use this book as a starting point in planning their trips. It would also make an interesting souvenir after the trip is over. Even armchair travelers will find the book a pleasure. For use on the road, more detailed information will be needed, both in the area of accommodations and restaurants and in actual information regarding the parks.

Traveling and Camping in the National Park Areas (Western States). See the review of this title under United States, National Parks.

PHOTOGRAPHY

The High West. Les Blacklock and Andy Russell. New York: Penguin Books, 3rd ed. 1978. 141 pp. pap. $6.95.

The most striking feature of *The High West* is its incredible color photography. Here are scenes of life in the mountains that are literally breathtaking: majestic mountains cloaked in snow, foliage exploding in every color imaginable, a barking wolf in the shade of a winter-clad pine forest, and bison grazing in a golden field as a summer thunderstorm approaches. Forty-five pages of text that provide background information on the area and describe life in the high country precede the photographs. Special sections include a list of notes on the plates, which briefly describe the scenes in the photographs, an informal discussion on how to take wildlife photographs, and a list of technical photographic data.

Evaluation: Les Blacklock is the unquestioned master of western wildlife photography. All the photographs in the book are suitable for framing, with color and clarity that is difficult to believe. They alone make the book well worth the price. Andy Russell's descriptions and background that precede the photographs are written in a smooth and entertaining style that conjures images of an ageless world just slightly removed from Paradise. The book can be appreciated equally by experienced travelers and those whose travel will be limited to their own imagination. It is an extraordinary celebration of outdoor living.

SIGHTSEEING

American Jewish Landmarks: Middle West and West. See the review of this series under United States, Museums and Historic Sights.

WILDLIFE

A Pilgrim's Notebook: Guide to Western Wildlife. Buddy Mays. San Francisco, CA: Chronicle Books, 1977. 219 pp. pap. $4.95.

A Pilgrim's Notebook is intended as a field guide to the wildlife of the western United States for beginning naturalists. The list of animals in the book is not exhaustive, but includes those most frequently encountered in the field, those of particular interest, and those whose existence is threatened. The entries are divided into small, medium, large, and aquatic mammals, birds of prey, waterfowl, ground and upland birds, venomous and nonvenomous snakes, and lizards. Each entry lists the physical identification, habitat, voice, food, enemies, and status of each creature, along with a short list of odd facts about it. Photographs and illustrations of most are included, as well as a glossary of animal tracks and skulls, a list of endangered species, and an extensive bibliography. The book is useful to anyone vacationing outdoors in the West who is interested in learning about the area's most intriguing inhabitants.

Evaluation: The quality of the science-for-the-layperson makes this an ideal field guide to the wildlife of the West for all budding naturalists, but especially for families with school-age children who plan to camp or hike in the area. The information is presented clearly and is as complete as it need be for the large audience. The descriptions of the animals and the large photographs and illustrations make it relatively easy to identify the different species. The book lacks the detail and scope of the Sierra Club guides (see above, under the Southwest, Science, and below under California, Sierra Nevada), but serves a larger audience and is much easier to use. It would be an excellent complement to a more complete camping or hiking guide to an area in the western states.

STATE GUIDES

Alabama

See also The South under Regional Guides.

AAA Tourbook: Alabama. See AAA Tourbook series under North America, Accommodations and Restaurants.

Alaska

See also Pacific Coast and The West under Regional Guides

COMPREHENSIVE GUIDES

Alaska: The Complete Travel Book. Norma Spring. New York: Collier Books, Macmillan Publishing Co., 3rd ed. 1979. 269 pp. pap. $5.95.

The book gives a feel for the Alaskan wilderness that cannot be found in other guides. The entries, particularly those for the area above the panhandle, describe the people and the land in detail. Each emphasizes outdoor sights and transportation, including air travel, trains, ferries, and cruise ships. The camping, accommodations, and food sections are sparse, offering suggestions rather than complete listings. The information is presented in a way that suggests the book's best use is as pretravel reading, providing ideas to be used while planning a trip.

Evaluation: Most guides to Alaska concentrate almost exclusively on the physical beauty of the land and have little to say about the inhabitants. *Alaska: The Complete Travel Book* introduces the reader to the land and the residents of the state, both recent arrivals and native Alaskans. The entries particularly shine when describing the more remote regions of the state. The information is less complete and harder to find than in *The Milepost* (see below), but it is presented in a much more entertaining style. The book is especially useful as a description of travel possibilities for those planning their first visit to the state.

The Milepost. Publishers of *Alaska* magazine. Anchorage, AK: Alaska Northwest Publishing Co., 1979. 498 pp. pap. $5.95.

The book is a series of mile-by-mile logs of all the highways in Alaska and the major travel routes through the Yukon, Northwest Territories, British Columbia, and Alberta. It includes detailed maps, beautiful color photography, advertisements for hotels, motels, and stores, complete camping information, and tips for hunters and fishermen. The book is organized in a magazine format, with special sections for cruise ships, bicycling, wild flowers, a calendar of events, boating, canoeing and kayaking, C.B. radios, customs regulations, emergency information, newspapers, a rock-hound's guide, and totem poles. It emphasizes automobile travel, but includes information on other methods of transportation.

Evaluation: This is the most complete and best-organized road guide for the area. The mile-by-mile logs escort the reader across thousands of miles of northern highways, describing the area and listing services, campgrounds, sights, histories, and driving tips. The text is fluid and clear, and the use of symbols is unambiguous. The format and use of color photographs give the book great eye appeal. This book may well be indispensable for anyone traveling through the area by car.

The Most Complete Guide on Alaska. Cliff Cross. Tucson, AZ: H. P. Books, 1969. 170 pp. pap. $4.95.

The book is primarily a description of travel routes through the state. Ferries, trains, and air travel are mentioned, but nearly all of the book is devoted to travel by car. There is a short general information section, followed by a listing of major parks. The entries include short references to wildlife, hiking, fishing, climate, accommodations and camping, services, directions (with small maps), and special restrictions.

Evaluation: The book is indeed complete, but the author seems to have sacrificed organization for general inclusion. The information is disheveled, uneven, and confusing. The entries are listed both geographically and by travel style, rendering the index useless. The hand-drawn maps, many different type faces, and small black-and-white photographs give it the appearance of a junior high school project. A book that treats the same subject matter in a much better way is *The Milepost* (see above).

ACCOMMODATIONS AND RESTAURANTS

AAA TourBook: Alaska. See AAA TourBook series under North America, Accommodations and Restaurants.

PRETRAVEL READING

Alaska. See Sunset Pictorial series under United States, Pretravel Reading.

Facts about Alaska: The Alaska Almanac. Editors of *Alaska* magazine. Anchorage, AK: Alaska Northwest Publishing Co., 3rd ed. 1978. 133 pp. pap. $3.95.

The book is a compendium of miscellaneous facts on Alaska. There are 129 topics organized alphabetically, averaging less than a page long. Entries include indigenous mushrooms, the meanings of certain Eskimo and Aleut terms, dog mushing, and volcanoes. More practical items include national forests, hostels, hunting and sport fishing, and air travel. The book is most useful for residents or those on an extended visit to the state.

Evaluation: This is not a tour guide, but rather a reference touching on many topics and detailing none. Most travelers would find little practical use for the book, though it would make a nice complement to a more inclusive guide.

THE OUTDOORS

A Tourist Guide to Mt. McKinley. Bradford Washburn. Anchorage, AK: Alaska Northwest Publishing Co., 3rd ed. 1976. 80 pp. pap. $4.95.

The book is a description and history of the area around Mt. McKinley National Park. It features a guided tour in the form of a 90-mile highway log that enumerates scenic vistas, plant and animal life, and general points of interest. There is also an extensive history of successful ascents of the mountain.

Evaluation: A Tourist Guide to Mt. McKinley is as much a souvenir as a practical tour guide. The most useful section of the book is the mileage log in which the author smoothly blends descriptions and directions. The listings of camping facilities are short and sketchy. The strong points of the book are its history and incredible photography, which points to its best use as pretravel reading.

Wild Rivers of Alaska. Sepp Weber. Anchorage, AK: Alaska Northwest Publishing Co., 1977. 169 pp. pap. $8.95.

Wild Rivers of Alaska outlines canoe and raft trips down 58 representatively selected rivers. Included are a short history of river exploration, a discussion of the encroachment of civilization and its effects upon the rivers, and detailed descriptions of five major rivers. There is substantial preparatory material for both novice and expert, as well as safety tips and river classifications.

Evaluation: The text blends the author's experiences with points of interest and histories in an entertaining and informative style. The rivers are presented as individuals, and each of their ever-changing personalities is examined. The color photography sparkles and the maps are precise and uncomplicated. The book is a solid introduction to Alaskan rivers and the challenges they present.

Arizona

See also The Southwest and The West under Regional Guides.

COMPREHENSIVE GUIDES

All about Arizona. Thomas B. Lesure. Floral Park, NY: Harian Books, 12th ed. 1978. 194 pp. pap. $4.95.

All about Arizona is exactly what the title says it is—an introduction to almost every facet of life in the state, intended as much for newcomers as visitors. It includes long sections on climate, business and job opportunities, retiring in the state, housing, and practical information (banks, laws, newspapers, voting, and so on), as well as vacation ideas, sightseeing routes, hunting and fishing, national parks and forests, and short trips into Mexico. The last third of the book lists the towns and cities alphabetically. Included in these entries are directions, points of interest, accommodations, and restaurants, though the last two are limited to a string of abbreviations. The emphasis is on car travel by visitors on a moderate budget.

Evaluation: The book is well-organized and clear in its presentation. It is best to read it while still planning the trip to make the most of its information and ideas. The reading is fluid. The book may be used alone by both first-time and experienced travelers. It is a solid introduction to the state.

ACCOMMODATIONS AND RESTAURANTS

AAA TourBook: Arizona. See AAA TourBook series under North America, Accommodations and Restaurants.

Menus of the Valley's Finest Restaurants. See *Menus of Tucson's Finest Restaurants,* below.

Menus of Tucson's Finest Restaurants. Lindi Laws and John V. Long. Paradise Valley, AZ: Quail Run Publications, 1979. 120 pp. pap. $3.95.

When approaching an unfamiliar restaurant, what is one of the first things diners will check to determine if the restaurant is for them? Often it is the menu hung conveniently near the door. Many restaurant guides show parts of the menus (Best Restaurants series, for one; see under United States, Accommodations and Restaurants), but in this guide to the restaurants of the Tucson area, the menus are the stars and solo performers. Nearly all the restaurants listed are in the moderate to high price range, though a few offer more economical meals. Along with the menus, the entries list the address, telephone, and hours of the restaurants, as well as credit cards accepted, the times when reservations are required, very brief descriptions, and the house specialties. The restaurants are listed alphabetically and indexed by specialty, and their locations are shown on a large map of the area. The book is most useful to residents of southern Arizona and travelers on moderate and above-average budgets planning an extended visit to the area.

Evaluation: However informative a restaurant's menu may be, still other considerations should be taken into account. Many times, impressive menus merely mask the quality of the food, and isn't this the most important reason for dining in any restaurant? The entries include all the practical information necessary, and the menus are well presented, but there are no evaluations of the restaurants or the food. For travelers who feel comfortable judging a restaurant by its menu, the book serves very well. Other diners should look for a guide with more evaluative restaurant listings.

Other titles in the series: Menus of the Valley's Finest Restaurants.

OUTDOOR RECREATION

Canyon Country Series. See the review of this series under Utah, Outdoor Recreation.

Woodall's Arizona Campground Directory. See *Woodall's Campground Directory: State Editions* under United States, Camping.

SIGHTSEEING

Visitor's Guide to Arizona Indian Reservations. Boye DeMente. Phoenix, AZ: Phoenix Book Publishers, 1978. 122 pp. pap. $3.

Arizona has the highest native American population in the country, and some of the best examples of past and present native American cultures are to be found there. The book tells of their land and culture as it was and is. It opens with the history of the area from "the days of the old ones" to the "Renaissance of the Red Man." The reservation listings are divided into five geographic regions. Included are the reservations of the Navajo, Hopi, Hualapai, Havasupai, Kaibab, Paiute, Apache, Yavapai, and Papago. Each entry includes a description of the land and people, special events, sights, tribal parks, fishing and hunting, camping, overnight facilities, weather, and annual festivals. Some also list recreational facilities, rules for visitors, skiing, and jewelry. The book would benefit anyone with even the slightest interest in the native Americans of the Southwest.

Evaluation: The author received much assistance from native Americans when compiling the book. It contains a great amount of information about the reservations that is unavailable elsewhere. The book is well organized, but there is little information on transportation, shopping, or eating. It would be best to use the book as a complement to a more comprehensive guide to the state.

Major Cities

Insider's Guide: Phoenix, Scottsdale, Tempe, Mesa, and Tucson. Boye DeMente. Phoenix, AZ: Phoenix Book Publishers, 1978. 174 pp. pap. $2.

Insider's Guide is sponsored by the Arizona Bank and is intended primarily for new residents. It includes chapters on house-hunting, moving, and finding a job, as well as more practical travel information on spectator and participant sports, cultural facilities, places for children, restaurants, and night clubs in the Phoenix and Tucson areas. There is a special list of practical information on business, social, and outdoor clubs, driving regulations, hospitals, and bus and taxi services and, of course, plenty of banking information. A short description of other Arizona communities is also included. The book serves newcomers to the area and travelers planning an extended visit.

Evaluation: The lack of information on accommodations and transportation and the short sights listings severely limit the book's usefulness to travelers. The restaurant listings are very short and do not include prices. The book features a wide range of practical information, not all of which is useful to travelers, and the lack of an index makes finding it difficult. More colorful and detailed background information on the state can be found in the *AAA TourBook* (see under North America, Accommodations and Restaurants) and in the *Mobil Travel Guide* (see under United States, Accommodations and Restaurants). It isn't that the author has failed in his purpose, but that his purpose is not to provide information particularly for travelers. For newcomers, the practical information included is useful, but most travelers will need more information than is contained in the book.

Arkansas

See also The South under Regional Guides.

AAA TourBook: Arkansas. See AAA TourBook series under North America, Accommodations and Restaurants.

Woodall's Arkansas/Missouri Campground Directory. See *Woodall's Campground Directory: State Editions* under United States, Camping.

California

See also Pacific Coast and The West under Regional Guides.

ACCOMMODATIONS AND RESTAURANTS

AAA TourBook: California. See AAA TourBook series under North America, Accommodations and Restaurants.

Country Inns of America: California. See Country Inns of America series under United States, Accommodations and Restaurants.

Historic Country Inns of California. Jim Crain. San Francisco, CA: Chronicle Books, 1977. 205 pp. pap. $4.95.

The history of the inns is the outstanding feature of this book. It lists 65 inns in every part of California, though most are in rural areas along the coast between Mendocino and Santa Barbara. The entries are arranged geographically and include address, phone, facilities, ratings, price, meals, hours, and reservations. There are a number of old photographs of the inns that complement the text well. Some of the inns included offer restaurant service only.

Evaluation: The emphasis on history does not preclude some descriptions of the inns' present conditions, furnishings, and table fare, though they are secondary to the stories of the inns' pasts. But the descriptions of the meals often outshine those of the inns themselves. The information is easy to find, and the listings of facilities and the directions to the inns are clear and complete. The book lists many more California inns than either the Country Inns series of 101

Productions (see under Regional Guides, The South and The West), or of Burt Franklin (see under United States, Accommodations and Restaurants), though both of these cover larger areas. It is a solid introduction to the inns of the area and the history of nineteenth-century California.

Mobil Travel Guide: California and the West. See Mobil Travel Guide series under United States, Accommodations and Restaurants.

CAMPING

Woodall's California Campground Directory. See *Woodall's Campground Directory: State Editions* under United States, Camping.

DRIVING TOURS

Roaming the Back Roads: Day Trips by Car through Northern California. Peter Browning and Carol Holleuffer. San Francisco, CA: Chronicle Books, 1979. 175 pp. pap. $5.95.

Roaming the Back Roads is a listing of 28 car tours around Northern California. The tours are divided into four geographic areas, with each entry about five pages long. The entries themselves combine history, points of interest, the conditions of the roads, a short description of the area, and ideas for side trips all mixed in with the directions. Each tour includes photographs and a large, clear map. It serves a wide audience and all budgets.

Evaluation: The authors stress a slow pace to get a good look at the countryside. What may help keep the pace slow is the fact that the directions are blended with the information, so that distinguishing the two is not easy. But a wide variety of sights are included in the book, and the style in the entries is very entertaining. It would be best to read the tour before leaving, refer to it along the way, and let the view speak for itself.

PRETRAVEL READING

Sunset Pictorial Series: Beautiful California, California Coast, and California Missions. See Sunset Pictorial series under United States, Pretravel Reading.

SCIENCE

Earthquake Country: How, Why, and Where Earthquakes Strike in California. Robert Iacopi. Menlo Park, CA: Lane Publishing Co. (dist. in the U.K. by Lunesdale Publishing Group), 1971. 160 pp. pap. $4.95 (£1.50).

California: land of sun, sand, movie stars, Disneyland, and earthquakes. Although it will rarely be found in the glossy travel brochures, to California falls the dubious distinction of having some of the most active fault lines in the world. *Earthquake Country* discusses where, how, and why earthquakes occur in the state. It describes general characteristics of earthquakes, where the fault lines are located, and how to recognize them and includes a series of tours to areas where fault activity is most observable. A number of photographs, maps, and illustrations are used to highlight information in the text. The book also describes past major earthquakes in the different areas, including a rather detailed account of the disturbance of 1906 in and around San Francisco. Special sections are included on earthquake prediction and preparation and "what to do when the next big one hits."

Evaluation: The book was intended primarily for residents of the state, but other travelers could conceivably plan an entire vacation around the tours in the book, supplementing them with more complete transportation and accommodation information. The entries are interesting without being trivial and informative without being too technical. The clear directions and the many maps and illustrations greatly facilitate finding the out-of-the-way areas of fault activity mentioned in the tours. The book is a useful reference for anyone interested in earthquake activity in California, though its use as a practical travel guide is limited by the narrow scope of the information.

SIGHTSEEING

Gold Rush Country: Guide to California's Colorful Mining Past. Editors of Sunset Books and *Sunset* magazine. Menlo Park, CA: Lane Publishing Co., 1972. 128 pp. pap. $3.95.

Gold Rush Country vividly recounts the history of California's gold country and the people who made it famous. It examines in detail the events in the last half of the nineteenth century and the traces of the era that can be seen today. The book begins with a description of the area and the travel possibilities it presents. The area is then divided into southern, central, and northern mines, with short histories and descriptions of the small towns and mining areas in each. Entries are interspersed throughout on a variety of subjects pertaining to travel in the area, including old-time playhouses, short biographies of many interesting characters, a listing of country inns, and the area's architecture. Special sections include a calendar of events, a historical chronology, a bibliography, and a glossary of mining terms. The book is useful as pretravel reading for families on modest to above-average budgets.

Evaluation: The book includes little practical travel information, and that which is included is likely to be out of date. However, the book is not meant to be a practical travel guide, but rather provides background information on the area, and should be used with another more complete transportation/accommodations guide. The information makes up in entertainment value what it lacks in completeness. The short essays on the people and activities of the mining era in the state are particularly colorful. Though most of its fortunes have been found and spent, the area is still a motherlode of historic fact and fantasy.

Hidden Country Villages of California. Frances Coleberd. San Francisco, CA: Chronicle Books, 1977. 178 pp. pap. $5.95.

Hidden Country Villages describes 17 small California towns in 12 different entries. The lure of these towns is their slow pace, their picturesque beauty, and their removal from the heavily traveled areas of the state. The entries are detailed descriptions of the towns and their histories only. They introduce the reader to some of the residents and describe some points of interest in each town. The practical travel information in the entries is minimal, and no addresses for more information are included. The book serves as pretravel reading for travelers looking for vacation destinations that lie well off the beaten path.

Evaluation: The information on the towns in the book is meant only as a description of the areas and their individual charms. The style of the entries is more conversational than informative, with many references to past residents and visitors, buildings of historical interest, and more recent changes in the towns. The entries provide complete background information, but more comprehensive travel information should be found before planning a trip. A major feature of the towns is that they are relatively undiscovered. The word is now out.

SPAS AND HOT SPRINGS

Hot Springs and Spas of California. Patricia Cooper and Laurel Cook. San Francisco, CA: 101 Productions, 1978. 156 pp. pap. $3.95.

Hot Springs and Spas is an introduction and guide to hot water soaking and steaming. It describes the medicinal and aesthetic benefits of hot water pools and tubs, saunas, massages, and mud baths. A variety of facilities are included, from luxurious resorts hidden deep in the back country to small family-run saunas on crowded city streets. Each of the 42 entries features a history and description of the spa, an illustration, its address and phone, accommodations, rates, meals, reservations, and credit cards accepted. The book is geared to travelers on moderate to above-average budgets, but includes options for those on a more limited budget. Because of the wide range of facilities described and the varied price range, it is suggested that bathers read the book while planning their trip.

Evaluation: The book offers a unique vacation alternative for travelers looking for the ultimate in relaxation. The information is presented clearly in an entertaining style, but it is limited to the spas. Travelers staying exclusively at the spas would need no other guide. Those wishing to combine sights, adventure, and more conventional accommodations along with their stay at a spa should use a guide with a broader range of information as a supplement.

WINE TOURS

Wine Tour Series. St. Helena, CA: Vintage Image, 1977, 1978. 200 pp. pap. $6.95.

The three books in the Wine Tour series explore the rich vineyard country of central and northern California. They begin with a history of the wine industry in the area, which concentrates on the people most responsible for the birth of the California vineyards in the nineteenth century. The food sections feature over 50 restaurants and specialty shops. Each entry includes a description, specialties, address, phone numbers, hours, credit cards accepted, and price ranges. The accommodations sections include 25 hotels, inns, and ranches with all the practical information needed. The wineries and vineyards in the books are divided geographically. The entries introduce the owners, give a short history of each vineyard, and include wine specialties and oenological points of interest. An appendix lists the particulars (address, phone, and so on) of each vineyard. The books are geared to travel by car through the areas. They best serve travelers on a moderate to high budget who plan on spending more than a few days touring the vineyards of the state.

Evaluation: For travelers whose vacation goals are limited to the California wine industry, the inclusion of food and lodging sections makes the series the only guides necessary. But those who plan on more traditional vacation activities should supplement these guides with one that includes more complete transportation and sights sections. The texts are entertaining and informative, and the maps and illustrations make these very attractive books. They serve both as travel guides and as introductions to the wine industry of the state.

Note: According to the publishers, the upcoming edition of the series will see a change in the books' format. The food and lodging sections will be included in a companion book to the series, which will feature more complete touring maps and other points of interest.

Included in the series: Central Coast Wine Tour: From San Francisco to Santa Barbara, by Richard Hinkle and William H. Gibbs, III; *Napa Valley Wine Tour,* by Michael Topolos and Betty Dopson; *Sonoma and Mendocino Wine Tour,* by Patricia Latimer, Deborah Kenly, and Michael Topolos.

Death Valley

Exploring Death Valley. Ruth Kirk. Stanford, CA: Stanford University Press, 3rd ed. 1976. 88 pp. pap. $3.45.

Death Valley is one of the most inhospitable places in North America, but for many travelers this only adds to the adventure. *Exploring Death Valley* is a complete guide to the area around Death Valley National Monument. It includes sections on the area's natural and social history, weather and desert survival, sights on the main roads and in the back country, trips by truck and jeep, hiking trails, and a directory of complete practical information. The directory lists the quality of the roads in the area, public transportation, lodging, campgrounds, facilities and services, programs and recreation, and desert driving suggestions. There are a number of photographs and first-rate maps, as well as a complete index. The book serves all travelers to Death Valley.

Evaluation: The book is the most complete travel guide to the area. The information is broad in scope, though less detailed than in other guides. The inclusion of lodging, sights, activities, and information on automobile services in the area make it the only guide most travelers would need, though some may be more interested in the more detailed science and desert camping information found in the Sierra Club guide, *The Deserts of the Southwest* (see under The Southwest, Sightseeing). It should be noted that the book was last updated in 1976, so that much of the information may be too old. Still, no other guide to the area is as well organized, and none includes such a wide range of practical information.

Los Angeles and Vicinity

COMPREHENSIVE GUIDES

Los Angeles on $500 a Day. Ferne Kadish and Kathleen Kirtland. New York: Macmillan Publishing Co., 1976. 193 pp. $8.95; pap. $4.95.

Los Angeles on $500 a Day was written to serve a small and definable audience—those travelers for whom money is limitless. The authors do not simply suggest a visit to Disneyland; they suggest renting it. Or perhaps a new Mercedes, as a nice souvenir of your visit to Beverly Hills. The self-indulgence does not stop there. The day's entertainment may include renting a small jet to Palm Springs to show off a new, custom-made wardrobe acquired while rubbing elbow-patches with the stars on Rodeo Drive. The book does include what might be called practical travel information on hotels (long descriptions of four of the classiest), night clubs and restaurants, shopping, transportation (limousine rentals), and arts and antiques. But don't look for any bargains.

Evaluation: The least that can be said about the book is that it is unique. The information, while narrow in scope, is complete for this particular travel style. The shopping and nightlife sections in particular describe areas and activities in the city that are not mentioned in other guides. The text is very stylized, reminiscent of the Suzy Knickerbocker school of journalism. The book is great fun to read, with names dropped ever so casually on nearly every page, but the practicality of the travel information is severely limited. The book makes for entertaining pretravel reading and is perhaps useful as a description of the upper extremes of the cost spectrum, though most travelers will find that a more humble guide will serve them better on the road.

Other titles in the series: London on $500 a Day; New York on $500 a Day; Paris on $500 a Day.

ARCHITECTURE

A Guide to Architecture in Los Angeles and Southern California. See *A Guide to Architecture in San Francisco and Northern California,* under San Francisco and Vicinity, above.

CHILDREN

In and Around L.A. for Kids. Stephanie Kegan. San Francisco, CA: Chronicle Books, 1978. 144 pp. pap. $4.95.

In and Around L.A. for Kids describes over 300 sights and activities of interest to the entire family throughout southern California. Few areas offer a wider range of year-round activities, most of which are free or have only a minimal admission charge. The entries are divided into geographic regions and include parks, zoos, museums, points of natural interest, missions, newspaper and television station tours, restaurants, beaches, and playhouses. Each entry lists the address, telephone, hours, and admission charge, along with short descriptions. A system of symbols is used to point out particular activities or services provided by the different establishments. A special list of annual events is included after the geographic listings. The book was written primarily for residents of the area and serves all budgets and family travel styles.

Evaluation: Few guides to sights and activities of interest to children include such a variety of entries in all price ranges—from expensive but irreplaceable Disneyland to the free and equally irreplaceable Death Valley Monument. The practical information in the entries is complete, but the descriptions are too short to provide a very clear picture. The book does not include transportation and accommodations information, maps, travel time from Los Angeles (or other major cities), or preparatory information on family travel. It is most useful to southern California residents or those already familiar with the area. Other travelers should supplement the information in this guide with a more comprehensive guide to the area.

HIKING

Trails of the Angeles. John W. Robinson. Berkeley, CA: Wilderness Press, 4th ed. 1979. 256 pp. pap. $6.95.

Few travelers are aware of the variety of hiking trips available within an hour's drive of Los Angeles. The San Gabriel Mountains ring the north and east sides of the city, providing a soothing respite from its choking smog and often frenzied inhabitants. *Trails of the Angeles* describes 100 hikes in this urban mountain range. The introduction discusses the natural and social history of the San Gabriels, basic hiking tips, mountain courtesy, and how to order National Forest Service and U.S. Geological Survey maps. Each hike entry includes the length and elevation gain, a rating of the difficulty, the seasons it is open, on which U.S.G.S. topographic map it can be found, its basic features, directions to the starting point, and a detailed description of the route. Special features include a section on organized trail systems in the area, a list of trail camps, a description of trails that were used formerly, and a complete bibliography. The book is most useful to residents of the Los Angeles area, but may also be used by hikers planning an extended visit to southern California.

Evaluation: Although the book is limited in scope, the hiking information and the descriptions of the trails are complete and clear. Few of the trips are more than day hikes, and fewer still call for much strenuous climbing. The photographs, maps, and illustrations complement the text nicely. The preparatory information in the introductory sections serves as a reminder for experienced hikers, but beginners should supplement this with more complete equipment, clothing, and safety information. Travelers wishing to combine hiking with more traditional vacation activities should use this book along with a more comprehensive transportation, accommodations, and sights guide to the Los Angeles area.

RESTAURANTS

Best Restaurants: Los Angeles and Southern California. See Best Restaurants series under United States, Accommodations and Restaurants.

Mammoth Lakes

Mammoth Lakes Sierra: A Handbook for Roadside and Trail. Genny Schumacher Smith, ed. Palo Alto, CA: Genny Smith Books, 4th ed. 1976. 147 pp. pap. $6.95.

Mammoth Lakes Sierra, like its sister publication *Deepest Valley: A Guide to Owens Valley* by the same author (see below, under Owens Valley), concentrates on scenic roads and trails in the area in the eastern shadow of the Sierra Nevada, south of Lake Tahoe. The first half of the book describes nearly every car route and hiking trail in the region, emphasizing the natural and social history of the area. Special sections are included on geology, climate and life zones, trees, wild flowers and shrubs, mammals, fish, and birds. Clear photographs and detailed illustrations are included throughout, as well as a large map of the area. The character of the area dictates that a visit to it be centered around outdoor activities. The book is useful as pretravel reading, but is especially handy on the road to identify the many natural sights.

Evaluation: Much of the science and outdoor information in the book is covered in more detail in the Sierra Club Naturalist's Guide (see below), but *Mammoth Lakes Sierra* includes a wider range of practical travel information and covers a smaller area. The information is just technical enough to be both interesting and understandable. The book is worthwhile for travelers with more than a passing interest in the natural science of the area who are planning either an extended visit to the area or a number of short visits.

Northern California

COMPREHENSIVE GUIDES

North of San Francisco. Robert W. Matson. Millbrae, CA: Celestial Arts, 1979. 257 pp. pap. $5.95.

Few guides are as difficult to categorize as *North of San Francisco*. At first it seems as if its emphasis is on restaurants, with a number of detailed descriptions and complete listings of practical information for each. But these are surrounded by pages of histories and descriptions of the different areas. Then there are the complete descriptions of the areas' inns, vineyards, and wineries. So where is the emphasis? Perhaps nowhere—and everywhere. The book has a unique method of organization. Histories, descriptions, and restaurant listings for the five counties directly north of San Francisco are divided roughly by geographic area or city. These are followed by the inn listings, and finally the section on the areas' vineyards. The restaurants, accommodations, and wineries are indexed, and there is a set of hand-drawn maps in the back of the book.

Evaluation: The two most striking features of the book are the large number of old photographs and beautiful illustrations, and the smooth and easy style of the text. The information on the restaurants, wineries, and accommodations is complete and clear, and the historical and descriptive entries are fun to read. It may take a while for travelers to get used to the unorthodox organization, but the indexes help make the book easier to use. Many travelers will be more than satisfied with this book's range of information, especially when it is coupled with more complete sights and transportation information.

Sunset Travel Guide to Northern California. Barbara J. Braasch and Julie Anne Gold, eds. Menlo Park, CA: Lane Publishing Co. (dist. in the U.K. by Lunesdale Publishing Group), 1980. 128 pp. pap. $4.95 (£1.50).

In this colorful book, eight areas of northern California are described: San Francisco, the Bay Area, Monterey Peninsula, the north coast, the wine country, the Sierra, the northern wonderland, and the central valley. General descriptions of the areas are given, with notes on history and particular towns or sites of interest. Only the most general driving directions are given. Usually practical information is minimal, although there are special sections on San Francisco dining, golfing, inns, wines, and apples, among others. The text dwells more on the appeal of each area to the traveler. Maps are provided, but it is usually not clear how they relate specifically to the text.

Evaluation: For those planning a trip to northern California, the *Sunset Travel Guide to Northern California* will certainly whet the appetite for travel. The photographs are outstanding, and the text is appealing, making the reader want to discover more. Unfortunately, in this book there isn't more. In spite of the pictures, the book can serve only as a collection of glimpses of possible travel routes and destinations. The one exception to this is the more complete treatment of San Francisco. For those already familiar with the area, it will be enough to get them on the road. For tourists, however, much more practical information and further guidebooks will be needed.

The What, When and Where Guide to Northern California. Basil C. Wood. Garden City, NY: Doubleday & Co., 1977. 150 pp. pap. $3.95.

The book lists sights and activities of interest to the entire family throughout northern California. The entries are divided into many geographic regions, and a unique system of organization is employed to present the information. Four vertical columns are used on each set of facing pages. The first column lists the name, address, and phone number of the sight, the second is a short description and history, the third lists the operating dates, the hours, and the admission charges, and the fourth shows the sight's location on a carefully drawn map. Major areas, such as Golden Gate Park and the Monterey Peninsula, are described in more detail. The sights and activities are indexed in the front of the book by type (museums, zoos, missions, and so on) and in the back of the book alphabetically. Special sections include a long list of winery and industrial tours, ghost towns, winter sports, and sites of interest on the campus of the University of California-Berkeley.

Evaluation: The most striking feature of the book is the unique method of organizing and presenting the information on the sights and activities. The use of vertical columns makes it very easy to find the information, and the complete indexes allow travelers to find a particular point of interest without paging through half the book. The large number and variety of sights listed in the entries almost guarantees something for every interest, although the lack of detail in some of the descriptions makes it difficult to distinguish between them. The book would be most useful to residents of northern California, who could use the information on many short trips. Travelers new to the area will also find the book useful when combined with more complete background, preparation, accommodations, and transportation information.

ARCHITECTURE

A Guide to Architecture in San Francisco and Northern California. See the review of this title below, under San Francisco, Architecture.

OVERNIGHT TRIPS

Weekend Adventures for City-Weary Families: A Guide to Overnight Trips in Northern California. Carole Terwilliger Meyers. Albany, CA: Carousel Press, 1977. 97 pp. pap. $3.95.

Most guides to short family trips in a particular area concentrate on sights and activities. *Weekend Adventures* is different in that it includes complete information on accommodations and restaurants for each city included, as well as baby-sitting services, a list of special annual events, and many addresses for further information. Other special sections include tips for traveling by car with children, suggestions for planning a trip, and a list of other travel books to the area. Written primarily for residents of the San Francisco Bay Area, the book serves families on modest to above-average budgets who are looking for a variety of activities in northern and central California.

Evaluation: Because the book has a wider range of information than other guides to short family trips, it would be possible for visitors unfamiliar with the area to use it with only a good set of maps when traveling in northern California. However, most will want to supplement the information in this book with a comprehensive guide to one of California's major cities. The cities and area included in the book are all small enough to see in a day or two. The information in the entries is complete, well organized, and easy to find. A major feature of the book is the advice on keeping children busy on long car trips. This alone would make the book worthwhile for many families.

RESTAURANTS

Best Restaurants: San Francisco and Northern California. See Best Restaurants series under United States, Accommodations and Restaurants.

SCIENCE

Field Guide Series: Northern California. See the review of this series under United States, Science.

Roadside Geology of Northern California. See Roadside Geology series under United States, Science.

WINE TOURS

Central Coast Wine Tour: From San Francisco to Santa Barbara. See Wine Tour series under California, Wine Tours.

Napa Valley Wine Tour. See Wine Tour series under California, Wine Tours.

Sonoma and Mendocino Wine Tour. See Wine Tour series under California, Wine Tours.

Owens Valley

Deepest Valley: A Guide to Owens Valley. Genny Schumacher Smith, ed. Los Altos, CA: William Kaufman, 6th ed., 1978. 239 pp. pap. $6.95.

The book describes California's Owens Valley (in the eastern shadow of the Sierra Nevada) in a variety of ways. Its history is recounted in depth, both before and after the arrival of the Europeans. There are sections on the geology of the area, plant and animal life, fish, major auto routes, and hiking trails. There are also a number of beautiful photographs and illustrations, and very legible maps. The book ends with a discussion of the water problem which arose with the creation of the Los Angeles aqueduct and which continues in the courts today. It serves low and moderate budgets and emphasizes outdoor activities.

Evaluation: The authors have packed the entries with a great amount of information on a wide variety of subjects pertaining to the valley. The road and trail entries combine practical information with descriptions in a way that complements both. The book is organized well and the information is very accessible. Two problems with the book are the lack of accommodations and restaurant listings and the few references to the towns in the valley. The star and solo performer is the great outdoors.

Point Reyes

The Visitor's Guide to Point Reyes National Seashore. Alice F. Dalbey. Old Greenwich, CT: The Chatham Press, 1974. 79 pp. pap. $1.95.

Point Reyes is a small peninsula about 100 miles up the coast from San Francisco. *The Visitor's Guide* describes the area's history and physical setting, with references to points of interest, protected coastal areas, hiking trails, park office locations, swimming, horseback riding, camping facilities and regulations, and nearby attractions. The book emphasizes inexpensive outdoor activities along one of the most beautiful coastlines in the world.

Evaluation: The quality and completeness of the entries make this a first-rate guide to the area. It includes a variety of activities for many interests in a limited space. The information is organized well and presented clearly. The area covered is small, but very much worth seeing. The low price of the book makes it ideal for all travelers planning a weekend visit to the area.

San Diego County

Backcountry Roads and Trails: San Diego County. Jerry Schad. Beaverton, OR: The Touchstone Press, 1977. 96 pp. pap. $3.95.

The mountains of San Diego County may be less spectacular than other ranges in the state, but *Backcountry Roads and Trails* shows that the area has many unique charms for hikers to discover. The book is divided into five car trips, with three to twelve hikes in each trip short enough to be taken comfortably in one afternoon. A short introduction discusses hiking preparation, seasonal changes, and general characteristics of the area. Each trip lists points of interest, campgrounds and picnic areas, and detailed descriptions of the route, and includes a large, hand-drawn map. The trail listings include distance, elevation at the trail head, low and high points, short descriptions of the trails, and a thumbnail sketch of each. Points of natural or historic interest are referred to throughout the entries, and a number of photographs are included of each area.

Evaluation: The road and trail descriptions are complete and clear, and the large maps make them easy to find. However, this guide differs from other hiking guides to various areas. All the hikes are about the same distance, and, though proper conditioning is always essential, they require no real mountain climbing skills. There is very little preparatory information, no practical information on the campgrounds listed, and no information on topographic maps to the different areas. The book is useful to day hikers and overnight campers, but hikers planning an extended backpacking trip in the area will need more information than is provided in the book.

San Francisco and Vicinity

COMPREHENSIVE GUIDES

An Opinionated Guide to San Francisco. Franz T. Hansell. Sausalito, CA: Comstock Editions, 3rd ed. 1976. 276 pp. pap. $1.95.

An Opinionated Guide to San Francisco is a different kind of city guide. It provides detailed background information on all sections of the city—both those likely to be cluttered with tourists and those whose charms would be known only to the city's long-term residents. Sections not likely to be found in other San Francisco guides include a long list and description of city views and scenic vistas, monuments throughout the city, bars, bookstores, and viewing the rich. More traditional topics include a long description of the Golden Gate Park, a list of museums and specialized collections, a series of walking tours, a long transportation section, and a calendar of annual events. The book does not list accommodations or restaurants, but suggests that travelers request this information from the Chamber of Commerce. The book serves travelers looking for the hidden San Francisco, the one that everyone sings about.

Evaluation: But for the lack of accommodation and restaurant information, the book is a complete guide to the city. It provides a wide range of sights and activities for travelers wishing to explore a bit deeper than the well-worn tourist paths. The author has spent years traversing the city from corner to corner. and he shares his discoveries and opinions in a clear and entertaining style. Although the book is much older than most guides to the city, it serves an audience that many guides fail to address—those with an urge to uncover all the aspects of the city, including some that may be less than positive. But it is all part of the discovery. The strength of the book is its openness and wide range of subjects. Its weakness is its age. Still, it is unlike any other guide to a city that is unlike any other city.

ARCHITECTURE

A Guide to Architecture in San Francisco and Northern California. David Gebhard et al. Layton, UT: Peregrine Smith, 1976. 557 pp. pap. $8.95.

This guide to the buildings of California is geared to the architectural connoisseur. It details the trends in architecture over the last 200 years that can be seen in the northern part of the state, using text, photographs, maps, and illustrations. The book begins with a historical overview of the architecture of the area. The entries are listed by city, with the cities arranged geographically. Each entry lists the name of the building, the year it was built, its address, and a short description. The locations of the buildings are shown on a series of large, clear maps, with photographs and floor plans of many of the buildings featured. A photographic history, a glossary of architectural terms, and a long bibliography are included. Special sections include a description of Bay Area planning, a complete discussion of the rapid transit system and the location of rapid transit stations.

Evaluation: The detailed and high-quality references to the many architectural trends in the state go beyond that found in many other architecture guides. In fact, there is so much detail that it would be difficult to view even a small percentage of the buildings in a one-week stay. The book is well organized and easy to use, considering the great amount of information included. The many photographs and illustrations complement the text well. The book serves both as a guide to the buildings and as an introduction to the study of architecture in general, but travelers who are not preapred to center their vacation around the study of buildings should look for another guide. *Other titles in the series: A Guide to Architecture in Los Angeles and Southern Calfornia.*

THE OUTDOORS

An Outdoor Guide to the San Francisco Bay Area. Dorothy L. Whitnah. Berkeley, CA: Wilderness Press, 1978. 401 pp. pap. $7.95.

Eighty-four hikes within 70 miles of the Golden Gate Bridge are described in *An Outdoor Guide*. They include easy strolls and more difficult trips, though all can be taken in a day. The introduction discusses the benefits of walking, describes the climate, geography, flora, and fauna of the area, gives a capsulated history, and tells where to get more information. It also briefly discusses hiking preparation, safety, etiquette, and regulations. The hikes are divided by county, with a short description of each area preceding the entries. Each hike entry lists the distance and grade of the hike, on which topographic map it can be found, and how to get to the trail head by bus and by car. The general features of the hikes are listed before more detailed descriptions of the routes, which include suggested side trips. The hikes are shown on a series of maps, and each hike is given a descriptive title (for thespians, for train buffs, for athletes, for the lazy, and so on). There is also a special list of outdoor organizations in the Bay Area, a complete index, and long lists of suggested reading. The book is most useful to Bay Area residents, though all hikers planning a visit to the area will find it a handy companion.

Evaluation: The hiking information is complete and very well presented, with a wide range of information provided in the entries. The author succeeds in showing the different personalities of the hikes, making it easy to choose a hike of particular interest from the many included. The descriptions of the trails are much more detailed than those in other hiking guides. The book is more expensive than most trail guides, but well worth the price for hikers who can plan on spending a number of days exploring the area. The preparatory and background information is very useful to beginning hikers and those making their first visit to the San Francisco area.

RESTAURANTS

Arthur Bloomfield's Guide to San Francisco's Restaurants. Arthur Bloomfield. Sausalito, CA: Comstock Editions, 2nd ed. 1977. 309 pp. pap. $2.95.

The 248 eateries described in Arthur Bloomfield's guide range from the finest in Continental cuisine to the corner bar and grill, with the widest variety of ethnic restaurants to be found outside of New York City. The restaurants are listed alphabetically and indexed by nationality or type, by location, and by dish (400 specialties are listed), with a special list for late-night dining. The entries include the address and phone number of each restaurant, a description of the atmosphere and menu specialties, the price range (no specific prices listed), hours, reservations, bar facilities, and formality level. A three-star rating system is used to denote the level of overall excellence. The book is most useful to travelers on moderate to above-average budgets who are spending more than a week in San Francisco.

Evaluation: The many restaurant indexes and the clear presentation of the information make the book very easy to use. The descriptions of the restaurants are both colorful and informative, providing a clear picture of what can be expected. No other guide to the city's restaurants includes the number and variety in this book, though nearly all of the establishments are in the medium or higher price range. A unique and very useful feature is the list of favorite dishes and where to find them. The book is inexpensive enough to be useful as a complement to a more thorough sights and accommodations guide.

Best Restaurants: San Francisco and Northern California. See Best Restaurants series under United States, Accommodations and Restaurants.

Eating Out with the Kids in San Francisco and the Bay Area. Carole Terwilliger Meyers. Albany, CA: Carousel Press, 1976. 72 pp. pap. $3.45.

For those unafraid of the challenge of family dining, there is *Eating Out with the Kids*. The author describes her experience with her son, who was just slightly better behaved than a tornado. She includes a list of helpful hints on children's seats, ordering, cleanup, and keeping the children occupied before and after the meal. The restaurants are listed alphabetically and indexed by category. Each entry includes the address, telephone, and hours of the restaurant, as well as parking and reservation information, the availability of highchairs and booster seats, credit cards accepted, and a half-page description of its specialties, atmosphere, and special services. Many of the restaurants included are not strictly family-oriented, but all have been tested and deemed suitable for children.

Evaluation: The preparatory information, especially the seating and "goodie bag" suggestions, would be useful reading for all families, whether dining in San Fransicso or in their home town. If their home town is San Francisco, all the better. The practical information on the restaurants is complete and easy to find, but the descriptions of the atmospheres and specialties lack the inimitable style of the Best Restaurants series and *Where to Eat in America* (see under United States, Accommodations and Restaurants). Families planning a trip to the Bay Area will find this a very useful book when combined with a sights and accommodations guide.

WALKING TOURS

Timeless Walks in San Francisco. Michelle Brant. Atlanta, GA: Lompa Press, 1979. 70 pp. pap. $3.50.

The book consists of nine walking tours in the city. The author claims they are "about an hour long," but with all there is to see in the tours, they could easily take the better part of an afternoon. The tours concentrate on the history of the city from its founding in 1776 to the fire of 1906. The tour entries average about five pages but contain a wealth of historical information in a crisp and clear style. There are a number of drawings and early photographs of the city that greatly complement the text.

Evaluation: Whether used alone or paired with a complete city guide, *Timeless Walks* is a valuable introduction to the city for both first-time visitors and residents. The tours are organized well and the maps are easy to read. The book is worthwhile for anyone with even the slightest interest in the history of San Francisco.

San Luis Obispo

An Uncommon Guide to San Luis Obispo County. Georgia Lee, Vicki Leon, and Lachlan MacDonald. San Luis Obispo, CA: Padre Productions, 1977. 160 pp. pap. $4.95.

What is uncommon about this guide is its organization—all the information is arranged alphabetically. The topics are many and varied. Among them are festivals, fairs and fiestas, abalone, rock hounds, picnics, lookouts, bicycling, strawberries, and the Hearst Castle. None of the entries except parks is longer than two pages, and the average length is two or three paragraphs. There is much history, including the history of the Indians of the area, and directions to out-of-the-way places of interest. The only index, however, is a very informal one on the inside of the front and back covers. The book serves as an introduction to the area for all budgets and travel styles, but is most useful when used with a more complete guide.

Evaluation: The information in the entries is inconsistent. Some are very good, while others seem incomplete. One highlight is the parks section, which includes plenty of listings, descriptions, camping areas, and beaches. A shortcoming is the restaurant section, which has no addresses and few descriptions—just names. After one becomes acclimated to the organization, however, it is a fairly good guide, offering a wide variety of sights and activities in a minimal amount of space. The book is worthwhile only to those spending more than a few days in the county.

Santa Barbara/Channel Islands

Cruising Guide to the Channel Islands. Brian M. Fagan and Graham Pomeroy. Santa Barbara, CA: Capra Press; Newport Beach, CA: Pacific Skipper. 1979. 206 pp. pap. $15.

Written for use with sail-powered pleasure craft in the Santa Barbara Channel, this carefully researched guide is divided into two conceptual parts. The introductory section covers general information regarding the channel: a basic description, history of its people and wildlife, winds and weather, boat equipment, and general cruising hints. Charts, graphs, and detailed information are included in abundance. The actual sailing directions make up the remaining 70 percent of the book, which refers specifically to points on the western offshore islands, mainland coasts, and eastern offshore islands. General descriptions of each of these are given, point by point. Approaches to anchorages, landings, facilities, hints, and warnings are given in such detail that sailors will have no problem matching the text and photographs with what they see before them.

Evaluation: The detail, both nautical and historical, in this book makes it a must for sailors in the Santa Barbara Channel. While it does not substitute for charts, which should be acquired and used, the detailed text and very helpful photographs make sailing without the *Cruising Guide* unthinkable. Sailors in the channel will use it so often that they will wish the binding were sturdier.

Sierra Nevada

Sierra Club Naturalist's Guide: The Sierra Nevada. Stephan Whitney. San Francisco, CA: Sierra Club Books, 1979. 526 pp. pap. $8.95.

The *Sierra Club Naturalist's Guide: The Sierra Nevada* is intended as a field guide for hikers and campers to the mountains west of the California-Nevada border. The book details the natural history and environmental characteristics of the area both in the text and with a great number of graphs, maps, and illustrations. After a geographic, geological, and climatic orientation, the mountains are divided into four general areas: the western foothills, the forest belt, the alpine communities, and the dry, rugged eastern slope. The land formation, plants, and wildlife of each area are examined extensively. Although the book includes no practical information on camping or hiking trails, addresses for further information and the location of park offices are listed in the back, with a complete reading list and index.

Evaluation: The quality and detail of the science information makes this book an excellent home reference as well as a field guide. The information is presented in a way that can be enjoyed and appreciated by both novice and experienced naturalists, but the great amount of material and the relatively high price of the book make it practical only for those who can plan to use it many times over. Experienced campers and hikers can enjoy many weeks of outdoor adventure with this guide alone, although beginners or those looking for more traditional vacation activities should supplement this book with a more complete camping guide.

Southern and Central California

BICYCLE TOURING

Fifty Southern California Bicycle Trips. Jerry Schad and Don Krupp. Beaverton, OR: The Touchstone Press, 1976. 112 pp. pap. $3.95.

Bicycling is a viable transportation alternative for travelers concerned with their health and the rising cost of gasoline. *Fifty Southern California Bicycle Trips* provides everything necessary for successful bicycle touring by beginning cyclists and experts, except road maps and a bicycle. The introductory sections explain how the trips were selected, how to read the entries, how to prepare for the terrain and road conditions, a short comparison and description of basic bicycle designs and equipment, clothing, repairs, rules of the road, and safety tips. The different trips range from one to eight hours and include easy and more challenging rides. Each entry lists road conditions, distance, riding time, facilities, and a difficulty rating, with a page-long description of the route and a graph that shows changes in elevation. Hand-drawn maps are included for each ride, though the authors suggest that more detailed maps be used on the road.

Evaluation: The completeness of the practical information on the rides and the clear descriptions of the different routes make the book ideal for both residents and travelers unfamiliar with the area, although visitors planning to spend some time on their feet as well would want to supplement the information with an accommodations and sights guide. The preparatory information is very useful for beginners, and the safety tips should be heeded by all cyclists. The information is much more complete than in most cycling guides to a particular area, and the rides included offer something for everyone. The book is an excellent example of what a cycling guide to a particular area should be.

SCIENCE

Field Guide Series: Coastal Southern California. See the review of this series under United States, Science.

Field Guide Series: Southern California. See the review of this series under United States, Science.

Colorado

See also Rocky Mountains and The West under Regional Guides.

ACCOMMODATIONS AND RESTAURANTS

AAA TourBook: Colorado. See AAA TourBook series under North America, Accommodations and Restaurants.

GHOST TOWNS

Ghost Trails to Ghost Towns. Inez Hund and Wannetta W. Draper. New York, NY: Sage Books, 1972. 48 pp. pap. $1.50.

If they could speak, the deserted and semideserted mountain towns of central Colorado would have many strange tales to tell. The characters that came and went left a legacy of unintended mystery on the streets and in the crumbling buildings. The authors of this book introduce travelers to 19 of these places of mysterious emptiness. Not all the small towns in the book are completely deserted, but none approach the vitality they possessed in the past. The entries for each town include a photograph, directions, a poem about the town, and a short history. This short book is an eerie introduction to the nineteenth-century mining towns of the area and could be used both as pretravel reading and on the road.

Evaluation: The book is most useful as a complement to a hiking or camping guide to the area. It is very short, but offers hours of interesting (and free) exploration far off the beaten track. The entries tell little more than how to find the town and one or two things to look for; the discovery is left to the traveler. The book serves all travel styles and budgets. Because of the low price, it would be worthwhile for anyone traveling in the area. *Ghost Trails to Ghost Towns* gives a unique view of life in the Old West as it was, and is.

MOUNTAINS

Exploring the Colorado High Country. Jeremy Agnew. Colorado Springs, CO: Wildwood Press, 1977. 156 pp. pap. $4.95.

Exploring the Colorado High Country is an overview of outdoor living in the mountains of central Colorado. It was written primarily for travelers planning their first visit to the area to give them an idea of the environment they can expect. The text blends history and science in the descriptions of the area, with sections on wildlife, parks, transportation, mining towns, and gold. The book includes very little practical information. It is strictly armchair reading.

Evaluation: This does not compare with other travel guides to the area because of the emphasis on history and description and the exclusion of any practical information. The book provides a view of the area in the mind's eye, as it were. The author writes in a lively and entertaining style that brings the people and places of the past to life. The book is no substitute for a complete motoring or camping guide to the Rockies, but is useful to travelers looking for more background information than is provided in those guides.

The Fourteeners—Colorado's Great Mountains. Perry Eberhart and Philip Schmuck. Chicago; IL: The Swallow Press, 1970. 127 pp. $12; pap. $5.95.

There are 53 mountains in Colorado that top the 14,000-foot mark—many more than in any other state except Alaska. *The Fourteeners* describes these mountains through text and photographs. A short introduction lists basic mountain terminology and describes some basic characteristics of the mountains. The entries for the mountains are arranged in no discernible order and include detailed background information and large photographs of each peak. They emphasize the stories of the mountains' pasts and the people who first named and explored them. In the back of the book is a special description of five mountains that are either just shy of the 14,000-foot line or whose correct elevation cannot be agreed upon by the different authorities.

Evaluation: The book's practical travel usefulness is limited by the emphasis on background and description, although it serves well as an introduction to the mountains of the state. The photographs are clear and inviting, but they lack the punch of those in *The High West* (see under The West, Photography). The descriptions of the mountains and their early inhabitants are entertaining and informative. The book's age is of little consequence because of the emphasis on background information. The book is a worthwhile pretravel reference for travelers planning their first visit to the area, but another practical guide for camping, accommodations, and transportation information should be acquired for use on the road.

Guide to the Colorado Mountains. Robert Ormes. Chicago, IL: The Swallow Press, 6th ed. 1970. 300 pp. $6.

The most unusual feature of the *Guide to the Colorado Mountains* is the large area it covers. Other guides to the mountains of the state concentrate on a particular area. This book includes descriptions and hiking information on all of the Colorado mountain ranges. It begins with a general description of the geology, wildlife, and vegetation of the area, and a discussion of past inhabitants, with safety tips and map and trail information sources. The descriptions of the mountains and trails are arranged informally north to south. Each entry includes the topographic maps on which it can be found, descriptions of the roads in the area, and the location of Forest Service campgrounds. The trail entries are simply short descriptions of the length of the trails and directions to the trail heads. Special sections are included on rock climbing, ski touring, caves and spelunking, and white-water boating. The book is useful to experienced hikers planning a trip or trips over a large area of the state.

Evaluation: The book covers a larger area than most hiking guides and includes a wider range of information, but the lack of detail in the entries and the emphasis on experienced hikers limit the book's audience. The trail directions are fairly clear, though the practical information on the hikes (distance, difficulty, elevation gain) is difficult to isolate in the text. The book sacrifices completeness for general inclusion, which makes it more useful as a pretravel reference than as a practical trail guide. First-time hikers and those planning a trip to a particular area in the state should look for a different guide.

OUTDOOR RECREATION

Canyon Country Series. See the review of this series under Utah, Outdoor Recreation.

Fifty West Central Colorado Hiking Trails. Don Lowe and Roberta Lowe. Beaverton, OR: The Touchstone Press, 1976. 111 pp. pap. $6.95.

The book describes hikes in a small area around Aspen, Colorado. The small area covered and the simplicity of the hike entries are the book's most striking features. A short introduction describes the area in general, explains how to use the book, briefly tells how to order and use topographic maps, and gives some safety precautions. The hike entries include the distance, elevation gain, elevation of the highest point, approximate time needed for the hike, the times of the year the trail is open, and on which topographic map it can be found. The trail descriptions are less than a page long and emphasize directions. The trails are shown on small cutouts of topographic maps, and photographs are included in each entry. The book is useful only to experienced hikers planning an extended visit to the area.

Evaluation: Because of the lack of preparatory or safety information, difficulty ratings, and descriptions of the different areas, the book's usefulness is limited. The trail directions and the directions to the trail heads are clear and uncomplicated, but the lack of any other information in the entries makes it difficult to find any difference between the hikes. The book is more expensive than most hiking guides, covers a smaller area, and includes less practical hiking information. It is a very attractive book, but it is useful only to hikers who live near the area or are frequent visitors and who have some previous hiking experience.

Hiking Trails of Northern Colorado. Mary Hagen. Boulder, CO: Pruett Publishing Co., 1979. 154 pp. pap. $5.95.

The 39 hikes described in *Hiking Trails of Northern Colorado* include easy and more challenging trips, all short enough to be completed in a day. The book begins with lists showing on which U.S.G.S. topographic map the trails can be located, the destination and distance of each hike, and the location of the trail head. The trail entries average three pages long and emphasize directions and descriptions. Each hike is shown on a cutout of a topographic sheet, with many photographs included of sights along the way. The book best serves residents of the area and experienced hikers planning an extended visit to the mountains of the area.

Evaluation: The trail directions and descriptions are clear and uncomplicated, and the maps are very useful, though most hikers would still want to use topographic maps on the trails. However, the lack of preparatory and background information and the incomplete practical information on the trails detract from the book's overall usefulness. The book is very difficult to use for travelers unfamiliar with the area because of the lack of an area map or an index. It covers a relatively small area and is more expensive than most hiking guides, and all the hikes included are day trips. Because of the narrow scope and the uneven distribution of the information, the book is recommended only to experienced hikers already familiar with the area.

Rocky Mountain National Park Trail Guide. Erik Nilsson. Mountain View, CA: World Publications, 1978. 187 pp. pap. $3.95.

Rocky Mountain National Park is one of the most frequently visited areas administered by the National Park Service. The *Rocky Mountain National Park Trail Guide* is the complete hiking and camping guide to the area. It includes a detailed history of the park and a description of its natural history and physical characteristics. The preparatory sections in the book include basic hiking and camping equipment, clothing, first aid information and safety tips, a discussion of mountain etiquette, campsite listings, and park regulations. Also featured are a series of topographic maps that show all the trails listed in the book. The trail entries are divided into areas and include mileage, elevation, trail directions, and descriptions. Appendixes list designated backcountry campsites and principal mountains of the park. There is also a bibliography and a complete index.

Evaluation: The detailed background and preparatory information in the book provide an excellent introduction to the area and hiking in general. The information in these sections is complete and clearly presented. The use of topographic maps in the book may save hikers the expense of buying them, though the ones in the book lack the clarity of those usually available to hikers. The trail directions are fairly clear, but complicated by being interwoven with the trail descriptions. The book serves both as a pretravel reference and as a trail guide. It is a solid introduction to hiking and camping in the mountains of north central Colorado.

Uphill Both Ways: Hiking Colorado's High Country. Robert L. Brown. Caldwell, ID: The Caxton Printers, 1978. 232 pp. pap. $5.95.

The book describes 78 hiking trails in the Colorado Rockies. The introduction outlines the preparation necessary (not an exhaustive list), tells what to do in an emergency (but does not list the location of park offices), gives a short history of the walking habits of U.S. presidents, and time and again stresses common sense. The hikes are divided into eight geographic areas, with each entry including a description of the location, some history, directions to the starting points, and a description of the trails. The author gives an idea of the different characteristics of the hikes and plenty of safety tips. The book is strictly for pretravel reading.

Evaluation: Anyone unfamiliar with the area will have a hard time figuring out where the hikes are from the maps in the book. The author gives no indication how or why the hikes were grouped as they are, or where the hikes are in relation to larger cities in the area. The poor organization makes the book difficult to use. The practical information included is little more than advice. There are many hiking guides to the area that are more usable than this. One that can be recommended, though it covers a smaller area, is *Rocky Mountain National Park Trail Guide* (see above).

Woodall's Colorado Campground Directory. See *Woodall's Campground Directory: State Editions* under United States, Camping.

SCIENCE

Field Guide Series: Northern Colorado Plateau and **Southern Colorado Plateau.** See the review of this series under United States, Science.

Roadside Geology of Colorado. See Roadside Geology series under United States, Science.

Connecticut

See also New England and The East under Regional Guides.

ACCOMMODATIONS AND RESTAURANTS

AAA TourBook: Connecticut. See AAA TourBook series under North America, Accommodations and Restaurants.

Myra Waldo's Restaurant Guide to New York City and Vicinity. See the review of this title under New York City, Accommodations and Restaurants.

ONE-DAY TRIPS

One-Day Adventures by Car. See the review of this title under New York City, One-Day Tours.

OUTDOOR RECREATION

Canoeing: Trips in Connecticut. Pamela Detels and Janet Harris. Chester, CT: The Pequot Press, 1977. 128 pp. pap. $4.95.

This is a guide for the novice. The information pertaining to preparation, technique, and equipment is geared to beginning canoeists, and the trips themselves are all over quiet water, whether on rivers or lakes or along the tidal marsh areas. The 20 trips in the book are divided both geographically and by river. There is a short preparatory section with diagrams on stroking techniques, a checklist of equipment, and advice in general. Each entry includes a hand-drawn map of the trip, where to put in and take out, a description of the area, and natural points of interest. In the back of the book are listings of renters and outfitters, equipment sales, and state camping areas. The book was written to be read before leaving to give a feel for the area and the sport.

Evaluation: The small area covered and the "basic" quality of both the text and the trips themselves limit the book's scope. *Whitewater; Quietwater* (see under The Midwest and the Great Lakes Region, Canoeing and Rafting) is broader in its approach to the subject (with challenging trips), while *Canoeing and Rafting* (see under United States, Canoeing) covers a wider area, but gives the reader much less information. This is a good introduction to canoeing in New England for the beginner. More experienced canoeists looking for more challenging trips in the area with less basic information should use *Canoe Camping Vermont and New Hampshire Rivers* (see under Vermont, Outdoor Recreation).

Fifty Hikes in Connecticut. See the review of *Fifty Hikes in New Hampshire's White Mountains* under New Hampshire, Outdoor Recreation.

Twenty-Five Ski Tours in Connecticut. See *Twenty-Five Ski Tours* series under Regional Guides, New England, Outdoor Recreation.

Hartford

A Guide to Hartford. Alyson B. Henning and Gwynne Maccoll. Chester, CT: The Pequot Press, 1978. 257 pp. pap. $4.95

A Guide to Hartford is a comprehensive city guide directed to travelers on a moderate budget. It introduces the reader to every facet of life in Hartford, Connecticut. Special sections include planned excursions with children, lover, or guest; the neighborhood story; where to park; the city's media; and social services. The practical information includes climate, all-night establishments, education, government contacts, laws, housing, and hot lines. The only shortcoming of the book is the accommodations section. Only nine hotels are listed, and they are all in the same price range.

Evaluation: This is an extremely attractive book. The printing, format, and illustrations make it easy and almost fun to use. The book is more than a guide for visitors. Long-time residents would find it informative and entertaining, as well as a useful item to have close at hand.

Delaware

See also The East, Middle Atlantic, and The South under Regional Guides.

AAA TourBook: Delaware. See AAA TourBook series under North America, Accommodations and Restaurants.

Factory Outlet Shopping Guide: Washington, D.C., Maryland, Virginia, Delaware. See Factory Outlet Shopping Guide series under United States, Shopping.

Woodall's Delaware/Maryland/Virginia/District of Columbia Campground Directory. See *Woodall's Campground Directory: State Editions* under United States, Camping.

District of Columbia

See also The East, Middle Atlantic, and The South under Regional Guides.

COMPREHENSIVE GUIDES

The Best of Washington. Publishers of *Washingtonian* magazine. Washington, DC: Washingtonian Books, 1977. 203 pp. pap. $2.50.

The most outstanding feature of this book is its completeness for both types and numbers of entries. There are over 90 hotels and motels listed, with short descriptions of each. The restaurant section is a treat to read. The restaurants are divided by type (American, Eastern, Middle

European, Beef and Lobster, and so on), and the descriptions give a good idea of what the restaurants are about. The book includes eleven walking and eight driving tours in and around the city. Other features include an intensive history, entertainment and spectator sports, outdoor fun with children, and shopping. The book serves a wide audience, but is of most use to those not severely limited by a tight budget.

Evaluation: The information in the book is handled well, but the large amount often seems unnecessary and leads to duplication (museums may be listed in any of three sections). The book was originally published for the Bicentennial, but a special section in the back updates some information.

Black Guide to Washington. Ron Powell and Bill Cunningham. Washington, DC: Washingtonian Books, 1975. 124 pp. pap. $2.

This specialty guide to the capital city highlights points of interest from black history such as the Frederick Douglass Home, the Snow riots of the nineteenth century, the auction block that stood in what is now Lafayette Park, and the contributions of Benjamin Banneker in the design and building of the city. The book features restaurants, nightspots, shopping, and special tours of the city with entries representing a sample of black-owned establishments in and around Washington. The listings for the different sections are not exhaustive, nor are they meant to be.

Evaluation: The perspective of the city offered from this book is both unique and enlightening. But the book itself is no substitute for a comprehensive guide to Washington. It is not a guide for blacks only; anyone interested in black American history will enjoy the insights the book offers.

ACCOMMODATIONS AND RESTAURANTS

AAA TourBook: District of Columbia. See AAA TourBook series under North America, Accommodations and Restaurants.

Washington, D.C. See Arthur Frommer's City Guide series under United States, Accommodations and Restaurants.

Washington, D.C. on $15 a Day. See Dollars a Day Guides under The World, Accommodations and Restaurants.

CHILDREN

Going Places with Children in Washington. Elizabeth Post Mirel, ed. Washington, DC: Washingtonian Books, 8th ed. 1976. 170 pp. pap. $3.

Going Places with Children is a guide for the entire family. It includes all the information that is needed in a good guide, with an emphasis on keeping children of all ages and adults equally satisfied. Tips are given on the types of activities to look for and what to avoid. There are special sections for foreigners and handicapped travelers, three walking tours at a slightly slower pace with variations on a theme, museums of special interest to children, and sections for parks, sports, neighborhoods, and nearby towns. The restaurant section has over 60 eateries and includes fast food and ice cream parlors. The book is geared to travelers on a moderate budget.

Evaluation: The information is both complete and easily accessible. This is the eighth edition, and it would appear that the authors (all with plenty of firsthand experience) have mastered the subject. The style is lively, clear, and informative. The only area not covered is accommodations. The book would be of great value to any family visiting the capital.

ONE- AND TWO-DAY TRIPS

The One-Day Trip Book. Jane Ockershausen Smith. McLean, VA: EPM Publications, 1978. 182 pp. pap. $4.95

This is a book for anyone wanting to break out of the tourist routine. It offers trips in or near Washington, D.C., for nature lovers, budding historians, families, sports enthusiasts, the handicapped, and just about everyone else. The variety of excursions in the book invite many exciting hours of discovery and adventure. The entries are arranged according to the best season to visit them, but the fact that a trip is listed under spring does not preclude taking it in the autumn. Each entry includes a description, points of interest, a little history, and directions. The trips are listed alphabetically and topically ("parks," "wildlife/animals") at the back of the book. Some of the trips stretch the self-imposed one-day limit (the trip to Assateague Island is close to 200 miles round trip), but this should not be a problem for the truly adventurous.

Evaluation: The two special features of the book are its uniqueness and its utility. The variety of excursions offers something for everyone in a usable format and enjoyable style. The book is a refreshing change from the more touristy tour guides and would be a valuable companion to all visitors to the capital. Because the book includes only sights and adventures, it should be used along with a more inclusive practical guide.

Weekender's Guide. Robert Shosteck. Washington, DC: Potomac Books, 7th ed. 1979. 406 pp. pap. $4.95.

The book was written primarily for residents of the Washington-Baltimore area. It provides hundreds of sights of all kinds, all within 200 miles of the capital. They include farm tours, historical sights, parks, universities, scenic drives, beaches, old homes, museums, nature centers, shops, and art galleries. The book divides the area into ten geographic regions, with special sections for weekend skiing and vineyards. The entries are rarely longer than two paragraphs and include a short description, directions, hours, and the price of admission. Hotels and restaurants are listed (addresses only) at the end of each section.

Evaluation: The number and variety of sights listed in the book are incredible. But the method of organization and the poor maps limit the book's usefulness to travelers familiar with the area. The information in the entries is short and to the point. The book is recommended only for residents or travelers on an extended visit to the area. *The One-Day Trip Book* (see above) provides ample activities and is much easier to use. It lists fewer sights, but includes more information on each.

OUTDOOR RECREATION

Potomac Trail Book. Robert Shosteck. Oakton, VA: Appalachian Books, 2nd ed. 1979. 179 pp. pap. $3.75.

Potomac Trail Book is the complete guide to hiking, bicycling, and short-term camping within 100 miles of Washington, D.C. The 34 camping areas listed include directions, facilities, and addresses and telephone numbers for fee and reservation information. The bicycle tours are divided into short trips (under ten miles) and longer ones (up to sixty miles), each with directions and points of interest. Two-thirds of the book is a listing of short hiking trails, averaging four miles in length. The trail entries combine science, history, and points of interest with practical information and are accompanied by maps. There is a special section on the geology and natural history of the area, with a list of mines and quarries. Other sections include outdoor organization, state and county park offices, hiking etiquette, and woodland pests.

Evaluation: The first edition of the book appeared in 1935. No doubt its longevity is attributable to its usefulness to a wide variety of outdoor enthusiasts. The information is complete and well organized, and the tour directions are easy to follow. Since the maps are small and cluttered, it would be best to acquire those available from the many park offices listed. The book can be used on its own by residents of the Washington, D.C., area, but others, especially first-time visitors interested in both outdoor activities and more traditional sightseeing, should use it along with a sights/accommodations guide to the capital.

Rand McNally National Park Guide. See the review of this title under United States, National Parks.

Woodall's Delaware/Maryland/Virginia/District of Columbia Campground Directory. See *Woodall's Campground Directory: State Editions* under United States, Camping.

SHOPPING

Factory Outlet Shopping Guide: Washington, D.C., Maryland, Virginia, Delaware. See Factory Outlet Shopping Guide series under United States, Shopping.

Florida

See also The South under Regional Guides.

COMPREHENSIVE GUIDES

A Kosoy Travel Guide to Florida and the South. Ted Kosoy. Washington, DC: Acropolis Books, 1979. 253 pp. pap. $6.95.

Kosoy provides basic but wide-ranging coverage of major travel destinations throughout Florida and six other southern states. The book begins with a section on preparation that includes brief information on state tourist offices, pretravel routines, health, packing, traveler's checks, motoring, car rental and drive car services, travel by plane, rail, and bus, annual festivals, travel photography, and weather. This is followed by background and descriptions of sights in each state and the major cities, complete with addresses, directions, dates, and hours of operation. The final section is a listing of hotels and motels by city and state, which includes the address, directions, a brief list of facilities, credit cards accepted, and a price rating of each. A special section is included for Canadian visitors. The book is useful to travelers planning their first visit to the South who are interested in seeing the major tourist sights and areas.

Evaluation: Kosoy guides sacrifice detail for general inclusion; they offer only superficial coverage of a large area. The areas the book describes are all popular tourist spots, and while the practical information included on each is complete, the descriptions and background are short and do little to inspire interest. However, the basic approach in the entries is useful to travelers with little past travel experience; such people will find the information in the guide useful. Experienced travelers looking for unique travel activities or destinations, and those planning an extended visit to one particular area of the South, should look for another guide.

ACCOMMODATIONS AND RESTAURANTS

AAA TourBook: Florida. See AAA TourBook series under North America, Accommodations and Restaurants.

Best Restaurants: Florida. See Best Restaurants series under United States, Accommodations and Restaurants.

OUTDOOR RECREATION

Diver's Guide to Florida and the Florida Keys. Jim Stachowicz. Miami, FL: Windward Publishing, 1976. 64 pp. pap. $2.95.

Florida offers divers some of the most intriguing and easy-to-reach diving areas in which to explore and cavort. A variety of underwater activities are available along the state's 1,800 miles of shoreline. The *Diver's Guide* is a comprehensive overview of diving in the state. It includes information on skin diving for beginners, fresh water diving, night diving, shipwrecks, treasure sites, air stations, hazardous marine life, sharks, and Florida diving laws. Twenty-six different diving sites are described along the Atlantic and Gulf shores, in the Keys, and at a few inland sites. Charts are provided for each area that show reefs, soundings, and underwater points of interest, most of which are also described in the entries. Special sections are included on spear fishing, tropical fish collecting, underwater photography, lobstering, shelling, artifacts, and fossils. The book serves all divers planning a plunge in Florida.

Evaluation: The diving information in the preparatory sections and in the diving area descriptions is complete and clear, though inexperienced divers may need more safety and equipment information than is provided here. The charts, maps, and color photographs add greatly to the book's usefulness and general appearance. The book includes no information on anything other than diving, so that travelers planning to spend some time out of the water may want to use in addition a more complete travel guide to the area. But on its own, the *Diver's Guide* is the total guide to underwater trips in and around Florida.

Florida by Paddle and Pack. Mike Toner and Pat Toner. Miami, FL: Banyan Books, 1979. 144 pp. pap. $5.95.

Florida by Paddle and Pack is divided into three distinct parts. The first of these covers the basics of being out-of-doors in Florida. Weather, mosquitoes, other insects, snakes, alligators, poisonous plants, and other practicalities are included. The second section is for canoeists. Very basic information is provided for beginners, including equipment, paddling strokes, safety, and tides. Twenty-eight canoe trips are mapped and described by length of river, time required, access, and source of further information. Excellent general one-page descriptions of the trips are provided. The third section is for hikers, and, similar to the canoe trips, contains one-page descriptions with maps, time required, lengths of trails, and reference locations.

Evaluation: This excellent book can serve as the perfect way to introduce people to nonurban Florida. Written for those without extensive experience, all the information needed is efficiently provided for pretravel reading. For travelers who want to see Florida as it was before development, or who want to get away from the urban sprawl, this hiking and canoeing guide is highly recommended.

Woodall's Florida Campground Directory. See *Woodall's Campground Directory: State Editions* under United States, Camping.

SCIENCE

Field Guide Series: Southern Florida. See the review of this series under United States, Science.

Everglades

The Everglades: Exploring the Unknown. Christopher Linn. Mahwah, NJ: Troll Associates, 1976. 32 pp. pap. $2.50.

The Everglades: Exploring the Unknown contains 32 pages of captioned color photographs of outdoor scenes in southern Florida. It takes the reader on an imaginary journey through the Everglades, viewing its wildlife in natural settings. A trip through the Everglades swamps and forests is compared to a journey through the past, to an area where modern man is still only a visitor. The book is useful only as pretravel reading to provide a feel for the area; its practical travel information is severely limited.

Evaluation: The photographs are beautiful and inviting, showing scenes from a world that sadly seems very remote from the gray-on-gray of city life. However, there is very little in the book other than the photographs. It is useful only as pretravel reading for travelers planning their first visit to the area. On the road, more comprehensive travel information is required.

Sanibel and Captiva

The Firestone/Morse Guide to Florida's Enchanting Islands—Sanibel and Captiva. Linda Firestone and Whit Morse. Richmond, VA: Good Life Publishers, 1978. 123 pp. pap. $3.95.

The islands in the title lie in the Gulf, a few miles off Florida's southwestern coast, and until recent years they have been relatively untouched by the development that has blanketed much of the state. The main pleasures of the islands are their wildlife and scenic beaches. *Florida's Enchanting Islands* describes the natural and social history of the islands and their present physical characteristics. It includes practical travel information on accommodations and restaurants, the weather, outdoor activities, food stores and other shops, bird and nature tours, entertainment, services, and emergencies. Special sections include annual and ongoing activities. A multicolored shell identification key, guide to native foods, and complete fishing information are also given.

Evaluation: The Firestone/Morse team seems to specialize in writing complete travel guides to small areas of particular interest, and their style and organizational formula work extremely well for these areas. The book includes a complete range of practical information on all aspects of travel on the islands, presented clearly and in a fairly easy-to-find manner. The entries show the strong feelings the authors have for the wildlife of the area and their deep concern for its preservation. The book is a comprehensive and very serviceable guide to the islands for all visitors, young and old, rich and poor, with years of travel or experiencing their first trip. It is a key to a relatively uncrowded vacation in the sun.

Georgia

See also The East and The South under Regional Guides.

AAA TourBook: Georgia. See AAA TourBook series under North America, Accommodations and Restaurants.

Hawaii

See also The West under Regional Guides.

COMPREHENSIVE GUIDES

Hawaii A to Z. See A to Z World Travel Guides under The World, Comprehensive Guides.

Hawaii: A Woman's Guide. Shirley Van Campen. Wheaton, IL: Merton House Publishing Co., 1979. 161 pp. pap. $5.95.

Hawaii: A Woman's Guide was written for women traveling to the islands for the first time, either alone or accompanied, on a moderate to high budget, though some bargains are listed. It includes the usual sections on preparation, transportation, climate, shopping, accommodations, restaurants, and sightseeing tours, with special sections on singles tours, singles clubs, and traveling alone and a full chapter devoted to medicine. Each chapter has tips on avoiding problems and offers addresses for further information. The book serves best as pretravel reading.

Evaluation: The book compares favorably with other guides to the islands for completeness of information, style, and variety of entries. What makes it of particular interest to women is more than just the addition of a few special sections. The recurring theme throughout the entries is providing enjoyable and safe opportunities to meet men. For many women, this may still be a prime criterion for a thoroughly successful vacation.

Hidden Hawaii: The Adventurer's Guide. Ray Rigert. Berkeley, CA: And/Or Press, 1979. 369 pp. pap. $8.95.

The purpose of the book is to make possible a low-cost vacation in paradise. The secret to achieving this is to get away from the well-worn tourist paths and into the secluded realms of the back country. This does not, however, necessarily preclude staying in hotels, traveling by car, and eating in restaurants. The author points out many available low-cost options and includes, for the sake of completeness, some sights and activities that are strictly touristy. The broad scope and variety of entries are two of the book's major features. Special sections cover drugs, whale watching, shell hunting, and gathering free fruit and seafood. There is also a special section for handicapped travelers. The book is primarily for young travelers on a low to moderate budget looking for a variety of outdoor sights and adventures.

Evaluation: The book's 369 pages are loaded with information, but, as the author states, the longer the stay, the cheaper it will be. Travelers who will be spending a week or less on the islands or who plan to stick with the more traditional tourist activities would be better off with a smaller, easier-to-use, and less-expensive guide. But for those who plan to head for the hills, forget the world, and soak up nature, this is the book.

The Maverick Guide to Hawaii. Robert W. Bone. Gretna, LA: The Pelican Publishing Co., 1979. 440 pp. pap. $7.95.

The Maverick Guide to Hawaii was written for both visitors and newcomers to the state. It is safe to say no other guidebook to the islands has more information on a wider range of topics. It covers preparation, transportation to and on the islands, a calendar of events, language, history, culture, social and economic conditions, a great number of sights, local flavor, land and water sports, parks, shopping, and nightlife. There is a special section on toll-free numbers and a complete index. The book best serves travelers on extended visits with moderate and above-average budgets. It should be read while planning a trip and may also be used as a reference on the road.

Evaluation: The major problem of the book is also the major feature—the huge amount of information may be more than some will need. But it is handled very well, being complete and usually easy to find. What truly makes the book worthwhile is that it is so much fun to read. The author writes in a lively and informative style that gets the reader involved in the subject. As a complete introduction to the state, no guide can match it.

ACCOMMODATIONS AND RESTAURANTS

AAA TourBook: Hawaii. See AAA TourBook series under North America, Accommodations and Restaurants.

Hawaii on $20 a Day. See Dollars a Day Guides under the World, Accommodations and Restaurants.

BEACHES

The Beaches of Maui County. John R. K. Clark. Honolulu, HI: The University Press of Hawaii, 1980. 161 pp. pap. $7.95.

This beach book is much more than a guide to beaches. The main body of the text features beach descriptions, with notes on safety, sand type, and access, but even more space is given to the history and stories relating to each beach, the background of its name, and the activities historically associated with it. Every beach on the islands of Maui, Molokai, Lanai, Kahoolawe, and Molokini is covered in a clockwise direction around each island. Excellent maps, both of the islands and individual beach areas, are found throughout the book. The book has several helpful photographs as well. Clear and easy-to-read tables indicate possible beach activities, public facilities, beach composition (sand, rock, and so on), and access. A section on water safety is included.

Evaluation: Many of the histories and stories associated with the beaches have never appeared in print before, making this book a unique offering to the traveler or resident. The total coverage of every beach assures that the user of this book will be well informed about all beach activities, including swimming, surfing, body surfing, and beachcombing. The safety suggestions are sound, reflecting the former lifeguard activities of the author. This book is all that is needed for the beach fan on the five islands included, if a hotel has already been secured. For those who will spend some time off the beach, an additional, more general-purpose guide is needed.

The Beaches of O'Ahu. John R. K. Clark. Honolulu, HI: The University Press of Hawaii, 1977. 193 pp. pap. $4.95.

The purpose of the book is to provide practical, historical, and emergency information on some of the most famous vacation beaches in the world. There is a 14-page general information section that describes particular characteristics of the surf and shoreline, snorkeling equipment, flotation gear, wave-riding sports, and emergency facilities. One hundred forty-two beaches and shoreline parks are included in the entries, which cover facilities, water activities, water conditions, public access, a history and description of the beach, and nearby attractions. The book is useful both as pretravel reading and on the road.

Evaluation: No other guide has as much practical and emergency information on the beaches as this. It is complete, organized well, and very easy to use. The maps are some of the best to be found in any specialty guide. When used with a sights/accommodations guide (for those spending some time off the beaches), it can be a valuable companion for beach bums of all ages and budgets.

BICYCLE TOURING

Bicycler's Guide to Hawaii. Linda McComb Rathbun. Hilo, HI: The Petroglyph Press, 1976. 62 pp. pap. $3.25.

The purpose of the book is to provide all the necessary information for bicycling on the islands for the novice and expert. Bicycling is one method of transportation few travelers consider when planning a trip to Hawaii, but the author shows that it can save both time and aggravation when the cyclist is properly prepared. The book includes pretravel exercise, flying your bicycle and yourself to the islands, repairs, packing, cycling itineraries, seasonal weather variations, and camping on each of the islands. Special sections include bicycling with children and renting a bicycle (which the author does not recommend). There is also a long and varied reading list and many addresses for further information. The book should be used as pretravel reading and as a reference on the road, although maps would have to be added.

Evaluation: A major feature of the book is the completeness and accessibility of the preparatory information. Few bicycling guides come close to matching the amount of practical information found in this short book. However, its scope is very narrow, with little information other than on bicycling and camping. Bicyclists with a little more money to spend may also wish to use a more detailed sights/accommodations guide along with it. But alone or paired, the book is a valuable companion to anyone bicycling on the islands.

PHOTOGRAPHY

Hawaiian Islands Traveler's Guide Series. Honolulu, HI: The Oriental Publishing Co. (dist. by ISBS), 1978. 40-100 pp. pap. $3.-$5.50.

The most striking feature of the series is the color photography—pages and pages of beautiful scenes around the islands. Between the photographs are listings of sights (no addresses, phone numbers, or hours), parks, beaches, camping, outdoor activities, weather, and Hawaiian phrases. Each of the books included in the series ends with five or six detailed maps.

Evaluation: The books in this series are not practical tour guides. The information included is sketchy and incomplete, which makes it seem that its inclusion is meant only to complement the photographs, instead of the other way round. Because the books are more pictorial essays than practical guides, they must be used along with other, more inclusive guides on the trip. However, they make excellent souvenirs.

Included in the series: *Big Island Traveler's Guide*, by Bill Gleasner and Diana Gleasner; *Hawaiian Gardens*, by Bill Gleasner and Diana Gleasner; *Hawaiian Scenes*, by Mark David Merlin; *Kauai Traveler's Guide*, by Bill Gleasner and Diana Gleasner; *Maui, Lanai, Molokai Traveler's Guide*, by Bill Gleasner and Diana Gleasner; *Oahu Environments*, by Joseph Morgan and John Street; *Oahu Traveler's Guide*, by Bill Gleasner and Diana Gleasner.

Sunset Pictorial Series: Beautiful Hawaii. See Sunset Pictorial series under United States, Pretravel Reading.

Honolulu and Oahu

A Native's Guide to Honolulu and the Island of Oahu. George S. Kanahele. Honolulu, HI: Topgallant Publishing Co., 1976. 193 pp. pap. $3.

This is the most basic guide to sights and activities on the most-visited island of the Hawaiian chain. It is geared to travelers on their first visit and emphasizes the major tourist routine. The book includes a short preparatory section, history from a native's point of view, three walking and two driving tours, and a directory of information. Hotels and restaurants are listed with name, address, phone, and price rating only. The book is recommended as pretravel reading, particularly for foreign visitors on a moderate budget whose stay in Hawaii will be limited to the island of Oahu.

Evaluation: The information on the sights and activities is both basic and complete. The book is organized well and is easy to use, but the emphasis on touristy activities and the skeletal hotel/restaurant listings limit its usefulness to those looking for the picture-postcard Hawaii of luaus, leis, and grass shacks. It is a good guide, when supplemented with more accommodations information, for the island's typical visitor.

Idaho

See also Rocky Mountains under Regional Guides.

AAA TourBook: Idaho. See AAA TourBook series under North America, Accommodations and Restaurants.

Winery Tours in Oregon, Washington, Idaho, and British Columbia. See the review of this title under Regional Guides, Pacific Coast, Wine Tours.

Woodall's Idaho/Oregon/Washington Campground Directory. See *Woodall's Campground Directory: State Editions* under United States, Camping.

Illinois

See also The Midwest under Regional Guides.

AAA TourBook: Illinois. See AAA TourBook series under North America, Accommodations and Restaurants.

Woodall's Illinois/Indiana Campground Directory. See *Woodall's Campground Directory: State Editions* under United States, Camping.

Chicago

RESTAURANTS

Best Restaurants: Chicago. See Best Restaurants series under United States, Accommodations and Restaurants.

ENTERTAINMENT

Dr. Night Life's Chicago: An Intimate and Informative Guide to the City's Best Entertainment. Rick Kogan. Chicago, IL: Chicago Review Press, 1979. 156 pp. pap. $6.95.

Dr. Night Life is a semimythical character who is frequently seen in Chicago's more jumping nighttime establishments. People who should know have called him one of the few qualified experts on the city's late-night entertainment. *Dr. Night Life's Chicago* describes a variety of indoor activities, most of which are centered around the consumption of alcohol. The book begins with a foreword that discusses the history of drink in Chicago, followed by an introduction to the good doctor. The bars, clubs, dance halls, and restaurants are divided both by area and by specialty, with addresses, telephone numbers, descriptions, and an overall rating. Practical information on the establishments is listed at the back of the book and includes hours, dress, price range, and major attractions. Each is also indexed by area.

Evaluation: Although there is a definite emphasis on the city's bars, the book includes entries on a variety of establishments, such as some restaurants, discos, places for teens, and polka halls. This broadens the audience slightly, but the book is still most useful to residents and frequent visitors with a regular thirst. The establishments are arranged in a haphazard way, which makes the book difficult to use. Some establishments are listed by area, some by type, and some are grouped together in a leftover "Party Down" section. The descriptions of the bars and clubs are clear and lively, with a directness and honesty that is refreshing and entertaining. Except for the poor organization, the book is an excellent guide to Chicago late-night entertainment.

The Great Chicago Bar and Saloon Guide. Dennis B. McCarthy. Chicago, IL: Chicago Review Press, 1978. 158 pp. pap. $3.25.

This guide, which describes over 200 of the "best" Chicago bars and saloons, shows that the city that works is also the city that drinks. How the author found it possible to limit himself to 200 establishments is unknown, though it is certain that his research was pleasurable. The bars are arranged alphabetically and indexed by area and by character (dives, ethnic bars, elegant, food, music, and so on). Each entry includes the name, address, telephone, and proprietor, a description of the bar, the prices for domestic and imported beer and the average mixed drink, games, cocktail hours, and music. The descriptions include references to food served, the neighborhood, the atmosphere of the bar, and sometimes a glimpse of its history. The book is useful to all serious drinkers who, for whatever reason, find themselves in Chicago.

Evaluation: The information on the bars is complete and accessible, and their descriptions all give a clear picture of what each bar is like. The book is most useful to Chicago residents and frequent visitors to the city. Its narrow scope makes it necessary for travelers spending some time outside of the bars to use in addition a more comprehensive Chicago guide. For visitors more interested in entertainment than in drinking, *Dr. Night Life's Chicago* (see above) would be more suitable. However, *The Great Chicago Bar and Saloon Guide* is the most complete and entertaining guide to the city's watering holes.

SIGHTSEEING

Chicago on Foot: Walking Tours of Chicago's Architecture. Ira J. Bach. Chicago, IL: Rand McNally & Co., 1977. 391 pp. $12.50; pap. $7.95.

Few American cities can boast of the variety of architectural trends to be found in Chicago. The city could almost be called the world's largest architectural museum, though curators would be difficult to find. *Chicago on Foot* describes the history and architecture of the city through a series of 32 walking tours, which combine maps, text, photographs, and illustrations to tell the stories of the city's buildings. The walks are arranged from the downtown area to the outlying districts and include walking time and directions by bus, train, and car to the starting point, along with the names and addresses of the many buildings described and their architects. Maps are provided for each walk that show the route and the locations of the buildings described. A symbol is used to denote buildings officially designated as architectural or historical landmarks.

Evaluation: The descriptions of the buildings in the entries are complete enough to give a solid impression of the site and simple enough to be understood and appreciated by travelers with little architectural background. The amount of information and the large area covered by the walks may be more than many travelers would want, but they serve to make the book an excellent reference to architecture throughout Chicago for students and residents of the city as well as visitors. The many large photographs and illustrations (including floor plans of many buildings) complement the text well. The book presents a unique perspective on the city and opens it to travelers as few other city guides can.

Norman Mark's Chicago: Walking, Bicycling and Driving Tours of the City. Norman Mark. Chicago, IL: Chicago Review Press, 1977. 225 pp. pap. $6.95.

The tours in *Norman Mark's Chicago* cover the city from top to bottom, with colorful stories, historic insights, and an unbridled sense of humor that brings the city's sights and inhabitants to life. The first 14 entries are walking tours, most of which are located near the lakeshore. Each tour includes a hand-drawn map that shows the route and the location of particular points of interest. The text of the tours gives the time necessary to complete the walks, directions by bus and car to the starting points, and descriptions and histories of the different sights. Margin headings are used to facilitate finding the description of a particular building or area. One bicycle tour is included along the lakefront; it includes information on bicycle rentals. The three driving tours have the same type of information as the walks, but the directions are more difficult to follow. An interesting feature, and one that shows much of the character of the city, is the six "Pub Crawls," with plenty of information on the city's nightlife.

Evaluation: Not the buildings, not the people, not the histories, but the city itself is the star of the tours. The book introduces the readers to Chicago in all its moods—laughing, crying, pitiful, proud, timid, and arrogant. No city can compare with it, and no guide mirrors the city as clearly as this. The descriptions and histories in the text are so entertaining that after reading them, some may consider it unnecessary to take the walks (and rides) at all. But that would be a shame. Few cities can be enjoyed like Chicago, and few books open the city to strangers like this one.

Indiana

See also The Midwest under Regional Guides.

ACCOMMODATIONS AND RESTAURANTS

AAA TourBook: Indiana. See AAA TourBook series under North America, Accommodations and Restaurants.

THE OUTDOORS

Dune Country: A Guide for Hikers and Naturalists. Glenda Daniel. Chicago, IL: The Swallow Press, 1977. 167 pp. pap. $4.95.

The book is a complete description and history of the dunes area in the shadow of Gary, Indiana. The emphasis of the book, as the title implies, is on nature. The formation and behavior of the dunes are explained and the plant and wildlife of the area are described in detail. Many different hikes are outlined at the back of the book, and the appendixes list the plants by habitat. The author also includes a long reading list. The subject of the book limits its usefulness to those with more than a passing interest in the natural sciences.

Evaluation: The text reads well for the number of botanical references it contains. The accompanying illustrations are beautifully done, and the maps are large and legible. It is hard to believe that residents of the upper Midwest could find an area so full of natural vitality in their own backyard. *Dune Country* invites hours of exploration in a unique natural environment.

Field Guide Series: Southern Ohio, Indiana, and Northern Kentucky. See the review of this series under United States, Science.

Woodall's Illinois/Indiana Campground Directory. See *Woodall's Campground Directory: State Editions* under United States, Camping.

Iowa

See also The Midwest under Regional Guides.

AAA TourBook: Iowa. See AAA TourBook series under North America, Accommodations and Restaurants.

Kansas

See also The Midwest under Regional Guides.

AAA TourBook: Kansas. See AAA TourBook series under North America, Accommodations and Restaurants.

Kentucky

See also The South under Regional Guides.

AAA TourBook: Kentucky. See AAA TourBook series under North America, Accommodations and Restaurants.

Field Guide Series: Southern Ohio, Indiana, and Northern Kentucky. See Field Guide series under United States, Science.

Woodall's Kentucky/Tennessee Campground Directory. See *Woodall's Campground Directory: State Editions* under United States, Camping.

Louisiana

See also The South under Regional Guides.

ACCOMMODATIONS AND RESTAURANTS

AAA TourBook: Louisiana. See AAA TourBook series under North America, Accommodations and Restaurants.

SIGHTSEEING

Pelican Guide to Gardens of Louisiana. Joyce Yeldell LeBlanc. Gretna, LA: Pelican Publishing Co. 1974. 64 pp. pap. $2.95.

Five gardens are described in detail in this book. Each entry emphasizes the history of the garden and the surrounding buildings and includes descriptions of seasonal changes and points of interest in the area. The entries are accompanied by maps and beautiful color photographs. In a special section at the back, brief descriptions of 15 other gardens in the state are given, along with the story of Louisiana gardens of the past.

Evaluation: The book is a garden-lover's delight. The information is complete, the descriptions are colorful, and the histories are entertaining. Because of the narrow scope of the book, it would be best to use it as a complement to a more general guide.

Pelican Guide to Plantation Homes of Louisiana. Nancy Harris Calhoun and James Calhoun. Gretna, LA: Pelican Publishing Co., 4th ed. 1977. 128 pp. pap. $2.95.

The book is a series of 19 car tours featuring old homes in Louisiana. That's it. No introduction, no conclusion, one map, and no directions with the tours. A typical entry is the name of the home, a paragraph about its history or architecture (rarely both), the current owner, the hours, and the address. None of the 240 entries is a full page, and most of the homes listed are private residences. The book is guaranteed to disappoint both historians and architecture enthusiasts. It is a specialty guide without an audience.

Evaluation: The one saving feature of the book is that the homes listed are probably worth seeing. But the lack of information and organization makes the book very difficult to use. One is hard pressed to describe an audience who might be pleased with this book.

New Orleans

PRETRAVEL READING

Frenchmen, Desire, Good Children, and Other Streets of New Orleans. John Churchill Chase. New York: Collier Books, Macmillan Publishing Co., 3rd ed. 1979. 272 pp. pap. $5.95.

The history of New Orleans and the stories behind the naming of its streets is a simple explanation of what is in the book, but in reality it is much more than that. Few American cities have had as colorful a past as New Orleans, and the stories behind its founding and development are delightfully reproduced in this guide. The author's knowledge and love of the city are clearly evident in the informative and entertaining entries. The book describes the journeys of the first European explorers in the area, the Native Americans they encountered, the founding of the city during the reign of Louis XIV, its growing pains, the famous battle in 1815, and other developments of interest to the present. Three new chapters have been added to the third edition, which update some of the material. Many illustrations highlight the text, and a complete index is included at the back of the book.

Evaluation: Although no practical travel information is included in the book, it is still a valuable and entertaining pretravel reference for visitors interested in the city's history and development. The stories of the area's past inhabitants and how they came together to fashion a city are told by a master storyteller who combines his knowledge of the city with a lively sense of humor. The result is a thoroughly enjoyable and remarkably informative book. For travelers planning a trip to New Orleans or those whose travels will be limited to their own imagination, no other guide brings the city's history to life as well as this one.

Pelican Guide to New Orleans. Thomas K. Griffin. Gretna, LA: Pelican Publishing Co., 3rd ed. 1978. 160 pp. pap. $3.95.

The book is directed primarily to travelers without budget restrictions. It is mostly a history and description of the city and includes sections on the river, Mardi Gras, entertainment, the French Quarter, sports, restaurants, and nightlife. The entries suggest only the "best" (most expensive), giving the reader very little choice in price range. Hotels and transportation around the city are untouched. The restaurants are not listed as they usually appear in a guide—there is no break in the text; the entry for one flows into the next with no warning.

Evaluation: The book has little apparent organization. Because of the unbroken text, the emphasis on history and descriptions, and the difficulty in finding any particular piece of information, it is best to read it before making the trip. The style of the book is smooth and fun, but it is of little use for most visitors. It may be useful as pretravel reading, as a description of vacation possibilities in the city.

Maine

See also The East and New England under Regional Guides.

ACCOMMODATIONS AND RESTAURANTS

AAA TourBook: Maine. See AAA TourBook series under North America, Accommodations and Restaurants.

THE OUTDOORS

Fifty Hikes in Maine. See *Fifty Hikes in New Hampshire's White Mountains* under New Hampshire, Outdoor Recreation.

Short Walks along the Maine Coast. Ruth Sadlier and Paul Sadlier. Chester, CT: The Pequot Press, 1977. 131 pp. pap. $3.50.

Thirty-three walks are included, ranging from less than a half mile to just under three miles. The entries are mostly descriptions of the natural environment and the location of the best views of the ocean. The book highlights the wildlife preserves along the coast and the plant life of the area. It contains little history or practical information.

Evaluation: The book is unpretentious. It has a simple subject, treated simply. The directions are clear and the maps are easy to read. The lack of practical information (accommodations, restaurants, and so on) suggests that the book's best use is as a complement to another, more inclusive guide. But there is little in the entries themselves (other than descriptions) that could not be found at a state or national park office. The authors write in a conversational style that tends to make one circuit indistinguishable from the next.

Maryland

See also The East, Middle Atlantic, and The South under Regional Guides.

ACCOMMODATIONS AND RESTAURANTS

AAA TourBook: Maryland. See AAA TourBook series under North America, Accommodations and Restaurants.

Country Inns of Maryland, Virginia, and West Virginia. Lewis Perdue. Washington, DC: Washingtonian Books, rev. 1978. 177 pp. $7.95; pap. $4.95.

It seems no author of a guide to country inns has a clear-cut definition of what an inn is. Some insist that both meals and lodging be provided, while others have a broader definition and will be satisfied with one or the other. In this book the author includes a variety of inns in the area, some with both rooms and meals, and some with either rooms or meals. Eighty inns are listed in northern and eastern Virginia, Maryland, and West Virginia. Each entry includes a drawing of the inn, its address and telephone, facilities, reservations, dress, and credit cards accepted. All the inns in the book are in the moderate to high price range. Because reservations are almost always required, it is best to use the book while planning your trip.

Evaluation: The book includes more inns in a smaller area than either the Burt Franklin or 101 Productions Country Inns series (see under United States, Accommodations and Restaurants, and under Regional Guides, The South and The West) and has livelier entries, more nearby attractions, and more of an emphasis on food, though the history and appearance of the inns is not neglected. The information is complete and easy to find. The book is as much an introduction to the area as a guide to its inns. It is most useful when used with a sights/transportation guide, such as the AAA TourBook series (see under North America, Accommodations and Restaurants) or one of the oil company guides, such as the *Mobil Travel Guide* (see under United States, Accommodations and Restaurants).

CAMPING

Woodall's Delaware Maryland/Virginia/District of Columbia Campground Directory. See *Woodall's Campground Directory: State Editions* under United States, Camping.

HISTORIC TOURS

Maryland: A New Guide to the Old Line State. Edward C. Papenfuse et al., eds. Baltimore, MD: Johns Hopkins University Press (dist. in the U.K. by I.B.E.G.), 1976. 463 pp. $16 (£12; pap. £3.75).

It is a good bet that no book contains more information about the state of Maryland than this. Over 6,500 miles of roads have been covered (some recovered) in the 49 tours it describes. The book opens with a short history of tour guides in general, with special entries from eighteenth- and nineteenth-century guides. This is followed by a short section of miscellaneous facts about the state. The emphasis of the tours themselves is on history, in which the area abounds. Interspersed throughout the tour directions are numerous short essays on various topics, which, though they attempt to enliven the text, fail to do so.

Evaluation: The biggest problem with the book is the difficulty in finding the information one is looking for. Any book this size needs solid organization to facilitate its usage. This book seems to be randomly organized. There is little break in the text, very small print, and few directions on how to use the book. Add to this the lack of any practical information (weather, shopping, emergencies) and what you have is 463 interesting but difficult-to-use pages that do not meet the traveler's needs.

SHOPPING

Factory Outlet Shopping Guide: Washington, D.C., Maryland, Virginia, Delaware. See Factory Outlet Shopping Guide series under United States, Shopping.

Massachusetts

See also The East and New England under Regional Guides

ACCOMMODATIONS AND RESTAURANTS

AAA TourBook: Massachusetts. See AAA TourBook series under North America, Accommodations and Restaurants.

OUTDOOR RECREATION

Fifty Hikes in Massachusetts. See *Fifty Hikes in New Hampshire's White Mountains* under New Hampshire, Outdoor Recreation.

The Launching Ramp Guide. Marine Educational Services. Boston, MA: Herman Publishing, 1975. 224 pp. pap. $5.95.

The book is a full description of over 150 public boat-launching sites along the coast of Massachusetts. The entry for each site includes its location, how to find it, the size and condition of the ramp, the fee, the hours of operation, parking, fuel, repairs, bait and tackle, access to a telephone, and comments on such things as tides, low clearances, and neighbors. There are a number of maps: street maps, boat maps, maps of small areas and large. Each is large and easy to read. The different launching sites are listed both geographically and alphabetically by town.

Evaluation: The book is incredibly complete, but for a very small area. The information is clear and accessible, with nearly every possible contingency planned for. The authors have done a great service for the trailer boating public, one that would be appreciated in many other parts of the country.

Short Bike Rides on Cape Cod, Nantucket, and the Vineyard. Jane Griffith and Edwin Mullen. Chester, CT: The Pequot Press, 1977. 131 pp. pap. $2.95.

The Cape Cod area is one of the major summer tourist centers along the east coast. One way of avoiding the city-sized traffic jams is to see the sights by bicycle. *Short Bike Rides* lists 30 bicycle tours in the area that range from six to twenty-six miles and are meant to be more relaxing than challenging. Each entry includes distance, time, terrain, the quality of the road surface, points of interest, and directions to the starting point. The ride directions are first listed step by step and are then repeated in the text. A brief discussion of safety is included, as well as an equipment checklist, but there is no information on repair shops, bicycle rentals, or other methods of transporting a bicycle.

Evaluation: The narrow scope of the book points to its best use as a supplement to a more inclusive guide to the area. The practical information in the book is minimal. The tour entries emphasize directions that are easy to follow and points of interest that seem less than interesting. The maps for each circuit are small and difficult to read. Because of the small area covered, the incompleteness of the information, and the lack of variety in the different rides, it is difficult to recommend the book to anyone but the most leisurely of cyclists. Experienced riders would be just as well off with no guide at all.

Twenty-Five Ski Tours in Western Massachusetts. See *Twenty-Five Ski Tours* series under Regional Guides, New England, Outdoor Recreation.

Boston

Boston. See Arthur Frommer's City Guide series under United States, Accommodations and Restaurants.

All about the Boston Harbor Islands. Emily Kales and David Kales. Boston, MA: Herman Publishing Co., 1976. 120 pp. pap. $5.95.

The book describes the islands that dot the Boston harbor. Each island's history and character are highlighted in the entries, and recreational facilities and directions are included. Much of the islands' recent history is a story of "neglect and misuse." The authors tell of the ravages of the past and the processes at work to restore the area. Interspersed throughout are short essays on a variety of topics pertaining to the islands, such as "The Life and Death of a Salt Marsh," "Island Flora," and "The Short Happy Life of a Clam." Other sections include harbor cruises, bus tours, boat launching sites, boat rentals, a fishing guide, and swimming areas—strictly outdoor activities.

Evaluation: The book features nearly every facet of life on and around the islands. The information is complete without being weighty. The maps in the book are only fair, but addresses are given of park services in the area where better maps are available. Both visitors and residents will find this book an entertaining and enlightening book.

Michigan

See also The Midwest under Regional Guides.

COMPREHENSIVE GUIDES

Rand McNally Guide to Michigan. Chicago, IL: Rand McNally & Co., 1979. 154 pp. pap. $4.95.

The *Rand McNally Guide to Michigan* provides travelers with information on what to see and do, where to eat, stay, and camp in Michigan, and many other specific features such as skiing, fishing, and hunting. The guide is organized into four regions, with a brief section on the part of Ontario, Canada, adjacent to the United States. Each section contains a brief introduction with major attractions followed by points of interest and an alphabetical listing of sights, museums, and so on. All entries have highway directions and map coordinates for easy location on the various maps throughout this guide. Accommodations and restaurant listings, with complete information, including prices, are also provided.

Evaluation: Rand McNally's guide offers the traveler a good, wide-ranging basis for traveling through Michigan. Many of the essential aspects of traveling are covered. Accommodations, restaurants, and sights are geared to the vacationing family, but information is complete and versatile enough for any traveler in Michigan.

ACCOMMODATIONS AND RESTAURANTS

AAA TourBook: Michigan. See AAA TourBook series under North America, Accommodations and Restaurants.

Dining and Delights. Neil E. Rand. Madison, WI: The Coda Press, 2nd ed. 1980. 518 pp. pap. $6.95. Revised annually.

Restaurants, sights, and activities in five cities in southern (lower) Michigan are described in *Dining and Delights.* The entries for each city are mostly restaurant menus and descriptions, arranged alphabetically, covering all price ranges. The restaurants are indexed by type and location, and all are shown on large, clear maps. Each section begins with short background information on the city and includes references to the development of its restaurant industry. Other sections for each city include information sources, nightlife, theater, concerts, dance, annual events, sights, shopping, parks and recreation, sports, and descriptions of particular areas in each city. Special sections include descriptions of the different types of foods and wines in the restaurants, the Ann Arbor Art Fairs, jazz in Detroit, day trips to Ohio, Ontario, and other parts of Michigan, plus interviews with single residents in each city about where the "action" is. Eleven pages of money-saving coupons are included at the back of the book.

Evaluation: The book's emphasis on restaurants and nightlife suggests that it is best used by young and young-at-heart travelers on moderate and above-average budgets. It was written primarily for residents of the area, but it also serves travelers well when supplemented with accommodations and transportation information. The book is well organized and presented clearly, with a complete index and maps that make it easy to locate the restaurants described. The wide range of sights and activities included, especially in the Ann Arbor and Detroit sections, guarantees something for almost every interest. The book is an excellent introduction to the cultural and social life of the area.

Meet, Eat, and Enjoy Greater Detroit. Mary Conway and Harry Satchwell. Detroit, MI: J. Well. 296 pp. $7.95. Revised annually.

Meet, Eat, and Enjoy Greater Detroit is the complete dining guide to southeastern Michigan. Eating experiences of every kind are described, and 200 menus are included. The introductory sections discuss how the restaurants were selected, dress codes, and dining tips, and there is a long description and listing of ethnic restaurants and special dining in the area (cafeterias, ice cream, health-food, pizza, and so on). The entries in these sections list addresses, telephone numbers, hours, and brief descriptions only. Most of the restaurants (those for which menus are included) are arranged alphabetically, and their locations are shown on a series of maps at the back of the book. Each entry includes complete practical information and a short description of the restaurant and its specialties, along with the menus. Special sections include current "ins" and "outs" on the restaurant trail, cider mills, dancing and entertainment, markets, ethnic festivals, parks and picnics, restaurants open very early, very late, and on Sundays, and a long list of special recipes.

Evaluation: Although the book was intended for Detroit-area residents, travelers will find it an excellent way to discover some of the unique charms of a city that many people who should know better insist is charmless. The restaurant information is up-to-date, complete, and clear, and the many special sections add greatly to the book's practical and enjoyment value. When used along with a guide that includes complete accommodations, transportation, and practical information, the book can be the beginning of an enjoyable vacation in a city that many, unfortunately, never expect to enjoy.

CAMPING

Woodall's Michigan Campground Directory. See *Woodall's Campground Directory: State Editions* under United States, Camping.

SCIENCE

Michigan: Heart of the Great Lakes. Richard A. Santer. Dubuque, IA: Kendall/Hunt Publishing Co., 1977. 364 pp. pap. $9.95.

Michigan's geography, geology, ecology, and history are described in detail in *Michigan: Heart of the Great Lakes.* The book resembles a textbook more than a travel guide, but the background information it includes on the state cannot be found elsewhere. Sections are included on the American Indian culture before and after contact with whites, the French explorers and colonists, the Spanish in Michigan, the political geography of the state, mining sites, the effect of glaciers, lumber resources, population and settlement, a description of fourteen development areas, the state's economic history, transportation and communication systems, and environmental management. Many maps, photographs, and illustrations are included in the book, along with a source list and a complete index.

Evaluation: Although the practical travel information in the book is severely limited, the text does offer detailed background information on the state that would not otherwise be available to travelers. There is a definite emphasis on science in the entries, but the information is presented in a way that is clear even to those with little science background. Many travelers will find the information in another more practical guide (such as The Great Lakes Guidebook series; see under Regional Guides) much more useful on the road, but those looking for complete historic and geographic background on the state will find it in this guide.

Minnesota

See also The Midwest under Regional Guides.

ACCOMMODATIONS AND RESTAURANTS

AAA TourBook: Minnesota. See AAA TourBook series under North America, Accommodations and Restaurants.

OUTDOOR ACTIVITIES

Whitman's Travel Guide to Minnesota. John Whitman. Minneapolis, MN: Nodin Press, 1977. 256 pp. pap. $2.95.

The book is divided into two major sections. After a brief history of the state, there is a list of state and national parks, major historical sights, the best walleye fishing lakes in the state (which is twice as long as the history), and parks near the Twin Cities. The second part is a series of driving and walking tours, with a short section for canoeists and backpackers. The tables used for the state parks are complete but cramped and very difficult to use. The national parks are listed with short descriptions and addresses for further information. If the book has a saving feature, it is its advice to backpackers and fishing enthusiasts. But even this includes nothing that could not be found in a better organized guide.

Evaluation: For most of the tours, the text reads like a succession of place-names. There are many references to points of interest and "breathtaking" views, but the practical information they contain is transparent. In considering a tour guide, this is one book that should be left on the shelf.

Mississippi

See also The South under Regional Guides.

ACCOMMODATIONS AND RESTAURANTS

AAA TourBook: Mississippi. See AAA TourBook series under North America, Accommodations and Restaurants.

SIGHTSEEING

Pelican Guide to Old Homes of Mississippi: Vol. 1—Natchez and the South; Vol. 2—Columbus and the North. Helen Kerr Kempe. Gretna, LA: Pelican Publishing Co., 1977. 158 pp. pap. $3.95.

The two volumes take the reader into the homes of eighteenth- and nineteenth-century Mississippi. Each divides the area into nine sections with a short introduction and a listing of 15 to 60 homes in each. The entries themselves are short (from a line to a page in length) and concentrate more on the history than the architecture of the homes. There is a wide variety of both private and public homes represented. The books include very few directions and fewer maps; for the most part, the readers are expected to find the homes on their own. There is sometimes a brief description of the surrounding area, but the homes are always the featured attractions.

Evaluation: The first problem with the books is the lack of addresses in the entries. The author depends on two hand-drawn maps to provide the locations of the homes and directions no longer than a phrase at the end of the entries, which are of no use to those not familiar with the area. The listings are short, but include some insights into the peculiarities of the homes in a light and easy style. The books are worthwhile only for those truly interested in the homes of the area; they must be paired with a guide that includes more practical information.

Missouri

See also The Midwest under Regional Guides.

AAA TourBook: Missouri. See AAA TourBook series under North America, Accommodations and Restaurants.

Woodall's Arkansas/Missouri Campground Directory. See *Woodall's Campground Directory: State Editions* under United States, Camping.

St. Louis

COMPREHENSIVE GUIDES

The Complete St. Louis Guide. Anne Fuller Dillon and Martha Mullally Donnelly. St. Louis, MO: The Dillon-Donnelly Press, 1976. 144 pp. pap. $3.25.

The first half of the book is a series of tours throughout St. Louis and nearby excursions. There is a nice mix of history, insights, and practical information in the entries, and the maps and directions are kept clear and simple. One drawback is the lack of space devoted to accommodations. There are 29 listings (name, address, phone, price) on a page and a half, and most of these are nationwide chains. The book is directed to a wide audience with the emphasis on travelers on a moderate budget.

Evaluation: St. Louis is usually not considered a hotbed of tourist activity. This guide shows it as a city with much more to offer visitors than a big arch and a bigger river. The book is organized well, and the information is clear and concise. The authors write in an informal style that keeps the entries lively. The book shows that good vacation ideas can sometimes be found where they are least expected.

SCIENCE

Field Guide Series: St. Louis Area. See Field Guide series under United States, Science.

Montana

See also Rocky Mountains and The West under Regional Guides.

AAA TourBook: Montana. See AAA TourBook series under North America, Accommodations and Restaurants.

Nebraska

See also The Midwest under Regional Guides.

AAA TourBook: Nebraska. See AAA TourBook series under North America, Accommodations and Restaurants.

Nevada

See also Rocky Mountains, The Southwest and The West under Regional Guides.

ACCOMMODATIONS AND RESTAURANTS

AAA TourBook: Nevada. See AAA TourBook series under North America, Accommodations and Restaurants.

PRETRAVEL READING

The Compleat Nevada Traveler. David W. Toll. Reno, NV: University of Nevada Press, 1976. 277 pp. pap. $3.50.

The book is a guide to the sights of Nevada, covering the state from corner to corner. The state is divided into four geographic regions, each section beginning with a history and description of the area. This is followed by a listing of the cities and towns. There is a short entry for each, the length of which depends on the size of the town. Each lists points of interest, campgrounds, directions, short descriptions, and the location of park offices. The four sections end with entries of state and national parks, historical monuments, and ghost towns. There are short essays interspersed throughout the book on a wide variety of topics, both practical and frivolous. They include highway tips, hunting, rock hounding, implied consent laws, the Chinese in Nevada, and the Nevada Highway Patrol. The book emphasizes history and outdoor sights and is meant primarily for pretravel reading.

Evaluation: The histories and descriptions of the rural areas truly shine. The different entries are lively, informative, and incredibly entertaining. The section on the city of Las Vegas does not do the town justice. Travelers spending most of their time in any of the larger cities would be better off with a more comprehensive city guide —perhaps Arthur Frommer's guide to Las Vegas (see under United States, Accommodations and Restaurants). The most outstanding feature of the book is that it is such great fun to read.

New Hampshire

See also The East and New England under Regional Guides.

ACCOMMODATIONS AND RESTAURANTS

AAA TourBook: New Hampshire. See AAA TourBook series under North America, Accommodations and Restaurants.

OUTDOOR RECREATION

Canoe Camping Vermont and New Hampshire Rivers. See the review of this title under Vermont, Outdoor Recreation.

Fifty Hikes in New Hampshire's White Mountains. Daniel Doan. Somersworth, NH: New Hampshire Publishing Co., 1977. 165 pp. pap. $4.95.

As a volume in the Fifty Hikes series, this book has all the information needed by either a beginning hiker or an expert. It covers preparation, safety tips, equipment, types of trails, clothing, shelters, and regulations. Information is included on trees and animals in the area, the seasons, unique physical characteristics, and addresses for further information. The hikes themselves range from easy afternoon walks over fairly flat ground to strenuous week-long hikes over some of the tallest peaks in the area. Each entry includes a description of the trail, a short history, and directions to the starting point.

Evaluation: The variety in the book is amazing. Each hike has its own peculiar characteristics—almost a personality of its own. The text is clear and informative, and good use is made of photographs. The maps in the book are only fair, but the book gives the location of park offices where proper hiking maps are available. It compares favorably with most other hiking guides, but covers a much smaller area than all but a few.

Included in the series: Fifty Hikes in Connecticut; Fifty Hikes in Maine; Fifty Hikes in Massachusetts; Fifty Hikes in New Hampshire; Fifty Hikes in Vermont.

Twenty-Five Ski Tours in the White Mountains. See Twenty-Five Ski Tours series under Regional Guides, New England, Outdoor Recreation.

Twenty-Five Walks Series. Somersworth, NH: New Hampshire Publishing Co., 1978. approx. 118 pp. pap. $4.95.

In contrast to the more strenuous trips in most hiking guides, the walks described in this series are meant to be enjoyed at one's ease. The entries for each walk are rarely longer than three pages and concentrate on the natural beauty of the area. Each hike is shown on a clear map, with trail directions that include points of interest along the way. Hikers and outdoor enthusiasts will find the books in the series rewarding, but because each covers such a small area, they are of most use to residents and travelers on an extended visit.

Evaluation: The books in the Twenty-Five Walks series are organized very simply. Little information is included other than trail directions and descriptions. The walks are easy to locate from the maps in the books, and the use of photographs brings added charm to the entries. The books in the series would be excellent supplements to camping guides to the different areas, though all travelers looking for free outdoor activities would benefit from them.

Included in the series: Dartmouth-Lake Sunapee Region (New Hampshire); Lakes Region (New Hampshire); Rhode Island; Finger Lakes (New York).

New Jersey

See also The East and Middle Atlantic under Regional Guides.

AAA TourBook: New Jersey. See AAA TourBook series under North America, Accommodations and Restaurants.

Bicycle Tours in and around New York. See the review of this title under New York City, Bicycle Touring.

Factory Outlet Shopping Guide: New Jersey and Rockland County. See Factory Outlet Shopping Guide series under United States, Shopping.

Myra Waldo's Restaurant Guide to New York City and Vicinity. See the review of this title under New York City, Accommodations and Restaurants.

One-Day Adventures by Car. See the review of this title under New York City, One-Day Tours.

Woodall's New Jersey/New York Campground Directory. See *Woodall's Campground Directory: State Editions* under United States, Camping.

New Mexico

See The Southwest and The West under Regional Guides.

AAA TourBook: New Mexico. See AAA TourBook series under North America, Accommodations and Restaurants.

Canyon Country Series. See the review of this series under Utah, Outdoor Recreation.

New York State

See also The East and Middle Atlantic under Regional Guides.

AAA TourBook: New York. See AAA TourBook series under North America, Accommodations and Restaurants.

Field Guide Series: Upstate New York. See Field Guide series under United States, Science.

Woodall's New Jersey/New York Campground Directory. See *Woodall's Campground Directory: State Editions* under United States, Camping.

Catskill Mountains

Guide to the Catskills and the Region Around. Arthur Gray Adams. Albuquerque, NM: Sun Publishing Co., 1977. 274 pp. pap. $12.

This is a guidebook in the traditional sense, dealing primarily with the geography and history of the region around the Catskill Mountains in southeastern New York State. The book is divided into three sections. The first describes geographic characteristics of the area's highlands, its rivers and creeks, its railroad lines, and the major highway routes passing through. The history of the region's buildings, places, and past residents is thoroughly examined in the second section, with many references to famous hotels and a chronology of the area's past political leaders. The third section is an alphabetical listing of all the region's towns and places of particular interest, with short descriptions and many accompanying photographs. Special sections include a complete reprint of Washington Irving's *Rip Van Winkle*, famous Hudson River steamboats, and complete population statistics of the area. The book serves travelers with more than a passing interest in the history of the area around the Catskills.

Evaluation: The book is not intended to be read like other guides, but rather to be browsed through. Its pages are filled with insights into the historic and geographic character of the area. The text is lively and evocative, creating a series of images that dance from page to page. The many photographs and old illustrations are excellent complements to the text and add greatly to the book's eye appeal. When used with a transportation/accommodations guide, such as the AAA *TourBook: New York* (see under North America, Accommodations and Restaurants) or one of the oil company guides such as the *Mobil Travel Guide* (see under United States, Accommodations and Restaurants), the book almost guarantees many days of enjoyment and discovery in the region around the Catskills.

Finger Lakes Region

Twenty-Five Walks in the Finger Lakes Region. See the Twenty-Five Walks series under New Hampshire, Outdoor Recreation.

Hudson River Area

Hudson River Tourway. Gilbert Tauber. New York: Doubleday & Co., 1977. 203 pp. pap. $4.95.

The book details eleven tours from New York City to the Adirondacks. Each entry includes a large map, mile-by-mile instructions, short histories, sights (including hours, prices, and telephones), and side trips. The tours are all for automobile and average over 100 miles, which can make for a long day. Also in the book are photographs of some of the sights and addresses for further information.

Evaluation: The information is presented clearly, with a good mix of instructions and descriptions. The book helps the traveler to see and become acquainted with Hudson River Valley sights, vistas, and histories. It would be best to use it along with a more general guide to the area that includes restaurants, accommodations, and practical information. But on its own the book is a nice introduction to the area.

New York City and Vicinity

COMPREHENSIVE GUIDES

Michelin Green Guide to New York City. Michelin Corp. New Hyde Park, NY: Michelin Tire Corp. (dist. in the U.K. by Michelin Tyre Co.), 1978. 148 pp. pap. $4.95 (£2.05).

The book lists the sights of New York City in general and Manhattan in particular. The city offers an incredible number of activities, and the *Green Guide* does an admirable job of distinguishing the imperative from the superfluous. It includes a great lode of practical information, a special subway map, two- and four-day programs, and a section on Long Island and environs. The book serves all budgets and travel styles.

Evaluation: Michelin guides have a tradition of quality, which is evident in their *Green Guide to New York City*. The descriptions of historical sights and museums are superb, and the maps and illustrations are as good as can be found in any guide. The small print may be hard to read, and the odd size hard to handle, but this book could be the hero of your trip.

New York. Carole Chester. London: B. T. Batsford (dist. in the U.S. by Hippocrene Books), 1978. 168 pp. $10.95 (£5.50).

Written by a Londoner and published in England, *New York* is a personable guide to the author's favorite Manhattan hotels, restaurants, sights, and shops. The book begins with a brief but colorful history of the city that includes references to many historic sites. The island is divided into seven areas, with each section including brief background and descriptions of selected restaurants, hotels, and shops. The descriptions include addresses and irregular references to approximate prices. For certain areas of the city there are long sections on nightlife, which describe the singles action and gay bar scene. Special sections include a list of twenty top museums, ten things to do in New York, the businessperson's New York, brief transportation and practical travel information, and trips outside of the city for a day or a weekend. The book is intended primarily for British travelers on moderate and above-average budgets.

Evaluation: The author writes in a style that is both informed and informal. She introduces the reader to the New York that she has grown to love. But it is a city with many faces, and the author's emphasis may not coincide with the viewpoints of all travelers. The book highlights selected "favorites" and gives complete descriptions and information only on certain Manhattan neighborhoods. The practical information does not provide the amount of detail first-time transatlantic travelers will need. Also, little information is included on the city's outlying boroughs. The long nightlife sections and the lack of touristy activities (Grant's Tomb, Statue of Liberty) make the book most useful to young travelers without major budget restrictions. The book is very enjoyable reading, but is less than the total travel guide to New York.

New York City Slicker: A Counterchic Guide to Manhattan. Didi Lorillard. New York: The Viking Press, 1979. 383 pp. pap. $7.95.

This is a specialized guide to New York City, concentrating on its more fashionable qualities. The introduction describes two different itineraries for a day in the city and sets the tone for the rest of the book. The emphasis throughout is on the "untouristy": unique and unusual restaurants, boutiques, handcrafts, and museums. Chapters are included on art, beauty, clothing, eating, home environment, nightlife, sightseeing, and specialty stores. The entries in each chapter include all the necessary practical information, with brief descriptions. A variety of topics are covered in each section, providing at least cursory coverage of all aspects of travel in the city. A series of walking tours and a few day trips are described in the sightseeing sections, and special references are made to those establishments open on Sundays.

Evaluation: New York City Slicker presents a view of the city not found in other guides. It is a city of style, of cool. It wears an imperturbable pout of humorous disdain that is mirrored in its people and its buildings. The information in the book is wide ranging, but less than complete. It lists sights, restaurants, hotels, and shops in Manhattan selected for their suitability to a particular travel style—untouristy and unpoor. Travelers can be certain that the establishments listed in the book may not be exclusive, but most lie far off the well-worn tourist paths. Art enthusiasts, fashion-conscious shoppers, and those who do most of their vacationing at night will find the book particularly useful. Budget-minded travelers and those looking for more traditional tourist activities should use another guide.

New York on $500 a Day. See *Los Angeles on $500 a Day* under California, Los Angeles and Vicinity.

ACCOMMODATIONS AND RESTAURANTS

The All New Underground Gourmet—New York. Milton Glaser and Jerome Snyder. New York: Simon & Schuster, 1977. 370 pp. pap. $3.95.

The Underground Gourmet specializes in budget dining in New York, with over 100 restaurants of every type described in detail and many more listed briefly. The restaurants are arranged alphabetically and indexed by location and by nationality. Each entry lists the address, telephone, days open, hours, bar, whether the place is air conditioned, and the best time and season to dine there. The entries also rate the food, service, clientele, and hygiene of the restaurants, along with detailed descriptions of the décor, selected menu items (with prices), and (sometimes) the neighborhoods and the usual crowd. The restaurants in the "short takes" section list the name, address, and telephone only, with brief descriptions.

Evaluation: The authors' major concern is good food at low prices, and because of their commitment to this principle a large and loyal audience has developed for their books and articles. The descriptions of the restaurants are clear and informative, and the listings of practical information and ratings are complete and easy to find. Although the authors limit themselves to low and moderately priced restaurants, the variety of eateries described guarantees something of interest for nearly every palate. Other New York City restaurant guides include a larger number of restaurants in a wider price range, but no other guide serves budget-minded travelers as well.

Best Restaurants: New York. See Best Restaurants series under United States, Accommodations and Restaurants.

Myra Waldo's Restaurant Guide to New York City and Vicinity. Myra Waldo. New York: Collier Books, Macmillan Publishing Co., 1978. 433 pp. pap. $5.95. Revised periodically.

Myra Waldo includes 800 restaurants of varying price ranges in her restaurant guide to New York City and nearby Connecticut, Long Island, and New Jersey. Restaurants are arranged alphabetically, with special alphabetical lists according to ratings, areas, and those serving Sunday brunch and after-theater meals, those suitable for children, and so on. Restaurants are rated in relation to the rates charged, and information includes quality of food and service, atmosphere and décor, hours of operation, and special menu recommendations.

Evaluation: This guide contains much of the essential information for a great many New York restaurants and includes a great variety—from luncheonettes to international cuisine. No price estimates are given, just general terms like "moderate" or "expensive," which mean different things to different readers. The alphabetic rather than regional organization would make this guide difficult to use when looking for a restaurant in a particular vicinity, but it is very useful once the restaurant is found.

New York on $15 and $20 a Day. See Dollars a Day Guides under The World, Accommodations and Restaurants.

The Restaurants of New York. Seymour Britchky. New York: Random House. 322 pp. pap. $6.95. Revised annually.

Dining in New York is not a subject most travelers wish to take lightly. The consequences of finding oneself in a bad restaurant are made worse by the fact that just a few doors away may be the restaurant of a lifetime. *The Restaurants of New York* colorfully points out both the pitfalls and the pleasures of Manhattan dining, with an opinionated honesty that leaves no doubt as to the impression of the author. The restaurants described are all in the moderate and above-average price range and represent a variety of restaurant types and dining experiences. Most of the reviews in this edition are of new restaurants. They are given an overall rating; the address, hours, telephone number, credit cards accepted, and price range are included for each. The restaurants are listed separately by type of food, by rating, and by neighborhood, with special lists of restaurants open on Sunday, open late, suitable for large family groups, with outdoor dining, enclosed gardens, and enclosed sidewalk cafés, and places where you bring your own wine. There is also a supplemental list of 163 Manhattan restaurants rated without comment. Most of them have been reviewed in earlier editions of this book.

Evaluation: The major features of the book are the large number of restaurants described and the detail of the descriptions. Whereas other restaurant guides to the city may be satisfied with one or two suggestions from the menu and a short paragraph describing the dining room, entries in this guide examine nearly all the menu items and provide a feel for the restaurants that goes far beyond the atmosphere. The information on the restaurants is complete and easy to find, and the special restaurant listings make the book easy to use. The author's opinions and impressions of the restaurants are readily apparent from the entries, and he writes in an informative and descriptive style. He strongly chastises the restaurant critics in the New York press for feeling a need to turn up wonderful new eateries with great regularity, selecting in desperation any place at all. Whether or not this criticism is justified, it is clear that the author will abide little sentiment standing in the way of an honest review. His opinions may contradict others who have judged the same restaurants, but unlike others, his views are always clear.

ARCHITECTURE

The City Observed: New York. Paul Goldberger. New York: Vintage Books/Random House, 1979. 337 pp. pap. $7.95.

This guide to the architecture of Manhattan is the author's first book in a planned series. In it, he describes the approximately 400 buildings or areas that catch his fancy as significant, distinguished, amusing, or instructive. *The City Observed* divides Manhattan into five geographic regions and identifies neighborhoods within each region. Individual entries are listed in a progression that enables, but does not require, the user to take a walking tour. Buildings, groups of buildings, whole streets, parks, and districts are included, accompanied by chatty descriptions not only of the technical features of architecture, but of the mood and flavor as well. Snapshot-size black-and-white photographs throughout the book illustrate and augment the text, often capturing the atmosphere the author seeks to present. Helpful maps are included.

Evaluation: This book facilitates the development of a real sense of New York as reflected in its architecture. The reader is led to see the architecture of Manhattan as part of the living heritage of the city. *The City Observed* is highly recommended for those willing to walk around Manhattan who want to acquire an intimate understanding of and familiarity with its people through their architecture.

New York: A Guide to the Metropolis. Gerard R. Wolfe. New York: Washington Mews Books—New York University Press, 1975. 434 pp. $22.50; pap. $8.95.

This guide was developed from a class taught by the author at New York University. It describes the city's architectural history through a series of 20 walking tours that wind from the Battery north and east as far as historic Flushing. Each tour begins with directions to the starting point by subway and bus and gives detailed descriptions of many historic buildings in each area. The tour directions are printed in boldface type and are isolated from the text. Large, clear maps and many photographs and illustrations of street scenes from New York's past bring the information in the entries to life. Many of the buildings described are no longer standing, though their beauty and historical significance may still be appreciated to a degree. The book is at least as useful for New York City residents as for visitors. The amount of information included in the entries may be more than most travelers would need—after all, there are many other things to do in the city besides walk.

Evaluation: The entries for the walking tours in the book include much more detailed descriptions of the buildings and their histories than are found in most city walking guides, but the scope of the information is limited to the buildings and their historical significance. No mention is made of other nearby sights or more recently constructed buildings. The directions in the tours are clear, and they, along with the maps, make the routes easy to follow. With the detailed information on the buildings and the long bibliography, the book would make an excellent reference for anyone interested in New

York's architectural history. Travelers planning a more traditional vacation to the city may find that the walking tours in a more comprehensive guide will suffice.

ATLASES

Hagstrom Pocket Atlas of New York's Five Boroughs. New York: Hagstrom Co., 7th ed. 1978. 144 pp. pap. $1.95.

The book is a series of 45 detailed street maps of Manhattan, the Bronx, Brooklyn, Queens, and Staten Island. There is a special subway map, a complete street index, and a short street number guide. The maps point out playgrounds, parks, cemeteries, airports, hospitals, golf courses, state and federal land, postal zones, and post office stations. The book would be useful to anyone doing much traveling by car through New York City.

Evaluation: The book is organized well and is easy to use. The maps are large and legible, with a color system that makes locating particular buildings or areas easy. The low price of the book makes it worthwhile for almost any traveler in the city. Some things that could have been included but were not are a discussion of driving hazards peculiar to the area, parking, bridge and tunnel tolls, and service stations. But these all go beyond what is expected in an atlas. It is a very useful book for visitors and residents alike.

BICYCLE TOURING

Bicycle Tours in and around New York. Dan Carlinsky and David Heim. New York: Hagstrom Co., 1975. pap. 87 pp. $2.95.

The book outlines 21 tours from the heart of Manhattan to the Connecticut and Pennsylvania borders. The trips range from two-hour sprints to overnight excursions, with ratings such as "easy" and "challenging ride." Safety tips and information for beginners are included, as well as detailed maps and precise directions. References are made to the best times to avoid traffic, special hazards, and bicycle repairs. The book is recommended for beginning and experienced bicyclers and offers a unique view of the New York City area.

Evaluation: The book is true to the subject. The information is complete and well presented. The maps are clear enough for those familiar with the area, but strangers should not depend on them alone.

HISTORY

The Street Book: An Encyclopedia of Manhattan Street Names and Their Origins. Henry Moscow. New York: Hagstrom Co., 1978. 119 pp. pap. $7.50.

The Street Book gives a unique and enlightening history of Manhattan Island through the origins of its street names. The introduction is an extensive history of the island. The entries for each street are organized alphabetically and range from a line to a page in length, featuring the stories of the streets and the people for whom they were named. Interspersed throughout are beautiful old maps, photographs, and illustrations that alone would make the book worth the cover price.

Evaluation: Travelers interested in the history of Manhattan will find this specialty guide an entertaining and educational complement to a more comprehensive guide to New York City, one that can be consulted long after the trip is over. The entries are delightful and the graphics make for an extremely attractive book. It provides insights into the city's history that cannot be found in other guides.

MUSEUMS

Museums in New York. Fred W. McDarrah. New York: Quick Fox (Music Sales Corp.), 3rd ed. 1978. 349 pp. pap. $5.95.

Along with the many museums listed, this book describes historic sites and old homes, zoos, libraries, international centers, exhibit halls, and planetariums. Each entry lists the address, telephone number, hours, dates, admission, tours, and restrictions, with complete directions to the sites by subway, bus, and auto. The descriptions include many historical references and highlight points of particular interest. Over 200 photographs of the buildings and exhibits surround the entries. A special landmarks checklist is featured at the back of the book, which briefly describes major sites of historical interest throughout the city. The book is useful to all travelers to New York with even a slight interest in the history of museums of the city.

Evaluation: The variety of sights and activities described in the book offers something for nearly every interest. The information on the museums and exhibits is complete, informative, and easy to find. The many photographs and illustrations are an excellent complement to the text. Both visitors and residents will find *Museums in New York* an excellent introduction to the cultural and historical aspects of the city. When used with a more comprehensive accommodations/restaurant guide, this is the only guide to the city's sights most travelers would need. It serves all budgets and travel styles and guarantees many fruitful hours of urban exploration.

ONE-DAY TOURS

Back Before Bedtime. Sandy Beram. New York: Quick Fox (Music Sales Corp.), 1978. 269 pp. pap. $6.95.

Written for residents of the New York City area, the book lists hundreds of sights and activities of interest to the entire family that can be enjoyed in a one-day trip. It begins with pointers for better day trips, followed by a 75-page listing of special annual events divided by month and area. The other entries are divided by city and state and include addresses, phone numbers, hours, and admission, with short descriptions and special features. At the back of the book are eight pages of money-saving coupons. The book is geared to travel by car and, though the author keeps an eye out for cost-cutters, is intended for travelers on modest and above-average budgets.

Evaluation: The major feature of the book is the number and variety of entries—so many, in fact, that travelers spending less than a week in the area would be able to see only a fraction of them. The book was meant to be used many times over and is worthwhile only for residents or those making a number of trips to the New York City area. It is well organized for the number of sights and activities included, with category indexes for each state and a detailed table of contents. The style is colorful and clear. The author includes many useful tips in the entries to facilitate harmony in the family. However, the book is no substitute for a comprehensive travel guide to the area.

One-Day Adventures by Car. Lida Newberry. New York: Hastings House Publishers, 3rd ed. 280 pp. pap. $4.95.

One-Day Adventures by Car describes short trips for a variety of interests within 100 miles of New York City. The book divides the area into eight sections that cover the Hudson River Valley, Connecticut, Long Island, Staten Island, and New Jersey. A number of trips are described in each area, with many side trips and possible deviations included. Each entry includes distance and tolls, driving directions, and location of restaurants along the way. The descriptions of the sights include the hours, operating dates, and facilities of each, and mention whether or not a fee is charged. Special references are included in the entries for handicapped travelers. A list of performing arts in the area is found at the back of the book along with complete category and general indexes. The book best serves residents of New York City or travelers planning an extended visit to the area.

Evaluation: The information on the sights is complete and easy to find. The driving directions are fairly clear, but travelers unfamiliar with the area should not rely on them alone. Although there is a historical emphasis in many of the entries, the wide variety of sights and activities described provide something for almost every interest. Because of the lack of preparatory and practical travel information and the limited restaurant information, the book is most useful to New

York City residents, particularly families, who could use the book on many short trips. The book is well organized and the information is presented clearly, but the many different typefaces, especially the small size used in the driving directions, may take some getting used to. However, this detracts very little from the book's general usefulness.

SCIENCE

Field Guide Series: Greater Metropolitan New York. See Field Guide series under United States, Science.

SHOPPING

The Book-Store Book: A Guide to Manhattan Booksellers. Robert Egan. New York: Avon Books, 1979. 376 pp. pap. $5.95.

The Book-Store Book is a bibliophile's dream come true. It lists over 750 Manhattan booksellers, large and small, dealing with every type of book published and some that no longer are. Along with the many entries for general bookstores, the guide lists specialty stores that stock books on a variety of subjects that include art, black culture, braille, chess, comics, cookbooks, dance, design, drama, film, flying saucers, genealogy, Judaica, magic, maps, medicine, music, mystery, occult, pets, philosophy, psychology, science fiction, sports, technical engineering, travel, women's interests, and many more. The entries include the name of the bookstore, the address, telephone, hours and dates, main sections, special services provided, and a short description. The book dealers are listed at the back of the book both alphabetically and by subject, and maps of Manhattan are provided. Special sections include a discussion of how bookstores work, how to use *Books in Print*, used bookstores, antiquarian booksellers, auction galleries, and antiquarian organizations.

Evaluation: The wide range of bookstores described almost guarantees something for every interest. The book invites hours, days, or even weeks of browsing through thousands of titles on a variety of subjects. The information on the stores is complete and easy to find, and the descriptions, though short, give a clear picture of what the different bookstores are like. The book would be most useful to residents of the New York City area who could use it many times over for years to come, though visitors to the city will find it an excellent complement to a more comprehensive guide. Anyone at all interested in bookstores will not want to miss the chance for discovery this guide provides.

Factory Outlet Shopping Guide: New York, Long Island, and Westchester. See Factory Outlet Shopping Guide series under United States, Shopping.

The Manhattan Clothes Shopping Guide. Elaine Louie. New York: Macmillan Publishing Co., 1978. 363 pp. $9.95.

Every area of Manhattan and every type of clothing store on the island are described in *The Manhattan Clothes Shopping Guide*. Geared to shoppers on moderate and above-average budgets (though some less expensive alternatives are included), the book lists the stores by neighborhood, with a short description of the area and a paragraph on where to eat and drink. The entry for each store includes the address, telephone number, store hours, credit cards accepted, when sales are likely, the price range, and the types of clothes available, with descriptions of the stores and their specialties. A map is provided of each area, and indexes are included of the stores and designers and the clothes.

Evaluation: Although the book is intended primarily for New York City residents, shoppers traveling to the city will find it a time- and money-saver. The variety of clothing stores listed in the entries guarantees something for every interest in a lively and informative style, and the colorful descriptions give a feel for the uniqueness of the different stores. The practical information on the stores is complete and accessible. Because of the geographic organization, it may be difficult for those unfamiliar with the area to use the book, though this is only a minor problem. The book is the most complete, best-organized, and most descriptive clothes shopping guide available.

North Carolina

See also The East, Middle Atlantic, and The South under Regional Guides.

AAA TourBook: North Carolina. See AAA TourBook series under North America, Accommodations and Restaurants.

Factory Outlet Shopping Guide: North and South Carolina. See Factory Outlet Shopping Guide series under United States, Shopping.

Woodall's North Carolina/South Carolina Campground Directory. See *Woodall's Campground Directory: State Editions* under United States, Camping.

North Dakota

See also The Midwest under Regional Guides.

AAA TourBook: North Dakota. See AAA TourBook series under North America, Accommodations and Restaurants.

Ohio

See also The Midwest under Regional Guides.

AAA TourBook: Ohio. See AAA TourBook series under North America, Accommodations and Restaurants.

Field Guide Series: Southern Ohio, Indiana, and Northern Kentucky. See Field Guide series under United States, Science.

Woodall's Ohio/Pennsylvania Campground Directory. See *Woodall's Campground Directory: State Editions* under United States, Camping.

Oklahoma

See also The Southwest under Regional Guides.

AAA TourBook: Oklahoma. See AAA TourBook series under North America, Accommodations and Restaurants.

Oregon

See also Pacific Coast and The West under Regional Guides.

ACCOMMODATIONS AND RESTAURANTS

AAA TourBook: Oregon. See AAA TourBook series under North America, Accommodations and Restaurants.

CHILDREN'S ACTIVITIES

Now Where? Places in Oregon to Go with Kids. Joyce Tuggle and Nancy Martin McCarthy. Portland, OR: Timber Press (dist. by ISBS), 2nd ed. 1977. 132 pp. pap. $3.45.

Intended primarily for residents of the state, the book describes 319 sights and activities of interest to the entire family. Many types of museums are included, as well as farms, railroads, factory tours, theaters and movie houses, a few parks and national monuments, wildlife refuges, county fairs, and annual festivals. The entries average a half page in length and include addresses, entrance prices, hours, and short descriptions of the special attractions of each. The sections are organized geographically, with most of the entries in and around Portland or along the coast. The book is geared to travel by car. The lack of maps and preparatory information suggests that its primary users will be those already familiar with the area.

Evaluation: Now Where? is very simply a list of sights and activities in Oregon. There are no introductory sections or practical information other than on the sights themselves. The entries pique the reader's interest, but are too short to give a clear picture. Travelers would need to supplement the book with a more inclusive guide to the area. The authors succeed in their goal of providing a wide variety of activities, but those unfamiliar with the area will have a hard time using the book.

DRIVING AND HIKING TOURS

Back Roads and Trails: The Willamette Valley. Susan E. Hawkins and Dennis Bleything. Beaverton, OR: The Touchstone Press, 1976. 80 pp. pap. $3.95.

Back Roads and Trails: The Willamette Valley was written primarily for residents of the area around Portland, Oregon. The 16 trips included are along forest roads "suitable for a family car" and combine hikes with many different possible routes, so that each trip can be taken more than once. The first seven provide alternative north-south routes to Interstate 5; the next seven are along rivers in the valley; and the last two feature old mines and covered bridges. Along with descriptions of the roads, the trips include references to parks, points of historic and natural interest, and camping information. It is possible for travelers unfamiliar with the area to use the book, but only after carefully studying a good road map.

Evaluation: The entries include all the information needed for day trips and short camping excursions, but only for a small area. The lack of preparatory and practical information limits the book's usefulness to experienced hikers and campers. The road and trail directions are clear and easy to follow, and the text handles the mix of directions and points of interest well. Many readers may be surprised by the lack of an emphasis on any one subject in the entries: neither science, sports, nor history. It seems the emphasis is simply on the joys of being outdoors.

Exploring Oregon's Central and Southern Cascades. William L. Mainwaring. Salem, OR: Westridge Press, 1979. 80 pp. pap. $7.95.

Like the author's guide to the Oregon coast (see below), *Exploring Oregon's Central and Southern Cascades* informally describes popular automobile and hiking routes through the area. The 18 different entries, averaging four pages in length, include capsule histories and spectacular color photographs along with the descriptions and irregularly include references to campgrounds and other outdoor activities. In the back are four maps that show all the routes and points of interest mentioned in the entries. The book was written primarily for Oregon residents who could use it on many short trips close to their homes, but it is also useful to travelers on an extended visit to the area.

Evaluation: The book has much less detail and a narrower scope of information than most outdoor guides. The author relies heavily on descriptions and history in the entries, giving little practical information. The book is most useful when used along with a more complete camping or hiking guide as an introduction to the area, or as a postvacation souvenir. The photographs and the lively text make the book enjoyable reading, but its practicality when used alone is limited.

Exploring the Oregon Coast. William L. Mainwaring. Salem, OR: Westridge Press, 1977. 63 pp. pap. $6.95.

The exploration in the book is limited to car travel along scenic coastal roads, with stops in some of the smaller, tourist-oriented towns, state parks, and beaches. The book describes 23 different coastal areas, arranged in a north-south line, with many color photographs of each. The text for each entry relies mainly on descriptions and directions, with irregular references to camping, hiking, side trips, nearby attractions, and picnic facilities. Each includes a small map of the area and an address for further information. The large size and the many photographs suggest that the book is best used as pretravel reading.

Evaluation: When used with a camping or accommodations guide, *Exploring the Oregon Coast* is a useful guide to sights and outdoor activities in the area. But many features limit the book's usefulness. It is a short book, with nearly as much space devoted to photographs as to text, and the practical information is sparse and unevenly distributed. For these reasons, the book is recommended for first-time travelers to the area without excessive budget restrictions.

OUTDOOR RECREATION

Columbia River Gorge: An Enjoyment Guide. Jack Grauer. Portland, OR: Jack Grauer, 1977. 32 pp. pap. $2.

This is a short (32-page) introduction to the area around Portland, Oregon. It emphasizes camping and hiking and features a variety of outdoor attractions, such as parks, waterfalls, campsites, trails, and rock climbs. The entries include little information other than names, addresses, and sketchy directions. The city entries are jumbled, with points of interest and accommodations barely listed. The key feature of the book is the colorful and detailed maps, which accentuate camping.

Evaluation: The camping and hiking sections are informative, clear, and complete. These and the maps make the book worthwhile for backpackers or trail campers. In other sections, it seems as if the author tried to incorporate as many bits of information as possible in a limited space. The result is a little confusing. The small area covered and the poor quality of the city entries limit the book's usefulness to campers in the area.

101 Best Fishing Trips in Oregon. Don Holm. Caldwell, ID: The Caxton Printers, 1976. 207 pp. pap. $4.95.

The fishing trips in the book are divided into ten geographic regions. They are well distributed throughout the state and represent fishing sites on the coastline, on rivers and streams, and a few on lakes. There is a short introduction that tells why the book was written, gives a little background on the state, and tells how the different sites were selected. The entries themselves are rarely longer than a page and include the types of fish in the area, the equipment needed to catch them, and a short description of the area. There are irregular references to alternate sites, seasonal changes, where to find detailed maps, and the best fishing spots. The book is of most use to experienced fishing enthusiasts who know their way around the outdoors.

Evaluation: The entries were meant to be short and to the point, and for the most part they are. But the information provided is uneven. Some entries include the location of stores and services; some do not. Some are mostly recollections and descriptions; some are strictly fish. Some include directions; most do not. The hit-or-miss quality of the entries and the narrow scope make the book less than an ideal guide.

Oregon River Tours. John Garren. Beaverton, OR: The Touchstone Press, 1979. 184 pp. pap. $6.95.

Geared to river enthusiasts with some previous experience, *Oregon River Tours* describes trips down 13 rivers selected as representative of the many possible trips in the state. The tour entries follow sections on river classification, general characteristics of the rivers and trips, an explanation of the river logbooks used on tours, a comparison of different drift crafts, and tips on planning the tour (car shuttling, campsites, and so on). The entries for each trip describe the river, give a detailed river log, graph the monthly river discharge, and provide a large map of each course. A special reference list is included at the back of the book.

Evaluation: The technical quality of the information, and the lack of information on preparation and technique, restrict the book's usefulness to experienced river runners. The amount of information on the rivers themselves goes beyond that in most other river guides. The book's best feature is the detailed river logs that provide at a glance the location of rapids, campgrounds, springs, bridges, islands, and side streams. *Whitewater; Quietwater* (see under The Midwest and the Great Lakes Region) is a better introduction to the sport in general and is easier to use, but it includes less information on the rivers.

Oregon River Tours is an excellent guide to river tours in the state for those who know the sport but not the rivers.

Woodall's Idaho/Oregon/Washington Campground Directory. See *Woodall's Campground Directory: State Editions* under United States, Camping.

SCIENCE

Field Guide Series: Western Washington and Oregon. See Field Guide series under United States, Science.

Roadside Geology of Oregon. See Roadside Geology series under United States, Science.

WINE TOURS

Winery Tours in Oregon, Washington, Idaho, and British Columbia. See the review of this title under Regional Guides, Pacific Coast, Wine Tours.

Portland

The Portland Guidebook. See *The Seattle Guidebook* under Washington, Seattle.

Pennsylvania

See also The East and Middle Atlantic under Regional Guides.

AAA TourBook: Pennsylvania. See AAA TourBook series under North America, Accommodations and Restaurants.

Best Restaurants: Philadelphia. See Best Restaurants series under United States, Accommodations and Restaurants.

Factory Outlet Shopping Guide: Pennsylvania. See Factory Outlet Shopping Guide series under United States, Shopping.

Woodall's Ohio/Pennsylvania Campground Directory. See *Woodall's Campground Directory: State Editions* under United States, Camping.

Puerto Rico

See The Islands series under The World, Pretravel Reading, Islands of the World.

Rhode Island

See also The East and New England under Regional Guides.

AAA TourBook: Rhode Island. See AAA TourBook series under North America, Accommodations and Restaurants.

Twenty-Five Walks in Rhode Island. See Twenty-Five Walks series under New Hampshire, Outdoor Recreation.

South Carolina

See also The East, Middle Atlantic, and The South under Regional Guides.

AAA TourBook: South Carolina. See AAA TourBook series under North America, Accommodations and Restaurants.

A Contemplative Fishing Guide to the Grand Strand. Donald Millus. Lexington, SC: The Sandlapper Store, 1977. 110 pp. pap. $2.95.

At first this may look like a guide to seasonal fishing along the South Carolina coast, but it is more a group of recollections by the author than a practical how-to guide. The listings for each type of fish are organized by the season. Each entry tells of some past fishing experience involving either the type of fish or the location listed in the entry. Tips on the best spots and times to fish are included irregularly. At the end of each entry is a listing of the different names of the fish, the best method of catching it, and where to look for more information. The book is useful to experienced fishing enthusiasts and should be read before the trip.

Evaluation: The essay style pushes the practical and incidental information together, making it difficult to find a particular item. There is no index of fish, no geographic organization, and one very sketchy map. The book is written to give the reader an impression of what the particular trip is like. The addresses for further information and the lists of other sources provide the means for acquiring more thorough detail.

Factory Outlet Shopping Guide: North and South Carolina. See Factory Outlet Shopping Guide series under United States, Shopping.

Woodall's North Carolina/South Carolina Campground Directory. See *Woodall's Campground Directory: State Editions* under United States, Camping.

South Dakota

See also The Midwest under Regional Guides.

AAA TourBook: South Dakota. See AAA TourBook series under North America, Accommodations and Restaurants.

Tennessee

See also The South under Regional Guides.

AAA TourBook: Tennessee. See AAA TourBook series under North America, Accommodations and Restaurants.

Woodall's Kentucky/Tennessee Campground Directory. See *Woodall's Campground Directory: State Editions* under United States, Camping.

Texas

See also The South and The Southwest under Regional Guides.

ACCOMMODATIONS AND RESTAURANTS

AAA TourBook: Texas. See AAA TourBook series under North America, Accommodations and Restaurants.

Best Restaurants: Texas. See Best Restaurants series under United States, Accommodations and Restaurants.

AUTOMOBILE TRAVEL

Texas Guidebook. Rex Z. Howard with F. M. McCarthy, ed. Austin, TX: The F. M. McCarthy Co., 5th ed. 1976. 313 pp. pap. $2.95.

The book is a guide to travel through Texas by car. It covers all the major state and U.S. highways and a few back roads. The book opens with a general information section that is a compilation of a series of brief essays on a wide variety of topics pertaining to Texas. They include cattle and cowboys, fishing, old-time foods, climate and weather, hunting, Mexico, quarterhorses, trees, and much, much history. The entries are limited to roads, sights, and history, so that many travelers will find that a more complete guide (with accommodations, emergency information, and other means of transportation) would serve them.

Evaluation: The sights in the entries are organized as they are found along the highway. Even with the index, particular sights are difficult to locate in relation to cities. The double columns, small photographs, and poor printing quality give the book an untidy appearance. The entries are usually brief, but complete for motorists, and interesting. It seems the author is a storyteller from way back. The text drags at times, but never for too long. The book is recommended for use on the road by those traveling through Texas by car on a low to moderate budget.

SCIENCE AND THE OUTDOORS

Field Guide Series: North Texas. See Field Guide series under United States, Science.

Roadside Geology of Texas. See Roadside Geology series under United States, Science.

Woodall's Texas Campground Directory. See *Woodall's Campground Directory: State Editions* under United States, Camping.

Utah

See also Rocky Mountains and The West under Regional Guides.

ACCOMMODATIONS AND RESTAURANTS

AAA TourBook: Utah. See AAA TourBook series under North America, Accommodations and Restaurants.

OUTDOOR RECREATION

Canyon Country Series. F. A. Barnes. Salt Lake City, UT: Wasatch Publishers, 1977. 80 pp. pap. $1.95.

The first book in this series is *Canyon Country: Scenic Roads.* It is a guide to the roads that traverse the southeastern corner of Utah and describes thirteen routes of various lengths (not always in the form of a tour), and seven state and national parks in the area. At the back of the book are special sections for off-season travel and facilities, services, and supplies. The different entries include the location of park offices, points of interest, scenic views, suggestions for hikes, and hazards to be avoided. The series stresses inexpensive outdoor activities in an area that covers most of Utah, northern Arizona, western Colorado, and northwestern New Mexico. It is suggested for those with some previous outdoor experience.

Evaluation: The books in the Canyon Country series have a narrow scope, but the information included is complete. The directions for both the walking and the driving tours are easy to follow and mention points of interest and precautions. The brevity of the entries sometimes compacts the information to a point that makes finding particulars difficult. The series is of most use when paired with a guide such as the AAA TourBook Series (see under North America, Accommodations and Restaurants). Because the books are short and inexpensive, it would be possible to pick one up and plan an afternoon excursion off the interstate, thereby enjoying the scenery while making time on the road. Another possible use for the *Scenic Roads* volume is by travelers driving across the country.

Included in the series: Camping; Canyon Country Exploring; Geology for the Layman and Rockhound; Hiking and Natural History; Off-Road Vehicle Trails (six different areas); *Paddles; Scenic Roads.*

Petzoldt's Teton Trails. Paul Petzoldt. Salt Lake City, UT: Wasatch Publishers, 1976. 160 pp. pap. $3.50.

The book is a hiker's guide to Grand Teton National Park. It opens with short stories by the author that combine his experiences with history, safety tips, amusing recollections, and observations on the world in general. This is followed by advice on conservation, clothing, time and energy control, weather, and summer snow. A short introduction to the park precedes the trail listings. Thirty-seven trails are included, with many suggestions for side-trail and off-trail hikes. The trails vary in length from short afternoon hikes to backpacking trips of up to two weeks. It is suggested at all times that hikers use U.S. Geological Survey maps available at park offices. Because of the sparse preparatory material, the book is recommended for those with some previous hiking experience.

Evaluation: The author has over 50 years of hiking experience and has made numerous first ascents of mountains around the world. It is doubtful that anyone knows more about the Tetons. Often, experience alone is no guarantee of a useful guide; but in this case, the author's experiences are translated into a complete, well-organized trail guide. The book is pleasurable reading in itself, but would be of most use when read before leaving and consulted on the road.

Wasatch Tours. Alexis Kelner and David Hanscom. Salt Lake City, UT: Wasatch Publishers, 1976. 233 pp. pap. $4.95.

Written primarily for residents of Utah, *Wasatch Tours* describes 67 snow tours in the Wasatch Mountains, near Salt Lake City. The introductory sections describe the area and include a detailed discussion of ski-touring equipment, skiing safety, and clothing. An entire chapter is devoted to avalanches—how to recognize and avoid possible avalanche areas, safety precautions, and rescue techniques. The first nine tours in the book are intended for beginners and include information of particular use to them. The rest of the tours are divided into five areas, with intermediate and advanced trips described in each area. The descriptions of the tours include distance, elevation gain, directions to the starting point, and possible side trips. The routes are shown in a series of clear photographs and illustrations.

Evaluation: The detailed preparatory and safety information and the inclusion of trips for beginners make the book an excellent introduction to winter touring as well as a practical guide to ski touring in the Wasatch Mountains. The many photographs and illustrations complement the information in the text well. Much of the practical information on the tours is embedded in the descriptions and is difficult to isolate, so that it is necessary to read the tour descriptions carefully before the trip. Of particular interest is the chapter on avalanches; no other ski-touring guide includes such a detailed discussion of this hazard. The equipment and safety sections are complete, clear, and very useful to skiers of all levels of expertise. Although it covers a small geographic area, the book may be the most complete guide to snow touring currently available.

Wasatch Trails: Vols. 1 and 2. Daniel Geery. Salt Lake City, UT: Wasatch Publishers, 1977. 112 pp. pap. $2.50.

The two volumes of *Wasatch Trails* describe a number of hikes in the mountains just east of Salt Lake City. The hikes in the first volume are intended for beginning and intermediate hikers, with the second volume describing hikes for those with more experience. The introductory sections explain how to read the trail entries and how to find U.S. Geological Survey maps, describe basic hiking techniques, and give some safety tips. The trail entries list the destination, distance, and elevation gain, give a difficulty rating, and tell on which U.S.G.S. maps the trails can be found. The trails and the area around them are described in detail, and each trail is shown on a large, hand-drawn map. The books serve all hikers planning a trip to the area, but are particularly useful to Utah residents.

Evaluation: All the information necessary for enjoyable hiking, except for preparatory and background information, is included in the entries. The practical information on the trails is complete and easily accessible, and the trail directions and the directions to the starting points are presented clearly. The books are small enough not to be cumbersome on the trails and are inexpensive compared to other hiking guides. With a good set of maps and basic camping information, the books can be the key to a number of enjoyable trips in some conveniently located mountains.

Vermont

See also The East and Middle Atlantic under Regional Guides.

ACCOMMODATIONS AND RESTAURANTS

AAA TourBook: Vermont. See AAA TourBook series under North America, Accommodations and Restaurants.

OUTDOOR RECREATION

Canoe Camping Vermont and New Hampshire Rivers. Roioli Schweiker. Somersworth, NH: New Hampshire Publishing Co., 1979. 92 pp. pap. $4.95.

The book describes canoe trips on 14 different ribers in Vermont and New Hampshire. The introduction includes a general information section, safety tips, hazards, equipment, clothing, canoeing with children, camping, fishing, hiking, addresses for further information, and how to get the most out of the entries. Even with this amount of preliminary information, the book is not a how-to guide. It is directed primarily to the intermediate and expert canoeist. Each river entry includes a number of canoe runs from under 20 to over 80 miles. These entries cover all the information needed to canoe the rivers. The book is meant for pretravel reading and as a reference on the trip.

Evaluation: The shining feature of the book is its completeness. The information is clear and concise, with enough style to keep it interesting. The audience for the book is limited by the emphasis on experienced canoeists and the small area it covers. A better introduction to canoeing in general is *Whitewater; Quietwater* (see under The Midwest and the Great Lakes Region). A book that covers a wider geographic area is *Canoeing and Rafting* (see under United States, Canoeing).

Favorite Vermont Ski Inns and Lodging Guide. Janet Colter and Rudyard Colter. New York: McGraw-Hill Book Co., 1977. 221 pp. pap. $5.95.

Skiing is not the most inexpensive of pastimes, but the authors of this book do a good job of providing a wide range of lodges and inns that serve every budget. The introduction covers food plans at the different lodges, price ratings, credit cards, deposits, discounts, a description of the different ski facilities, and local driving distances (travel by car is emphasized throughout). The state is divided into six sections. Each includes a description and listing of ski runs in the area, transportation, activities, and restaurants (with name and city only). The inn listings in each section include all the necessary practical information, the distance from the slopes, and a short comment. The inns are grouped in low, medium, and expensive price ranges. The appendixes list the inns by special feature. The book's large size and the emphasis on reservations at the inns suggest that it is best used as pretravel reading.

Evaluation: This is a well-organized, complete, and easy-to-use guide. The information is clear and accessible. The authors have had years of experience with skiing in the area and have translated that experience into a first-rate guide that serves all budgets. It is a worthwhile investment for everyone planning a ski vacation in Vermont.

Fifty Hikes in Vermont. See *Fifty Hikes in New Hampshire's White Mountains* under New Hampshire, Outdoor Recreation.

Outsiders Inside Vermont. T. D. Seymour Bassett, ed. Canaan, NH: Phoenix Publishing, 1967. 148 pp. pap. $4.95.

Outsiders Inside Vermont employs thirty-one essays and three poems to recount over three centuries' worth of visitors' opinions of the state. The authors include both famous and obscure men and women, whose impressions range from sublime infatuation to contemptuous disgust. The essays are divided chronologically into five major eras: Indian Days; Frontier Days; Stagecoach and Steamboat Days; Railroad Days; and Automobile Days. In the afterword is a contemporary essay on Vermont's landscape and people's impact upon it, as well as poems by John Updike, William Jay Smith, and Genevieve Taggard. A long source list is included along with a brief index. The book is useful background reading for both first-time travelers and life-long Vermont residents.

Evaluation: The opinions of past visitors is a unique approach to the history of the state and one that makes for interesting reading. Many aspects of the state's history are most evident when they are viewed through the eyes of those who have lived it. The essays tell much more than the history of one state; the growth and development of Vermont is representative of the process that shaped the entire country. The book is valuable reading for anyone with ever the slightest interest in the history of Vermont in particular and the United States in general.

Twenty-Five Ski Tours in the Green Mountains. See the review of this title under Regional Guides, New England, Outdoor Recreation.

Virginia

See also The East, Middle Atlantic, and The South under Regional Guides.

AAA TourBook: Virginia. See AAA TourBook series under North America, Accommodations and Restaurants.

Country Inns of Maryland, Virginia, and West Virginia. See the review of this title under Maryland, Accommodations and Restaurants.

Factory Outlet Shopping Guide: Washington, D.C., Maryland, Virginia, Delaware. See Factory Outlet Shopping Guide series under United States, Shopping.

Woodall's Delaware/Maryland/ Virginia/District of Columbia Campground Directory. See *Woodall Campground Directory: State Editions* under United States, Camping.

Alexandria

Old Alexandria. Nettie Allen Voges. McLean, VA: EPM Publications, 1975. 208 pp. pap. $5.95.

The book is a detailed account of the history of Alexandria, Virginia, from the founding of the colony by Sir Walter Raleigh to the close of the eighteenth century. Four walking tours are included, the texts of which describe at length the histories and unique features of the buildings to be visited—reading the entries may almost take longer than taking the tours. An interesting section near the back of the book tells of the archaeological restorations both completed and in progress throughout the city. The audience for this book is limited by the small area it covers and by its historical emphasis.

Evaluation: This book was written for the semi-serious student of American history; it excludes the practical information most travelers expect from a guide for such a small area. It is extremely well written, but is recommended only for those with more than a passing interest in the history of the area.

Charlottesville and Albemarle Counties

Jefferson's Country: Charlottesville and Albemarle Counties. Whit Morse and Linda Firestone. Richmond, VA: Good Life Publishers, 1977. 151 pp. pap. $3.95.

The emphasis of the book is on the history of the area around Thomas Jefferson's home, Monticello. The first two-thirds and much of the last third of the book recount the events and catalog the sights of eighteenth- and nineteenth-century central Virginia. Included are walking tours of the university and of old Charlottesville, art galleries and museums, shopping, and information centers. The accommodations section is a disappointment, with only 18 listings (names, addresses, and phone numbers only), most of them nationwide chains. The book is as much for students of history and newcomers to the area as for visitors and serves all budgets equally.

Evaluation: The authors blend histories and descriptions in a smooth and easy style. The use of photographs, maps, and illustrations accentuate the text well. Anyone with the slightest interest in the area will find that interest fanned by the book. It is recommended for those spending more than a few days in the area who may desire a thinking vacation.

Chincoteague and Assateague

Virginia's Favorite Islands: Chincoteague and Assateague. Linda Firestone and Whit Morse. Richmond, VA: Good Life Publishers, 1978. 84 pp. pap. $2.95.

This book describes two of the larger islands lying off Virginia's northern coast. The most famous feature of the islands is the wild ponies, and the book includes a section on their history and the annual summer festival. The islands described are relatively undeveloped, and their economy depends greatly on tourism. Activities featured in the book include bird watching, sport fishing, backpacking, shopping, and special events. The book lists restaurants, accommodations, visitor's centers, and emergency information and best serves travelers on a low or moderate budget looking for an outdoor vacation close to home.

Evaluation: The area described in the book is very small, and many travelers would have their fill of the islands in a day. But they offer much more for those who will but look. This book introduces the reader to a variety of outdoor adventures, with entries that inform and interest without becoming bogged down in detail. A book such as this can stretch a weekend vacation into a week or longer. Its value increases with the price of gasoline.

Washington

See also Pacific Coast and The West under Regional Guides.

ACCOMMODATIONS AND RESTAURANTS

AAA TourBook: Washington. See AAA TourBook series under North America, Accommodations and Restaurants.

PRETRAVEL READING

Adventures in Washington. Archie Satterfield. Mercer Island, WA: The Writing Works, 1978. 138 pp. pap. $6.95.

Adventures in Washington is based on the experiences of the author and his family in and around the state. It offers short histories and legends of intriguing out-of-the-way sights and includes a variety of outdoor activities, such as skiing, hiking, clamming, and crabbing. The book emphasizes the rugged—fishing, camping, hiking, and trips to the back country. Many natural phenomena of the state are described, and a small section is included on the city of Seattle.

Evaluation: The first-person narrative style and the neighborly, storytelling quality of the text give the book a distinctive down-home feeling. It most often reads like a novel, which tends to blur the information. It will give you a feeling for the area before you take your trip, but another more general guide would be of more use on the road.

OUTDOOR RECREATION

121 Free Campgrounds in Washington State. Ed Bedrick and Christina Bedrick. Seattle, WA: Superior Publishing Co., 1977. 103 pp. pap. $4.95.

The emphasis of the book is on trailer and recreational vehicle camping, mostly outside of national and state parks. Often the location described is a spot off the road (near a river or lake) that is large enough to accommodate an RV. The short introduction gives basic camping information and tips on the seasons and road conditions. Many of the sights are free only in the off-season. The entries themselves are arranged geographically and include descriptions, directions, sporting activities in the area, and points of interest. The locations of the sites are marked on skeleton maps that precede each section. The book serves a small audience, but for that audience, it may be worthwhile.

Evaluation: The authors claim that you can save the price of the book on your first night out. This statement is true, but only for a limited number of travelers. The scope of the book is narrow—directed at tent and trailer campers in Washington State. The practical information in the book is at a minimum. The authors rely on descriptions in most entries, and more concrete information is sketchy and unevenly distributed.

Roads and Trails of Olympic National Park. Frederick Leissler. Seattle, WA: University of Washington Press (dist. in the U.K. by International Book Distributors), 4th ed. 1976. 84 pp. pap. $4.95 (£2.75).

Few guidebooks are this simple—a mere collection of descriptions of the many roads and trails that traverse Olympic National Park in the northwest corner of the state of Washington. A short preface describes the park, tells how to use the guide, and gives general hiking advice. The trails are divided into 15 areas, each with a description of one to five roads and five to sixteen trails of varying length. The trails and roads are shown on a series of maps of the area, and a mileage chart is included for each. The book has no practical information on camping, park services, or supplies, and the discussion on preparation is very informal.

Evaluation: Like many special-use guides, the book is most useful to residents of the Seattle area, who would be able to use the book on a number of visits to the park. Travelers unfamiliar with the area would need to use a complete sights/accommodations guide to the area in addition. There is little information in the entries other than road and trail directions and short descriptions of the terrain. This is all some hikers need, but those looking for more detailed information should look elsewhere.

Snow Tours in Washington. Mary Ann Cameron, ed. Edmonds, WA: Signpost Books, rev. 1979. 96 pp. pap. $4.95.

Recent years have seen a boom of sorts in outdoor winter sports activity. As an alternative to often crowded and usually expensive ski slopes, and the shattering frenzy of a herd of snowmobiles, there is now the snow tour. *Snow Tours in Washington* includes information for both cross-country skiers and snowshoers, whether novice or expert, with more than 125 tours described and many suggested side tours. The entries for each tour include short descriptions with references to possible hazards, directions to the starting point, distance, elevation gain, and on which topographic map the routes can be found. Each tour is rated for difficulty and is shown on a series of hand-drawn maps. Information is included on park permits and commercial facilities for snow travelers in the state.

Evaluation: The tour descriptions and directions are clear and easy to find on the maps provided, although better maps are necessary on the trails. The information on the tours is complete, but the lack of preparatory and emergency information calls for some previous snow-touring experience. The book is intended primarily for residents of the state. Travelers unfamiliar with the area would need to use an accommodations/transportation guide along with it.

Woodall's Idaho/Oregon/Washington Campground Directory. See *Woodall's Campground Directory: State Editions* under United States, Camping.

SCIENCE

Field Guide Series: Western Washington and Oregon. See Field Guide series under United States, Science.

WINE TOURS

Winery Tours in Oregon, Washington, Idaho and British Columbia. See the review of this title under Regional Guides, Pacific Coast, Wine Tours.

Seattle

The Seattle Guidebook. Archie Satterfield and Merle E. Dowd. Mercer Island, WA: The Writing Works, 3rd ed. 1977. 212 pp. pap. $3.95.

The Seattle Guidebook is a comprehensive city guide that describes nearly every facet of the city's people and places. It best serves those not limited by a tight budget, but the variety of information will be useful even to rock-bottom travelers. Special sections are included for foreign visitors, newcomers, singles, and senior citizens.

Evaluation: The book is a relaxed introduction to the city. It handles a wide range of information clearly and succeeds at being both practical and entertaining. The accommodations section falls short of the quality of the book's other sections, but with the fantastic number of sights and activities in the book, you may have no need for a room.

Other books in the series: The Portland Guidebook; The Spokane Guidebook.

Spokane

The Spokane Guidebook. See *The Seattle Guidebook* under Seattle, above.

West Virginia

See also Middle Atlantic and The South under Regional Guides.

AAA TourBook: West Virginia. See AAA TourBook series under North America, Accommodations and Restaurants.

Country Inns of Maryland, Virginia, and West Virginia. See the review of this title under Maryland, Accommodations and Restaurants.

Wisconsin

See also The Midwest under Regional Guides.

AAA TourBook: Wisconsin. See AAA TourBook series under North America, Accommodations and Restaurants.

Woodall's Wisconsin Campground Directory. See *Woodall's Campground Directory: State Editions* under United States, Camping.

Wyoming

See also Rocky Mountains under Regional Guides.

ACCOMMODATIONS AND RESTAURANTS

AAA TourBook: Wyoming. See AAA TourBook series under North America, Accommodations and Restaurants.

THE OUTDOORS

Field Book Series. Orrin H. Bonney and Lorraine G. Bonney. Chicago, IL: The Swallow Press, 2nd ed. 1977. approx. 200 pp. pap. $5.95.

The books in this series are selected chapters from a larger work, *Guide to the Wyoming Mountains and Wilderness Areas.* They are complete hiking and climbing guides to the mountains of the state. Each includes long preparatory sections, safety tips, a description of the American Rating System, a chapter on hunting and fishing, campgrounds, and climbing histories. A major feature of the books is the detailed descriptions of the trails and climbing routes. The books were meant to be used along with topographic or forest maps, and information is included on how to acquire them. They serve both as pretravel reading and as references while on the trip. Information is included for beginners, but most of the trails and climbs in the area require some expertise.

Evaluation: The information in the Field Book series is complete and well presented. The entries emphasize history and practical information much more than descriptions, with directions and points of interest kept short and clear. Each of the series covers a smaller area than most hiking guides, but few others are as complete. Their completeness and ease of use make them ideal hiking and climbing guides.

Included in the series: Field Book: The Big Horn Range; Field Book: The Teton Range and the Gros Ventre Range; Field Book: The Wind River Range; Field Book: Yellowstone and the Absaroka Range.

A Guide to Geyser Gazing. John S. Rinehart. Santa Fe, NM: Hyper-Dynamics, 1976. 64 pp. pap. $1.40.

Many travelers, when viewing a natural wonder such as Niagara Falls, the Grand Canyon, or the Old Faithful geyser, see as much as they care to see after a few minutes. They watch passively, perhaps take a photograph or two, and move on. Others, however, have their interest fanned by such sights and crave answers to some of the questions these wonders pose. *A Guide to Geyser Gazing* is for travelers who are not satisfied to watch and wonder. It explains the mechanisms behind all types of active geysers in the world, with an emphasis on those found in Yellowstone National Park. The short book includes references to their histories and geological settings, the effects of weather, tides, and earthquakes, cold water geysers, and geothermal power. Charts and illustrations help clarify the information, and a complete reading list is included. The book is particularly useful to those visiting Yellowstone, but anyone with the least interest in geysers will appreciate the book.

Evaluation: The technical information is handled clearly, although some previous science background is useful when reading the book. It has a very narrow scope of information, but that which is included covers the subject of geysers completely. The book serves as an excellent complement to a more complete camping guide to different areas in the West, particularly to the area around Yellowstone National Park.

DIRECTORY OF PUBLISHERS

Abelard-Schuman Ltd.
10 E. 53 St.
New York, NY 10022

Acropolis Books Ltd.
2400 17 St. N.W.
Washington, DC 20009

Alaska Northwest Publishing Co.
130 Second Ave. S.
Edmonds, WA 98020

American Adventures Association
444 N.E. Ravenna Blvd., Suite 301
Seattle, WA 98115

American Automobile Association
8111 Gatehouse Rd.
Falls Church, VA 22042

American Federation of Teachers
11 Dupont Circle N.W.
Washington, DC 20036

American Map Co. Inc.
1926 Broadway
New York, NY 10023

American Youth Hostels Inc.
Delaplane, VA 22025

Anchor Press
See Doubleday & Co. Inc.

And/Or Press Inc.
Box 2246
Berkeley, CA 94702

Appalachian Books
Box 249
Oakton, VA 22124

Arco Publishing Co. Inc.
219 Park Ave. S.
New York, NY 10003

Ariel Publications
Box 255
Mercer Island, WA 98040

Atheneum Publishers
597 Fifth Ave.
New York, NY 10017

Automobile Association
Fanum House
Basingstoke, Hampshire RG21 2EA, England

Avon Books
The Hearst Corp.
959 Eighth Ave.
New York, NY 10019

Banyan Books
7575 S.W. 62 Ave., Suite B
South Miami, FL 33143

19 Aberdeen Rd.
London N5 2UG, England

B. T. Batsford Ltd.
Box 57
North Pomfret, VT 05053

Box 4
Braintree, Essex CM7 7QY, England

Ernest Benn Ltd.
Sovereign Way
Tonbridge, Kent TN9 1RW, England

Berkshire Traveller Press
Pine St.
Stockbridge, MA 01262

The Bobbs-Merrill Co. Inc.
Box 558
4300 W. 62 St.
Indianapolis, IN 46206

Bookpeople
2940 Seventh St.
Berkeley, CA 94710

Bradt Enterprises
409 Beacon St.
Boston, MA 02115

Branden Press
Box 843, 21 Station St.
Brookline, MA 02147

British Tourist Authority
Queen's House
64 Saint James's St.
London SW1A 1NF, England

Burns & MacEachern Ltd.
62 Railside Rd.
Don Mills, ON M3A 1A6, Canada

Jonathan Cape Ltd.
30 Bedford Square
London WC1B 3EL, England

Capra Press
Box 2068
Santa Barbara, CA 93120

Caroline House Publishers
Box 978
Edison, NJ 08817

Carousel Press
Box 6061
Albany, CA 94706

The Caxton Printers Ltd.
Box 700
Caldwell, ID 83605

Celestial Arts
231 Adrian Rd.
Millbrae, CA 94030

Chatham Press Inc.
143 S. Beach
Old Greenwich, CT 06870

Chatham Square Press Inc.
401 Broadway
New York, NY 10013

Chicago Review Press Inc.
820 N. Franklin St.
Chicago, IL 60610

China Books
2929 24 St.
San Francisco, CA 94110

China Publications
2700 Mariposa Dr.
Burlingame, CA 94010

Chronicle Books
870 Market St., Suite 915
San Francisco, CA 94102

Clio Press Inc.—The American Bibliographical Center
Box 4397, 2040 Alameda Padre Serra
Santa Barbara, CA 93103

The Coda Press
700 W. Badger Rd., Suite 101
Madison, WI 53713

Collet's Holdings Ltd.
Denington Estate
Wellingborough, Northamptonshire
NN8 2QT, England

Collier Books
See Macmillan Publishing Co. Inc.

William Collins Sons & Co. Ltd.
14 St. James's Place
London SW1A 1PS, England

Comstock Editions Inc.
3030 Bridgeway Blvd.
Sausalito, CA 94965

Thomas Congdon Books
See E. P. Dutton

Contemporary Books Inc.
180 N. Michigan Ave.
Chicago, IL 60601

Frank Cook Travel Guides
8 Wykeham Court
Old Perry St.
Chislehurst, Kent BR7 6PN, England

Cornerstone Library Inc.
See Simon & Schuster Inc.

Council on International Educational Exchange
205 E. 42 St.
New York, NY 10017

Creative Communications
3430 W. Main
Kalamazoo, MI 49007

Thomas Y. Crowell Co.
521 Fifth Ave.
New York, NY 10017

Dance Books Ltd.
9 Cecil Court
London WC2N 4EZ, England

Dance Horizons
1801 E. 26 St.
Brooklyn, NY 11229

David & Charles Inc.
Box 57
North Pomfret, VT 05053

David & Charles Ltd.
Brunel House
Newton Abbott, Devon TQ12 2DW, England

The Dillon-Donnelly Press
7058 Lindell Blvd.
St. Louis, MO 63130

Dodd, Mead & Co.
79 Madison Ave.
New York, NY 10016

Doubleday & Co. Inc.
501 Franklin Ave.
Garden City, NY 11530

E. P. Dutton
2 Park Ave.
New York, NY 10016

E. P. Group of Cos.
Bradford Rd.
East Ardsley
Wakefield, W. Yorkshire WF3 2JN, England

EPM Publications Inc.
1003 Turkey Run Rd.
McLean, VA 22101

The East Woods Press
See Fast & McMillan Publishers Inc.

Eurasia Press Inc.
16 Fulton Place
Fair Lawn, NJ 07410

Evergreen Paddleways
1416 21 St.
Two Rivers, WI 54241

Exposition Press
325 Kings Highway
Smithtown, NY 11787

F. O. S. G. Publications
Box 239
Oradell, NJ 07649

Far Eastern Economic Review
G.P.O. Box 47
Tong Chong St.
Hong Kong

Farm & Ranch Vacations
36 E. 57 St.
New York, NY 10022

Fast & McMillan Publishers Inc.
820 East Blvd.
Charlotte, NC 28203

George Wright Ferguson
Box 2033, 2000 W. Henderson Rd.
Columbus, OH 43220

Field Research Projects
3551 Main Highway
Miami, FL 33133

Fielding Publications
105 Madison Ave.
New York, NY 10016

Fleet Press Corp.
160 Fifth Ave.
New York, NY 10010

Henry Fletcher Services Ltd.
304 Taylor Rd.
West Hill, ON M1C 2R6 Canada

Follett Publishing Co.
1010 W. Washington Blvd.
Chicago, IL 60607

Ford's Travel Guides Inc.
Box 505, 22030 Ventura Blvd., Suite B
Woodland Hills, CA 91365

Burt Franklin & Co.
235 E. 44 St.
New York, NY 10017

Frommer/Pasmantier Publishing Corp.
380 Madison Ave.
New York, NY 10017

Gambit
27 N. Main St.
Meeting House Green
Ipswich, MA 01938

The Globe Pequot Press Inc.
Box Q, Old Chester Rd.
Chester, CT 06412

David R. Godine, Publisher Inc.
306 Dartmouth St.
Boston, MA 02116

Good Life Publishers
713 N. Courthouse Rd.
Richmond, VA 23235

Jack Grauer
1220 S.W. 66, Apt. 2228
Portland, OR 97225

The Stephen Greene Press
Box 1000, Fessenden Rd., Indian Flat
Brattleboro, VT 05301

Greey de Pencier Publications Ltd.
59 Front St. E.
Toronto, ON M5E 1B3, Canada

H. P. Books
Box 5367
Tucson, AZ 85703

Hagstrom Co. Inc.
450 W. 33 St.
New York, NY 10001

Robert Hale Ltd.
Clerkenwell House
Clerkenwell Green
London EC1R OHT, England

Hammond Inc.
515 Valley St.
Maplewood, NJ 07040

Harian Books
One Vernon Ave.
Floral Park, NY 11001

Harmony Books/Crown Publishers Inc.
One Park Ave.
New York, NY 10016

Harper & Row, Publishers Inc.
10 E. 53 St.
New York, NY 10022

Hastings House, Publishers Inc.
10 E. 40 St.
New York, NY 10016

Herman Publishing Inc.
45 Newbury St.
Boston, MA 02116

Hippocrene Books
171 Madison Ave.
New York, NY 10016

Hodder & Stoughton Services
Box 6, Mill Rd., Dunton Green
Sevenoaks, Kent TN13 2XX, England

Hutchison Publishing
99 Main St.
Salem, NH 03079

HyperDynamics
Box 392
Santa Fe, NM 87501

IBEG Ltd.
2-4 Brook St.
London W1Y 1AA, England

I.S.B.S.
Box 555, 2130 Pacific Ave.
Forest Grove, OR 97116

International Book Distributors Ltd.
66 Wood Lane End
Hemel Hempstead, Herts. HP2 4RG, England

International Intertrade Index
Box 636, Federal Square
Newark, NJ 07101

International Visitors Information Service
801 19 St. N.W.
Washington, DC 20006

International Youth Hostel Federation
Midland Bank Chambers, Howardsgate
Welwyn Garden City, Herts. England

David Jamieson & Associates Ltd.
c/o Middle East Review Co. Ltd.
21 Gold St.
Saffron Walden, Essex CB10 1EJ, England

Jansen Publishing
Box 21
Pinedale, CA 93650

The Johns Hopkins University Press
Baltimore, MD 21218

William Kaufman Inc.
One First St.
Los Altos, CA 94022

Kendall/Hunt Publishing Co.
2460 Kerper Blvd.
Dubuque, IA 52001

Key Publishers Ltd.
59 Front St. E.
Toronto, ON, Canada

The Knapp Press
5900 Wilshire Blvd.
Los Angeles, CA 90036

Kosoy Travel Guides
See St. Martin's Press

Lane Publishing Co.
Willow & Middlefield Rds.
Menlo Park, CA 94025

Roger Lascelles
3 Holland Park Mansions
16 Holland Park Gardens
London W14 8DY, England

Les Femmes Publishing
See Celestial Arts

Charles Letts & Co. Ltd.
3 Woodhollow Lane
Huntington, NY 11743

Dairy House
Borough Rd.
London SE1 1DW, England

Lompa Press
100 Colony Square
Atlanta, GA 30361

Lonely Planet Publications
Box 88
South Yarra
Victoria 3141, Australia

Robert P. Long
634 Bellmore Ave.
East Meadow, NY 11554

Lotus Press Ltd.
Chofu Box 15
Tokyo 182-91, Japan

Lunesdale Publishing Group Ltd.
Lunesdale House
Hornby, Lancaster LA2 8NB, England

The F. M. McCarthy Co.
4527 Clawson Rd.
Austin, TX 78745

Macmillan Publishing Co. Inc.
866 Third Ave.
New York, NY 10022

McGraw-Hill Book Co.
1221 Avenue of the Americas
New York, NY 10020

David McKay Co. Inc.
2 Park Ave.
New York, NY 10016

Paul Maitland
2/16 Mount Sion
Tunbridge Wells, Kent TN1 1UF, England

Meadowbrook Press Inc.
16648 Meadowbrook Lane
Wayzata, MN 55391

Merrimack Book Service
99 Main St.
Salem, NH 03079

Merton House Publishing Co.
937 W. Liberty Dr.
Wheaton, IL 60187

Michelin Guides & Maps
Michelin Tire Corp.
Box 5022
New Hyde Park, NY 11042

Michelin Tyre Co. Ltd.
Maps & Guides Dept.
81 Fulham Rd.
London SW3 6RD, England

Mongolia Society
Box 606
Bloomington, IN 47401

Moon Publications
Box 9223
Berkeley, CA 94709

William Morrow & Co. Inc.
105 Madison Ave.
New York, NY 10016

Mountain Press Publishing Co.
Box 2399
Missoula, MT 59801

John Muir Publications
Box 613
Santa Fe, NM 87501

New Hampshire Publishing Co.
Box 70, Nine Orange St.
Somersworth, NH 03878

New Republic Books
1220 19 St. N.W., Suite 205
Washington, DC 20036

Nodin Press
c/o The Bookmen Inc.
519 N. Third St.
Minneapolis, MN 55401

Omega Books
428 Tamal Plaza
Corte Madera, CA 94925

101 Productions
834 Mission St.
San Francisco, CA 94103

The Oriental Publishing Co.
Box 22162
Honolulu, HI 96822

Oxford University Press
200 Madison Ave.
New York, NY 10016

Pacific Skipper
Box 1698
Newport Beach, CA 92663

Padre Productions
Box 1275
San Luis Obispo, CA 93406

Pan American Airways Inc.
Pan Am Bldg.
New York, NY 10017

Pelican Publishing Co. Inc.
630 Burmaster St.
Gretna, LA 70053

Penguin Books
625 Madison Ave.
New York, NY 10022

Penguin Books Ltd.
Bath Rd.
Harmondsworth, Middlesex UB7 0DA, England

The Pequot Press Inc.
Old Chester Rd.
Chester, CT 06412

Peregrine Smith Inc.
Box 667
Layton, UT 84041

The Petroglyph Press
211 Kinoole St.
Hilo, HI 96720

Phoenix Book Publishers
1641 E. McLellan Blvd.
Phoenix, AZ 85016

Phoenix Publishing
Canaan, NH 03741

Pilot Books
347 Fifth Ave.
New York, NY 10016

Potomac Books Inc., Publishers
4418 MacArthur Blvd. N.W.
Washington, DC 20007

Prentice-Hall Inc.
Englewood Cliffs, NJ 07632

Project Press
710 Wilshire Blvd.
Santa Monica, CA 90401

Pruett Publishing Co.
3235 Prairie Ave.
Boulder, CO 80301

Quail Run Publications Inc.
5221 N. Quail Run Place
Paradise Valley, AZ 85253

Quick Fox (Music Sales Corp.)
33 W. 60 St.
New York, NY 10023

Rail-Europe
Box 3255
Alexandria, VA 22302

Rand McNally & Co.
Box 7600
Chicago, IL 60680

Random House
201 E. 50 St.
New York, NY 10022

Egon Ronay Organization Ltd.
Greencoat House
Francis St.
London SW1P 1DH, England

Sage Books Inc.
216 E. 45 St.
New York, NY 10017

St. Martin's Press
175 Fifth Ave.
New York, NY 10010

The Saltzman Cos.
27450 Pacific Coast Highway
Malibu, CA 90265

The Sandlapper Store Inc.
Box 841, 101 West Main
Lexington, SC 29072

Scottish Development Agency
102 Telford Rd.
Edinburgh EH4 2NP, Scotland

Charles Scribner's Sons
597 Fifth Ave.
New York, NY 10017

Selpress Books
16 Berkeley St.
London W1X 6AP, England

Seymour Press Ltd.
334 Brixton Rd.
London SW9 7AG, England

Shufunotomo Co. Ltd.
1-Chome, Surugadai, Kanda,
Chiyoda-ku
Tokyo 101, Japan

Sierra Club Books
530 Bush St.
San Francisco, CA 94108

Signpost Books
8912 192 St. S.W.
Edmonds, WA 98020

Simon & Schuster Inc.
The Simon & Schuster Bldg.
1230 Avenue of the Americas
New York, NY 10020

Doug Smith
Box 260
Corvallis, OR 97330

Genny Smith Books
1304 Pitman Ave.
Palo Alto, CA 94301

Southwest Parks & Monuments Association
Box 1562
Globe, AZ 85501

Stackpole Books
Box 1831, Cameron and Keller Sts.
Harrisburg, PA 17105

Standing Orders
Box 183
Patterson, NY 12563

Stanford University Press
Stanford, CA 94305

Stone Wall Press Inc.
5 Byron St.
Boston, MA 02108

The Stonehill Publishing Co.
10 E. 40 St., Suite 2109
New York, NY 10016

Sun Publishing Co.
Box 4383
Albuquerque, NM 87106

Superior Publishing Co.
Box 1710, 708 Sixth Ave. N.
Seattle, WA 98111

The Swallow Press Inc.
811 W. Junior Terrace
Chicago, IL 60613

Thorsons Publishers Ltd.
Denington Estate
Wellingborough, Northamptonshire
NN8 2RQ, England

Timber Press
Box 10766
Portland, OR 97210

Topgallant Publishing Co.
Elizabeth Bldg.
845 Mission Lane
Honolulu, HI 96813

The Touchstone Press
Box 81
Beaverton, OR 97005

Trade & Travel Publications Ltd.
The Mendip Press
Parsonage Lane
Bath BA1 1EN, England

Transatlantic Arts Inc.
North Village Green
Levittown, NY 11756

Travel Aid Services Ltd.
7A Belsize Park
London NW3, England

Travel Digests
Paul Richmond & Co.
73-465 Ironwood
Palm Desert, CA 92260

Travel Information Bureau
Box 105
Kings Park, NY 11754

Travelaid Publishers
Box 38
Southwater Industrial Estate
Southwater, Sussex, England

Travelwise Inc.
411 Crest Dr.
Holland, MI 49423

Troll Associates
320 Route 17
Mahwah, NJ 07430

Charles E. Tuttle Co.
28 S. Main St.
Rutland, VT 05701

The Two Continents Publishing Group Inc.
171 Madison Ave.
New York, NY 10016

The University of Michigan Press
Box 1104
Ann Arbor, MI 48106

University of Nevada Press
Reno, NV 89557

University of Oklahoma Press
1005 Asp Ave.
Norman, OK 73019

University of Washington Press
Seattle, WA 98105

The University Press of Hawaii
2840 Kolowalu St.
Honolulu, HI 96822

Vacation-Work
9 Park End St.
Oxford OX1 1HJ, England

Vanguard Press Inc.
424 Madison Ave.
New York, NY 10017

Vantage Press Inc.
516 W. 34 St.
New York, NY 10001

The Viking Press Inc.
625 Madison Ave.
New York, NY 10022

Vintage Books
See Random House

Vintage Image
1335 Main St.
St. Helena, CA 94574

Volunteers in Asia Inc.
Box 4543
Stanford, CA 94305

Wasatch Publishers Inc.
4647 Idlewild Rd.
Salt Lake City, UT 84117

Washington Mews Books—New York University Press
Washington Square
New York, NY 10003

Washingtonian Books
1828 L St. N.W., Suite 200
Washington, DC 20036

Waxwing Productions
139 Scarborough Rd.
Toronto, ON M4E 3M4, Canada

Wayne State University Press
Leonard N. Simons Bldg.
5959 Woodward Ave.
Detroit, MI 48202

George Weidenfeld & Nicolson Ltd.
91 Clapham High St.
London SW4 9TA, England

J. Well Inc.
Box 15194
Detroit, MI 48215

Westridge Press Ltd.
1090 Southridge Place S.
Salem, OR 97302

Wexas (World Expeditionary Association) International Inc.
Graybar Bldg., Suite 354
420 Lexington Ave.
New York, NY 10017

45 Brompton Rd.
Knightsbridge
London SW3 1DE, England

The Wheelchair Traveler
Ball Hill Rd.
Milford, NH 03055

Wilderness Press
2440 Bancroft Way
Berkeley, CA 94704

Wildwood Press
2110 Wood Ave.
Colorado Springs, CO 80907

Wilton House Gentry Ltd.
Wilton House
Hobart Place
London SW1, England

Windward Publishing Inc.
Box 371005, 105 N.E. 25 St.
Miami, FL 33137

Woodall Publishing Co.
500 Hyacinth Place
Highland Park, IL 60035

Woodbridge Press Publishing Co.
Box 6189
Santa Barbara, CA 93111

World Expeditionary Association
See Wexas

World Publications Inc.
1400 Stierlin Rd.
Mountain View, CA 94043

Writer's Digest Books
9933 Alliance Rd.
Cincinnati, OH 45242

The Writing Works Inc.
7438 S.E. 40 St.
Mercer Island, WA 98040

YHA Services Ltd.
14 Southampton St.
London WC2E 7HY, England

TITLE–SUBJECT INDEX

S0-AYY-469

THE LITERATURE OF DEATH AND DYING

This is a volume in the Arno Press collection

THE LITERATURE OF DEATH AND DYING

See last pages of this volume for a complete list of titles

THE

FEAR OF THE DEAD IN PRIMITIVE RELIGION

JAMES GEORGE FRAZER

Volumes One,
Two and Three

ARNO PRESS

A New York Times Company

New York / 1977

Reprint Edition 1977 by Arno Press Inc.

THE LITERATURE OF DEATH AND DYING
ISBN for complete set: 0-405-09550-3
See last pages of this volume for titles.

Manufactured in the United States of America

Library of Congress Cataloging in Publication Data
Frazer, James George, Sir, 1854-1941.
The fear of the dead in primitive religion.

(The Literature of Death and dying)
Reprint of the ed. published by Macmillan, London, which was issued as the 1932-1933 Lectures delivered on the William Wyse Foundation.
Includes bibliographical references.
1. Dead (in religion, folk-lore, etc.)--Addresses, essays, lectures. 2. Ancester worship--Addresses, essays, lectures. 3. Religion, Primitive--Addresses, essays, lectures. I. Title. II. Series. III. Series: Cambridge. University. Trinity College. William Wyse Foundation. Lectures delivered on the William Wyse Foundation ; 1932-1933.

BL470.F7 1977 291.2'3 76-19571
ISBN 0-405-09566-X

THE FEAR OF THE DEAD IN PRIMITIVE RELIGION

MACMILLAN AND CO., LIMITED
LONDON · BOMBAY · CALCUTTA · MADRAS
MELBOURNE

THE MACMILLAN COMPANY
NEW YORK · BOSTON · CHICAGO
DALLAS · ATLANTA · SAN FRANCISCO

THE MACMILLAN COMPANY
OF CANADA, LIMITED
TORONTO

THE FEAR OF THE DEAD IN PRIMITIVE RELIGION

LECTURES DELIVERED ON
THE WILLIAM WYSE FOUNDATION
AT TRINITY COLLEGE, CAMBRIDGE
1932–1933

BY

SIR JAMES GEORGE FRAZER
O.M., F.R.S., F.B.A.

FELLOW OF TRINITY COLLEGE, CAMBRIDGE
ASSOCIATE MEMBER OF THE *INSTITUT DE FRANCE*

MACMILLAN AND CO., LIMITED
ST. MARTIN'S STREET, LONDON
1933

PRINTED IN GREAT BRITAIN
BY R. & R. CLARK, LIMITED, EDINBURGH

PREFACE

THESE lectures were delivered on the William Wyse Foundation at Trinity College, Cambridge, in the Michaelmas Term of 1932 and the May Term of 1933. They are printed almost exactly as they were spoken, except that a few passages, including a long one at the end of the Sixth Lecture, which were omitted for the sake of brevity in oral delivery, are here retained in the text. It was my intention to pursue the subject in subsequent lectures, and ultimately in a systematic treatise which should embrace the substance of all the lectures, together with a good deal of additional matter. But circumstances oblige me to defer for a time, perhaps indefinitely, the execution of this design. Meanwhile, I publish these introductory lectures as an instalment of the larger work in the hope that they may draw the attention of readers to a side of primitive thought which hitherto has hardly attracted the notice it deserves, for there can be little doubt that the fear of the dead has been a prime source of primitive religion.

On the question of how far the almost universal belief in the survival of the human spirit after death, which is implied by the fear of the dead, can be regarded as evidence of the truth of that survival, opinions will doubtless always be divided. From the crudities, inconsistencies and absurdities in which the belief commonly clothes itself, an impartial observer might be tempted to conclude that the spirits of the dead exist only in the imagination of the fond and foolish portion of mankind; but this conclusion, so little consonant with the natural wishes, and perhaps the instincts, of humanity, is not likely to be ever popular, and it seems probable that the great majority of our species will continue to acquiesce in a belief so flattering to human vanity and so comforting to human sorrow. And it cannot be denied that the champions of eternal life have entrenched themselves in a strong, if not impregnable, position; for if it is impossible to prove the immortality of the soul, it is, in the present state of our knowledge, equally impossible to disprove it. But the batteries of science have an ever longer range, and on this side they may yet make a deep breach in the frowning bastions of faith.

I cannot close this preface without thanking my beloved College of Trinity for the honour it has done me by associating me in these lectures with the memory of my ever dear and honoured friend, William Wyse, who, by his noble Foundation, has not only created an instrument for the advancement of knowledge, but has erected for himself a monument to a life unswervingly devoted to the pursuit of truth and to all that is good and beautiful in humanity. I could wish that my own contribution to the monument were less unworthy of it and of him.

J. G. FRAZER

7th June 1933

CONTENTS

LECTURE I

LECTURE I

Men commonly believe that their conscious being will not end at death, but that it will be continued for an indefinite time or for ever, long after the frail corporeal envelope which lodged it for a time has mouldered in the dust. This belief in the immortality of the soul, as we call it, is by no means confined to the adherents of those great historical religions which are now professed by the most civilized nations of the world; it is held with at least equal confidence by most, if not all, of those peoples of lower culture whom we call savages or barbarians, and there is every reason to think that among them the belief is native; in other words, that it originated among them in a stage of savagery at least as low as that which they now occupy, and that it has been handed down among them from generation to generation without being materially modified by contact with races at higher levels of culture. It is therefore a mistake to suppose that the hope of immortality after death was first revealed to mankind by the founders of the great historical religions, Buddhism, Christianity and Islam; to all appearance, it was cherished by men all over the world thousands of years before Buddha, Jesus Christ and Mohammed were born. Indeed, it is safe to conjecture that these great religious revolutionaries were not in this respect innovators, but that they owed in some measure the rapid success which attended their teaching to the circumstance that they accepted the current and popular belief in immortality and built on it, as on a sure foundation, their towering structures of theology which would topple over and crash to the ground if the belief in immortality were to be proved baseless. No doubt the founders of the historic faiths modified the existing belief in many respects, particularly by giving it an ethical character as the ultimate and supreme sanction of morality. This was a very important innovation; for in the lower religions, as a rule, the belief in immortality is entirely divested of any ethical significance; in them the virtuous are not rewarded and the bad are not punished in the life after death; all goes on in the other world much as in this; there is no awful judgment to be anticipated by all, no blissful eternity to be hoped for by the good, no eternity of torture to be dreaded by the wicked.

But in these lectures I am not concerned with the belief in immortality as it is taught in the higher religions; I shall confine myself strictly to that momentous belief as it meets us in what I call primitive religion, by which, roughly speaking, I mean the religion of the backward or uncivilized races; in other words, savages and barbarians.

When I speak of their religion as primitive I use the word primitive in a relative, not an absolute, sense; elsewhere I have expressly disclaimed, and I desire here again to disclaim, any knowledge whatever of absolutely primitive man and his religion; existing savages are doubtless highly developed physically, intellectually and morally, by comparison with their ancestors in the remote past, but by comparison with the civilized nations of the present time they may fairly be described as primitive in a relative sense, and it is in that relative sense alone that I speak of their religion as primitive.

But in treating of the fear of the dead I shall not confine myself strictly to evidence drawn from the customs and beliefs of savages in the ordinary sense of the word; I shall occasionally, or even frequently, borrow my examples from the beliefs and practices of civilized nations, among whom many primitive practices and ideas concerning the dead exist in the form of survivals, in short, as folklore. For it is one of the most assured results of the study of folklore that the customs and beliefs of the uneducated classes in civilized society often present a surprising analogy to those of savages, and therefore deserve to be similarly described as primitive by comparison with the customs and beliefs of the educated and cultured members of the community; in short, under the polished surface of civilized society there exists a deep stratum of savagery, which finds vent in eruptions of crime as well as in the comparatively, or even wholly, harmless and generally picturesque form of folklore.

I have defined the sense in which I employ the term primitive as applied to religion. I wish now to define the sense in which I use the phrase, "the immortality of the soul". By "the soul" I mean simply the unknown principle of life about which philosophers have disputed from the days of Plato and Aristotle to the present time, and to all appearance are likely to dispute till life on earth is extinguished by some final cosmic catastrophe, unless in the meantime science should crown its long series of victories over nature by discovering the origin of life. And with regard to the word immortality, I employ it somewhat loosely, for the sake of brevity, to include the conception of the prolongation of life after death for a longer or shorter period, or for a wholly indefinite time, not necessarily for ever. Strictly speaking, the term immortality implies the conception of eternity or infinite time, and such a conception is beyond the reach of uncivilized man; indeed we may perhaps doubt whether even the mind of the most accomplished philosopher and mathematician is capable of grasping it. In any case I shall speak of the immortality of the soul in a much humbler sense as the indefinite persistence of personality after death.

In that sense the belief in immortality has been remarkably widespread and persistent among mankind from the earliest times down to the present. Scepticism on the subject is rare and exceptional;

it is hardly found among savages but seems to grow commoner with the advance of civilization and the progress of thought. Still, even among savages there have been hardy spirits who doubted or denied the immortality of the soul. The inhabitants of the Tonga Islands in the Pacific thought that the souls of noblemen were immortal, but that the souls of commoners were not.[1] But this aristocratic faith appears to be unique; at all events I do not remember to have met with any other instance of such a spiritual privilege accorded to nobility. The generality of the Tongan lower orders, I may add, acquiesced in the belief that their souls perished with their bodies, though some of them were presumptuous enough to imagine that they had immortal souls like their betters.[2] Of the primitive tribes inhabiting the southern slopes of Mount Kenya in East Africa it is said, by one who has lived among them and administered them, that they appear to have no idea of a future life and that their general belief seems to be "that a man once dead is completely finished".[3] The Margi of Northern Nigeria believe in immortality through reincarnation of the souls of the dead in human infants; but they restrict this privilege to the souls of the good and deny it to the souls of the bad, which, they say, are destroyed by fire.[4] The Roba and northern

[1] W. Mariner, *Account of the Natives of the Tonga Islands* (London, 1818), ii. 99.

[2] W. Mariner, *op. cit.* ii. 128 *sq.*

[3] Major G. St. J. Orde Browne, *The Vanishing Tribes of Kenya* (London, 1925), pp. 205 *sq.*

[4] C. K. Meek, *Tribal Studies in Northern Nigeria* (London, 1931), i. 223.

Yungur of the same region seem to deny immortality impartially to good and bad alike.[1] The Binjhwar, a Dravidian tribe in the Central Provinces of India, are of a different opinion; they think that only the wicked survive death, becoming malignant ghosts, while the souls of well-behaved people are, to all appearance, simply snuffed out.[2] Thus the beliefs of primitive peoples on the subject of immortality present a considerable variety of choice to any one who might undertake to found a new religion; he might adopt the democratic doctrine of immortality for everybody; or the aristocratic doctrine of immortality only for noblemen; or the moral doctrine of immortality only for the good; or the immoral doctrine of immortality only for the bad; or lastly, the blighting doctrine of immortality for nobody. One of these alternatives must surely be right, since taken together they seem to exhaust the possibilities of survival after death; but which of them is the true solution of this profound problem it is not for the simple-minded anthropologist to decide.

The Assiniboin Indians of North America generally believed that the human soul lives after death, but some of them denied it, holding that death is the end of soul and body alike;[3] and the same negative belief is said to be held by the Central

[1] C. K. Meek, *Tribal Studies in Northern Nigeria*, ii. 462.

[2] R. V. Russell, *Tribes and Castes of the Central Provinces of India* (London, 1916), ii. 334.

[3] E. T. Denig, "The Assiniboin", *Forty-sixth Annual Report of the Bureau of American Ethnology* (Washington, 1930), pp. 498 *sq*.

Caribs of South America.[1] According to the Lakhers, a hill tribe of South-Eastern India, on the borders of Arakan, there is no second life for the dead, but when the dead man's spirit has been for a very long time in Athiki, the underground abode of the departed, the spirit dies again, and after this second death a chief's spirit is turned into a heat mist, and a poor man's spirit becomes a worm ; the heat mist goes up to heaven and vanishes, while the worm is eaten by a chicken, and that is an end of it.[2] Here again we are met by the aristocratic distinction between the fate of nobles and commoners in the after life, and though we are told that for the Lakhers there is no second life for the dead, yet at the same time we learn that the souls of the departed are supposed to exist in Athiki for a very long time, which may be regarded as nearly equivalent to immortality in the loose general sense in which I employ that term. Similarly the eminent Finnish scholar, Professor Karsten, a high authority on the South American Indians, tells us that the Tobas of the Bolivian Gran Chaco " certainly do not believe in the immortality of the soul, an expression often abused especially by Christian missionaries ", but he immediately adds : " On the other hand, the conviction of the continued existence of the soul after death is a positive dogma in their religion ".[3] What Professor Karsten here affirms

[1] W. C. Farabee, *The Central Caribs* (Philadelphia, 1924), p. 82.

[2] N. E. Parry, *The Lakhers* (London, 1932), p. 395.

[3] R. Karsten, *The Toba Indians of the Bolivian Gran Chaco* (Abo, 1923), p. 89.

of the Toba Indians of Bolivia might probably, if we knew all the facts, be affirmed with truth of all primitive races without distinction: they do not believe in the immortality of the soul in the strict sense of the word, for the simple reason that they lack the conception of eternity which that word implies; but they do most strongly believe in the continued existence of the human spirit after death, and they act on that belief with logical consistency in everyday life by seeking to gain from the spirits of the dead all the benefits, and to avert all the evils, which these ghostly powers are supposed to bestow or to inflict upon mankind. Of this attitude of primitive man towards the dead I shall adduce ample evidence elsewhere in these lectures; here I will only say a few words as to it by way of introduction to what follows. The general attitude of primitive man—and by primitive man I mean the savage—towards the spirits of the dead is very different from ours in that, on the whole, it is dominated by fear rather than by affection. We think of our beloved dead with sorrow and fond regret, and we can hardly conceive of any greater happiness than that of being reunited to them for ever in a better world beyond the grave. It is far otherwise with the savage. While it would be foolish and vain to deny that he often mourns sincerely the death of his relations and friends, he commonly thinks that their spirits undergo after death a great change, which affects their character and temper on the whole for the worse, rendering them touchy, irritable, irascible, prone to take offence on the slightest pretext and to visit their displeasure on the survivors by inflicting on them troubles of many sorts, including accidents of all kinds, drought, famine, sickness, pestilence and death. For it must always be borne in mind that in primitive religion the spirits of the dead are regularly supposed not only to exist but to exert an active and persistent influence on the life of the survivors by virtue of the very extensive powers which they are believed to possess in their disembodied state. These powers they are thought to put forth either for the good or the ill of their living friends and enemies; and as they are very jealous of their rights and very revengeful of any neglect or slight on the part of their friends or any injury done them by their enemies, the living have to be constantly on their guard against the dead; they must do everything in their power to please and nothing to offend these touchy spirits, who are only too ready to pick a quarrel even with the friends whom they loved and cherished in life. This belief in the continued power of the dead to affect the life of the survivors for good or ill is one of the most marked differences between the primitive and the civilized conceptions of life after death. In Protestant religion it has little or nothing to correspond to it, but in Catholicism it has a close analogy in the worship of the saints, those blessed spirits of the dead, who in virtue of their good deeds and their sufferings on earth are believed to possess in heaven the power of aiding and protecting the faithful in this world who submit themselves to their gracious keeping. The saints in glory, therefore, whom the Church commemorates to-day, answer to the spirits of the dead in primitive religion so far as these spirits are conceived in their beneficent aspect as the helpers and patrons of the living.

From what I have said you will have gathered that in the opinion of primitive man the life hereafter is very different from the conception which civilized man frames to himself of that awful subject. The savage in general imagines that life in the next world hardly differs in essentials from life in this world, and that dead men continue to feel the same passions and to experience the same needs which they felt and experienced in life. On this subject the eminent African explorer, Joseph Thomson, observes that by almost all the tribes of Eastern Africa "after death a person was supposed to feel pain, hunger, disease, just the same as before; he only took a new material existence, which differed from the present in that, like the wind, it could not be seen, though it was known to exist. They had not as yet grasped the idea of a pure spirit."[1] To the same effect a good authority on the Kafir tribes of South Africa tells us that in the opinion of these people the spirits of the dead "are intensely human. . . . The Kafir worships a magnified *very natural man*. The ancestral spirits love the very things they loved before they passed through the flesh;

[1] Joseph Thomson, in *Proceedings of the Royal Geographical Society* (1882), p. 212.

they cherish the same desires and have the same antipathies. The living cannot add to the number of the wives of ancestral spirits; but they can kill cattle in their honour and keep their praise and memory alive on earth. Above all things, they can give them beef and beer. And if the living do not give them sufficient of these things, the spirits are supposed to give the people a bad time; they send drought, and sickness and famine, until people kill cattle in their honour. When men are alive they love to be praised and flattered, fed and attended to; after death they want the very same things, for death does not change personality."[1] Similarly by the Thonga, a Bantu tribe of South Africa, the life of the other world is regarded as an exact reproduction of this terrestrial existence; the spirits of the dead are supposed to depart to a great village under the earth, where they till the fields, reap great harvests and live in abundance, and they take of this abundance to give to their descendants on earth; they have also a great many cattle.[2]

Like most rules, the rule that primitive folk regard the spirits of the dead with more fear than affection appears to be subject to exceptions; and as I do not wish to prejudge the case in favour of fear by overlooking the contrary instances, I will notice a few exceptions which I have met with before I adduce the mass, or rather a small part of the mass, of the evidence which seems to me con-

[1] Dudley Kidd, *The Essential Kafir* (London, 1904), pp. 88 *sq.*

[2] Henri A. Junod, *The Life of a South African Tribe*, Second Edition (London, 1927), ii. 375 *sq.*

clusively to establish the rule. The first exception I shall cite is that of the Trobriand Islanders, to the east of New Guinea. Speaking of them, Professor Malinowski, who knows them intimately, observes: "The main thing that struck me in connection with their belief in the spirits of the dead, was that they are almost completely devoid of any fear of ghosts, of any of those uncanny feelings with which we face the idea of a possible return of the dead. All the fears and dreads of the natives are reserved for black magic, flying witches, malevolent disease-bringing beings, but above all for sorcerers and witches. The spirits migrate immediately after death to the island of Tuma, lying in the north-west of Boyowa, and there they exist for another span of time, underground, say some, on the surface of the earth, though invisible, say others. They return to visit their own villages once a year, and take part in the big annual feast, *milamala*, where they receive offerings. Sometimes, at this season, they show themselves to the living, who are, however, not alarmed by it, and in general the spirits do not influence human beings very much, for better or worse. In a number of magical formulae, there is an invocation of ancestral spirits, and they receive offerings in several rites. But there is nothing of the mutual interaction, of the intimate collaboration between man and spirit which are the essence of religious cult." [1]

[1] Bronislaw Malinowski, *Argonauts of the Western Pacific* (London, 1922), pp. 72 *sq.* For full details as to the beliefs of the Trobriand

In this passage, which I have quoted entire, Professor Malinowski does not affirm that the Trobriand Islanders are absolutely devoid of fear of the dead, and as he tells us that the spirits of the dead are sometimes invoked and receive offerings, it is natural to suppose that if these marks of respect were withheld the spirits would be displeased and might find some means of visiting their displeasure on their undutiful relations. In the sequel we shall meet with many examples of such ghostly visitations. However, we may accept it on the high authority of Professor Malinowski that in comparison with many other savage races the Trobriand Islanders are remarkably free from the fear of the dead.

Another people who are reported to enjoy the same happy immunity are the Macheyenga of Eastern Peru, of whom we are told "that they 'have no fear of the dead', that is, of the ghost or soul of the departed. Nevertheless when one member of the family dies the others desert the home, and build another some distance away. 'They leave the house because they are afraid of the disease that took away the other member of the family, and for no other reason.'"[1] On this statement I would remark that the desertion of a house in which somebody has died is often expressly

Islanders on this subject see Professor Malinowski's article, "Baloma; the Spirits of the Dead in the Trobriand Islands", *Journal of the Royal Anthropological Institute*, xlvi. (1917) pp. 353-430.

[1] R. Karsten, *The Civilization of the South American Indians* (London, 1926), p. 479, quoting Farabee, *Indian Tribes of Eastern Peru*, pp. 12, 13, a work which I have not seen.

said to be due to the fear of the ghost of the deceased, and it may be so in the case of the Macheyenga, though the writer who reports the case gives another explanation of the custom. To that custom I shall return elsewhere in these lectures and will illustrate it by examples which seem to put its connexion with the fear of the dead beyond the reach of doubt.

Again, with regard to the natives of some parts of British New Guinea we are told by Dr. W. M. Strong that "it does not seem that there is ever any fear of the ghost of a dead relative. The native has a most intense desire to keep the remains of his dead relative near him. The old custom on the coast, both on the south and on the north coast, was for a dead body to be buried in or under the house or in the village. The government have forcibly compelled the natives to give up this custom. At Maiva, on the south coast, it once became the custom for the natives to openly bury the body in the appointed cemetery, and for them to secretly exhume it afterwards and to bury it in or under the house. In Mekeo it became the custom for the natives to go and live for two or three weeks in the cemetery after a relative had been buried. Special houses were built in the cemetery for this purpose. In the North-Eastern Division I found similar sentiments existing. The native usually places some belongings of the deceased near the grave. The Mekeo natives were anxious that the cemetery shall not be liable to be flooded because 'they do not like their relatives to be in the wet and cold'. I could never find in all this a belief that the ghost would resent any lack of proper treatment, but merely the continuation of the kindly way in which they previously regarded their relatives when living." [1] So far Dr. Strong.

The custom of burying the dead or preserving portions of them, particularly their skulls, in the houses which they inhabited in life has been widespread; it has prevailed in many parts of Africa, South America and some parts of Micronesia; and wherever it has prevailed and the survivors have continued to occupy the house containing the relics, we may take it as good evidence that the survivors did not greatly fear the ghost of their dead kinsman, but rather desired to keep him near them. But it is to be observed that many people who bury the dead in the house are in the habit of immediately thereafter abandoning or even destroying the house, which seems a clear indication of a fear of the ghost who may be supposed to haunt it. I shall return to this custom elsewhere; but here I will only observe that the custom of burying the dead in the house and continuing to inhabit it afterwards appears to have prevailed at an early date in some parts of Italy and Greece. The old writer Servius, whose commentary on Virgil is a gold-mine of folklore, tells us that the ancient Romans were always buried in their houses, and to this custom he traced the worship of the

[1] W. M. Strong, "Some Personal Experiences in British New Guinea", *Journal of the Royal Anthropological Institute*, xliv. (1919) p. 297.

domestic gods, the Lares, which in his opinion were clearly no other than the spirits of the dead.[1] A later Latin writer, who records the custom in similar terms, informs us that it was afterwards forbidden by law, in order to protect the bodies of the living from the noxious exhalations of the dead,[2] exactly as in our own time the native custom of burying the dead in the house has been forbidden by the British Government, for the same reason, in some parts of Africa [3] and New Guinea. Modern excavations in various parts of Greece, including Aegina, Attica, Argolis, Melos and Crete, prove that the burial of the dead in the house, particularly in jars interred beneath the floor, was practised by the Greeks, or rather by their predecessors, in Mycenaean, Minoan or earlier times. Young children especially seem to have been thus buried in jars under the floor of the house.[4] On this custom Dr. Farnell has justly remarked that "one important reflection is at once suggested: the earlier people, whoever they were, did not fear the contagion of the dead; believing in the continuance of the soul as we know that they did, they must have regarded the ghost with affection rather than with terror and desired to keep it in or near the family".[5]

This conclusion can be confirmed by a modern

[1] Servius, on Virgil, *Aen.* v. 64, vi. 151.

[2] Isidore, *Origines*, xv. 11. 1.

[3] A. B. Ellis, *The Tshi-speaking Peoples of the Gold Coast* (London, 1887), p. 239; P. Amaury Talbot, *Life in Southern Nigeria* (London, 1923), pp. 142, 146.

[4] See my note on Ovid, *Fasti*, ii. 615 (vol. ii. pp. 467 *sq.*), to which I may refer for fuller details as to house-burial.

[5] L. R. Farnell, *Greek Hero Cults and Ideas of Immortality* (Oxford, 1921), p. 4.

custom of house-burial which was practised till lately by the Gilbert Islanders, a Micronesian people in the Pacific. With them the grave was generally dug in the floor of the house; and a near relative would make a bed of the grave and open it from time to time to look on the beloved remains. The skull was very often removed and kept in a box; and the widow or child of the deceased would sleep and eat beside it, carry it about in all excursions, and frequently anoint it with coconut oil. Rarely the whole skeleton would be dug up from the grave and the bones hung to the ridge-pole of the family meeting-house, from which they were lowered from time to time and anointed for good luck in fishing, war or love.[1] Clearly the Gilbert Islanders did not fear the ghosts of their dead kinsfolk, but desired to keep them at hand in the expectation of receiving help from them in the practical affairs of life. In the sequel we shall see that the spirits of the dead are often supposed to aid their surviving kinsfolk both in peace and war. Similarly the Kingsmill Islanders, another Micronesian people in the Pacific, used sometimes to bury their dead in the house of the nearest relative; sometimes they stowed away the body in the loft of the building, and when the flesh was nearly gone they detached the skull, cleaned it and kept it as an object of worship.[2]

[1] A. Grimble, "From Birth to Death in the Gilbert Islands", *Journal of the Royal Anthropological Institute*, li. (1920) pp. 46 *sq.*

[2] Horatio Hale, *Ethnography and Philology of the United States Exploring Expedition* (Philadelphia, 1846), pp. 99 *sq.*

A different motive for the burial of the dead in the house is suggested by a tradition of the Gonds, the principal Dravidian tribe of India. It is said that formerly they buried the dead " in or near the house in which they died, so that their spirits would thus the more easily be born again in children, but this practice has now ceased ".[1] This Gond tradition, with the motive which it assigns for burying the dead in the house, is confirmed by a practice, still observed in some parts of India, of burying children, especially still-born infants, under the threshold of the house, for which the reason sometimes assigned is that in consequence of the daily passage of the parents across the threshold the child will be born again in the family.[2] The Andaman Islanders bury very young children under the floor of the hut, beneath the hearth, believing that the souls of the dead babies may re-enter their mothers' wombs and be born again.[3] In the light of these customs and beliefs it seems possible that the practice of burying adults in the houses in which they died may sometimes have been prompted by a desire to secure their rebirth in the family. Both the practice of house-burial and the belief in reincarnation are very common in Africa,[4] and the

[1] R. V. Russell, *Tribes and Castes of the Central Provinces of India* (London, 1916), iii. 89.

[2] W. Crooke, *Religion and Folklore of Northern India* (Oxford University Press, 1926), pp. 149 *sq.*, 345 ; further references in my note on Ovid, *Fasti*, ii. 573 (vol. ii. p. 447).

[3] A. R. Brown, *The Andaman Islanders* (Cambridge, 1922), p. 109.

[4] Much evidence of the belief in reincarnation in Africa has been collected by Mr. Theodore Besterman. See his paper, " The Belief in Rebirth among the Natives of Africa (including Madagascar) ", *Folklore*, xli. (1930) pp. 43-94.

coincidence seems to favour the theory that the two things may be vitally connected.

But perhaps nothing proves the absence of the fear of the dead more plainly than the habit which some people have of bringing back the soul of the deceased to the house after they have buried or otherwise disposed of the body elsewhere. The custom seems to be particularly common in India. Thus in some places the Gonds perform on the fifth day after a death the ceremony of bringing back the soul. The relatives go to the river-side and call aloud the name of the dead person, and then enter the river, catch a fish or insect and, taking it home, place it among the sainted dead of the family, believing that the spirit of the dead person has in this manner been brought back to the house. The brother-in-law or son-in-law of the deceased then makes a miniature grass hut in the compound (courtyard) and places the fish or insect inside it. He next sacrifices a pig, which is eaten, and next morning he breaks down the hut and throws away the earthen pots from the house. Further, they spread some flour on the ground and in the morning bring a chicken up to it. If the chicken eats the flour, they say that the soul of the deceased has shown his wish to remain in the house, and he is enshrined there in the shape of a stone or copper coin. If the chicken does not eat the flour, they say that the spirit will not remain in the house. So they take the stone or coin, which represents his spirit, outside the village, sacrifice a chicken to it, and bury it under a heap of stones to prevent the spirit from returning.[1] Thus we see that after the burial the Gonds bring back the soul of the dead to the house and give it the option of remaining there or outside the village. We have also seen that according to tradition the Gonds used to bury their dead in the house in order that their souls might be reborn in the family; and the same motive may underlie their present practice of bringing back the souls of the dead to the house, for they still believe that the spirits of ancestors are reincarnated in children or in animals. Sometimes they mark a corpse with soot or vermilion, and if afterwards a similar mark is found on any newborn child they think that the dead man's spirit has been reborn in it.[2]

The Ahirs, a caste of cowherds in the Central Provinces of India, similarly bring back the souls of their dead to the house in the form of fish, after they have buried or burnt the bodies elsewhere. The ceremony takes place on the third day after death. The women go with a lamp on a red earthen pot at night to a tank or stream. The fish are attracted by the light, and one of them is caught and put in the pot, which is then filled with water. The pot is brought home and set beside a small heap of flour, and the elders sit round it. The son of the deceased or other near relative anoints himself with turmeric and picks up a stone. The stone

[1] R. V. Russell, *Tribes and Castes of the Central Provinces of India*, iii. 94.

[2] R. V. Russell, *l.c.*

is then washed with water from the pot and placed on the floor, and a cock or a hen is sacrificed to it according as the deceased was a man or a woman. The stone is then enshrined in the house as a family god, and the sacrifice of a fowl is repeated annually. Apparently it is supposed that the dead man's spirit is brought back to the house in the fish and then transferred to the stone by washing it with the water which was in the pot, which held the fish, which contained the soul of the dead.[1]

When a man has been killed by a tiger, the Halbas, a caste of cultivators in the Central Provinces of India, think it absolutely essential to bring back his spirit to the house. The help of a hedge-priest (a Baiga) is invoked to perform the rite. To do this the priest suspends a copper ring on a long thread above a vessel of water and then burns butter and sugar on the fire, muttering incantations, while the people sing songs and call on the spirit of the dead man to return. The thread swings to and fro, and at length the copper ring falls into the pot, and this is taken as a sign that the spirit has come and entered into the vessel. The mouth of the pot is immediately covered and the pot is buried or kept in some secure place. Thus the soul of the dead man is kept in safe custody. The people believe that if the soul were left on the loose to wander at will, it would accompany the tiger which killed the man, and in that bad company it would lure solitary travellers to

[1] R. V. Russell, *Tribes and Castes of the Central Provinces of India*, ii. 28 *sq*.

their doom by calling out their names and offering them a quid of tobacco to smoke, and when the unwary wayfarer put out his hand to take the quid, the tiger would spring on him and gobble him up.[1] Thus we see how the spirit of a perfectly innocent man may, as a victim of circumstances over which he has no control, become a most dangerous ghost, and how necessary it is, in the public interest, to keep his ghost, if I may say so, under lock and key.

The Kharia, a primitive Kolarian tribe of the Central Provinces in India, bury their dead at a distance from the house, but bring back their souls on the tenth day after death. For this purpose they set a lighted wick in a vessel at a cross-road which the man's corpse had passed on its way to the grave, and at which consequently his ghost might naturally be supposed to loiter. There they call on the dead man, and when the flame of the lamp wavers in the wind they break the vessel that holds the lamp, saying that his soul has come back and joined them; so they go home together.[2] These people also believe that the dead are reborn in children;[3] hence one of their motives for bringing back the soul of a dead kinsman to the old home may be a hope that he will be born again in the family.

The Khonds, a Dravidian tribe of India, who were formerly notorious for their cruel human sacrifices, also believe that the dead are reborn in children, and like other tribes which cherish that

[1] R. V. Russell, *Tribes and Castes of the Central Provinces of India*, iii. 195 *sq*.

[2] R. V. Russell, *op. cit.* iii. 450.

[3] R. V. Russell *op cit.* iii. 451.

fond belief they strive to bring back the souls of the departed on the tenth day after the burial or cremation of their bodies. For that purpose outside the village at a cross-road, which is everywhere the favourite haunt of disembodied spirits, they offer rice to a cock, and if the bird eats it they accept it as a sign that the soul has come. So they beg the soul to ride on a bowstick covered with cloth, and mounted on that vehicle the spirit is brought back to the house and installed in a corner with the souls of other dead kinsfolk who are supposed to be awaiting reincarnation.[1]

Similarly the Lohars, a caste of blacksmiths in the Central Provinces of India, believe in the reincarnation of the dead and call their spirits home when they have buried or burnt their bodies. For this purpose rice-flour is spread on the floor of the cooking-room and covered with a brass plate. The women retire and sit in an adjoining room, while the chief mourner, with a few companions, goes outside the village and sprinkles some more rice-flour. They call to the deceased person, saying, "Come! Come!" and then wait patiently till some worm or insect crawls on to the flour. A pinch of dough is then applied to the creature, and, thus caught, the worm or insect is carried home and let loose in the house. The flour under the brass plate is now examined, and it is said that they usually discern the footprints of a person or an animal, indicating the body of the man or beast in which the

[1] R. V. Russell, *Tribes and Castes of the Central Provinces of India*, iii. 469.

wandering soul of the deceased has found another place of rest.[1]

The Taonla, a small non-Aryan caste of the Uriya States in India, hold similar beliefs and practise similar customs. They believe in the re-incarnation of the dead, and when a child is born they try to ascertain which ancestor has come back by dropping coloured grains of rice, one by one, in water, and naming an ancestor at every grain; the first grain that floats gives the desired name. They both bury and burn the dead, and observe a ceremony for bringing back their souls. Outside the village an earthen pot is placed upside down on four legs as a chair for the soul of the dead to sit on, and on the eleventh day after the death they go to the spot, ringing a bell. Arrived at the place, they spread a cloth before the upturned pot on which the ghost is believed to be sitting, and there they wait till an insect alights on the cloth. The creature is thought to be the soul of the dead, and it is carefully wrapped up in the cloth and carried back to the house. There the cloth is unfolded and the insect allowed to go; some rice-flour spread on the ground is inspected, and if any mark is found on it they are sure that the dead man's spirit has come home.[2]

Among the Khasis of North-Eastern India, when a man has died in a distant village or district every attempt is made by his family to lead back his spirit,

[1] R. V. Russell, *Tribes and Castes of the Central Provinces of India*, iv. 124.

[2] R. V. Russell, *op. cit.* iv. 541.

with or without his calcined bones, to his native place. Emissaries are sent to the village where he died to bring home his mortal remains if possible, but certainly his soul. On their return journey they take great pains to guide the soul on the right road, lest haply it should wander by the way and be lost. They pluck leaves and place them with rice at the wayside as offerings to lure the spirit onward. And when they come to a river, through which the spirit cannot wade, they stretch a cotton thread across it from bank to bank to serve as a bridge for the soul. If the river is broad, they plant notched sticks in its bed and attach the string to their tops, lest the string should droop into the water and the poor soul should fall into it and be drowned or swept away by the current. But if the stream should be very narrow, a stick or even a simple stalk of grass laid across it is deemed a bridge sufficient for the passage of the soul.[1]

A ceremony of bringing back the soul of a dead person after the burial of his body is also practised by the Mailu people of British New Guinea. Three or four days after the burial, eight or ten young men, generally led by the particular comrade (*isigoina*) of the deceased, remain behind at the grave, when the other mourners, who have been engaged in the obsequies at it, have left for the village. They go off into the forest near one of the pieces of

[1] H. H. Godwin-Austen, "On the Stone Monuments of the Khasi Hill Tribes", *Journal of the Anthropological Institute*, i. (1872) pp. 132 *sq*. Compare Capt. T. H. Lewin, *Wild Tribes of South-Eastern India* (London, 1870), pp. 209 *sq*.

land owned by the deceased, there to call back his spirit to the village. While the others hide behind trees or bushes, the special comrade of the deceased calls out to the dead man's spirit, " We are about to sail for sago. Come ! " Meantime all those in hiding put their hands to their ears to catch the reply of the spirit. Again the cry rings out, " We are about to sail to Uri to get pigs. Come, because we are sailing. Oh, companion, we are sailing to Uri to get that pig. Come ! " Sometimes the men in hiding hear an *o* sound which they take to be the voice of some one who died long ago, and not that of their recently departed brother. So they give up that spot and go off to another piece of the deceased's land, where the same calls to his spirit are repeated till they hear a feeble " *oooooo* " in response. Pricking up their ears at that, they cry, " He has come ! " So they run to the path and stand in line on either side of it, while two of them rush off to the village to help the spirit to find his way correctly to his old house. They have to make haste, for the spirit runs fast and leaps as he goes. The other eight men follow at leisure.[1]

The Abchases, a people of the Caucasus, have a remarkable way of recovering the soul of a drowned man after his body has been rescued from the water and buried. Men and women assemble on both banks of the river where the accident took place. A silken thread is stretched across the river, from which a leathern bag is hung so that its lower

[1] W. J. V. Saville, *In Unknown New Guinea* (London, 1926), p. 231.

end just touches the surface of the water. The men and women then begin to sing to the accompaniment of lutes. The soul of the drowned man, lingering in the water, is lured by the sweet strains and, emerging from the water, clambers into the bag. No sooner has he done so than one of the company assembled on the bank plunges into the river, ties up the mouth of the bag and carries it, with the captured soul of the drowned man in it, to the grave, where he opens the bag and lets down the soul through a hole in the earth to rejoin its body.[1] In this case the strayed soul is not indeed brought back to the house, but the kindly intention of laying it to rest with its mortal remains is not less conspicuous.

In one way or another the foregoing customs exhibit a tender regard for the spirits of the dead which is very different from that fear and scrupulous avoidance which often, if not generally, characterize the attitude of primitive man to the souls of the departed. This is the brighter aspect of the subject with which we are here concerned. In subsequent lectures I shall have to deal at some length with the darker side of the picture. Here it must suffice to have shown that in primitive religion the fear of the dead is often tempered with affection.

[1] N. v. Seidlitz (Tiflis), " Die Abchasen ", *Globus*, lxvi. (1894) p. 43.

LECTURE II

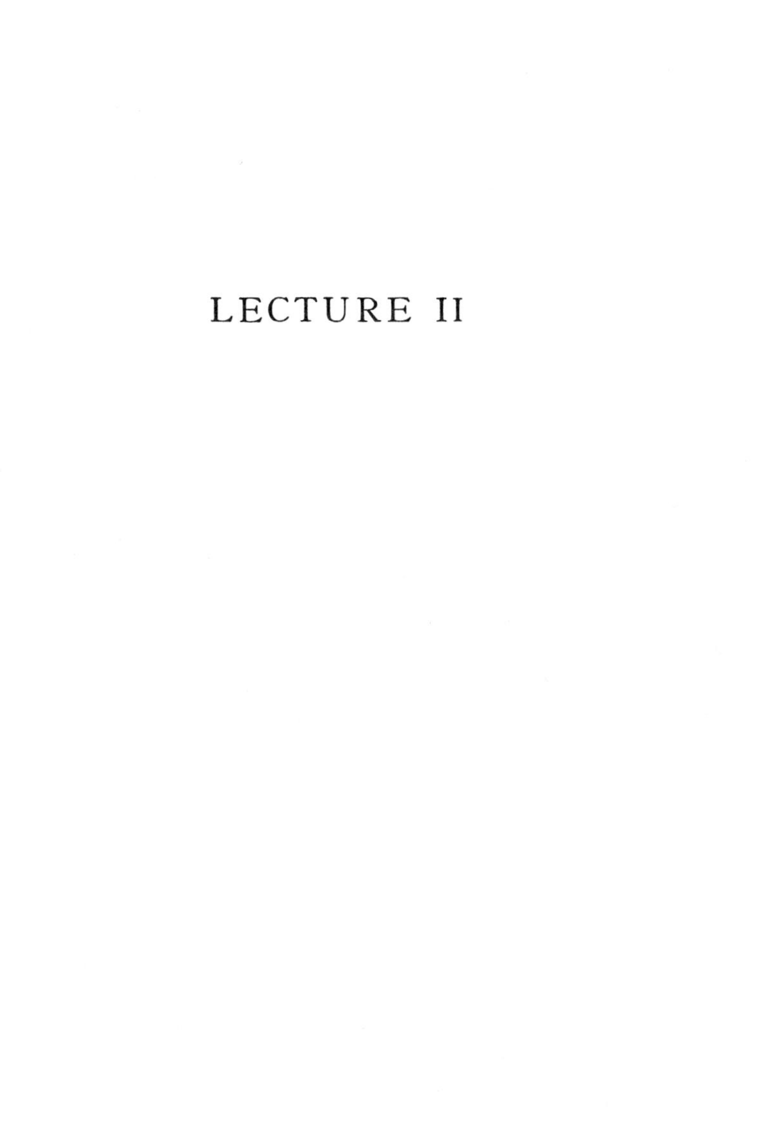

LECTURE II

At the close of the last lecture I showed that primitive man sometimes exhibits a respectful regard for his dead kinsfolk by bringing their souls back to the house and installing them there after he has buried or burnt their bodies elsewhere. But this respectful treatment of the ghost is exceptional. The general attitude of primitive man to ghosts, even of his own kinsfolk, is one of fear, and far from attempting to retain them in the dwelling or to facilitate their return, he is at great pains to drive them away, to keep them at a distance, and to bar the house against their unwelcome intrusions. The means to which he resorts for the sake of thus keeping the spirits of the dead at bay are very various and often display an ingenuity and resourcefulness worthy of a better cause. I shall describe some of them presently; but before I come to details I think it may be well to adduce some evidence as to the general attitude of primitive peoples to the spirits of the dead in order to familiarize you, to some extent, with a mode of thought which is so alien to our own.

For this purpose we may begin with the Melanesians, the dark-skinned, frizzly-haired people who inhabit the long chain of islands stretching along the eastern coasts of New Guinea and Australia, from New Britain on the north to New Caledonia on the south. Speaking of them, the late Rev. Dr. Codrington, one of our highest authorities on the people, observes that "in the Solomon Islands the ghost, being the principal object of worship, occupies . . . a much higher place in the religious world of the natives than it does in the islands which lie to the eastward, and on that account it is desirable, before entering upon details, to draw the distinction between the two classes of ghosts which is generally recognized in the former islands. The distinction is between ghosts of power and ghosts of no account, between those whose help is sought and their wrath deprecated, and those from whom nothing is expected and to whom no observance is due. Among living men there are some who stand out distinguished for capacity in affairs, success in life, valour in fighting, and influence over others; and these are so, it is believed, because of the supernatural and mysterious powers which they have, and which are derived from communication with those ghosts of the dead gone before them who are full of those same powers. On the death of a distinguished man his ghost retains the powers that belonged to him in life, in greater activity and with stronger force; his ghost therefore is powerful, and so long as he is remembered the aid of his powers is sought and worship is offered him; he is the *tindalo* of Florida, the *lio'a* of Sa'a. In every society again, the multitude is composed of insignificant persons, *numerus fruges consumere nati*; of no particular account for valour, skill or prosperity. The ghosts of such persons continue their insignificance, and are nobodies after death as before; they are ghosts because all men have souls, and the souls of dead men are ghosts; they are dreaded because all ghosts are awful, but they get no worship and are soon only thought of as the crowd of the nameless population of the lower world."[1] And again, speaking of San Cristoval ghosts, Dr. Codrington observes: "Here, as elsewhere, a man's ghost has in greater force the power which the man had in his lifetime, when he had it from his communication with the ghosts that went before him; and those who have lately died have most power, or at least are the most active sources of it. The ghost of the great man lately dead is most regarded; as the dead are forgotten their ghosts are superseded by later successors to the unseen power."[2]

What Dr. Codrington here says of Melanesian ghosts might probably be said of ghosts everywhere; they rank in the other world according to the status which the men or women had in this world; equality exists as little among the dead as among the living; the power of the ghost is proportioned to the power which the man had in life; or rather it is at first

[1] R. H. Codrington, D.D., *The Melanesians* (Oxford, 1891), pp. 253 *sq*.

[2] R. H. Codrington, *The Melanesians*, p. 258.

increased by his transference to the other sphere, though it gradually dwindles with lapse of time, till at last ghost and man are alike forgotten.

Dr. Codrington's testimony as to the essential inequality and transitory nature of Solomon Island ghosts is confirmed by a later observer, Dr. Ivens, who says that "the ghosts of ordinary persons are just mere ghosts, and are doubtless invoked by their own people, but their names do not abide permanently, nor are they invoked generally. At Sa'a, the chiefs of the main branch were all invoked in sacrifice and their names mentioned, but even with them the elder ones of the line gave place to the later."[1]

When from the Melanesians we pass eastward to the Polynesians, the fairer-skinned people who occupy the far-scattered islands of the Central and Eastern Pacific, we find that they also stood in great fear of the spirits of the dead. Thus the Society Islanders believed that these restless souls haunted their old homes and visited the abodes of the living, but seldom on errands of mercy or benevolence. They woke the survivors from sleep by squeaking noises to upbraid them for their past wickedness or to reproach them with the neglect of some ceremonial observance, for which the ghosts had to suffer. Thus the inhabitants of these lovely islands imagined that they lived in a world of disembodied spirits, which, though invisible, sur-

[1] W. G. Ivens, *The Melanesians of the South-East Solomon Islands* (London, 1927), p. 179.

rounded them by night and by day, watching every action of their lives and ready to revenge the smallest slight or the least disobedience to their injunctions, as these were revealed to them by the priests. Convulsions and hysterics, for example, were ascribed to the maleficent action of these spirits, which seized the sufferer, scratched his face, tore his hair and otherwise maltreated him.[1]

In our progress round the world we now pass from the Pacific Ocean to the great island of New Guinea, which forms, as it were, a stepping-stone between the Pacific Ocean and the continent of Asia. Speaking of the natives of British New Guinea in the neighbourhood of Port Moresby, two early missionaries, with one of whom I was personally acquainted before he died a martyr's death, have recorded that "each family has a sacred place, where they carry offerings to the spirits of deceased ancestors, whom they terribly fear. Sickness in the family, death, famine, scarcity of fish, etc.—these terrible spirits are at work and must be propitiated."[2] With reference to the Kiwai Papuans of British New Guinea, the Finnish ethnologist, Professor Landtman, who has made a careful and very complete study of them, tells us that "on the whole the natives stand in great dread of the spirits of the dead, whoever the person may have been in his lifetime. Ghosts are known to carry away the souls of living people and also to cause illness, and

[1] W. Ellis, *Polynesian Researches*, Second Edition (London, 1832–1836), i. 402.

[2] James Chalmers and W. Wyatt Gill, *Work and Adventure in New Guinea* (London, 1885), p. 84.

must therefore be carefully kept away."[1] A somewhat more favourable opinion of the character of ghosts appears to be held by the Roro-speaking tribes of British New Guinea, for we learn that they are believed to haunt the villages of their people, and if they deserted the village the inhabitants would have no luck at all; so if they are suspected of having forsaken a village, measures are taken to bring them back. However, it is said that their benevolence is not unconditional; for if they are annoyed, as for instance by too many quarrels among the women, they will send bad luck in hunting and fishing, and in these circumstances it might even be necessary to drive them out of the village. Moreover, the ghosts make people ill by stealing their souls, and the natives stand in such fear of them that, in order not to encounter a ghost, they will not go out of the village after dark, unless they are accompanied by a friend to keep them in countenance, if it were only for a distance of a few yards.[2] On the whole we seem compelled to admit that the virtues of Roro ghosts are dashed with some serious defects.

The ghosts of Orokaiva people, in the east of British New Guinea, appear to be very little better, or rather a good deal worse. True, every Orokaiva gardener and hunter thinks that the spirits of the dead can send him success in the garden and the chase, but such benevolent conduct on the part of

[1] G. Landtman, *The Kiwai Papuans of British New Guinea* (London, 1927), p. 282.

[2] C. G. Seligman, *The Melanesians of British New Guinea* (Cambridge, 1910), p. 310.

the ghosts is, we are told, " to say the least unusual, and it must be confessed that on the whole the Orokaiva regards his relatives and friends after death as enemies. Any failure of the crops may be attributed to them; they may baffle the hunter; they may send the pigs to break through the fences and despoil the gardens." Sickness appears to be attributed by the Orokaiva to the malevolence of ghosts oftener than to any other cause. In short, according to Mr. F. E. Williams, our principal authority on the people, the Orokaiva inherits a body of beliefs regarding the ghosts (*sovai*) which picture them in a variety of horrible and dangerous forms, so that he cannot help regarding them with aversion, and especially with fear.[1] So much for ghosts in New Guinea.

Still moving westward, we come to the Indian Archipelago or Indonesia, which by its long chain of islands links up New Guinea with Asia. The Indonesians, who inhabit the Archipelago, appear to have developed the theory of animism—that is, the doctrine of souls—more fully and with greater logical consistency than any other people on earth; it is therefore particularly interesting to learn what these people think about the souls of the dead. On this subject the highest living authority, the Dutch missionary, Dr. Albert C. Kruijt, who has laboured for many years in the Archipelago, writes as

[1] F. E. Williams, *Orokaiva Society* (Oxford University Press, London, 1930), pp. 283, 284; compare *id.*, p. 285, " It is certain that the Orokaiva goes in real fear of the power of the *sovai* " (ghosts); *ib.*, " the genuine fear of the *sovai* which motivates so much of an Orokaiva's conduct ".

follows: "Now and then we meet with instances of the love for the dead one overcoming the fear of his soul; this happens especially with dead children. But as a rule the Indonesians feel great fear of the soul of a dead person. They naturally think that the dead person resents leaving this earth, and in his resentment wishes to have his fate shared by others. He therefore tries to carry off the soul-substance of the surviving people into the grave, which will cause them to die." [1]

In these words I believe that Dr. Kruijt has laid his finger on the true cause of the fear, the almost universal fear, of the spirits of the dead. Man fears them because he feels instinctively that they are angels and ministers of death hovering about him in the air and ready to bear away his own soul with them to the unknown world beyond the grave. In the early days of the Crimean war John Bright declared in the House of Commons that the Angel of Death had been abroad throughout the land, you might almost hear the beating of his wings. A like declaration might be made by almost any savage, with this difference, that he imagines himself to be compassed about by a whole host of such gloomy angels, all the spirits of all his dead friends and foes, who lie in wait to clutch him in their cold embrace and to snatch him away from this sweet life on earth. No wonder that he looks on these Harpy spirits with fear and abhorrence.

[1] Alb. C. Kruijt, *s.v.* "Indonesians", in J. Hastings, *Encyclopaedia of Religion and Ethics*, vii. (Edinburgh, 1914) p. 250.

In our progress westward from New Guinea, the first of the great islands which stud these tropic seas is the fantastically shaped island of Celebes. Its centre is inhabited by a race called the Toradyas, who were hardly known in Europe till the Dutch missionaries, Dr. Albert C. Kruijt and N. Adriani, settled among them. As a result of the devoted labours of these two men we now possess a full and exact account of the Toradyas, who accordingly rank among the best known of primitive races, though they are less familiar than they should be out of Holland because the description of them is mostly written in the Dutch language. In regard to the old native religion of the Toradyas, we are informed that their gods fall into two classes: first, gods who have always been gods; and secondly, the souls of dead men who have only gradually, in the opinion of the Toradyas, attained to the rank of godhead. In the gods of the first class, who have always been gods, may be recognized personifications of natural phenomena or forces. One of these natural deities who is most frequently invoked is the Sun-god, who is said to have come down to earth in human form and instructed mankind in everything that relates to agriculture. The invocations to the Sun-god always begin with an address to him "who is in the east and in the west". However, we are told that in the life of the Toradyas it is the human gods, the deified spirits of dead men, who play the greatest part. But not all human souls become gods after death. As in daily life a freeman is esteemed above a slave, a chief above an ordinary freeman, so the souls of the dead are conceived to differ in power and standing. The souls of very brave and honoured chiefs are revered as gods; offerings are brought to them, and their help is implored in war as well as in the chase and in the rice-field. And the more generations have elapsed since the death of the brave who have won for themselves a place in popular legend, the greater is the confidence reposed in their godhead. In honour of these human gods a house is built in the village; all these human gods were once men; men need a house, and so do these men-gods. And we can only understand these Toradya men-gods, so Dr. Kruijt tells us, when we know the Toradya himself, for the Toradya imagines his gods to be exactly like himself. The Toradya himself seeks, or rather used to seek, his glory by cutting off the heads of his enemies and bringing back these gory trophies to the village; hence he believes that the gods delight in these proofs of valour, and that they will make him sick if he does not go head-hunting at the proper time. Again, the Toradya is quick to take offence if any one wrongs him in anything; so he thinks that his gods are equally touchy, and that they will manifest their displeasure by blasting the rice, by sending sickness, or by causing mishaps on a journey if a man has done anything contrary to customary law.[1] Elsewhere Dr. Kruijt tells us

[1] A. C. Kruijt, "Het wezen van het heidendom te Posso", *Mededeelingen van wege het Nederlandsche Zendelinggenootschap*, xlvii. (Rotterdam, 1903) pp. 24-26.

that the Toradya conceives life after death to be exactly like life on earth, for he can imagine no other. In his opinion the souls of the dead eat and drink; they till the fields and keep cattle; and men have every motive for treating them well, for on a good understanding with them depends the success or failure of the harvest.[1]

Still moving westward from Celebes, we come to the great island of Borneo. In it the Sea Dyaks of Sarawak, as we learn from a very good authority—the Rev. J. Perham—"attribute to the dead a disposition of mixed good and evil towards the living, and so alternately fear and desire any contact with them. . . . They do not speak of taking a 'corpse' to the grave, but an *antu*, a spirit; as though the departed had already become a member of that class of capricious unseen beings which are believed to be inimical to men. They think the dead can rush from their secret habitations, and seize invisibly on any one passing by the cemetery, which is, therefore, regarded as an awesome, dreaded place. But yet this fear does not obliterate affectionate regard, and many a grave is kept clean and tidy by the loving care of the living; the fear being united with the hope of good, as they fancy the dead may also have the will and the power to help them."[2] "In times of peril and of need the dead

[1] N. Adriani en Alb. C. Kruijt, *De Bare-sprekende Toradjas van Midden-Celebes* (Batavia, 1912), ii. 118.

[2] Rev. J. Perham, "Sea Dyak Religion", *Journal of the Straits Branch of the Royal Asiatic Society*, No. 14 (December, 1884), p. 300; *id.*, in H. Ling Roth, *Natives of Sarawak and British North Borneo* (London, 1896), i. 210 *sq.*

are called upon; and on the hilltops or in the solitudes of the jungle a man often goes by himself and spends the night in the hope that the spirit of some dead relative may visit him, and in a dream tell him of some charm by means of which he may overcome difficulties and become rich and great."[1]

Passing still westward from Borneo, we come to the last and largest island of the Indian Archipelago, the great island of Sumatra. In it the Bataks, an important people of the interior, are said to share the universal human belief in a life after death. Their ideas about that life, however, are as usual vague, but they seem to think of it as not very different from the present life on earth. From their stories and their custom of invoking the dead it appears that weaving, plaiting, fetching the water, tilling the ground and so forth, are supposed to go on in the other world just as in this one. But they prefer to have nothing to do with the dead, except in so far as the dead can tell them of means to avert or heal sickness. The souls of the dead are believed, indeed, to exercise an influence on the life of the survivors, but on the whole that influence is thought of as unfavourable, and the living endeavour to restrict it and keep it within bounds by the performance of certain ceremonies designed to arm themselves against the malignity of the dead.[2]

The natives of Nias, an island lying off the

[1] E. H. Gomes, *Seventeen Years among the Sea Dyaks of Borneo* (London, 1911), p. 142.

[2] M. Joustra, "Het leven, de zeden en gewoonten der Bataks", *Mededeelingen van wege het Nederlandsche Zendelinggenootschap*, xlvi. (Rotterdam, 1902) pp. 415, 417.

western coast of Sumatra, are reported to go in fear of the spirits of the dead, which are believed often to make the living sick for the purpose of drawing away their souls with them to the other world. The spirits of dead chiefs are thought to possess this power in a higher than ordinary degree. Hence the natives of Nias do all they can to humour and propitiate the souls of the dead in order that these dreaded spirits may leave the living in peace, and many are the devices to which they resort for this purpose.[1]

Our brief preliminary survey of these ghostly beliefs must now pass from the islands of the Pacific and the Indian Ocean to the continent of Asia. Concerning the Kachins, a tribe of Burma, we are told that the belief in the ancestral spirits has undoubtedly the strongest hold on the popular imagination. Every individual at death becomes a ghost (*tsu*), and at the final obsequies is solemnly dismissed to the region where the ancestral spirits reside. If he stays there, all is well; the living are left in peace. But if he decides to return, as he may do, to the land of the living, there is apt to be trouble for his surviving relatives. For death is believed by the Kachins to work a radical change for the worse in the spirits of the dead. " The affectionate mother will return from the spirit land and in the shape of a chirping cricket entice the ghost of the still living child to wander away, and death will

[1] J. P. Kleiweg de Zwaan, *Die Heilkunde der Niasser* (Haag, 1913), pp. 17 *sq*.

follow in a few months. A departed friend will return and leave his fingermarks on the boiling rice with the result that most of the partakers will sicken and die. An old respected chief, if not properly buried, will cause a drought or deluge, destroying the crops of the whole community. There is apparently no case on record where a departed spirit has improved in company with the shades." [1]

Of the Chukchis, a people of low culture, living under severe natural conditions at the north-eastern extremity of Siberia, we are told that " one of their most prevalent notions is that the dead become wicked spirits, the enemies of mankind. The funeral rites of the Chukchis abound in incantations intended to prevent the return of the dead in the form of wicked spirits. Even the spirit of the nearest relation, returning with the best intentions in the world, cannot but frighten the living and do them harm. A shaman said to me, " The spirit of a (dead) father is no better than the *ivmetoun* (the spirit of epilepsy). He who sees the spirit of his deceased father will suffer from convulsions and die a sudden death." [2]

The Birhors are a primitive jungle tribe of Chota Nagpur in India. Of them it is said by the eminent Indian ethnologist Mr. Sarat Chandra Roy, who has made a special study of the tribe, that so long as he lives the Birhor stands in

[1] O. Hanson, *The Kachins* (Rangoon, 1913), pp. 157 *sq.*

[2] W. Bogaraz, " Idées religieuses des Tchouktchis ", *Bulletins et Mémoires de la Société d'Anthropologie de Paris*, Ve Série, vol. v. (Paris, 1904) pp. 351 *sq.*

continuous fear of the spirit-world ; but as soon as he is dead, and until a certain ceremony, called *Umbul-ader*, has been performed, "it is he, or rather his disembodied spirit, that becomes the prime object of fears and concern to his relatives and other people of his settlement. And the observances and ceremonies customary during this period appear to have for their main object the prevention of harm to the *tāndā* (settlement) through his spirit, on the one hand, and, on the other hand, of harm to his spirit through stray, malignant spirits. Even the offering of food laid out for the spirit of the deceased appears to be prompted less by a feeling of affection for him than from a fear of his spirit and a desire to keep it agreeably engaged at a safe distance."[1] And speaking of the Oraons, another tribe of Chota Nagpur, the same high authority similarly observes that some of their funeral ceremonies "would appear to indicate that their original object was to keep the spirits of the dead out of harm's way, to cut off all connection with them so as to avoid all chance of their evil attentions being directed to their living relatives. As a matter of fact, all departed spirits would appear to have been originally conceived of as evil spirits,—all of them, though regarded as ancestral spirits (*Pāch-bā'lār*), were at one time regarded by the Oraons as mischievous spirits or *nāsan bhuts* as well."[2]

The Kunbis, a great agricultural caste of the

[1] Sarat Chandra Roy, *The Birhors* (Ranchi, 1925), pp. 265 *sq.*

[2] Sarat Chandra Roy, *Oraon Religion and Customs* (Ranchi, 1928), p. 38.

Maratha country in India, are firm believers in the action of ghosts, and never omit the attentions due to the ancestral spirits. On the appointed day the Kunbi calls on the crows, who represent the spirits of ancestors, to come and eat the food which he sets out for them ; and if no crow appears, he is disturbed at the thought of having incurred the displeasure of the dead. So he changes the food and goes on calling till a crow comes and eats the food. From this the Kunbi infers that the first food he offered was not to the taste of his ancestors; hence, taking the lesson to heart, he continues to offer the other food to the spirits so long as a crow responds to his first invitation to partake of it. The reason why crows are taken to represent the spirits of the dead is probably connected with the widespread notion of the crow's longevity. The Hindoos believe that a crow lives a thousand years, and others think that it never dies except by violence.[1] But while the Kunbi is thus careful to keep on good terms with the spirits of his dead ancestors, he is apparently far from thinking that the action of these spirits is purely beneficent ; for his people have a proverb that Brahmans die of indigestion, goldsmiths (Sunars) die of bile, and Kunbis die of ghosts.[2] In the sequel we shall meet with many examples of the belief that ghosts are often responsible for sickness and death ; it is indeed one of the commonest articles of savage religion, and in the mind of

[1] R. V. Russell, *Tribes and Castes of the Central Provinces of India,* iv. 37.

[2] R. V. Russell, *op. cit.* iv. 40.

primitive man throws a dark shadow on the bright vision of immortality.

The Kolhatis of Central India believe that the spirits of dead ancestors enter the bodies of the living and work evil to them unless they are appeased with offerings. The Dukar Kolhatis sacrifice a boar to male ancestors and a sow to female.[1] The Korkus, a Munda or Kolarian tribe of the Central Provinces of India, believe that the spirits of their dead are not finally laid to rest until a ceremony has been performed which may not take place for many months or even years after the death. In the interval the disembodied and unquiet spirits are thought to possess the power of sending aches and pains to molest the bodies of their surviving relatives.[2]

With these few notices of Asiatic ghosts we must content ourselves for the present and pursue our journey ever westward to Africa, only touching for a moment at Madagascar on the way. The Sakalavas, a tribe or nation who occupy all the western portion of that great island, are firm believers in the existence and almost omnipresence of their ancestral spirits, to the influence of which they trace most of the events of life, whether good or bad, but oftener the bad than the good. In their opinion, spirits (*lolo*) are everywhere—under the earth, on the earth, in the water and on the water, in the river, in the forest, in the air; some trees and mountains are especially haunted by them, and

[1] R. V. Russell, *Tribes and Castes of the Central Provinces of India*, iii. 530.

[2] R. V. Russell, *op. cit.* iii. 565.

almost always the spirit is that of an ancestor. Any unusual event is set down to the action of one of these spirits, who has produced it either to punish some breach of ancestral custom (*fady*) or to attract the attention of the living to himself. All sickness is referred to that cause, and even vice finds an excuse in it. A drunkard has been known to apologize for his drunkenness by laying the blame on the thirsty ghost (*lolo*) who possessed him.[1]

Holding as they do this unfavourable, or at best ambiguous, view of the spirits of the departed, we are not surprised to learn that the Sakalavas "generally like to get rid of their dead at once, and will have nothing to do with corpses unless they are obliged, for they are doubtful as to how their dead relatives will conduct themselves towards those still living; whether they will act as friends or enemies is not known to anybody. But to secure them as friends, they pour out at least once a year a quantity of rum on the graves of their deceased relatives, and especially on those of their ancestors. This they suppose to be a means of averting the feelings of enmity which they probably might keep up towards some one of the living members of the family; for, as they were always fond of rum during their lifetime, they also must be so after death."[2] What is here said of Sakalava ghosts might probably be said with equal truth of primitive ghosts in

[1] H. Rusillon, *Un Culte dynastique avec Evocation des Morts chez les Sakalaves de Madagascar* (Paris, 1912), pp. 43 *sq*.

[2] Rev. A. Walen, "The Sakalava", *The Antananarivo Annual and Madagascar Magazine*, viii. (Antananarivo, 1884) p. 67.

general; they all retain the tastes and passions, the weaknesses and frailties which they had in life; death produces no amelioration, if it does not effect a distinct deterioration, in their moral character.

We now pass to Africa, where the belief in the power of ancestral spirits for good and evil is perhaps more widely spread and more deeply rooted than in any other part of the world. Out of the immense mass of evidence available I can here only pick out, almost at random, a few typical specimens to indicate the depth and diffusion of the belief, which in many tribes takes the form of the worship of ancestors.

We may begin with the Thonga, a Bantu tribe of South-Eastern Africa which has been thoroughly studied by a Swiss missionary, Dr. Henri A. Junod, who has devoted his life to it and given us a masterly account of his dusky flock. Speaking of their religion, he says that in their opinion any man who has departed this earthly life becomes a *shikwemba*, which Dr. Junod does not scruple to translate "a god",[1] though sometimes he uses the more explicit term "ancestral god". But the character of these ancestral gods, as it is described by Dr. Junod, hardly squares with our conceptions of divinity; at all events it is of a very mixed sort. He tells us that "the gods can *bless*: if the trees bear plenty of fruit, it is because they have made it grow; if the crops are plentiful, it is because they

[1] Henri A. Junod, *The Life of a South African Tribe*, Second Edition (London, 1927), ii. 372.

forced wizards to increase them, or hindered them from spoiling them ; if you come across a pot of palm wine, it is your god who has sent you that windfall. . . . Often when a man has narrowly escaped drowning, or spraining his ankle on a stump which has caught his foot, he will say : ‘ The gods have saved me ’. But they (the gods) can also *curse*, and bring untold misfortune on their descendants. If the rain fails, it is owing to their anger ; if a tree falls on you, they have directed its fall ; if a crocodile bites you, the gods have sent it ; if your child has fever and is delirious, they are in him, tormenting his soul ; if your wife is sterile, they have prevented her from child-bearing ; perhaps the gods of your mother have done this because you had not given your maternal uncle ‘ the part of your daughter's marriage price (*lobolo*) ’ which he has the right to claim ; in fact any disease, any calamity may come from them." [1]

On the whole Dr. Junod finds that these ancestral spirits of the Thonga have not improved by being raised to the rank of divinities. In fact, he says plainly " they are not better than they were as men. Their *character* is that of suspicious old people, who resent any want of respect, or attention, on the part of their descendants. They wish to be thought of, and presented with offerings. It would seem that they are not actually in need of anything, for they live in abundance, but they exact a punctual observance of the duties of their descendants in

[1] H. A. Junod, *The Life of a South African Tribe*[2], ii. 386.

regard to them. They must eat the first fruits, and have their share of the tobacco leaves. They are jealous, and avenge themselves when forgotten. The only sin which seems to be deserving of punishment is to neglect them."[1] Notwithstanding this very dubious character which Dr. Junod gives to the deified ancestors of the Thonga, he tells us that the people do not stand in perpetual fear of them; their attitude to these jealous and testy spirits is rather that of indifference; "natives ask for one thing only: that they may live in peace, and that their gods may interfere with them as little as possible".[2]

The Bavenda, a Bantu tribe of the Northern Transvaal, recognize a certain mysterious deity named Raluvhimba, who is supposed to live somewhere in the heavens and to be connected with all astronomical and physical phenomena.[3] But he plays only a secondary part in the religious life of the Bavenda. "The direct relationship with their dead ancestors is a much more personal factor in their lives and is the basis of their religious ideas. Their attitude is quite rational; to them death is a transition between life on this earth and life in the spirit-world, where the dead continue the lives begun on earth, still exerting a powerful influence on their living relatives. The ancestor spirits have themselves experienced ordinary mortal life and so understand the daily trials and difficulties which

[1] H. A. Junod, *The Life of a South African Tribe*², ii. 426.

[2] H. A. Junod, *op. cit.* ii. 428.

[3] H. A. Stayt, *The Bavenda* (London, 1931), p. 230.

beset all humanity and their own descendants in particular. The ancestor spirits, *medzimu* (sing. *mudzimi*), have many idiosyncrasies, and if they think that they have been slighted by their descendants, take their revenge by bringing misfortune to them; they are therefore feared rather than loved. There seems to be a fairly fundamental conception among the Bavenda as to the inherent good of most worldly things, all trouble being associated with the evils of witchcraft or the jealousy and spitefulness of their ancestors." [1] The ancestral spirits which can affect the life of an individual are divided by the Bavenda into two groups—those of the father's lineage and those of the mother's lineage, and curiously enough the ancestral spirits of the mother's lineage are believed to be much more personally and intimately connected with their descendants than those of the father's line; they cause far more trouble and are consequently more feared and respected than those of the father.[2]

The Bechuana (singular Mochuana) are a great Bantu tribe who inhabit the interior plains of central South Africa, including what used to be called Bechuanaland and parts of the Western Transvaal and the Kalahari desert. Concerning their religion a missionary, who laboured among them for about forty years and has given us a valuable account of their customs and beliefs, writes as follows: "Fear of the dead, whether one's own

[1] H. A. Stayt, *The Bavenda*, p. 240.
[2] H. A. Stayt, *op. cit.* pp. 240 *sq.*, 246.

relatives or others, does, however, play an important part in the life of the living Mochuana, who believes that the dead have power over the lives of the living to bless or to curse, to send prosperity or the reverse to their relatives and members of their clan; especially is this fear potent when the living are conscious of any reason why the deceased should bear ill-will. Many forms of sickness, the onslaught of adversity and ills in general, are laid at the door of the offended spirit, and what may appear to be ancestor worship is simply acts of propitiation, sacrifices of atonement, which are intended to reconcile, and to bring back into harmonious fellowship the severed kinship. . . . The attitude of the Mochuana at the grave of his ancestor, immediate or more remote, is one of reverence and awe. Fear fills mind and heart—fear of the unknown powers—fears lest they be inimical. So far as I have been able to gather, it is never love, never thanksgiving, never the desire for communion with the deceased, never even a longing for a renewal of fellowship, that calls forth their offerings and sacrifice, but always the fear that kinship with all it connotes has been severed and must be recovered." [1]

The Ba-ila are a Bantu people of Northern Rhodesia. Like all Bantu tribes, they revere or worship their ancestral spirits as divinities, but their attitude to them is somewhat ambiguous. The spirits are regarded generally as beneficent or

[1] J. Tom Brown, *Among the Bantu Nomads* (London, 1926), pp 98, 99.

neutral, though they may be induced by neglect to make people sick. But some ghosts are incorrigibly bad and do much mischief, either at the bidding of witches and wizards or of their own free will. Not only do these maleficent spirits cause disease by entering the bodies of the living, but they waylay people and strike them dead. Or, without going so far as that, sometimes out of sheer devilry they will play all sorts of pranks, knocking burdens off people's heads, breaking hoes, unhandling axes, upsetting pots of beer and so forth. On the whole Ba-ila ghosts, in putting off the flesh, have not divested themselves of human frailties and weaknesses. As ordinary people in life may at times be jealous, touchy and fickle, so it is with the ghosts; you can never be quite sure of them; any omission on your part to do them reverence will be visited by them on your head or on the head of some one dear to you, and when that happens they must be placated by offerings. Hence the attitude of the Ba-ila towards the spirits of their dead resembles their attitude towards their chiefs; it is a blending of trust and fear; in a word, it is awe.[1]

The Banyamwezi are a large Bantu tribe of Central Africa, inhabiting the great tableland to the south of Lake Victoria Nyanza. Like all Bantu tribes, they believe that the spirits of their dead ancestors (the *misambwa*) exercise a very great influence on all the events of this mortal life. Hence

[1] Rev. Edwin W. Smith and Captain Andrew Murray Dale, *The Ila-speaking Peoples of Northern Rhodesia* (London, 1920), ii. 132, 167 *sq.*

they are prompted to do all they can to keep on good terms with these touchy spirits in order to escape from the troubles which it is in their power to inflict on the living. Thus the whole concern of the native in regard to the dead is to avert the anger of his ancestors and to gain their good graces, and this he does by offering them sacrifice and prayer and thanks. So long as the ancestral spirits are in a good humour, all goes well with the people and there is nothing to fear; but when trouble comes and affairs go ill, it is a sign that the ancestors are displeased, and then it is necessary to propitiate them and to restore friendly relations with their spirits.[1]

The Konde are a Bantu people who inhabit the country about the northern end of Lake Nyasa. Concerning them we are told that the importance of the spirits of the dead in the daily life of the Konde can hardly be exaggerated. From the day when the infant is presented by the head of the family to the spirits of its ancestors until the day of death, when the parting spirit is directed to go in peace to meet his forefathers, the living and the dead are mingled in one stream, they form one community, and are dependent on each other for many of the best things here on earth and in the world below, where the spirits of the dead reside.[2] For though at death the souls of the dying are dismissed to that subterranean region, they are

[1] Fr. Bösch, *Les Banyamwezi* (Münster i. W., 1930), p. 166.

[2] D. R. Mackenzie, *The Spirit-ridden Konde* (London, 1925), p. 190.

usually believed to be able to return to earth and to exert themselves there very energetically; indeed, the dead are conceived to obtain a great accession of power on passing into the spirit-world, a power both for good and for evil, and to placate them is one of the chief preoccupations of Konde life.[1] As usual, the conditions of life below the earth are thought to be much the same as of life above it. The dead chief is a chief still, and the dead slave is still a slave in the underworld. The rich man is still rich, and the poor man is still poor. The dead wife goes to her dead husband, and the dead children go to their dead parents.[2] The motives which the spirits of the dead have for returning to the land of the living are mainly two.

First, they wish to assure themselves that they still have descendants on earth; for if the family dies out, it is a dreadful calamity for the ghosts, because in that case they are turned into frogs. Second, the dead desire to make certain that they are not forgotten by the survivors, for the departed spirit who receives no attention from his living kinsfolk becomes of no account in the underworld. Hence the illness or other misfortune which overtakes the survivors is set down by them to the anger of the dead at the slight put upon them.[3] We need not wonder, then, that the spirits of the dead are a matter of anxious concern to the Konde.

The Barundi are another Bantu tribe who in-

[1] D. R. Mackenzie, *The Spirit-ridden Konde* (London, 1925), pp. 191, 192.

[2] D. R. Mackenzie, *op. cit.* p. 193.

[3] D. R. Mackenzie, *op. cit.* p. 195.

habit a district on the western side of Lake Victoria Nyanza. In their belief the dead are always more or less wicked and hostile to the living, even when they had been comparatively good in life. For the dead man has been forced to abandon all that he held dear in life and is therefore filled with envy of the living, who now possess what he has lost. Hence these envious and malicious spirits (*abasimu* or *imisimu*) inflict sickness, dearth, cattle-plague and other evils on the living, who dread them accordingly, and much of the daily life of the Barundi is taken up with the efforts to ward off, restrain, appease and propitiate these dreadful beings. For that purpose the Barundi offer sacrifices to the dead, and these sacrifices, we are told, are merely insurances against the damage that would otherwise be done them by these dangerous spirits; they are not the expression of disinterested affection for departed kinsfolk. The Marundi sacrifices to the dead only because he fears them.[1]

Of the Basoga, a Bantu people inhabiting a district called Busoga on the northern shore of Lake Victoria Nyanza, Canon Roscoe, our best authority, writes as follows: "In all parts of Busoga worship of the dead forms a most important part of the religion of the people, and the belief in ghosts and the propitiation of them are the chief features of their most constant and regular acts of worship. The gods, with fetishes and amulets, are able to do great things for the living; but, after all, it is

[1] H. Meyer, *Die Barundi* (Leipzig, 1916), p. 119.

the ghost that is most feared and obtains the most marked attention. In childbirth, in sickness, in prosperity, and in death, ghosts materially help or hinder matters ; hence it behoves the living to keep on good terms with them. It is because of this belief that people frequently make sacrifices of fowls and other animals to the dead and constantly seek their help. First and foremost, it is because of the firm conviction of the presence of ghosts that the elaborate funeral ceremonies are performed. . . . In the beliefs of these primitive people we must relegate the gods to a secondary place after the worship of the dead." [1]

The principal Bantu tribe, or rather nation, of Uganda in Central Africa are the Baganda, who have given their name to the province. Among this interesting and once powerful people my honoured friend, the Rev. Canon Roscoe, laboured for many years and has published the fullest and best account of their customs and beliefs. Speaking of their religion he says, "The last, and possibly most venerated, class of religious objects were the ghosts of departed relatives. The power of ghosts for good or evil was incalculable." [2] "The belief in ghosts, both malevolent and benevolent, was firmly held by all classes, from the highest to the lowest. Existence in another world was a reality to them, and all looked forward to living and moving in the next state. The horrors of mutilation were in-

[1] John Roscoe, *The Northern Bantu* (Cambridge, 1915), p. 245.

[2] John Roscoe, *The Baganda* (London, 1911), p. 273.

creased by their ideas of the after-world; for not only would the maimed person be inconvenienced and made to suffer in this life, but in the next world his ghost would in like manner be maimed. Hence the idea of amputation was so dreaded by men, that a person preferred to die with a limb rather than to live without it, and so lose his chance of possessing full powers in the ghost world. The loss of an eye was not only the sign which marked an adulterer in this life, but the loss would hold good in a future state and mark the man there; the thief who had been caught and deprived of his hand was for ever maimed, and his ghost bore the stigma of a thief."[1] So exactly, in the opinion of the Baganda, does the ghost resemble the living man, and so unquestioning is their faith in immortality.

[1] John Roscoe, *The Baganda*, pp. 281 *sq*.

LECTURE III

LECTURE III

IN the last lecture I adduced some evidence of the fear and worship of the dead in the southern, eastern and central regions of Africa. To complete this portion of our subject, it remains to give some specimens of a similar attitude towards the spirits of the departed in the western and more northern parts of the continent.

Thus, speaking of the natives of the Gaboon district in French West Africa, an experienced missionary observes: "That they had a belief in a future world is evidenced by survivors taking to the graves of their dead . . . boxes of goods, native materials, foreign cloth, food, and formerly even wives and servants, for use in that other life to which they had gone. Whatever may have been supposed about the locality or occupations of that life, the dead were confidently believed to have carried with them all their human passions and feelings, and especially their resentments. Fear of those possible resentments dominated the living in all their attempts at spiritual communication with the dead." [1]

[1] Rev. R. H. Nassau, *Fetichism in West Africa* (London, 1904), p. 237.

In the neighbouring province of Loango the relations of the living to the dead are reported to be friendly up to the time when the ceremony of mourning is performed at the grave, or at all events till the moment when the grave is dug, but after the mourning rites have been duly observed or the body interred, the relations between the living and the dead are said to be decidedly hostile. The mourning rites are the last farewell, the last testimony of affection to the soul of the departed, if indeed he was a person of sufficient importance to merit this token of esteem. Afterwards everybody seeks to keep the spirit of the deceased at arm's length or at a greater distance, and they do not scruple to resort to magical arts to protect themselves against the ghost.[1]

Among the tribes of Northern Nigeria, as we learn from Mr. C. K. Meek, our best authority on the subject, the predominant religious influence is the worship of ancestors, or, in more general terms, the cult of the dead. The tribal god is generally a deified ancestor. As usual, the worship is based on the almost universal belief in the persistence of the human soul after death. In the opinion of these Nigerian people a man who lives to a good old age has a vigorous soul, and when he goes to the next world he takes his spiritual power with him. Hence in his disembodied state he can assist and protect his tribe. He is the intermediary between his

[1] E. Pechuel-Loesche, *Die Loango-Expedition*, iii. 2 (Stuttgart, 1907), p. 308.

family and the unknown powers that control the universe. When he leaves the world he must therefore be sent off with due respect and equipped with all that he may need in the far country and on the journey thither. Hence he is commonly provided with a meal on the day of his funeral, and part of his property is buried with him in the grave; and before the advent of the British Government, if he were a great man or chief, his favourite wife, slave, horse and boy and girl attendants were buried with him; for one who is great in this world will be great also in the next. The social position which he had on earth must be fully maintained in the life hereafter. To ensure his good-will it is necessary to make periodical offerings at his grave. If these are neglected he will remind his relatives by appearing to them in dreams, and if they were to continue the neglect he would assume a malevolent attitude towards them. For, as usual, the Nigerian dead are said not to divest themselves of their human attributes, nor do they cease to take an interest in mundane affairs. Indeed, their interest is so far kept up that many of them return to earth and are born again in the bodies of their grandchildren.[1] Concerning the Jukun in particular, an important tribe of Northern Nigeria, we are told that their workaday religion is the cult of ancestors. A Jukun regards his dead ancestors as ever present with him; he never eats food with-

[1] C. K. Meek, *The Northern Tribes of Nigeria* (London, 1925), ii. 12 *sq*.

out making an offering to their spirits, and when things go wrong he is directed by the divining apparatus to some particular ancestor deceased who is in need of sustenance. If he even dreams of an ancestor he will go to his household shrine with an oblation of beer and porridge and address his dead forefather by name, saying, " I have seen you in my sleep. Whether it is good or evil I know not. But I remember you now with these gifts and beseech you to give me and mine health." The ancestral spirits, so thinks the Jukun, can prevent the rain from falling and children from being conceived in the womb; they can ensure a successful season for the extraction of salt, which is a principal article of commerce; and when a man finds a dead game animal in the forest, he ascribes the windfall to his ancestors. The ancestors are, indeed, the dominating influence in the life of a Jukun.[1]

This must conclude what I have to say for the present about the fear and worship of the dead in Africa. Brief and fragmentary as is the evidence which I have laid before you, it may suffice to give you some conception of the firm hold which the belief in immortality has on the mind of the native African, and of the deep influence it exercises on his life. Far more than the ordinary civilized man, he is occupied with thoughts of death and the dead; in the events of daily life, in good and evil fortune he traces the handiwork of these awful beings; and to them he turns in seasons of distress and danger

[1] C. K. Meek, *A Sudanese Kingdom* (London, 1931), pp. 217 *sq.*

for help and deliverance from the troubles that beset this our mortal life on earth. No wonder that he looks on the spirits of the departed with mingled feelings of hope and fear, of affection and abhorrence. Indeed, it is hardly too much to say that in Africa, so far as it has not been affected by Europe, the living exist in perpetual bondage to the spirits of the dead.

Among the aborigines of America, to whom we must now turn for a few minutes, the fear and worship of the dead have apparently far less importance and extension than among the natives of Africa; yet they have had their place in the religion of the New World as well as of the Old. A few specimens must suffice to complete this rapid and very imperfect survey of ghost worship in primitive religion.

Thus, among the Nootka Indians of British Columbia, there is, or used to be, "great reluctance to explain their funeral usages to strangers; death being regarded by this people with great superstition and dread, not from solicitude for the welfare of the dead, but from a belief in the power of departed spirits to do much harm to the living".[1] Again, concerning the Dacota or Sioux, a great Indian tribe of the United States, we are told that "they have very little notion of punishment for crime hereafter in eternity: indeed, they know very little about whether the Great Spirit has anything to do with their affairs, present or future. All the fear they

[1] H. H. Bancroft, *The Native Races of the Pacific States* (London, 1875–1876), i. 206.

have is of the spirit of the departed. They stand in great awe of the spirits of the dead, because they think it is in the power of departed spirits to injure them in any way they please; this superstition has, in some measure, a salutary effect. It operates on them just as strong (*sic*) as our laws of hanging for murder. Indeed, fear of punishment from the departed spirits keeps them in greater awe than the white people have of being hung." [1]

Again, the Assiniboin, another Indian tribe of the Upper Missouri, "most sincerely believe in the theory of ghosts, that departed spirits have the power to make themselves visible and heard, that they can assume any shape they wish, of animals or men, and many will affirm that they have actually seen these apparitions and heard their whistlings and moanings. They are much afraid of these appearances, and under no consideration will go alone near a burial-place after dark. They believe these apparitions have the power of striking the beholder with some disease, and many complaints are attributed to this cause. They therefore make feasts and prayers to them to remain quiet. Smaller evils and misfortunes are caused by their power, and a great many stories are nightly recounted in their lodges of the "different shapes in which they appear". [2] Hence the Assiniboin used

[1] Philander Prescott in H. R. Schoolcraft's *Indian Tribes of the United States* (Philadelphia, 1853–1856), ii. 195 *sq*.

[2] E. T. Denig, "Indian Tribes of the Upper Missouri", *Forty-sixth Annual Report of the Bureau of American Ethnology* (Washington, 1930), p. 494.

to lament the death of their friends for years, perhaps so long as any relatives of the deceased were living; they instituted feasts in honour of the dead, invoked their spirits, and offered them sacrifices and prayers. And if they neglected thus to pay respect to the souls of their departed kinsfolk, the angry ghosts would visit them in dreams and trouble them with whistling sounds and startling apparitions.[1]

The Tarahumare Indians of Mexico, we are told, "certainly believe in a future life, but they are afraid of the dead, and think that they want to harm the survivors. This fear is caused by the supposition that the dead are lonely, and long for the company of their relatives. The dead also make people ill, that they too may die and join the departed. When a man dies in spite of all efforts of the shamans to save his life, the people say that those who have gone before have called him or carried him off. The deceased are also supposed to retain their love for the good things they left behind in the world, and to be trying every way to get at them. So strong is the feeling that the departed still owns whatever property he once possessed that he is thought to be jealous of his heirs who now enjoy its possession. He may not let them sleep at night, but makes them sit up by the fire and talk."[2]

The attitude of the South American Indians

[1] E. T. Denig, *op. cit.* p. 318.

[2] C. Lumholtz, *Unknown Mexico* (London, 1903), i. 380 *sq.*

towards the spirits of the dead has been carefully examined by the eminent Finnish ethnographer, Professor Rafael Karsten, who spent five years in close contact with savages in different parts of the continent and learned their language. Speaking of the subject which here concerns us, Professor Karsten mentions "as an indisputable fact that the dead are feared",[1] but he would distinguish the fear of the ghost from the fear of the demon who is supposed to have caused the death of a person. However, he tells us that in his belief a careful examination of the two, that is, of the ghost and the demon, would lead to the conclusion that the demons who cause death "have originally been nothing but ghosts of dead men which for one reason or another have assumed a positively evil nature. This, indeed, can in some cases be strictly proved, and it is a well-known fact that certain disembodied souls, especially the souls of wizards, murdered persons, etc., are changed into evil demons who visit other people with sickness and death. The disease- and death-demons, moreover . . . have a tendency to identify themselves with the souls of the departed in a way which, in some cases, makes it practically impossible to distinguish them from each other. The disease-spirit, such seems to be the general belief, having once got possession of the patient and caused his death, will thereafter remain in his body and seize his soul

[1] Rafael Karsten, *The Civilization of the South American Indians* (London, 1926), p. 243.

as well, with the result that he is himself altogether changed into an evil demon independently of what has been his character in life. This belief naturally makes the ideas of the Indians about the spirits of the dead more complicated and also explains why persons who in their lifetime have perhaps been loved and esteemed, after death are feared as malignant and dangerous beings. The change is due to the operation of the strange demon who invaded the deceased. The more power a person had in life, the more dangerous he will become after death, for the obsessing demon lays hold of that power. This is the true reason why old people, and particularly medicine-men, are so greatly feared after death."[1]

Thus, while Professor Karsten distinguishes the soul of a dead person from the demon who has caused his death, he admits that the soul and the demon are sometimes indistinguishable and sometimes actually identical, and he thinks that originally the demon was nothing but the ghost of the dead. Thus on Professor Karsten's theory the ultimate factor in the attitude of the South American Indian to the dead is the fear of their ghosts. The conclusion tallies perfectly with the result of our present inquiry.

That must conclude my brief survey of the general attitude of primitive man to the spirits of the dead in different parts of the world. We must now consider that attitude more in detail and endea-

[1] R. Karsten, *The Civilization of the South American Indians*, pp. 480 *sq.*

vour to understand more fully why primitive man both fears and reverences the spirits of the dead.

From what has preceded you will have gathered that in the opinion of the savage the spirits of the dead not only exist but in their disembodied state retain great powers, by virtue of which they are believed sometimes to benefit, but often to injure, the survivors. That is the root cause of the ambiguous attitude which uncivilized man commonly adopts towards the spirits of the departed. What, then, are the powers for good or evil which he commonly attributes to these potent but dangerous beings? what benefits does he hope for from their favour? what evils does he fear from their ill-will? In what follows I will endeavour to answer these questions; and as I am anxious to do no injustice to the primitive ghost by creating a prejudice against him, I will begin by enumerating some of the benefits he is supposed to confer on the living before I go on to describe some of the troubles and distresses which he is believed to inflict upon them.

In the first place, then, the ghosts are often thought to render a great variety of services to their surviving kinsfolk. Thus, for example, we are told of the Kiwai of British New Guinea that they "are all firm believers in the existence of their ancestors' spirits, that these take an interest in their daily lives, and that they are able to help or mar their undertakings. In all their ceremonies—for fighting, hunting, fishing, gardening—offerings are made and toasts drunk to their ancestors, who are earnestly and solemnly entreated to come to their aid on the projected enterprise. There is never a garden site chosen, a garden fence built, a yam planted or any fishing expedition undertaken without these spirits being called upon to bless and prosper the enterprise."[1]

Thus we see that the spirits of the dead are believed to be able, amongst other things, to aid the living in hunting and fishing, which are industries of capital importance for primitive man, who indeed subsisted mainly by them before he learned to till the ground. It is therefore not surprising to learn that among the benefits which the savage hopes to receive from his ancestral spirits help in hunting and fishing takes a foremost place. Hence at the opening of the turtle-fishing season, when the Kiwai perform a ceremony for the multiplication of turtle, they begin by cleaning up the burial-ground and placing food and pouring coconut milk on the graves for the dead, while they address the spirits, saying, "Give us turtle; we give you food".[2] And if a canoe returned unsuccessful from the turtle-fishing, the captain would at once go to his father's grave, clean it up, and pour coconut milk on it, saying, "We have cleaned your grave and given you a drink. Come with us." After that it was thought that next morning he would catch plenty of turtle.[3]

[1] E. Baxter Riley, *Among Papuan Headhunters* (London, 1925), p. 293.

[2] G. Landtman, *The Kiwai Papuans of British New Guinea*, p. 398; compare *id.*, p. 296; W. N. Beaver, *Unexplored New Guinea* (London, 1920), p. 305.

[3] E. Baxter Riley, *Among Papuan Headhunters*, pp. 125 *sq.*

And before they go out to harpoon dugong, the Kiwai invoke the spirits of their fathers and forefathers, saying, " Bring the dugong along for us to-morrow and do not let them return again to the sea ".[1]

In the Trobriand Islands, to the east of New Guinea, a magician who professes to control the fishing will sometimes make an offering of food to the spirits of the dead (*baloma*), saying, " Partake, O spirits, and make my magic thrive " ; or he will dream of an ancestral spirit and say in the morning, " The ancestral spirit has instructed me in the night, that we should go to catch fish ".[2] The natives of the South-East Solomon Islands believe that the ghosts control the bonito fishing, and that they will punish with bodily swellings the fishermen who neglect their worship. To avert this misfortune the fishermen offer coconuts to the ghosts.[3] The Belep, a tribe of New Caledonia, used to make offerings to the skulls of their ancestors and to invoke their spirits before they went out to fish on the reefs.[4]

The Galelarese of Halmahera, an island to the west of New Guinea, revere the souls of their dead ancestors as house-spirits or domestic deities, to whom they make offerings of food. Before a man goes out hunting he prays to these house-spirits, saying, " O spirits of my fathers, pray drive a little

[1] E. Baxter Riley, *Among Papuan Headhunters*, p. 131.

[2] B. Malinowski, *Argonauts of the Western Pacific*, pp. 422 *sq.*

[3] W. G. Ivens, *The Melanesians of the South-East Solomon Islands*, p. 373 ; compare *id.*, pp. 234, 311.

[4] Father Lambert, " Mœurs et Superstitions de la tribu Bélep ", *Les Missions Catholiques*, xii. (1880) p. 239.

herd or flock together towards us that we may find a little food, and we shall, if need be, at once bring you an offering from it ". But if the hunters come back with an empty bag, they are angry and say, " The house-spirits sit still there and do not drive the least herd together for us ".[1]

The Gonds of Gandla in Central India from time to time organize fishing expeditions in which all the men of a village take part. On such an occasion the women make a mound or platform in front of the house of the leader of the party, and on this platform the fish caught are afterwards laid. The leader thereupon distributes the fish among the people, leaving one fish on the platform. Next morning this fish is taken away and placed on the grave of the leader's ancestor, doubtless as a thank-offering to the dead man's spirit for the fish which he is supposed to have sent to the people. But if no fish are caught for several days, the villagers act very differently. The women go and dig up the platform in front of the leader's house and level it with the ground. Then early next morning all the people go to another village and there dance a certain dance, called the Sela dance, before the tombs of the ancestors of that village. The head-man of that village then levies a contribution on his people and gives the visitors food and drink and a present of money, with which the visitors buy liquor and, going home to their village, offer the liquor in

[1] M. J. van Baarda, " Fabelen, Verhalen en Overleveringen der Galelareezen ", *Bijdragen tot de Taal- Land- en Volkenkunde van Nederlandsch - Indie*, xlv. (1895) p. 524.

front of the platform which they had demolished. Next morning they go fishing again. Apparently in this elaborate ritual the platform represents the forefathers of the village, whose spirits are supposed to give success in fishing. If the fishers are unsuccessful, they demolish the platform to show their displeasure to the spirits, and then go and dance before the ancestors of another village to intimate the transference of their allegiance from their own ancestors to those of that other village. Their own ancestors will then feel themselves properly snubbed and discarded for their ill-nature in not giving success to the fishing-party. But when they have been in this chastened frame of mind for a few days, the headman of the other village sends them a present of liquor, which suffices to restore their good humour. Thus the spirits of the forefathers receive a salutary lesson, and the people hope that in future the spirits will be more careful of the welfare of their descendants.[1]

Before some of the mountain people of Formosa go out hunting, they invoke the spirits of their ancestors to give them good sport.[2] In Africa, when the Thonga are about to catch a certain fish in water infested by crocodiles, they make an offering to the spirits of their ancestors for protection against the crocodiles. And sometimes they employ a man of an aboriginal tribe to offer a fish to his ancestors, after which the Thonga chief proclaims in a loud

[1] R. V. Russell, *Tribes and Castes of the Central Provinces of India*, iii. 105-107.

[2] Shinji Ishii, "The Life of the Mountain People in Formosa", *Folk-lore*, xxviii. (1917) p. 125.

voice, " Let the fish abound, and kill them all, but do not bewitch each other ".[1] When a party of Thonga hunters return to a village after killing a lion, the headman meets them and sacrifices a hen to the ancestral spirits to thank them for having saved the hunters from the maw of the lion.[2] And when a Thonga hunter has killed a hippopotamus, he prays to the ancestral spirits to give him many more such beasts.[3]

Before the Bakongo, a tribe of the Lower Congo, go out hunting they visit the grave of a great hunter. There the leader or advocate, as he is called, goes first and kneels with his back to the grave and his face to the hunters. They approach him slowly, and on reaching him as he kneels they spread themselves out and dance round the grave to the rub-a-dub of a drum. They have brought with them a calabash of palm wine, which they place on the grave. Then the advocate turns towards the grave, and, shaking his rattle, he prays, saying : " You are blind, but your ears are not deaf. O ears, hear well ! We have come to you, we come kneeling. While you lived in the town, you ate and you drank, now we who are left die of hunger ; give us male and female animals." Then he takes a cup of the palm wine and pours it out on the grave as an oblation to the famous hunter who sleeps the last sleep there. The rest of the wine is drunk by the hunters sitting round the

[1] Henri A. Junod, *The Life of a South African Tribe*[2], ii. 88.

[2] Henri A. Junod, *op. cit.* ii. 62.

[3] Henri A. Junod, *op. cit.* ii. 71.

grave.[1] When a party of Bakongo hunters have killed an antelope, they catch the blood in a bladder and take it to the advocate, who pours it out on the grave of the great hunter, who is supposed to have heard their prayer and sent them the game.[2] And in this tribe a widow has been known to kneel on her husband's grave and tell him that the people were short of game, apparently in the hope that the ghost would take the hint and send the desired animals to the hunters.[3]

The Jen, a tribe of Northern Nigeria, believe that the spirits of their ancestors return to plague their living relatives who have not given them a proper burial or not kept their graves tidy. So at the beginning of the hunting season a hunter will go to the grave of his father or his paternal uncle, clean away the weeds, and pray to the following effect: "May the ghost (*ijang*) of you, my father, look after me well; if I did evil in your lifetime I implore your forgiveness; I have cleaned your grave. I am going on the morrow to the bush to hunt. The bush is not the town; it is a place of death. Grant that I may have success in my hunting, or, at least, that I may return in safety."[4] And when a Jen hunter has killed a lion, he and his helpers take the lion's body to the graves of famous ancestors and laying it down there engage in a dance, apparently as a token of gratitude to

[1] John H. Weeks, *Among the Primitive Bakongo* (London, 1914), p. 182.

[2] John H. Weeks, *op. cit.* p. 183.

[3] R. P. van Wing, S.J., *Études Bakongo* (Bruxelles, N.D.), p. 282.

[4] C. K. Meek, *Tribal Studies in Northern Nigeria*, ii. 526.

the spirits of the dead for granting them this victory over the king of beasts.[1] Among the Teme, another tribe of Northern Nigeria, before a man goes out hunting he visits the grave of an ancestor and lays some porridge on it with a prayer for success in the chase.[2]

Far away from Africa, on the bleak shores of Bering Strait, the Eskimo believe that the souls of infants who have died at birth can render great services to the hunter in the chase. To secure such a ghostly helper a man will sometimes not hesitate to kill a child. But the murder must be secret, and he must contrive to steal the body so that no one knows of the foul play. Having secured the little corpse, he dries it, puts it in a bag, and wears it on his person, or carries it with him in the canoe when he is at sea. When a hunter carries one of these ghastly relics, it is believed that the ghost of the child, which is very sharp-sighted, will assist him in finding game and direct his spear in its flight so that it shall not miss the animal.[3]

So much for the help which the spirits of the dead are commonly believed by primitive man to give to the hunter and the fisher. They are further supposed, at a more advanced stage of culture, to aid the husbandman by promoting the fertility of the earth, whether in the shape of cereals or of fruit. To this branch of our subject we must now turn our attention for a short time.

[1] C. K. Meek, *Tribal Studies in Northern Nigeria*, ii. 522.

[2] C. K. Meek, *op. cit.* i. 494.

[3] E. W. Nelson, "The Eskimo about Bering Strait", *Eighteenth Annual Report of the Bureau of American Ethnology*, Part I. (Washington, 1899) p. 429.

Thus when the natives of British New Guinea, in the neighbourhood of Port Moresby, begin planting, "they first take a bunch of bananas and sugar-cane, and go to the centre of the plantation, and call over the names of the dead belonging to their family, adding, 'There is your food, your bananas and sugar-cane; let our food grow well, and let it be plentiful. If it does not grow well and plentiful, you all will be full of shame, and so shall we.'"[1] When the Kiwai of British New Guinea are making a yam-garden in ground which had been cultivated by their people in years gone by, they call on the spirits of their ancestors to help in making the fence and to produce an abundant harvest of yams.[2] And when every man has finished a ceremonial planting of four yams, they all stand erect alongside the garden fence, with bow and arrow in hand, and earnestly implore the assistance of the spirits of all their neighbours from north, south, east and west, concluding their appeal with the mention of their ancestors, who are requested to come and produce a good crop of yams. During this invocation an arrow is placed on every bow-string and held aloft as if the shaft were about to be shot away. Then the weapons are laid down and bull-roarers are whirled with a deafening noise.[3] When the Orokaiva of British New Guinea are burying a member of the tribe, before the body is

[1] J. Chalmers and W. Wyatt Gill, *Work and Adventure in New Guinea*, p. 85.

[2] E. Baxter Riley, *Among Papuan Headhunters*, p. 93.

[3] E. Baxter Riley, *op. cit.* pp. 95 *sq.*

lowered into the grave, an elderly man addresses the deceased to the following effect: "Go now to a good place, not an evil one; go to the road of the sunshine, not to the road of the rains; go where there are neither mosquitoes nor marsh-flies, but where there are pigs in plenty and taro in plenty. Send us pigs and send us taro, and we shall make a feast in your honour."[1]

Similar beliefs and practices prevail in the northern portion of New Guinea which formerly belonged to Germany; nor is this surprising, for the natives of New Guinea in general are settled people, subsisting by the cultivation of the ground and believing in the pervading influence of ancestral spirits. Thus the Yabim believe that in their field or garden labours they are dependent on the favour of the spirits of the dead (the *balum*). Before they plant taro in the ground which has been freshly cleared from the forest they pray to the spirits of the dead, saying, "Come not so often into the field, remain in the forest. Let the taro of the people who have helped us in clearing the field thrive well. Let the taro of everybody be very great; and when we now plant our taro in the earth let it all grow luxuriantly." At first they plant only a few shoots of taro, and at the next planting they again invoke the spirits of the dead and seek to win their favour by offering them valuable objects, such as boars' tusks and dogs' teeth, with which the ghosts, like living men, are supposed to ornament themselves.

[1] F. E. Williams, *Orokaiva Society*, p. 214.

And to satisfy their more material wants they offer taro porridge to the spirits. Later in the season they swing bull-roarers in the field, uttering the names of the dead as they do so, in the belief that thereby they ensure especially good crops of all the fruits of the field.[1]

However, in this case there seems to be some ground for thinking that the help of the spirits in cultivating the land is conceived as rather negative than positive; we have seen that the spirits are invited to stay in the forest and not to come so often into the field, which suggests that they are expected to abstain from injuring, rather than actively to promote, the growth of the crops. This is confirmed by other good evidence concerning the Yabim, from which it appears that their offerings to the ghosts are made for the purpose of inducing them to keep away and refrain from harming the growing crops.[2] The same conclusion is also suggested by the beliefs of the natives near Cape King William in what used to be German New Guinea. These people try to persuade the souls of the dead to avert all injurious influences that might hinder the growth of the yams, which are their staple food; in particular, the spirits are expected to guard the fields against the incursions of wild boars and the devouring locusts.[3]

The Toradyas of Central Celebes believe that the

[1] H. Zahn, "Die Jabim", in R. Neuhauss, *Deutsch Neu-Guinea* (Berlin, 1911), iii. 332 *sq.*

[2] See my *Belief in Immortality and the Worship of the Dead*, i. (London, 1913) pp. 247 *sq.*

[3] Stoltz, "Die Umgebung von Kap König Wilhelm" in R. Neuhauss, *Deutsch Neu-Guinea*, iii. 245.

success or failure of the harvest depends on maintaining a good understanding with the souls of the dead ;[1] but here again the help of the spirits would seem to be conceived as of a negative sort, for we are told that the offerings of rice, maize, sugar-cane and so forth which the Toradyas make to the spirits of the dead at planting their rice-fields are intended to induce the spirits not to injure the crops.[2]

The mountain tribes of Formosa worship the spirits of their ancestors both at sowing and at harvest.[3] Thus in regard to the Atayals or Taiyals, a notorious tribe of head-hunters, we are told that "after the rice or millet has been harvested, the Atayals select a day, during the period of a full moon, and worship their ancestors. A similar ceremony occurs when seed is sown. The first is to express their gratitude for a bountiful harvest, which they attribute to the spirits of their dead ancestors; and the second is to beseech a continuance of favour in respect of the coming harvest. In such case the ceremony is as follows. Every family makes from the rice or millet they have harvested, cakes, which they take during the darkness of night into the thick wood and, wrapping them in leaves, suspend them from the branches of trees. The spirits of their ancestors are expected to partake of their offerings."[4] Further details concerning the Atayal worship of

[1] N. Adriani en Alb. C. Kruijt, *De Bare-sprekende Toradjas van Midden-Celebes*, ii. 118.

[2] N. Adriani en Alb. C. Kruijt, *op. cit.* ii. 249.

[3] James W. Davidson, *The Island of Formosa* (London, 1903), pp. 567, 569, 571, 575, 579.

[4] J. W. Davidson, *op. cit.* p. 567.

ancestors at sowing and harvest have been furnished by a Japanese gentleman, Mr. Shinji Ishii, now deceased, who spent some years in Formosa studying the wild and little-known tribes of the mountains. I was personally acquainted with him during his stay in London, and from the abundant ethnological materials which he had collected in the island he furnished me with a number of legends of a great flood which he had taken down from the lips of the natives.[1] On the subject with which we are here concerned he tells us that among the Taiyals (Atayals) the ceremony of sowing marks the beginning of the new year. It is usually held between February and March of our calendar, when the moon is on the wane; a dark night is selected for the ceremony. When the day, or rather night, has been fixed by the chief, the men go out hunting, and the game they kill is kept for the coming feast, while the women are busy pounding rice and millet and brewing liquor. New fire is kindled by the friction of a drill and must be kept alight till the feast days are over. On the first day of the feast hundreds of small round cakes are baked at the chief's house, and when the night has come, men, one from each family, assemble at the chief's house. Accompanied by one or two of them the chief goes forth. The party carries torches and a basket containing seeds of rice, millet and sorghum, also a piece of boar's flesh and a tub of spirits. The chief himself carries a small hoe. At a short distance

[1] J. G. Frazer, *Folk-lore in the Old Testament*, i. 225 *sqq*.

from the house he digs a hole in the ground in which he buries the seed and covers it up with earth. Close beside it he digs another hole and deposits in it some of the cakes and meat, after which he pours the liquor on them. The spirits of the ancestors are then worshipped with the following prayer: "We now bury seed and meat; kindly give us good crops and plenty of game". The party then return to the chief's house with the remainder of the liquor and cakes. When they reach the house, the people who had remained behind come out to receive them, while the chief pronounces the words, "A good crop and plenty of game". He then gives to each person a portion of the cakes and liquor.[1]

After the harvest a ceremony is performed by the Atayals which is called the worship of the spirits of ancestors, because its intention is to offer the new crop to them. On the morning of the day appointed the chief cooks some millet, which is made into dumplings, and each family sends a man to the chief's house. Each of these men wraps one of the dumplings in an oak leaf and ties it to a branch of a tree which the chief had cut the day before; the branch is thus made to look as if it were bearing a bunch of fruit. Carrying the branch and followed by all the men, the chief then goes a little way from the house and there ties the branch to the bough of a big tree, while he prays to the spirits of the dead, saying, "O spirits of our an-

[1] Shinji Ishii, "The Life of the Mountain People of Formosa", *Folk-lore*, xxviii. (1917) pp. 120-122.

cestors, come and help yourselves!"[1] The reason for performing this ceremony at a big tree is apparently to convey the new millet of the harvest to the ancestral spirits who live in the tree. Similarly the Tsous, another mountain tribe of Formosa, believe that the spirits of their ancestors inhabit a big tree which grows near the entrance of each of their villages.[2]

In most Naga tribes of North-East India "the ancestral souls are regarded as directly responsible for the crops if indeed they are not immanent in the grain itself".[3] The Lakhers, another tribe of that region on the borders of Arakan, perform a sacrifice in October to the spirits of their ancestors to induce them to make the crops abundant, the domestic animals fertile and healthy, and to give good hunting. At the same time the sacrifice is intended to please the spirits of the rice and maize and to prevent them from leaving the village. For this ceremony the Lakhers make a broad road in front of the village for the spirits of the dead to come along, and when it is ready the men of the village march in procession up and down the road, with drums and gongs beating, to meet the unseen visitors and escort them to the house where the sacrifice is to take place. After this solemn march the Lakhers of one particular village (Chapi) visit the graves of all people who have died within the last three years

[1] Shinji Ishii, "The Life of the Mountain People of Formosa", *Folk-lore*, xxviii. (1917) p. 124.

[2] J. W. Davidson, *The Island of Formosa*, p. 571.

[3] J. H. Hutton, note in N. E. Parry, *The Lakhers*, p. 445.

and place handfuls of every kind of food and flour on the graves for the spirits of the dead to eat. The sacrifice to the dead on this occasion consists of seeds of every kind of food crop anointed with the blood of a fowl. It is deposited at the foot of the main post at the back of the house.[1] The Savars, a primitive tribe of the Central Provinces in India, "believe that the souls of those who die become ghosts, and in Bundelkhand they used formerly to bury the dead near their fields in the belief that the spirits would watch over and protect the crops".[2]

The same belief in the power of the spirits of the dead to promote the fertility of the ground is common in Africa. We have seen that, in the opinion of the Thonga, these potent spirits cause the fruit-trees to bear fruit and the crops to be plentiful.[3] An old Portuguese writer has recorded that the Kafirs of South-East Africa, on the morning after a burial "proceed to the grave of the deceased, and pronouncing certain words they throw upon it millet, beans and rice flour, with which they also powder one cheek and an eye, and go about without washing their faces until the flour has entirely disappeared. By this ceremony they say that they recommend their crops to the deceased, and they believe that in this their souls can be of use to them and grant good harvests."[4]

[1] N. E. Parry, *The Lakhers* (London, 1932), pp. 445 *sq.*

[2] R. V. Russell, *Tribes and Castes of the Central Provinces of India*, iv. 507.

[3] H. A. Junod, *Life of a South African Tribe*[2], ii. 386. See above, p. 51.

[4] J. Dos Santos, "Ethiopia Oriental", in G. McCall Theal, *Records of South-Eastern Africa*, vii. (London, 1901) pp. 308 *sq.*

The Bavenda of the Northern Transvaal invoke and propitiate the ancestral spirits before sowing and reaping the corn. In October or November, when the land is ready for sowing, a pot, containing seeds of eleusine, Kafir corn and all the other crops that are to be sown, is carried to the corn-field where the family has assembled. There a priestess, who is usually the father's sister (*makhadzi*) of the head of the family, addresses the ancestral spirits, saying, "Here is food for you, all our spirits; we give you of every kind of grain, which you may eat. Bring to us also crops in plenty and prosperity in the coming season."[1] And at the harvest-thanksgiving the priestess, in presence of the assembled family, again addresses the ancestral spirits, saying, "I offer you the first grain of the new year that you may eat and be happy; eat all of you; I deprive none amongst you. What remains in the ground belongs to me and your little ones. Let them eat and be happy."[2]

The Barea of East Africa celebrate a festival in honour of the dead by way of thanksgiving every year in November after the harvest. Every household brews much beer for the day, and a small pot of the beer is set apart for every dead member of the family and kept for two days, after which the beer is drunk by the living.[3]

The Kam, a tribe of Northern Nigeria, believe that the dead ancestors of their chief are the life

[1] H. A. Stayt, *The Bavenda* (London, 1931), pp. 252 *sq.*

[2] H. A. Stayt, *op. cit.* p. 255.

[3] W. Munzinger, *Ostafrikanische Studien* (Schaffhausen, 1864), p. 473.

and soul of the crops; hence the chief performs a daily ritual for the purpose of feeding these his royal forefathers, addressing them thus: "You are my forefathers. Once upon a time you did as I now do. If it were not so, then may my offering be of no account before you. But if you did as I now do, then accept this offering, that I and my people may be blessed with corn and health." So saying, he spits into a ladleful of beer and passes it to an official, who pours the beer as a libation into a well in the shrine. It is said that if this ritual were not observed daily the crops would wither.[1] In like manner the Namas, another tribe of Northern Nigeria, believe that the success of agricultural operations depends on the good-will of the royal ancestors, especially of the chief who died last. Hence after sowing, and also in times of drought, it is the Nama custom to perform rites at the graves of former chiefs. The duties are delegated by the chief to a priest in whose family the priesthood is hereditary. The priest goes to the graves and, after a prayer for a successful season and general prosperity, pours a libation on each of the gravestones.[2]

In some tribes of Northern Nigeria the power of promoting the growth of the crops is not restricted to the ancestors of chiefs; it is attributed to the ancestral spirits of commoners as well. Thus among the Abo, at the ripening of the Guinea-corn crops,

[1] C. K. Meek, *Tribal Studies in Northern Nigeria*, ii. 540 *sq.*
[2] C. K. Meek, *op. cit.* ii. 559.

the head of a household takes some porridge and fish-stew to the family graveyard and attracts the attention of his dead forefathers by smacking a leaf in the hollow of his left hand. Having thus got their ear, he pours a libation of beer, deposits some of the porridge and stew on the ground, and prays the ancestors that the harvest may be bountiful.[1] The Mumuye, another tribe of the same region, preserve the skulls of their dead forefathers in pots, and just before the harvest the head of the household brings out the skulls and pours a libation of chicken's blood and beer on them, praying for a good harvest.[2] Again, among the Yendang, another tribe of this region, when the crops have been gathered, the priest prepares a special brew of beer and goes to the grave of his father, where he pours a libation, saying, "The food which we sought at your hand has been given to us in plenty. We thank you, and we bring you your share." He goes also to the grave of his mother and pours a libation there. All heads of households do likewise.[3] Once more, the Hona, another tribe of Northern Nigeria, make offerings to their ancestors at sowing and harvest; but if the year has been a bad one the offerings may be withheld. In that case the head of the family enters the shrine of the defaulting ghosts and upbraids them, saying, "This year I will give you nothing, as you have hindered us. We did well by you, but you have done ill by us."[4]

[1] C. K. Meek, *Tribal Studies in Northern Nigeria*, ii. 565 *sq.*

[2] C. K. Meek, *op. cit.* i. 469 *sq.*

[3] C. K. Meek, *op. cit.* i. 486.

[4] C. K. Meek, *op. cit.* ii. 403.

In their worship of ancestors these people clearly go on the principle of payment by results.

A similar faith in the power of the ancestral spirits to make or mar the fruits of the earth prevails widely also among the tribes of the French Sudan, and it finds similar expression in ceremonies of prayer, thanksgiving and worship offered to these spirits at sowing and harvest. The belief and the worship have been recorded by a French administrator, but I will spare you the details, which would be substantially a repetition of the evidence I have adduced from the neighbouring province of Northern Nigeria.[1]

[1] L. Tauxier, *Le Noir du Soudan, pays Mossi et Gourounsi* (Paris, 1912), pp. 70 *sq.*, 104, 189 *sq.*, 191, 237, 270, 322, 323, 356

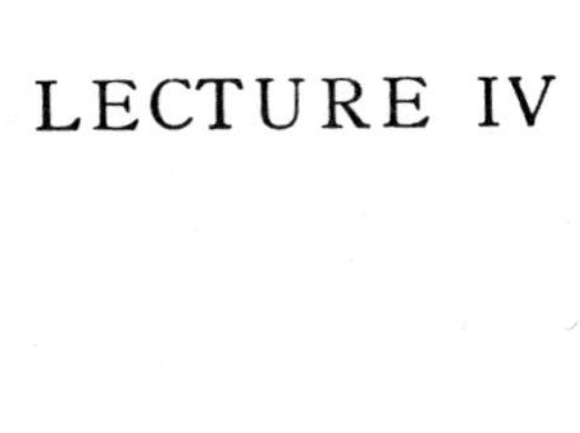

LECTURE IV

LECTURE IV

In the last lecture I showed that the spirits of the dead are believed by many peoples to promote the fertility of the ground, either positively by the generative virtue they possess, or negatively by guarding the crops against the noxious influences which might otherwise injure or destroy them. Where such beliefs prevail, the spirits of the dead are naturally supposed to possess a proprietary right in the fruits of the earth which entitles them to receive an offering of the first-fruits before the living may partake of the new crop. Elsewhere I have collected some evidence of the custom of offering first-fruits to the dead.[1] I will not repeat it all here but shall content myself with citing a few typical examples.

The South-East Solomon Islanders are among the peoples who strive to keep the souls of the dead beside them in the house. For this purpose, when a death has taken place, they angle for the ghost of the deceased with a sort of little fishing-rod, and, having caught it, they put it, together with some bodily relic of the dead man, such as his

[1] *Spirits of the Corn and of the Wild*, ii. 109 *sqq.*

skull or jawbone or a tooth or a lock of hair, in a case which is deposited in a corner of the dwelling-house. Each householder hangs up offerings of first-fruits beside these cases, which are supposed to contain the souls as well as the bodily relics of his dead kinsfolk.[1] In these islands, when the Canarium nuts were ripe, nobody might eat of them till the first-fruits had been sacrificed to the dead.[2] Similarly when the yams are ripe, the people fetch some of them from the gardens to offer to the ghosts. A man goes to the sacred place and cries with a loud voice to the ghost, "This is yours to eat". So saying, he lays down the yam beside the dead man's skull.[3]

In Viti Levu, the largest of the Fijian Islands, there was a Sacred Place, called the Nanga, where the ancestral spirits were to be found by their worshippers, and whither offerings were taken on all occasions when the aid of the spirits was to be invoked. Thither accordingly the first-fruits of the yam harvest were carried and presented to the ancestors with great ceremony before the bulk of the crop was dug for the people's use, and no man might taste of the new yams until the presentation had been made to the dead. If any one were impious enough to appropriate the yams to his own use before the ancestors had received their proper share, it was thought that he would be smitten with madness.[4]

[1] W. G. Ivens, *The Melanesians of the South East Solomon Islands*, p. 178; compare *id.*, pp. 210, 216.

[2] R. H. Codrington, *The Melanesians*, pp. 132 *sq.*

[3] R. H. Codrington, *op. cit.* p. 138.

[4] Lorimer Fison, "The Nanga, or Sacred Stone Enclosure of Wainimala, Fiji", *Journal of the Anthropological Institute*, xiv. (1885) pp. 26 *sq.*

The Oraons of India offer the first-fruits of the upland rice and of *Panicum miliare* to the ancestral spirits at their two annual festivals ; these offerings must be made to the dead before the living may partake of the new crops.[1] Among the Birhors, a primitive jungle tribe of India, no man will eat certain edible flowers and fruits and upland rice till he has offered the first-fruits of the season to his ancestral spirits. Similarly he will not sip honey from certain first flowers of the season till he has offered a few drops to the souls of his forefathers.[2]

Among the Thonga of South-East Africa the regular national offering is that of the first-fruits to the ancestral spirits. The Bantu conception of hierarchy is clearly illustrated by this custom; the ancestral spirits or gods, as M. Junod calls them, must be the first to enjoy the produce of the new year, then the chief, the sub-chiefs, the counsellors, the headmen, then the younger brothers in order of age. There is a stringent taboo directed against anybody who presumes to precede his superiors in the enjoyment of the first-fruits. The law applies to Kafir corn or Kafir plums in certain clans, and to sorghum, pumpkin leaves, beer and so forth in others.[3] In offering the first-fruits of the Kafir corn to his ancestral spirits the chief addresses these august beings, saying, " Here has the new

[1] Sarat Chandra Roy, *Oraon Religion and Customs*, p. 33. Compare F. Hahn, " Some Notes on the Religion and Superstitions of the Orãos ", *Journal of the Asiatic Society of Bengal*, lxxii. Part iii. (Calcutta, 1904) p. 13.

[2] Sarat Chandra Roy, *The Birhors*, pp. 112, 520.

[3] H. A. Junod, *The Life of a South African Tribe*[2], ii. 403 *sq*.

year come! Precede us, you gods, and eat the first-fruits (*luma*), so that for us also Kafir corn shall help our body, that we may become fat, not thin, that the witches may increase the corn, make it to be plentiful, so that, even if there is only a small field, big baskets may be filled!"[1] And when the first ripe Kafir plums are gathered, the sour liquor obtained from them is poured out on the graves of the dead Thonga chiefs in the sacred wood, and the souls of the chiefs are invoked to bless the new year and the feast which is about to be celebrated.[2]

The Ba-ila of Northern Rhodesia have not, like the Thonga and other Bantu tribes, a tribal or national festival of first-fruits, but before eating of the new maize every man offers some of the fresh cobs privately to his ancestral spirits, placing them above the door and in the rafters of his hut, thereby expressing his gratitude to the spirits, and his hope of similar blessings in the future.[3] But before he makes this domestic offering he takes some new ripe cobs of maize to the grave of an ancestor and kneeling before it says, "So-and-so, here is some of the maize which is ripe first and which I offer to thee".[4]

Among the Yombe of Northern Rhodesia nobody might eat of the first-fruits of the new crops until the chief had sacrificed a bull before the grave of

[1] H. A. Junod, *The Life of a South African Tribe*[2], i. 396.

[2] H. A. Junod, *op. cit.* i. 397.

[3] E. W. Smith and A. M. Dale, *The Ila-speaking Peoples of Northern Rhodesia*, i. 139 *sq.*

[4] E. W. Smith and A. M. Dale, *op. cit.* ii. 179 *sq.*

his grandfather, and had deposited pots of beer and porridge, made from the first-fruits, in front of the shrine. After thanking the ghost of his grandfather for the harvest, and praying him to partake of the first-fruits, the chief and his followers withdrew to feast on the fresh porridge and beer at the village.[1] Among the Konde of Lake Nyasa the first cobs of maize of the new harvest are taken to the chief, who offers them to his ancestors, usually at the place where the trees of the village stand. The heads of families then offer some of the new maize to their own ancestors and, curiously enough, to twins. Not until these offerings have been made to the spirits of the dead may the people eat the new season's crops.[2]

The A-Kamba, a tribe of Kenya, in East Africa, offer the first-fruits of every crop to their ancestral spirits before anybody dare eat of the new crop. Sometimes the offerings are piled on the graves of chiefs; sometimes they are deposited in a clearing under the sacred wild fig-tree, for the A-Kamba think that the spirits of the dead dwell in wild fig-trees, and they build miniature huts at the foot of the trees for the ghosts to dwell in. The clearing under the fig-tree is called the Place of Prayer. When any crop is ripe, the people assemble, and an old man and woman go to the Place of Prayer, and there calling aloud to the spirits of the dead, ask their permission to eat of the new crop. The people

[1] C. Gouldsbury and H. Sheane, *The Great Plateau of Northern Rhodesia* (London, 1911), pp. 294 *sq*.

[2] D. R. Mackenzie, *The Spirit-ridden Konde*, p. 120.

then dance, and during the dance some woman is sure to be seized with a fit of shaking and to cry out, which is taken to be an answer of the spirits to the people's prayer.[1]

Among the Bura of Northern Nigeria, at the maize harvest, every man who has lost a father or mother chooses three heads of corn, dresses them carefully, and places them on a tray, which he sets by his head at night, and during the night the spirits of the dead father and mother are thought to come and eat the soul of the corn. No man of the tribe will eat fresh corn till he has performed this rite with the first-fruits.[2] The Igbiras, a pagan tribe at the confluence of the Niger and the Benue, bury, or used to bury, their dead in their houses and have great faith in the power of ghosts, to whom they offer the first-fruits of their crops, hanging bunches of the new grain over the burial-places in their huts.[3]

Closely connected with the belief that the spirits of the dead possess the power of fertilizing the earth and promoting the growth of the crops is the belief that these spirits can give or withhold rain at their pleasure; for everywhere vegetation depends for its very existence on water, and in most countries water is, in the last resort, obtained mainly or exclusively in the form of rain. Hence in dry and

[1] C. W. Hobley, *Ethnology of A-Kamba and other East African Tribes* (Cambridge, 1910), pp. 66, 85 *sq.*

[2] C. K. Meek, *Tribal Studies in Northern Nigeria*, i. 161.

[3] A. F. Mockler-Ferryman, *Up the Niger* (London, 1892), pp. 141 *sq.*

arid regions, where the rainfall is scanty and precarious, and where often not a drop falls for months together, the coming of the rain is a matter of the most anxious concern to the natives, to whom a long drought may bring famine, suffering and death. Accordingly, when they believe that the rain is controlled by the spirits of the dead, we need not wonder that the inhabitants are eager to cultivate the good graces of the departed and appeal to them earnestly for help whenever the expected rain is long delayed.

For example, among the Toradyas of Central Celebes there is a certain village where there is the grave of a famous chief. When the land suffers from unseasonable drought, the people go to the grave, pour water on it, and say, " O grandfather, have pity on us ; if it is your will that this year we should eat, then give rain ". After that they hang a bamboo full of water over the grave ; in the lower end of the bamboo there is a small hole, from which the water drips continually. The bamboo is always refilled with water till rain falls.[1] In this ceremony the religious appeal to the compassion of the dead chief is reinforced by dripping water on his grave, which is essentially a magical rite supposed to produce the desired effect by imitating it.

But it is in Africa, where the belief in the power of ancestral spirits is most deeply felt and most widely acknowledged, that we find these spirits most

[1] A. C. Kruijt, " Regen lokken en regen verdrijving bij de Toradjas van Central Celebes ", *Tijdschrift voor Indische Taal- Land- en Volkenkunde*, xliv. (1901) p. 6, citing v. Baarda.

commonly looked to for a due supply of rain. Thus, for example, the Thonga believe that the spirits of the ancestors cause the rain to fall. So, if the spring showers do not come in due time, the first thought of the people will be to offer a sacrifice to their ancestors, especially if the diviner, by means of his divining bones, has announced that the anger of the ancestors is the real cause of the drought. Thereupon men will go to the sacred wood where the ancestors are buried, and there they will chant an ancient mourning song, and some of them will beat the graves with sticks. Also, they will sacrifice a black ram, without any white spot on it, and shed its blood all over the ground. In many of these sacred woods human victims are said to have been formerly offered to the ghosts of chiefs on these occasions.[1]

Among the Bechuanas, when rain is long delayed, it is deemed necessary to sacrifice a sheep or goat or a more costly victim at the grave of a distinguished and still revered or dreaded ancestor. The sacrifice is accompanied by a prayer to the spirit of the dead man, begging him to look on the distress of his children and to come to their aid.[2] Similarly, when a drought had lasted a long time, the Herero of South-West Africa used to go in a body with their cattle to the grave of some eminent man, it might be the father or grandfather of the chief. There they would lay offerings of milk and

[1] H. A. Junod, *The Life of a South African Tribe*[2], ii. 316, 405.

[2] J. Tom Brown, *Among the Bantu Nomads*, p. 131.

flesh on the grave and pray, saying, "Look, O Father, upon your beloved cattle and children; they suffer distress, they are so lean, they are dying of hunger. Give us rain." But the voice of the supplicant was almost drowned in the lowing of the cattle, the bleating of the flocks, the barking of dogs, the shouts of the herdsmen, and the screams of the women.[1]

In like manner the Bavenda of the Northern Transvaal usually trace the failure of rain to the anger of their ancestors. When the identity of the particular ancestor who is causing the drought has been discovered by divination, the people are summoned to dance a certain sacred dance, either in a village within hearing of the grave of the offended forefather or in the forest near his tomb. The chief, accompanied by his kinsfolk, then repairs to the grave, and after laying the stomach of a sacrificed ox on it, beseeches the spirit to stay his anger, and not to let the earth grow hot, and cause his descendants to perish for want of water.[2]

So, again, among the Banyamwezi, when the rain is unduly delayed and the crops are in danger, the official rain-maker or diviner will visit the king and propose to appease the wrath of the royal ancestors by offering bloody sacrifices on their tombs. If the king consents, the sacrifice of a bull

[1] P. H. Brincker, "Beobachtungen über die Deisidämonie der Eingeborenen Deutsch-Südwest-Afrikas", *Globus*, lviii. (1890) p. 323; *id.*, in *Mitteilungen des Seminars für orientalische Sprachen zu Berlin*, iii. (1900) Dritte Abteilung, p. 89.

[2] H. A. Stayt, *The Bavenda*, p. 310.

or a he-goat is solemnly performed at the royal graves, which are often under the shadow of great trees.[1] Similarly many tribes of Northern Nigeria ascribe a prolonged drought to the displeasure of the royal ancestors. When that calamity happens in the country of the Zumu, the grave-diggers and custodians of the royal tombs are called on to inspect the graves of former chiefs, and if they find, as they commonly do, that one of the graves has been neglected, the head of the grave-diggers takes immediate steps to repair the neglect. When that has been done, he lays an offering of pumpkins on the grave of the chief who died last, apologizes to him for the neglect, and prays him to send the needed rain.[2]

The Malabu, another tribe of Northern Nigeria, are wont to detach the skull of a dead chief in the spring after the burial, and to preserve it, with the other royal skulls, in a hut set apart for that purpose. When a fresh skull has thus been added to the collection in the royal charnel-house, the head of a certain kindred addresses it, saying, "To-day we have brought you home, so that you may not be left abandoned in the bush. Hinder us not, therefore, from obtaining sufficient rain this season, and send not sickness amongst us." He then pours a libation of beer over the skull, and all hasten home; for it is believed that on the conclusion of these rites, which coincide with the beginning of the rainy

[1] Fr. Bösch, *Les Banyamwezi*, pp. 149 *sqq*.

[2] C. K. Meek, *Tribal Studies in Northern Nigeria*, i. 75.

season, rain will immediately fall. If this does not happen for several days, resort is had to a professional diviner to ascertain the cause. The sage generally declares that the people had offended the late chief on some occasion during his life, and that therefore the angry ghost is holding up the rain. All the seniors, accordingly, accompanied by the new chief, go to the royal skull-hut and tender a formal apology to the ghost, after which rain is sure to follow sooner or later.[1] In the Gola tribe of the same region it is a custom for some senior man, acting on behalf of the community, to offer a prayer for rain before the skull of a man who was reputed to have been a centenarian. The petitioner holds a chicken up to the midday sun and addresses the ghost of the centenarian as follows: "God gave you food so that you lived a hundred years. May we also have food and live to a ripe old age. Behold, our crops are parched for want of rain. We beseech you to ask God to send us rain, so that we and our children may not perish. You cannot speak to us, but you can see us; so help us, we beseech you." He then kills the chicken and pours the blood over the pot containing the skull.[2]

Thus we see that the spirits of the dead are commonly supposed to possess the power of quickening or blasting the fruits of the earth by giving or withholding rain. Sometimes it is believed that

[1] C. K. Meek, *Tribal Studies in Northern Nigeria*, i. 109.
[2] C. K. Meek, *op. cit.* i. 478.

they can also render a woman barren or make her the joyful mother of children. Among the Lakhers of North-Eastern India, when a wife whose parents are dead is childless, the misfortune is ascribed to the displeasure of her deceased father and mother, who are preventing her from having offspring. So to appease their angry spirits a fowl is sacrificed and cooked with rice, and the meat and rice are placed on the graves of the barren woman's parents. And if a wife's father-in-law and mother-in-law are dead, their spirits can also prevent her from having children should they happen to have a grudge at her. In that case it is necessary to propitiate their spirits also with the sacrifice of a fowl.[1] Similarly in Imerina, a province of Madagascar, when a woman does not conceive for a certain time after marriage, she consults a diviner, who, after examining his divining apparatus, informs her which of the ancient inhabitants of the land, or which of her own ancestors is offended with her, and what sacrifice she must offer to appease the angry spirit of the dead in order to obtain a child. For the Merina believe, we are informed, that the commerce of the sexes is by no means essential to the birth of children, which is the work of God and of the ancestors. So after praying and anointing with fat the tomb of an ancestor or of one of the aboriginal inhabitants of the land, the woman who desires to have a child takes a little of the fat from the grave home and rubs it on her belly, believing that in this way the

[1] N. E. Parry, *The Lakhers* (London, 1932), p. 380.

wish of her heart will be granted.[1] The Kwottos of Northern Nigeria, who believe in the reincarnation of the dead, think that unless an ancestral spirit consents to enter a woman's womb she cannot conceive a child. Hence a barren woman consults a medicine-man and begs him to mediate for her with the ancestral spirits who are supposed to be responsible for the calamity; or at least she asks him to ascertain the cause and prescribe the remedy, whether that is to be effected by penitence or propitiation.[2] In this tribe the male ancestor who is believed to be reborn in a woman is usually a deceased grandfather.[3] Holding this view of the spiritual origin of childbirth, a Kwotto woman will sometimes make a pilgrimage to a sacred place known to be haunted by ghosts, in the hope of persuading some ghost to enter into her womb and be born again.[4] Hence, too, before a child is born, the Kwottos sacrifice fowls and beer to the ancestral ghosts to induce them to aid the expectant mother in her hour of need.[5] Similar beliefs as to the essential part played by ancestral spirits in the birth of children appear to be held by the Banyamwezi. Once when a missionary asked a member of the tribe, "Why do you worship your ancestral spirits as if they were your gods and you were their creatures?" the man replied, "Do you think that

[1] A. Grandidier et G. Grandidier, *Ethnographie de Madagascar*, ii. (Paris, 1914) pp. 245 *sq*.

[2] J. R. Wilson-Haffenden, *The Red Men of Nigeria* (London, 1930), pp. 185 *sq*.

[3] J. R. Wilson-Haffenden, *op. cit.* p. 236.

[4] J. R. Wilson-Haffenden, *op. cit.* p. 237.

[5] J. R. Wilson-Haffenden, *op. cit.* p. 245.

a woman could bear a child if the ancestral spirits did not wish it ?" [1]

Another important service which the spirits of the dead are believed to be able to render to the living is success or victory in war. When war threatened the country of the Thonga, the general of the army used to take a large thorn of a certain kind of tree (*Acacia horrida*) and after sucking it he would spit out, saying, "You, the ancestor-gods, So-and-so, enemies wish to take your country! Give us valour ! May we stab them with this thorn, with the assegai !" [2] Speaking of the Bantu tribes of South Africa in general, a good authority says that "the ancestral spirits are interceded with, and begged to help in the war ; indeed many natives seem to think that there is far more real warfare among the ancestral spirits than among the actual warriors. . . . These ancestral spirits are sometimes supposed to be fighting in the air just above the heads of the people, and if only the warriors can be persuaded that their ancestral spirits are with them they will fight with immense bravery and confidence." [3] In the old days, when the Awemba of Northern Rhodesia were about to go to war, the king and the elders used to pray daily for victory to the spirits of the dead kings, his predecessors. In the dusk of the evening, on the day before the army set out, the king and the elderly women, who passed for the wives of the dead kings and tended their

[1] Fr. Bösch, *Les Banyamwezi*, p. 161.

[2] H. A. Junod, *The Life of a South African Tribe*[2], ii. 405.

[3] Dudley Kidd, *The Essential Kafir* (London, 1904), p. 307.

shrines, went and prayed at their shrines that the souls of the departed monarchs would keep the war-path free from foes and lead the king in a straight course to the enemy's stockade. These solemn prayers the king led in person, and the women beat their breasts as they joined in the earnest appeal to the dead.[1]

The natives of New Caledonia used to catch the soul of a famous warrior after death and enclose it in a stone which the priest was supposed to carry with him to battle; but as the stone was heavy the priest contented himself with attaching to his wrist a small round stone which represented the big one that contained the dead warrior's soul. Thus borne to battle by deputy, the spirit of the deceased champion was no doubt supposed to nerve his people to fresh deeds of courage in the fight.[2] Among the Sea Dyaks of Borneo the bodies of mighty warriors were sometimes buried for a time and then exhumed, and their remains kept as sacred relics by their descendants in or near their houses, or it might be on the spur of a neighbouring hill, for the purpose of securing the dead heroes as guardian spirits, whose protection might naturally be looked for above all in time of war.[3] For of the Sea Dyaks in general we are told that "before going forth on an expedition against the enemy, the dead are invoked, and

[1] J. H. West Sheane, "Wemba Warpaths", *Journal of the African Society*, No. xli. (October 1911) pp. 25 *sq.*

[2] M. Leenhardt, *Notes d'Ethnologie Néo-Calédoniennes* (Paris, 1930), pp. 214 *sq.*

[3] Rev. J. Perham, "Sea Dyak Religion", *Journal of the Straits Branch of the Royal Asiatic Society*, No. 14 (December 1884), p. 293.

are begged to help their friends on earth, so that they may be successful against their foes ".[1] In Tobelo, a district in the north of Halmahera, an island to the west of New Guinea, when the people are going to war, the soothsayer prepares a warrior for the combat by supplying him with the soul of a brave ancestor. In order to do this he throws the man into a sort of swoon, combined with a fit of shivering, and while the patient is in this state, the sage attaches the soul of the deceased warrior to his living descendant. The soul does not enter into his body nor pass into his blood, but sits astraddle on his neck with its legs hanging down in front on the man's shoulders. It is not seen or felt by the man himself, and after the battle it flies away, still invisible. A soldier who is thus reinforced by the soul of a gallant ancestor is sure to kill his adversary in the fight.[2]

But it is not merely to the souls of dead ancestors that the savage resorts for help in war ; he can press the souls of his dead enemies into the same service. The Kiwai of British New Guinea know how to recruit their forces by these unwilling allies. In the central hall of any one of their club-houses, which are reserved for the use of the men, may be seen two small holes, and in each of the holes is the dried eye of an enemy killed in battle. Spirits of slain

[1] E. H. Gomes, *Seventeen Years among the Sea Dyaks of Borneo* (London, 1911), p. 142.

[2] F. S. A. de Clercq, " Dodads Ma-taoe en Goma Ma-taoe, of Zielenhuisjes in het district Tobélo op Noord-halmahera ", *Internationales Archiv für Ethnographie*, ii. (1889) p. 210 ; W. Kükenthal, *Forschungsreise in den Molukken und in Borneo* (Frankfurt a. M., 1896), p. 177.

foes are supposed to inhabit the two eyes, and when the builders of the house go forth to war these spirits are thought to possess the power of capturing the souls of the enemy, thus making them weak and impotent, and giving the attacking party an easy victory. In the discharge of this useful office the spirits are supposed to precede the fighting men and to prepare the way for them.[1]

The Bataks, a barbarous people living in the interior of the great island of Sumatra, have, or rather perhaps formerly had, a still stranger and more tragic mode of pressing spiritual recruits into the fighting line. They believed that if anybody made a solemn promise to aid them in battle and died immediately after giving the promise, his disembodied soul would prove a powerful ally in war, striking terror into the breasts of the foe. To procure such an ally they proceeded thus. A lad of some twelve or fifteen years was procured by purchase or violence, and outside the village, generally in the neighbouring forest, he was buried in the ground up to the neck with his arms at his sides. There for four days he was fed with rice strongly seasoned with pepper and salt to make him very thirsty. From time to time his tormentors asked him whether he would bless them and help them in war. At first he naturally refused and threatened rather to curse and injure them. On the fourth day the principal men gathered about him and sought by all sorts of flattering words to wheedle the desired

[1] E. Baxter Riley, *Among Papuan Headhunters*, pp. 88, 90.

promise of blessing and help out of him. Meantime a man at the lad's back was busy melting lead. At last, driven to despair by his intolerable sufferings, the victim yielded and said, "My spirit or soul shall guard you". No sooner were the words uttered than the man behind the boy drew back the victim's head and poured the molten lead into his open mouth. Thus the lad died a sudden death and was prevented from retracting his promise. After dying such a death his soul, it was supposed, would become a mischievous demon, but, bound by his promise not to injure his murderers, he would wreak his vengeance only on their enemies. That he might do so with greater effect, portions of his brain, heart and liver were extracted from his body, and a salve compounded from them was inserted in a magical staff, which was entrusted to a sorcerer. When a war broke out, a sacrifice was offered to the soul of the murdered lad, represented by the magical staff, which was carried to battle at the head of the troop, the soul of the dead lad marching grimly with them against the enemy.[1]

Far less barbarous than this was the custom of the Muyscas, an Indian tribe in the ancient province of Cundinamarca, which now forms part of the State of Colombia in South America. Marching to battle, the Muyscas used to carry, at the head of their regiments, the embalmed bodies of their ancient heroes. This custom, we are told, pre-

[1] J. M. Meerwaldt, "De Bataksche Tooverstaf", *Bijdragen tot de Taal- Land- en Volkenkunde van Nederlandsch-Indie*, liii. (1901) pp. 302-304.

vented them from retreating, for they esteemed it the height of infamy to allow the bodies of their ancestors to fall into the hands of the enemy.[1] We are not told, but may reasonably presume, that the souls of these dead heroes were supposed to accompany their bodies to the fight. The idea that the spirits of the fathers rise from their graves to fight the battles of their children is one that naturally occurs to primitive man: it is not entirely alien to Englishmen of to-day, or at least of yesterday. In the poet's address to the mariners of England he says,

> The spirits of your fathers
> Shall start from every wave—
> For the deck it was their field of fame,
> And Ocean was their grave.

That concludes what I have to say as to the aid which the souls of the dead are thought to give to their descendants in war.

We now pass to a service of a different kind which the spirits of the dead are commonly supposed to render to their surviving kinsfolk by giving them counsel and advice in times of doubt, danger or distress. In short, the spirits of the dead are often consulted as oracles by the living. Elsewhere I have treated this part of our subject at some length.[2] Here it must suffice to cite a few typical cases.

The oracles of the dead are commonly supposed

[1] H. Ternaux-Compans, *Essai sur l'ancien Cundinamarca* (Paris, Librairie A. Bertrand, N.D.), pp. 66 *sq*. Compare A. de Herrera, *The General History of the Vast Continent and Islands of America*, translated by Captain Stevens (London, 1725), v. 86.

[2] *Folk-Lore in the Old Testament*, ii. 517 *sqq*.

to be imparted either directly by the ghost or indirectly by a medium, a living person who is believed to be possessed by the spirit of the dead and to speak with his voice or at least in his name. Sometimes the communication is effected by means of an image of the dead, sometimes by means of one of his bodily relics, especially the skull, less often a jawbone.

The oracular function of ghosts may be illustrated by the beliefs and practices of the Melanesians. These people believe that the knowledge of future events is conveyed to them by a spirit or ghost speaking with the voice of a living man, one of the wizards, who is himself unconscious while he speaks. In the island of Florida, for example, men might be sitting in their canoe-house discussing an expedition, perhaps to attack some unsuspecting village. One among them, known to have his ghost of prophecy, would sneeze and begin to shake, a sign that the ghost had entered into him ; his eyes would glare, his limbs twist, his whole body be convulsed, and foam would burst from his lips ; then a voice, apparently not his own, would be heard from his throat, approving or disapproving of what was proposed. Such a man used no means of bringing the ghost on him ; it came on him, as he believed, of its own free will ; its ghostly power overmastered him, and when it departed it left him quite exhausted.[1] Again, we are told that, in the belief of the Melanesians, ghosts make known to men who

[1] R. H. Codrington, *The Melanesians*, p. 209.

use them secret things which the unaided human intelligence could not find out. In the Solomon Islands, for instance, when an expedition has started in a fleet of canoes, there is sometimes a hesitation whether they shall proceed, or a question in what direction they shall go. While they are hesitating, a man who knows the ghosts may say that a ghost has just stepped on board, for did not the canoe tip over to one side, weighed down by the invisible passenger? So he asks the ghost, "Shall we proceed? Shall we go to such and such a place?" If the canoe rocks, the answer is yes; if it lies on an even keel, the answer is no.[1]

In the Solomon Islands both men and women can be possessed and inspired by ghosts, and there are professional mediums whose services are employed when any one wishes to ascertain the cause of sickness in a particular case. A deputation is sent to such a person on behalf of the sick, and the sage straightway falls into a trance, and speaks with the voice of the ghost that has taken possession of him or her, saying, "I am So-and-so", naming the person whose ghost is supposed to be speaking. For instance, at Sa'a there was a man named Soiolo who used to be possessed by the ghost of a woman called the Twin's Wife. The paroxysms would come on him quite suddenly, but they were generally associated with bad health or nervous prostration. The utterances of the Twin's Wife by his mouth were all of trouble and confusion and

[1] R. H. Codrington, *The Melanesians*, p. 210.

death. During the time of possession he would swallow hot coals or chew up the cockle-shells used for scraping yams. As a rule, whatever is said by a person thus possessed by a ghost is believed and followed, be it never so foolish, since his utterances are supposed to be inspired by the ghost. The same thing is more or less true of the utterances of a mad person, who is similarly supposed to be possessed and inspired by a ghost. His wild whirling words and the convulsive movements of his body are attributed to the action of the ghost who has entered into him.[1] Indeed, it may be laid down as a general rule that in primitive society there is no sharp distinction between inspiration and insanity. On this point, Dr. Codrington, speaking of the Melanesians, says that " the possession which causes madness cannot be quite distinguished from that which prophesies, and a man may pretend to be mad that he may get the reputation of being a prophet ".[2]

The natives of Ambrym, a Melanesian island in the New Hebrides, carve wooden images of their ancestors, by means of which they communicate with their spirits and consult them oracularly. If a man is in trouble, he blows his whistle at nightfall near the image of his ancestor, and if he hears a noise he thinks that the spirit of the ancestor has approached and entered the image. So he proceeds to tell the image his sorrows and asks the spirit for

[1] W. G. Ivens, *The Melanesians of the South-East Solomon Islands*, pp. 191 *sq*.

[2] R. H. Codrington, *The Melanesians*, p. 219.

help. Occasionally sacrifices are offered to the ancestral images, as is shown by the pigs' jaws which are often found tied to these venerable figures.[1]

The belief in the survival of the soul after death and in the power of the dead to affect the living is deeply rooted in the minds of the Mortlock Islanders, a Micronesian people in the Pacific. Every man believes himself to be surrounded by the souls of his departed forefathers, who hover about him unseen, protect him from danger, and foresee what will befall him. But the spirits cannot speak with everybody, only with the seers or necromancers who have learned the art of communing with the dead. So when a man desires to consult the ancestral spirits, he betakes himself to one of the wizards, acquaints him with his business, and makes him a present. The wizard then sits down on the ground and invokes the spirits. They come and light upon him; they take possession of him; he becomes a man inspired. The signs of inspiration are a convulsive twitching of the hands, a violent nodding of the head, and other equally plain tokens of ghostly possession. The spirits now open his mouth and speak through him. Now one spirit announces his presence and now another; for every spirit can at pleasure give his answer to the seer, though the answer is always couched in a special language, quite different from the speech of daily life. The state of possession or

[1] Felix Speiser, *Two Years with the Natives in the Western Pacific* (London, 1913), p. 206.

inspiration does not last very long, and on awakening from his trance the seer communicates to his hearers the message which he has received from the oracular spirits of the dead.[1]

In New Guinea also the spirits of the dead are frequently supposed to impart oracular information to their surviving kinsfolk. At Mawatta, a village of British New Guinea near the mouth of the Fly River, the skulls of the dead were not uncommonly kept by their relatives. When an important man died, the corpse would be buried up to the neck until the flesh of the head had decayed, leaving the bones bare. The skull was then detached from the body and preserved. The skulls of relatives, thus treasured, are often consulted on the temporal affairs of life. The owner places them by his pillow at night, and in sleep each dead man's spirit comes and communicates with the sleeper in a dream. All sorts of valuable information about gardens or wizards or hunting may thus be imparted by the ghost.[2] The Kiwai, a Papuan people of British New Guinea, believe that they can obtain oracular communications directly from the ghost by questioning the dead man at his grave or by sleeping on the grave, in which case the soul of the departed will visit the sleeper in a dream and give the desired answer. And in order to obtain advice from his

[1] Max Girschner, "Die Karolineninsel Namōluk und ihre Bewohner", *Baessler Archiv*, ii. (1912) pp. 193 *sq.* Compare J. G. Frazer, *The Belief in Immortality and the Worship of the Dead*, iii. 120 *sq.*

[2] W. N. Beaver, *Unexplored New Guinea* (London, 1920), p. 63.

dead parents a Kiwai will sometimes dig up their skulls from the grave, wash them clean, rub them with sweet-scented herbs, and sleep close to them, apparently with one skull in each armpit. Sometimes in so doing he will provide himself with a stick and threaten to smash the skulls, if the ghosts of his parents do not appear promptly. In a Kiwai folk-tale the laggard ghosts excuse themselves for being late by pleading that they are old and cannot move fast.[1]

The Mailu, a Papuo-Melanesian people of British New Guinea, keep the skulls of their dead in their houses and believe that the ghosts continue to reside in the skulls. The family accordingly consults the ghosts in the skulls and invokes them in all incantations, as when they are setting up a mark of taboo on coconuts to protect them against thieves.[2]

The Papuans of Geelvink Bay, in the northern part of Dutch New Guinea, believe that the spirits of the dead not only exist but possess superhuman power and exercise great influence over the affairs of life on earth, being able to protect the survivors in danger, to stand by them in war, and to grant success in hunting and fishing. In order to communicate with these powerful beings they make wooden images of their dead, which they keep in their houses and consult from time to time. Every family has at least one such

[1] G. Landtman, *The Kiwai Papuans of British New Guinea*, p. 295.

[2] B. Malinowski, " The Natives of Mailu ", *Transactions of the Royal Society of South Australia*, xxxix. (1915) pp. 583, 653.

ancestral image, which forms the medium whereby the soul of the departed communicates with his or her surviving kinsfolk. These images are not only kept in the houses but carried in canoes on voyages, in order that they may be at hand to help and advise their relatives. At these consultations the inquirer may either take the image in his hands or crouch before it on the ground, on which he places his offerings. The spirit of the dead is thought to be in the image and to pass from it into the inquirer, who thus becomes inspired by the soul of the deceased and so gains supernatural knowledge. The sign of inspiration in the medium is that he shivers and shakes. It is especially in cases of sickness that these oracular images are consulted.[1]

In preparing a body for burial the Betsileo of Madagascar are careful to place a piece of money in the mouth of the corpse for the purpose, as they say, of "opening the lips of the dead" when his ghost comes to visit the family. For the appearance of a ghost who could not speak and give them advice would be a presage of misfortune.[2]

[1] J. G. Frazer, *The Belief in Immortality and the Worship of the Dead*, i. 307-309, where I have cited the authorities.

[2] G. Grandidier, "La Mort et les funérailles à Madagascar", *L'Anthropologie*, xxiii. (1912) p. 330.

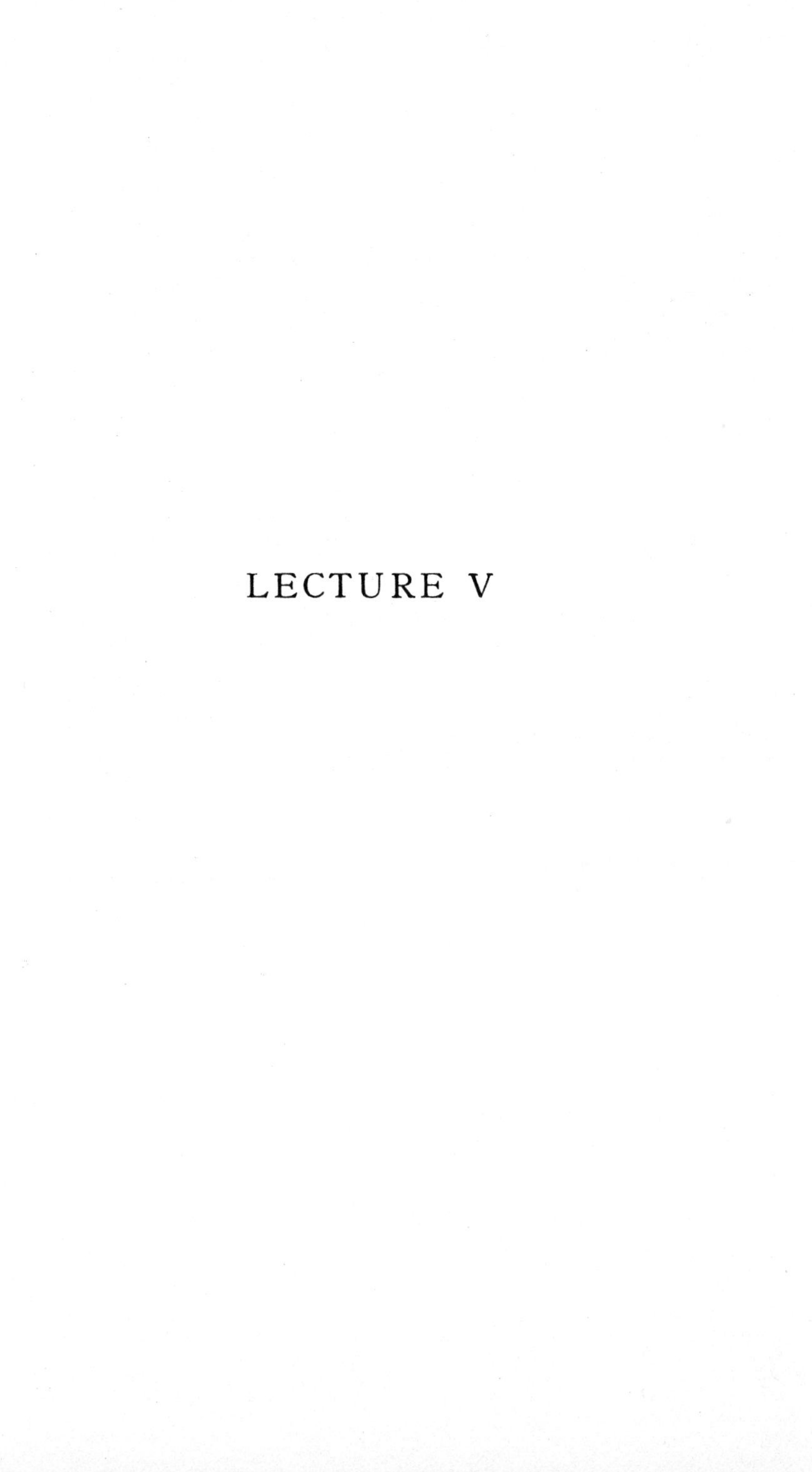

LECTURE V

LECTURE V

In the last lecture I dealt with the oracular function of the ghost, that is, with the belief that the spirits of the dead can communicate with the living and convey to them valuable information which otherwise might not be accessible to the unassisted human intelligence; and I showed that the communication is often made by a medium, whether a man or woman, who is supposed to be possessed by the ghost and to speak with his voice and in his name. This oracular function of ghosts I illustrated from the beliefs and practices of the Melanesians and other islanders of the Pacific.

In Africa similar beliefs and practices are widespread among the native races, especially the Bantu. Thus with regard to the Ba-ila of Northern Rhodesia we are told that the prophets who claim to be inspired by the ghosts of the dead play a very important part in the life of the people. As the mouthpieces of the worshipful spirits, they are the legislators of the community and, generally speaking, receive a great deal of credit. The word of the prophet is enough to condemn to death for witchcraft a perfectly innocent man or woman. And such is the extraordinary credulity of the people that often they will destroy their grain or kill their cattle at the bidding of a prophet. The ghost is supposed to enter into the chest of the prophet and to speak from it. He tells who he is, saying, "I am So-and-so". The matter of the prophecy may be very various. It may be a prediction of famine or drought or a plentiful harvest; it may foretell a ravening by a lion or the rebirth of the ghost himself in a woman known to be with child.[1]

But in Africa it is, above all, the ghosts of dead chiefs or kings which are consulted as oracles of the highest authority. Thus among the Barotse, a Bantu tribe of the Upper Zambesi, the souls of dead kings are inquired of and give responses by the mouth of a priest. Each royal tomb is, indeed, an oracle of the dead. It stands within a sacred enclosure which only the priest may enter. For it is he who acts as intermediary between the royal ghost and the people who come to pray and sacrifice at the shrine. All over the country these temple-tombs may be seen, each in its shady grove, where the spirits of the dead kings are consulted on matters of public concern as well as by private persons on their own affairs.[2]

Among the Bantu tribes of Northern Rhodesia the spirits of dead chiefs or kings sometimes take possession of the bodies of living men or women and prophesy through their mouths. When the

[1] E. W. Smith and A. M. Dale, *The Ila-speaking Peoples of Northern Rhodesia*, ii. 140-142.

[2] Eugène Beguin, *Les Marotsé* (Lausanne et Fontaines, 1903), pp. 120-123.

spirit of a dead chief comes over a man, he begins to roar like a lion, whereupon the women gather together and beat the drums, shouting that the chief has come to pay them a visit. The man thus temporarily possessed and inspired may prophesy of future wars or impending attacks by lions. While the inspiration lasts he may eat nothing cooked by fire, but only unfermented dough. However, the spirit of a departed chief takes possession of women oftener than of men. "These women assert that they are possessed by the soul of some dead chief, and when they feel the 'divine afflatus', whiten their faces to attract attention, and anoint themselves with flour, which has a religious and sanctifying potency. One of their number beats a drum, and the others dance, singing at the same time a weird song, with curious intervals. Finally, when they have arrived at the requisite pitch of religious exaltation, the possessed woman falls to the ground, and bursts forth into a low and almost inarticulate chant, which has a most uncanny effect. All are silent at once, and the *bashing'anga* (medicine-men) gather round to interpret the voice of the spirit."[1]

Among the Basoga of the Central District, in the Uganda Protectorate, the souls of dead chiefs are in like manner consulted as oracles through the medium of women who act as their interpreters or prophetesses. When a chief has been dead and

[1] C. Gouldsbury and H. Sheane, *The Great Plateau of Northern Rhodesia* (London, 1911), p. 83.

buried for some months, his ghost appears to one of his kinsmen and says, "I wish to move". On learning of the ghost's wish the new chief orders the grave of his predecessor to be opened and the skull removed. When the skull has been cleansed, it is wrapped up in the skins of a cow, a sheep and a gazelle, the eye-sockets having previously been filled in with the beads which the deceased chief wore round his neck in life. The new chief now sends for a woman, who must be a member of the clan to which the nurse of the late chief belonged. To her he commits the duty of guarding the skull, acting as the medium of the ghost, and attending to its wants. A special escort then conducts the woman to a place where a large house is built for her reception. There the skull is deposited in a shrine or temple, which is deemed the house of the ghost, and there the woman becomes possessed by the ghost and reveals his wishes. Thither, too, the new chief sends offerings to the spirit of his father. However, the skull and the ghost remain in this place of honour only during the lifetime of the ghost's successor. When he, too, has gone the way of all flesh, the old skull and the old ghost are forced to vacate the premises and to shift their quarters to a wooded island in the river, where the skulls and ghosts of all former chiefs are permanently lodged. No house there shelters them from the inclemency of the weather. Each skull is simply deposited in the open, with a spear stuck in the ground beside it. The prophetess who waited on it in the temple accompanies it to its long home in the island, and there she may continue to interpret the oracles of the royal ghost to anybody who may care to consult him. But few people think it worth while to ask the advice of the old ghost in the island when they can get the latest information from the new ghost in the temple.[1] *Sic transit gloria mundi.*

Such is, or was till lately, the practice as to oracular ghosts among the Basoga of the Central District. But among the Basoga of the North-Western District the custom is somewhat different, for there it is not the skull but the lower jawbone of a dead chief which is kept to serve as the means of communicating with his spirit. It is cleansed, wrapped in a skin decorated with cowry shells, and sent to a temple in a remote part of the district, where the jawbones of all former chiefs are preserved. The guardian is a priest and medium, who holds converse with the ghost and conveys any message from him to the ruling chief.[2]

Among the Baganda, the powerful neighbours of the Basoga on the west, it was also the jawbone of a dead king rather than his skull which was deemed the vehicle of his ghost and the instrument of his oracular utterances; for, curiously enough, the Baganda think that the part of their bodies to which the ghost cleaves most constantly is the jawbone. So in the temple which was built for each dead king of Uganda his lower jawbone was rever-

[1] John Roscoe, *The Northern Bantu* (Cambridge, 1915), pp. 227 *sq.*

[2] J. Roscoe, *op. cit.* pp. 226 *sq.*

ently preserved. The temple, a large conical hut of the usual pattern, was divided into two chambers, an outer and an inner, and in the inner chamber or holy of holies the precious jawbone was kept for safety in a cell dug in the floor. The prophet or medium, whose business it was to be inspired from time to time by the ghost of the dead king, dedicated himself to his holy office by drinking a draught of beer and a draught of milk out of the royal skull, which thus served as a means of putting him in intimate relations with the spirit of the deceased monarch. When the ghost gave an audience, the jawbone, wrapped in a decorated packet, was brought forth from the inner shrine and set on a throne in the outer chamber, where the people gathered to hear the oracle. On such occasions the prophet stepped up to the throne, and addressing the royal ghost informed him of the business in hand. Then he smoked one or two pipes of home-grown tobacco, and the fumes bringing on the prophetic fit he began to speak in the very voice and with the characteristic turns of speech of the departed monarch. However, his rapid utterances were hard to understand, and a priest was in attendance to interpret them to the inquirer. The living king thus consulted his dead predecessors periodically on affairs of state, visiting first one and then another of the temples in which their sacred relics were preserved with religious care.[1]

[1] John Roscoe, "Notes on the Manners and Customs of the Baganda", *Journal of the Anthropological Institute*, xxxi. (1901) pp.

Similarly among the Banyoro, another great tribe of Uganda, the ghosts of dead kings used to be consulted as oracles by their living successors. Over the king's grave a mound of earth was raised with a flat top, which was covered with a grass carpet and overlaid with the skins of cows and leopards. This mound was the throne where the king's ghost was said to take its seat at any ceremony. Before the throne offerings were presented to the ghost, and there, too, requests were made when the reigning king wished to consult his deceased father upon matters of state or when sickness appeared in the royal household. The late king was commonly spoken of as being asleep, but never as dead.[1]

So much for the oracular function of ghosts. That concludes what I had to say about the spirits of the dead in their beneficent aspect. I have shown that these spirits are commonly believed by primitive or savage man to help him in many ways, particularly by enabling the hunter to kill game and the fisherman to catch fish; by making trees to bear fruit and the earth to produce crops of various kinds; by sending rain to refresh and fertilize the thirsty ground; by enabling women to bear children; by granting success and victory in war; and by imparting precious information and advice on all the

129 *sq.*; *id.*, "Further Notes on the Manners and Customs of the Baganda", *Journal of the Anthropological Institute*, xxxii. (1902) pp. 44 *sqq.*; *id.*, *The Baganda* (London, 1911), pp. 109-113, 283-285; *id.*, "Worship of the Dead as practised by some African Tribes", *Harvard African Studies*, i. (1917) pp. 39 *sq.*

[1] John Roscoe, *The Northern Bantu*, p. 53.

affairs of life to such as apply to them in the proper way either directly or through the appointed intermediaries. These are, indeed, very substantial benefits, since they appear to secure a supply of food, protection against enemies, and the continuation of the species. We need not wonder, therefore, that people who hold these beliefs should revere the spirits of the dead and that they should take all the means in their power to ensure the favour and to avoid the displeasure of these potent beings, on whom they imagine themselves to be dependent not only for the support, the security and the comforts of life, but even for existence itself. Their feelings towards the spirits are naturally, therefore, of a mixed sort; for while they are grateful for the benefits received, they are uncertain how long these may continue, since they are conceived to be liable at any moment to be forfeited by any neglect or oversight in the marks of attention which the souls of the dead expect to receive from the survivors. Thus the gratitude and affection of the living are strongly tinged with anxiety and fear. For though the spirits of the dead are thought to confer many benefits on the survivors, they are also believed to bring on them evils and calamities of many sorts, including the last evil, death. To this, the gloomy side of the belief in ghosts, we must now turn our attention.

To begin with, ghosts are sometimes thought to disturb the ordinary course of nature in various alarming ways, as by causing earthquakes, thunderstorms, drought and famine. Thus, for example, the Kiwai of British New Guinea attribute earthquakes to the action of ghosts walking underneath the ground in a party with their women and children. They say that just as big strong men drag heavy burdens through the forest, so do big strong ghosts push their way through the earth; and that if you look at the reflections on the surface of pools you can see these earthquake spirits passing along.[1] A similar belief is entertained by the Orokaiva of British New Guinea, who further think that an earthquake presages sickness,[2] which accordingly they set down to the account of the ghosts. The Kai of Northern New Guinea believe that the entrance to the subterranean world of the dead is at a certain cave at the mouth of which there stands a tree. When a ghost arrives at the cave on his way to his long home, he perches on the tree for a time, waiting for a favourable moment to plunge into the abyss. So when the Kai feel the earth shaking under them or hear a rumbling noise down below, they say that a ghost has just jumped from the tree, causing the earth to quake.[3]

The natives of Timor, an island in the Indian Archipelago, think that an earthquake is produced by the spirits of the dead underground who are struggling to force their way up to the surface of the earth. So when a shock of earthquake is felt,

[1] G. Landtman, *The Kiwai Papuans of British New Guinea*, p. 281.

[2] F. E. Williams, *Orokaiva Society*, p. 184.

[3] Ch. Keysser, "Aus dem Leben der Kaileute", in R. Neuhauss, *Deutsch-Neu-Guinea* (Berlin, 1911), iii. 149.

the Timorese knock on the ground and call out, "We are still here", to let the unquiet spirits of the dead know that there is no room for them on the surface of the earth.[1] The Andaman Islanders in like manner hold that earthquakes are caused by some mischievous male spirits of their deceased ancestors, who, impatient at the delay of the resurrection, combine to shake the palm-tree on which the earth is thought to rest, hoping thus to destroy the cane bridge which stretches between this world and heaven and is the only prop of the sky. However, these impious resurrectionists down below are careful not to play their pranks during the dry season, because, the surface of the earth being then much cracked with heat, they fear that it might collapse and bury them under the ruins instead of toppling over in one solid block and thus, so to say, lifting up the hatches which now batten down the dead. That is why in the Andaman Islands earthquakes only occur in the rainy season. Such is the Andaman theory of earthquakes as reported by Mr. E. H. Man, an excellent authority.[2] A somewhat different version of the theory is reported by another good authority, Professor Radcliffe-Brown. The account which he received from a native was that an earthquake is caused by the spirits of the dead dancing underground at the reception of a newcomer from the upper world. On such an occasion the spirits of the dead hold a ceremony

[1] A. Bastian, *Indonesien*: II. *Timor und umliegende Inseln* (Berlin, 1885), p. 3.

[2] E. H. Man, *On the Aboriginal Inhabitants of the Andaman Islands* (London, N.D.), p. 86.

to welcome or initiate the raw ghost into the mysteries of the new life down below. The ceremony includes a dance at which the rainbow serves as a screen for the dancers, which they shake by their jumps; and this shaking of the rainbow produces an earthquake.[1]

The Lakhers of North-Eastern India also give more than one explanation of earthquakes. According to one view, the earth is attached to the sky by cords so close together that of all birds only the martin and the swallow can fly between them. But spirits can also fly between them; and when a chief dies, his soul flies between the cords, and as it passes it cuts one of the cords with a dagger, which causes an earthquake.[2] The Lusheis, another tribe of the same region, say that the people of the lower world shake the upper world in order to know if any one is still alive there. So when an earthquake happens, some Lushei villages resound with shouts of "Alive! alive!" to reassure the people down below and so induce them to stop the earthquake.[3]

In Africa the Banyoro think that earthquakes are produced by dead kings moving about underground, which causes the earth to shake.[4] They also attribute earthquakes to the struggles of a dead king named Isaza to escape from Dead-land and return home to the land of the living.[5] The

[1] A. R. Brown, *The Andaman Islanders* (Cambridge, 1922), pp. 147 *sq*.

[2] N. E. Parry, *The Lakhers*, pp. 486 *sq*.

[3] J. Shakespear, *The Lushei Kuki Clans* (London, 1912), p. 184.

[4] J. Roscoe, *The Northern Bantu*, p. 93.

[5] J. Roscoe, *The Bakitara or Banyoro* (Cambridge, 1923), p. 325.

Baluba, a large tribe in the upper valley of the Congo, imagine that earthquakes are produced by the spirits of the dead fighting among themselves underground just as living people fight with each other above ground.[1] In antiquity a precisely similar opinion was attributed to the great philosopher Pythagoras,[2] whose so-called symbols, whoever may have been their author, are little more than a collection of popular superstitions which furnish a rich harvest to reapers in the field of folklore.[3]

Again, storms of thunder and lightning are thought by some savages to be caused by the spirits of the dead. Thus, concerning the Bantu tribes of South Africa we are told that "the Kafirs have strange notions concerning the lightning. They consider that it is governed by the *umshologu*, or ghost, of the greatest and most renowned of their departed chiefs, and who is emphatically styled the *inkosi*; but they are not at all clear as to which of their ancestors is intended by this designation. Hence they allow of no lamentation being made for a person killed by lightning; for they say that it would be a sign of disloyalty to lament for one whom the *inkosi* had sent for, and whose services he consequently needed; and it would cause him to punish them, by making the lightning again to descend and do them another injury."[4] The savage

[1] Le R. P. Colle, *Les Baluba*, ii. (Bruxelles, 1913) p. 428.

[2] Aelian, *Var. Hist.* iv. 17.

[3] J. G. Frazer, *Garnered Sheaves* (London, 1931), pp. 130 *sqq.*; Fr. Boehm, *De symbolis Pythagoreis, Dissertatio Inauguralis* (Berlin, 1905).

[4] Mr. Warren's Notes, in Col. Maclean's *Compendium of Kafir Laws and Customs* (Cape Town, 1866), pp. 82 *sq.*

Conibos, of the Ucayali River in Eastern Peru, imagine that thunder is the voice of the dead,[1] and among them when parents who have lost a child within three months hear thunder they go and dance on the grave, howling turn about.[2] Apparently they fancy that in a peal of thunder they hear the voice of their dead child calling to them from the grave.

The Choroti Indians of the Gran Chaco believe that thunder and lightning are caused by a great number of evil spirits rushing through the air and making their onset on the village. Every time that a peal of thunder is heard, these Indians, sitting in their huts, shout and scream loudly to frighten the demons away. These demons appear to be conceived of as the souls of old men of the tribe, who in their lifetime were skilled in the magic art.[3] Thus in the opinion of the Chorotis it is the spirits of the dead who are responsible for thunder and lightning. Similarly the wild Jibaros, an Indian tribe of Ecuador, think that thunder and lightning are caused by a band of dead warriors, who, under cover of the noise, are attacking the Indians. So during a violent thunderstorm the Jibaro men may be seen brandishing their lances against the sky, leaping and shouting defiance at their invisible foes. Hence they call thunder by a name which means, " The

[1] W. Smyth and F. Lowe, *Journey from Lima to Para* (London, 1836), p. 240.

[2] De St. Cricq, " Voyage du Pérou au Brésil ", *Bulletin de la Société de Géographie*, IVme Série, vi. (Paris, 1853) p. 294.

[3] R. Karsten, *The Civilization of the South-American Indians*, p. 359.

enemies are fighting". Lightning they imagine to be an old Jibaro warrior, one of their ancestors.[1] That storms of thunder and lightning are the work of the spirits of the dead is the belief also of the warlike Araucanians, an Indian tribe of Chili. Concerning them a Spanish historian of Chili tells us that not a storm bursts upon the Andes or the ocean which these Indians do not ascribe to a battle between the souls of their fellow-countrymen and the dead Spaniards. In the roar of the wind they hear the trampling of the spectral horses, in the peal of the thunder the roll of the ghostly drums, and in the flashes of lightning the fire of the ghostly artillery.[2]

Further, the souls of the dead are sometimes believed to cause drought and famine. This belief is held by the Chinese, who, though certainly not a primitive people, retain many primitive superstitions under their ancient civilization; in particular they cherish a strong faith in the existence and power of their ancestral spirits, whose worship, indeed, forms the main feature of their religion. The Chinese are convinced that when human bodies or bones are left unburied and exposed to the air, the souls of their late owners feel the discomfort of showers of rain, just as living men would do if they were exposed without shelter to the inclemency of the weather. Accordingly these unhappy souls do all in their power to prevent the rain from falling,

[1] R. Karsten, *The Civilization of the South-American Indians*, p. 360.

[2] J. I. Molina, *Geographical, Natural and Civil History of Chili* (London, 1809), ii. 92 *sq.*

and often their efforts, according to the Chinese, are only too successful. Then drought ensues, the most dreaded of all calamities in China, because bad harvests, dearth, and famine follow in its train. Hence it has been a common practice of the Chinese authorities, in time of drought, to order the burial of the dry bones of the unburied dead for the purpose of putting an end to the scourge and conjuring down the rain. For example, in the year A.D. 108, after a long drought, the Governor of Honan caused to be interred the bones of ten thousand strangers which were bleaching outside the walls of the city, whereupon rain fell abundantly and the harvest was very fine that year. Again, in the year A.D. 481 the Emperor issued a decree as follows: "The rains of the season do not trickle down, so that the tender sprouts of spring hang heavily. Wherever human bones lie, orders must be issued by the authorities to have them buried, and none may be left uncovered, in order that the spirits may become aware of these acts and the catastrophe be deprecated."[1]

The Lakhers of North-Eastern India similarly believe in the power of the spirits of the dead to create a famine by blighting the crops. They are in the habit of erecting memorials to their dead, ordinarily in the shape of a flat stone accompanied by a wooden post, but for chiefs and persons of importance pyramids and small stone walls are set up in addition. The erection of such a memorial

[1] J. J. M. de Groot, *The Religious System of China*, iii. (Leyden, 1897) pp. 918 *sq*.

marks the final separation of the dead man's spirit from his living kinsfolk. The day after the ceremony the whole village is tabooed ; no one may do any work, and the women may neither spin nor weave. It is thought that, if this taboo were not observed, the dead man's spirit would carry off with it to the other world the spirits of rice and of all other edibles, and that consequently there would be a famine.[1]

Similar beliefs in the power of the dead to cause famine by withholding the rain are held by Bantu tribes in South Africa, for example, by the Pondomisi tribe. In 1891 it happened that there was a time of intense heat and severe drought. So the tribe ascribed the calamity to the wrath of a dead chief, named Gwanya, at the treatment of one of his descendants, who had been arrested and sent before a colonial court for a criminal offence. The departed chief had been buried in a deep pool of a river ; so to appease his angry spirit cattle were slaughtered as a peace-offering on the banks of the pool and the flesh was thrown into the water, together with new dishes full of beer. Apparently the soul of the offended chief was mollified by these attentions and he withdrew his ban on the rain. At all events copious showers fell a few days later, which naturally confirmed the belief of the tribe that they had done the right thing, and that the spirit of the late chief was appeased.[2]

[1] N. E. Parry, *The Lakhers*, pp. 414 *sq*.

[2] G. McCall Theal, *Records of South-Eastern Africa*, vii. (Cape Town, 1901) p. 400.

In these various ways the spirits of the dead are believed by primitive man to trouble and afflict the living. But the standing accusation which he levels against them is that they are the causes, often the most general causes, of sickness and death. This is the great damning blot on their character: this is their one unforgivable sin: their other faults, their frailties and weaknesses, might perhaps be overlooked and excused, or at least palliated, but this one cannot. Not that all savages believe sickness and death to be the work of the spirits of the dead exclusively or mainly; many tribes think that these dreaded evils are wrought for the most part not by the ghosts but by living sorcerers; and where this belief prevails its effects on the life of the people are much more disastrous. For while people cannot normally punish a ghost for his offences, since he is beyond their reach, they can punish a living sorcerer, who is well within the reach of tribal law and justice. Hence in tribes who firmly believe that every death is brought about by sorcery, every natural death is commonly followed by the judicial murder of the sorcerer who is supposed to have caused the death by his nefarious arts; and the murders may easily be multiplied when suspicion falls on several persons, all of whom must clear their character by submitting to a poison ordeal which may prove fatal to many. Thus, while a belief in ghosts has slain its victims by thousands, a belief in sorcery has slain its victims by tens of thousands, or rather by millions; for this fatal error, or rather obsession, is still rampant in some parts of the world, above all in Africa, where it has prevailed from time immemorial, and where tribes are known to have actually extinguished themselves by their blind faith in sorcery and their infatuated devotion to the poison ordeal as an infallible test of truth. Hence, strange as it may seem, the recognition of ghosts or spirits of the dead, apart from sorcery, as causes of disease and death marks a real and important step in the moral and social, if not in the intellectual, progress of our species, for it has saved countless human lives by preventing countless judicial murders.[1]

The evidence for the belief of primitive man in the spirits of the dead as the causes of disease and death is immense. In these lectures I can only give a small selection from it.

Thus, to begin with the Melanesians, we are told that by them "any sickness that is serious is believed to be brought about by ghosts or spirits; common complaints such as fever and ague are taken as coming in the course of nature. . . . Generally it is to the ghosts of the dead that sickness is ascribed in the eastern islands as well as in the western; recourse is had to them for aid in causing and removing sickness; and ghosts are believed to inflict sickness not only because some offence, such as a trespass, has been committed against them, or because one familiar with them has

[1] Compare my book, *The Belief in Immortality and the Worship of the Dead*, i. 31-58.

sought their aid with sacrifice and spells, but because there is a certain malignity in the feeling of all ghosts towards the living, who offend them by being alive."[1] Sometimes a man will fancy that he has offended his dead father, uncle or brother. In that case he needs no special intercessor; he or one of his kinsfolk will sacrifice to the offended ghost and beg him to take the sickness away; it is a family affair. But if he does not know to what ghost he has given umbrage, he will call in a wizard to ascertain the truth and prescribe the remedy. This the sage may do by divination. For example, he may hang a stone by a string which he holds in his hand, while he calls over the names of the persons who died lately. When the stone swings at the mention of a certain name, that is the name of the ghost who is causing the sickness. Then it remains to ask what shall be given to appease the anger of the ghost—a mash of yams, a fish, a pig or what not. The answer is given in the same way; and whatever the ghost may express his preference for is offered on the dead man's grave, and the sickness is expected to depart.[2] Sometimes the wizard ascertains the identity of the offended ghost in a dream. For example, he may meet the ghost in his dream, and the ghost may inform him that the sick man had offended him by trespassing on his preserves, and that to punish the trespass he, the ghost, had taken away the man's soul and im-

[1] R. H. Codrington, *The Melanesians*, p. 194.

[2] R. H. Codrington, *op. cit.* pp. 195 *sq.*

pounded it in a magic fence in the garden. The dreaming wizard then begs for the restoration of the lost soul and asks the ghost's pardon on behalf of the sick man, who meant no disrespect. So the mollified ghost accepts the apology, pulls up the fence in which the soul of the sick man was impounded, and lets it out. So the released soul returns to the sick man, who of course recovers.[1] The natives of San Cristoval, one of the Solomon Islands, think that if a man was gentle and killed nobody in his life, he will be cruel and kill many people after his death. Hence all persons who are taken ill in the first months after the death of such a man put down their illness to the account of his ghost; so they quit their houses and flee to the mountains, where they hide, hoping thus to give the slip to the bloodthirsty ghost and so to recover their health.[2]

The Orokaiva of British New Guinea appear to ascribe sickness to the malevolence of ghosts oftener than to any other cause.[3] Of these people we are told that by them no agency is more readily made responsible for human illness than are the ghosts (*sovai*), who are so often regarded as dangerous and spiteful. Strange as it may seem, it is especially the ghosts of near relations who are blamed for sickness, and they are sometimes thought to enter the bodies of their victims at the very funeral when the

[1] R. H. Codrington, *The Melanesians*, p. 208.

[2] L. Verguet, "Arossi ou San-Christoval et ses habitants", *Revue d'Ethnographie*, iv. (1885) p. 211.

[3] F. E. Williams, *Orokaiva Society*, p. 283.

mourners are embracing the corpse.[1] To induce a ghost to quit the body of the sufferer the Orokaiva make offerings to it.[2] The Mailu of British New Guinea in like manner sometimes attribute sickness to the ghosts of the sick man's relations who are trying to draw his soul away. The wizard can see the ghost at his deadly work; it may be the ghost of the patient's father or brother. So the watchers over the sick or dying man address the spirit, saying, "Go away! Don't call him! Leave him alone!"[3]

In like manner the Kiwai of British New Guinea think that, when a child is made sick by ghosts who are trying to carry off its soul, it is oftenest the ghosts of the child's dead grandparents who are engaged in this attempt on its life. But the wily wizard spits the juice of a certain plant over the ghosts, which stupefies them and drives them away; so the sick child is made whole. Hence among the Kiwai it is necessary to guard all little children against the ghosts of their dead relatives, but especially against the ghosts of their grandparents, who are apt to come in the night and snatch away the baby's soul, prompted, we are told, by their solicitude as to how the little one is cared for.[4] Similarly, again, in Tumleo, a small island off the north coast of New Guinea, sickness is sometimes attributed to the agency of the ghosts of the sick man's grandfather and father, who have entered into his body. So in

[1] F. E. Williams, *Orokaiva Society*, p. 293.

[2] F. E. Williams, *op. cit.* p. 304.

[3] W. J. V. Saville, *In Unknown New Guinea*, p. 219.

[4] G. Landtman, *The Kiwai Papuans of British New Guinea*, p. 271.

order to expel the ghostly intruders, two men strike the body and legs of the patient lightly with certain plants, inviting the ghosts to come out of the sufferer, and praying that he may be made whole.[1]

The natives of Nias, an island to the west of Sumatra, believe that the spirits of the dead often try to make men sick in order that they too may die and so bear the ghosts company to the land of the dead. It is especially the souls of dead chiefs which are credited with this fatal power.[2] The wild tribes in the mountains of Formosa attribute disease to the displeasure of the spirits of the dead, and they engage a priestess to pray for the favour of these dangerous beings.[3] The Khmers of Cambodia think that sickness is caused by a ghost who is hovering near the sufferer or has entered into his body. And since a ghost can only be combated by a ghost, they invoke the aid of the patient's ancestral spirits, especially the spirit of one particular friend, usually a doctor, who died long ago and is thought to have constituted himself the spiritual patron and protector of his former clients in this world. So a sorceress is called in to exorcise the ghost who has taken possession of the sick man. This she does with the help of water, oil and rice-spirit, to the accompaniment of noisy music. Sometimes the doctor questions the ghost as to his reason for afflict-

[1] M. J. Erdweg, "Die Bewohner der Insel Tumleo, Berlinhafen, Deutsch-Neu-Guinea", *Mittheilungen der anthropologischen Gesellschaft in Wien*, xxxi. (1901) pp. 284 *sq.*

[2] J. P. Kleiweg de Zwaan, *Die Heilkunde der Niasser* (The Hague, 1913), p. 17.

[3] J. W. Davidson, *The Island of Formosa*, p. 580.

ing the sufferer, and the ghost answers that in his lifetime he had been injured or insulted by the sick man, who had dirtied his house, thrown stones into his yard to frighten his family, or passed him in the street with an air of disdain. So to appease the resentment of the ghost the doctor fashions a rude clay image, which he offers to the ghost as a substitute for his victim. If the ghost graciously accepts the exchange all is well, and the patient may expect to recover.[1] Similar theories as to the causes of disease appear to be held and similar practices to be observed for the cure of it in Siam and the Shan States of Burma.[2]

The Birhors, a jungle tribe of India, revere their ancestral spirits, which each family installs in an inner tabernacle or shrine of the hut and propitiates with offerings of food and drink. But if their descendants neglect to make these offerings, the ancestral spirits may punish them by inciting the demons (*bhuts*) to cause sickness in the family. It is said that out of a touch of natural affection the ancestral spirits do not generally themselves cause sickness to their surviving relatives, they only instigate other spirits thus to avenge the neglect of their undutiful kinsfolk.[3] Among the Korkus, a Munda or Kolarian tribe of the Central Provinces in India, when a person is sick his friends attribute the sickness to the anger of some god or ancestral

[1] J. Moura, *Le Royaume du Cambodge* (Paris, 1883), i. 175 *sq*.

[2] H. S. Hallett, *A Thousand Miles on an Elephant in the Shan States* (Edinburgh and London, 1890), pp. 105-108, 276.

[3] Sarat Chandra Roy, *The Birhors*, pp. 305 *sq*.

spirit. So they wave a handful of grain over the patient and then carry it to the village priest (*bhumka*). The priest thereupon makes a heap of it on the floor, and, sitting over it, swings a lighted lamp suspended by four strings from his fingers. He then repeats slowly the names of the village deities and the sick man's ancestors, pausing after each name, and the name at which the lamp stops swinging is that of the offended god or ancestral spirit. He next inquires in a similar manner whether the god or ancestor is to be appeased by the sacrifice of a pig, a chicken, a goat, a coconut, or what not.[1]

In Africa also sickness is often traced to the anger of ancestral spirits who are offended with their surviving kinsfolk for some real or imaginary injury and take this mode of punishing them for their undutiful behaviour. The Thonga, for example, think that the ancestral spirits are incarnate in certain little harmless snakes, of a bluish-green colour, which are often seen crawling in the thatch of the roof or along the walls. These the Thonga suppose to be their ancestral spirits paying them a visit; so they will not kill the reptiles, imagining that were they to do so the ancestral spirits would punish them with disease. Hence, when disease has broken out, a soothsayer may declare by means of his divining bones that somebody has hurt one of the sacred snakes, and that the offended spirit must be appeased by a sacrifice.[2] The diviner ascertains by

[1] R. V. Russell, *Tribes and Castes of the Central Provinces of India*, iii. 560 *sq*.

[2] H. A. Junod, *The Life of a South African Tribe* [2], ii. 384.

his divining bones what particular ancestral spirit is causing the sickness, and how he is to be propitiated. The propitiatory sacrifice may consist, for example, of a hen or a bracelet. If it is a fowl, after killing it and addressing the ancestral spirits, the priest takes a feather and a claw of the bird, ties them together, and fastens them to the wrist or ankle of the patient. If the offended ghost is an ancestor on the mother's side of the house, the feather and claw are attached to the sufferer's left wrist or ankle ; but if the angry spirit is an ancestor on the father's side, the feather and claw are attached to the right wrist or ankle. If the offering consists of a bracelet, the priest will pour consecrated beer over it and say his prayers. Then the bracelet will be fastened to the patient's foot, and he may not remove it or exchange it for anything ; it belongs to the ancestral spirits.[1] The Bavenda similarly believe that sickness may be caused by the spirit of a dead ancestor either on the father's or the mother's side of the house, but they think that it is oftener a ghost on the mother's side than on the father's that is causing the trouble. As usual, the diviner ascertains the particular ghost who is causing the illness, and having done so he prescribes the appropriate offering ; in some cases a black goat has to be sacrificed at the grave of the angry ancestor.[2]

The Ba-ila ascribe many sicknesses and deaths to the direct action of the ancestral spirits who are

[1] H. A. Junod, *The Life of a South African Tribe*[2], ii. 395-397.

[2] H. A. Stayt, *The Bavenda*, pp. 247 *sq.*, 251 *sq.*

offended by neglect. Delirium is supposed to be caused by ghosts speaking from within the sufferer; and if the patient dies, they say that the ghosts have taken him away.[1] In this tribe, when a man wastes away without any visible cause he is thought to have a malevolent ghost within him which is devouring the food he takes. So his friends put him in a hut, where young girls under puberty make a new fire in order that the smoke may drive out the intruding ghost.[2] Should a child fall sick, the parents will go to a diviner, who may pronounce that the sickness is caused by ancestral spirits either on the father's or on the mother's side of the house. If he lays the blame on the mother's ancestors, the father will wax exceeding wroth, roundly declaring that they have no right to sicken his child.[3] When a man is thought to be possessed by a particularly troublesome and dangerous ghost, his friends will sometimes attempt to heal him by holding his head forcibly over a potsherd full of burning coals and medicinal herbs in order that the pungent fumes may drive away the ghost that is obsessing him; and should the patient break away from his captors, they follow him with the potsherd till he falls down. Then they throw away the potsherd, and he gets up and goes home, free from the tormenting ghost.[4]

Similar beliefs and practices concerning ghosts

[1] E. W. Smith and A. M. Dale, *The Ila-speaking Peoples of Northern Rhodesia*, i. 245.

[2] E. W. Smith and A. M. Dale, *op. cit.* i. 235.

[3] E. W. Smith and A. M. Dale, *op. cit.* ii. 166.

[4] E. W. Smith and A. M. Dale, *op. cit.* ii. 168 *sq.*

as the causes of disease prevail among the Nyanja-speaking tribes of Nyasaland. Thus a diviner may ascribe a child's illness to the anger of the ghost of the child's grandmother, who thinks that she is not duly kept in mind by her grandchild, and demands a fowl to soothe her ruffled feelings. So the father of the child will offer a fowl to the grandmother's ghost, saying, "Grandmother, there is the fowl for which you are causing a person to be ill; you harden your heart all for the sake of a fowl; go, let your little child alone, that he also shall walk about as his companions do; you must not see fit to take a man, only for the sake of a fowl". With these words he kills the fowl, and, having cooked the flesh, offers some of it to the grandmother's ghost, saying, "Here is the fowl we have killed for you. Eat of it."[1]

[1] R. Sutherland Rattray, *Some Folk-lore Stories and Songs in Chinyanja* (London, 1907), pp. 120 *sq.*

LECTURE VI

LECTURE VI

In the last lecture I dealt with the belief of primitive man that sickness and death are often caused by the spirits of the dead, and I illustrated the belief and the practices to which it gives rise by examples drawn from savage races in various parts of the world. Towards the end of the lecture I dealt with the belief and the practices as they are found among the Bantu tribes in the more southerly parts of Africa. I now resume the subject at the point where I broke off.

The theory that sickness is often caused by the spirits of the dead is widely held by the Bantu tribes of the Uganda Protectorate, and in order to effect a cure these tribes sometimes exorcise the ghost instead of propitiating him by sacrifice, the treatment varying with the nature of the particular ghost who is supposed to be doing the mischief.

Thus, to begin with the Bambwa, who were a wild and turbulent mountain tribe living on the western slopes of the great Ruwenzori range, these savages, like so many others, attributed illness to the action of ghosts. When a medicine-man, on being consulted, declared that a particular case of sickness was caused by an angry ghost of a member of the sick man's own family, the ghost had to be appeased by the offering of a goat, which was killed by having its throat cut near a shrine built at the spot where the ghost was supposed to reside. The blood was allowed to run on the ground by the shrine, and prayers were put up to the ghost that in return for the sacrifice he would refrain from causing further trouble.[1] If, however, the ghost that was inflicting the sickness was judged to belong to a hostile clan, he met with a very different reception. The medicine-man began by killing a fowl and letting the blood flow over various medicines which he had brought with him and spread out in front of the patient. He then proceeded to make incisions in the flesh of the sick man's chest, arms, legs and back, and, after powdering some of the medicines, which had an irritating effect, in the palm of his hand, he spat on his thumb, dipped it into the powder, and rubbed the powder into the incisions in the patient's body. As if this was not enough to expel the ghost, a small hut was built near-by and the sufferer was laid in it, after which the hut was set on fire. A strong man was deputed to stand by, and as soon as the sick man was in danger of burning alive he was snatched from the flames by his stalwart friend. By this time the ghost was thought to have found the place too hot for him and to have fairly taken to his heels, leaving

[1] J. Roscoe, *The Bagesu and other Tribes of the Uganda Protectorate* (Cambridge, 1924), pp. 153 *sq.*

the sick man to recover. To complete the cure the medicine-man then took the fowl which he had killed, and, having cooked the flesh, offered it to the ghost, praying him not to harm the man again.[1]

The Banyankole, a pastoral tribe inhabiting the south-western district of the Uganda Protectorate, think that the spirits who cause sickness are either the ghosts of people belonging to other clans, or else the ghosts of relatives, but never the ghost of a father, who is deemed too tender-hearted to molest his surviving progeny. But a widower may be troubled by the jealous ghost of his late spouse, who resents his taking a second wife and may kill her rival if she is not appeased by offerings. If the ghost of the late wife obstinately refused to accept an atonement, the new wife might not remain in the house of her husband but had to go back to her parents.[2]

In this tribe, when a ghost proved unusually obstreperous, it was sometimes necessary to eject him from the patient's body by cunning or force. In that case the diviner told the relatives what medicine-man to send for and what preparations to make. A goat of a particular colour, always either black or black and white, was tied to the head of the patient's bed during the night, so that the ghost might pass from the sufferer into the animal. In the morning the medicine-man came dancing and singing and passed a bunch of sticks and herbs all

[1] J. Roscoe, *The Bagesu*, p. 154.

[2] J. Roscoe, *The Banyankole* (Cambridge, 1923), p. 138.

round the house by way of sweeping together all the evil influences into one place. Next he killed the goat which had been tied to the bed, and which was now supposed to contain the troublesome ghost. After that, a fowl was brought and passed round the goat, and when the ghost had incautiously vacated the goat and passed into the fowl, the bird was buried alive in the gateway through which the cows entered the kraal, thus preventing the ghost from returning to make fresh trouble.[1] Sometimes, in order to expel the ghost, the medicine-man rubbed the patient down with his hands, pressing the ghost from his head out at his feet and the tips of his fingers, and when the ghost sought to escape it was caught in a pot and burned or drowned.[2]

Among the Banyoro or Bakitara, a great tribe of Uganda to the north of the Banyankole, the treatment of sick people supposed to be infested by ghosts was similar, though with some differences. With them, also, the treatment varied according to whether the ghost was hostile and determined to destroy the patient, or whether it was the ghost of some member of the sufferer's own clan. In the latter case, as among the Banyankole, a goat was tied up near the patient's bed, and the medicine-man besought the ghost to pass from the sick person into the animal ; but when the ghost was supposed to have complied with the request and entered into the goat, the animal was not killed ; on the contrary it became sacred and lived near the bed ever after-

[1] J. Roscoe, *The Banyankole*, p. 139.

[2] J. Roscoe, *op. cit.* p. 141.

wards. It might not be killed, and nobody might strike or ill-use it. Should it die, the owner must replace it with another at once. If it had kids, the man had to ask the ghost's leave before he might use any of the young animals, and one of them had always to be left for the ghost. But when the ghost would not accept an animal as the price of quitting the sick person, a girl or woman-slave was offered him instead. She took the place of an animal, slept all night near the patient's bed, and was said to receive the ghost, after which she became a favoured member of the family. She might not be sold or sent away, nor dared the family ill-treat her, because of her connexion with the ghost. These family-ghosts seem invariably to have attacked women; Canon Roscoe, who is our authority for these customs of the Banyoro, never heard of a case of a man's illness being treated in this way.[1]

But when the ghost who was causing the sickness was of another clan and hostile, a very different treatment was meted out to him. The medicine-man took a black goat, which he kept with him all night, and early in the morning he made his preparations to capture and destroy the ghost. The patient, wearing a black bark-cloth, lay on a bed near the door, and the medicine-man prepared a heap of herbs near the bed. The black goat was thrown on the heap and killed, and pieces of the flesh were roasted on spits over a fire which was kindled for the purpose near the bed. When a little

[1] J. Roscoe, *The Bakitara or Banyoro* (Cambridge, 1923), pp. 285 *sq.*

of the flesh was cooked it was put into a pot near the bed, and some blades of grass were arranged over the mouth of the pot in such a way that the least disturbance of the air set them in motion. Some of the patient's friends were now set to watch this pot with instructions to inform the medicine-man if the grass moved. The reason for these preparations was that ghosts were thought to be shy creatures, shunning the light of day in the presence of spectators. A place of retreat in the pot was therefore prepared for the ghost who was afflicting the patient. The medicine-man sat on the other side of the fire, shaking his rattle and chanting incantations to persuade the ghost to come out of the patient and eat the meat. Smelling the savoury odour of the roast flesh, the ghost did come out, and, peering about for some place where it could eat unseen, it descried the pot and entered it. But in doing so it disturbed the blades of grass on the mouth of the pot, causing them to wave. The movement did not escape the watchers, and they at once reported it to the medicine-man. Quick as thought he seized a skin which he had ready to hand, clapped it on the mouth of the pot and tied it down, thus securing the ghost inside the pot in durance vile. Sometimes the ghost would call out from the pot, but his remonstrances were vain. The medicine-man was adamant. To make assurance doubly sure he smeared clay over the skin and carried away the pot with the imprisoned ghost in it to waste land, where he burned pot and ghost together, or he threw them into running water. But the attempt to drown the ghost was thought dangerous, because the pot might break in the water, and the ghost, thus rescued from a watery death, might return and renew his attack on the patient.[1]

In this tribe another mode of dealing with a hostile ghost was to smoke him out of the patient's body. The sick man, wearing fetishes, was laid on his bed, and a pot full of hot embers was put on the floor beside him. Sheep's wool or cock's tail-feathers, together with certain herbs, were thrown on the embers, causing the place to reek with foul smoke. Sometimes a bark-cloth was spread over the patient, and the pot with the smouldering embers was put under it. When the sufferer, sweating freely and more dead than alive, was at last uncovered, the ghost was supposed to have left him, driven out by the stinking fumes. But the medicine-man saw it lurking somewhere in the room, and he gave chase, making frantic efforts to catch it and holding a pot in which he sought to entrap it. But sometimes the ghost escaped from the house, and the medicine-man pursued it, screeching and hitting about in the air and trying to drive it back. The struggle might last some time, but in the end the medicine-man was sure to be successful in catching the ghost and covering up the pot with the struggling ghost inside of it. Then he carried the pot to waste land, where he burned it and the ghost. That was the end of the ghost; so the sick man and his clan were rid of him.[1]

[1] J. Roscoe, *The Bakitara or Banyoro*, pp. 286 *sq.*

Among the Bagesu, a cannibal tribe living on the slopes of the lofty Mount Elgon in Kenya, a medicine-man sometimes attributes sickness to ghostly possession and declares that it must be cured by propitiating the ghost. He may say that the ghost is that of some relative which has been offended by his living kinsman and takes this mode of wreaking his revenge. Should the patient be a rich man, a hut is built as a shrine for the ghost with a long pole projecting through the apex of the thatched roof. The patient gives the medicine-man a goat or an ox to offer to the ghost ; the animal is killed near the shrine, the blood is caught in a vessel and put into the shrine with a portion of the meat. The people assemble in numbers to take part in the ceremony. After making the offering of blood, the medicine-man climbs the roof of the hut, and spikes a large piece of meat on the pole. Then he cuts it into small morsels which he throws among the crowd, who scramble for them and eat them. The sickness is supposed to be widely scattered by this ceremony and thus rendered harmless, while the patient quickly regains his usual health.[2]

The Nilotic Kavirondo in Kenya are quite different racially from the Bantu tribes who occupy most of the Uganda Protectorate, in which till lately Kavirondo was included. But their theory of disease caused by ghostly possession does not differ essentially from that of their Bantu neighbours. It is

[1] J. Roscoe, *The Bakitara or Banyoro*, pp. 287 *sq*.

[2] J. Roscoe, *The Northern Bantu*, p. 177.

true that they seem to trace sickness oftener to black magic than to ghosts, but when they see the hand of a ghost in a case of illness, their treatment of it conforms to what we may call the orthodox pattern. As usual, a medicine-man is consulted, and his ordinary verdict is that the ghosts of grandparents are afflicting their grandchildren because their father failed to perform the duties of a son to his father in his old age. The sage will now order a shrine to be built at the grave of the grandparent concerned, and the sick person's father offers a sheep or a goat at the grave, pouring out the blood as a libation on the ground and then eating the meat on the spot with a few relatives. The medicine-man can afterwards treat the sufferer with reasonable hope of restoring him to health, because the offended ghost has now been pacified and will allow the sick man to benefit by the treatment.[1]

Among the Bantu tribes in the valley of the Congo similar views are current as to sickness and disease caused by the spirits of the dead, and similar methods of cure are adopted. Thus, for example, among the Baluba, a large tribe in the Belgian Congo, the sickness of a child is sometimes thought to be due to the displeasure of his dead mother, because she thinks that her child has not received his proper share of the goods which she bequeathed at her death. When this has been revealed to the father by the medicine-man, he hastens to place in his child's hand a lance-head or a hoe, according as

[1] J. Roscoe, *The Northern Bantu*, pp. 285 *sq.*

the child is a boy or a girl, enjoining the little one to hold it tight. Then he takes a white fowl or a small she-goat and gives it as a present to the sick child. Next morning he goes out into the forest and addressing the spirit of his dead wife, the mother of the sick child, he cries, "O thou who wast my wife, leave my child, torment him no more! Go, return to thine abode in the underworld!" The dead mother hears the father's cries, and content that her child has now received something she leaves him in peace. So the sick child recovers.[1]

So among the Baholoholo, another Bantu tribe of the Belgian Congo, when a man falls sick, the medicine-man may tell him that the sickness is due to the anger of his dead paternal grandmother. When he learns this melancholy truth, the sick man cries aloud to his grandmother's ghost, beseeching her not to let him die, and next morning he sends his sons to his grandmother's grave. They go and erect a little hut on the grave, and bury a fowl at the foot of the hut, and pour out a libation of beer. Mollified by these attentions the grandmother's ghost leaves her grandson alone, and he naturally recovers.[2]

But sometimes in this tribe the medicine-man declares that it is not the grandmother's ghost but the ghost of the patient's own father that is making him ill and calling him away to the spirit-land. This

[1] Le R. P. Colle, *Les Baluba*, ii. (Bruxelles, 1913) pp. 786 *sq.*

[2] R. Schmitz, *Les Baholoholo* (Bruxelles, 1912), p. 214.

case is much more serious than the other, because it is much more difficult to appease the ghost of a father than the ghost of a grandmother. So in the evening the medicine-man, accompanied by the brothers or sons of the patient, goes to the father's grave and digs up the body or the mouldering bones. Of these relics he burns a part, keeping only the skull and a few bones for his own future use. If the body has entirely disappeared, the medicine-man catches a rat, a lizard or any other little animal he may have found in digging up the grave. Whatever the animal may be, the sage declares that the soul of the sick man's father has entered into it; so he burns the creature solemnly, which is thought to render the father's ghost impotent, and the patient accordingly recovers.[1]

Among the Ewe-speaking peoples of the Slave Coast, in West Africa, sickness is often thought to be caused by some ancestral ghost, who requires the services of his descendant in Dead-land, and so is hastening his departure from the land of the living. In such a case the sick man sends for a priest, pays him a fee, and begs him to dispatch his soul to Dead-land to stop the importunities of the family ghost. The priest professes to send his soul on this mission by falling into a trance, and on coming to himself again he informs the patient that he has been to Dead-land and has seen the ghost who is causing the trouble. If he thinks that the patient is not very ill and in no risk of his life, he comforts

[1] R. Schmitz, *Les Baholoholo*, p. 215.

him with the assurance that the unquiet ghost has been pacified ; but if he judges the case to be serious and the issue doubtful, he confines himself to cautious ambiguities.[1]

Among the Yungur-speaking peoples of Northern Nigeria, if a person falls sick, he consults a diviner, who may declare that the sickness is due to an ancestral spirit. In that case the sick man has a small representation of the dead ancestor made for him in pottery, it may be either a figurine or simply a pot. Having obtained his figurine or pot, the owner kills a chicken and sprinkles the blood over the symbol with a prayer that, if it is indeed the ancestral spirit who is causing his illness, he will graciously accept the sacrifice and leave his descendant alone. The chicken is then cooked and eaten by the patient in the company of his relatives. If the sickness continues, the patient may again consult the diviner, who may this time prescribe the sacrifice of a goat. As most people have at various times been attacked by sickness, most possess pots or figurines for the abode of the spirits of dead grandfathers, fathers or even brothers. These pots are placed close to the owner's head at night, and when beer is brewed for any festival, libations are poured on the pots.[2]

That concludes what I have to say as to the belief that the spirits of the dead are often the causes of sickness and death. The evidence which I have

[1] A. B. Ellis, *The Ewe-speaking Peoples of the Slave Coast of West Africa* (London, 1890), pp. 109 *sq.*

[2] C. K. Meek, *Tribal Studies in Northern Nigeria*, ii. 460.

thus far adduced may suffice to prove that in the opinion of primitive or savage man the spirits of the dead are the sources of many of the ills which beset this our mortal life on earth; in particular that he sees their handiwork in earthquakes, thunderstorms, drought, famine, disease and death. No wonder that he regards the supposed authors of such evils with awe and fear, and seeks to guard himself against them by all the means at his command. These means are various, and the devices to which he resorts in self-defence are manifold. Their general aim is, first, to send the spirits away, and next, to keep them at a distance; for so long as he believes them to be hovering near him the savage can never feel himself safe from their attacks; in short, he desires, as far as possible, to rid himself of their dangerous neighbourhood. That this is his real wish and intention will appear, I think, from the many shifts and expedients which he adopts in order to banish the ghost from his old home and to prevent him from returning to it. These shifts and expedients are exceedingly various, some of them are very extraordinary, and taken altogether they exhibit in primitive man, as I have observed before, a resourcefulness and ingenuity worthy of a better cause. Regarded from the point of view of their intention, these expedients fall into two classes, according as they are meant to send the ghost away, or to keep him away and prevent him from returning. Regarded from the point of view of the means adopted to effect these purposes, the expedients fall into two general classes according as they are either fair or foul, in other words, according as they tend to propitiate or to compel the ghost. For, roughly speaking, the means employed to guard against ghosts are either persuasion, fraud or force, of which persuasion may be said to be fair, and fraud and force to be foul. All these means of guarding the living against ghosts I propose to illustrate by examples in what follows, and as I desire to place the character of ghosts and of primitive man in the best light possible, I will begin with what I have called the fair means of dealing with ghosts before I pass on to the foul, which must be reserved for subsequent lectures.

In the first place, then, when a death has taken place, primitive man often asks the ghost to go away and not to come back. This is the method of persuasion; an appeal is made to what we may call the better feelings of the ghost.

Thus, for example, in the Kakadu tribe of Northern Australia, when a woman was buried, the women and children, led by an elderly female, marched round the grave in single file singing words to the following effect, which were supposed to be addressed to the spirit of the deceased: "You lie down quietly, do not come back, lie down all right —if the children see your spirit, later on they will be sick".[1] At the conclusion of mourning the natives of New Caledonia, who make images of

[1] Baldwin Spencer, *Native Tribes of the Northern Territory of Australia* (London, 1914), pp. 240 *sq.*

their dead as memorials, accost the spirit of the deceased, saying, " Return now to your maternal kinsfolk in the forest. Leave us. We have loved you and made your portrait."[1] The Kiwai of British New Guinea think that the ghost is apt to haunt the neighbourhood of his old home for some days after his decease; so for a few nights after a death all the doors of the houses are kept carefully barred, and no one ventures out in the dark. If the people in the house fancy that they hear the prowling ghost whistling outside or tapping at the barred door, they throw out food for the importunate spirit and beg him to go away, saying, " You go back, do not come. You belong to the dead; there is no use of your coming."[2] Among the natives of the Purari Delta, in British New Guinea, when the detached heads of the departed kinsfolk are finally buried, the master of the ceremonies is said to address their spirits somewhat as follows: " Depart now for good and all. Never return to our village. All these bodies of pigs and dogs are for you; so, too, all these coconuts and garden stuff (*talo*). Now I bury you under the ground. You are done with for ever."[3]

Among the Toradyas of Central Celebes, when a married person is buried, a rattan is placed on the coffin and cut in two, with these words: " Your marriage is cut off, your relation to your children

[1] M. Leenhardt, *Notes d'Ethnologie Néo-Calédoniennes* (Paris, 1930), p. 9.

[2] G. Landtman, *The Kiwai Papuans of British New Guinea* (London, 1927), pp. 281 *sq.*

[3] F. E. Williams, *The Natives of the Purari Delta* (Port Moresby, 1924), pp. 222 *sq.*

is cut off. Go away and look no more after them." [1] And among the same people, when the deceased was the last of a group of brothers and sisters, they throw a handful of rice after the corpse, when it is being carried out of the house, and say, "Come not back. You have no longer any brothers or sisters here, and we do not yet wish to follow you." If the funeral procession passes other houses, the people in the houses call out to the dead man, "Go away. Look no more round at us", and they throw out ashes to blind the ghost and prevent him from seeing his way back. And at the grave, when the body is being lowered into it, they cry out to the dead person, saying, "Go straight on. Call us not, for we are still well off here. Go to your fathers and mothers and your kinsfolk (who are dead) and plant bananas and sugar-cane for us." [2] Among the Alfoors of Minahassa in Northern Celebes, when a wife has died before her husband, the widower is led by a woman, with his head muffled, from the house to the place where his marriage was celebrated, there to take a last farewell from his departed spouse. The children and nearest relations follow, lamenting. Arrived at the place, the woman beseeches the spirit of the dead wife to go away and not to come and trouble the widower and children and make them ashamed.[3] In the Tumbuluh tribe

[1] N. Adriani en Alb. C. Kruijt, *De Bare-sprekende Toradjas van Midden-Celebes*, ii. 95.

[2] N. Adriani en Alb. C. Kruijt, *op. cit.* ii. 98.

[3] "De godsdienst en godsdienst plegtigheden der Alfoeren in de Menahassa op het eiland Celebes", *Tijdschrift voor Nederlandsch Indië*, December 1849 (Groningen, 1849), p. 400.

of Minahassa, when a man has died, his spirit is solemnly invited to set out on the journey to the spirit-land and not to look back, for the way is now open. And some time afterwards the relatives go to the garden of the deceased, where a bamboo platform has been set up, laden with specimens of all the fruits which the dead man had cultivated. They all gather round the platform, while one of the eldest calls out in a loud voice, "O So-and-so, take something of all this produce for your journey. We also are going away."[1] Among the Southern Amis, a tribe of Formosa, at a burial it is customary for one of the family to throw a handful of earth on the grave and, addressing the deceased, to say, "You shall not return".[2] In the Nicobar Islands, when a corpse is being carried out to burial, a medicine-man (*menluana*) commands the disembodied spirit to go quietly to the grave and remain there till the memorial feast takes place, when it will be required to proceed to the land of the dead. The spirit is further exhorted not to wander about in the meantime and frighten the living with its ghostly presence.[3]

The Kachins of Burma think that after a burial the spirit of the dead seeks to re-enter the house, but being foiled in the attempt, he finds the entrance to the pig-pen under the floor open, so he passes in

[1] J. G. F. Riedel, "Alte Gebräuche bei Heirathen, Geburt und Sterbefällen bei dem Toumbuluh-Stamm in der Minahassa (Nord-Selebes)", *Internationales Archiv für Ethnographie*, viii. (1895) pp. 108, 109.

[2] J. W. Davidson, *The Island of Formosa* (London, 1903), p. 579.

[3] E. H. Man, "Notes on the Nicobarese", *The Indian Antiquary*, xxviii. (1899) p. 258; *id.*, *The Nicobar Islands and their Inhabitants* (Guildford, N.D.), p. 137.

by it and takes up his abode for a time there on the ground. At the final obsequies the priest takes a spear in his hand, gives a terrific yell and, thrusting the spear into the floor, orders the ghost, who is lurking under it, to quit the house through the door of the pig-pen by which it had entered.[1] The Karens of Burma stand in great fear of the apparitions of the dead, so to appease the ghosts and prevent them from returning to haunt the living, the people go to the forest and there deposit a little basket of coloured rice, saying, "Ghosts of those who died by falling from a tree, ghosts of those who died of hunger or thirst, ghosts of those who died by a tiger's tooth or a serpent's fang, ghosts of those who perished of small-pox or cholera, ghosts of those who died of leprosy, do not molest us, do not catch us, do not do us any harm. Stay here in this wood. We will take care of you; we will bring you red, yellow and white rice for your subsistence."[2] The Karieng are the aboriginal inhabitants of Siam, who, when the Siamese or Thai invaded the country from the north, retreated to the mountains on the east and west, where they still remain.[3] They burn their dead, after which they detach a bone from the skull and hang it on a tree, together with the clothes, ornaments and weapons of the deceased. After performing dances and pantomimes accompanied by

[1] W. J. S. Carrapiett, *The Kachin Tribes of Burma* (Rangoon, 1929), pp. 40, 44.

[2] Bringaud, "Les Karins de la Birmanie", *Les Missions Catholiques*, xx. (1888) p. 208.

[3] Mgr. Pallegoix, *Description du royaume Thai ou Siam* (Paris, 1854), i. 54.

mournful songs, some of the elders carry away the bone and the belongings of the departed and bury them secretly at the foot of a distant mountain, begging the ghost not to return and torment his family, since everything that he owned has been buried with him.[1]

Under the surface of their ancient civilization the Chinese have retained many primitive beliefs and customs concerning the dead. In some places on the eve of a burial tables covered with viands are placed before the tablet in the house which represents the deceased, and a priest addresses the spirit of the departed as follows: "We are now about to move your remains to the tomb; and as you must of necessity accompany them to the tomb, and there remain with them in perpetuity, we have prepared for you a parting feast. Partake of it, we pray you."[2] And when the body has been lowered into the grave, the geomancer or the priest again addresses a few words to the soul of the deceased, telling it to remain with the corpse.[3] The Goldi are a primitive people of Eastern Asia, on the banks of the Amoor River. A Russian traveller has described one of their funerals, which he witnessed. The corpse was buried in a grave outside the village. Though the distance was short, the funeral procession halted thrice on the way, brandy was poured on the coffin, and the mourners called out to the dead, "Drink! A happy journey to the land of souls! Come not

[1] Mgr. Pallegoix, *Description du royaume Thai ou Siam* (Paris, 1854), i. 57 *sq.*

[2] J. H. Gray, *China* (London, 1878), i. 299 *sq.*

[3] J. H. Gray, *op. cit.* i. 304.

back, and take none of thy children with thee!" After the body was interred, a little hut was erected at the grave, and the women called out to the dead man, "We have built you a beautiful house. Farewell! Take not thy wife and children to thee when they come to pay thee a visit."[1]

The primitive Birhors of India bury with a dead man a miniature hunting-net, an axe and two small sticks used to support a net, and accosting his spirit one of the elders says, "Go thou and hunt that way. Do not come this way again." But if the deceased was a woman, they bury with her a bundle of fibres and say to her, "Do thou work with these. Do not come back to us."[2] Among the Oraons of India, when a corpse has been carried to the cremation-ground to be burnt, women put rice in the dead man's mouth, saying, "Take, eat. Now you have given us up. Now you have seen your way. Go, taking with you all your sicknesses and sins."[3] The Limbus, a tribe of Bengal, who are probably of Mongolian descent, sometimes burn, but oftener bury, their dead. A shaman or medicine-man (*phedangma*) attends at the funeral and delivers a brief address to the departed spirit, concluding with a command to go whither his fathers have gone before and not to come back to trouble the living with dreams.[4]

[1] "Schimkjewitschs Reisen bei den Amurvölkern", *Globus*, lxxiv. (1898) p. 272.

[2] Sarat Chandra Roy, *The Birhors* (Ranchi, 1925), p. 270.

[3] Sarat Chandra Roy, *Oraon Religion and Customs* (Ranchi, 1928), pp. 173 *sq.*

[4] (Sir) H. H. Risley, *Tribes and Castes of Bengal, Ethnographic Glossary* (Calcutta, 1891–1892), ii. 19; W. Crooke, *Popular Religion and Folk-lore of Northern India* (Westminster, 1896), ii. 57 *sq.*

When the Bana, a negro tribe of the Cameroons in West Africa, have buried one of their members, the men brandish their clubs threateningly at the soul (*lauona*) of the deceased, saying, " Soul, remain in the grave. Come not out of it. Every man must die. Give us no trouble." [1] The Kpelle, a negro tribe of Liberia, dislike the notion of the return of the ghost and think that only a bad ghost takes that liberty. After a death they always beg the spirit of the departed not to visit the living.[2] When the Verre, a tribe of Northern Nigeria, have laid a dead body in the grave, a priest addresses the deceased, saying, " You have lived long. Go now to the Sun and declare that you are the last of living men, and that it is useless to send for any more of us. And do you bear us no malice—return not to earth to interfere with our crops or prevent our women bearing children." [3]

At the burial of a North American Indian it used to be customary to address a few words to his departed spirit, asking him to remain in his own place and not to disturb his surviving friends and relatives.[4] Among the Tarahumare Indians of Mexico, when a man dies his weeping widow tells him that, " now that he has gone and does not want to stay with her any longer, he must not come back to frighten her or his sons or daughters or any one else.

[1] G. von Hagen, " Die Bana ", *Baessler-Archiv*, ii. (Leipzig and Berlin, 1912) pp. 108 *sq*.

[2] D. Westermann, *Die Kpelle* (Göttingen and Leipzig, 1921), p. 179.

[3] C. K. Meek, *Tribal Studies in Northern Nigeria*, i. 435.

[4] H. R. Schoolcraft, *Indian Tribes of the United States*, iv. 65.

She implores him not to carry any of them off, or do any mischief, but to leave them all alone. A mother says to her dead infant, 'Now go away! Don't come back any more, now that you are dead. Don't come at night to nurse at my breast. Go away, and do not come back!' And the father says to the dead child, 'Don't come back to ask me to hold your hand, or to do things for you. I shall not know you any more. Don't come walking around here, but stay away.'"[1]

But not content with requesting or commanding the souls of the dead to go away and not to come back, primitive man is often at pains to facilitate their departure and to speed them on their long journey to the spirit-land. Thus, for example, the Garos of Assam believe that the journey to the spirit-land, which they call Mangru-Mangram, "is a long one and the spirit is provided with a guide, the necessary eatables for the journey, and money for his requirements, exactly as if he were about to set out on a long journey on earth. These requirements are provided by the sacrifice of the necessary animals, and the offering of food and liquor at the shrines which form the last resting-place of the deceased."[2] The provisions thus made for securing a safe passage of the soul to the other world may no doubt be sometimes dictated by an affectionate regard for the spirit of the deceased, but taken along with the often repeated requests or commands to the

[1] C. Lumholtz, *Unknown Mexico* (London, 1903), i. 382.

[2] A. Playfair, *The Garos* (London, 1909), p. 103.

spirit to go away and stay away, they are probably prompted rather by fear of the ghost and a desire to get rid of him once and for all. Whatever their motive, the measures taken by the survivors for speeding the ghost on his way are varied in kind and shed an interesting light on the conceptions which primitive man forms of the life after death. It is therefore worth while to consider them in some detail.

In the first place, then, the savage sometimes furnishes the soul of the deceased with elaborate instructions as to the route he is to follow to the other world. Thus, for example, among the Kachins of Burma, at the final obsequies a priest, holding a spear before him and stepping on a sword, exhorts the spirit of the dead to leave its place in the house and to follow the central post up to the house-ridge and then depart by the front gable. Thence over grass, brush and trees, hills and mountains, brooks and rivers, the road is shown, until finally the White River is reached, which is the boundary between the land of the living and the land of the dead. The priest conducts the soul of the deceased across the rueful stream, exhorting it not to fear the wild boars on either bank, but, disguising itself by putting on the mask or forehead of a monkey, to pass nine cross-roads and at the tenth to turn off to the realm of the ancestral spirits. This is only a brief summary of the directions with which, as with a vade-mecum, the soul of a dead Kachin is provided to guide him to his long home.

We are told that to rehearse the formula at full length would occupy a whole night.[1] However, the route of Kachin souls to Dead-land varies with the particular tribe and clan to which the deceased belonged. On one of the routes the soul encounters a formidable caterpillar which seems to bar the road, raising and lowering its long body alternately. The priest instructs the dead man to wait till the body of the caterpillar is at its lowest point, and then to jump over it and pursue his way to where the spirits of his forefathers are waiting for him in the sacred grove (*numshang*) of the Happy Land.[2]

When the Kayans, a tribe in the interior of Borneo, are conveying a corpse in a coffin to its final place of rest, whether in a tree or on a pole, they repeatedly caution the dead man not to lose his way, but to be sure to take the middle road of three, avoiding the right-hand road, which leads to Borneo, and the left-hand road, which leads to the sea.[3]

But primitive man does not confine himself to telling the ghost the way he should go; he helps to open the path for him. Thus, for example, it is conceivable that after death the soul may be lingering in the skull, unable to find its way out; so among the Kurmis, a caste of cultivators in the Central Provinces of India, a son will sometimes strike his dead father's skull seven times with a log on the

[1] Rev. O. Hanson, *The Kachins* (Rangoon, 1913), p. 207.

[2] J. S. Carrapiett, *The Kachin Tribes of Burma* (Rangoon, 1929), p. 44 *sq.*

[3] James Brooke, *Journals*, i. 265.

funeral pyre, in order to crack his crown and so let out his soul.[1] The Kirars, another caste of cultivators in the same province, content themselves with touching the head of a corpse with a bamboo before it is laid on the funeral pyre, " by way of breaking it and allowing the soul to escape if it has not already done so ".[2]

When a Birhor is dying, all persons present in the chamber of death stand aside or walk out of the hut, leaving the door open so that the parting soul may meet with no obstacle in setting out on its last journey.[3] To clear the way for the soul of a dying man the Karens of Burma will sometimes make a hole in the thatched roof of the house, leaving it to the discretion of the soul to take its departure by the hole, by the door, by a window or by any other aperture it may prefer.[4] Similarly among the Basutos of South Africa, when a native died within a hut, it used to be the practice to make a hole in the thatch of the roof to let his soul go out by it, since the Basutos think that the spirits of the dead cannot pass through any openings that are used by living people.[5] In many parts of Germany it is said to be still customary after a death to open doors and windows in order to let the soul fly away ; in some places people even wave cloths to hasten its

[1] R. V. Russell, *Tribes and Castes of the Central Provinces of India*, iv. 75.

[2] R. V. Russell, *op. cit.* iii. 491.

[3] Sarat Chandra Roy, *The Birhors*, p. 261.

[4] J. B. Bringaud, " Un chapitre de l'ethnographie des Birmans Karins ", *Les Missions Catholiques*, xxviii. (Lyons, 1896) p. 521.

[5] T. Lindsay Fairclough, " Notes on the Basuto ", *Journal of the African Society*, iv. (1904–1905) p. 204.

departure.[1] In some parts of the Highlands of Scotland, when a person is dying, the door of the room is left slightly ajar to let his soul escape, but not wide enough to permit foul fiends to enter;[2] from which we seem bound to infer that, in the opinion of these Highlanders, a fiend is more corpulent than a ghost. In the north-east of Scotland, "in the very moment of death all the doors and windows that were capable of being opened were thrown wide open, to give the departing spirit full and free egress, lest the evil spirits might intercept it in its heavenward flight".[3] In some parts of England, at a death every bolt and lock in the house is unfastened, that the soul of the dying man or woman may fly freely away.[4]

When the body of a king of Michoacan, in Central America, was borne at midnight to the funeral pyre, it used to be preceded by torch-bearers and by men who swept the road, crying, "Lord, here thou hast to pass. See that thou dost not miss the way."[5] In Kan-Sou, a province of China, they place chairs at intervals along the road where a funeral procession passes, and the soul of the deceased is popularly believed to sit and rest on them

[1] R. Wuttke, *Sächsische Volkskunde*[2] (Dresden, 1901), p. 319. See further my essay, "On certain Burial Customs as illustrative of the Primitive Theory of the Soul", *Garnered Sheaves* (London, 1931), p. 9. The references given there could easily be multiplied.

[2] Ch. Rogers, *Social Life in Scotland* (Edinburgh, 1884–1886), iii. 234.

[3] Rev. Walter Gregor, *Folk-lore of the North-East of Scotland* (London, 1881), p. 207.

[4] T. F. Thiselton Dyer, *English Folk-lore* (London, 1884), p. 230; J. Brand, *Popular Antiquities of Great Britain* (London, 1882–1883), ii. 231.

[5] H. H. Bancroft, *Native Races of the Pacific States* (London, 1875–1876), ii. 620 *sq*.

before pursuing his weary way to the grave.[1] In Europe similar attentions to the comfort of the poor ghost on his last journey are not unknown. Thus in Masuria people think that the soul of a deceased person always follows his body to the grave; so if the corpse is to be buried in another village, when the funeral procession comes to the boundary a handful of straw is thrown out from the hearse that the ghost may sit on it and rest.[2]

A ghost notoriously experiences a difficulty about crossing water; hence some people considerately provide a bridge for his use when he has to pass a stream on his way to his last resting-place. Thus, among the Khasis of Assam, when a funeral procession is conveying the calcined bones of a deceased person to a cairn, where they are to repose, a man walks in front strewing leaves of a certain sort to guide the soul of the dead to the cairn, and if a stream has to be crossed, a rough bridge of branches and grass is thrown over it for the passage of the ghost.[3] A similar custom is observed by the Chins of Burma. They burn their dead and inter the bones in the ancestral burial-ground, which is generally situated in the depths of the jungle. When they convey the bones to the cemetery they take with them some cotton-yarn, and "whenever they come to any stream or other water, they stretch a thread across, whereby the spirit of the deceased, who

[1] J. Dols, "La vie chinoise dans la province de Kan-sou", *Anthropos*, x.-xi. (1915–1916) p. 744.

[2] M. Toeppen, *Aberglauben aus Masuren* (Danzig, 1867), p. 109.

[3] P. R. T. Gurdon, *The Khasis* (London, 1914), p. 134.

accompanies them, may get across it too. When they have duly deposited the bones and food for the spirit in the cemetery they return home, after bidding the spirit to remain there, and not to follow them back to the village."[1] For some time after a death the Karens of Burma stretch threads beside the footbridges in order to enable the spirit of the dead to pass by them without meeting the living folk who cross the bridges.[2] When the Trung Cha, a tribe in the mountains of Tonquin, are conveying a dead body to the place of burial and have to cross a stream, they fasten a band or ribbon of white cloth from bank to bank to serve as a bridge for the soul of the deceased, lest it should fall into the water and be swept away by the current.[3] The Chinese believe that the souls of the dead, on their way to the other world, have to cross a certain river by a bridge, but that the souls of the wicked fall from the bridge into the stream, where they are tormented by serpents and crocodiles. However, the Buddhist monks have a way of guarding against these painful accidents. They set up a miniature bridge of paper or cloth, and while some of them are mumbling prayers, one of them passes the memorial tablet of the deceased across the bridge, thus securing for the poor sinner a safe passage over the sombre stream to the other world.[4]

[1] Rev. G. Whitehead, "Notes on the Chins of Burma", *The Indian Antiquary*, xxxvi. (1907) pp. 214 *sq.*

[2] Max and Bertha Ferrers, *Burma* (London, 1900), p. 153.

[3] E. Diguet, *Les Montagnards du Tonquin* (Paris, 1908), pp. 102 *sq.*

[4] J. Dols, "La vie chinoise dans la province de Kan-sou", *Anthropos*, x.-xi. (1915–1916) p. 742.

Savages who dwell beside the sea sometimes provide their dead with canoes in which their souls may sail away to their final place of rest. Thus in Mille, one of the Marshall Islands in the Pacific, it used to be customary to wrap the dead in mats and bury them ; after which a little canoe, fitted with a sail and laden with pieces of coconuts or other food, was taken down to the shore and sent off with a fair wind "to bear far away from the island the spirit of the deceased, that it may not afterwards disturb the living".[1] In Nukahiva, one of the Marquesas Islands in the Pacific, the American seaman, Captain David Porter, who spent some months in the island in 1813, was told by the natives that they believed the abode of the dead "to be an island, somewhere in the sky, abounding with everything desirable ; that those killed in war and carried off by their friends, go there, provided they are furnished with a canoe and provisions ; but that those who are carried off by the enemy, never reach it, unless a sufficient number of the enemy can be obtained to paddle his canoe there".[2] Near a grave in a sacred grove of the island Captain Porter saw four fine war canoes, provided with outriggers and decorated with human hair and streamers. In the stern of each of them was the effigy of a man holding a paddle as if in the act of steering. On inquiry of the natives Captain Porter learned that the dignified figure

[1] H. Hale, *Ethnography and Philology of the United States Exploring Expedition* (Philadelphia, 1846), p. 89.

[2] Captain David Porter, *Journal of a Cruise to the Pacific Ocean* (New York, 1822), ii. 113.

seated in the stern of the most magnificent canoe represented a priest who had been killed not long before by their enemies, the Happahs. In the bottom of the priest's canoe were the putrefying bodies of two natives (Typees) whom the Americans had recently killed in battle, and lying about the canoe were many other corpses of men with the flesh still on them. The three other canoes, Captain Porter was informed, belonged to different other warriors who had been killed or had died not long before. " I asked them ", continues Captain Porter, " why they had placed their effigies in the canoes, and also why they had put the bodies of the dead Typees in that of the priest? They told me (as Wilson interpreted) that they were going to heaven, and that it was impossible to get there without canoes. The canoe of the priest, being large, he was unable to manage it himself, nor was it right that he should, he being now a god. They had therefore placed in it the bodies of the Happahs and Typees, which had been killed since his death, to paddle him to the place of his destination; but he had not been able yet to start, for the want of a full crew, as it would require ten to paddle her, and as yet they had only procured eight. They told me also that the taboo, laid in consequence of his death, would continue until they had killed two more of their enemies, and by this means completed the crew. I inquired if he took any sea stock with him. They told me he did, and pointing to some red hogs in an enclosure, said that they were intended for him, as well as a quantity of bread-fruit, coconuts, etc., which would be collected from the trees in the grove. I inquired if he had to go far; they replied, no; and pointing to a small square stone enclosure, informed me that was their heaven, that he was to go there. This place was tabooed, they told me, for every one except their priests."[1]

The Kiwai of British New Guinea are accustomed to leave a canoe, or at all events a piece of one, beside a grave, to enable the soul of the dead to voyage to Adiri, the land of departed spirits.[2] The Melanaus of Borneo "build picturesque boats, decorated with flags and other embellishments, which are dedicated to the use of departed spirits, who are supposed to travel in them on marine migrations. These crafts are placed near their graves." Sometimes these boats, laden with a supply of clothes and food for the use of the dead, were sent floating out to sea on a strong ebb tide to waft the spirit to its long home. In former times a slave-woman was often chained to the boat to serve her dead master on his last voyage.[3]

Sometimes the canoe which conveys the spirit of the dead to the other world, is like the spirit itself, invisible. It was so in the funeral ceremony which the Nakelo tribe of Fiji used to perform for their dead chiefs. While the body of the chief was lying

[1] Captain David Porter, *Journal of a Cruise to the Pacific Ocean* (New York, 1882), ii. 109-111. Compare J. G. Frazer, *The Belief in Immortality and the Fear of the Dead*, ii. 364-366.

[2] G. Landtman, *The Kiwai Papuans of British New Guinea*, p. 264; E. Baxter Riley, *Among Papuan Headhunters*, p. 166.

[3] Charles Brooke, *Ten Years in Sarawak* (London, 1866), i. 78 *sq.*

in state in his house, surrounded by a silent multitude of his subjects, three old men of a certain clan approached, holding fans in their hands. One of them entered the house, while the other two waited in the doorway. He flourished his fan over the dead man's face and called him, saying, "Rise, sir, the chief, and let us be going. Broad day has come over the land." And the soul of the dead man was believed to rise up at the call. Holding his fan horizontally a little above the floor, and walking backwards, the old man led the spirit from the house. The other two old men joined him at the doorway, holding their fans in like manner about two feet above the ground as a shelter for the spirit, who was clearly supposed to be of short stature. Thus they went along the path, followed in reverential silence by a multitude of men, no women being allowed to join the procession. When they came to the bank of the river, one of the three old men who were escorting the chief's spirit climbed a tree and cried in a loud voice, "Themba, bring over the canoe!" This call he repeated thrice, whereupon the people fled in all directions and hid themselves. For Themba was the Nakelo Charon who ferried departed souls across the river. After summoning the ghostly ferryman the three old men waited by the riverside until they saw a wave rolling in towards the shore, which they believed to be the surge of the approaching canoe. They said that a blast of wind accompanied it, and that the wave dashed the spray over the bank. At that sign they averted their faces, pointed their fans suddenly to the river, and cried aloud, " Go on board, sir ! " After that they ran for their lives, for no eye of living man might look on the embarkation of the dead chief's soul.[1]

Some people who bury their dead obligingly furnish them with ladders on which to climb up to heaven, or to wherever the place of bliss may be. Thus when the Mangars, one of the fighting tribes of Nepaul, have buried one of their number, two bits of wood, about three feet long, are set up on either side of the grave, and in one of them are cut nine steps or notches forming a ladder for the spirit of the dead to ascend to heaven. The maternal uncle officiates as priest at the burial, and as he steps out of the grave he bids a solemn farewell to the dead and calls upon him to ascend to heaven by the ladder which stands ready for him.[2] It is a popular belief in Russia that the soul of a dead person has to rise from the grave ; hence to assist him in rising it is, or used to be, customary with the peasants to bury certain utensils with him in the grave, such as little ladders and plaited thongs. Even at the present day, when many of them have forgotten the origin of the custom, the peasants of some districts make little ladders of dough and have them baked for the benefit of the dead. " In the

[1] Rev. Lorimer Fison, " Notes on Fijian Burial Customs ", *Journal of the Anthropological Institute*, x. (1881) pp. 147 *sq.*

[2] Sir H. H. Risley, *Tribes and Castes of Bengal, Ethnographic Glossary*, ii. 75 ; W. Crooke, *Popular Religion and Folk-lore of Northern India*, ii. 60 *sq.*

Government of Voroneja a ladder of this sort, about three feet high, is set up at the time when a coffin is being carried to the grave; in some other places similar pieces of dough are baked in behalf of departed relatives on the fortieth day after their death, or long pies marked cross-wise with bars are taken to church on Ascension Day and divided between the priest and the poor. In some villages these pies, which are known as *Lyesenki* or 'Ladderlings', have seven bars or rungs, in reference to the 'Seven Heavens'."[1] Clearly nothing could be more appropriate than that the souls of the dead should ascend to the Seventh Heaven on Ascension Day by swarming up a long pie as a ladder marked with seven rungs. But the custom need not be, and probably is not, of Christian origin. In many graves of ancient Egypt, belonging to the later period, ladders have been found, and it is a reasonable conjecture of Professor Adolf Erman that they were intended to help the souls of the dead to clamber out of the sepulchral shafts.[2] The Shans of Burma, though they do not provide the dead man with a ladder, sometimes supply its place with a rope, which hangs down into the grave until the coffin has been finally lowered into it. Then the rope is pulled out in the direction of the north, "to help the spirit of the dead person to begin his journey to Mount Meru, the great spirit moun-

[1] W. R. S. Ralston, *The Songs of the Russian People* [2] (London, 1872), pp. 110 *sq.* Compare J. N. Smirnov, *Les Populations finnoises des bassins de la Volga et de la Kamma* (Paris, 1898), p. 141.

[2] Adolf Erman, *Die ägyptische Religion* [2] (Berlin, 1909), pp. 210 *sq.*

tain, which lies, it is believed, north of our world ".[1]

Some people think that the soul of a dead person needs an animal or bird to guide or carry him to the spirit-land, and they obligingly provide him with the necessary creature. A dog is often employed as the guide of the soul. Thus among the Greenlanders, " when little children die and are buried, they put the head of a dog near the grave, fancying that children having no understanding, they cannot by themselves find the way, but the dog must guide them to the land of souls ".[2] Similarly the Catios Indians of Colombia, in South America, think that a dead man needs a dog to conduct him to the spirit-land, and apparently (though this is not expressly stated) they furnish him with a canine guide.[3] Some of the Garos of Assam believe that the souls of the dead could never find their way unaided to the spirit-land; so at the cremation-ground they kill a dog and burn it with the corpse to guide the dead man's soul to Chikmang, the land of souls.[4] Among the Lakhers, when a child dies who has not yet learned to talk, a dog must be killed in order that the child's soul may hold on to the dog's tail and so find its way to Athiki, the land of the dead.[5] The Meo, a tribe of mountaineers in Tonquin, dress

[1] Mrs. Leslie Milne, *Shans at Home* (London, 1910), p. 95.

[2] Hans Egede, *Description of Greenland* (London, 1818), p. 153.

[3] Fr. Severino de Santa Teresa, " Religion und soziale Verhältnisse der Catios-Indianer in Kolumbien ", *Archiv für Religionswissenschaft*, xxiii. (1925) p. 296.

[4] W. W. Hunter, *Statistical Account of Assam* (London, 1879), ii. 154; A. Playfair, *The Garos* (London, 1909), p. 109.

[5] N. E. Parry, *The Lakhers*, p. 388.

a dead man in his best clothes, taking care to undo all the fastenings in them in order to let his soul fly freely away; and to the right hand of the corpse they tether a dog, which is to guide the departed spirit to the other world.[1] According to one account, the dog in question is made of lacquer,[2] but no doubt in that case he serves the purpose quite as well as the living animal.

Some people prefer a pig to a dog as the guide of the departed soul to its long home. Thus among the Lolos, a primitive aboriginal people of Southern China, as soon as a death has taken place, a pig is led to a fountain, where it is killed. They think that in the other world the soul of the deceased person, being a newcomer, will not know where to find water to slake his thirst, but that the soul of the dead pig, fresh from its slaughter at the fountain, will be sure to guide its master's spirit to some spring or stream.[3] On the day after a death the Khyeng of Arakan tie a dead fowl to the big toe of the deceased, and a priest addresses the dead man as follows: "O spirit, thou hast a long and wearisome journey before thee, so a hog has been killed upon whose spirit thou mayest ride, and the spirit of the dead fowl will so terrify the worm guarding the portals of paradise that thou wilt find an easy entrance".[4]

[1] E. Diguet, *Les Montagnards du Tonquin* (Paris, 1908), pp. 143 *sq.*

[2] H. Baudesson, *Au pays des superstitions et des rites* (Paris, 1932), p. 129; *id.*, *Indo-China and its Primitive People* (London, N.D.), p. 174.

[3] A. Liétard, *Au Yun-nan. Les Lo-lop'o* (Münster i.W., 1913), p. 171.

[4] Major G. E. Fryer, "On the Khyeng People of the Sandoway District, Arakan", *Journal of the Asiatic Society of Bengal*, xliv. (1875) p. 43.

The Bhils, a primitive people of Central India, appear to choose the horse, if it be only a clay horse, as the best vehicle for wafting the human soul to heaven. On the tops of high hills they are said to erect images of horses made of burnt clay and arranged in rows on platforms. An English surgeon, who inquired the meaning of the custom, received the following explanation: "Heaven is supposed to be but a short distance from earth, but the souls of the dead have to reach it by a very painful and weary journey, which can be avoided to some extent during life by ascending high hills, and there depositing images of the horse, which in addition to reminding the gods of the work already accomplished, shall serve as chargers upon which the soul may ride a stage to bliss". The surgeon adds that "the more modest (of the Bhils) make a hollow clay image, with an opening in the rear, into which the spirit may creep. An active Bhil may, in this fashion, materially shorten the journey after death. Both men and women follow the custom."[1]

In India the favourite animal for the conveyance of the soul to heaven is the sacred cow. Hence, when a Brahman dies, a calf is allowed to wander in the name of the deceased, in order that, by grasping its tail, the dead man may cross the dreaded river Virja nadi, which divides the land of the dead from the land of the living.[2] But it is

[1] T. H. Hendley, Surgeon, "An Account of the Maiwar Bhils", *Journal of the Asiatic Society of Bengal*, xliv. (1875) pp. 347 *sq.*

[2] J. Abbott, *The Keys of Power* (London, 1932), p. 397.

not Brahmans alone who find salvation in this quaint fashion. When a Kir, member of a caste of cultivators in the Central Provinces of India, is about to die, he makes a present of a cow to a Brahman in order that, by catching hold of the animal's tail, he may cross in safety the horrible River of Death.[1] A similar custom is observed by the Kurmis, another caste of cultivators in the same province.[2]

Some people choose a bird as the vehicle to waft the soul of the dead to the realms of bliss. On the evening of a burial the Iroquois used to release a bird over the grave "to bear away the spirit to its heavenly rest".[3] Among the Yorubas of West Africa, after a death the deceased is called thrice by name and adjured to depart and no longer to haunt the dwellings of the living; and to facilitate his departure a fowl is sacrificed, "which, besides a right-of-way for his soul, is supposed also to guide it".[4] At a death the Khasis of Assam sacrifice a cock, which is called "The cock that scratches the way", because it is thought to scratch a path for the spirit of the dead to the next world.[5] The Karens of Burma cremate their dead and deposit the calcined bones in a shrine consisting of a miniature hut, on which there is always the rude carving of a bird. This bird represents a certain mythical creature which is supposed to convey the spirit of

[1] R. V. Russell, *Castes and Tribes of the Central Provinces of India*, iii. 483.

[2] R. V. Russell, *op. cit.* iv. 74.

[3] Lewis H. Morgan, *League of the Iroquois* (Rochester, 1851), p. 174.

[4] A. B. Ellis, *The Yoruba-speaking Peoples of the Slave Coast of West Africa* (London, 1894), p. 160.

[5] R. T. Gurdon, *The Khasis* [2] (London, 1914), p. 132.

the deceased on its wanderings over rivers and chasms.[1] The Tho of Tonquin fasten duck's feathers to the clothes of a dead person in order to enable his spirit to fly over the streams that may cross his path in the other world.[2]

Many peoples have been in the habit of supplying their dead with money or its equivalent to enable them to defray the expenses of the journey to the other world. Elsewhere I have given many examples of the custom,[3] which might easily be multiplied; here I must content myself with citing a few typical specimens. Thus the Khasis of Assam place money in the coffin beside the corpse, "so that the spirit of the deceased may possess the wherewithal to buy food on its journey".[4] The Lolos insert money and rice in the mouth of the corpse, thus providing him both with food and travelling expenses for his last journey.[5] Among the Mosquito Indians of Central America every child soon after birth has a bag of seeds tied round its neck "in order to pay the price of being ferried across a certain river that separates this from the next world, should it die young".[6] The Kakhyens of Burma put a piece of silver in

[1] Max and Bertha Ferrers, *Burma* (London, 1900), p. 153.

[2] Baudesson, *Au pays des superstitions et des rites* (Paris, 1932), pp. 128 *sq.* In the English translation of this book the bird is incorrectly described as a goose. The French word is *canard*. See H. Baudesson, *Indo-China and its Primitive People* (London, N.D.), p. 172.

[3] J. G. Frazer, "On certain Burial Customs as illustrative of the Primitive Theory of the Soul", *Journal of the Anthropological Institute*, xv. (1886) pp. 77-79; *id.*, *Garnered Sheaves* (London, 1931), pp. 19 *sq.*

[4] P. R. T. Gurdon, *The Khasis*[2] (London, 1914), p. 133.

[5] A. Liétard, *Au Yun-nan. Les Lo-lop'o* (Münster i.W., 1913), p. 172.

[6] Chas. N. Bell, "The Mosquito Territory", *Journal of the Royal Geographical Society*, xxxii. (1862) p. 254; H. H. Bancroft, *Native Races of the Pacific States*, iii. 543.

the mouth of a corpse "to pay ferry dues over the streams the spirit may have to cross ",[1] and a similar custom is observed by the Burmese generally; between the teeth of the dead they insert a piece of gold or silver called *kado akah*, that is, "ferry toll", to pay for the passage of the mystic river which is known to exist, but concerning which it is difficult to extract any definite information from the Burmese.[2] The coin which the ancient Greeks inserted in the mouth of the dead to pay Charon for ferrying them across the Styx[3] is the most familiar case of a ferry-toll provided by survivors for the comfort and convenience of the ghosts.[4] But it is not so commonly known that in antiquity at the city of Hermion there was a short cut to hell down through a chasm, which avoided the necessity of going round by the Styx; so the thrifty people of Hermion put no money in the mouths of their dead to pay for their passage across the river, which would have been a perfectly needless expense. According to the local legend, it was through this chasm that Hercules dragged up Cerberus, the hound of hell,[5] so that he had no ferry-toll to pay to Charon either for himself or for the dog. The pawky hero might almost have been a Scotchman.

[1] J. Anderson, *Mandalay to Momien* (London, 1876), p. 143.

[2] C. J. F. S. Forbes, *British Burma* (London, 1878), p. 93; Shway Yoe (Sir J. G. Scott), *The Burman* (London, 1882), ii. 338.

[3] Lucian, *De luctu*, 10.

[4] Strabo, viii. 6. 12, p. 373.

[5] Pausanias, ii. 35. 10.

INDEX

Printed in Great Britain by R. & R. Clark, Limited, *Edinburgh*

THE FEAR OF THE DEAD IN PRIMITIVE RELIGION

VOL. II

MACMILLAN AND CO., LIMITED
LONDON · BOMBAY · CALCUTTA · MADRAS
MELBOURNE

THE MACMILLAN COMPANY
NEW YORK · BOSTON · CHICAGO
DALLAS · ATLANTA · SAN FRANCISCO

THE MACMILLAN COMPANY
OF CANADA, LIMITED
TORONTO

THE FEAR OF THE DEAD IN PRIMITIVE RELIGION

LECTURES DELIVERED ON
THE WILLIAM WYSE FOUNDATION
AT TRINITY COLLEGE, CAMBRIDGE

BY

SIR JAMES GEORGE FRAZER
O.M., F.R.S., F.B.A.

FELLOW OF TRINITY COLLEGE, CAMBRIDGE
ASSOCIATE MEMBER OF THE *INSTITUT DE FRANCE*

VOL. II

MACMILLAN AND CO., LIMITED
ST. MARTIN'S STREET, LONDON
1934

PRINTED IN GREAT BRITAIN
BY R. & R. CLARK, LIMITED, EDINBURGH

TO

THE MASTER, THE WARDEN

AND THE

BROTHERS AND SISTERS

OF THE

DRAPERS' COMPANY

THIS VOLUME IS GRATEFULLY

AND RESPECTFULLY DEDICATED

BY

THE AUTHOR

PREFACE

In this second course of lectures on the " Fear of the Dead in Primitive Religion " I resume the subject at the point at which I left off at the end of the first course. I said there that primitive man attempts to get rid of the dangerous spirits of the dead by one or other of two methods, either the method of persuasion and conciliation or the method of force and fraud. In the first course I illustrated the former method, that of persuasion and conciliation, by a variety of examples. I now take up the second method, that of force and fraud, or deception. For primitive man imagines that the spirits of the dead are not only amenable to physical force, but that they can be deceived or cheated into doing his will. In the present course I have dealt mainly with the method of force, showing how primitive man attempts to drive away the spirits of the dead by sheer physical force, and to keep them at a distance by interposing physical obstacles between him and them. The method of fraud or deception practised on the spirits of the dead has been incidentally illustrated ; but this curious aspect of primitive religion must be reserved for fuller treatment in a subsequent work, in which I shall hope to discuss many other important sides of the subject, which the limitations of time have compelled me to pass over at present. Meanwhile this volume concludes the second course of my lectures on the William Wyse Foundation at Trinity College.

J. G. FRAZER

April 1934

CONTENTS

LECTURE I

LECTURE I

In my former lectures on the fear of the dead in primitive religion, I reached or anticipated certain general conclusions which it may be well to recapitulate before I proceed to develop the subject in further detail. We saw that the belief in immortality, or to speak more correctly, the belief in the survival of human personality for an indefinite time after death, has been widespread if not universal among mankind, being shared by the races of lower culture, whom we call savages or barbarians, as well as by the civilized nations who now cherish the belief as a fundamental article of their religious creed. But among the races of lower culture, who may be called primitive in a relative sense by comparison with the civilized nations, the spirits of the dead appear to be predominantly feared rather than loved, for they are believed to be the sources of many evils which afflict humanity, including the last evils, sickness and death. Hence, primitive man is often at great pains to send these dangerous spirits away and to keep them at a safe distance from him. At the same time, I pointed out in my lectures, and I desire now to repeat, that this fear of the dead appears to be by no means characteristic in the same degree of all the races of men, even those of lower culture, for many of them observe customs which appear to be inconsistent with such a fear, and to indicate rather respect and affection for the souls of the departed. Thus, for example, many peoples have been accustomed to welcome home the spirits of the dead and entertain them at a great festival once a year, of which the rites of All Souls' Day in Europe have furnished a conspicuous instance down to modern times.[1] Again, many peoples have been in the habit of burying their dead in their houses; a practice which is hardly consistent with a deep-seated fear of the dead and a dread of close contact with them. Other peoples, again, though they do not bury the dead in the house, attempt to bring back their spirits to the house and to install them there, which incontestably proves that they expect to reap some benefit from the presence of the spirits in the dwelling. For it is commonly supposed that the spirits of the dead can confer many benefits on the living, if only they are duly propitiated, and kept in good humour, though they are quick to resent any fancied slight or neglect on the part of the survivors. Among the benefits so anticipated appears to be the hope that the spirits will ultimately be reborn in the infants of the family. Once more, the practice of embalming the bodies of the dead, as has been well pointed out by Mr. Warren Dawson,[2]

[1] I have collected many examples of such festivals in *The Golden Bough*, Part IV. *Adonis, Attis, Osiris*, ii. pp. 51 *sqq*.

[2] Warren R. Dawson in *Folk-Lore*, xliv. (December 1933) p. 416.

undoubtedly aims at preserving the bodies of the dead, and presumably, therefore, their spirits, for an indefinite time after death, which would certainly not be done if the living did not expect to receive some benefit from the continued existence of the dead. The classic land of embalming was ancient Egypt, and in its extant literature, as I am informed by our eminent English Egyptologist, Mr. Alan H. Gardiner, there is very little trace of a fear of the dead. To sum up : the attitude of primitive man to the spirits of the dead is complex ; it is a compound of hope and fear, of affection and aversion, of attraction and repulsion, and in any attempt to analyse it, full account should be taken of all these conflicting emotions and tendencies. But in investigating our complex subject it is legitimate, I trust, to single out some one particular element of the compound for special examination. That must be my justification for here concentrating attention on the element of fear in the attitude of primitive man towards the spirits of the dead.

In my last lecture, I dealt with the means which primitive man adopts for banishing the dangerous spirits of the dead and keeping them at a distance. I said that these means fall into two classes, which may be distinguished respectively as fair or foul, according as they are based on either persuasion and conciliation, or on force and fraud. When the method of persuasion and conciliation is adopted, the ghost is invited or entreated to go quietly away to the spirit-land and to stay there, not returning to torment the living with his unwelcome attentions. He is provided with directions for the journey to the spirit-land and with a guide to conduct him thither: he receives food to eat and money to defray his expenses on the road; and he is furnished with a bridge or a boat to enable him to cross any rivers or seas which he may encounter on his passage to the far country. But in the opinion of many primitive peoples, there are obdurate and obstreperous spirits who, turning a deaf ear to blandishments and a blind eye to the accommodations obligingly offered them for the journey, obstinately persist in haunting their old home, and persecuting their surviving kinsfolk in a great variety of ways. In the case of such incorrigible spirits nothing remains but to drive them away by sheer force, and to force in such circumstances primitive man does not hesitate to have recourse. This introduces us to the foul treatment of the spirits of the dead to which we must now turn our attention.

Thus, for example, at a burial in Melville Island, North Australia, all the men present have been seen to charge at the invisible spirit of the dead man, throwing sticks and spears at it in order to drive it into the grave.[1] The Arunta of Central Australia believe that after his death a man's ghost is free to walk the earth for a period of twelve or eighteen months, but that after that time it is necessary to confine his restless spirit within narrower bounds.

[1] Baldwin Spencer, *Native Tribes of the Northern Territory of Australia* (London, 1914), p. 233.

The favourite haunt of the ghost is believed to be the burnt and deserted camp where he died. Here accordingly, on a certain day, a band of men and women, the men armed with shields and spear-throwers, assemble and begin dancing round the charred and blackened remains of the camp, shouting and beating the air with their weapons and hands in order to drive away the lingering spirit from the spot he loves too well. When the dance is over the whole party proceeds at a run to the grave, chasing the ghost before them. In vain the poor ghost makes a last bid for freedom and doubles back towards the camp; the leader of the party, making a long circuit, cuts off the retreat of the fugitive. Finally, having run the ghost to earth they trample him down into the grave, dancing and stamping on the heaped-up soil, while with downward thrusts through the air they beat and force him underground.[1] After a series of deaths a band of the Kamilaroi tribe in New South Wales used to scour the country, dancing and beating the air with branches to drive away the dangerous spirits of the dead, while a chorus of women and girls helped them by their songs.[2] The natives of the Banks' Islands believe that after a death the spirit of the deceased does not at once depart, but continues to haunt the neighbourhood for five or ten days; but as they

[1] Baldwin Spencer and F. J. Gillen, *The Native Tribes of Central Australia* (London, 1899), pp. 498-508.

[2] Rev. Wm. Ridley, *Kamilaroi, and other Australian Languages* (Sydney, 1875), p. 149; *id.* "Report on the Australian Language and Traditions", *Journal of the Anthropological Institute*, ii. (1873) p. 269.

think it undesirable that the ghost should linger for more than five days they drive it away with shouts and blowing of conches, and sometimes with the booming sound of bull-roarers.[1] At Ureparapara in these islands, the ceremony of ghost-driving is peculiar and remarkable. "Bags of small stones and short pieces of bamboo are provided for the people of the village, and are charmed by those who have the knowledge of the magic chaunt appropriate for the purpose. Two men, each with two white stones in his hands, sit in the dead man's house, one on either side. These men begin to clink the stones one against the other, the women begin to wail, the neighbours—who have all assembled at one end of the village—begin to march through it in a body to the other end, throwing the stones into the houses and all about, and beating the bamboos together. So they pass through till they come to the bush beyond, when they throw down the bamboos and bags. They have now driven out the ghost, who up to this time has been about the house, in which the widow has for these five days never left the dead man's bed except upon necessity; and even then she leaves a coconut to represent her till she returns. At Motlav the ghost is not driven away unless the man who has died was badly afflicted with ulcers and sores, either a *gov* covered with sores, or a *mamnagita* with a single large ulcer or more. When such a one is dying the people of his village send word in time to the next village westwards, as the

[1] R. H. Codrington, *The Melanesians* (Oxford, 1891), p. 267.

ghost will go out following the sun, to warn them to be prepared. When the *gov* is dead they bury him, and then, with shell-trumpets blowing and the stalks of coconut fronds stripped of some of the leaflets beating the ground, they chase the ghost to the next village. The people of that village take up the chase, and hunt the ghost further westward ; and so on till the sea is reached. Then the frond stalks are thrown away and the people return, sure that the ghost has left the island, and will not strike another man with the disease."[1]

In San Cristoval, one of the Solomon Islands, when a burial is taking place, a man goes to the hut of the deceased, and, standing at the door, fishes for the soul of the dead man with a fishing-rod baited with betel nut ; and when he has caught it, puts the ghost with the bait into a little bag. Later on the bag will be put with the skull of the dead man wherever it is kept. After the soul of the deceased has thus been caught and deposited in the bag, other men come to the door of the hut and fish for the ghosts who may have come to the hut to prey on the flesh of the corpse. The bait in this case is a dracaena leaf. The other men come, some with torches, some with sticks, and entering the hut dash their torches and sticks against the walls to drive out the lingering and dangerous ghosts.[2] In this custom it will be observed that though the ghost of the dead man is carefully removed from the hut

[1] R. H. Codrington, *The Melanesians*, pp. 270-271.

[2] C. E. Fox, *The Threshold of the Pacific* (London, 1924), p. 212.

which he inhabited, it is not driven away to a distance, but is deposited with the skull wherever that may be kept, obviously in order that the spirit of the deceased may abide with his mortal remains. So far, therefore, the custom does not conform to the general type of driving away ghosts to the bourne from which no traveller returns.

Among the Sulka of New Britain, after a death has taken place, a deep hole is dug in the hut of the deceased and the corpse is placed over it, and kept there for some time. Then follows the ceremony of driving out the ghost from the hut. The time for performing the ceremony is communicated secretly to the men who are appointed to carry it out, lest the ghost should overhear and prepare to resist. The time is always in the early morning when the first cry of a certain bird is heard. At that moment the natives raise a great shout, and the ghost-drivers, entering the hut, beat and shake the walls, and set fire to coconut leaves with which they dance wildly about, thus expelling the ghost of the deceased. When they have done their work, they throw away the burning leaves on the path. Thereby the ghost is believed to be frightened and to be driven finally away.[1]

In Fiji the old custom of driving away the spirit of the dead has been described as follows by Captain Erskine, who witnessed it about the middle of the nineteenth century. "As soon as this feast was

[1] M. S. C. Rascher, "Die Sulka, ein Beitrag zur Ethnographie Neu-Pommern", *Archiv für Anthropologie*, xxxiv. (1904) p. 214; R. Parkinson, *Dreissig Jahre in der Südsee* (Stuttgart, 1907), p. 185.

over (it was then dark) began the dance and uproar which are always carried on either at natural or violent deaths. All classes then give themselves up to excess, especially at unnatural deaths of this sort, and create all manner of uproar by means of large bamboos, trumpet-shells, etc., which will contribute to the general noise which is considered requisite to drive away the spirit and to deter him from desiring to dwell or even to hover about his late residence. The uproar is always held in the late habitation of the deceased, the reason being that as no one knows for a certainty what reception he will receive in the invisible world, if it is not according to his expectations, he will most likely repent of his bargain and wish to come back. For that reason they make a great noise to frighten him away, and dismantle his former habitation of everything that is attractive, and clothe it with everything that to their ideas seems repulsive."[1]

In the Marquesas Islands of the Pacific, after a death, the ghost was believed not to abandon the corpse definitely for the first two nights. On the third night, a priest, stepping out on the terrace in front of the house, implored the wandering soul of the deceased to depart; and by way of enforcing the request, a band of men, armed with spears and other lethal weapons, went about in the outer darkness, beating the bushes and stabbing the thatched roofs of the houses in order to drive the lingering

[1] J. E. Erskine, *Journal of a Cruise among the Islands of the Western Pacific* (London, 1853), pp. 475-477.

ghost away. If, roused by the clamour, the dogs began to bark, the priest would say, " The soul is departing ".[1]

In the Gilbert Islands of the Pacific " on the three nights following a death the ceremony of *bo-maki* was performed. All the people irrespective of their kinship to the deceased, gathered together in the darkness, with sticks of pandanus wood and the butt ends of coconut leaves in their hands, at the southern extremity of the village, and forming a line abreast from east to west, slowly advanced northwards, beating the ground and trees before them with their staves. Not a word was uttered. When the line had swept through the settlement from south to north it stopped, and the participants disbanded in silence. All pedestrians who happened upon the party while it was at work would seize a staff without a word, join in and when it was finished pass on their way. The object of the ceremony was to encourage the soul to leave the neighbourhood of the body and also to drive away any evil spirits that might wish to possess it. Immediately life was extinct the family began a great wailing and yelling which was kept up by relays for three days without intermission, except when the ceremony of *bo-maki* was being performed ; to have sustained it during that rite would have been to encourage the soul of the dead to linger about the body and haunt the living."[2] In these same islands it was customary at

[1] M. Radiguet, *Les Derniers Sauvages* (Paris, 1882), pp. 284 *sqq.*

[2] Arthur Grimble, " From Birth to Death in the Gilbert Islands ", *Journal of the Royal Anthropological Institute*, ii. (1921) p. 44.

a burial to place two coconuts in the hands of the corpse, as an additional precaution to prevent the ghost from returning to haunt his kinsfolk. "The body was kept for three or nine days, being buried on the fourth or tenth, as the case might be. Those who kept it for the shorter period were of the opinion that, as the soul had finally been driven away from its neighbourhood on the third repetition of the *bo-maki* ceremony, it might safely be laid to rest on the fourth day. But many families, and particularly those of Tarawa and Butaritari, believed that the soul might reinhabit the body at any time during the nine days after death, and so, though they took the greatest pains to prevent it, still kept its fleshly tenement available until the last moment."[1]

The Kiwai of British New Guinea believe that the spirits of the dead normally depart to Adiri, the far-off spirit-land, in the west; but some of them are thought to linger behind, and to haunt the villages intent on mischief. So it becomes necessary to drive away these malignant spirits with blasts of the conch shell.[2]

The Kiwai are also accustomed to burn the platform on which a corpse has been exposed and gifts which have been deposited on the grave. Moreover, they chew ginger in order to drive away the lingering spirit of the dead.[3]

In the Purari delta of British New Guinea, at a death some of the natives wave branches of the

[1] A. Grimble, *op. cit.* p. 45.

[2] W. N. Beaver, *Unexplored New Guinea* (London, 1920), p. 177.

[3] G. Landtman, *The Kiwai Papuans of British New Guinea* (London, 1927), p. 259.

coconut palm over the corpse in the house to waft the spirit of the deceased to spirit-land, before they carry out the corpse to burial.[1]

The natives about Hood Bay and Port Moresby in British New Guinea "believe, too, in the deathlessness of the soul, but their ideas as to its abode or condition are very vague and indefinite. A death in the village is the occasion of bringing plenty of ghosts to escort their new companion and perhaps fetch some one else. All night the friends of the deceased sit up and keep the drums going to drive away the spirits. When I was sleeping one night at Hood Bay a party of young men and boys came round with sticks, striking the fences and posts of houses all through the village. This I found was always done when any one died, to drive back the spirits to their own quarters on the adjacent mountain tops."[2]

Among the Roro-speaking peoples of British New Guinea when a corpse has been laid in the grave a near relative takes a branch of a tree and strokes the body from foot to head, in order to drive away the spirit. In Yule Island similarly two men stroke the corpse from head to foot with a certain herb to drive away the spirit. After the spirit has been thus swept from the corpse the same two men, shouting and brandishing sticks and torches, chase the spirit beyond the bounds of the village into the bush,

[1] J. H. Holmes, *In Primitive New Guinea* (London, 1924), pp. 218, 219.

[2] The Rev. W. G. Lawes, "Notes on New Guinea and its Inhabitants", *Proceedings of the Royal Geographical Society*, ii. (1880) p. 615.

where, with a last curse, they hurl at it the sticks or torches they have in their hands.[1]

After a death or a series of deaths, the Orokaiva of British New Guinea celebrate a drama, a dance and a feast in honour of the recently deceased. At the conclusion of the ceremonies, the paraphernalia of the dancers are placed on a raft, and the spirit or the spirits of the dead are supposed to embark along with them and to float down the river to its mouth: meanwhile, the chief man of the village calls out the names of all the deceased and bids them go right down to the sea and there to turn into crocodiles, sharks and snakes.[2]

Among the Papuans of Geelvink Bay in Dutch New Guinea after the burial, you may hear about sunset a great uproar in all the houses of the village: the people are yelling and throwing sticks about with the object of driving away the dreaded ghost. They have given him all that he can expect to get: to wit, a grave, a banquet and funeral ornaments; and now they beseech him not to intrude upon the survivors, and not to kill them or fetch them away, as the Papuans put it.[3]

In some of the Turki tribes of Siberia it is believed that after a death the soul of the deceased is free to roam about for forty days, after which, if

[1] C. G. Seligman, *The Melanesians of British New Guinea* (Cambridge, 1910), p. 275.

[2] F. E. Williams, *Orokaiva Society* (Oxford, 1930), pp. 253 *sqq.*, pp. 279 *sq.*

[3] J. L. van Hasselt, "Die Papuastämme an der Geelvinkbai (Neu-Guinea)", *Mitteilungen der Geographische Gesellschaft zu Jena*, ix. (1891) p. 101; cf. J. B. van Hasselt, "Die Noeforezen", *Zeitschrift für Ethnologie*, viii. (1876) p. 196.

it is still hanging about, the *shaman* drives it out and drums it down to hell. To secure a favourable reception for the dead man in his new abode, the *shaman* is said, after conducting the soul personally thither, to serve out brandy to the devils all round.[1]

Among the Western Bhotias of Thibet there is performed on the last day of the obsequies a final ceremony for getting rid of the soul of the deceased. A venerable sage gives his last instructions to the departing spirit. The clothes of the deceased are taken and placed upon an animal which represents the dead man. A man then leads forth the animal to a spot far from the village, while all the villagers beat the poor creature to drive it away and prevent its return. In Chaudans the animal is allowed to go free, but elsewhere low-caste Bhotias, or Thibetans, speedily dispatch it and eat its flesh. So glad are the villagers that the spirit has departed, that they return singing and dancing, and after this, the men and women shave, cut their hair, wash their heads and wear rings on their ears and hands.[2]

Among the Kunbis, a great agricultural caste of the Central Provinces of India, after all the other funeral rites have been performed, the chief mourner goes to the door of the house and, breaking an areca-nut on the threshold and placing it in his mouth, spits it out of the door, signifying the final ejectment of the spirit of the deceased from the

[1] W. Radloff, *Aus Siberien* (Leipsig, 1884), ii. p. 52.

[2] Charles A. Sherring, *Western Tibet and the British Borderland* (London, 1906), pp. 129, 130.

dwelling.[1] Among the Savara, a hill tribe of Southern India, as soon as a death has taken place in a house, a gun is fired at the door in order to drive away the spirit of the deceased.[2]

Among the Kachins of Burma, after a death in a house a priest attempts to lure the soul of the deceased out of the dwelling by means of a bait attached to the end of a string, of which he, sitting in the house, holds one end, while a man seated at the door holds the other and baited end of the string. If the soul is judged not to take the bait, as a further inducement to the soul to depart, the priest throws a spear at it, and tells it that the house is full of caterpillars, serpents and wild boars, which will bite the poor soul if it does not at once make off. When the priest feels sure that the ghost has really departed from the house, he takes his spear in his hand, and harangues the spirit as follows: "We have made solemn funeral rites for you; we have offered you fowls and pigs and buffaloes, and we give you now these two images of birds to sell on the road; take all these objects, these provisions for the journey and especially all evil omens, and go to your great-grandfather, by way of your tomb and those of your father and grandfather".[3]

It is believed by the Malagasy that the spirits of

[1] R. V. Russell, *The Tribes and Castes of the Central Provinces of India* (London, 1916), iv. p. 36.

[2] E. Thurston, *Castes and Tribes of Southern India* (Madras, 1909), vi. p. 324; Fred. Fawcett, "On the Soaras (or Savaras), an aboriginal Hill People of the Eastern Ghats of the Madras Presidency", *Journal of the Anthropological Society of Bombay*, i. (1886) p. 248.

[3] P. Ch. Gilhodes, "Mort et funérailles chez les Katchins (Birmanie)", *Anthropos*, xiii. (1917–1918) pp. 264, 265

the dead hover about the towns and even revisit their former homes, "and it is customary in great floods or downpours of rain for the people to beat the sides of their houses with great violence to drive away, as they say, the *angatra* or spirits who may be seeking to re-enter and shelter themselves beneath the ancestral roof".[1]

After a death the Bari of the Nilotic Sudan carry burning grass round the house to drive away the soul of the deceased, which otherwise would worry the survivors.[2] Among the Bakarewe, who inhabit an island of the Victoria Nyanza, on the fifth day after a burial, a relative of the deceased enters the house and turns everything upside down in the chamber where the dead man breathed his last. This he does in order to expel the ghost lest he should return to haunt and molest the survivors. The service which the kinsman thus renders to the family is a dangerous one, and no sooner has he performed it than he demands his reward, which is at once given him in the shape of a hoe, or a goat. Having got it, the ghost-driver departs quickly to his own house.[3]

Speaking of the natives of the Gabun district of West Africa, a very experienced American missionary tells us that "the feelings in the hearts of the mourners are very mixed. The outcry of affection, pleading with the dead to return to life, is sincere, the

[1] Henry W. Little, *Madagascar* (Edinburgh and London, 1854), p. 84.

[2] C. G. Seligman and Brenda Z. Seligman, *Pagan Tribes of the Nilotic Sudan* (London, 1932), p. 291.

[3] P. Eugène Hurel, "Religion et vie domestique des Bakarewe", *Anthropos*, vi. (1911) p. 299.

survivor desiring the return to life to be complete; but almost simultaneously with that cry comes a fear that the dead may indeed return, not as the accustomed embodied spirit, helpful and companionable, but as a disembodied spirit, invisible, estranged, perhaps inimical, and surrounded by an atmosphere of dread imparted by the unknown and unseen. The many then ask, not that the departed may return, but that, if it be hovering near, it will go away entirely. Few were those who during the life of the departed had not on occasion had some quarrel with him, or had done him some injustice or other wrong, and their thought is, 'His spirit will come back to avenge itself!' So guns are fired to frighten away the spirit and to cause it to go far off to the far world of spirits, and not take up residence in or near the town to haunt and injure the living."[1]

Among the Ewe-speaking people of Togoland in West Africa, when the relatives of a dead man visit his fields for the first time after his death, they are careful to drive away his spirit by shouts and gun shots.[2]

In Loango, when many spirits of the dead are believed to be haunting and troubling a village, the inhabitants resort to strong measures for expelling them. Fires are kindled everywhere; houses are swept and cleaned out; the people rush about shouting and screaming, and men fire guns and brandish chopping knives to drive away the spirits.[3]

[1] R. H. Nassau, *Fetichism in West Africa* (London, 1904), pp. 223-224.

[2] J. Spieth, *Die Ewe-Stämme* (Berlin, 1906), p. 121.

[3] E. Pechuel Loesche, *Die Loango-Expedition*, iii. 2 (Stuttgart, 1907), p. 309.

In aboriginal America, also, the custom of expelling the spirit of the deceased has often been observed and recorded. Thus, for example, among the Eskimo of Bering Strait, the ceremony has been described by an eye-witness as follows. On the evening of the second day after the death, the men in every house in the village took their domestic buckets and, turning them bottom upwards, went about thrusting the bottom of the vessel into every corner and into the smoke-hole and the doorway. This, it was said, was done to drive out the shade or ghost if it should be in the house, and from this custom the second day is called *a-hun-ig-ut*, or "the bottom day". After this was done, and the people were ready to retire for the night, every man took a long grass stem and, bending it, stuck both ends into the ground in a conspicuous place in the middle of the doorway. They said that this would frighten the spirit off, for should it come about and try to enter the house, it would see this bent grass, and believing it to be a snare, would go away, fearing to be caught. On the lower Yukon, below Ikogmut, "the housemates of the deceased must remain in their accustomed places in the house during the four days following the death, while the shade is believed to be still about. During this time all of them must keep fur hoods drawn over their heads to prevent the influence of the shade from entering their heads and killing them. At once, after the body is taken from the house, his sleeping-place must be swept clean and piled full of bags and other things, so as not to leave any room for the shade to return and reoccupy it. At the same time, the two persons who slept with him upon each side must not, upon any account, leave their places. If they were to do so the shade might return and, by occupying the vacant place, bring sickness or death to its original owner, or to the inmates of the house. For this reason none of the dead person's housemates are permitted to go outside during the four days following the death. The deceased person's nearest relatives cut their hair short along the forehead in sign of mourning. During the four days that the shade is thought to remain with the body, none of the relatives are permitted to use any sharp-edged or pointed instrument for fear of injuring the shade and causing it to be angry and to bring misfortune upon them. One old man said that should the relatives cut anything with a sharp instrument during this time, it would be as though he cut his own shade and would die."[1]

Among the Shuswap of British Columbia, often after a death the *shaman* is called in by the relatives of the deceased. It is believed that the ghost of the dead person is eager to take one of his nearest relatives with him to the spirit-land. The *shaman* is called in to drive away the ghost. He sees the ghost and orders all the members of the mourning family to stay in the house, which the ghost cannot enter. Then he addresses the ghost, telling him that he

[1] E. W. Nelson, "The Eskimo of Bering Strait", *18th Annual Report of the Bureau of American Ethnology* (1899), pp. 314, 315.

cannot have the person he wants. Thus he induces the ghost to go away and not to trouble the family any more.[1] Some of the Canadian Indians, whom the Jesuits called the Mountaineers, believed that when a man died in a hut his soul passed out of it by the smoke-hole in the roof, and they beat the walls of the hut with sticks to hasten its departure.[2] Among the Ojebway Indians, on the evening after a burial when it began to grow dark, the men used to fire their guns through the smoke-hole in the roof, while the women beat the walls of the hut with sticks in order to drive away the lingering ghost. As a further precaution against the return of the ghost, they cut thin strips of birch bark and hung them inside the walls of the hut, as scarecrows to frighten away the poor soul if nevertheless it should come back to disturb their slumbers.[3]

Among the Cora Indians of Mexico after a death wizards were engaged to hunt out and drive away the soul of the deceased. This they did by smoking their pipes and poking branches into all the corners of the house, until they pretended to find the lurking ghost, whom thereupon they summarily ejected.[4]

Thus we have seen that, in many parts of the world, primitive man has been in the habit of driving

[1] *Sixth Report on the North-Western Tribes of Canada* (*Report of the British Association for 1890*, separate reprint); Second General Report on the Indians of British Columbia, by Dr. Fr. Boas, p. 85.

[2] *Relations des Jésuites* (Canadian reprint) (Quebec, 1858), i. Année 1634, p. 23; cf. *id.*, 1633, p. 11; *id.*, 1639, p. 44.

[3] Peter Jones, *History of the Ojebway Indians* (London, 1861), pp. 99-100.

[4] H. H. Bancroft, *The Native Races of the Pacific States of North America* (London, 1875–1876), i. p. 744.

forcibly away the dangerous ghosts of the dead. In civilized Europe similar usages have not been unknown. Thus, the Germans sometimes wave towels about or sweep the ghost out with a besom,[1] just as in old Rome the heir solemnly swept out the ghost of his predecessor with a broom specially made for the purpose.[2] So like is human nature in all latitudes and under all varieties of culture.

[1] A. Wuttke, *Der deutsche Volksaberglaube*, Second Edition (Berlin, 1869), §§ 725, 737; F. Schmidt, *Sitten und Gebräuche bei Hochzeit, Taufen und Begräbnissen in Thüringen*, p. 85; J. A. E. Kohler, *Volksbrauch, Aberglauben, Sagen und andre alte Überlieferungen im Voigtlande* (Leipsic, 1867), p. 254.

[2] Festus, *s.v. everriator*, p. 68, ed. W. M. Lindsay: "Everriator vocatur, qui iure accepta hereditate iusta facere defuncto debet; qui si non fecerit, seu quid in ea re turbaverit, suo capite luat. Id nomen ductum a verrendo. Nam exverriae purgatio quaedam domus, ex qua mortuus ad sepulturam ferendus est, quae fit per everriatorem certo genere scoparum adhibito, ab extra verrendo dictarum." In this passage the ghost is not expressly mentioned, but on the analogy of the customs described above he may be inferred with a high degree of probability.

LECTURE II

LECTURE II

IN the last lecture we saw that in many parts of the world, after deaths have taken place, primitive man has been in the habit of driving away the spirits of the departed because he believes that the continued presence of these spirits in their old haunts might bring many calamities on the living. But once he succeeded to his satisfaction in banishing these dangerous spirits to a distance, his anxiety is by no means over ; for he thinks that the spirits can return and persecute the survivors ; especially by carrying off their souls with them to dead land. Hence, having banished the spirits of the dead to what he conceives to be a safe distance, he nevertheless adopts a great many precautions to prevent their return. To these precautions, which are very varied and often very curious, we must now direct our attention.

Thus, to begin with, failing to distinguish the immaterial and spiritual from the material and corporeal, he imagines that the spirits of the dead can be arrested by physical obstacles, and accordingly he proceeds to erect such obstacles in the way of the returning spirits, in the hope that the spirits will be unable to surmount them and to reach him and his fellows ; in short, he attempts to barricade the road against them.

Thus, for example, some of the Tungus are said to make a barrier of snow and trees.[1]

Amongst the Mangars, one of the fighting tribes of Nepal, when the mourners are returning from the grave, " one of their party goes ahead and makes a barricade of thorn bushes across the road, midway between the grave and the house of the deceased. On the top of the thorns he puts a big stone on which he takes his stand, holding a pot of burning incense in his left hand and some woollen thread in his right. One by one the mourners step on the stone and pass through the smoke of the incense to the other side of the barrier. As they pass, each takes a piece of thread from the man who holds the incense, and ties it round his neck. The object of this curious ceremony is to prevent the spirit of the dead from coming home with the mourners and establishing itself in its old haunts. Conceived of as a miniature man, it is believed to be unable to make its way on foot through the thorns, while the smell of the incense, to which all spirits are highly sensitive, prevents it from surmounting this obstacle on the shoulders of one of the mourners."[2] The Chins of Burma burn their dead and collect their bones in an earthen pot. Afterwards, at a convenient

[1] T. de Pauly, *Description ethnographique des peuples de la Russie* (St. Petersburg, 1862), Peuples ouralo-altaïques, p. 71.

[2] H. H. Risley, *Tribes and Castes of Bengal, Ethnographic Glossary*, ii. (Calcutta, 1891) pp. 95-96.

season, they carry away the pot containing the bones to the ancestral burial place. "When the people convey the pot of bones to the cemetery, they take with them some cotton-yarn, and whenever they come to any stream or other water, they stretch a thread across, whereby the spirit of the deceased, who accompanies them, may get across it too. When they have duly deposited the bones and food for the spirit in the cemetery they return home, after bidding the spirit to remain there and not to follow them back to the village. At the same time they block the way by which they return by putting a bamboo across the path."[1] Thus the mourners make the way to the grave as easy as possible for the ghost, but obstruct the way by which he might return from it.

Among the Kachins, another tribe of Burma, when the mourners are returning from the grave precautions have to be taken against any onslaughts by the spirit of the dead. A long bamboo is procured and split in half for about half-way or more up its length. One half is fixed in the ground, the other lying loose. Between the two halves a wedge is inserted about three or four inches off the ground, thus forming a triangle with the wedge as base. All those who have attended the funeral pass through the triangle, the priest and the butcher bringing up the rear. Either of these two knocks away the wedge after having passed over it and the two halves

[1] Rev. G. Whitehead, "Notes on the Chins of Burma", *Indian Antiquary*, xxxvi. (1907) pp. 214 *sqq*.

of the bamboo close with a snap. Those who have guns fire as many shots as they can into the bamboo to frighten away the dangerous spirit of the deceased. In this custom the split bamboo is the obstacle interposed between the mourners and the pursuing ghost; while the two pieces of the bamboo are held apart the gateway is open to let the mourners pass through; but when the two pieces are allowed to come together with a snap the gate is closed in the face of the baffled ghost and the mourners feel themselves to be safe from his pursuit.[1]

Among the Moïs, a primitive tribe of Tonkin, when the mourners are returning from a burial, they make their way through a narrow passage constructed of reeds on trees, hoping thus to rid themselves of the ghost who will be brushed off by contact with the reeds or trees.[2]

Among the Lakhers, a tribe of Assam, when a death has taken place in a village all the people are very much afraid lest the spirit of the dead should enter their houses during the night and do them harm. To prevent this each householder places his paddy pestle across the doorway. When the dead person's spirit arrives at the door it sees the pestle, and, mistaking it for a huge serpent, retreats in terror. More intelligent spirits are said to recognize the pestle, but, fearing that it might fall and crush them if they attempt to enter, return whence they came. In Tisi, a village of the Lakhers, to prevent

[1] W. J. S. Carrapiett, *The Kachin Tribes of Burma* (Rangoon, 1929), p. 47.

[2] H. Baudesson, *Au pays des superstitions et des rites* (Paris, 1932), p. 130.

the ghost of the deceased from re-entering his house on the night of the funeral, they take a hen, and standing on the ladder leading to the house, cut off its feathers, allowing them to fall on each side of the ladder. These feathers are supposed to form a barrier which the ghost cannot cross. The cutting of the feathers is meant to intimate to the ghost that if he ventures to return to the house they will cut him up just as they cut off the feathers.[1]

Among the Dhobas, a primitive tribe of the Central Province of India, on the ninth, eleventh or thirteenth day after a death, when the ceremonial impurity ends, the male members of the sept are shaved on the banks of a river and their hair is left lying there. When they start home they spread some thorns and two stones across the path. Then, as the first man steps over the thorns, he takes up one of the stones in his hand and passes it behind him to the second, and each man successively passes it back as he steps over the thorns, the last man throwing the stone behind the thorns. Thus the dead man's spirit in the shape of the stone is separated from the living and prevented from accompanying them home.[2] In this custom the ghost is apparently supposed to adhere to the hair of the mourners, till the hair has been shorn off and left on the bank of the river ; and though the ghost attempts to pursue the mourners home, he is stopped on his way by the barrier of thorns.

[1] N. E. Parry, *The Lakhers* (London, 1932), p. 403.

[2] R. V. Russell, *The Tribes and Castes of the Central Provinces of India*, ii. (London, 1916) pp. 516, 517.

Again, when the Aheriyas of the North-Western Provinces of India burn the corpse they fling pebbles in the direction of the pyre to prevent the spirit accompanying them. In the Himalayas when a man is returning from the cremation ground, after the burning of a corpse, he places a thorny bush on the road wherever it is crossed by another path, and the nearest male relative of the deceased on seeing this, puts a stone on it, and pressing it down with his feet, prays the spirit of the dead man not to trouble him.[1] Here again the thorns serve as a barrier against the pursuing spirit. In India the custom of erecting barriers against the return of the ghost appears to be by no means confined to the wild tribes of the present day, but to go back to a remote antiquity. It was the ancient rule that when the mourners left the cremation ground the officiating priest raised a barrier of stones between the dead and the living.[2] In the *Satapatha-Brâhmana*, an ancient Indian book of religious ritual, it is said that the officiating priest, having fetched a clod from the boundary, deposits it midway between the grave and the village, saying: "This I put up as a bulwark for the living, lest another of them should go unto that thing; may they live for a hundred plentiful harvests, and shut out death from themselves by a mountain". The priest is said thus to make a

[1] W. Crooke, *The Popular Religion and Folklore of Northern India*, ii. (London, 1896) p. 57.

[2] W. Crooke, *Religion and Folklore of Northern India* (edited by R. E. Enthoven) (London, 1926), p. 237, referring to *Rajendralala Mitra*, ii. 123, 136; E. J. Atkinson, *The Himalayan Districts of the North-Western Provinces of India*, ii. (Allahabad, 1884) p. 832.

boundary between the dead forefathers and their living descendants.[1] The great Marātha leader Śivaji is said to have crawled through a perforated stone, to escape from the ghost of the Mogul General he had killed.[2]

Among the Sea Dyaks of Borneo the mourners who are the last to leave the grave plant sharpened stakes in the ground, so that the spirit of the dead may not follow them to the house, the stakes planted in the ground being supposed to prevent its return.[3] Similarly the Kiwai of British New Guinea put up sticks on the path which the ghost is supposed to have taken, in order to block the road against its return.[4]

Among the Kpelle, a negro tribe of Liberia, ropes are stretched round the base of a house or the walls of a town to ward off evil spirits, among whom mischievous ghosts are no doubt included. Between one of the villages and a graveyard two posts used to be planted in the ground with wattle-work stretched between them, in order to prevent the ghosts from coming from the graveyard to molest the villagers.[5]

In Loango, similarly, a cord protected by an

[1] *Satapatha-Brâhmana*, translated by J. E. Egeling (Oxford, 1900), Part V. p. 440; *Sacred Books of the East*, vol. xliv.

[2] J. Abbott, *The Keys of Power* (London, 1932), p. 504.

[3] E. H. Gomes, *Seventeen Years among the Sea Dyaks of Borneo* (London, 1911), p. 138; cf. J. Perham, "Sea Dyak Religion", *Journal of the Straits Branch of the Royal Asiatic Society*, No. 14 (1884), p. 291.

[4] G. Landtman, *The Kiwai Papuans of British New Guinea* (London, 1927), p. 282.

[5] D. Westermann, *Die Kpelle; ein Negerstamm in Liberia* (Leipsic, 1921), pp. 203-204.

appropriate charm is stretched and a furrow is traced all round a village. Further, a sacrificial victim, generally a goat, is carried round the whole circumference and is afterwards sacrificed. If these precautions fail to keep out the ghosts the inhabitants are at their wits' end, and think of abandoning the site altogether.[1]

Like the inhabitants of the Old World, the aborigines of America have sometimes been wont to erect barriers as a protection against the intrusion of unwelcome ghosts. Thus among the Shuswap of British Columbia mourners use thorn-bushes for pillow and bed in order to keep away the ghost of the deceased. They also lay thorn-bushes all round their beds for the same purpose.[2] So among the Bella Coola Indians, another tribe of British Columbia, the bed of a mourner must be protected against the ghost of the deceased. The relatives of the dead stick a thorn-bush at each corner of their bed. After four days these bushes are thrown into the water. Mourners must rise early and go into the woods, where they stick four thorn-bushes into the ground, at the corners of a square, in which they must cleanse themselves by rubbing their bodies with cedar branches. They also swim in ponds. After swimming they cleave four small trees and creep through the clefts, following the course of the

[1] E. Pechuel-Loesche, *Die Loango-Expedition*, iii. 2. (Stuttgart, 1907) p. 310.

[2] Fr. Boas, Second General Report on the Indians of British Columbia, *Sixth Report on the North-Western Tribes of Canada* (*Report of the British Association for 1890*), separate reprint, p. 91.

sun. This they do on four subsequent mornings, cleaving new trees every day.[1] In this latter custom the passage of the mourner through cleft trees is another mode of evading the pursuit of the ghost, just as we have seen that Kachin mourners returning from the grave creep through a split bamboo for a similar purpose. Among the Thompson Indians, another tribe of British Columbia, after a death, a string of deer-hoofs with a short line attached was hung across the inside of the winter house, to prevent the ghost from entering. During four successive nights an old woman pulled at the string frequently to make the hoofs rattle. Branches of juniper were also placed at the door of the house, or were burned in the fire for the same purpose.[2] Some of the Algonkin Indians of Canada used to stretch nets round their huts in the meshes of which they sought to catch any spirits of the dead who might attempt to enter from the wigwams of their neighbours.[3] Among the Huichol Indians of Mexico no strong liquor is drunk at burial feasts. Instead, a cross, made from a kind of *salvia*, is hung up in the house to prevent the soul of the deceased from re-entering the house and to keep him from getting into the

[1] *Seventh Report on the North-Western Tribes of Canada* (*Report of the British Association for 1891*, separately paged extract), Third Report on the Indians of British Columbia, by Dr. Fr. Boas, p. 13. On the custom of creeping through cleft trees or other narrow openings to escape from a ghost, see *The Golden Bough*, Part VII. *Balder the Beautiful*, ii. pp. 174 *sqq*.

[2] James Teit, "The Thompson Indians of British Columbia" (*Memoirs of the American Museum of Natural History*, ii. Anthropology I.; *The Jessup North Pacific Expedition*, iv. (April, 1900) p. 331.

[3] *Relations des Jésuites* 1639, vol. i. (Quebec, 1858) p. 44.

distillery and spoiling the wine. For the same purpose branches are put upon the paths leading to the distillery and the jars of liquor are covered.[1]

As usual, savage custom has its counterpart in civilized Europe. In Savoy there is a curious belief attached to the custom of closing all doors and windows when a funeral is about to pass. The peasants say that if this were not done the soul of the dead might escape into a house through some open door or window.[2] This belief probably gives the clue to the common European custom of lowering the blinds of all windows in a house of mourning.

Among the barriers which primitive man attempts to interpose between himself and the dreaded spirits of the dead, a prominent place is taken by water and fire. Thus, to begin with water, after burying a body the Ngarigo of South-east Australia were wont to cross a river in order to prevent the ghost from pursuing them.[3] Obviously they shared the common opinion that ghosts for some reason are unable to cross water.

The natives of Nias, an island to the west of Sumatra, attribute contagious diseases to the ill-will of the spirits of the dead : hence, the bodies of persons who die of such diseases do not receive regular obsequies, but are either thrown away in the forest or are buried in an island, to prevent the return of their dangerous ghosts.[4]

[1] C. Lumholz, *Unknown Mexico*, ii. (London, 1903) pp. 243-244.

[2] Estella Canziani, *Costumes, Traditions and Songs of Savoy* (London, 1911), p. 136.

[3] A. W. Howitt, *Native Tribes of South-east Australia* (London, 1904), p. 461.

[4] Elio Modigliani, *L' Isola delle Donne* (Milan, 1895), p. 198.

The use of water as a barrier against a ghost may be illustrated from a practice of the Ainu of Japan, as it is described from personal experience by the Rev. John Batchelor, our principal authority on these primitive people. He had visited the grave of an old woman, in the company of the woman's son. The son would by no means approach within fifty yards of the grave for fear of his mother's ghost. "Upon returning to the hut, the man, together with the women, brought a bowl of water to the door, and requested me to wash my face and hands. Whilst at my ablutions the women commenced to beat me and brush me down with *inao* (sacred whittled sticks). Upon inquiring into the ideas which moved the people to act in this manner, I discovered that the washing was to purify me from all uncleanness contracted at the grave through contact with the ghost of the deceased, and that the beating and brushing with *inao* was to drive away all evil influences and diseases she may have aimed at me. The water and *inao* were the antidote against, and the corrective for, the evil intentions the spirit is supposed to have directed towards me out of her wicked spite for trespassing on her domain."[1]

Among the Taungthu of Upper Burma, when the corpse is carried outside the house, the chief mourner, widow or widower, son or daughter, pours water over the body and says: "As a stream divides

[1] Rev. John Batchelor, *The Ainu and their Folk-lore* (London, 1901), pp. 549, 550.

countries so may the water poured now divide us ".[1]

In the *Satapatha-Brâhmana* it is prescribed that seven furrows should be dug on the north side of the grave and filled with water, for sin not to pass beyond, for indeed sin cannot pass beyond seven rivers. The mourners returning from the grave throw three stones each into these northern furrows and pass over them, saying: " Here floweth the stony one; hold on to each other, rise and cross over, ye friends: here will we leave behind what unkind spirits there be, and will cross over to auspicious nourishments ". On this custom a commentator observes: " These seven furrows are straight, running from west to east; thus separating the grave from the north, the world of men ". In the text just quoted the seven furrows are represented as a barrier which sin cannot cross, but this moral explanation of the custom is probably a priestly interpretation. We may suspect that the water of the seven furrows was originally intended to prevent the ghost from following the mourners on their return from the grave.[2]

In Africa, among the Bangala of the Upper Congo, the Rev. John H. Weeks witnessed a good example of the use of water as a barrier to divide the dead from the living. He says: " Walking one day in Monsembe I saw an incident that re-

[1] G. W. Scott and J. P. Hardiman, *Gazetteer of Upper Burma and the Shan States*, Part I. vol. i. (Rangoon, 1900) p. 554.

[2] *Satapatha-Brâhmana*, translated by Julius Egeling, Part V. (Oxford, 1900) pp. 437 *sqq*.

called Burns' 'Tam o' Shanter' to my mind. There had been a death in a family and the relatives had just performed all the necessary rites and ceremonies and were returning to their homes. A small trench some twenty feet long was dug with a hoe. The relatives took up their position on the side of the trench nearest to the grave, the medicine-man stood on the other side, and his assistant was placed at the end of the trench with a large calabash of water. At a signal the water was poured into the trench, and while it was running the medicine-man took each person by the hand, and mumbling an incantation pulled him or her over the running water. When all had been pulled over, one by one, the water was allowed to run until the calabash was empty. I asked the reason of the ceremony, and they told me that it was to keep the spirit of their deceased, and buried, relative from following them. It was very evident from the rites observed that they thought the spirits could not cross running water."[1]

With regard to the natives of the Gabun district we are told by the Rev. Robert Nassau that "when they have finished the work of burial, they are in great fear, and are to run rapidly to their village, or to the nearest body of water, river or lake or sea. If in their running one should trip and fall it is a sign that he will soon die. They plunge into the

[1] John H. Weeks, *Among Congo Cannibals* (London, 1913), pp. 102-103; cf. *id.*, "Anthropological Notes on the Bangala of the Upper Congo River", *Journal of the Royal Anthropological Institute*, xxxix. (1909) p. 454.

water, as a means of 'purification' from possible defilement. The object of this purification is not simply to cleanse the body, but to remove the presence or contact of the spirit of the dead man or of any other spirit of possible evil influence, lest they should have ill-luck in their fishing, hunting and other work."[1]

A much attenuated form of the water barrier against ghosts is observed amongst the Basutos; a man with holy water follows the funeral, sprinkling with the holy water the footprints of the men who carry the corpse.[2]

Widows and widowers are often supposed to be peculiarly liable to be haunted by the ghosts of their deceased spouses, and special precautions are accordingly taken to protect them from these importunate spirits. The Bakongo of the Lower Congo River resort to the water barrier as the means of guarding both widows and widowers in these melancholy circumstances. In the case of the widow, "if it is the woman's first husband who has died, she must take his bed, and one or two articles he commonly used, to a running stream. The bed is put in the middle of the stream and the articles placed on it. The woman washes herself well in the stream and afterwards sits on the bed. The medicine-man goes to her and dips her three times in the water and dresses her. Then the bed and articles are broken and the pieces thrown down-stream to float away. She is

[1] Rev. Robert H. Nassau, *Fetichism in West Africa* (London, 1904), pp. 218-219.

[2] *Verhandlungen der Berliner Gesellschaft für Anthropologie* (1877), p. 84.

now led out of the stream, and a raw egg is broken and given to her to swallow. A toad is killed and some of its blood is rubbed on her lips, and a fowl is killed and hung by the roadside. These sacrifices having been made to the spirit of the departed one, she is free to return to her town."[1] Clearly, the Bakongo suppose that by placing the widow in her bed in the middle of a river they oppose an insuperable obstacle to the attentions of her husband's ghost; but to make assurance doubly sure, they afterwards seek to pacify the ghost by a sacrifice. The treatment of a widower among the Bakongo is somewhat similar, if the woman was his first wife. He must stay in his house for six days, but on the morning of the seventh day the male relatives of his deceased wife come to escort him to a running stream. On arrival at the stream one of the kinsmen takes the bed and throws it into the water. Then he scrapes the widower's tongue, shaves him, pares his nails, makes three cuts in his arm, and finally immerses him three times in the river, to "wash away the death", or rather, as we may suppose, his wife's ghost.[2]

With this African application of the water barrier to protect the widow we may compare a somewhat similar custom observed by the Papuans of Geelvink Bay in Dutch New Guinea. A widow must not leave her dwelling for several months, for the spirit of her dead husband is still associated with her, and

[1] J. H. Weeks, *Among the Primitive Bakongo* (London, 1914), pp. 172, 173.

[2] J. H. Weeks, *op. cit.* p. 173.

if she went about the men who met her might be taken ill or die. Her hair is shorn in sign of mourning. After her hair is shorn, she is bathed, and in order that she may not meet any one in taking her bath, a canoe is brought under the house, a hole is made in the floor and she descends into the boat.[1] Thus these Papuan widows, like their African sisters, are surrounded by water as a barrier against their husbands' ghosts.

Among peoples of the lower culture, it is a common custom for mourners after a burial or a funeral to plunge completely into water. The custom is usually interpreted as a mode of cleansing the mourner from the impurity which he has contracted by contact with the dead. But in all such cases it is safe to conjecture that the original motive was fear of the ghost, and a wish to interpose a barrier of water between the living and the dead. And even when the custom has degenerated into a simple ablution of some part of the mourner's person, or into a still slighter contact with water, it seems probable that the underlying motive has been a desire to wash off the clinging ghost, or otherwise to get rid of him by the interposition of water. With regard to the Hindoos, we are told that they regard themselves as defiled by simple presence at a funeral, and immediately after contracting this defilement they go and plunge into water, and no

[1] J. L. van Hasselt, "Eenig Aanteekeningen arngaande de bewoners der Nord-Westkust van Nieu Guinea, meer bepaaldeligk de Stam der Noefoorezen", *Tijdschrift voor Indische Taal- Land- en Volkenkunde*, xxxii. (1889) p. 591

one dare enter his house before he has thus purified himself.[1]

Among the people of Ambaca in Angola, the surviving relative, whether husband or wife, is carried from the grave on the back of a person of the same sex and thrown into the river for ablution or purification. On returning to his house, the person so purified is secluded ; he may not converse with any person of the opposite sex, nor eat anything that has been boiled, nor wash himself[2] for eight days.

In some parts of the Cameroons all present at a burial throw handfuls of earth on the grave and then run away lest they should die the same death as the deceased. Those who live near the coast afterwards throw themselves into the sea, but the inland people in the like circumstances plunge into a river.[3]

A traveller in the Cameroons tells us how, after witnessing the execution of a man accused of witchcraft, the whole population of the village, men, women and children, ran to the shore, and stripping themselves of their clothes, bathed in the sea to wash off, as he says, the witchcraft, but probably rather the dangerous spirit of the sorcerer just set free from its earthly tenement.[4]

Among the Kaffirs of South Africa all persons who touched a corpse or any of the dead man's

[1] J. A. Dubois, *Mœurs, institutions et cérémonies des peuples de l'Inde* (Paris, 1825), i. p. 244.

[2] F. T. Valdez, *Six Years of a Traveller's Life in Western Africa* (London, 1861), p. 296 *sq*.

[3] C. Cunym, "De Libreville au Cameroun", *Bulletin de la Société de Géographie*, xvii. (1896) pp. 340-341.

[4] R. Buchholz, *Reisen in West-Afrika* (Leipsic, 1880), p. 143.

effects were obliged to go through certain ceremonies and then to bathe in running water before they might associate with their companions.[1]

Among the Ba-Ila-speaking tribes of Northern Rhodesia, when the grave has been filled up and before the diggers have stepped off from it, water is brought and all who have handled the corpse wash their hands over the grave. This they do, it is said, to cleanse them from the defilement they have contracted.[2]

Among the Fangs of West Africa, after the death of a chief, his wives are shut up in a hut, where they have to stay five days mourning for him. On the evening of the fifth day they lie down on the felled trunks of banana trees laid side by side, and all the people of the village, from the youngest to the oldest, pour water over them. The women have to lie there all night without stirring, and next morning their heads are carefully shaved with bits of broken glass. Afterwards the villagers form a double line, men on one side, women on the other, armed with swords and other weapons, and the women have to run the gauntlet between these two rows, being well belaboured in their passage.[3] In this custom the beating of the widows is doubtless a secondary precaution to rid them of their husband's ghost, lest

[1] G. McCall Theal, *Ethnography and Condition of South Africa* (London, 1919), p. 222; Dos Santos, in *Records of South-Eastern Africa*, edited by G. McCall Theal, vii. (1901) p. 401.

[2] E. W. Smith and A. M. Dale, *The Ila-Speaking Peoples of Northern Rhodesia*, ii. (London, 1920) p. 106.

[3] P. Trilles, "Chez les Fangs: leurs mœurs, leur langue, leur religion", *Missions Catholiques*, xxx. (1898) pp. 521, 522.

he should be clinging to their persons, despite the sousing of their bodies with water.

Among the Nyanja-speaking peoples of the Nyasaland Protectorate, when a grave has been filled in the mourners go to a river and bathe in it, the men up-stream and the women down-stream.[1]

When the Damara or Herero of South-West Africa have buried a body they pour bowls of water on the grave before retiring from it.[2]

In North Guinea, after a corpse has been buried, the bearers rush to the water and wash themselves thoroughly before they return to the town.[3]

Among the Bare-speaking Toradjas of Central Celebes the mourners in returning from a burial step in vessels of water, doubtless in order to escape from the ghost.[4] In New Zealand, among the Maoris, all who had attended a funeral used to betake themselves to the nearest stream and plunge several times head under in the water.[5] In Tahiti all who had assisted at a burial fled precipitately and plunged into the sea, casting also in the sea the garments they had worn.[6]

Among the Singhalese of Ceylon the funeral party bathe before returning to the house, and are

[1] R. Sutherland Rattray, *Some Folk-Lore, Stories and Songs in Chinyanja* (London, 1907), p. 94.

[2] C. J. Andersson, *Lake Ngami* (London, 1856), p. 467.

[3] J. Leighton Wilson, *Western Africa* (London, 1856), ch. 17.

[4] N. Adriani in A. C. Kruijt, *De Bare'e-sprekende Toradjas van Midden Celebes*, ii. pp. 98, 99.

[5] W. Yate, *An Account of New Zealand* (London, 1835), p. 137; R. Taylor, *Te Ika A Maui, or New Zealand and its Inhabitants*, Second Edition (London, 1870), p. 224; *Annales de la Propagation de la Foi*, xv. (1843) pp. 23-24.

[6] Rev. William Ellis, *Polynesian Researches*, Second Edition (London, 1832–1836), i. p. 403.

supplied by the washerwoman with newly washed clothes; during their absence the house is well cleansed and purified by the sprinkling of water mixed with cow-dung.[1] The Oraons of Bengal after attending a burial always bathe before they return to the village.[2] In the Shan States of Burma, it is said that similarly all persons who have handled a corpse are obliged to bathe before they return to the village.[3]

Among the Kiwai of British New Guinea, mourners returning from a burial swim in the sea. Those who have carried the dead body spit ginger over their hands and afterwards rub them with a sweet-smelling herb. Until they have done so, nobody will touch his own body with his hands. After washing they smear face and body with clay, which is renewed from time to time.[4] In this custom the water, the ginger and the clay are probably alike regarded as protectives against the ghost. Similarly the natives of Rook, an island off the north-east coast of New Guinea, go and purify themselves in the sea immediately after a burial.[5]

Among the aborigines of America the use of water as a barrier against the dead appears to be familiar. Thus of the Songish Indians of Van-

[1] A. Perera, "Glimpses of Singhalese Social Life", *Indian Antiquary*, xxi. p. 382.

[2] E. T. Dalton, *Descriptive Ethnology of Bengal* (Calcutta, 1872), p. 262; Sarat Chandra Roy, *Oraon Religion and Customs* (Ranchi, 1928), p. 175.

[3] "Notes on the Manners, Customs, Religion and Superstitions of the Tribes inhabiting the Shan States", *Indian Antiquary*, xxi. p. 119.

[4] G. Landtman, *The Kiwai Papuans of British New Guinea* (London, 1927), p. 265.

[5] P. Ambrosoli, "Extrait d'une notice sur l'Ile de Rook", *Annales de la Propagation de la Foi*, xxvii. (1855) p. 363.

couver Island we are told that after a burial the whole tribe used to go down to the sea and bathe, wash their heads and cut their hair.[1] Among the Tarahumare Indians of Mexico on the occasion of a death by suicide all the women, after bidding farewell to the dead body, ran quickly into a deep waterhole, splashing into it, clothes and all, that nothing from the dead might attach itself to them.[2] In ancient Mexico all those who had helped to bury a king of Michoacan bathed afterwards.[3] Amongst the Mosquito Indians all persons returning from a funeral undergo a lustration in the river.[4] Among some of the Indians of Peru ten days after a death, the relatives of the deceased used to assemble and conduct the next of kin to a river or its springs where they thoroughly washed and scrubbed him to rid him, no doubt, of the contagion of death, or rather, as we may surmise, of the ghost of the deceased, who might be adhering to him.[5]

In civilized Europe also the barrier of water has sometimes been resorted to as a protection against the spirits of the dead. Thus, for example, in some parts of Transylvania "it is usual for the procession returning from a funeral to take its way through a river or stream of running water, sometimes going

1 *Sixth Report of the North-Western Tribes of Canada* (*Report of the British Association for 1890*), Second General Report on the Indians of British Columbia, by Dr. Fr. Boas, p. 23.

2 C. Lumholtz, *Unknown Mexico* (London, 1903), p. 389.

3 H. H. Bancroft, *Native Races of the Pacific States*, ii. p. 621; Brasseut de Bourbourg, *Histoire des nations civilisées de Mexique et de l'Amérique Centrale* (Paris, 1857–1859), iii. p. 85.

4 H. H. Bancroft, *op. cit.* i. p. 744.

5 Padre Pablo de Arriaga, *Extirpación de la Idolatria del Peru* (Lima, 1621), p. 33.

a mile or two out of their way to avoid all bridges, thus making sure that the vagrant soul of the beloved deceased will not follow them back to the house".[1] The Wends of Geislitz make a point of passing through running water after a burial; in winter, if the river is frozen, they break the ice in order to wade through the water.[2] In modern Mytilini and Crete if a man will not rest in his grave they dig up the body, ferry it across to a little island, and bury it there.[3] The Kythniotes of the Archipelago have a similar custom, except that they do not take the trouble to bury the body a second time, but simply tumble the bones out of a bag and leave them to bleach on the rocks, trusting to the "silver streak" of sea to imprison the ghost.[4] In many parts of Germany, in modern Greece and in Cyprus, water is poured out behind the corpse as it is being carried from the house, in the belief that, if the ghost returns, he will not be able to cross it.[5] Sometimes,

[1] E. Gerard, *The Land beyond the Forest* (Edinburgh and London, 1888), p. 316.

[2] K. Haupt, *Sagenbuch der Lausitz* (Leipsic, 1862–1863), i. p. 254.

[3] B. Schmidt, *Das Volkleben der Neugriechen* (Leipsic, 1871), p. 168.

[4] J. T. Bent, *The Cyclades* (London, 1885), p. 441 sq.

[5] A. Kuhn, *Märkische Sagen und Märchen* (Berlin, 1843), p. 368; J. D. H. Temme, *Die Volkssagen in Altmark* (Berlin, 1839), p. 77; F. Nork, *Sitten und Gebräuche der Deutschen und ihrer Nachbarvölker*, p. 479; A. Wuttke, *Der deutsche Volksaberglaube* (Berlin, 1869), p. 737; C. M. Rochholz, *Deutscher Glaube und Brauch* (Berlin, 1867), i. p. 177; G. Lammert, *Volksmedizin und medizinischer Aberglauber aus Bayern* (Wurzburg, 1869), p. 105; M. Toppen, *Aberglauben aus Masuren* (Danzig, 1867), p. 108; A. Witschel, *Sagen, Sitten und Gebräuche aus Thüringen* (Vienna, 1878), ii. p. 258; Panzer, *Beiträge zur deutschen Mythologie* (Munich, 1848–1855), i. p. 257; *Folk-Lore Journal*, ii. p. 170; C. Wachsmuth, *Das alte Griechenland im neuen* (Bonn, 1864), p. 119; Tettau und Temme, *Die Volkssagen Ostpreussens, Litauens und Westpreussens* (Berlin, 1837), p. 286; A. Kuhn, *Sagen, Gebräuche und Märchen aus Westphalen* (Leipsic, 1848), ii. p. 49.

by night, the Germans pour holy water before the door; the ghost is thought to stand and whimper on the further side.[1] In some parts of the North-East of Scotland after a death the neighbours did not yoke their horses unless there was a stream of running water between them and the house in which the dead body lay.[2]

In ancient Greece the relations washed themselves after the funerals.[3] So long as a corpse was in the house a vessel of water stood before the street door, that all who left the house might sprinkle themselves with it.[4] Sometimes after a death the house of mourning was sprinkled with salt water.[5] In old Rome the barrier of water after a death survived in a much attenuated form: it sufficed to carry water three times round the persons who had been engaged in the funeral and to sprinkle them with the water.[6] The ancient Scythians in mourning washed themselves and took a vapour bath.[7] A very peculiar case of our water barrier is recorded by Plutarch; he says that when a man had died of dropsy or consumption his children had to sit with their feet in water till the corpse had decayed.[8] Apparently,

[1] Wuttke, *op. cit.* § 748; Rochholz, *op. cit.* i. p. 186.

[2] Rev. Walter Gregor, *Notes on the Folk-Lore of the North-east of Scotland* (London, 1881), p. 207.

[3] Scholia on Aristophanes, *Clouds*, 838.

[4] Pollux, viii. 65; Hesychius and Suidas, *s.v.* ἀρδάνιον; cf. Wachsmuth, *op. cit.* p. 109.

[5] H. Roehl, *Inscriptiones Graecae Antiquissimae* (Berlin, 1883), No. 395; G. Dittenberger, *Sylloge Inscriptionum Graecarum*, No. 468; P. Cauer, *Delectus Inscriptionum Graecarum propter dialectum memorabilium*, 2 (Leipsic, 1883), No. 530.

[6] Virgil, *Aeneid*, vi. 228. Servius on this passage speaks of carrying *fire* round similarly. We shall return presently to the barrier of fire.

[7] Herodotus, iv. 73, 75.

[8] Plutarch, *De sera numinis vindicta*, c. 14.

although Plutarch does not say so, this was a precaution to prevent the ghost of a man who had died of dropsy from attacking his surviving children and afflicting them with the malady which had proved fatal to him. We have seen that among the Toradjas of Celebes mourners on returning from a funeral planted their feet in vessels of water, apparently to evade the pursuit of the ghost. For a similar purpose apparently, when a man has died of dropsy among the natives of Rajamahall in India, they do not bury the body but throw it into a river and then bathe themselves in another part of the river.[1] Thus they adopt in a double form the barrier of water against the ghost of a man who has died of dropsy; first they throw his body into a river and then they bathe themselves in another part of the same river, so making assurance doubly sure. Alike in the Greek and the Indian custom the notion seems to be that on homoeopathic principles water is the best preservative against death by dropsy. So similar is the rut in which error has flowed in ancient Greece and in modern India.

[1] Th. Shaw, "On the Inhabitants near Rajamahall", *Asiatic Researches*, iv. (Calcutta, 1795).

LECTURE III

LECTURE III

In the last lecture I dealt with some of the barriers which primitive man erects to prevent the spirits of the dead from returning to haunt and trouble the living; in particular I described the barrier of water which he sometimes adopts for that purpose. Often with the same object he has recourse to a barrier of fire.[1]

Thus, for example, among some of the Tartars it used to be customary for all persons returning from a burial to leap over a fire made for the purpose, "in order that the dead man might not follow them; for apparently in their opinion he would be afraid of the fire".[2]

In the like circumstances some Tartars instead of leaping over a fire used to pass between two fires, but the object of the passage was no doubt the same.[3]

Among the Yakut no one but the gravediggers accompanies a corpse to the grave, and even they hasten to complete their work and return home; on

[1] On the barrier of fire against the spirits of the dead, cf. *The Golden Bough*, Part IV. *Balder the Beautiful*, ii. pp. 17-19.

[2] J. G. Gmelin, *Reise durch Sibirien* (Göttingen, 1751-1752), i. 333.

[3] Johannes de Plano de Carpini, *Historia Mongolorum* (d'Avezac edition) (Paris, 1838), c. iv.

their way back they do not stop or look behind, and when they enter the gate of the village, they and the animals which drew the coffin to the grave must pass through a fire made of the straw on which the dead man lay and the wood left from the making of the coffin. Other things which have been in contact with the dead, such as the shovel, are also broken and burnt.[1] According to another authority, " the Yakut bury their dead as a rule on the day of the death, and in order not to take the demon of death home with them, they kindle fires on the way back from the burial and jump over them in the belief that the demon of death, who dreads fire, will not follow them, and that in this way they will be freed from the persecutions of the hated demon of death ".[2] In this passage the demon of death is probably a mistake of the writer for the ghost of the deceased ; the conception of a demon of death is by no means primitive. In Sikkim, when members of the Khambu caste have buried a corpse, all persons present at the burial " adjourn to a stream for a bath of purification, and, on re-entering the house, have to tread on a bit of burning cloth, to prevent the evil spirits who attend at funerals from following them in ".[3] Here again, the barrier of fire is probably directed not so much against evil spirits in general as against the spirit of the dead. It will be observed

[1] M. A. Czaplicka, *Aboriginal Siberia* (Oxford, 1914), p. 160.

[2] W. L. Priklonski, " Über das Schamanthum bei den Jakuten " in A. Bastian's *Allerlei aus Volks- und Menschenkunde* (Berlin, 1888), i. 319 ; cf. V. Priklonski, " Todtengebräuche der Jakuten ", *Globus*, lix. (1891) p. 85.

[3] J. A. H. Louis, *The Gates of Thibet* (Calcutta, 1894), p. 116.

that these people seek to protect themselves against the spiritual danger by a barrier of water as well as by a barrier of fire.

In China, after a corpse has been interred fires are kindled at the four corners of the cemetery to prevent the soul of the deceased from wandering away from the grave.[1] And when the funeral party returns to the house a fire of straw is kindled at the door, and all the members of the family pass over it and through the flames, after which they believe themselves to be safe from the pursuit of the ghost.[2] But sometimes as an additional precaution on entering the house, they wash their eyes with water in which the leaves of the pomeloe tree have been boiled.[3] Thus they reinforce the barrier of fire by a barrier of water. Again in China, when a coroner has been holding an inquest on a dead body, the mandarins who have attended the inquest step over a small fire before they enter their palanquins to be carried home, and the ceremony is repeated at the door of their house.[4]

Among the Oraons of Bengal on the return of a funeral party to the house a fire of chaff is kindled in the courtyard and oil poured on it to create a smoke. Over this smoke every one of the party places the palms of his or her hands by way of ceremonial purification.[5] Among the Birhors, a

[1] P. J. Dols, " La Vie chinoise dans la province de Kan-sou (Chine)", *Anthropos* x.-xi. (1915–1916) p. 756.

[2] Dols, *op. cit.* p. 741.

[3] J. H. Gray, *China* (London, 1878), i. p. 305; cf. p. 287.

[4] J. J. M. de Groot, *The Religious System of China* (Leyden, 1892), p. 137; cf. *id.* p. 32.

[5] Sarat Chandra Roy, *Oraon Religion and Customs* (Ranchi, 1928), p. 175.

primitive tribe of Chota Nagpur in India, after a body has been buried, standing at the grave the son or grandson of the deceased takes up a lighted torch in his right hand and some one stands beside him pressing his left eye with one hand. With his left eye thus closed, he walks round the grave three times, and then puts the torch over the corpse's mouth.[1] Thus the heir appears to place a barrier of fire between himself and the dead. And among the same people, when the funeral party has returned from the grave they bathe and have to undergo a further ceremony of purification by fire. In their absence a fire of charcoal has been prepared by the women, and on the approach of the funeral party a quantity of aromatic resin of the *sal* tree is sprinkled on the fire to produce a strong-smelling smoke. Arriving there each one of the party touches the fire with his left great toe and waves his left hand over the fire.[2] Thus, once more a barrier of fire reinforces a barrier of water. Among the Lakhers of Assam, when a dead man has been buried in another village, before leaving the lands of the village in which the funeral has taken place, a fire is kindled, and the visitors step over the fire. A disease-bearing spirit cannot pass over a fire and so is unable to follow the visitors home.[3] Among the Lhota Nagas, another tribe of Assam, when a death by accident has taken place, the friends of the dead man build a little shed and put some clothes and

[1] Sarat Chandra Roy, *The Birhors* (Ranchi, 1925), pp. 270, 271.

[2] Sarat Chandra Roy, *op. cit.* p. 272.

[3] N. E. Parry, *The Lakhers* (London, 1932), p. 405.

food in it. On the day after the death, an old man lights a fire in front of the house and sacrifices a cock. All the members of the family come out of the house stark naked and, after stepping over the fire, enter the shed, where they remain six days without speaking to any one, their food being provided by friends.[1] As we shall see later on, the ghosts of all persons who die by accident or violence are particularly dreaded, and special precautions have to be taken against them. The example of the Lhota Nagas is a case in point. Among these same Lhota Nagas, when a man has been drowned on a fishing expedition the accident is announced in the village before the return of the fishers. An old man thereupon comes forth from the village and lights a fire on the path by which the fishers are returning; and every one of the fishers must step over the fire before he returns to the village.[2] Among the lower castes of Upper India, when the mourners return from a funeral they touch a stone, cow-dung, iron, fire and water, which have been placed outside the house in readiness when the corpse was removed, and after a cremation the officiating Brahman touches fire in order to purify himself and to bar the return of the ghost.[3] In these latter cases the mere touching of fire is probably a later substitute for an older custom of stepping over it. In the Nicobar

[1] W. Crooke, *Religion and Folk-lore of Northern India*, edited by R. E. Enthoven (London, 1926), p. 239 *sq.*

[2] J. P. Mills, *The Lhota Nagas* (London, 1922), p. 162.

[3] W. Crooke, *The Popular Religion and Folklore of Northern India* (London, 1896), ii. p. 59.

Islands, while a dead body is lying in a house, a fire is kindled and maintained at the foot of the house ladder. The intention of the fire is said to be partly to keep the disembodied spirit far off, partly to apprise friends at a distance of the sad occurrence. The fire is either kindled directly by the friction of sticks or is obtained from another fire, which is known to have been so ignited.[1] From this account it appears that the soul of the deceased is supposed to have quitted the house before the burial, and the object of the fire is to prevent it from re-entering the dwelling.

In Africa also the barrier of fire against the spirits of the dead meets us in a variety of forms. Thus we read of a Bushman who, fearing to be haunted by the ghost of his dead wife, first dashed the head of the corpse to pieces, and after burying the body, lighted a fire upon the grave, as an additional precaution to prevent the return of her spirit.[2] Among the Tumbuka of Nyasaland, when a burial party is returning from the grave, they are met by a medicine-man who has kindled a great fire on the path into which he has thrown some roots; each member of the party must pass through the flames before he returns to the village.[3] Among the Atonga of what used to be called British Central Africa, mourners returning from the grave bathe in water. Then the chief undertaker fetches a torch of grass pulled from the

[1] E. H. Man, *The Nicobar Islands and their People* (London, n.d.), p. 133.

[2] Henry Lichtenstein, *Travels in Southern Africa* (London, 1815), ii. p. 61.

[3] D. Fraser, *Winning a Primitive People* (London, 1914), p. 159.

roof of the dead man's hut, lights it at the fire in the same hut, jumps over it himself, and then holds it a few inches from the ground for the whole party to jump over, one by one. After being rubbed with certain roots on back and front by a woman they are deemed to be sufficiently purified to return home.[1] Among the Boloki of the Upper Congo, a good instance of the barrier by fire was witnessed by Mr. Weeks; he says: "One day I saw an old woman whom I knew very well sitting in the centre of a ring of fire, and upon inquiry I found that she had had much to do with preparing a corpse for burial, and at the close of the ceremony she had to be purified. A ring of fire made of small sticks encircled her; she took a leaf, dried it, crunched it in her fist, and sprinkled it on the fire, moving her hands, palms downwards, over the fire ring. When the fire had died out a witch-doctor took hold of the little finger of her left hand with the little finger of his right hand, and, lifting her arm, he drew her out of the fire circle purified. She was now supposed to be cleansed from all contamination with the dead."[2] Among the Fangs of West Africa, after a month of mourning, the widows of the deceased are obliged to step across a fire in the middle of the village; and while some leaves are still burning under their feet, they sit down and their heads are shaved. From this moment they are purified from mourning, or, as the writer who reports it suggests, delivered from the

[1] A. Werner, *The Natives of British Central Africa* (London, 1906), pp. 162-163.

[2] J. H. Weeks, *Among Congo Cannibals* (London, 1913), p. 102.

ghost of their husband and they now can be passed on to his heirs.[1]

Among the Ewe-speaking people of the Slave Coast, "in Agweh a widow is supposed to remain shut up for six months in the room in which her husband is buried, during which time she may not wash or change her clothes. Food is carried to her by the family. According to report, in bygone days widows underwent a kind of fumigation in these burial chambers, a fire being lighted on the floor and strewn with red peppers, till they were nearly suffocated by the fumes. At the end of the period of mourning the widows wash, shave the head, pare the nails, and put on clean cloths; the old cloths, the hair and the nail-parings being burned. At Agweh men who have lost their head wives do this also, after having remained shut up in a room of the house for eight days."[2] The purification of widows by fire and water on the Gold Coast has been described as follows by Miss Mary Kingsley. "To the surf and its spirits the sea-board dwelling Tschwis bring women who have had children and widows, both after a period of eight days from the birth of the child, or the death of the husband. A widow remains in the house until this period has elapsed, neglecting her person, eating little food, and sitting on the bare floor in the attitude of mourning. On the Gold Coast they bury very quickly, as they are

[1] E. Allegret, "Les Idées religieuses des Fañs (Afrique Occidentale)", *Revue de l'Histoire des Religions*, i. (1904) p. 220.

[2] A. B. Ellis, *The Ewe-Speaking Peoples of the Slave Coast of West Africa* (London, 1890), p. 160.

always telling you, usually on the day after death, rarely later than the third day, even among the natives, and the spirit, or *srah*, of the dead man is supposed to hang about his wives and his house until the ceremony of purification is carried out. This is done, needless to say, with uproar. The relatives of each wife go to her house with musical instruments —I mean tom-toms and that sort of thing—and they take a quantity of mint, which grows wild in this country, with them. This mint they burn, some of it in the house, the rest they place upon pans of live coals and carry round the widow as she goes in their midst down to the surf, her relatives singing aloud to the *srah* of the departed husband, telling him that now he is dead and has done with the lady, he must leave her. This singing serves to warn all the women who are not relations to get out of the way, which of course they always carefully do, because if they were to see the widow their own husbands would die within the year." Arrived at the surf, they strip every rag off the widow and throw it into the surf; and the widow is arrayed in a suit of dark blue baft in which she returns home.[1]

The Goajire Indians of Colombia keep up great fires at night in the village to ward off the ghosts of their dead enemies, who are apt to come and attack them with knives in the darkness; but protected by this barrier of fire they feel themselves quite safe from their invisible foes.[2] And in the same tribe

[1] Mary H. Kingsley, *Travels in West Africa* (London, 1897), p. 515.

[2] H. Candelier, *Rio Hacha et les Indiens Goajires* (Paris, 1893), p. 171.

when a man has been buried custom requires that his nearest relatives should keep up a great fire near the grave for nine days after the burial, to protect their deceased kinsman from the ghosts of their dead enemies, who would otherwise come to molest him ; for according to their belief life is not really extinct until nine days after death.[1] In this case it will be observed that the barrier of fire is directed not against the ghost of a dead friend, but against the ghosts of dead enemies, who might come by night to injure him.

In Europe also the barrier of fire against ghosts has not been unknown. In Mecklenburg, if fire and water are thrown after the corpse as it is being carried out the ghost will not afterwards appear in the house.[2] In ancient Rome, no doubt for a similar purpose, mourners returning from a funeral used to step over fire.[3] Some South Slavonians returning from a funeral are met by an old woman carrying a vessel of live coals. On these they pour water, or else take a live coal from the hearth and fling it over their heads.[4] In Ruthenia the barrier of fire against a ghost is still more attenuated ; mourners merely look steadfastly on the stove or place their hands upon it.[5]

So much for the barriers which primitive man erects to protect himself against the return of the spirit of the dead, but even when he has driven away

[1] *Op. cit.* p. 220.

[2] Bartschl, *Sagen, Märchen und Gebräuche aus Mecklenburg* (Vienna, 1879–1880), ii. p. 96.

[3] Festus, *s.v. aqua et igne.*

[4] W. R. Ralston, *Songs of the Russian People* (London, 1872), p. 320.

[5] W. R. Ralston, *loc. cit.*

these dangerous spirits and placed obstacles in the way of their return, he is still far from feeling easy, he still fears that they may break through the obstacles and return to haunt and torment the living. He is not, however, at the end of his resources, he has still many devices by which he hopes to bar the return of the ghosts, or at all events to render them impotent for mischief. Thus, for instance, failing as usual to distinguish the spiritual from the corporeal, he imagines that by tying up or mutilating and maiming a corpse he simultaneously ties up or mutilates and maims the dead person's ghost in exactly the same manner. To take instances: the Dieri of Central Australia used to tie the great toes and the thumbs of a corpse together to prevent the ghost from walking. The ceremony was witnessed by a constable, who describes it as follows: "Some of the younger men went off to dig a grave, and the elder ones proceeded to tie the great toes of the body together very securely, with strong, stout string, and then tied both the thumbs together behind the back, the body being turned face downwards whilst the latter operation was going on. From the manner in which the strings were tightened and the care taken over that part of the business, one would think that even a strong, healthy living man could not break or rise from such bonds. In reply to me they said that the tying was to prevent him from 'walking'."[1] Among the natives of the Herbert River in South-

[1] R. Brough Smyth, *The Aborigines of Victoria* (London, 1878), i. p. 119.

East Australia a near relative of the deceased used to beat the corpse with a mallet so violently as often to break the bones. Incisions were also generally made in the stomach, on the shoulder and in the lungs and filled with stones. The legs were generally broken for the express purpose of preventing the dead man from walking at night. The beating of the body, we are told, was for the sake of so frightening the ghost as to prevent it from haunting the camp, and the stones were put in the body to prevent it going too far afield.[1] Speaking of the natives of Queensland the Swedish traveller Lumholtz says: "The fact that the natives bestow any care on the bodies of the dead is doubtless owing to their fear of the spirits of the departed. In some places I have seen the legs drawn up and tied fast to the bodies, in order to hinder the spirits of the dead, as it were, from getting out to frighten the living. Women and children, whose spirits are not feared, receive less attention and care after death."[2] And speaking of the Australian aborigines in general another authority observes: "When a man dies, it is a very widely-spread custom for the relations to tie up the limbs of the corpse securely, so as to prevent his coming out of the grave in the shape of a ghost".[3] The same writer describes as follows the usual mode of burial among the Australian aborigines: "Shortly after death, the body, in the

[1] A. W. Howitt, *The Native Tribes of South-Eastern Australia* (London, 1904), p. 474.

[2] C. Lumholtz, *Among Cannibals* (London, 1889), pp. 277-278.

[3] E. M. Curr, *The Australian Race* (Melbourne and London, 1886), i. p. 44.

case of a man, is reduced as nearly as possible to the shape of a ball. To effect this the knees are forced up to the neck and firmly tied to it; the heels are then pressed against the hams, the arms lie flat along the sides, and are secured in each instance in these positions by cords. Some tribes tie the thumbs together; others burn the thumb nails besides. . . . The object sought in tying up the remains of the dead is to prevent the deceased from escaping from the tomb and frightening or injuring the survivors. The more nearly related and more influential in life, the more the deceased is feared." [1] To take some particular examples, concerning the natives near Newcastle in Western Australia, we are told that, "in burying the dead, besides taking off the finger nails, the thumb and forefinger of each hand are tied tightly together, with the object of preventing the corpse from escaping from the tomb and frightening the survivors. The more nearly an individual is related to the deceased the greater is his fear of the ghost." [2] Again, about the natives near Perth in Western Australia it is recorded that: "The limbs of the corpse are securely tied together with bands of rushes or bark, so as, if possible, to hinder it from getting out of the grave and wandering about in the shape of a ghost, of which the Australian Black in all parts is perpetually apprehensive".[3] Again, concerning the Whajook tribe in Western Australia, we read that: "Before interment the hair is cut off

[1] E. M. Curr, *op. cit.* i. p. 87.

[2] G. Whitfield in E. Curr's *The Australian Race*, i. p. 324.

[3] E. M. Curr, *op. cit.* i. p. 330.

and the nails burnt. This, and the binding of the corpse into the shape of a ball, are to prevent its escape from the grave."[1] Once more, concerning the natives in the neighbourhood of King George's Sound we are informed that at burial "the knees of the corpse are doubled up and tied; the forefinger and thumb of the right hand are tied together, the thumb nail is burnt off, to prevent, as they say, the deceased digging his way out and using his spears".[2]

It is reported that, in most parts of Central Borneo, when a death has taken place the corpse is brought out from the chamber into the common room of the house and there securely fastened down to the floor by bandages, tightened by pegs, which are passed round the arms and legs, the neck, the chest, and the trunk, constricting the body in such a way that even a strong living man would not be able to get up. The object of this constriction is said to be to prevent the ghost from returning to the body and doing harm to the living.[3] Among the Taungthu, a widely spread race of Upper Burma, when a man dies the thumbs and great toes of the corpse are tied together, and this is said by some to be intended to hinder the dead man from walking.[4] With a similar object we are told the ancient Indians used to put fetters on the feet of their dead, in order to prevent their ghosts from returning to the land of

[1] E. M. Curr, *op. cit.* i. p. 339.

[2] E. M. Curr, *op. cit.* i. p. 348.

[3] Oscar von Kessel, "Über die Volksstämme Borneos", *Zeitschrift für allgemeine Erdkunde*, N.F. iii. (1857) pp. 377-410.

[4] J. G. Scott and J. P. Hardiman, *Gazetteer of Upper Burma*, Part I. i. (Rangoon, 1900) p. 554.

the living and molesting the survivors.[1] Among the Chuvash of Russia, when a very ugly man has died, they fasten his corpse down into the grave with iron, lest his ghost should come back to scare living folk by his ungainly appearance.[2]

And whenever a wicked and quarrelsome man dies they think that his ghost will certainly return to wreak its spite upon the living. In order to obviate this danger they take strong measures to hinder the man, or rather his ghost, from escaping from the coffin ; they drive nails through the heart and soles of the feet of the corpse ; they nail the coffin securely down, and to make assurance still surer they constrict it with iron hoops.[3] Similarly, among the Cheremiss, a neighbouring tribe of Russia, when a bad man dies they drive nails through his heart and the soles of his feet to prevent his ghost from coming back and harming the survivors.[4] Among the Barundi of Central Africa when a person has died the men tie the limbs of the corpse tightly together on purpose, it is said, to prevent the return of the ghost, which they greatly fear.[5]

In America among the Tupinambas of Brazil the custom at burial is said to have been as follows: " The corpse had all its limbs tied fast, that it might

[1] H. Zimmer, *Altindisches Leben* (Berlin, 1879), p. 402.

[2] H. Vambéry, *Das Türkenvolk* (Leipsig, 1885), p. 462.

[3] A. Erman, " Briefliche Nachrichten über die Tschuwaschen und die Tscheremisen des Gouvernments Kaspan ", *Archiv für wissenschaftliche Kunde von Russland*, i. (1841) p. 376.

[4] A. F. von Haxthausen, *Studien über die innern Zustände, das Volksleben und inbesondere die ländlichen Einrichtungen Russlands* (Hannover, 1847), i. p. 449m.

[5] Hans Meyer, *Die Barundi* (Leipsic, 1916), p. 113.

not be able to get up and infest its friends with its visits ".[1] A custom curiously different from the foregoing is reported of some of the Eskimo at Bering Strait. The corpse is tied up in a bundle with cord, the head being forced down between the knees, and in this state it is drawn up through the smoke hole in the roof and carried to the graveyard till the coffin is ready for it. Just before the body is placed in the coffin the cords that bind it are cut, in order, they say, that the ghost may return and occupy the body and move about if necessary.[2] In this case the cords which bind the body are clearly supposed to bind the ghost also, but the custom of untying them before placing the body in the coffin indicates that these Eskimo do not greatly dread a possible return of the ghost to its mortal remains in the grave.

So much for the custom of tying up the corpse in order to prevent the ghost from roving and doing a mischief to the survivors, but for the same purpose primitive man sometimes resorts to still stronger measures. He breaks the bones of the dead body, or otherwise mutilates it in such a fashion as would disable a living man, thinking thus to disable the ghost in a precisely similar manner. We have seen that some of the Australian aborigines break the legs of the dead to hinder their ghosts from walking.

A tribe of the Cameroons in West Africa adopted still more forcible measures for accomplishing the

[1] Robert Southey, *History of Brazil*, i. (1817) (London, 1817) p. 258.

[2] E. W. Nelson, " The Eskimo about Bering Strait", *18th Annual Report of the Bureau of American Ethnology* (1896–1897), Part I. (1899) p. 314.

same purpose; as described by Dr. Nassau, an excellent authority, the custom was as follows. "Of one tribe in the upper course of the Ogowe, I was told, who, in their intense fear of ghosts, and their dread of the possible evil influence of the spirits of their own dead relatives, sometimes adopt a horrible plan for preventing their return. With a very material idea of a spirit, they seek to disable it by beating the corpse until every bone is broken. The mangled mass is hung in a bag at the foot of a tree in the forest. Thus mutilated the spirit is supposed to be unable to return to the village, to entice into its fellowship of death any of the survivors."[1] Among the Afars, a Danakil tribe on the southern borders of Abyssinia, all the bones of a corpse are broken before it is buried.[2] The motive for doing so is not mentioned by our authority, but we may conjecture that the object is thereby to render the ghost helpless. Among the Herero or Damara of South-West Africa, the backbone of a corpse is broken immediately after death. "The Herero say that in the spinal cord lives a small worm (maggot) which becomes after death the ghost of the deceased. This can be killed by fracturing the backbone: hence the proceeding here mentioned."[3] Thus it would appear that the Herero adopt the radical expedient of not merely

[1] Rev. R. H. Nassau, *Fetichism in West Africa* (London, 1904), p. 234.

[2] Ph. Paulitsche, *Ethnographie Nordost Afrikas. Die materielle Cultur der Danâkil, Galla und Somâl* (Berlin, 1893), p. 205.

[3] The Rev. G. Viehe, "Some Customs of the Ovaherero", *South African Folk-Lore Journal*, i. Part III. (May 1879) p. 55; cf. C. J. Anderson, *Lake Ngami* (London, 1856), p. 226; P. H. Brincker, "Beobachtungen über die Deisidämonie der Eingeborenen Deutsch-Südwest-Afrikas", *Globus*, lviii. (1890) p. 322.

disabling but killing the ghost. To this practice of killing the ghost we shall return later on.

Among the Kissi on the borders of Liberia the souls of dead witches and wizards are greatly dreaded. And when one of these folk dies the people smash his or her skull with heavy blows of a stone, believing that if this precaution is not adopted the ghost would issue from the grave on the third day after death and returning to the houses would beat the inhabitants and carry off their goods.[1] Of the Indians of the Californian Peninsula in North America we are told that formerly they had broken the spine of the deceased before burying them, and had thrown them into the ditch rolled up like a ball, believing that they would rise up again if not treated in this manner.[2]

But the breaking of the bones of the corpse is not the only mutilation of the body to which primitive man resorts for the purpose of disabling the ghost. He sometimes maims or mangles the body in other ways at least as radical. Thus with regard to the Kwearriburra tribe of Queensland in Australia we are told "that unless strong preventive measures are taken, the spirits of departed members of the tribe rise from their graves and continually haunt and otherwise annoy those who are still in the flesh. Accordingly, elaborate precautions are adopted, to keep the unfortunate ghosts confined in the grave

[1] H. Néel, "Note sur deux peuplades de la frontière Libérienne, les Kissi et les Toma", *L'Anthropologie*, xxiv. (1913) p. 462.

[2] *Account of the Aboriginal Inhabitants of the Californian Peninsula, etc. Report of the Smithsonian Institution for 1864*, p. 387.

which holds their mortal clay. The *modus operandi* is as follows: On the death of a member of the tribe, his or her head is cut off and the trunk placed in a grave in the usual squatting position, and covered up. A fire is then lighted on the top, in which the head is roasted; when it is thoroughly charred it is broken up into little bits amongst the hot coals, and the fire is then left to die gradually out. The theory is that the spirit rising from the grave to follow the tribe misses its head, and goes groping about to find it; but being bereft of its head, it is of course blind, and therefore, not being able to see the fire, gets burnt. This frightens it so terribly that it retires into the grave again with all expedition, and never again presumes to attempt a renewal of social intercourse with the human denizens of this world."[1] Among the natives of Australia others cut off the thumbs of their dead enemies in order that their ghosts may not be able to throw spears.[2]

For a similar purpose apparently when the Tupi Indians of Brazil killed and ate a prisoner they cut off his thumb because of its use in archery, but they did not eat it with the rest of the body.[3] Other Australian aborigines put hot coals in the ears of a corpse to keep the soul in the body and prevent it from following them till they have got a good start away from him. As a further precaution they bark the

[1] F. C. Urquhart, "Legends of the Australian Aborigines", *Journal of the Anthropological Institute*, xiv. (1885) p. 88.

[2] A. Oldfield, "On the Aborigines of Australia", *Transactions of the Ethnological Society of London*, N.S. iii. (1865) p. 287.

[3] R. Southey, *History of Brazil*, vol. i. Second Edition (London, 1822), p. 231.

trees in a circle round the spot, so that when the ghost succeeds in extricating himself from the body and setting off in pursuit of his friends, he may wander round and round in a circle and never overtake them.[1]

The Toradjas of Central Celebes believe that men can become werewolves. When a man has been found guilty of this horrible crime they take him to a lonely spot and hack him to pieces, but they fear that if they were bespattered with his blood they would themselves be turned into werewolves. Further, they place the severed head of the werewolf beside his hinder-quarters, with the avowed intention of hindering his soul from coming to life again and pursuing his depredations.[2]

The Birhors of Bengal believe that the ghost of a woman who dies within a short time of childbirth is very dangerous, and to prevent her ghost from issuing from the grave they prick the soles of her feet with thorns.[3] Similarly the Sântals, another primitive people of Bengal, believe that the ghosts of a certain class of women are very dangerous. They are supposed to lick their victims to death, filing off their flesh with their rough tongues. When any of these women die, the survivors slide thorns into the soles of their feet, thus rendering them lame and powerless to pursue their victims.[4]

[1] A. W. Howitt, *Native Tribes of South-East Australia* (London, 1904), p. 473.

[2] A. C. Kruijt "De weerwolf bij de Toradja's van Midden-Celebes", *Tijdschrift voor Indische Taal-, Land- en Volkenkunde*, Deel xli. (1899) p. 559.

[3] S. Chandra Roy, *The Birhors* (Ranchi, 1925), p. 267.

[4] Rev. F. T. Cole, "Sântâl Ideas of the Future Life", *Indian Antiquary*, vii. (1878) p. 274.

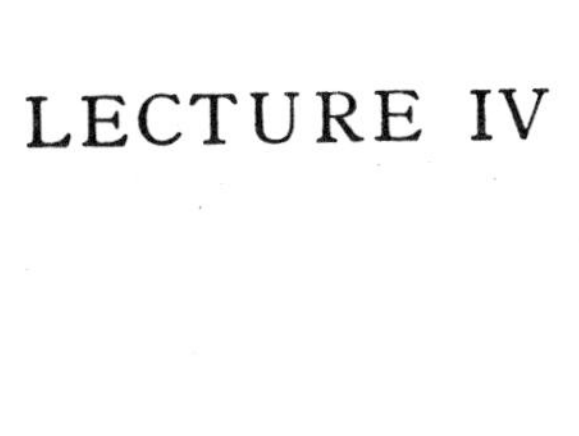

LECTURE IV

LECTURE IV

In the last lecture I dealt with some of the devices to which primitive man resorts for preventing the dangerous spirits of the dead from returning to attack the living. I illustrated the barrier of fire which he seeks to interpose between himself and the ghosts. Further I described some of the other very different ways in which he attempts to achieve the same object by tying up or mutilating the corpse, in the belief that by so doing he disables the ghost from doing any harm to the survivors. I propose now to illustrate this custom further by examples drawn from Africa, America and Europe.

In Africa, among the natives of the Gabun district of West Africa, "people who while they were living were supposed to have witch power are believed to be able to rise in altered form from their graves. To prevent one who is thus suspected from making trouble, survivors open the grave, cut off the head, and throw it into the sea,—or in the interior, where there is no great body of water it is burned; then a decoction of the bolondo bark is put into the grave. (The bolondo is a poison; even a little of it may be fatal.)"[1] Thus these natives appear to

[1] R. H. Nassau, *Fetichism in West Africa* (London, 1904), p. 220.

think that if decapitation should fail to disable the ghost poison will have the desired effect. An old writer of the eighteenth century has described these West African practices in more detail. He tells us that when a case of sickness was ascribed to the action of the malignant ghost of a man who had lately died, they used to dig up the body and cut off the head, from which they asserted that blood flowed : this blood they collected and made out of it plasters which they applied to the body of the sick man and mixed with his food, and drink, assuring him of a speedy recovery, since the dead man, having had his head cut off, had no longer strength to come and disturb him. But the case was deemed much more difficult when the man whose spirit was tormenting the patient had not been buried, because he had been killed and eaten by his enemies or by wild beasts. In that case the medicine-man spread nets round the house of the sick man and even into the forest, in order that the soul of the dead man might be caught in the net when he came to annoy the sufferer. When a bird, rat, lizard, ape or other animal was caught in the net it was taken to be the incarnation of the dead man's soul. The medicine-man took it to the sick man and said : " Rejoice ; we've got him ; he shan't escape ". But before he killed the animal he demanded another fee. When this was agreed to he killed the animal, to the sick man's joy. But to prevent the soul returning the animal must be ground to powder and swallowed by the sick man. When the man had swallowed it, digested it and voided it they thought that he was finally rid of the tormenting ghost.[1] The Mossi of the Western Sudan have a great respect for their chiefs during their life but treat their bodies with something less than respect after their death. As soon as a chief has died they pierce his hands and feet with large thorns to prevent his ghost from returning to catch and carry off one of his relatives, for they think that if he attempted to seize somebody the thorns would hurt him so grievously that he would at once relinquish his intended prey. The corpse is then thrown into a ditch.[2] The Ba-Ila-speaking people of Northern Rhodesia regard with great contempt any man who dies childless. When such a one dies " they cut off his little finger and little toe, and enclose a piece of charcoal in his fist, before burying him. Their reason for doing this is obscure. They suppose that it will either prevent his being reborn, or if it fails to that extent, at least they will be able to recognize him by the absence of those members should he return to earth."[3] Among the Wawanga of the Mount Elgon district in Kenya, when a case of illness is attributed to the action of a malignant ghost, they will sometimes dig up the body of the suspected man and burn the bones over a nest of red ants, and the ashes are swept into a basket and thrown into a river. But sometimes instead of digging up the body the relatives of the

[1] J. B. Labat, *Relation historique de l'Éthiopie Occidentale* (Paris, 1732), ii. pp. 209-212.

[2] P. E. Mangin, " Les Mossi ", *Anthropos*, ix. (1914) p. 732.

[3] E. W. Smith and A. M. Dale, *The Ila-Speaking Peoples of Northern Rhodesia*, ii. (London, 1920) p. 1.

sick man drive a stake into the head of the grave, and, to make assurance doubly sure, pour boiling water down after it.[1] This is no doubt thought to give a final quietus to the ghost who is causing the illness. Among the Ovambo of South-West Africa, the souls of dead magicians are especially dreaded. Hence, when a magician dies it is customary to dismember the body and to cut the tongue out of the mouth. They think that if these precautions are adopted the soul of the dead man cannot become a dangerous ghost; the mutilation of the body has practically disarmed his spirit.[2]

The custom of decapitating a corpse in order to disable the dangerous ghost which we have seen practised in Australia and Africa, is observed also by the Armenians. They not only cut off the head but smash it or stick a needle into it or into the dead man's heart.[3]

In America, among the Eskimo about Bering Strait, when a man of evil reputation died they used to cut the sinews of his arms and legs to prevent his ghost from returning to the body and causing it to walk about at night as a ghoul.[4] The Rev. J. Owen Dorsey, our highest authority on the Omahas, was told by these Indians that "when a man was killed by lightning, he ought to be buried face downwards and the soles of his feet had to be slit. When this

[1] Hon. K. R. Dundas, "The Wawanga and Other Tribes of the Elgon District of British East Africa", *Journal of the Royal Anthropological Institute*, xliii. (1913) p. 38.

[2] Herman Tönjes, *Ovamboland, Land, Leute, Mission* (Berlin, 1911), pp. 193-197.

[3] M. Abeghian, *Der armenische Volksglaube* (Leipsic, 1899), p. 11.

[4] E. W. Nelson, "The Eskimo about Bering Strait", *18th Annual Report of the Bureau of American Ethnology*, 1896–97 (1899), p. 423.

was done, the spirit went at once to the spirit land, without giving further trouble to the living. In one case (that of a Wejinecte man, Jadegi, according to George Miller and Frank La Fléche) this was not done, so it was said that the ghost *walked*, and he did not rest in peace till another person (his brother) was slain by lightning and laid beside him."[1]

The Lengua Indians of the Paraguaian Chaco inflict on the bodies of the dead or dying certain strange mutilations, the exact object of which is not clear, though some of them appear certainly to be directed not so much against the ghost of the deceased as against the sorcerer who is suspected of having caused the death. These mutilations are described as follows by the Rev. W. Grubb, our best authority on these Indians. "In some cases the only peculiar rite is the placing of hot embers beneath the feet of the corpse and on the head. If, however, the seat of trouble has been in the head, after the body has been placed in the grave they batter the skull with clubs; if in the region of the heart, arrows are shot into it, and sometimes a stake is driven through the shoulder and slanting out below the ribs, thus pinning the body to the side of the grave. In the case of dropsy, the body is shot at, and a bunch of herbs is held by the man conducting the burial. This is afterwards burnt, and each of the party swallows some of the smoke. The meaning of these and many more rites which are

[1] J. O. Dorsey, "A Study of Siouan Cults", *11th Annual Report of the Bureau of American Ethnology*, 1889–90 (1894), p. 420.

used I do not fully understand, and I have had opportunities of witnessing only some of them. A very common rite, however, is the cutting open of the side, and the insertion into the wound thus made of heated stones, an armadillo's claw, some dog's bones, and occasionally red ants. The wound is then closed. In cases where haste is necessary, as it always is if the funeral takes place towards sunset, the sick person is not always dead when this operation is performed. In any case, to be efficacious, it must be performed, if not before actual death, certainly immediately afterwards, and before the spirit is supposed to have left the vicinity of the body. The stones are thought to have knowledge communicated by the soul of the dying or dead person, who, being freed from the limitations of the body, is able to recognize more clearly the originator of the trouble. They are supposed to ascend to the Milky Way, and there remain until they find an opportunity to descend on the author of the evil in the form of shooting stars. Consequently the Indians are very frightened when they see a falling star. They have all been guilty in their time, or are supposed to have been guilty, of causing some evil to others, and they are never sure when vengeance in this form may be wreaked on them from some distant quarter."[1]

On these mutilations it may be observed that they are clearly intended to effect the soul of the dead or

[1] W. B. Grubb, *An Unknown People in an Unknown Land* (London, 1911), pp. 162, 163.

dying man since they must be inflicted on his body before the soul has quitted it. Apparently they are intended to enable the ghost to avenge himself upon the supposed author of his death rather than to prevent him from injuring other people. So far therefore they differ from most of the other mutilations which we have passed in review, but in them as in the other preceding cases is involved the fundamental fallacy of imagining that you can influence a disembodied spirit by inflicting certain injuries on its mortal remains. It is the old, the ever recurring confusion of body and spirit.

In civilized Europe itself the custom of mangling a dead body for the purpose of maiming and disabling the dangerous ghost of the deceased has not been unknown. Ancient Greek murderers used to cut off the extremities, such as the ears and noses, of their victims, fasten them on a string, and tie the string round the necks and under the armpits of the murdered man. One motive assigned for this custom, and probably the original one, was the wish to weaken him so that he, or rather his ghost, could not take vengeance on his murderer. According to one account (a Scholiast on Sophocles, *Electra*, 445) the murderer fastened the extremities of his victim about his own person, but the better attested and more probable account is that he tied them about the mutilated body of his victim.[1] The practice is

[1] Scholiast on Sophocles, *Electra*, 445; Suidas, *s.v* *μασχαλισθῆναι*. Hesychius and Photius, *Lexicon*, *s.v.* *μασχαλίσματα*; Scholiast on Apollonius Rhodius, *Argon*. iv. 477; cf. E. Rohde, *Psyche*, i. 322-326. R. C. Jebb, on Sophocles, *Electra*, 445, with the Appendix, pp. 211 *sqq*.

perhaps illustrated by an original drawing in the Ambrosian manuscript of the *Iliad*, which represents the Homeric episode of Dolon;[1] in the drawing the corpse of the slain Dolon is depicted shorn of its feet and hands, which lie beside it, while Ulysses holds Dolon's severed head in his hand.[2]

"'The greatest marvel that I know', says Walter Map, concerned a Welsh malefactor and unbeliever. He died in the house of William Laudun, a brave soldier, who told the Bishop of Hereford how the Welshman returned night by night, and summoned his fellow-lodgers by name, when they became ill and died in three days. Now only a few survived. The Bishop thought that God might have given permission to the evil angel of the man to make his dead body restless. He advised Laudun to dig up the corpse, cut the neck, sprinkle the body and grave with holy water, and rebury it. In spite of this being done, the survivors were still assailed, and finally Laudun himself was summoned. He drew his sword and pursued the malefactor to the grave and clave its head to the neck. The trouble now ceased, and Laudun did not die as a result of the summons."[3]

The medieval Danish historian Saxo Grammaticus has recorded how, when a pestilence was raging, the misfortune was attributed to the angry

[1] *Iliad*, x. 314.

[2] *Annali dell' Instituto di Corrospondeza Archeologica* (Rome, 1875), tav. d' agg. R.; A. Baumeister, *Denkmäler des klassichen Altertums*, i. 460 *sq.*, Fig. 506.

[3] J. A. MacCulloch, *Medieval Faith and Fable* (London, 1932), p. 90, referring to Walter Map, ii. 27.

ghost of a man who had been killed in a popular tumult shortly before. To remedy the evil they dug up his body, cut off the head and ran a sharp stake through the breast of the corpse. The remedy proved effectual, for the plague ceased.[1] In 1710 when a great pestilence was raging in East Prussia the authorities gave orders that the graves should be opened and the bodies dug up in order to detect the malefactor whose ghost was causing the mischief. Suspicion at last fell upon one, who seems to have inflicted some wounds upon himself, so the corpse was decapitated and the headless body thrown back into the grave with a live dog to keep it company. But strange to say, even after these strong measures had been taken, the plague still continued.[2]

In Eastern Europe from Prussia on the north to Macedonia and Greece on the south, the belief in vampires has been and still is rampant. Vampires are malicious ghosts who issue from their graves to suck the blood of the living, and stringent measures are deemed necessary to hinder or arrest this horrible proceeding. In East Prussia when a person is believed to be suffering from the attacks of a vampire and suspicion falls on the ghost of somebody who died lately, the only remedy is thought to be for the family of the deceased to go to his grave, dig up his body, behead it and place the head between the legs of the corpse. If blood flows from the severed head the man was certainly a vampire,

[1] Saxo Grammaticus, *Historia Danica*, lib. I. ed. P. E. Müller (Havniae, 1836), i. p. 43.

[2] M. Toeppen, *Aberglauben aus Masuren* (Danzig, 1867), p. 114.

and the family must drink of the flowing blood, thus recovering the blood which had been sucked from their living bodies by the vampire.[1] Thus the vampire is paid out in kind.

In Serbia and Bulgaria, to prevent a man from becoming a vampire they stick a whitethorn into the navel of his corpse, and burn off all the hair on his body except on the head. Further, they slit the soles of his feet and drive a nail into the back of his head to prevent the skin from being blown up by the devil.[2] These measures are preventive, but to put an end to a vampire his corpse is staked and burned. The stake with which his body is pierced should be of hawthorn. If a butterfly escapes from the grave while the corpse is being stabbed the people run after it, catch it and throw it on a fire. That is the end of the vampire. But if the butterfly escape, woe to the village, for the vampire will avenge himself on the inhabitants till his seven years are up. Some say the vampire should be stabbed with a knife that has never been used to cut bread. Some say the stab should be given through the dried hide of a young bull, for they believe that whoever is sprinkled with the blood of a vampire will himself become a vampire and will soon die. In the Drina district of Bosnia, on the borders of Bosnia, the priest goes at the head of the peasantry to the graveyard; they open the grave,

[1] W. J. U. Tettau und J. D. H. Temme, *Die Volkssagen Ostpreussens, Litauens und Westpreussens* (Berlin, 1835), p. 275.

[2] F. S. Krauss, "Vampyre in südslawischen Volksglauben", *Globus*, lxi. (1892) p. 326.

fill it with straw; stab the corpse through the straw with a stake of hawthorn, and set fire to the straw. The fire is kept up till the vampire is reduced to ashes. That prevents his return to plague people.[1] In Wallachia to prevent a man from becoming a vampire they run a long nail through the skull of the corpse, and lay a thorny rose bush on his body, in the hope that should he struggle to emerge from the grave the thorns will so entangle him in his shroud that he will not be able to extricate himself from it and so will remain quietly in the grave.[2] Among the Roumanians of Transylvania the custom and belief concerning vampires are similar. They think that there are two sorts of vampires, either living or dead. The living vampire is generally the illegitimate offspring of two illegitimate persons; but even a flawless pedigree will not ensure any one against the intrusion of a vampire into the family vault, since every one killed by a vampire becomes likewise a vampire after death, and will continue to suck the blood of other innocent persons until the ghost has been exorcised by opening the grave and either driving a stake through the corpse or else firing a pistol shot into the coffin. To walk smoking round the grave on each anniversary of the death, is also supposed to be effective in confining the vampire; this is clearly a mild form of the barrier by fire. In very obstinate cases of vampirism it is recommended to cut off the head and replace it in

[1] F. S. Krauss, "Südslavische Schutzmittel gegen Vampyre", *Globus*, lxii. (1892) p. 203 *sq*.

[2] Arthur und Albert Schott, *Walachische Mährchen* (Stuttgart, 1845), p. 298.

the coffin with the mouth filled with garlic; or to extract the heart and burn it, strewing the ashes over the grave. Every Roumanian village has some old woman versed in the modes of laying vampires. Sometimes she drives a nail through the forehead of the deceased, or she rubs the body with the fat of a pig which has been killed on the Feast of Ignatius, five days before Christmas. It is also very usual to place the thorny branch of a wild-rose bush across the body to prevent it leaving the coffin.[1]

The belief in the blood-sucking ghost which we call vampires is also widely spread amongst the modern Greeks, who may possibly have borrowed it from their northern neighbours the Slavs. To put an end to the depredations of a vampire they dig up the body of the suspected person, cut out the heart and burn it over the corpse, or as an alternative they burn it with the whole body.[2] "The accordance between the Greek and Slavonic conceptions of the vampire", says Mr. G. F. Abbott, "is nowhere more apparent than in Macedonia, a province which for many centuries past has been the meeting-point of Slav and Hellene. It is believed that a dead person turns into a vampire (*βρυκολακιάζει*), first, if at the unearthing of the body the latter is found undecayed and turned face downwards. In such an emergency the relatives of the deceased have recourse to a ceremony which fills the beholder with sickening horror. I was credibly informed of a

[1] E. Gerard, *The Land beyond the Forest* (Edinburgh and London, 1888), i. p. 13.

[2] B. Schmidt, *Das Volksleben der Neugriechen* (Leipzig, 1871), p. 167.

case of this description occurring not long ago at Alistrati, one of the principal villages between Serres and Drama. Someone was suspected of having turned into a vampire. The corpse was taken out of the grave, scalded with boiling oil, and was pierced through the navel with a long nail. Then the tomb was covered in, and millet was scattered over it, that, if the vampire came out again, he might waste his time in picking up the grains of millet and be thus overtaken by dawn. For the usual period of their wanderings is from about two hours before midnight till the first crowing of the morning cock."[1]

In some of the foregoing cases the treatment of the body of a vampire appears to be intended not merely to disable but to destroy the blood-sucking ghost. There is other evidence pointing to the conclusion that primitive man has clearly conceived the possibility of actually killing a dangerous ghost and so putting an end to it once and for all. From his point of view this mode of dealing with the spirit is clearly the most satisfactory of all ; for the ghost once dead can give no more trouble.

To take examples, the Mori-oris, the inhabitants of the Chatham Islands off New Zealand, believed that " after death, the spirit of the departed had power to return to earth and haunt the living, and that a person visited by the *kiko-kiko* (or evil spirit of the dead), and touched on the head by it, would die very soon after such visitation. To prevent the

[1] G. F. Abbott, *Macedonian Folklore* (Cambridge, 1903), pp. 218, 219.

dead from troubling them, they had a curious custom. As soon as breath had left the body, they would all assemble at midnight in some secluded spot, and proceed to kill the *kiko-kiko*. First, kindling a large fire, they would sit round in a circle, each person holding a long rod in his hand ; to the end of each rod a tuft of spear grass was tied ; they would then sway their bodies to and fro, waving the rods over the fire in every direction, jabbering strange and unintelligible incantations." By this means they appear to have imagined that they killed the dangerous ghost.[1]

In the island of Mangaia, in the Central Pacific, the ceremony of killing the ghosts used to be carried out with great pomp in a series of mock battles which have been described as follows by a missionary long resident in the island. The ceremony, he tells us, was called *Ta i te mauri*, or Ghost-Killing. " Upon the decease of an individual, a messenger (' bird ', so called from his swiftness) was sent round the island. Upon reaching the boundary line of each district, he paused to give the war-shout peculiar to these people, adding ' So-and-so is dead '. Near relatives would start off at once for the house of the deceased, each carrying a present of native cloth. Most of the athletic young men of the entire island on the day following united in a series of mimic battles designated '*ta i te mauri*', or slaying the ghosts. The district where the corpse lay represented the ' mauri '

[1] W. T. L. Travers, " Notes of the Traditions and Manners and Customs of the Mori-oris ", *Transactions and Proceedings of the New Zealand Institute*, ix. (1876) p. 26.

or ghosts. The young men belonging to it early in the morning arrayed themselves as if for battle, and well armed, started off for the adjoining district, where the young men were drawn up in battle array under the name of 'aka-oa', or friends. The war-dance performed, the two parties rush together, clashing their spears and wooden swords together in right earnest. The sufferers in this bloodless conflict were supposed to be malignant spirits, who would thus be deterred from doing further mischief to mortals. The combatants now coalesce, and are collectively called 'mauri', or ghosts, and pass on to the third district. Throughout the day their leader carries the sacred 'iku kikau', or cocoa-nut leaf, at the pit of his stomach like the dead. Arrived at this third village, they find the young men ready for the friendly conflict, and bearing the name of 'aka-oa'. 'The battle of the ghosts' is again fought, and now with swelling numbers they pass on to the fourth, fifth and sixth districts. In every case it was supposed that the ghosts were well thrashed. Returning with a really imposing force to the place where the corpse was laid out in state, a feast was given to the brave ghost-killers, and all save near relatives return to their various homes ere nightfall. So similar was this to actual warfare, that it was appropriately named 'e teina no te puruki', *i.e.* 'a younger brother of war'."[1]

In Fiji it was believed to be possible to kill a

[1] W. W. Gill, *Myths and Songs from the South Pacific* (London, 1876), pp. 268, 269.

troublesome ghost. Once it happened that many chiefs feasted in the house of Tanoa, King of Ambau. In the course of the evening one of them related how he had slain a neighbouring chief. That very night, having occasion to leave the house, he saw, as he believed, the ghost of his victim, hurled his club at him, and killed him stone dead. On his return to the house he roused the king and the rest of the inmates from their slumbers and recounted his exploit. The matter was deemed of high importance, and they all sat on it in solemn conclave. Next morning a search was made for the club on the scene of the murder ; it was found and carried with great pomp and parade to the nearest temple, where it was laid up for a perpetual memorial. Everybody was firmly persuaded that by this swashing blow the ghost had been not only killed but annihilated.[1]

In Africa, as we have seen, the Herero believe that they can kill a person's ghost by breaking his backbone after death.[2] The Bura and Pabir tribes of Northern Nigeria regard with great fear the ghost of a man who has been killed by lightning and they think that they can kill it. The ceremony of killing it must be performed by the members of a certain clan, the Lasama. Seven days after the burial the men of the clan assemble at the dead man's haunts and there dance and toss up in the air a goat which, as it falls, is caught on the sacred staves. Suddenly one of the men espies the wicked soul, and catching it

[1] Charles Wilkes, *Narrative of the United States Exploring Expedition*, New Edition (New York, 1851), iii. 85.

[2] See above, p. 69.

wraps it in grass and deposits it in the dead man's grave. A fee is paid to the men of the clan for rendering this dangerous service by destroying the dangerous ghost.[1] Among the Banyankole of Uganda sickness was sometimes attributed to the action of a malignant ghost. In order to drive out the obsessing ghost who had taken possession of the sufferer's body, a medicine-man made scratches on the patient's body and rubbed some pungent powder into them, till the patient writhed with pain. Smarting from the pain the ghost was now ready to quit the sufferer, and to hasten his departure the medicine-man rubbed the sick man's body down with his hands, pressing the ghost from his head out at his feet and the tips of his fingers. When the ghost sought to escape it was caught in a pot which was placed ready to receive it, and the pot was thrown either into fire or into water, thus either burning or drowning the ghost. In either case there was an end of the ghost.[2] Similarly among the Banyoro of Uganda, when a case of sickness was ascribed to the influence of a ghost who had taken possession of a patient's body, a medicine-man used to lure the ghost out of the body of the sufferer into a pot which he had baited with savoury meat. When the ghost thus tempted entered into the pot, the medicine-man shut it up and carried it to waste land, where he either burned it or threw it into running water, thus

[1] C. K. Meek, *Tribal Studies in Northern Nigeria* (London, 1931), i. p. 169.

[2] J. Roscoe, *The Banyankole* (Cambridge, 1923), p. 141; compare J. G. Frazer, *The Fear of the Dead in Primitive Religion* (London, 1933), pp. 157-158.

burning or drowning the ghost.[1] Again, amongst the Baganda the "evil-disposed ghost which attacks people of its own accord, uninfluenced by some living person, is usually thought to be the ghost of the aunt on the male side. These ghosts are sometimes most troublesome, causing the man's wife or his children constant sickness, and nothing will appease them. In such a case the *Mandwa* (priest) has to capture the ghost and destroy it; he comes to the house bringing either a cow or buffalo horn into which he puts a cowrie or snail shell with a seed of the wild plantain; this he places on the end of a long stick and passes up the central post of the hut until he reaches the top near the roof. The spirits always take up their abode in the highest part of the conical-shaped huts on the central pole. During the process of capturing the spirit the house is kept in darkness and only two or three people are permitted to be present. When the *Mandwa* (priest) has got the horn to the top of the pole he works it about until the shells and seed make a squeaking noise; this he pronounces to be the voice of the ghost which has entered the horn; he then rapidly lowers the horn, covers it with a bit of bark cloth and plunges it into a pot of water; the ghost thus secured is carried off in triumph to the nearest river and plunged into it; if there is no river near the priest secures the mouth of the pot, and carries it off into a place where there is some unreclaimed land where he deposits it, and

[1] J. Roscoe, *The Bakitara or Banyoro* (Cambridge, 1923), pp. 286 *sq.*; compare J. G. Frazer, *The Fear of the Dead in Primitive Religion*, pp. 159-161.

leaves it to be destroyed by the next grass fire."[1] Thus if the ghost escapes death by drowning he is sure to perish in the end by fire. Among the Bavenda of the Northern Transvaal a diviner will sometimes declare that the death of a member of a tribe has been caused by the wicked ghost of an ancestral spirit who must therefore be destroyed in order to protect his descendants against his further attacks. In order to effect this destruction the spear of the wicked spirit is tied round the neck of a black goat; a heavy stone is attached to it, and the goat with the spear and the stone is thrown into a deep pool. With the goat the ancestral spirit is believed to be thrown into the water and drowned, thus ridding his descendants of any danger from him for ever.[2] Speaking of West African negroes in general, Miss Mary Kingsley observes: "Destroying the body by breaking up or cutting up is a widely diffused custom in West Africa in the case of dangerous souls, and is universally followed with those that have contained wanderer-souls, *i.e.* those souls which keep on turning up in the successive infants of a family. A child dies, then another child comes to the same father or mother and that dies, after giving the usual trouble and expense. A third arrives, and if that dies, the worm—I mean the father—turns, and if he is still desirous of more children he just breaks one of the legs of the body before throwing it in the bush. This

[1] J. Roscoe, "Further Notes on the Manners and Customs of the Baganda", *Journal of the Royal Anthropological Institute*, xxxii. (1902) p. 43.

[2] H. A. Stayt, *The Bavenda* (Oxford, 1931), p. 252.

he thinks will act as a warning to the wanderer-soul and give it to understand that if it will persist in coming into his family, it must settle down there and give up its flighty ways. If a fourth child arrives in the family, and if it dies, the justly irritated parent cuts its body up carefully into very small pieces, and scatters them, doing away with the soul altogether."[1] Thus the total destruction of a child's body is believed to involve the total destruction of its soul.

[1] Mary H. Kingsley, *Travels in West Africa* (London, 1897), p. 480.

LECTURE V

LECTURE V

In the last lecture I dealt with some of the means which primitive man employs to prevent the spirits of the dead from coming back to trouble and plague the living. In particular I described some of the mutilations which he inflicts on a corpse in the belief that he thereby maims and disables the ghost in like manner. Later, I showed that going still further he imagines that he can not only disable the ghost but kill it and annihilate it. But apart from these strong measures he resorts to a great variety of less severe devices to effect the same object. I propose now to illustrate some of these devices by a series of miscellaneous examples. They display on the part of primitive man an ingenuity and resourcefulness which might, perhaps, have been turned to better account in a better cause; at least they serve to set in a strong light that obsessing fear of the spirits of the dead which has played an enormous part in the history of humanity.

Thus, for example, among the natives of Halmahera or Gilolo, a large island to the west of New Guinea, when any one dies, the members of his household must change their names; else the dead man knows their names and calls them, to keep him company in the grave; so that they die. When any one dies and his eyes remain wide open, they say that he is looking round for a companion; hence, some one else will die soon. So they are always careful to weight the eyelids of a corpse, generally with a rijksdollar, in order to keep them shut. When a corpse is buried, the stem of a banana-tree must be buried with it to keep it company, in order that the dead person may not seek a companion among the living. Hence, when the coffin is lowered into the ground, one of the bystanders steps up and throws a young banana-tree into the grave saying: "Friend, you must miss your companions of this earth; here, take this as a comrade". When any one dies and his coffin is made, they must take the measure of the corpse and make the coffin fit it exactly; otherwise, they say (if there is room and to spare in the coffin) some one else will soon die. For the same reason the grave must fit the coffin exactly. A grave must not be dug in a place all by itself, else the dead person buried in it will seek to have a companion. (Graves are dug behind the house, and generally there are old graves there already.) When a mother has a child that dies young she must wear the *slendang*, or cloth in which the child is carried, continually for more than a month; otherwise she will have another loss. When a man who was a werewolf dies, it is necessary to strew lime on his eyes and to cover his head with a pan ; for then, they say, his eyes are dim and he cannot see to come and visit the survivors with sickness or death. When some woman dies and they say that she was a *pontianak* (evil spirit), they stick needles under all her nails, and under her armpits they place two hen's eggs : this, they say, is a plaything for her child and therefore she will not spread out her arms to fly about else she would lose the eggs ; and the reason for sticking needles under her nails is that she may not go about as a *pontianak*, for her nails will be sore and thus she will not be able to seize with them.[1]

In the Island of Nias, to the west of Sumatra, at a burial " when they have come to the grave, whither they have proceeded with loud lamentations, the nearest relatives, and not least the women, behave as if they were frantic. When the coffin is lowered into the grave, they make as if they would leap into the grave, stab themselves, and so forth, customs which have their ground in the fear of the ghost of the deceased ; for by so doing they make it clear to him that his death is mourned, in order that his spirit may not, out of revenge, bring misfortune on the surviving relatives. For these reasons, before they go to the grave, the dead man's golden ornaments are shown to him in order that he may take the shadow of them with him to the land of souls ; and from the same consideration some gold is placed

[1] M. J. van Baarda, " Fabelen, Verhalen en Overleveringen der Gabelareezen ", collected by H. van Dijken, published and translated by M. J. van Baarda, *Bijdragen tot de Taal- Land- en Volkenkunde van Nederlandsch-Indie*, xlv. (1895) pp. 538-541.

in the mouth of the corpse.[1] In South Nias the corpse is coffined outside of the village, in order that the spirit of the dead may not find the way back to the village to fetch somebody there. For this reason there is, also in North Nias, no regular path to the cemeteries, but on each occasion of a burial a path is cleared to the cemetery.[2] Clearly these people count upon the inability of the ghost to find his way back to the house by a new and unfamiliar path through the forest.

Among the Papuans of Geelvink Bay in Dutch New Guinea, it is a rule that while a burial is proceeding no noise may be made and no work done in the village, for any noise would excite the anger of the ghost, and he would take his revenge on the survivors who show so little regard for his feelings. And after the burial is completed they fasten leaves and branches to the houses and trees as scarecrows to frighten away the ghost, if he should venture to return.[3] The Kiwai of British New Guinea always carry a dead body to the grave head foremost, because they believe that if they carried it in the reverse position the ghost would return to the village.[4] A contrary rule was observed in the neighbouring island of Mabuiag to the south of New Guinea, for there the corpse was always carried out to burial feet foremost, else it was believed that the ghost would

[1] Th. C. Rappard, " Het eiland Nias en zijne bewoners ", *Bijdragen tot de Taal- Land- en Volkenkunde van Nederlandsch-Indie*, lxii. (1909) p. 571.

[2] Th. C. Rappard, *op. cit.* p. 573.

[3] J. B. van Hasselt, " Die Noeforezen ", *Zeitschrift für Ethnologie*, viii. (1876) pp. 188-189.

[4] G. Landtman, *The Kiwai Papuans of British New Guinea* (London, 1927), p. 257.

return and trouble the survivors. As a further precaution to prevent his wandering the thumbs and great toes of the corpse were tied together.[1] The same rule of carrying out a corpse feet foremost to prevent the return of the ghost has been observed by other peoples, as we shall see presently. In the Society Islands of the Pacific, after an elaborate ceremony for the burial of the sins of the deceased, a priest used to step up to the side of the corpse, and taking some small slips of plantain leaf-stalk he fixed two or three of them under each arm, placed a few on the breast, and then, addressing the dead body, said: "There are your family, there is your child, there is your wife, there is your father, and there is your mother. Be satisfied yonder (that is, in the world of spirits). Look not towards those who are left in this world." This concluding ceremony was designed to impart contentment to the deceased, and to prevent his spirit from repairing to the places of his former resort, and so distressing the survivors.[2] Among the Subanos of Mindanao, when men return home after a burial they thrust their chopping knives deeply into the rungs of the house ladder, doubtless to prevent the ghost from returning and climbing up the ladder into the house.[3]

[1] A. C. Haddon, "Funeral Ceremonies", *Reports of the Cambridge Anthropological Expedition to the Torres Straits*, v. (Cambridge, 1904) p. 248; *id.*, "The Secular and Ceremonial Dances of Torres Straits", *Internationales Archiv für Ethnographie*, vi. (1893) p. 152.

[2] W. Ellis, *Polynesian Researches* (London, 1836), Second Edition, i. pp. 401-403.

[3] F. Blumentritt, "Neue Nachrichten über die Subanon (Insel Mindanao) (nach P. Francisco Sanchez)", *Zeitschrift der Gesellschaft für Erdkunde zu Berlin*, xxxi. (1896) p. 371.

The dwarf tribes of the Malay Peninsula, the Semang, the Orang Utan and the Kenta, shift their camp immediately after a death, often removing to a great distance, because they fear that the ghost might attack and kill them. They are careful to place a river between them and the old camp, believing apparently that the ghost cannot cross water.[1] This is obviously a case of the water barrier with which we are already familiar.

In Siam a corpse is sometimes placed in the coffin face downwards, in order that the ghost may not find its way back to the house; and for the purpose of rendering his return to the old home still more difficult, the coffin is carried out of the house not by the door but through an opening specially made in the wall. As if this were not enough to baffle the ghost the coffin is carried by the bearers at a run several times round the house, till the ghost may be presumed to be giddy and quite unable to retrace his steps to the familiar dwelling.[2] A similar mode of baffling the ghost and preventing his return to the house is practised by the Shans of Burma. They greatly dread the ghost of a woman who has died in child-bed and take great pains to prevent it from returning, in the form of a malignant spirit, to attack her husband, and torment him. Hence, when the bodies of the dead mother and child are being removed from the house part of the

[1] Paul Schebesta, *Among the Forest Dwarfs of Malaya* (London, n.d.), pp. 106, 143, 236.

[2] E. Young, *The Kingdom of the Yellow Robe* (Westminster, 1898), p. 246; Mgr. Pallegoix, *Description du royaume Thai ou Siam* (Paris, 1854), p. 245.

mat wall in the side of the house is taken down, and the dead woman and her baby are lowered to the ground through the aperture. The hole through which the bodies have passed is immediately filled with new mats, so that the ghost may not know how to return.[1] The Palaungs, another tribe of Burma, entertain a similar dread of the ghost of the woman dying in childbirth and adopt a similar precaution to prevent her spirit from returning. The body is lowered through a hole in the floor of the room in which she died, then the floor is washed and the hole is closed with new boards. This, they hope, will prevent the return of the spirits of the unfortunate mother and child, to Palaungs, the most terrifying of unhappy spirits.[2] This mode of preventing a ghost from returning to the house by carrying out his corpse through a special opening which is afterwards immediately closed, is by no means peculiar to Burma and Siam; it has been practised by many other peoples in many other parts of the world. Elsewhere I have collected the evidence for its diffusion, but I cannot linger over it now.[3] Among the Kakhyen of Upper Burma, mourners returning from the grave strew ground rice along the path and cleanse their legs and arms with fresh leaves. Before re-entering the house they are purified with water by the medicine-man with a sprinkler of grass,

[1] Mrs. Leslie Milne, *Shans at Home* (London, 1910), p. 96.

[2] Mrs. Leslie Milne, *The Home of an Eastern Clan* (Oxford, 1924), pp. 304, 305.

[3] J. G. Frazer, *Garnered Sheaves* (London, 1931), p. 10 *sqq.*; J. G. Frazer, *Belief in Immortality* (London, 1913), i. pp. 452 *sqq.*

and step over a bundle of grass sprinkled with the blood of a fowl sacrificed during their absence to the spirit of the dead. A few days later the ghost of the deceased, who is supposed to be still lingering about his old home, is finally expelled from the house by a great dance.[1]

Among the tribes in the Aracan Mountains in Burma, if a woman who has had children gives birth to a still-born infant a piece of iron is placed in the cradle-coffin, a relation saying: "Return not into the womb of thy mother until this iron is soft as cotton".[2]

Among the Karens of Burma, when a funeral party is returning from the grave, "each person provides himself with little hooks made of branches of trees, and calling his spirit to follow him, at short intervals, as he returns, he makes a motion as if hooking it, and then thrusts the hook into the ground. This is done to prevent the spirit of the living from staying behind with the spirit of the dead."[3]

In Chittagong, a district of North-Eastern India, when a funeral is taking place a man follows the body, pouring out water behind it all the way from the house to the boundaries; this is clearly another case of the water barrier. Formerly, when the corpse had been carried out of the house, they used to drive a nail into the threshold to prevent the ghost from returning and entering the dwelling.[4]

[1] J. A. Anderson, *Mandalay to Momien* (London, 1876), p. 144; cf. p. 77.

[2] *The British Burma Gazetteer*, i. (Rangoon, 1879–1880) p. 387.

[3] F. Mason, "Physical Characters, etc., of the Karens", *Journal of the Asiatic Society of Bengal*, Part II. No. 1 (1866), p. 28.

[4] Th. Bérangier, "Les funérailles à Chittagong", *Les Missions Catholiques*, xiii. (1881) pp. 503, 504.

Primitive man fears the spirits of the dead not only while he is awake but while he is asleep, for in sleep he may dream of a ghost, and to his thinking a dream is as real as a waking reality. Hence he deems it very dangerous to dream of the ghost of a dead man on the night after his burial; for he fancies that the ghost has come in person to disturb him and perhaps to carry off another soul from the house. To avoid these dangers the Lakhers of Assam take elaborate precautions. After a burial when the dead man's relations return home and are about to enter the house, they step on to a sieve containing a little rice, which has been placed ready for the purpose, and go on into the house. This is to show that the soul of the dead has gone to *Athikhi*, the spirit-land, and that his relations are again clean, rice being an emblem of purity. That evening the mother's brother's wife brings a fowl and some *sahmahei* (fermented rice), and sacrifices the fowl to console the souls of the surviving members of the deceased's family, and anoints the big toe of each with the fowl's blood; she then gives each of them a little fermented rice and returns home. This is an important sacrifice, for it is essential that the souls of the deceased's family should be at peace; because if any member of it sees any one in his dreams on the night of the funeral, the person dreamed of will soon die also. The belief is that on the night of the funeral the spirit of the deceased comes to visit his family, and if they are dreaming of any one, the deceased's spirit meets the spirit of the person dreamed of and seizes it and carries it off with him to *Athikhi*. On the morning after the funeral one of the neighbours always asks the deceased's relatives whether they had any dreams during the night or not ; if the answer is " No ", all is well, but if one of the family dreamt of any one that night he must say so, as it is very unlucky for the person dreamed of. If the dream was that the dead man appeared again alive in the house, it means that another member of the family will die. A further precaution is often taken to prevent the deceased's relations or other villagers from dreaming on the night of the funeral. Each householder, before going to sleep, puts a little cooked rice in a pot, and each member of the household says, " May my spirit not wander about to-night, let it remain within this pot " ; having said this, each person puts his hand inside the pot and touches the rice. By this means the spirits are kept imprisoned inside the pots, and as they cannot wander about and meet other people's spirits, the owners of the imprisoned spirits do not dream of any one that night, and so cause no one any harm. Another way of preventing the soul from escaping from its owner's house is to place a paddy pestle across the door, as the soul will fear to go under it, lest the pestle should fall on it.[1] We have already seen that these people sometimes place a paddy pestle at the door of a house to prevent the ghost from entering ; we now see that they also place a paddy pestle at the door to prevent their

[1] N. E. Parry, *The Lakhers* (London, 1932), pp. 402, 403.

own souls from going out. Clearly the pestle is regarded as an effectual barrier against the passage of a spirit in either direction.

Among the Kawar, a primitive tribe of the Central Provinces in India, after the funeral the mourners bathe and return home walking one behind the other in Indian file. When they come to a cross-road the foremost man picks up a pebble with his left foot, and it is passed from hand to hand down the line of men until the hindmost throws it away. This is thought to sever their connexion with the spirit of the deceased and prevent it from following them home.[1] Among the Korku, a Munda people of the Central Provinces of India, " in order to lay to rest the spirit of a dead person, who it is feared may trouble the living, five pieces of bamboo are taken as representing the bones of the dead man, and these with five crab's legs, five grains of rice and other articles, are put into a basket and thrust into a crab's hole under water. The occasion is made an excuse for much feasting and drinking, and the son or other representative who lays the spirit works himself up into a state of drunken excitement before he enters the water to search for a suitable hole."[2] Among the Pabia, a small caste in the Bilaspur District of India, " when any one dies in a family, all the members, as soon as the breath leaves his body, go into another room of the house; and across the door they lay a net opened into the room

[1] R. V. Russell, *The Tribes and Castes of the Central Provinces of India* (London, 1916), iii. p. 397.

[2] R. V. Russell, *op. cit.* iii. p. 564.

where the corpse lies. They think that the spirit of the dead man will follow them, and will be caught in the net. Then the net is carried away and burnt or buried with the corpse, and thus they think that the spirit is removed and prevented from remaining about the house and troubling the survivors."[1] In the Punjab the ghosts of sweepers are thought to be malevolent and are much dreaded; and their bodies are therefore always buried or burnt face downwards to prevent their spirits from escaping. Riots have taken place, and the magistrates have been appealed to, in order to prevent a sweeper being buried face upwards.[2]

The Koryak, a primitive people in the extreme north-eastern corner of Asia, appear to regard the spirits of the dead as hostile to the living from the moment that their bodies have been removed from the house. They burn their dead. At the cremation of the body of a girl, her grandfather "took a pole and thrusting it into the body said, 'Of yonder magpie pricked' . . . or, in a free translation, 'This is the magpie of the underworld which pricked'. He imitated the actions of the magpie of the world of the dead, in order to inform the deceased that she was passing to another world, and must not return to the house. The further actions of the dead girl's grandfather had the same end in view. When the flames of the pyre were dying away, he broke

[1] R. V. Russell, *op. cit.* i. p. 395.

[2] R. V. Russell, *op. cit.* iv. p. 221; W. Crooke, *The Popular Religion and Folk-Lore of Northern India* (Westminster, 1896), i. p. 269, referring to Ibbetson, *Punjab Ethnography*, p. 117.

some twigs from the alder and willow bushes that were growing near-by, and strewed them around the pyre. These twigs represented a dense forest that was supposed to surround the burning-place. We left the place while the pyre was still burning. Before leaving the grandfather went round the pyre, first from right to left and then from left to right, in order to so obscure his tracks that the deceased would not be able to follow him. Then stepping away from the pyre toward the houses, he drew a line with his stick on the snow, jumped across it and shook himself. The others followed his example. The line was supposed to represent a river which separated the village from the burning-place."[1] The line on the snow was clearly regarded as representing a water barrier which divided the living from the dead.

In the Bari tribe of the Nilotic Sudan "the body of the rain-maker is submitted to special treatment as soon after death as possible, all the orifices of the body being plugged, lest his spirit should escape by one of these and bring sickness or, becoming a lion or leopard, constitute a danger to the people. The corpse is then ruddled with the usual ochre mixture. As a comment on this, Mr. Whitehead sends the following very interesting account, which further indicates the importance of the process as enabling the new rain-maker to control the spirits of his rain-making ancestors: 'When the rain-maker is

[1] *The Jesup North Pacific Expedition* (*Memoir of the American Museum of Natural History*, New York), vi. *The Koryak, Religion and Myths*, by W. Jochelson (Leyden and New York, 1905), p. 112.

dead, he is plugged, his ears are plugged, his nose is plugged, his eye is plugged, his mouth is plugged, he is plugged, his fingers are plugged. And then he is buried. It is done so that . . . the spirits may not go out, so that the son may manage the father so that he obeys (him), so that the spirits obey the son.' "[1] In the Bachama and Mbula tribes of Northern Nigeria, a new king undergoes a period of seclusion for fifteen days; he then takes possession of the palace by stepping over a cow killed at the threshold. Two explanations of this rite are given: (1) that in crossing over the body of the cow he left behind him all conduct of a kind which would be inconsistent with his new position; and (2) that the sacrifice of the cow at the threshold secured the palace against invasion by the late chief's ghost.[2] Of these alternative explanations we cannot doubt that the second is the true one; the first is too vague and sentimental to be primitive. Among the Wajagga of Mount Kilimanjaro, in East Africa, when the body of a man is carried out to burial, the son of the deceased places a bean in the left ear of the corpse in order that the ghost may take no further part in earthly life and may not come back to plague the house. By way of further precaution, a leaden ornament such as women wear in their ears is attached to the ear of the corpse, as a symbol of the peace which is henceforth to reign between the

[1] C. G. Seligman and Brenda Z. Seligman, *Pagan Tribes of the Nilotic Sudan* (London, 1932), p. 292.

[2] C. K. Meek, *Tribal Studies in Northern Nigeria* (London, 1931), i. p. 4.

living and the dead.[1] In the Tumbuka tribe of Nyasaland a corpse was carried out of the hut not by the door but by a special opening made in the wall. All the dishes, pots, clothes and articles of personal use belonging to the deceased were buried with him. But no metal goods were buried, whether hoes, or arrows, or brass ornaments, because it was feared that these would give the ghost opportunity to return with anger to hurt the friends. The nearest relatives then threw pounded cinders into the grave, that they might not chatter in their sleep or death come to them.[2] The Bana of the Cameroons of West Africa believe that the ghost even of a good man is malignant; hence they take many precautions to prevent it from issuing from the grave, and returning to cause sickness or death in the family. The body is tied up, the eyes are bandaged and it is carried out of the hut feet foremost, because otherwise the ghost might know its way back to the house. In the grave heavy logs are placed on the body to keep it down, and the men brandish their clubs threateningly at the ghost, disclaiming any responsibility for the death.[3] In the Niger Delta, when a woman has died in giving birth to a child, it used to be customary to kill the infant and bury it with the dead mother; but if they decided to keep the child alive they performed a ceremony to prevent

[1] B. Gutmann (Madschame), "Trauer und Begräbnissitten der Wadschagga", *Globus*, lxxxix. (1906) p. 197; *id.*, *Dichten und Denken der Dschagganeger* (Leipsig, 1909), p. 133.

[2] D. Fraser, *Winning a Primitive People* (London, 1914), p. 158.

[3] G. van Hagen, "Die Bana", *Baessler-Archiv*, ii. (1912) p. 109.

the mother's ghost from returning to fetch away her child. A piece of a plantain stem (that portion which has the fruit clustered round it) was procured and forced into the womb of the dead mother. This according to native ideas prevents her spirit coming back to fetch the child, and the mother thinks she has the child with her. This account has been confirmed by an English lady who was present on two occasions when this ceremony was being performed.[1]

In Southern Nigeria, where the belief in the rebirth of the dead is prevalent, dead children are usually buried lying on their side as in sleep. But if for any reason it is deemed undesirable that its soul should be born again the little body is buried face downward, to prevent the return of its soul. Grown men, on the other hand, are buried face upwards in order that they may see straight before them and find their way back again to earth.[2] In the Ho tribe of Togoland in West Africa, on the fourth day after the burial of a woman or the fifth day after the burial of a man, a relative goes to the grave and sprinkles water on it for the purpose of quietening the spirit of the dead and preventing it from returning to cause another death.[3]

Among the Eskimo of Alaska, near St. Michael, when a *shaman* died no one did any work for three

[1] Le Comte C. N. de Cardi, "Ju-Ju Laws and Customs in the Niger Delta", *Journal of the Anthropological Institute*, xxix. (1899) p. 58.

[2] P. Amaury Talbot, *Life in Southern Nigeria* (London, 1923), pp. 144-145.

[3] J. Spieth, *Die Ewe Stämme* (Berlin, 1906), p. 704.

days afterwards. The following night, when the people prepared to retire, each man in the village took his urine-tub and poured a little of its contents before the door, saying, "This water is our water; drink"—believing that should the ghost return during the night and try to enter, it would taste this water, and, finding it bad, would go away.[1] Among the Skuñgen Indians of Vancouver Island, as soon as a death has taken place the body is immediately taken out of the house by an opening in the wall from which the boards have been removed, because it is believed that the ghost would kill every one if the body were to stay in the house. The implements of the deceased are deposited close to the body, else his ghost would come and get them. Sometimes even his house is broken down.[2] The Déné-Dindjie Indians of North-West America surround the tombs of the dead with long poles to which ribands of different colours are fastened. The intention is to amuse the soul of the deceased and thus keep it beside the corpse.[3]

Among the Araucanians of Chili when a corpse is being carried out to a place of burial a woman walks behind it, strewing ashes on the path to prevent the spirit of the dead from returning to its late abode.[4]

[1] E. W. Nelson, "The Eskimo about Bering Strait", *18th Annual Report of the Bureau of American Ethnology* (1896–97) (1899), p. 312.

[2] *Sixth Report on the North-Western Tribes of Canada* (*Report of the British Association for 1890*, separate reprint), Second General Report on the Indians of British Columbia, by Dr. Fr. Boas.

[3] E. Petitot, *Monographie des Déné-Dindjies* (Paris, 1876), p. 47.

[4] J. Ignatius Molina, *The Geographical, Natural and Civil History of Chili*, translated from the original Italian (London, 1809), ii. p. 91.

With regard to the Pehhuenches, an Indian tribe of Chili, speaking an Araucanian dialect, we are told that they greatly fear the spirits of the dead, and the nearer the relation of the survivor to the deceased the greater is his fear of the ghost. To prevent a ghost from returning they carry the corpse out of the tent feet foremost, for if they carried it out in any other posture they believe that the ghost will return. Further, when they are shifting camp, abandoning a site where they have tarried for some time and where several of their number have died and been buried, they take elaborate precautions to obscure their tracks by crossing them in various directions for the purpose of baffling the pursuit of the ghosts who might be following their comrades to their new home.[1] Among the Lengua Indians of the Paraguaian Chaco a witch-doctor had been persuaded by the missionary to build a superior hut with a small opening for a door. But after an old man had died and been buried the witch-doctor's wife and family made very considerable alterations in the hut; in particular they blocked up the little door of the new hut, making it appear like a part of the wall, and opened a small gap on the opposite side instead. The reason for this alteration was explained to the missionary by the wizard himself. He said that this was done on purpose to puzzle the ghost. He, while in the body, knew the house well, but the alterations were so considerable that it was supposed his ghost

[1] E. Poeppig, *Reise in Chile, Peru und auf dem Amazonenstrome während der Jahre 1827–1832* (Leipsig, 1835–1836), i. p. 393.

would not recognize it and would be particularly nonplussed when it made for the entrance to find it a solid wall.[1] The Indians of Brazil, in the neighbourhood of Rio de Janeiro, used greatly to fear lest the spirit of the dead should return and do them harm. To prevent the return of a dead man's ghost they rolled up his body and tied it tightly; but lest he, or rather his ghost, should undo the fastenings and come back to haunt them they adopted the further precaution of confining the corpse in a great earthenware jar, battened down with an earthenware lid.[2]

In civilized Europe itself, if, in spite of all precautions, the ghost should make his way back from the grave, steps were taken to barricade the house against him. Thus, in some parts of Russia and East Prussia an axe or a lock is laid on the threshold, or a knife is hung over the door,[3] and in Germany as soon as the coffin is carried out of the house all the doors and windows are shut, whereas so long as the body is still in the house, or at least immediately after the death, the windows (and sometimes the doors) are left open for the soul to escape.[4] In the

[1] W. B. Grubb, *An Unknown People in an Unknown Land* (London, 1911), pp. 165, 166.

[2] A. Thevet, *La Cosmographie Universelle* (Paris, 1575), ii. p. 959.

[3] W. Ralston, *Songs of the Russian People* (London, 1872), p. 318; A. Wuttke, *Der deutsche Volksaberglaube* (Berlin, 1869), §§ 736, 766; M. Töppen, *Aberglauben aus Masuren* (Danzig, 1867), p. 108.

[4] C. L. Rochholz, *Deutsche Glaube und Brauch* (Berlin, 1867), i. p. 171; A. Schleicher, *Volkstümliches aus Sonnenberg* (Weimar, 1858), p. 152; W. Sonntag, *Tödtenbestattung*, p. 169 (Halle, 1878); A. Wuttke, *op. cit.* §§ 725, 737; A. Gubernatis, *Storia comparata degli usi funebri in Italia e pressi gli altri popoli Indo-Europei*, p. 47; G. Lammert, *Volksmedizin und medizinischer Aberglaube aus Bayern* (Würzburg, 1869), pp. 103, 105, 106; F. Schmidt, *Sitten und Gebräuche*, pp. 85, 92; L. Strackerjan, *Aberglaube und Sagen aus dem Herzogthum Oldenburg* (Oldenburg, 1867), ii. p. 129;

Hebridean Islands of Mull and Tiree the barricade against the ghost assumes an easy and gentle form ; a sprig of pearlwort fastened over the lintel of a door from which a corpse has been carried is thought sufficient to deter the poor ghost from passing the threshold and re-entering his old home.[1]

W. Tettau und J. D. H. Temme, *Die Volkssagen Ostpreussens, Litauens und Westpreussens* (Berlin, 1837), p. 285 ; A. Kuhn, *Märkische Sagen und Mährchen* (Berlin, 1843), p. 367 ; F. Nork, *Die Sitten und Gebräuche der Deutschen und ihrer Nachbarvölker* (1845), pp. 479, 482 ; J. A. E. Köhler, *Volksbrauch, Aberglauben, Sagen und andere alte Überlieferungen in Voigtlande* (Leipsig, 1867), pp. 251, 254 ; F. Panzer, *Beiträge zur deutschen Mythologie* (Munich, 1848–1855), i. 263 ; A. Kuhn und W. Schwartz, *Norddeutsche Sagen, Märchen und Gebräuche* (Leipsig, 1848), p. 435.

[1] J. G. Campbell, *Superstitions of the Highlands and Islands of Scotland* (Glasgow, 1900), p. 241.

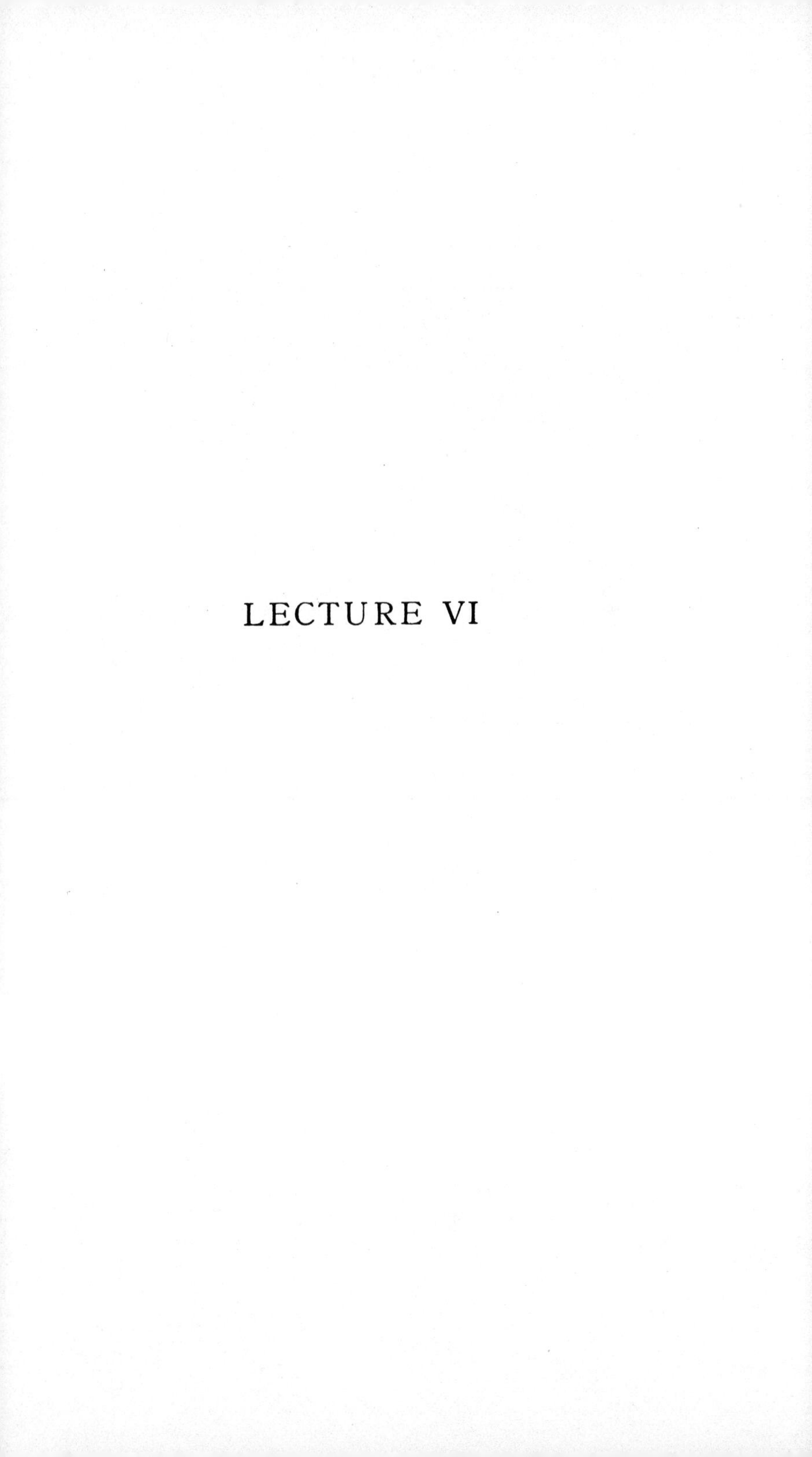

LECTURE VI

LECTURE VI

In the last lecture I gave some miscellaneous examples of the devices which primitive man adopts to prevent the spirits of the dead from returning to molest the living. To-day we turn to a device of another kind, which has had different and very important consequences. With many primitive peoples it has been customary to destroy all a dead man's property in order to prevent his ghost from returning to claim and enjoy it. Wherever this custom has been rigorously observed it has proved a fatal bar to economic progress, by preventing that accumulation and transmission of property which is essential to the advance of industry, and indeed to the very life of civilized society. Hence the tribes which have practised the custom have remained in a state of poverty and savagery from which they can never emerge so long as they adhere to this wasteful and ruinous practice.

Thus, for example, speaking of the natives of Melville and Bathurst Islands to the north of Australia, Baldwin Spencer observes: "The paper bark in which the body had been wrapped and all the dead woman's belongings were burnt in the fire, and afterwards the ashes were completely and carefully covered over. In the case of a man his weapons are broken up and then burnt in the same way. In most tribes all the belongings of a dead person are the property of some special individual, such as a mother's brother, but here they are all destroyed." [1] From this statement we may infer that most Australian tribes preserve the belongings of the dead and pass them on to their next of kin; they are therefore in a more hopeful condition for economic progress than the natives of Melville and Bathurst Islands, who systematically destroy all the property of the dead.

Among the Wonkonguru of the Lake Eyre district of Central Australia, as soon as a man dies his body is brought out of the hut by the men. It is then tightly bound up with hair or fibre rope until it is a stiff package, when it is deposited in a grave about three feet deep. All the personal belongings of the dead person are broken at the grave of a man so that his spirit will not come back and use them. Women's belongings are not broken. The covering of his hut and the sticks to make it are also put on the grave, and then wood is piled on top. The wood is provided so that when the dead person "jumps up"—that is, rises from the grave—he will have a supply of firewood handy, and the sticks and hut covering are put there so that, in case it is cold when the dead man comes back, he can build a shelter.[2]

[1] Baldwin Spencer, *Native Tribes of the Northern Territory of Australia* (London, 1914), p. 243.

[2] G. Horne and G. Aiston, *Savage Life in Central Australia* (London, 1924), pp. 162-163.

Thus the attitude of these people towards the spirit of a dead man exhibits a mixture of fear and tender regard. They break his personal belongings because they fear that the ghost will come back and use them, but they provide the ghost with the means of obtaining warmth and shelter on cold nights at the grave.

Among the natives of San Cristoval, one of the Solomon Islands, after a man's death his property is destroyed; his trees are cut down, his nuts and yams strewn about the ground, his bowl broken. The broken property is placed on the grave. A favourite dog or pig is also buried in a grave and their belongings are also broken; in the case of a pig the bowl from which it fed will be broken, and in the case of a dog its owner's pig-hunting spear will be stuck up on the grave and never used again.[1] In some of the Solomon Islands a chief's fruit trees are cut down after his death.[2] Among the Sulka of New Britain, when a man died his plantations were laid waste, his fruit trees were cut down, the fruits themselves hacked in pieces, his pigs were killed and cut up and his weapons were broken. In the case of a wealthy or distinguished man his wives would also be killed after his death.[3] The motive for all this destruction is not assigned by our authority, but we may conjecture that it was a fear lest the ghost of the dead man should return and attempt to enjoy his property and his wives.

[1] C. E. Fox, *The Threshold of the Pacific* (London, 1924), p. 211.

[2] W. G. Ivens, *Melanesians of the South-east Solomon Islands* (London, 1927), p. 215.

[3] R. Parkinson, *Dreissig Jahre in der Südsee* (Studgart, 1907), p. 185.

The natives of Niue, or Savage Island, in the Pacific disposed of the dead by setting their bodies adrift in canoes, or by laying the body on a pile of stones in the bush and covering it over with coconut leaves. After a time the bones were gathered and deposited in family caves or vaults. All the plantations, coconut trees, and other fruit trees of a person who died, were destroyed and thrown into the sea that they might go with him to the world of spirits.[1] Among the Kiwai Papuans of British New Guinea, after a burial some of the most valuable ornaments of the deceased are usually, but not always, kept by the heir, while the rest are destroyed or given away to people outside his or her group, sometimes to other villages. The near relatives do not want to keep the things of everyday use which have belonged to the dead person, lest they should themselves die, no doubt at the hands of the ghost, coming back to reclaim his property from the new owner. Even the harpoon-shaft of a man is often broken to pieces, out of which the people manufacture harpoon-heads or daggers. The people say that a harpoon-shaft is sometimes broken in two, and the butt end kept, to which a new shaft of bamboo is attached, so that the weapon can be used again.[2] Apparently they think that the ghost will not recognize his harpoon when once it has been broken or cut in pieces. At the same time they show a dawning sense of the permanent value of property by occasionally allow-

[1] G. Turner, *Samoa* (London, 1884), p. 306.

[2] G. Landtman, *The Kiwai Papuans of British New Guinea* (London, 1927), p. 263.

ing some of the most valuable ornaments of the deceased to be kept by his heir.

In the Nicobar Islands after a death, if the stores of food belonging to the deceased or other occupants of his hut were not removed prior to the death they are at once carried away to another hut for issue after the burial. Some of the coconut-shell water-vessels are taken with their contents to the entrance of the hut, where an uneven number (generally 3, 5 or 7 pairs) are violently dashed against a post so as to crack the shells. In like manner all of the bulk of the portable property of the deceased, such as (in the case of a man) his spears, pots, baskets, paddles, plates and a great variety of other articles, are broken or otherwise rendered unserviceable; and then the whole are conveyed to the cemetery in order to be deposited at the proper time on the grave or at the head-post, this being one of the essential sacrifices prescribed by time-honoured custom. The motive for depositing the broken property on the grave or at the head-posts is variously explained by the natives. Some say that it is done in order that all may see how sincere the mourners are in their intention of denying themselves the use or benefit of any of the property, notwithstanding its undoubted value in their eyes. "Another reason given for this wholesale destruction of property is that strangers who have no respect for the sacredness of tabued or sacrificed articles might appropriate uninjured and serviceable objects regardless of the displeasure of the disembodied spirit, who would unquestionably resent any such token of indifference and disrespect by wreaking vengeance probably on those through whose remissness such misconduct had been rendered possible." [1] However, we may surmise that here as elsewhere the true original motive for destroying a dead man's property was to prevent his ghost from returning to make use of it.

The Banar in Tonquin are said to burn all objects used by the deceased in order that he may not return and trouble the living by asking for his property.[2]

The Koryaks of North-Eastern Asia cremate their dead and burn with the body the weapons and household furniture of the deceased, such as spears, quivers and arrows, knives, hatchets and kettles; and they kill the deer which drew the corpse to the cremation ground and throw the fragments into the fire.[3]

The Savara of Southern India burn their dead, and with the body they burn everything that the dead man had: his bows and arrows, his dagger, his necklaces, his reaping-hook for cutting paddy, his axe, some paddy and rice, and so forth. Mr. Fawcett was told that all a man's money was burnt with him, but he thought that the statement was doubtful, though perhaps a little of the money might be so destroyed. When he asked the reason why a man's property is thus destroyed with his body he

[1] E. H. Man, *The Nicobar Islands and their People* (London, n.d.), pp. 131, 132, 138.

[2] E. Reclus, *Nouvelle Géographie Universelle*, viii. p. 869.

[3] S. Krasheninnikov, *The History of Kamtschatka and the Kurilski Islands*, translated into English by James Grieve, M.D. (Gloucester, 1764), p. 233.

was told that, if they did not destroy it, the man's spirit would come back and demand it of them, and trouble them.[1]

In Africa among the Yoruba-speaking peoples of the Slave Coast, on the day after a burial, all the articles which the deceased had in daily use, such as his pipe, his mat, his calabashes, and other things of small value, are carried out into the bush and burnt. Up to this point the soul of the deceased is supposed to be lingering near his old home, and the destruction of his property is to signify that there is no longer anything belonging to him. In former times the destruction of property was carried much further. Usually the room in which the deceased is buried is closed and never used again; sometimes the roof is removed. Rich families even abandon the house altogether. The deceased is then called thrice by name and adjured to depart and no longer to haunt the dwellings of the living. After this a fowl is sacrificed, which, besides securing a right-of-way for the soul, is supposed also to guide it. The feathers of the fowl are scattered round the house, and the bird itself carried out to a cross-roads, where it is cooked and eaten.[2] In a former lecture I gave other examples of a bird or an animal employed to conduct the souls of the dead to the spirit-land.[3]

[1] E. Thurston, *Castes and Tribes of Southern India*, vi. (Madras, 1909) p. 325; Fred. Fawcett, "Notes on the Soaras (or Savaras), an Aboriginal Hill People of the Eastern Ghats of the Madras Presidency", *Journal of the Anthropological Society of Bombay*, i. (1886) p. 249.

[2] A. B. Ellis, *The Yoruba-Speaking Peoples of the Slave Coast of West Africa* (London, 1894), p. 159.

[3] J. G. Frazer, *The Fear of the Dead in Primitive Religion* (London, 1933), pp. 189 *sqq*.

In the African kingdom of Gingiro the old custom of destroying the property of the dead has been reported as follows by Jesuit travellers of the seventeenth or eighteenth century. After describing the death of a king and the installation of his successor, they proceed: "The new king calls all the dead one's favourites and orders them to be killed to bear the dead king company in the other world. Then they burn the house the old king lived in, with all his moveables, goods and furniture, not sparing anything, though never so valuable; and even when any private man dies, they burn not only his house, but the very trees and plants that are about it, and being asked why they do so, they answer, to the end, that the dead man, who was us'd to those places, do not return to them, invited by his former habitation, and delight in walking among those trees."[1] Among the Bogos of Central Africa, as reported by the French traveller, R. Caillié, when the head of a family dies it is common to burn everything that is in the house. At the foot of his bed the corpse is buried; a fire is kindled over his head every night, and the relations come and talk to him. The family of the deceased who are ruined by this act of superstition are supported till the next harvest by the village, for even their rice is not saved from the flames.[2]

With regard to the Kaffirs of South-East Africa, an old Portuguese writer says that after the death

[1] F. B. Tellez, S.J., *The Travels of the Jesuits in Ethiopia* (London, 1710), p. 199.

[2] R. Caillié, *Travels through Central Africa to Timbuctoo* (London, 1830), p. 164.

and burial of a man "they burn the thatched house in which he resided with all it contains, so that no one may possess anything that the deceased made use of during his lifetime, or may even touch it, and if it so happens that some one touches anything belonging to the deceased he does not enter his house until he has washed in the river. The ashes of the burnt house with any pieces of wood not quite consumed they put on the top of the grave."[1] Summing up the evidence of earlier writers on this subject, the historian of South Africa, Dr. McCall Theal, says that: "There was an idea that something connected with death attached to the personal effects of the deceased, on which account whatever had belonged to him that could not be placed in the grave, his clothing, mats, head-rest, etc., was destroyed by fire. The hut in which he had lived was also burned, and no other was allowed to be built on the spot. If he had been the chief, the whole kraal was removed to another site. Those who touched the corpse or any of the dead man's effects were obliged to go through certain ceremonies, and then to bathe in running water before associating again with their companions."[2] Speaking of the Kaffirs of Natal, that is the Zulus, a good authority says that "the deceased's personal articles are buried with him, the assegais being broken or bent, lest the ghost, during some

[1] Fr. J. dos Santos, *Eastern Ethiopia*, in G. McCall Theal, *Records of South-Eastern Africa*, vol. vii. (London, 1901) Book II. p. 307.

[2] G. McCall Theal, *Ethnography and Condition of South Africa before A.D. 1505* (London, 1919), i. 221-222.

midnight return to air, should do injury with them".[1]

Among the aborigines of America also the custom of destroying a dead man's property, or at all events of refusing to make use of it, from a fear of his ghost has been widely diffused, especially in South America. Thus, among the Ahts of Vancouver Island after a death, the whole of a dead man's personal effects that had not been given away before his death were deposited with him—except his best canoes, his house-planks, and fishing and hunting instruments, which, with any slaves he may have had, were inherited by his eldest son. But if his friends were very superstitious they burnt the dead man's house with all its contents, or they removed the materials, and built the house in another place.[2] Thus, with regard to the Ahts it would appear that while the people as a whole had advanced to the stage of inheriting a dead man's most valuable property, the more superstitious members of the community adhered to the ancient custom of destroying it utterly by fire. Among the Knisteneaux Indians, if a dead man's property was not buried with him his ghost was supposed to return and sit on a tree near the house, armed with a gun, ready to shoot the frugal relatives who had thus deprived him of the use of his goods.[3] The Digger Indians of California burn all the property of the deceased, so

[1] J. Shooter, *The Kafirs of Natal and the Zulu* (London, 1857), p. 240.

[2] G. M. Sproat, *Scenes and Studies of Savage Life* (London, 1868), pp. 159, 160.

[3] A. Mackenzie, *Voyages through the Continent of North America*, p. cvi.

that the spirit of the dead man may have all that he needs in the other world, and not return to look for it among his surviving friends.[1] Similarly, the Kutchan Indians of the Colorado regarded the property of a dead man as fraught with danger, and accordingly they burned it with fire together with the hut in which he had died.[2] With regard to the Maidu of California who systematically burned the property of the dead, Professor Roland B. Dixon observes that "owing to the general custom of burning most, if not all, of the property of a man at his death, there was little that could be inherited. Such things as were not destroyed seem to have generally been regarded as the property of the eldest son, although other children and relatives often shared with him." [3]

Thus, while the Maidu destroyed the great bulk of the dead man's property, they seem to have had a faint beginning of a custom of allowing some of it to pass by inheritance to his surviving kinsfolk, especially to his eldest son. In that tribe the custom of burning the property of the dead was a solemn annual ceremony carried out by the whole body of the people collectively on a special burning ground set apart for the purpose. The property to be destroyed was first attached to tall poles or collected at their foot; after being thus exposed to public view for a time it was thrown on the fire, until the flames were almost choked by the weight of the

[1] M. Macfie, *Vancouver Island and British Columbia*, p. 449.

[2] *Zeitschrift für Ethnologie*, ix. p. 348.

[3] R. B. Dixon, "The Northern Maidu", *Bulletin of the American Museum of Natural History*, xvii. (1902) p. 226.

superincumbent property. At the burning held at Mooretown in 1900 there were about a hundred and fifty poles filled with objects, so the amount of property sacrificed was not small. "The purpose of the whole ceremony is to supply the ghosts of the dead with clothing, property and food in the other world. Each family gives to its dead what it can afford; and the whole ceremony is distinctly individual, in that there is no general offering for the dead as a body, but each family offers directly to its own relatives only . . . there is considerable property placed with the body in the grave, and sometimes some is burnt at the time of burial. The main reliance is, however, placed on the supplies offered at the annual burning. After sacrificing thus for three or four years it seems to be felt that enough has been done; and, as a rule, the family does not continue to offer property for a relative at the burnings for more than four or five years."[1]

The practice of the Mosquito Indians as regards the property of the dead appears to be inconsistent. "When a death takes place, they generally bury a bow and arrows, a gourd calabash, and knife, and sundry other articles with the body, and carefully keep in repair a small hut built over the grave, in which they deposit from time to time such little offerings as a yard or two of cloth, a bunch of plantains, a bottle of rum, etc. They have also the custom of destroying everything belonging to a dead

[1] R. B. Dixon, *op. cit.* pp. 241 *sqq.*, 254. (The quotation is from pp. 253, 254.)

person, burning his clothes, splitting his canoes, and, worst of all, cutting down his fruit trees."[1]

Similarly, at a man's death the Indians of Nicaragua destroy all the property that he had earned or otherwise acquired in his lifetime; they destroy also his trees and all his banana plantations. The writer who records the custom adds that in consequence these Indians never prosper.[2]

The Catio Indians of Colombia in South America carry a corpse out of the hut not by the usual door but by another opening, in order that the ghost may not be able to find his way back to his old dwelling. And they bury the dead man's property with him in the grave, because they fear that otherwise his ghost would come back to reclaim it, but apparently they do not break or destroy the articles which they deposit with the dead.[3]

Speaking of the Indian tribes in the valley of the Orinoco the great German traveller Humboldt says: "Some tribes, for instance the Tamanacs, are accustomed to lay waste the fields of a deceased relative, and cut down the trees which he has planted. They say 'that the sight of objects which belonged to their relation makes them melancholy'. They like better to efface than to preserve remembrances. These effects of Indian sensibility are very detri-

[1] C. N. Bell, "The Mosquito Territory, its Climate, People, Productions, etc.", *Journal of the Royal Geographical Society*, xxxii. (1862) p. 254.

[2] Dr. Bruno Mierisch, "Eine Reise nach den Goldgebieten im Osten von Nicaragua", *Petermann's Mitteilungen*, xxxix. (1893) p. 31.

[3] Joseph und Maria Schilling, "Religion und soziale Verhältnisse der Catios-Indianer in Kolumbien", *Archiv für Religionswissenschaft*, xxiii. (1925) p. 296.

mental to agriculture, and the monks oppose with energy these superstitious practices, to which the natives converted to Christianity still adhere in the missions."[1] While we can accept Humboldt's statement as to the destruction of the property of the dead among these Indians, we may doubt the truth of the motive which he puts in the mouth of the people. They seem to have been converted to Christianity, and were probably unwilling to reveal to a traveller that fear of the spirits of the dead which we can hardly doubt was the true original motive of the practice.

Among the Kobeua Indians of North-West Brazil on the borders of Colombia the dead are buried in the communal house. On the closed grave are burned the bow and arrows, the fish-traps and other implements of a man or the baskets and sieve of a woman, and her pots are smashed and the fragments thrown away in the forest, in order that nothing of the goods of the dead may remain behind, and that the soul be not compelled to return to claim the property and to punish the survivors for their negligence or avarice.[2]

The Macusi Indians of British Guiana burn the property of the dead.[3]

After a death the Conibos Indians of the Ucayale River in North-Eastern Peru break everything in the

[1] F. H. A. von Humboldt, *Personal Narrative of Travels to the Equinoctial Regions of America*, English translation (London, 1852), ii. p. 487.

[2] T. Koch-Grünberg, *Zwei Jahre unter den Indianern* (Berlin, 1909–1910), ii. p. 150.

[3] R. Schomburgk, *Reisen in Britisch-Guiana* (Leipsic, 1847–1848), p. 422.

house and then set it on fire; afterwards they cover the whole site of the burnt hut with a thick layer of ashes to receive the tracks of the ghost if he should come to revisit his old dwelling.[1] The Yaguas on the upper waters of the Amazon destroy everything that a dead man possessed or even touched; they kill his domestic animals and they lay waste his gardens.[2]

In the Bororo tribe of Central Brazil it is the rule that all the things which a dead man had made use of should be either burnt or thrown into a river or deposited in the basket which contains his bones, in order to give his ghost no inducements to return and fetch or enjoy his property. Professor von den Steinen witnessed the destruction of the property which had belonged to a dead woman; indeed the property of all the members of her family who had lived in the same hut with her was destroyed. A man decked with green leaves represented the dead woman, who lay buried under a covering of green leaves. This leaf-decked representative of the dead took part in a dance. A man with two rattles led the dance, behind him followed the leaf-decked man, and next came four others. After dancing and singing in chorus they ran away into the wood. The representative of the dead woman then blew a flute to summon two persons who had long been dead and buried. It was deemed necessary that their ghosts should be present at the ceremony of

[1] F. de Castelnau, *Expédition dans les parties centrales de l'Amérique du Sud*, iv. (1851) p. 384.

[2] F. de Castelnau, *op. cit.* v. (Paris, 1851) p. 19.

making over the property to the dead woman, in order that they should welcome their new comrade in the spirit-land and convince her that nothing that belonged to her had been withheld, so that she should have no excuse for coming back as a ghost to reclaim the missing articles. These two dead persons were represented by two men covered with mud, who came out of the wood carried on the bodies of two others. They jumped about, while bull-roarers were swung. A fire was kindled and the property of the deceased and her family was collected and burned, while the men danced round the fire. The leaf-decked man was held down by the two mud-covered men. Afterwards he was released and danced about with another man in a feather head-dress, throwing the things about and stepping into the flames.[1]

Yuracares are a tribe of Indians inhabiting the Cordilleras of Santa Cruz de la Sierra to the north east of Cochobamba. They bury with the dead his clothes, his bow and arrows, and presents for dead relatives in the other world, and they inter with him all the movable property which he had used and not given away in his lifetime. They break his wife's kitchen utensils on the grave. The writer who reports the custom adds that " they burn everything that he has not given away, for fear of his soul returning to the house to look for it and to terrify the survivors or touch them with the stick which a

[1] K. von den Steinen, *Unter den Naturvölkern Zentral-Brasiliens* (Berlin, 1894), pp. 502, 506 *sqq*.

ghost is supposed to carry and the touch of which brings death ".[1]

The Araucanians of the Pampas and the Puelches and the Patagonians burn all a dead man's possessions on his grave and slaughter his domestic animals, his horses and dogs, that they may accompany him to the other world.[2] Among the Lengua Indians of the Paraguaian Chaco "the personal belongings and animals of the deceased are destroyed at his death, evidently with the idea that they may prove useful to him in the after-life. The reason given by the Indian for doing this is that the ghost would otherwise haunt the relatives."[3] For the same reason they not only abandon but destroy by fire the village in which a death has taken place, believing that the site is haunted by the hovering spirit of the deceased for about a month, after which they suppose that the spirit will depart and no longer trouble them.[4] In like manner at the southern extremity of the continent the Onas of Tierra del Fuego destroy all a dead man's property at his death except his dogs, and they shun the place of his death and burial, making a long detour to avoid it, whenever their nomadic life has brought them once more into the neighbourhood.[5]

The disastrous economic and moral effects of this systematic destruction of the property of the dead

[1] A. d'Orbigny, *Voyage dans l'Amérique Méridionale* (Paris, 1835), iii. Ire Partie, 209.

[2] A. d'Orbigny, *L'Homme américain* (Paris, 1839), i. pp. 196, 238.

[3] W. B. Grubb, *An Unknown People in an Unknown Land* (London, 1911), p. 122.

[4] W. B. Grubb, *op. cit.* pp. 122, 160 *sqq.*

[5] C. R. Gallardo, *Los Onas* (Buenos Aires, 1910), pp. 321 *sqq.*

which has prevailed so widely among the Indians of South America have been well pointed out by the French traveller, Alcide d'Orbigny, who witnessed and has described the practice of the custom in several tribes of that continent.

Speaking of the Patagonians who practise the custom, this discerning traveller observes: "They have no laws, no punishments inflicted on the guilty. Each lives as he pleases, and the greatest thief is the most highly esteemed, because he is the most dexterous. A motive which will always prevent them from abandoning the practice of theft, and at the same time will always present an obstacle to their ever forming fixed settlements, is the religious prejudice which, on the death of one of their number, obliges them to destroy his property. A Patagonian who has amassed during the whole of his life an estate by thieving from the whites or exchanging the products of the chase with neighbouring tribes, has done nothing for his heirs; all his savings are destroyed with him, and his children are obliged to rebuild their fortunes afresh—a custom which, I may observe in passing, is found also among the Tamanaques of the Orinoco who ravage the field of the deceased and cut down the trees which he has planted;[1] and among the Yuracares, who abandon and shut up the house of the dead, regarding it as a profanation to gather a single fruit from the trees of his field. It is easy to see that with such customs they can nourish no real ambition since their needs

[1] F. H. A. von Humboldt, *Voyage aux régions équinoxiales*, viii. 273.

are limited to themselves; it is one of the causes of their natural indolence, and it is a motive which, so long as it exists, will always impede the progress of their civilization. Why should they trouble themselves about the future when they have nothing to hope from it? The present is all in all in their eyes, and their only interest is individual; the son will take no care of his father's herd, since it will never come into his possession; he busies himself only with his own affairs and soon turns his thoughts to looking after himself and getting a livelihood. This custom has certainly something to commend it from the moral point of view in so far as it destroys all the motives for that covetousness in heirs which is too often to be seen in our cities. The desire or the hope of a speedy death of their parents cannot exist, since the parents leave absolutely nothing to their children; but on the other hand if the Patagonians had preserved hereditary properties, they would without doubt have been to-day in possession of numerous herds, and would necessarily have been more formidable to the whites, since their power in that case would have been more than doubled, whereas their present habits will infallibly leave them in a stationary state, from which nothing but a radical change will be able to deliver them."[1]

Here, for the present, I must bring these lectures to a close, but I am far from having exhausted the subject; there remain large and important aspects

[1] Alcide d'Orbigny, *Voyage dans l'Amérique Méridionale*, ii. (Paris and Strasburg, 1839–1843) pp. 99 *sq.*; compare *id.*, *L'Homme américain* (Paris, 1839), ii. p. 74.

of it on which I have hitherto said little or nothing. In future I shall hope to supply some at least of these omissions. Meantime, perhaps, even in these short lectures I have said enough to give you an idea, however imperfect, of the extent and depth of that fear of the spirits of the dead which, for good or evil, has played a great part in the development of religion.

INDEX

Printed in Great Britain by R. & R. Clark, Limited, *Edinburgh.*